Fantastic Four

VISIONARIES

BY john byrne

Fantastic Four

VISIONARIES

Fantastic Four Visionaries: John Byrne Vol. 2

STORY & ART:
john byrne

LETTERS:
jim novak, rick parker & joe rosen

COLORS:
glynis wein, bob sharen, george roussos & christie scheele

COLOR RECONSTRUCTION:
jerron quality color

COVER COLORS:
avalon's andy troy

EDITORS:
jim salicrup & tom deFalco

COLLECTIONS EDITOR:
jeff youngquist

ASSISTANT EDITOR:
jennifer grünwald

BOOK DESIGNER:
carrie beadle

EDITOR IN CHIEF:
joe quesada

PUBLISHER:
dan buckley

SPECIAL THANKS TO
pond scum

fantastic four # 241

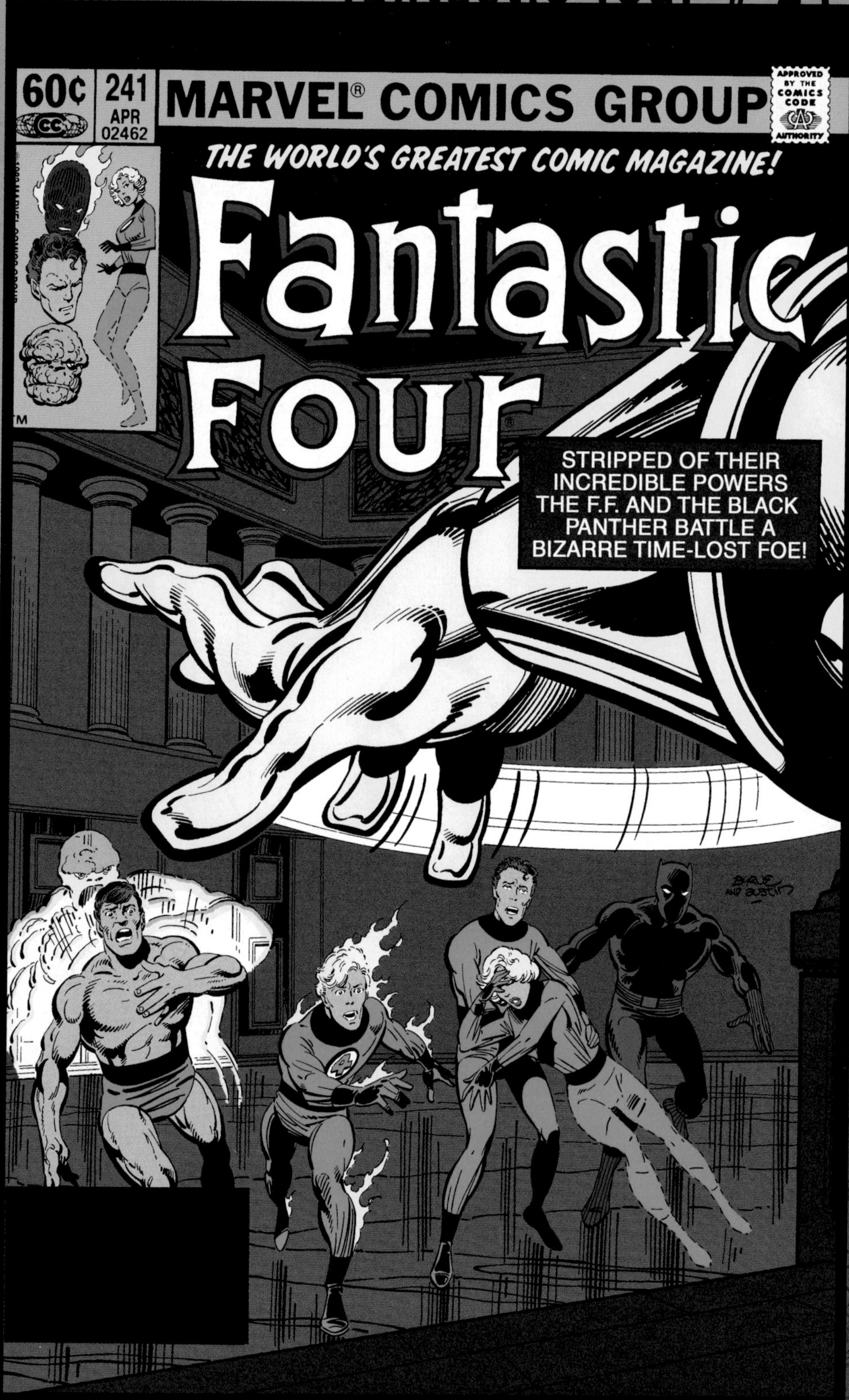
60¢
241
APR
02462
MARVEL® COMICS GROUP
APPROVED BY THE COMICS CODE AUTHORITY
THE WORLD'S GREATEST COMIC MAGAZINE!
Fantastic Four
STRIPPED OF THEIR INCREDIBLE POWERS THE F.F. AND THE BLACK PANTHER BATTLE A BIZARRE TIME-LOST FOE!

APRIL 1982

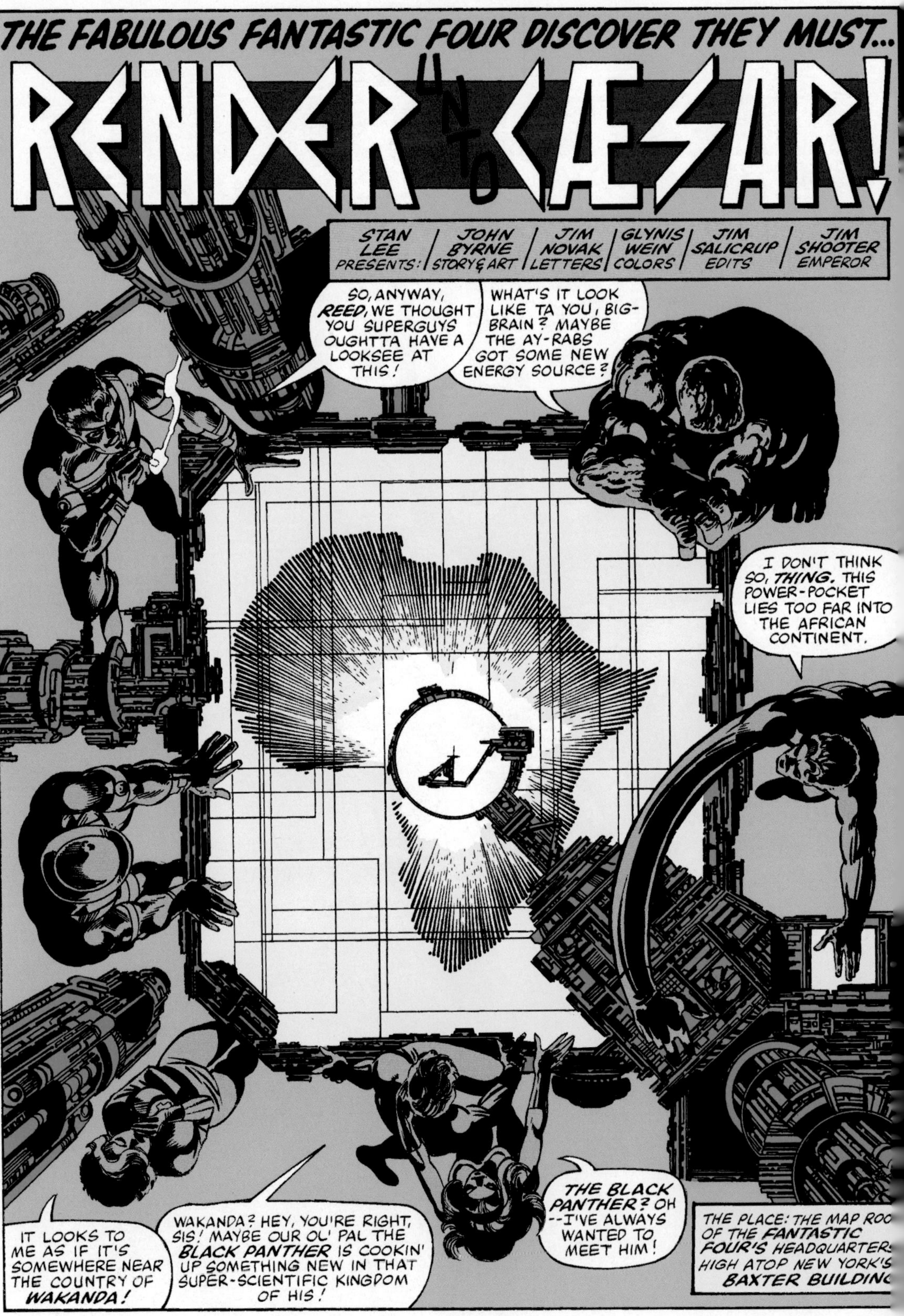

THE FABULOUS FANTASTIC FOUR DISCOVER THEY MUST...
RENDER UNTO CÆSAR!
STAN LEE PRESENTS: | JOHN BYRNE STORY & ART | JIM NOVAK LETTERS | GLYNIS WEIN COLORS | JIM SALICRUP EDITS | JIM SHOOTER EMPEROR
SO, ANYWAY, REED, WE THOUGHT YOU SUPERGUYS OUGHTTA HAVE A LOOKSEE AT THIS!
WHAT'S IT LOOK LIKE TA YOU, BIG-BRAIN? MAYBE THE AY-RABS GOT SOME NEW ENERGY SOURCE?
I DON'T THINK SO, THING. THIS POWER-POCKET LIES TOO FAR INTO THE AFRICAN CONTINENT.
IT LOOKS TO ME AS IF IT'S SOMEWHERE NEAR THE COUNTRY OF WAKANDA!
WAKANDA? HEY, YOU'RE RIGHT, SIS! MAYBE OUR OL' PAL THE BLACK PANTHER IS COOKIN' UP SOMETHING NEW IN THAT SUPER-SCIENTIFIC KINGDOM OF HIS!
THE BLACK PANTHER? OH --I'VE ALWAYS WANTED TO MEET HIM!
THE PLACE: THE MAP ROO OF THE FANTASTIC FOUR'S HEADQUARTERS HIGH ATOP NEW YORK'S BAXTER BUILDING

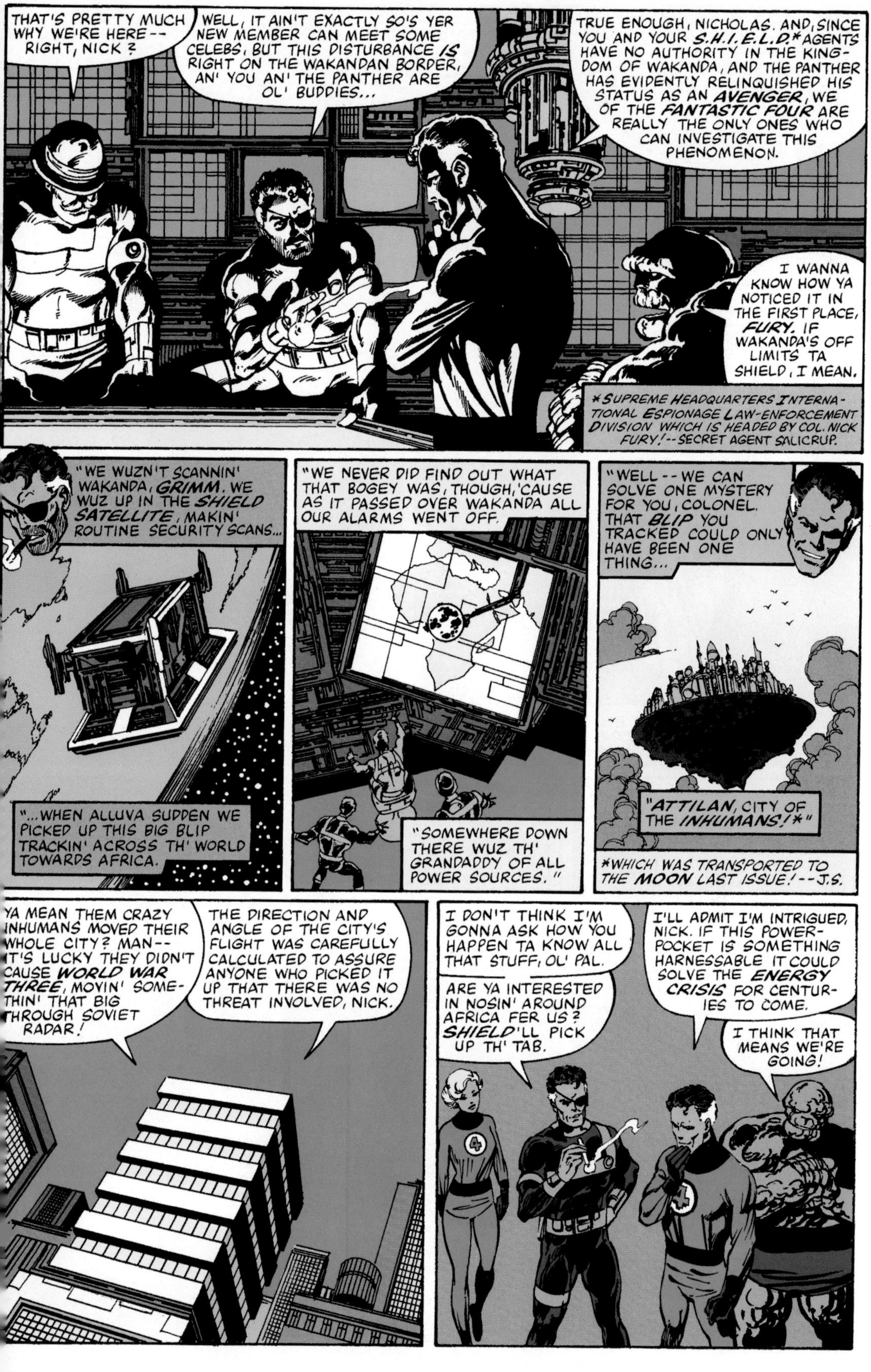
THAT'S PRETTY MUCH WHY WE'RE HERE-- RIGHT, NICK ?
WELL, IT AIN'T EXACTLY SO'S YER NEW MEMBER CAN MEET SOME CELEBS, BUT THIS DISTURBANCE IS RIGHT ON THE WAKANDAN BORDER, AN' YOU AN' THE PANTHER ARE OL' BUDDIES...
TRUE ENOUGH, NICHOLAS. AND, SINCE YOU AND YOUR S.H.I.E.L.D.* AGENTS HAVE NO AUTHORITY IN THE KINGDOM OF WAKANDA, AND THE PANTHER HAS EVIDENTLY RELINQUISHED HIS STATUS AS AN AVENGER, WE OF THE FANTASTIC FOUR ARE REALLY THE ONLY ONES WHO CAN INVESTIGATE THIS PHENOMENON.
I WANNA KNOW HOW YA NOTICED IT IN THE FIRST PLACE, FURY, IF WAKANDA'S OFF LIMITS TA SHIELD, I MEAN.
*SUPREME HEADQUARTERS INTERNATIONAL ESPIONAGE LAW-ENFORCEMENT DIVISION WHICH IS HEADED BY COL. NICK FURY!--SECRET AGENT SALICRUP.
"WE WUZN'T SCANNIN' WAKANDA, GRIMM. WE WUZ UP IN THE SHIELD SATELLITE, MAKIN' ROUTINE SECURITY SCANS...
"...WHEN ALLUVA SUDDEN WE PICKED UP THIS BIG BLIP TRACKIN' ACROSS TH' WORLD TOWARDS AFRICA.
"WE NEVER DID FIND OUT WHAT THAT BOGEY WAS, THOUGH, 'CAUSE AS IT PASSED OVER WAKANDA ALL OUR ALARMS WENT OFF.
"SOMEWHERE DOWN THERE WUZ TH' GRANDADDY OF ALL POWER SOURCES."
"WELL -- WE CAN SOLVE ONE MYSTERY FOR YOU, COLONEL. THAT BLIP YOU TRACKED COULD ONLY HAVE BEEN ONE THING...
"ATTILAN, CITY OF THE INHUMANS!*"
*WHICH WAS TRANSPORTED TO THE MOON LAST ISSUE!--J.S.
YA MEAN THEM CRAZY INHUMANS MOVED THEIR WHOLE CITY? MAN-- IT'S LUCKY THEY DIDN'T CAUSE WORLD WAR THREE, MOVIN' SOMETHIN' THAT BIG THROUGH SOVIET RADAR!
THE DIRECTION AND ANGLE OF THE CITY'S FLIGHT WAS CAREFULLY CALCULATED TO ASSURE ANYONE WHO PICKED IT UP THAT THERE WAS NO THREAT INVOLVED, NICK.
I DON'T THINK I'M GONNA ASK HOW YOU HAPPEN TA KNOW ALL THAT STUFF, OL' PAL.
ARE YA INTERESTED IN NOSIN' AROUND AFRICA FER US? SHIELD'LL PICK UP TH' TAB.
I'LL ADMIT I'M INTRIGUED, NICK. IF THIS POWER-POCKET IS SOMETHING HARNESSABLE IT COULD SOLVE THE ENERGY CRISIS FOR CENTURIES TO COME.
I THINK THAT MEANS WE'RE GOING!

SHORTLY, AFTER NICK FURY AND AGENT *DUM DUM DUGAN* HAVE DEPARTED...

COURSE SET AND LOCKED. ALL WE HAVE TO DO IS SIT BACK AND IN NINETY MINUTES WE'LL BE IN WAKANDA.

THAT'S GREAT PROFESSOR RICHARDS, BUT, WHERE'S THE THING? I HAVEN'T SEEN HIM SINCE WE CAME ABOARD.

I'M RIGHT HERE, FRANKIE! AS LONG AS WE'RE GOIN' TA AFRICA I THOUGHT I MIGHT AS WELL LOOK THE PART!

MISTER GRIMM!

I DON'T BELIEVE IT! IT'S *IDAHO SMITH* HIMSELF!

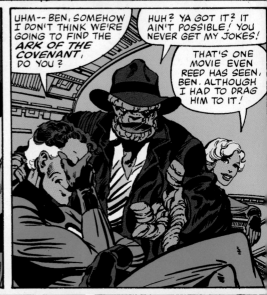

UHM-- BEN, SOMEHOW I DON'T THINK WE'RE GOING TO FIND THE *ARK OF THE COVENANT*, DO YOU?

HUH? YA GOT IT? IT AIN'T POSSIBLE! YOU NEVER GET MY JOKES!

THAT'S ONE MOVIE EVEN REED HAS SEEN, BEN. ALTHOUGH I HAD TO DRAG HIM TO IT!

AND SO, LESS THAN TWO HOURS LATER... THE PRINCIPAL *TRIBAL CENTER* OF WAKANDA IS A MILE OR SO THROUGH THIS UNDERBRUSH.

I THOUGHT IT MORE PRUDENT TO LAND HERE AS WE HAVE NO OFFICIAL INVITATION.

NUTS! SINCE WHEN DO WE NEED AN INVITE TA DROP IN ON OUR OL' PAL *T'CHALLA?*

BUT AS THE MIGHTY MUSCLED THING PLOWS THROUGH THE DENSE JUNGLE...

I WOULDA THOUGHT I'D HAVE COME UP ON TH' VILLAGE BY NOW. AN' WHERE DID THE OTHERS GO?

HOPE THEY AIN'T GONE AN' GOT THEMSELVES LOST --OR WORSE-- IN ALL THIS...

HOPE *I* AIN'T THE ONE WHO'S LOST!

SUDDENLY...

HEY, WHAT TH'...!

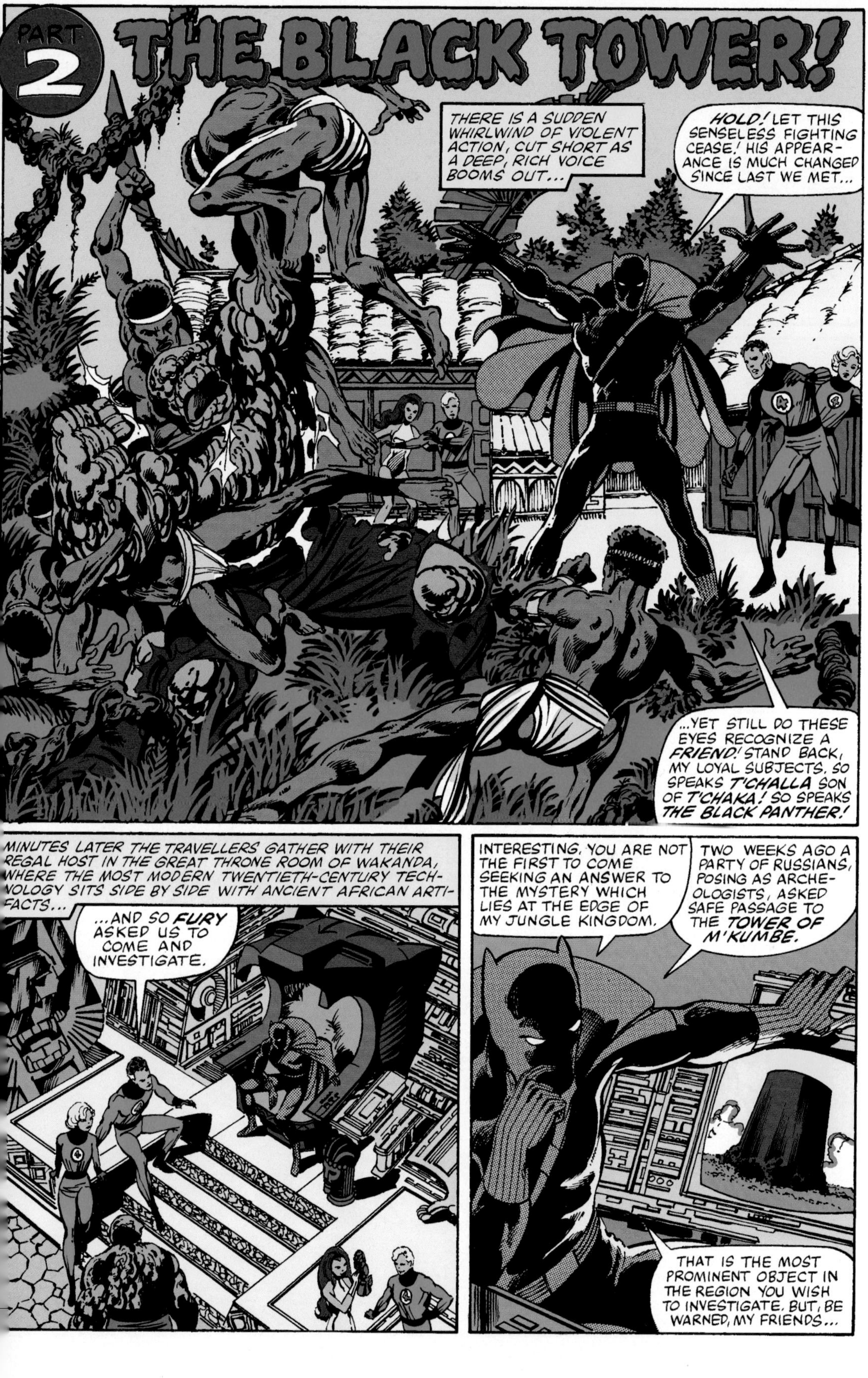
PART 2
THE BLACK TOWER!
THERE IS A SUDDEN WHIRLWIND OF VIOLENT ACTION, CUT SHORT AS A DEEP, RICH VOICE BOOMS OUT...
HOLD! LET THIS SENSELESS FIGHTING CEASE! HIS APPEARANCE IS MUCH CHANGED SINCE LAST WE MET...
...YET STILL DO THESE EYES RECOGNIZE A FRIEND! STAND BACK, MY LOYAL SUBJECTS. SO SPEAKS T'CHALLA SON OF T'CHAKA! SO SPEAKS THE BLACK PANTHER!
MINUTES LATER THE TRAVELLERS GATHER WITH THEIR REGAL HOST IN THE GREAT THRONE ROOM OF WAKANDA, WHERE THE MOST MODERN TWENTIETH-CENTURY TECHNOLOGY SITS SIDE BY SIDE WITH ANCIENT AFRICAN ARTIFACTS...
...AND SO FURY ASKED US TO COME AND INVESTIGATE.
INTERESTING. YOU ARE NOT THE FIRST TO COME SEEKING AN ANSWER TO THE MYSTERY WHICH LIES AT THE EDGE OF MY JUNGLE KINGDOM.
TWO WEEKS AGO A PARTY OF RUSSIANS, POSING AS ARCHEOLOGISTS, ASKED SAFE PASSAGE TO THE TOWER OF M'KUMBE.
THAT IS THE MOST PROMINENT OBJECT IN THE REGION YOU WISH TO INVESTIGATE. BUT, BE WARNED, MY FRIENDS...

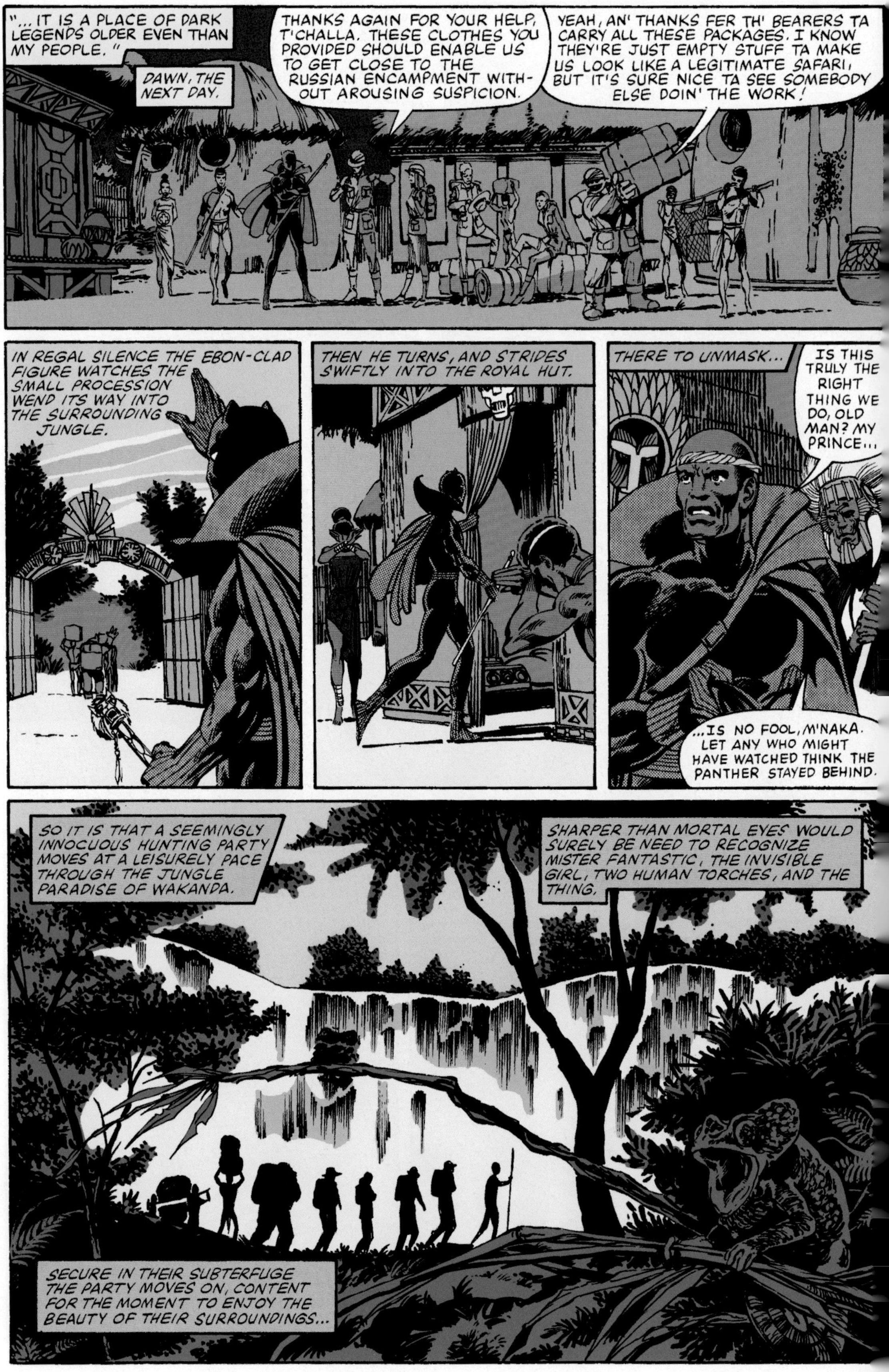
"... IT IS A PLACE OF DARK LEGENDS OLDER EVEN THAN MY PEOPLE."
DAWN, THE NEXT DAY.
THANKS AGAIN FOR YOUR HELP, T'CHALLA. THESE CLOTHES YOU PROVIDED SHOULD ENABLE US TO GET CLOSE TO THE RUSSIAN ENCAMPMENT WITHOUT AROUSING SUSPICION.
YEAH, AN' THANKS FER TH' BEARERS TA CARRY ALL THESE PACKAGES. I KNOW THEY'RE JUST EMPTY STUFF TA MAKE US LOOK LIKE A LEGITIMATE SAFARI, BUT IT'S SURE NICE TA SEE SOMEBODY ELSE DOIN' THE WORK!
IN REGAL SILENCE THE EBON-CLAD FIGURE WATCHES THE SMALL PROCESSION WEND ITS WAY INTO THE SURROUNDING JUNGLE.
THEN HE TURNS, AND STRIDES SWIFTLY INTO THE ROYAL HUT.
THERE TO UNMASK...
IS THIS TRULY THE RIGHT THING WE DO, OLD MAN? MY PRINCE...
...IS NO FOOL, M'NAKA. LET ANY WHO MIGHT HAVE WATCHED THINK THE PANTHER STAYED BEHIND.
SO IT IS THAT A SEEMINGLY INNOCUOUS HUNTING PARTY MOVES AT A LEISURELY PACE THROUGH THE JUNGLE PARADISE OF WAKANDA.
SHARPER THAN MORTAL EYES WOULD SURELY BE NEED TO RECOGNIZE MISTER FANTASTIC, THE INVISIBLE GIRL, TWO HUMAN TORCHES, AND THE THING.
SECURE IN THEIR SUBTERFUGE THE PARTY MOVES ON, CONTENT FOR THE MOMENT TO ENJOY THE BEAUTY OF THEIR SURROUNDINGS...

AND THUS, AFTER TWO DAYS JOURNEY...

THE BLACK TOWER OF M'KUMBE, FEARED THROUGHOUT WAKANDA AS A PLACE OF DARK MAGIC AND GREAT EVIL. NOT EVEN THE INFLUX OF EUROPEAN CULTURE HAS SERVED TO DISPEL ITS TERRORS.

INCREDIBLE! IT MUST BE A THOUSAND FEET HIGH! AND THE SIDES APPEAR AS SMOOTH AS POLISHED GLASS. WHAT COULD HAVE FORMED SUCH A STRUCTURE?

I'D WORRY A LITTLE LESS ABOUT THAT AN' A LITTLE MORE ABOUT THE REDS, IF I WUZ YOU, REED.

DESCENDING FROM THE GRASSY KNOLL THE PARTY MOVES CLOSER TO THE STRANGE TOWER, UNTIL...

ON YOUR TOES, EVERYONE! THE RUSSIAN ENCAMPMENT IS JUST AHEAD!

THEY MAY BE HERE FOR LEGITIMATE REASONS, BUT UNTIL WE CAN BE CERTAIN...

MAYBE FRANKIE AN' ME SHOULD FLAME ON AN' GIVE 'EM A QUICK BUZZ, REED, JUST TO SHOW 'EM WE MEAN BUSINESS.

NO, JOHNNY-- I DON'T WANT ANY OF US USING OUR POWERS UNTIL WE KNOW WHAT WE'RE UP AGAINST...

HEY, WHAT IS THIS? COMMIE SIESTA TIME OR SOMETHING? THEY AIN'T EVEN NOTICED US! I THINK I'M INSULTED!

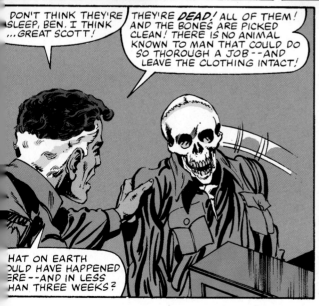

DON'T THINK THEY'RE [A]SLEEP, BEN. I THINK ...GREAT SCOTT!

THEY'RE DEAD! ALL OF THEM! AND THE BONES ARE PICKED CLEAN! THERE IS NO ANIMAL KNOWN TO MAN THAT COULD DO SO THOROUGH A JOB--AND LEAVE THE CLOTHING INTACT!

[W]HAT ON EARTH [SH]OULD HAVE HAPPENED [H]ERE --AND IN LESS [T]HAN THREE WEEKS?

UHM... I DUNNO, STRETCH. WHY DON'TCHA ASK THESE GUYS?

9

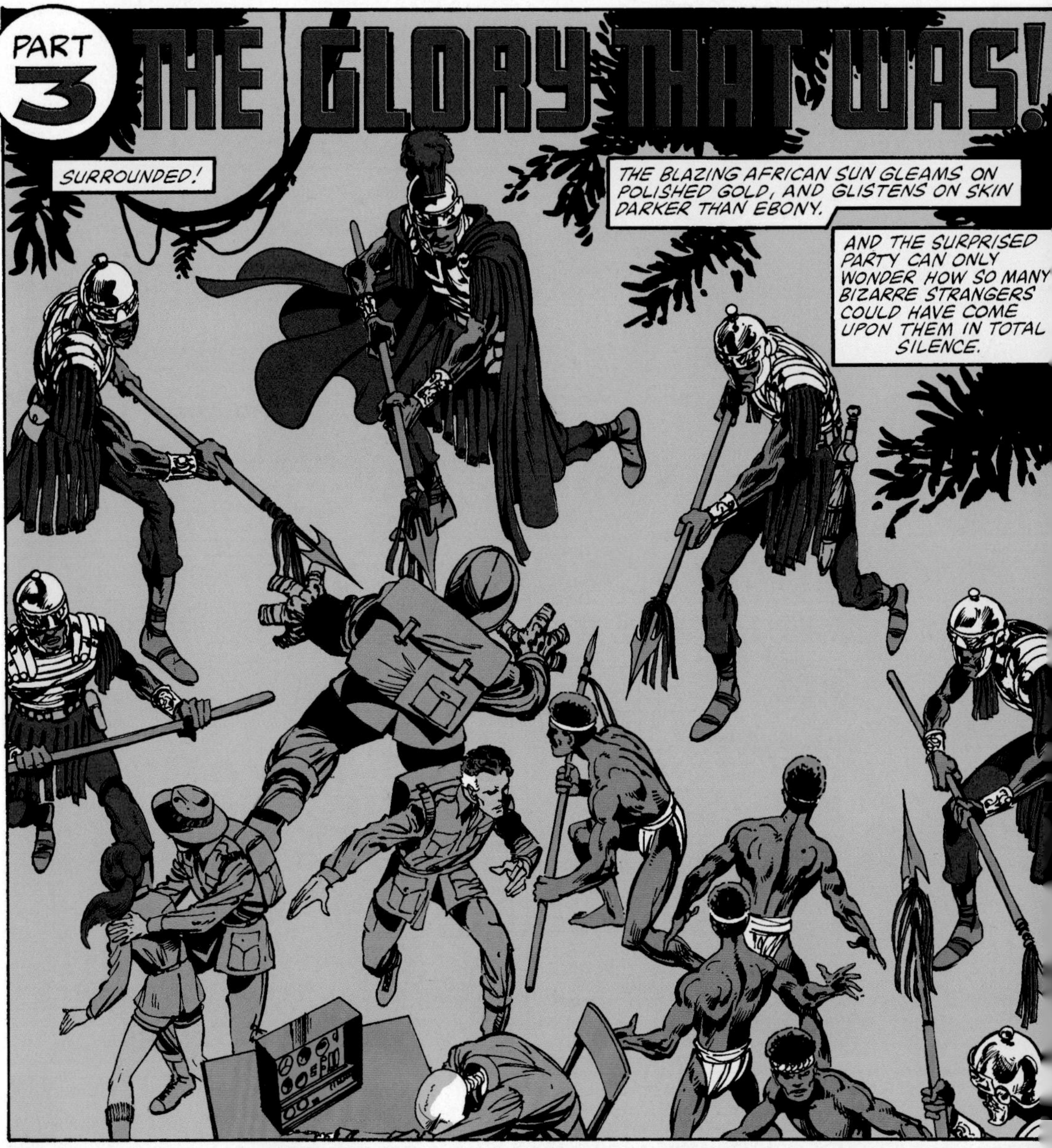
PART 3 THE GLORY THAT WAS!
SURROUNDED!
THE BLAZING AFRICAN SUN GLEAMS ON POLISHED GOLD, AND GLISTENS ON SKIN DARKER THAN EBONY.
AND THE SURPRISED PARTY CAN ONLY WONDER HOW SO MANY BIZARRE STRANGERS COULD HAVE COME UPON THEM IN TOTAL SILENCE.

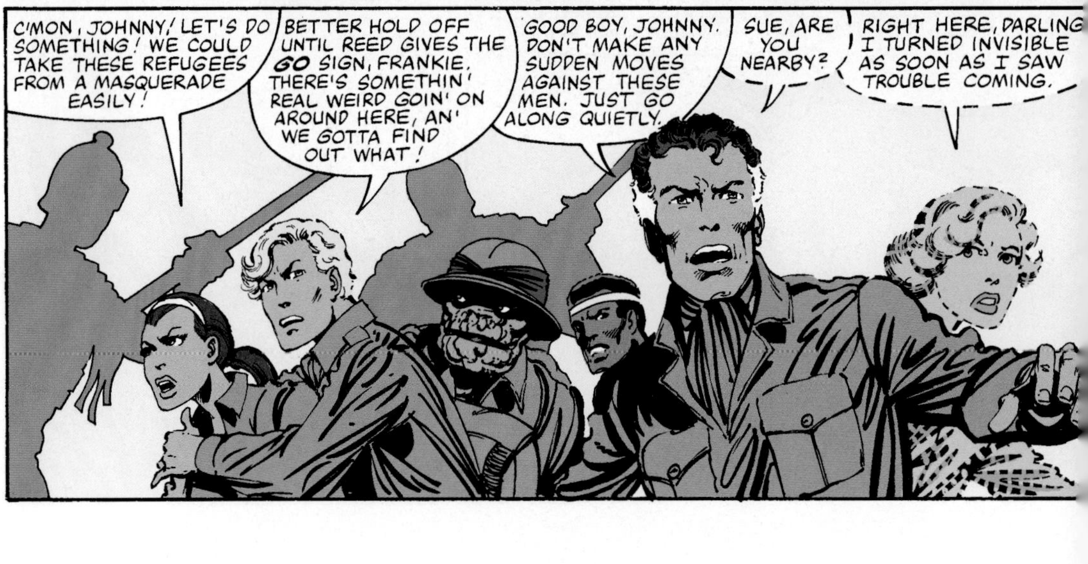
C'MON, JOHNNY! LET'S DO SOMETHING! WE COULD TAKE THESE REFUGEES FROM A MASQUERADE EASILY!
BETTER HOLD OFF UNTIL REED GIVES THE GO SIGN, FRANKIE. THERE'S SOMETHIN' REAL WEIRD GOIN' ON AROUND HERE, AN' WE GOTTA FIND OUT WHAT!
GOOD BOY, JOHNNY. DON'T MAKE ANY SUDDEN MOVES AGAINST THESE MEN. JUST GO ALONG QUIETLY.
SUE, ARE YOU NEARBY?
RIGHT HERE, DARLING. I TURNED INVISIBLE AS SOON AS I SAW TROUBLE COMING.

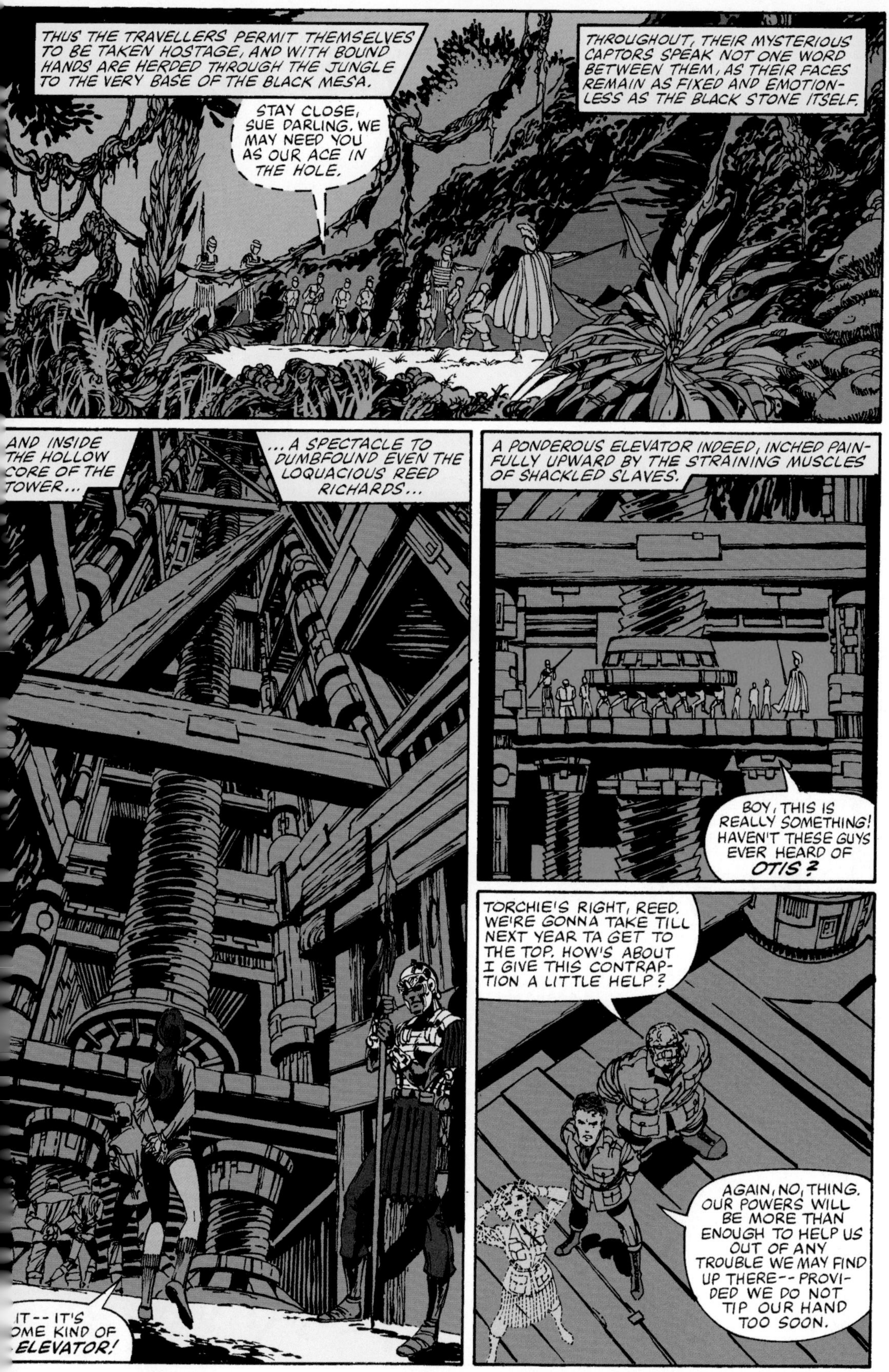
THUS THE TRAVELLERS PERMIT THEMSELVES TO BE TAKEN HOSTAGE, AND WITH BOUND HANDS ARE HERDED THROUGH THE JUNGLE TO THE VERY BASE OF THE BLACK MESA.
THROUGHOUT, THEIR MYSTERIOUS CAPTORS SPEAK NOT ONE WORD BETWEEN THEM, AS THEIR FACES REMAIN AS FIXED AND EMOTIONLESS AS THE BLACK STONE ITSELF.
STAY CLOSE, SUE DARLING. WE MAY NEED YOU AS OUR ACE IN THE HOLE.
AND INSIDE THE HOLLOW CORE OF THE TOWER...
...A SPECTACLE TO DUMBFOUND EVEN THE LOQUACIOUS REED RICHARDS...
IT-- IT'S OME KIND OF ELEVATOR!
A PONDEROUS ELEVATOR INDEED, INCHED PAINFULLY UPWARD BY THE STRAINING MUSCLES OF SHACKLED SLAVES.
BOY, THIS IS REALLY SOMETHING! HAVEN'T THESE GUYS EVER HEARD OF OTIS?
TORCHIE'S RIGHT, REED. WE'RE GONNA TAKE TILL NEXT YEAR TA GET TO THE TOP. HOW'S ABOUT I GIVE THIS CONTRAPTION A LITTLE HELP?
AGAIN, NO, THING. OUR POWERS WILL BE MORE THAN ENOUGH TO HELP US OUT OF ANY TROUBLE WE MAY FIND UP THERE-- PROVIDED WE DO NOT TIP OUR HAND TOO SOON.

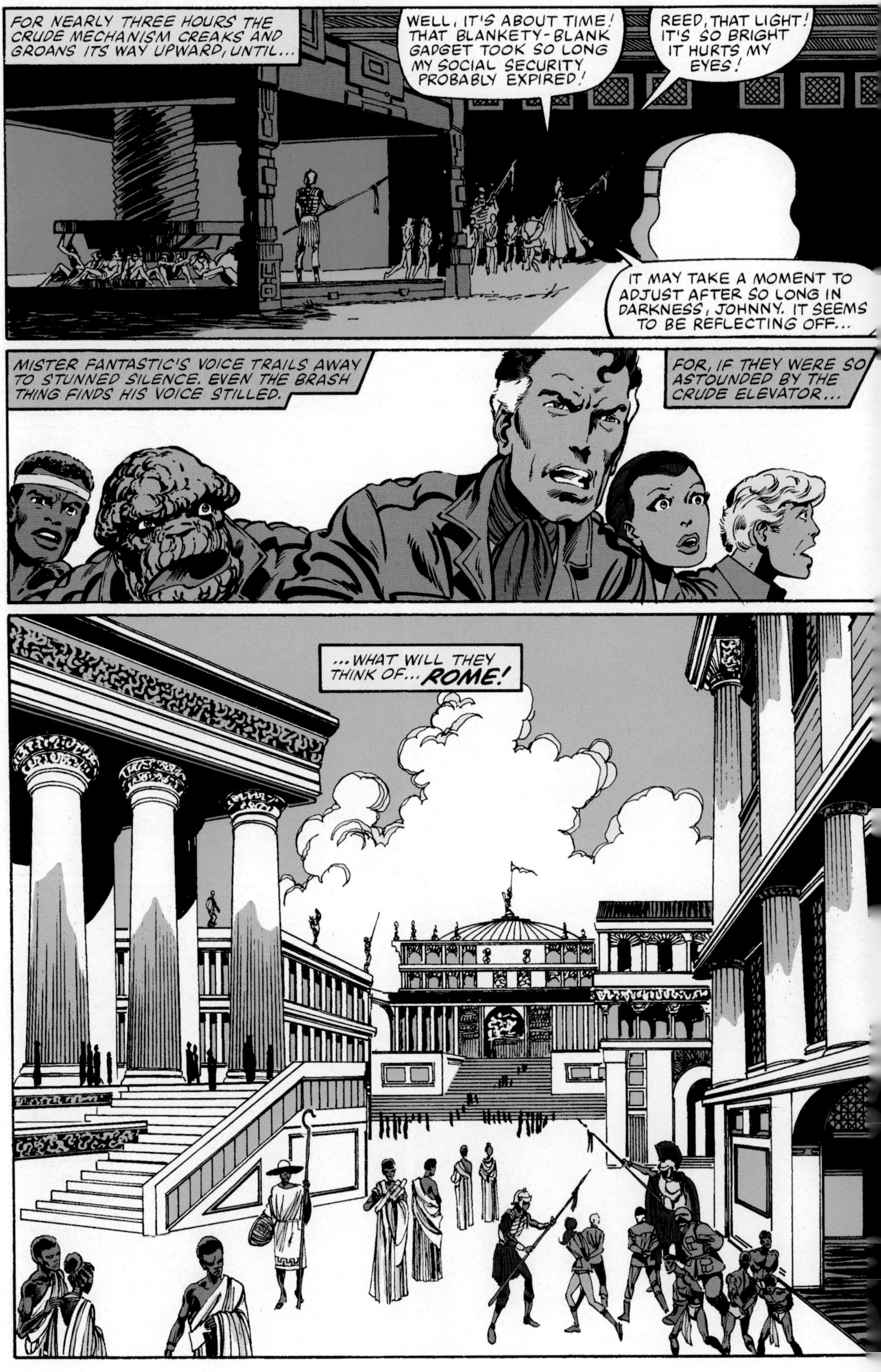
FOR NEARLY THREE HOURS THE CRUDE MECHANISM CREAKS AND GROANS ITS WAY UPWARD, UNTIL...
WELL, IT'S ABOUT TIME! THAT BLANKETY-BLANK GADGET TOOK SO LONG MY SOCIAL SECURITY PROBABLY EXPIRED!
REED, THAT LIGHT! IT'S SO BRIGHT IT HURTS MY EYES!
IT MAY TAKE A MOMENT TO ADJUST AFTER SO LONG IN DARKNESS, JOHNNY. IT SEEMS TO BE REFLECTING OFF...
MISTER FANTASTIC'S VOICE TRAILS AWAY TO STUNNED SILENCE. EVEN THE BRASH THING FINDS HIS VOICE STILLED.
FOR, IF THEY WERE SO ASTOUNDED BY THE CRUDE ELEVATOR...
...WHAT WILL THEY THINK OF... ROME!

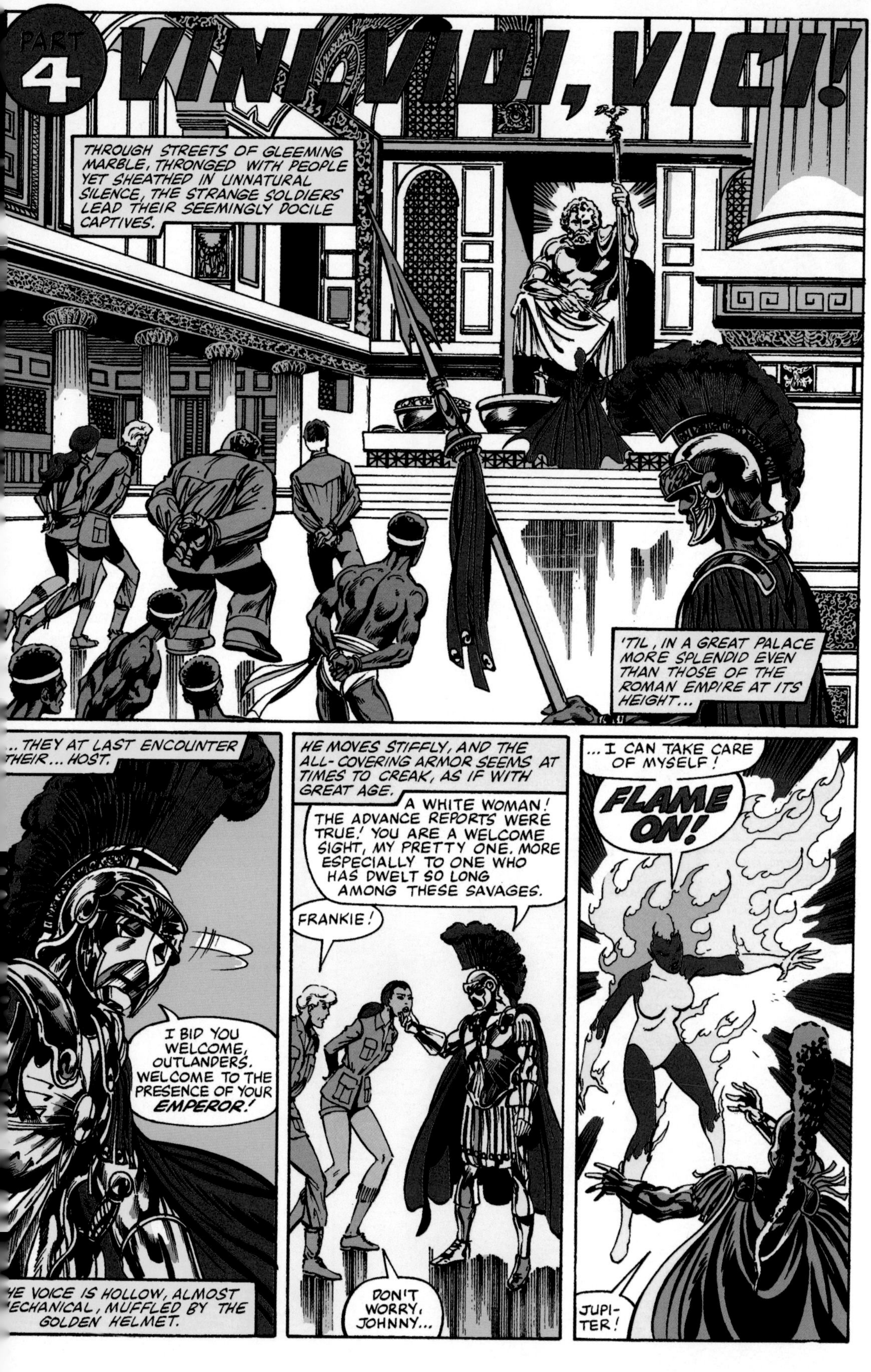
PART 4
VINI, VIDI, VICI!
THROUGH STREETS OF GLEEMING MARBLE, THRONGED WITH PEOPLE YET SHEATHED IN UNNATURAL SILENCE, THE STRANGE SOLDIERS LEAD THEIR SEEMINGLY DOCILE CAPTIVES.
'TIL, IN A GREAT PALACE MORE SPLENDID EVEN THAN THOSE OF THE ROMAN EMPIRE AT ITS HEIGHT...
...THEY AT LAST ENCOUNTER THEIR... HOST.
I BID YOU WELCOME, OUTLANDERS. WELCOME TO THE PRESENCE OF YOUR EMPEROR!
HE VOICE IS HOLLOW, ALMOST ECHANICAL, MUFFLED BY THE GOLDEN HELMET.
HE MOVES STIFFLY, AND THE ALL-COVERING ARMOR SEEMS AT TIMES TO CREAK, AS IF WITH GREAT AGE.
A WHITE WOMAN! THE ADVANCE REPORTS WERE TRUE! YOU ARE A WELCOME SIGHT, MY PRETTY ONE. MORE ESPECIALLY TO ONE WHO HAS DWELT SO LONG AMONG THESE SAVAGES.
FRANKIE!
DON'T WORRY, JOHNNY...
...I CAN TAKE CARE OF MYSELF!
FLAME ON!
JUPI-TER!

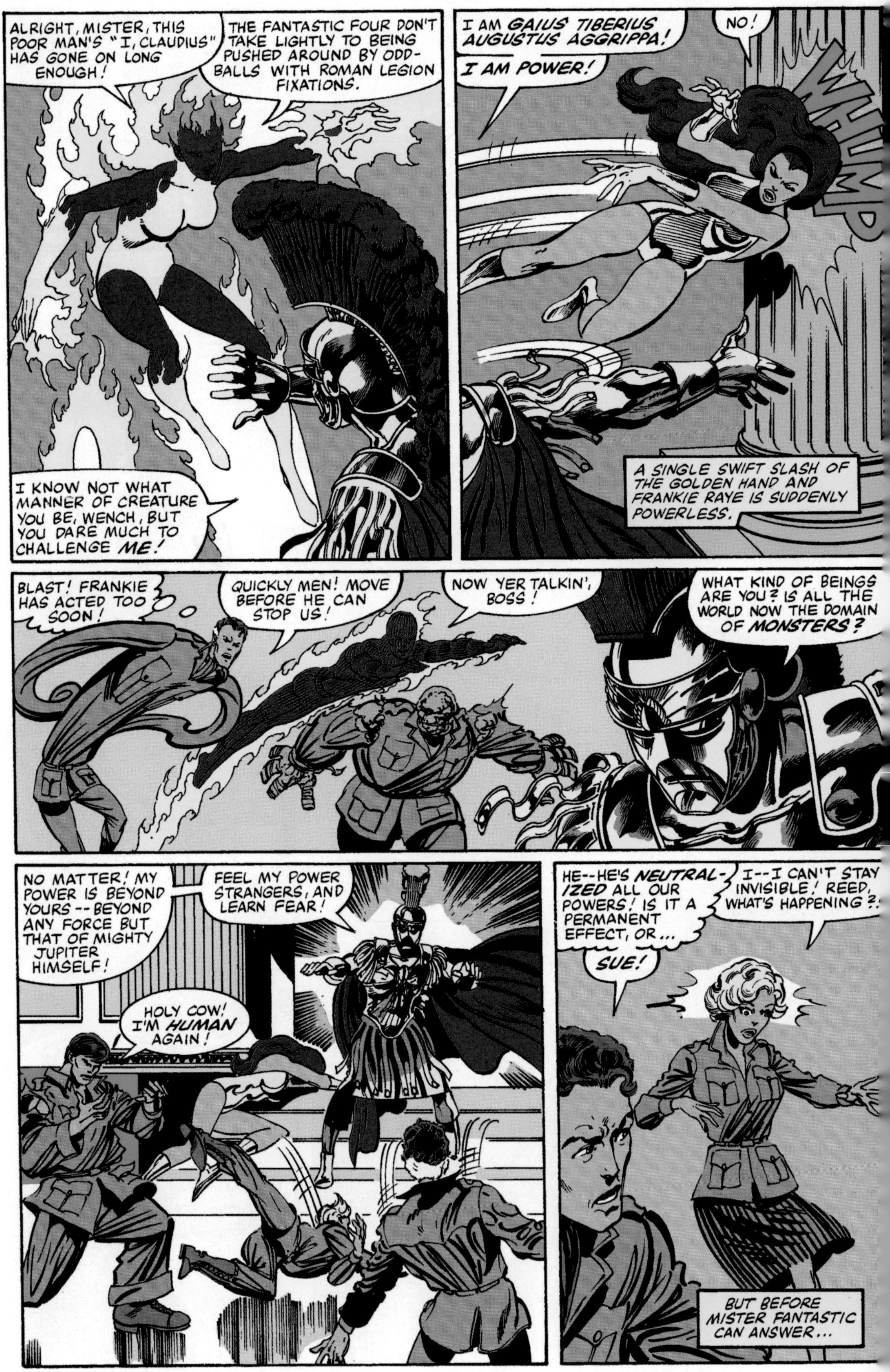

ALRIGHT, MISTER, THIS POOR MAN'S "I, CLAUDIUS" HAS GONE ON LONG ENOUGH!
THE FANTASTIC FOUR DON'T TAKE LIGHTLY TO BEING PUSHED AROUND BY ODD-BALLS WITH ROMAN LEGION FIXATIONS.
I KNOW NOT WHAT MANNER OF CREATURE YOU BE, WENCH, BUT YOU DARE MUCH TO CHALLENGE ME!
I AM GAIUS TIBERIUS AUGUSTUS AGGRIPPA!
I AM POWER!
NO!
WHUMP
A SINGLE SWIFT SLASH OF THE GOLDEN HAND AND FRANKIE RAYE IS SUDDENLY POWERLESS.
BLAST! FRANKIE HAS ACTED TOO SOON!
QUICKLY MEN! MOVE BEFORE HE CAN STOP US!
NOW YER TALKIN', BOSS!
WHAT KIND OF BEINGS ARE YOU? IS ALL THE WORLD NOW THE DOMAIN OF MONSTERS?
NO MATTER! MY POWER IS BEYOND YOURS -- BEYOND ANY FORCE BUT THAT OF MIGHTY JUPITER HIMSELF!
FEEL MY POWER STRANGERS, AND LEARN FEAR!
HOLY COW! I'M HUMAN AGAIN!
HE--HE'S NEUTRAL-IZED ALL OUR POWERS! IS IT A PERMANENT EFFECT, OR...
I--I CAN'T STAY INVISIBLE! REED, WHAT'S HAPPENING?!
SUE!
BUT BEFORE MISTER FANTASTIC CAN ANSWER...

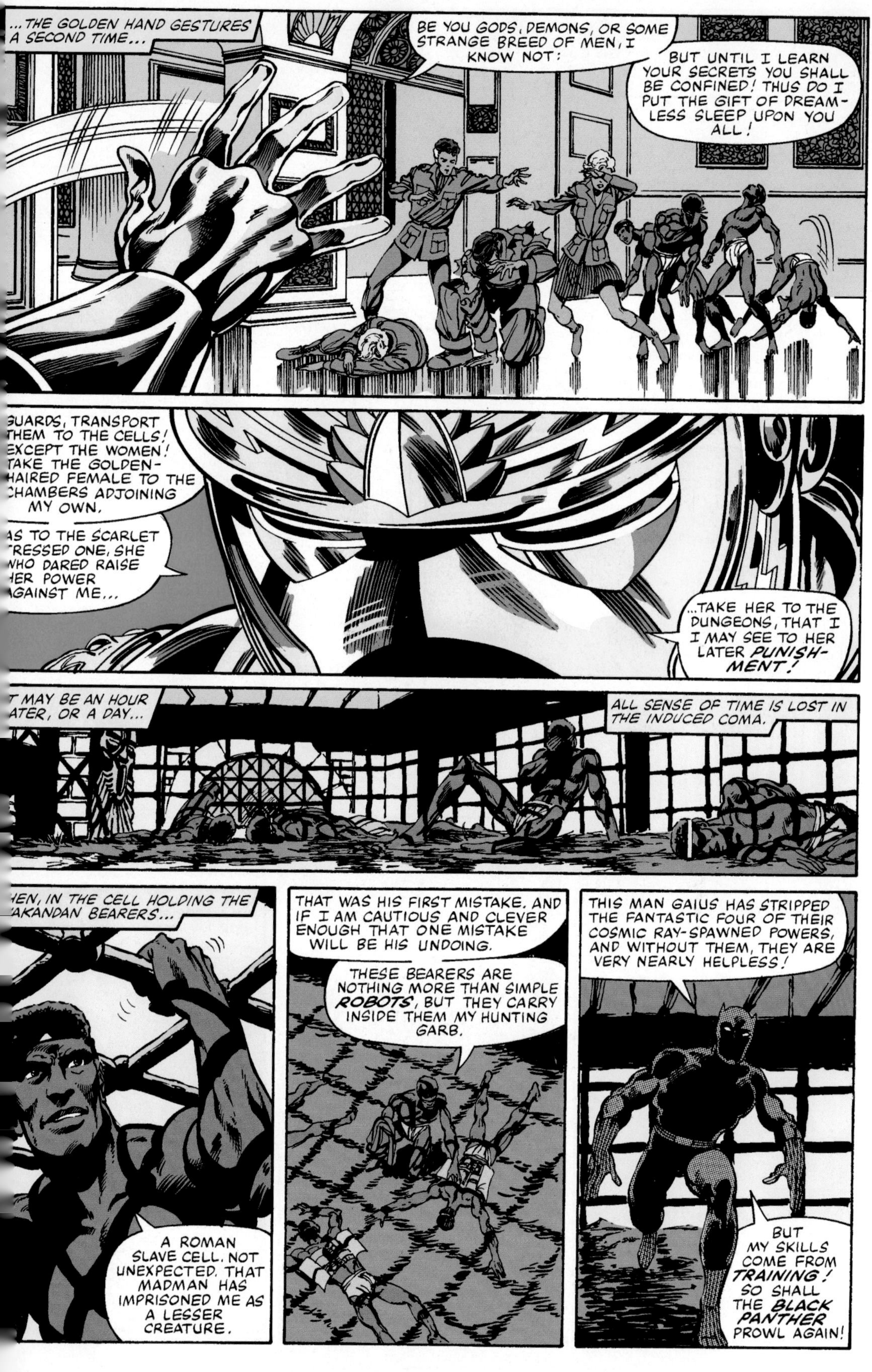

...THE GOLDEN HAND GESTURES A SECOND TIME...
BE YOU GODS, DEMONS, OR SOME STRANGE BREED OF MEN, I KNOW NOT:
BUT UNTIL I LEARN YOUR SECRETS YOU SHALL BE CONFINED! THUS DO I PUT THE GIFT OF DREAMLESS SLEEP UPON YOU ALL!
GUARDS, TRANSPORT THEM TO THE CELLS! EXCEPT THE WOMEN! TAKE THE GOLDEN-HAIRED FEMALE TO THE CHAMBERS ADJOINING MY OWN.
AS TO THE SCARLET TRESSED ONE, SHE WHO DARED RAISE HER POWER AGAINST ME...
...TAKE HER TO THE DUNGEONS, THAT I I MAY SEE TO HER LATER PUNISHMENT!
IT MAY BE AN HOUR LATER, OR A DAY...
ALL SENSE OF TIME IS LOST IN THE INDUCED COMA.
THEN, IN THE CELL HOLDING THE WAKANDAN BEARERS...
A ROMAN SLAVE CELL. NOT UNEXPECTED. THAT MADMAN HAS IMPRISONED ME AS A LESSER CREATURE.
THAT WAS HIS FIRST MISTAKE. AND IF I AM CAUTIOUS AND CLEVER ENOUGH THAT ONE MISTAKE WILL BE HIS UNDOING.
THESE BEARERS ARE NOTHING MORE THAN SIMPLE ROBOTS, BUT THEY CARRY INSIDE THEM MY HUNTING GARB.
THIS MAN GAIUS HAS STRIPPED THE FANTASTIC FOUR OF THEIR COSMIC RAY-SPAWNED POWERS, AND WITHOUT THEM, THEY ARE VERY NEARLY HELPLESS!
BUT MY SKILLS COME FROM TRAINING! SO SHALL THE BLACK PANTHER PROWL AGAIN!

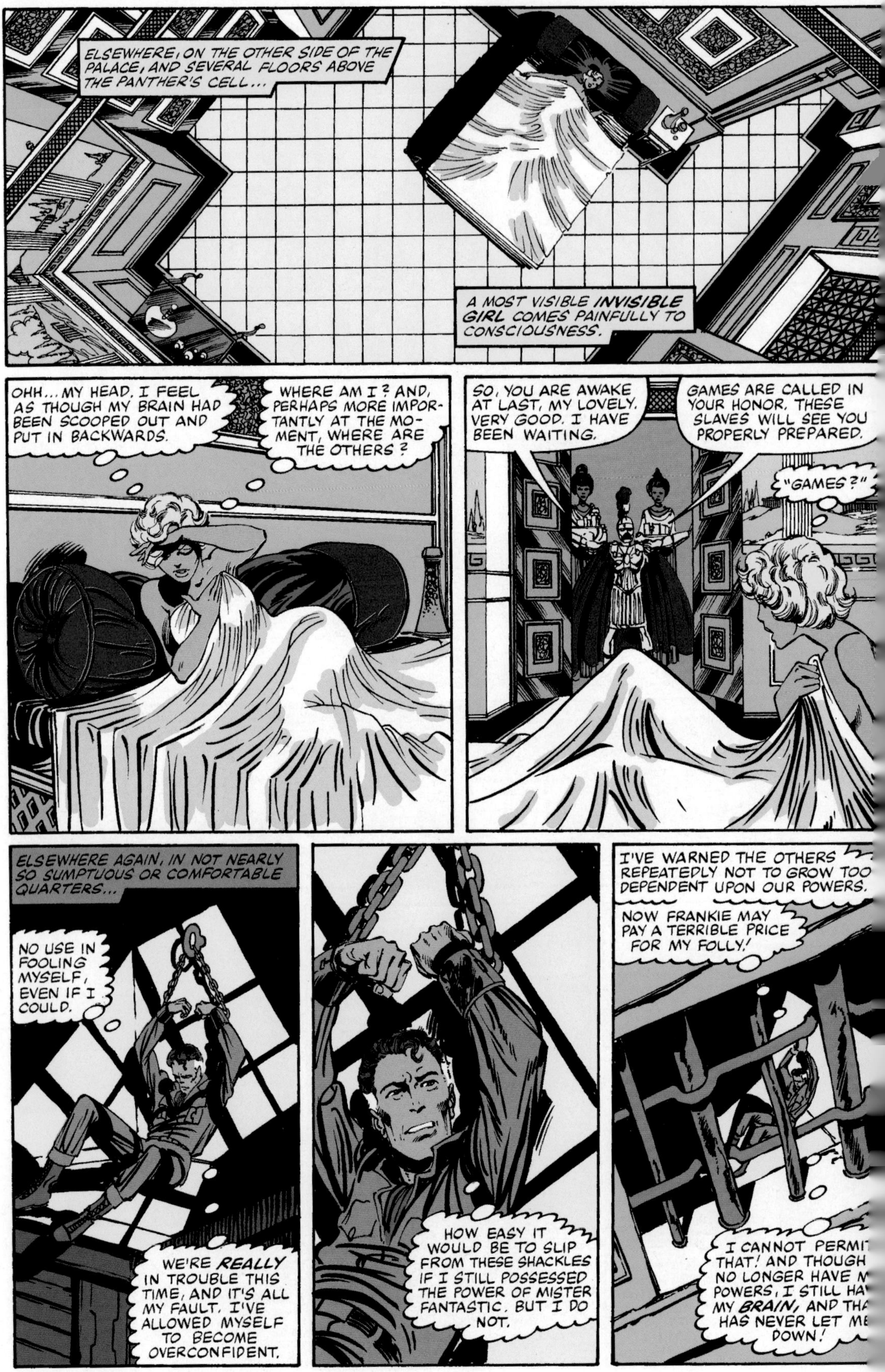
ELSEWHERE, ON THE OTHER SIDE OF THE PALACE, AND SEVERAL FLOORS ABOVE THE PANTHER'S CELL...
A MOST VISIBLE INVISIBLE GIRL COMES PAINFULLY TO CONSCIOUSNESS.
OHH... MY HEAD. I FEEL AS THOUGH MY BRAIN HAD BEEN SCOOPED OUT AND PUT IN BACKWARDS.
WHERE AM I? AND, PERHAPS MORE IMPORTANTLY AT THE MOMENT, WHERE ARE THE OTHERS?
SO, YOU ARE AWAKE AT LAST, MY LOVELY. VERY GOOD. I HAVE BEEN WAITING.
GAMES ARE CALLED IN YOUR HONOR. THESE SLAVES WILL SEE YOU PROPERLY PREPARED.
"GAMES?"
ELSEWHERE AGAIN, IN NOT NEARLY SO SUMPTUOUS OR COMFORTABLE QUARTERS...
NO USE IN FOOLING MYSELF, EVEN IF I COULD.
WE'RE REALLY IN TROUBLE THIS TIME, AND IT'S ALL MY FAULT. I'VE ALLOWED MYSELF TO BECOME OVERCONFIDENT.
HOW EASY IT WOULD BE TO SLIP FROM THESE SHACKLES IF I STILL POSSESSED THE POWER OF MISTER FANTASTIC. BUT I DO NOT.
I'VE WARNED THE OTHERS REPEATEDLY NOT TO GROW TOO DEPENDENT UPON OUR POWERS.
NOW FRANKIE MAY PAY A TERRIBLE PRICE FOR MY FOLLY!
I CANNOT PERMIT THAT! AND THOUGH NO LONGER HAVE POWERS, I STILL HA MY BRAIN, AND THA HAS NEVER LET ME DOWN!

NOT FAR AWAY THE BLACK PANTHER MOVES IN UTTER SILENCE THROUGH THE DANK CATACOMBS...

IT IS HERE--THE LOW MOANING I DETECTED SEVERAL MINUTES AGO.

THERE IS SOMEONE IN PAIN BEHIND THIS DOOR, AND MOST LIKELY IT IS ONE OF THE F.F.!

NOT QUITE, T'CHALLA. AT LEAST, NOT YET...

IT IS THE GIRL CALLED FRANKIE RAYE! THAT MONSTER GAIUS HAS STRUNG HER OVER A SLOW FIRE, AN ANCIENT ROMAN METHOD OF PAINFUL EXECUTION!

BUT WHY WAS THIS DOOR LEFT UNLOCKED?

PERHAPS BECAUSE SHE IS NOT UNATTENDED...

GUARDS!

HEAR ME, GUARDIANS OF THIS PIT OF HORRORS! I AM T'CHALLA, SON OF T'CHAKA! LAY DOWN YOUR WEAPONS AND SHOW OBEISANCE TO ME!

THE GUARDS REACTION IS SWIFT...

...AND TO T'CHALLA TOTALLY UNEXPECTED.

INCREDIBLE! THEY DEFY ME! YET THE NAME OF THE BLACK PANTHER IS HONORED AND FEARED THROUGHOUT AFRICA, AND HAS BEEN FOR GENERATIONS.

NO MATTER. IF THEY HAVE NOT HEARD OF MY POWER, THEY SOON SHALL!

WITH SPEED AND FEROCITY TO RIVAL HIS NAMESAKE, THE PANTHER LEAPS...

PART 5

BLOOD AND CIRCUSES!

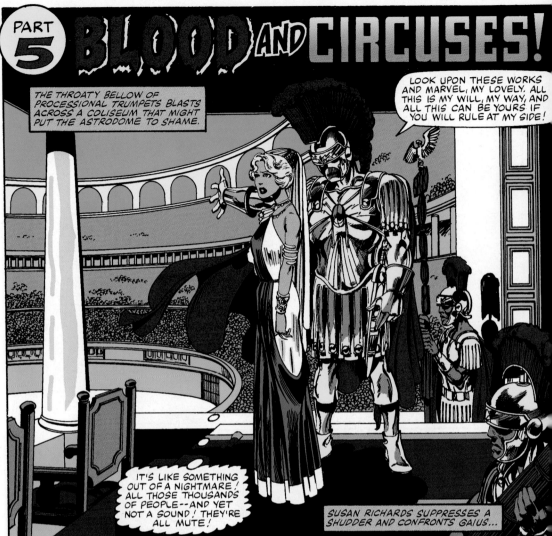

THE THROATY BELLOW OF PROCESSIONAL TRUMPETS BLASTS ACROSS A COLISEUM THAT MIGHT PUT THE ASTRODOME TO SHAME.

LOOK UPON THESE WORKS AND MARVEL, MY LOVELY. ALL THIS IS MY WILL, MY WAY, AND ALL THIS CAN BE YOURS IF YOU WILL RULE AT MY SIDE!

IT'S LIKE SOMETHING OUT OF A NIGHTMARE! ALL THOSE THOUSANDS OF PEOPLE--AND YET NOT A SOUND! THEY'RE ALL MUTE!

SUSAN RICHARDS SUPPRESSES A SHUDDER AND CONFRONTS GAIUS...

YOU ARE A STRANGE EMPEROR, GAIUS TIBERIUS, TO WISH TO BE RULER OF A SILENT KINGDOM. IS THIS BY YOUR HAND?

WHEN FIRST I CAME HERE I GRANTED TO THESE PRIMITIVES THE ABILITY TO SPEAK NOBLE LATIN, JUST AS I HAVE GIVEN YOU UNDERSTANDING!

BUT, IT OFFENDED ME TO HEAR THEM GIBBER IN THEIR MONKEY VOICES, AND SO I SILENCED THEM.

MONSTROUS!

WHEN YOU FIRST CAME HERE, GAIUS? WHEN WAS THAT? HOW DID YOU CREATE ALL THIS?

SPQR

"SINCE YOU ARE TO BE M QUEEN IT IS ONLY FITTIN YOU SHOULD KNOW. ONC I WAS BUT FLAVIUS SCOLLIO, A SOLDIER I A DISTANT OUTPOST OF THE EMPEROR CALIGULA

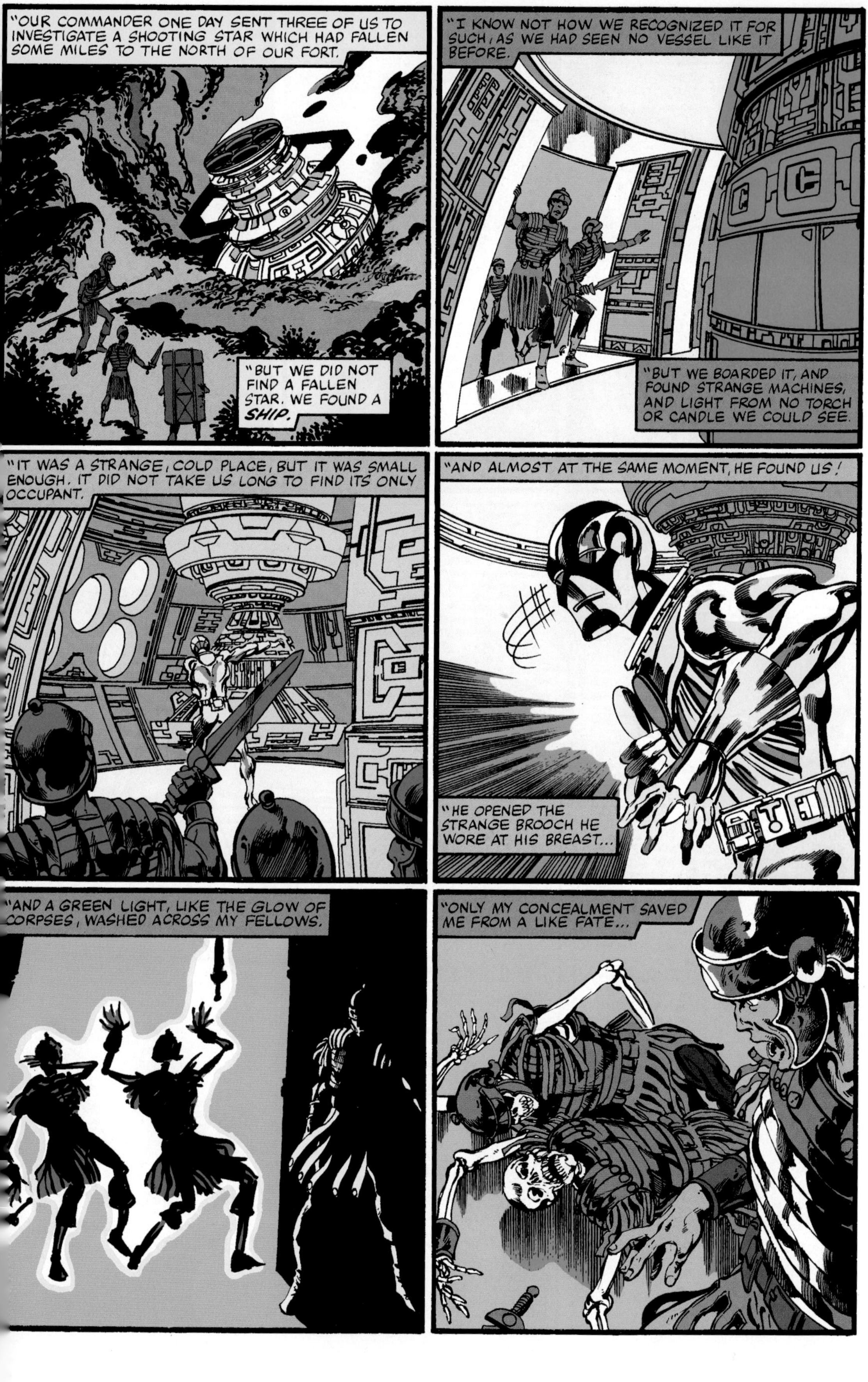
"OUR COMMANDER ONE DAY SENT THREE OF US TO INVESTIGATE A SHOOTING STAR WHICH HAD FALLEN SOME MILES TO THE NORTH OF OUR FORT.
"BUT WE DID NOT FIND A FALLEN STAR. WE FOUND A SHIP.
"I KNOW NOT HOW WE RECOGNIZED IT FOR SUCH, AS WE HAD SEEN NO VESSEL LIKE IT BEFORE.
"BUT WE BOARDED IT, AND FOUND STRANGE MACHINES, AND LIGHT FROM NO TORCH OR CANDLE WE COULD SEE.
"IT WAS A STRANGE, COLD PLACE, BUT IT WAS SMALL ENOUGH. IT DID NOT TAKE US LONG TO FIND ITS ONLY OCCUPANT.
"AND ALMOST AT THE SAME MOMENT, HE FOUND US!
"HE OPENED THE STRANGE BROOCH HE WORE AT HIS BREAST...
"AND A GREEN LIGHT, LIKE THE GLOW OF CORPSES, WASHED ACROSS MY FELLOWS.
"ONLY MY CONCEALMENT SAVED ME FROM A LIKE FATE...

"THEN, WHEN THE MAN-CREATURE CAME TO CHECK ON HIS HANDIWORK...

"...I SLEW HIM WITH A SWIFT JAB OF MY SWORD."

"REALIZING I HAD FOUND A WEAPON WHICH COULD GIVE ME DOMINION OVER THE EMPIRE ITSELF I DONNED HIS STRANGE ROBES AND AMULET.

"BUT WHEN I TRIED ON HIS HELMET, MY BRAIN WAS SET AFIRE WITH IMAGES AND THOUGHTS BEYOND HUMAN COMPREHENSION.

"FOR TIME OUT OF MEMORY I WRESTLED IN MY MIND WITH THE FLAMING HOSTS THAT MARCHED THERE."

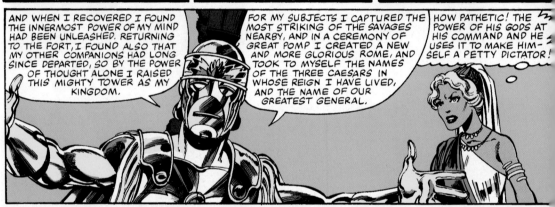

AND WHEN I RECOVERED I FOUND THE INNERMOST POWER OF MY MIND HAD BEEN UNLEASHED. RETURNING TO THE FORT, I FOUND ALSO THAT MY OTHER COMPANIONS HAD LONG SINCE DEPARTED, SO BY THE POWER OF THOUGHT ALONE I RAISED THIS MIGHTY TOWER AS MY KINGDOM.

FOR MY SUBJECTS I CAPTURED THE MOST STRIKING OF THE SAVAGES NEARBY, AND IN A CEREMONY OF GREAT POMP I CREATED A NEW AND MORE GLORIOUS ROME, AND TOOK TO MYSELF THE NAMES OF THE THREE CAESARS IN WHOSE REIGN I HAVE LIVED, AND THE NAME OF OUR GREATEST GENERAL.

HOW PATHETIC! THE POWER OF HIS GODS AT HIS COMMAND AND HE USES IT TO MAKE HIMSELF A PETTY DICTATOR!

BUT, THERE WAS ONE THING MISSING IN MY KINGDOM, MY LOVELY. A QUEEN TO REIGN BY MY SIDE. I WOULD AS SOON TAKE A GORILLA AS MY BRIDE AS ONE OF THESE SAVAGES, BUT NOW MY PATIENCE HAS BEEN REWARDED.

THE GODS HAVE SENT ME YOU!

THINK AGAIN, FLAVIUS. HERE YOU HAVE RECREATED NOT THE GLORY THAT WAS ROME, BUT ALL THAT WAS WRONG ABOUT IT--THE BLOODSHED AND INHUMANITY, THE BIGOTRY AND SLAVERY!

EVEN IF YOUR OFFER WAS IN ANY WAY APPEALING, I WOULD NOT ACCEPT IT.

DO NOT BE TOO QUICK TO DEFY ME, PRETTY ONE. I AM NOT SLOW TO SHOW MY CONTEMPT FOR THOSE BENEATH ME. BUT I WOULD AS SOON HAVE YOU WILLINGLY...

...AND AS AN INCENTIVE, LOOK YOU THERE...

20

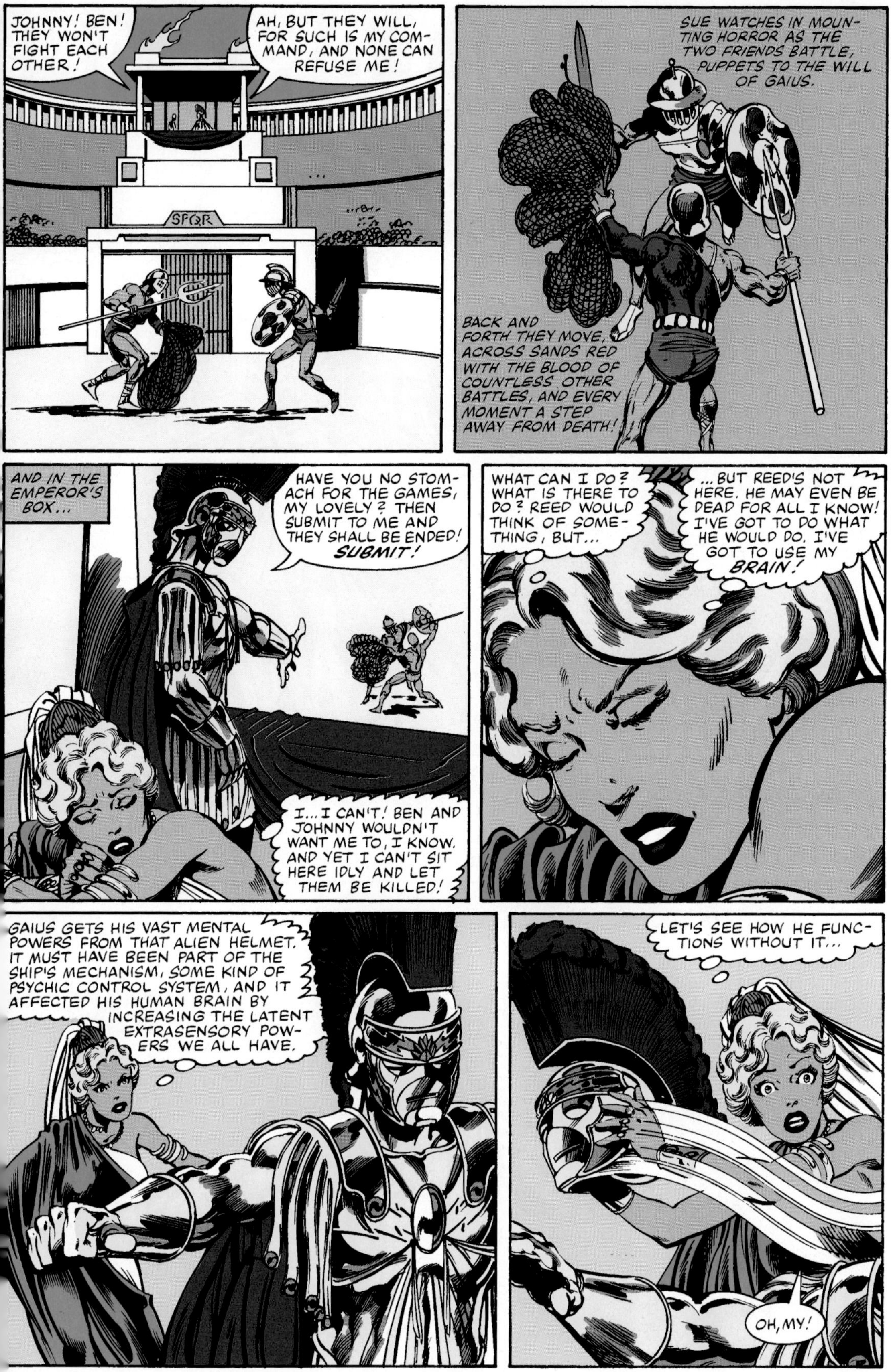

JOHNNY! BEN! THEY WON'T FIGHT EACH OTHER!
AH, BUT THEY WILL, FOR SUCH IS MY COMMAND, AND NONE CAN REFUSE ME!
SPQR
SUE WATCHES IN MOUNTING HORROR AS THE TWO FRIENDS BATTLE, PUPPETS TO THE WILL OF GAIUS.
BACK AND FORTH THEY MOVE, ACROSS SANDS RED WITH THE BLOOD OF COUNTLESS OTHER BATTLES, AND EVERY MOMENT A STEP AWAY FROM DEATH!
AND IN THE EMPEROR'S BOX...
HAVE YOU NO STOMACH FOR THE GAMES, MY LOVELY? THEN SUBMIT TO ME AND THEY SHALL BE ENDED! SUBMIT!
I... I CAN'T! BEN AND JOHNNY WOULDN'T WANT ME TO, I KNOW. AND YET I CAN'T SIT HERE IDLY AND LET THEM BE KILLED!
WHAT CAN I DO? WHAT IS THERE TO DO? REED WOULD THINK OF SOMETHING, BUT...
...BUT REED'S NOT HERE. HE MAY EVEN BE DEAD FOR ALL I KNOW! I'VE GOT TO DO WHAT HE WOULD DO. I'VE GOT TO USE MY BRAIN!
GAIUS GETS HIS VAST MENTAL POWERS FROM THAT ALIEN HELMET. IT MUST HAVE BEEN PART OF THE SHIP'S MECHANISM, SOME KIND OF PSYCHIC CONTROL SYSTEM, AND IT AFFECTED HIS HUMAN BRAIN BY INCREASING THE LATENT EXTRASENSORY POWERS WE ALL HAVE.
LET'S SEE HOW HE FUNCTIONS WITHOUT IT...
OH, MY!

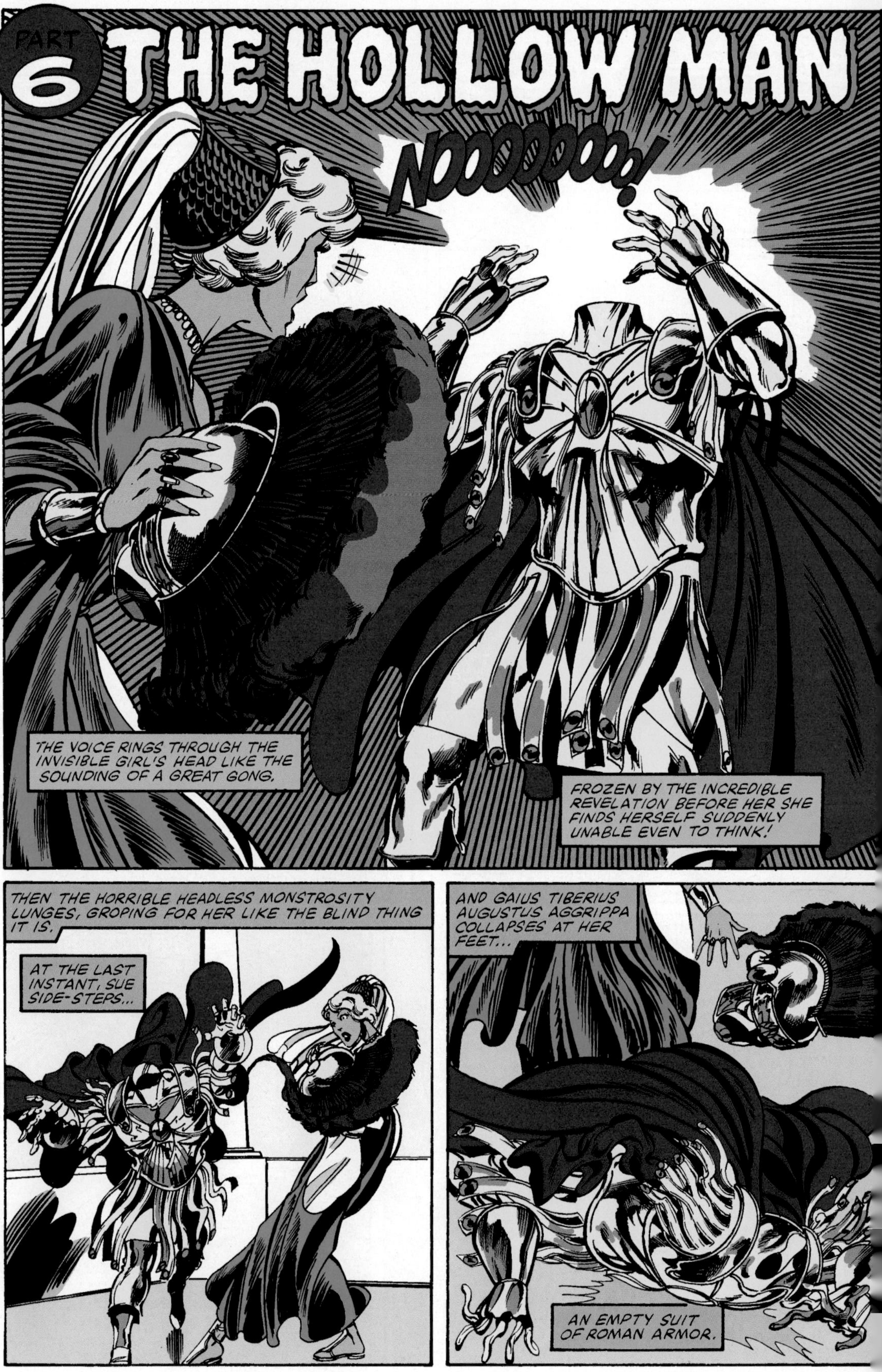
PART 6
THE HOLLOW MAN
NOOOOOOOO!
THE VOICE RINGS THROUGH THE INVISIBLE GIRL'S HEAD LIKE THE SOUNDING OF A GREAT GONG.
FROZEN BY THE INCREDIBLE REVELATION BEFORE HER SHE FINDS HERSELF SUDDENLY UNABLE EVEN TO THINK!
THEN THE HORRIBLE HEADLESS MONSTROSITY LUNGES, GROPING FOR HER LIKE THE BLIND THING IT IS.
AT THE LAST INSTANT, SUE SIDE-STEPS...
AND GAIUS TIBERIUS AUGUSTUS AGGRIPPA COLLAPSES AT HER FEET...
AN EMPTY SUIT OF ROMAN ARMOR.

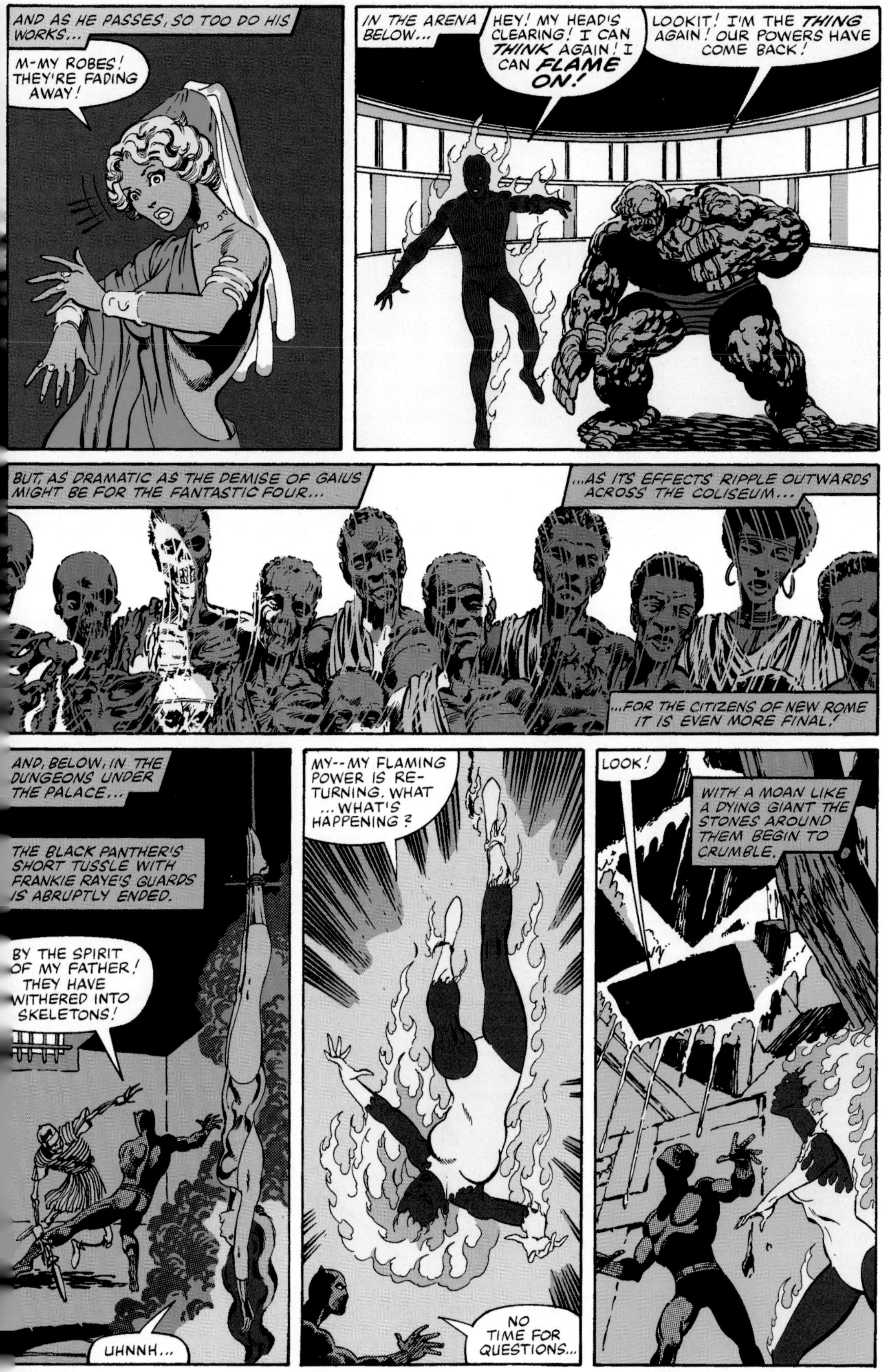
AND AS HE PASSES, SO TOO DO HIS WORKS...
M-MY ROBES! THEY'RE FADING AWAY!
IN THE ARENA BELOW...
HEY! MY HEAD'S CLEARING! I CAN THINK AGAIN! I CAN FLAME ON!
LOOKIT! I'M THE THING AGAIN! OUR POWERS HAVE COME BACK!
BUT, AS DRAMATIC AS THE DEMISE OF GAIUS MIGHT BE FOR THE FANTASTIC FOUR...
...AS ITS EFFECTS RIPPLE OUTWARDS ACROSS THE COLISEUM...
...FOR THE CITIZENS OF NEW ROME IT IS EVEN MORE FINAL!
AND, BELOW, IN THE DUNGEONS UNDER THE PALACE...
THE BLACK PANTHER'S SHORT TUSSLE WITH FRANKIE RAYE'S GUARDS IS ABRUPTLY ENDED.
BY THE SPIRIT OF MY FATHER! THEY HAVE WITHERED INTO SKELETONS!
UHNNH...
MY--MY FLAMING POWER IS RE-TURNING. WHAT ...WHAT'S HAPPENING?
NO TIME FOR QUESTIONS...
LOOK!
WITH A MOAN LIKE A DYING GIANT THE STONES AROUND THEM BEGIN TO CRUMBLE.

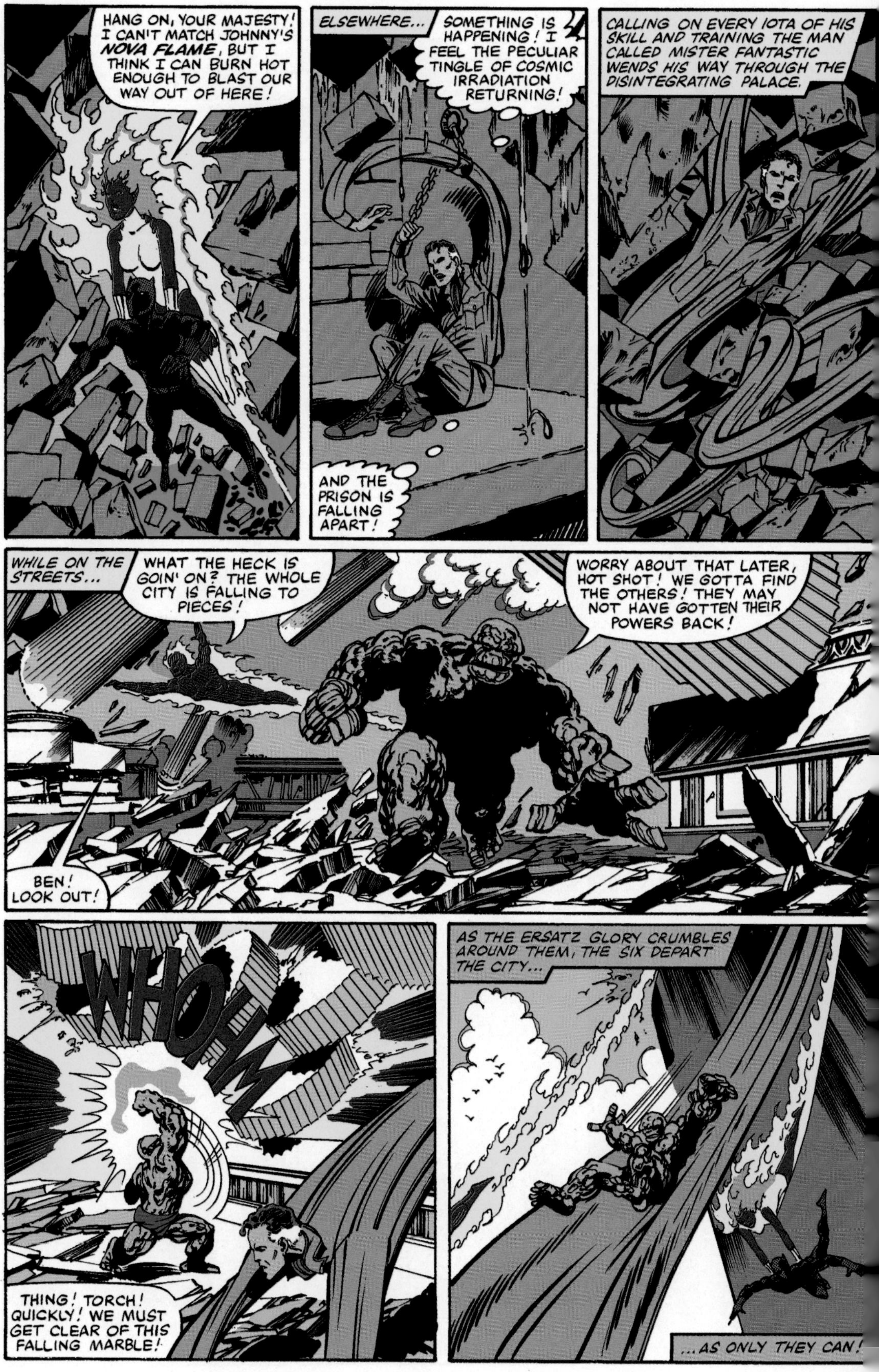
HANG ON, YOUR MAJESTY! I CAN'T MATCH JOHNNY'S NOVA FLAME, BUT I THINK I CAN BURN HOT ENOUGH TO BLAST OUR WAY OUT OF HERE!
ELSEWHERE...
SOMETHING IS HAPPENING! I FEEL THE PECULIAR TINGLE OF COSMIC IRRADIATION RETURNING!
AND THE PRISON IS FALLING APART!
CALLING ON EVERY IOTA OF HIS SKILL AND TRAINING THE MAN CALLED MISTER FANTASTIC WENDS HIS WAY THROUGH THE DISINTEGRATING PALACE.
WHILE ON THE STREETS...
WHAT THE HECK IS GOIN' ON? THE WHOLE CITY IS FALLING TO PIECES!
WORRY ABOUT THAT LATER, HOT SHOT! WE GOTTA FIND THE OTHERS! THEY MAY NOT HAVE GOTTEN THEIR POWERS BACK!
BEN! LOOK OUT!
WHOHM
THING! TORCH! QUICKLY! WE MUST GET CLEAR OF THIS FALLING MARBLE!
AS THE ERSATZ GLORY CRUMBLES AROUND THEM, THE SIX DEPART THE CITY...
...AS ONLY THEY CAN!

AND NOT A MOMENT TOO SOON!

WITH A BLAST TO RIVAL LEGENDARY **KRAKATOA** THE BLACK TOWER CEASES TO EXIST.

AND, WATCHING IN HORROR FROM A SAFE DISTANCE...

SUE! SUE! LET GO OF ME BEN! I HAVE TO GET TO HER! I HAVE TO FIND HER!

REED! NO! THAT WHOLE PLACE IS COMIN' DOWN! YOU'LL GET KILLED TOO!

NOT SO **PLURAL**, IF YOU PLEASE, MR. GRIMM!

S-SUSAN? SUE, YOU'RE HERE? YOU'RE ALL RIGHT? BUT, WHERE ARE YOU? WHY DON'T YOU SHOW YOUR-SELF?

I'M ABOUT SIX FEET TO YOUR LEFT, DARLING, AND IF YOU'LL LEND ME YOUR JACKET, I'LL BE HAPPY TO RESUME VISIBILITY.

MY JACKET? CERTAINLY... BUT I DON'T UNDERSTAND...

THE ROMAN COSTUME GAIUS PUT ME IN HAS GONE THE SAME ROUTE AS HIS CITY, REED. AND I DON'T THINK BEN AND T'CHALLA ARE QUITE THAT **INTIMATE** FRIENDS, DO YOU?

THAT'S BETTER! I GOT OUT OF THE CITY ON AN INVISI-BLE FORCE-FIELD SLIDE, BUT IT WAS A TERRIFIC STRAIN KEEPING MYSELF INVISI-BLE, TOO.

YOUR MODESTY AMAZES ME, SIS. ONE WOULD THINK YOU HAD SOMETHIN' **WORTH** HIDING!

THANKS FOR THE VOTE OF CONFIDENCE, BABY BROTHER!

AND, AFTER NOTES ARE COMPARED...

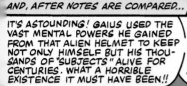

IT'S ASTOUNDING! GAIUS USED THE VAST MENTAL POWERS HE GAINED FROM THAT ALIEN HELMET TO KEEP NOT ONLY HIMSELF BUT HIS THOU-SANDS OF "SUBJECTS" ALIVE FOR CENTURIES. WHAT A HORRIBLE EXISTENCE IT MUST HAVE BEEN!!

AND HE MUST HAVE USED THE POWER OF THE AMULET TO DE-STROY THE RUSSIAN PARTY. THAT WOULD HAVE BEEN THE POWER SHIELD DETECTED. BUT HE DID NOT REALIZE THE GOLDEN SUIT HE TOOK FROM THE ALIEN WAS ALSO A PROTECTION AGAINST THE AMULET'S POWER SOURCE.

OVER NEARLY TWO THOU-SAND YEARS THE POWER MUST HAVE SLOWLY SEEPED INTO THE SUIT AND LITERALLY EATEN AWAY GAIUS'S PHYSI-CAL FORM! ALL THAT RE-MAINED WAS HIS AMPLIFIED INTELLECT. AND WHEN SUE REMOVED THE HELMET...

HE WENT BYE-BYE! AN' GOOD RIDDANCE, I SAY!

COME, MY FRIENDS. OUR TASK HERE IS ENDED. IT IS TIME TO GO HOME.

YEAH, I COULD USE ME A LITTLE NEW YORK SMOG AFTER ALL THIS CLEAN AIR.

I JUST WANT TO SLEEP FOR A WEEK!

TERRAX UNTAMED!

25

fantastic four # 242

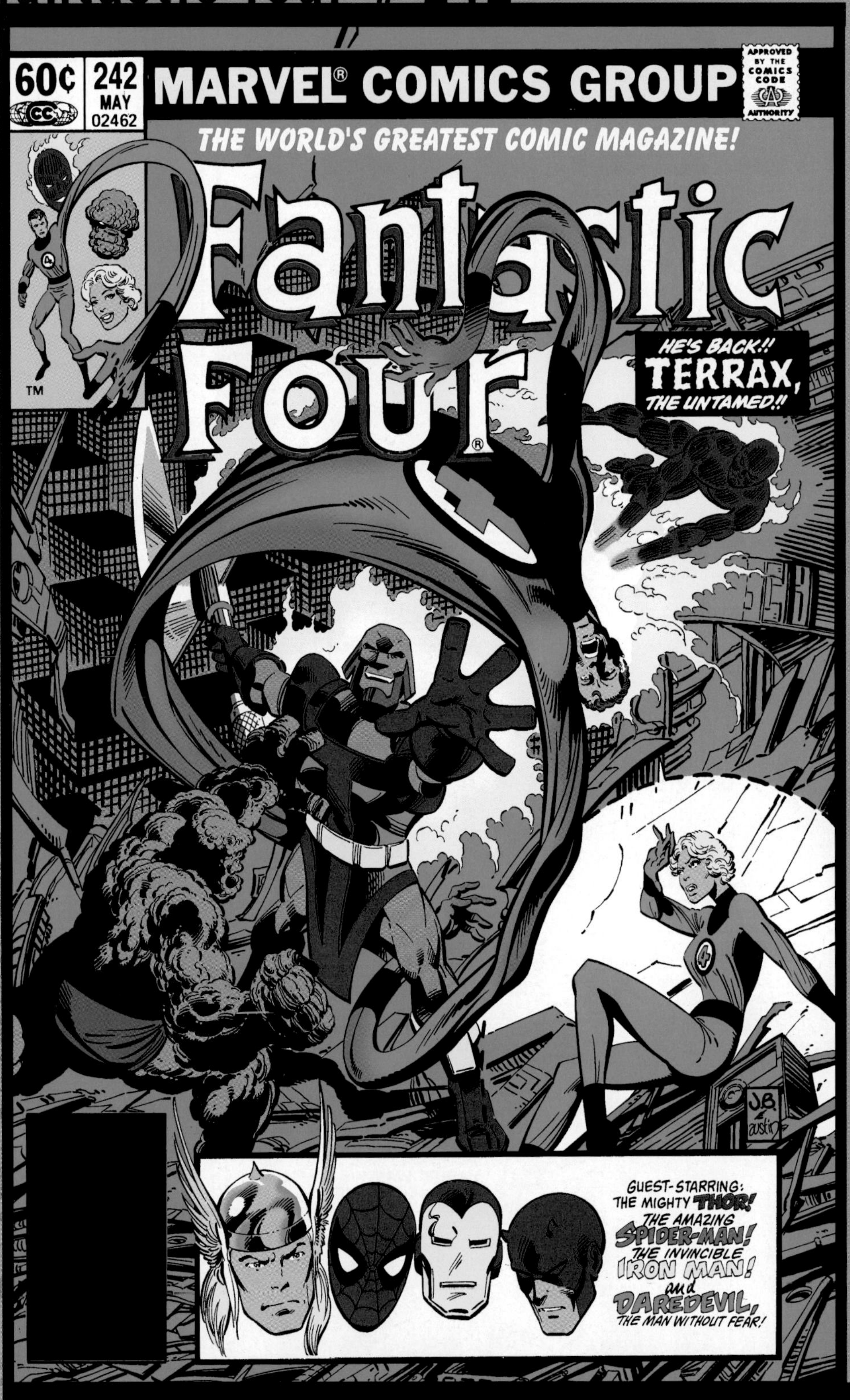
60¢
242
MAY
02462
MARVEL® COMICS GROUP
APPROVED BY THE COMICS CODE AUTHORITY
THE WORLD'S GREATEST COMIC MAGAZINE!
Fantastic Four®
HE'S BACK!!
TERRAX,
THE UNTAMED!!
GUEST-STARRING:
THE MIGHTY THOR!
THE AMAZING
SPIDER-MAN!
THE INVINCIBLE
IRON MAN!
and
DAREDEVIL,
THE MAN WITHOUT FEAR!

MAY 1982

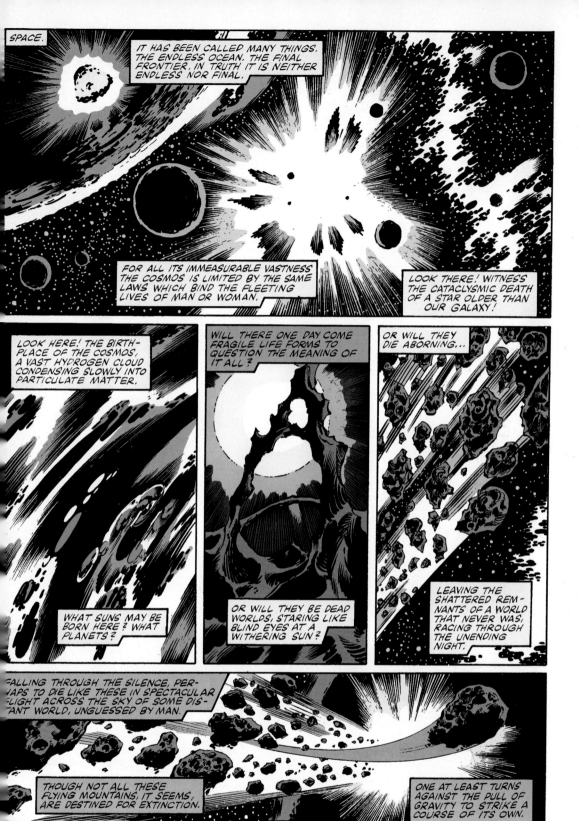

SPACE.

IT HAS BEEN CALLED MANY THINGS. THE ENDLESS OCEAN. THE FINAL FRONTIER. IN TRUTH IT IS NEITHER ENDLESS NOR FINAL.

FOR ALL ITS IMMEASURABLE VASTNESS THE COSMOS IS LIMITED BY THE SAME LAWS WHICH BIND THE FLEETING LIVES OF MAN OR WOMAN.

LOOK THERE.! WITNESS THE CATACLYSMIC DEATH OF A STAR OLDER THAN OUR GALAXY!

LOOK HERE.! THE BIRTH- PLACE OF THE COSMOS, A VAST HYDROGEN CLOUD CONDENSING SLOWLY INTO PARTICULATE MATTER.

WILL THERE ONE DAY COME FRAGILE LIFE FORMS TO QUESTION THE MEANING OF IT ALL?

OR WILL THEY DIE ABORNING...

WHAT SUNS MAY BE BORN HERE? WHAT PLANETS?

OR WILL THEY BE DEAD WORLDS, STARING LIKE BLIND EYES AT A WITHERING SUN?

LEAVING THE SHATTERED REM- NANTS OF A WORLD THAT NEVER WAS, RACING THROUGH THE UNENDING NIGHT.

FALLING THROUGH THE SILENCE, PER- HAPS TO DIE LIKE THESE IN SPECTACULAR FLIGHT ACROSS THE SKY OF SOME DIS- TANT WORLD, UNGUESSED BY MAN.

THOUGH NOT ALL THESE FLYING MOUNTAINS, IT SEEMS, ARE DESTINED FOR EXTINCTION.

ONE AT LEAST TURNS AGAINST THE PULL OF GRAVITY TO STRIKE A COURSE OF ITS OWN.

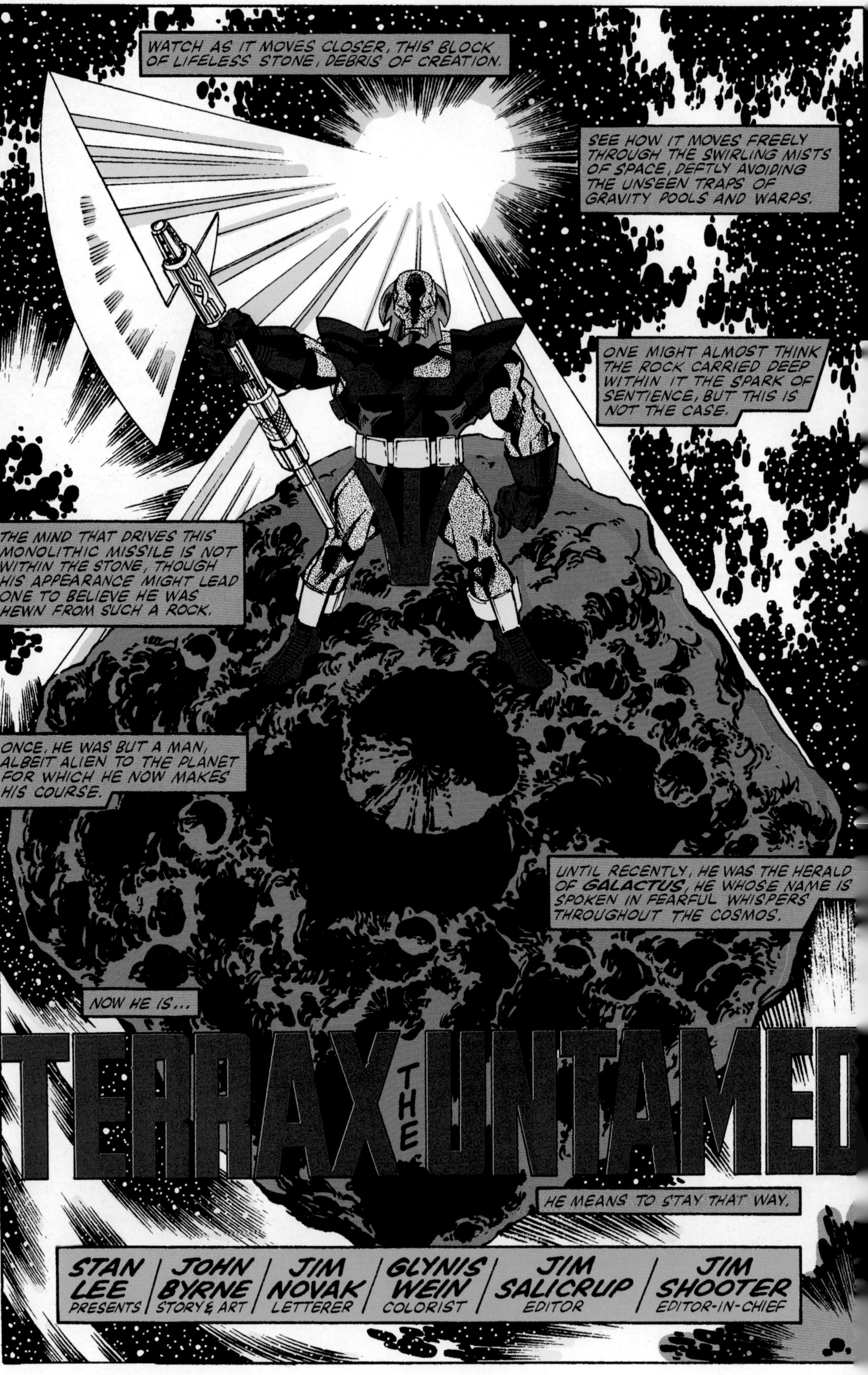
WATCH AS IT MOVES CLOSER, THIS BLOCK OF LIFELESS STONE, DEBRIS OF CREATION.
SEE HOW IT MOVES FREELY THROUGH THE SWIRLING MISTS OF SPACE, DEFTLY AVOIDING THE UNSEEN TRAPS OF GRAVITY POOLS AND WARPS.
ONE MIGHT ALMOST THINK THE ROCK CARRIED DEEP WITHIN IT THE SPARK OF SENTIENCE, BUT THIS IS NOT THE CASE.
THE MIND THAT DRIVES THIS MONOLITHIC MISSILE IS NOT WITHIN THE STONE, THOUGH HIS APPEARANCE MIGHT LEAD ONE TO BELIEVE HE WAS HEWN FROM SUCH A ROCK.
ONCE, HE WAS BUT A MAN, ALBEIT ALIEN TO THE PLANET FOR WHICH HE NOW MAKES HIS COURSE.
UNTIL RECENTLY, HE WAS THE HERALD OF GALACTUS, HE WHOSE NAME IS SPOKEN IN FEARFUL WHISPERS THROUGHOUT THE COSMOS.
NOW HE IS...
TERRAX THE UNTAMED
HE MEANS TO STAY THAT WAY.
STAN LEE PRESENTS
JOHN BYRNE STORY & ART
JIM NOVAK LETTERER
GLYNIS WEIN COLORIST
JIM SALICRUP EDITOR
JIM SHOOTER EDITOR-IN-CHIEF

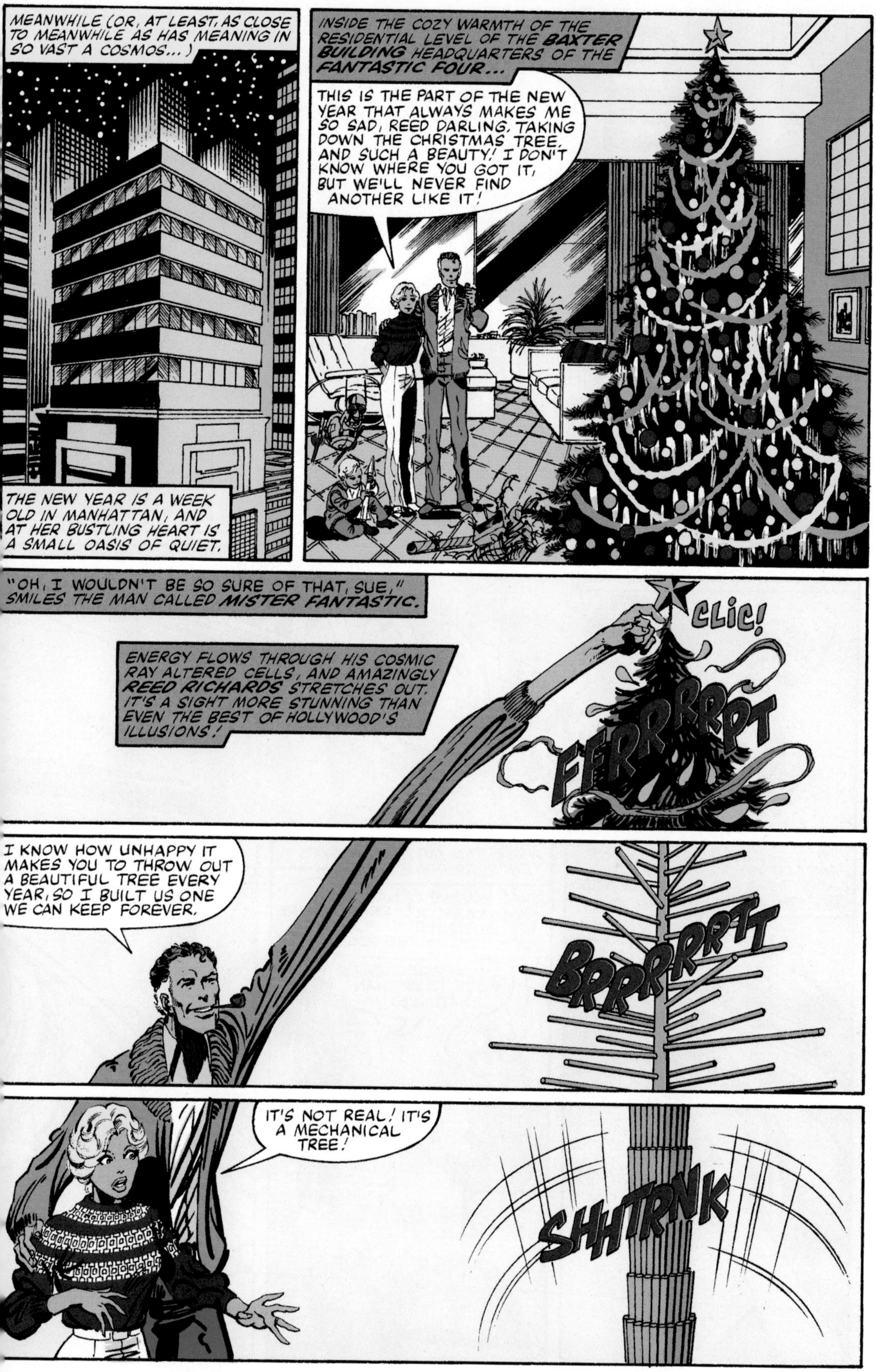
MEANWHILE (OR, AT LEAST, AS CLOSE TO MEANWHILE AS HAS MEANING IN SO VAST A COSMOS...)
THE NEW YEAR IS A WEEK OLD IN MANHATTAN, AND AT HER BUSTLING HEART IS A SMALL OASIS OF QUIET.
INSIDE THE COZY WARMTH OF THE RESIDENTIAL LEVEL OF THE BAXTER BUILDING HEADQUARTERS OF THE FANTASTIC FOUR...
THIS IS THE PART OF THE NEW YEAR THAT ALWAYS MAKES ME SO SAD, REED DARLING, TAKING DOWN THE CHRISTMAS TREE. AND SUCH A BEAUTY! I DON'T KNOW WHERE YOU GOT IT, BUT WE'LL NEVER FIND ANOTHER LIKE IT!
"OH, I WOULDN'T BE SO SURE OF THAT, SUE," SMILES THE MAN CALLED MISTER FANTASTIC.
ENERGY FLOWS THROUGH HIS COSMIC RAY ALTERED CELLS, AND AMAZINGLY REED RICHARDS STRETCHES OUT. IT'S A SIGHT MORE STUNNING THAN EVEN THE BEST OF HOLLYWOOD'S ILLUSIONS!
CLIC!
FFRRRRRPT
I KNOW HOW UNHAPPY IT MAKES YOU TO THROW OUT A BEAUTIFUL TREE EVERY YEAR, SO I BUILT US ONE WE CAN KEEP FOREVER.
BRRRRRRTT
IT'S NOT REAL! IT'S A MECHANICAL TREE!
SHHTRNK

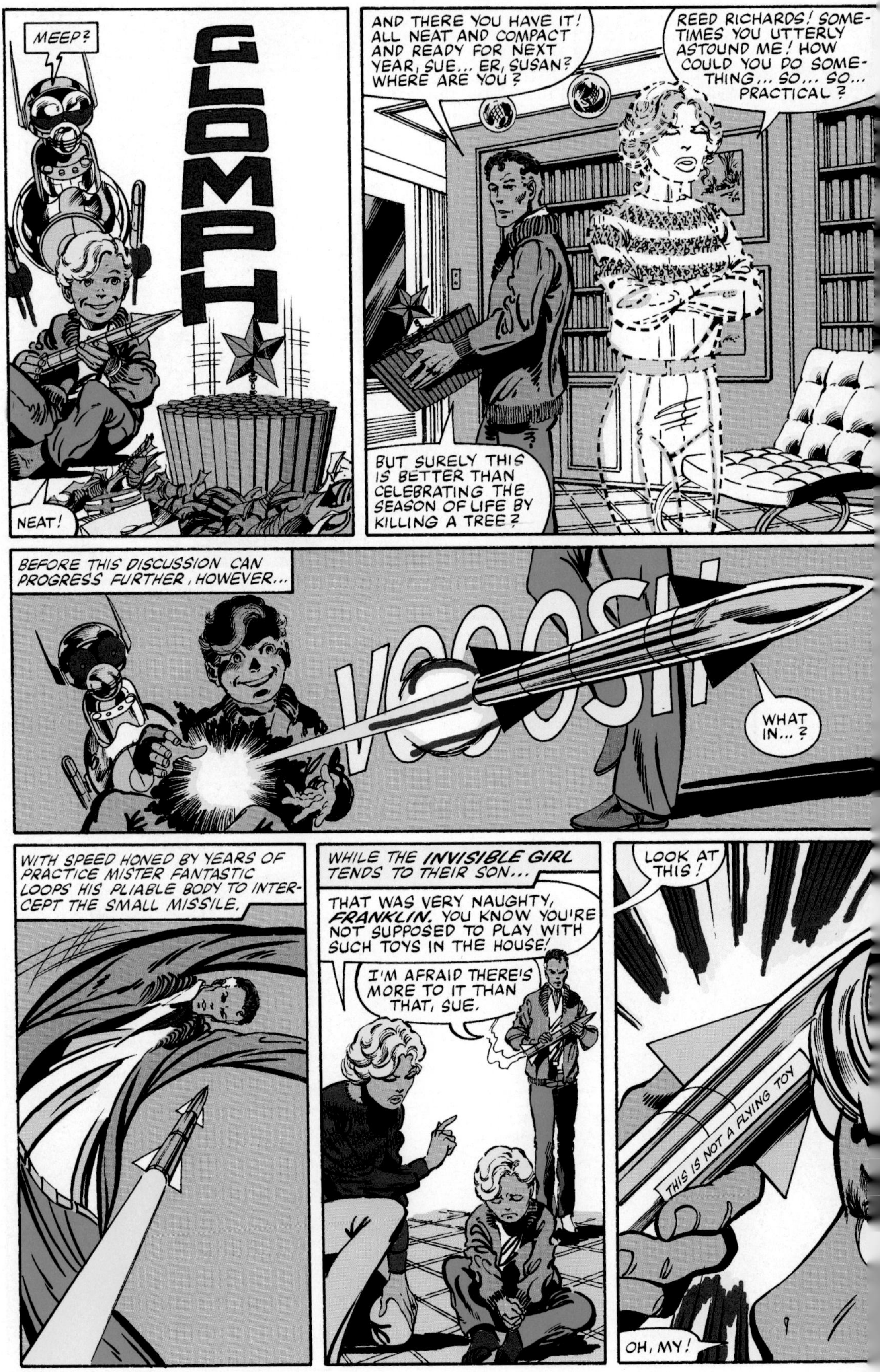
MEEP?
GLOMPH
NEAT!
AND THERE YOU HAVE IT! ALL NEAT AND COMPACT AND READY FOR NEXT YEAR, SUE... ER, SUSAN? WHERE ARE YOU?
REED RICHARDS! SOMETIMES YOU UTTERLY ASTOUND ME! HOW COULD YOU DO SOMETHING... SO... SO... PRACTICAL?
BUT SURELY THIS IS BETTER THAN CELEBRATING THE SEASON OF LIFE BY KILLING A TREE?
BEFORE THIS DISCUSSION CAN PROGRESS FURTHER, HOWEVER...
VOOOSH
WHAT IN...?
WITH SPEED HONED BY YEARS OF PRACTICE MISTER FANTASTIC LOOPS HIS PLIABLE BODY TO INTERCEPT THE SMALL MISSILE.
WHILE THE INVISIBLE GIRL TENDS TO THEIR SON...
THAT WAS VERY NAUGHTY, FRANKLIN. YOU KNOW YOU'RE NOT SUPPOSED TO PLAY WITH SUCH TOYS IN THE HOUSE!
I'M AFRAID THERE'S MORE TO IT THAN THAT, SUE.
LOOK AT THIS!
THIS IS NOT A FLYING TOY
OH, MY!

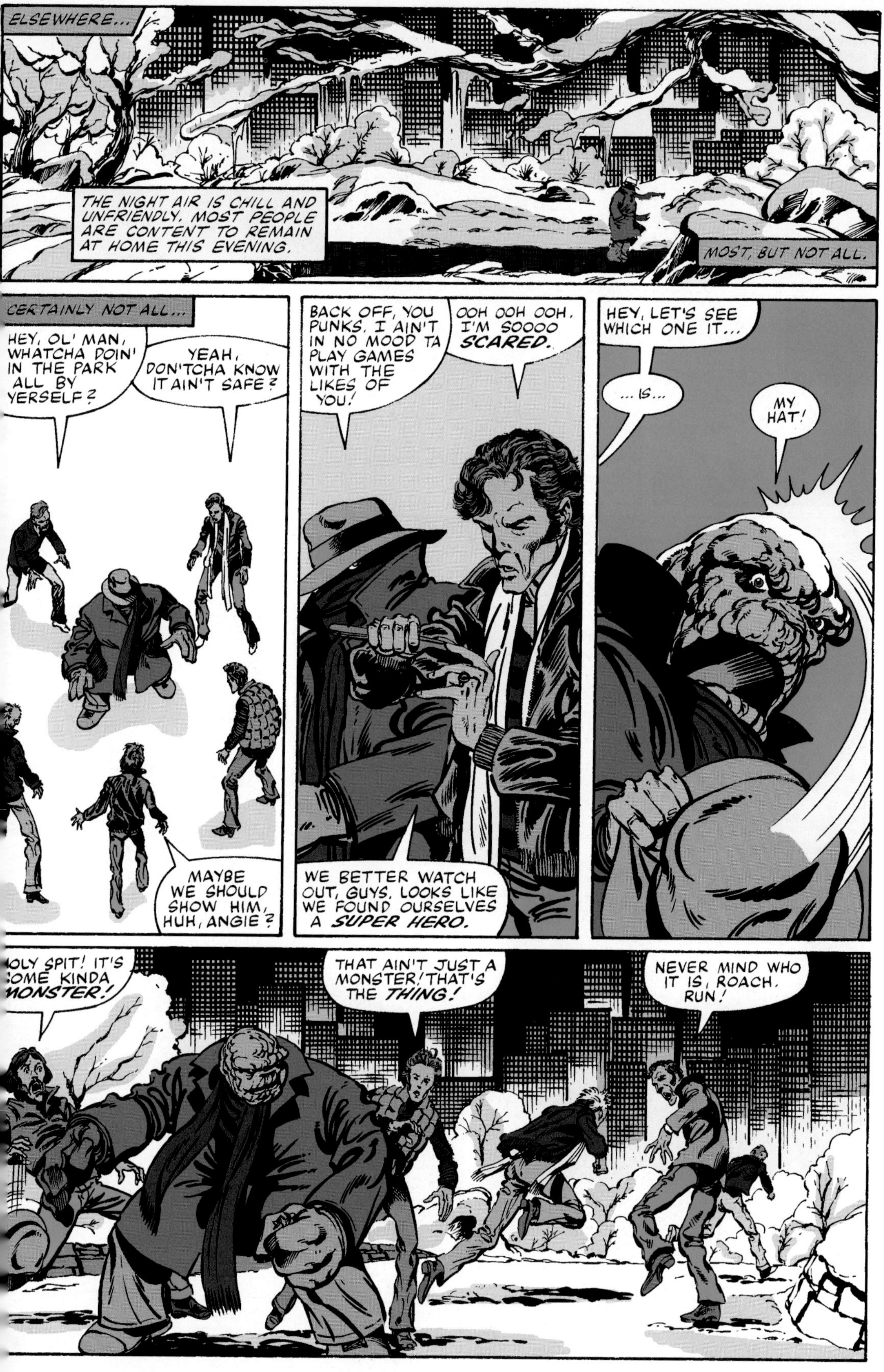
ELSEWHERE...
THE NIGHT AIR IS CHILL AND UNFRIENDLY. MOST PEOPLE ARE CONTENT TO REMAIN AT HOME THIS EVENING.
MOST, BUT NOT ALL.
CERTAINLY NOT ALL...
HEY, OL' MAN, WHATCHA DOIN' IN THE PARK ALL BY YERSELF?
YEAH, DON'TCHA KNOW IT AIN'T SAFE?
MAYBE WE SHOULD SHOW HIM, HUH, ANGIE?
BACK OFF, YOU PUNKS. I AIN'T IN NO MOOD TA PLAY GAMES WITH THE LIKES OF YOU!
OOH OOH OOH. I'M SOOOO SCARED.
WE BETTER WATCH OUT, GUYS. LOOKS LIKE WE FOUND OURSELVES A SUPER HERO.
HEY, LET'S SEE WHICH ONE IT...
...IS...
MY HAT!
OLY SPIT! IT'S OME KINDA MONSTER!
THAT AIN'T JUST A MONSTER! THAT'S THE THING!
NEVER MIND WHO IT IS, ROACH. RUN!

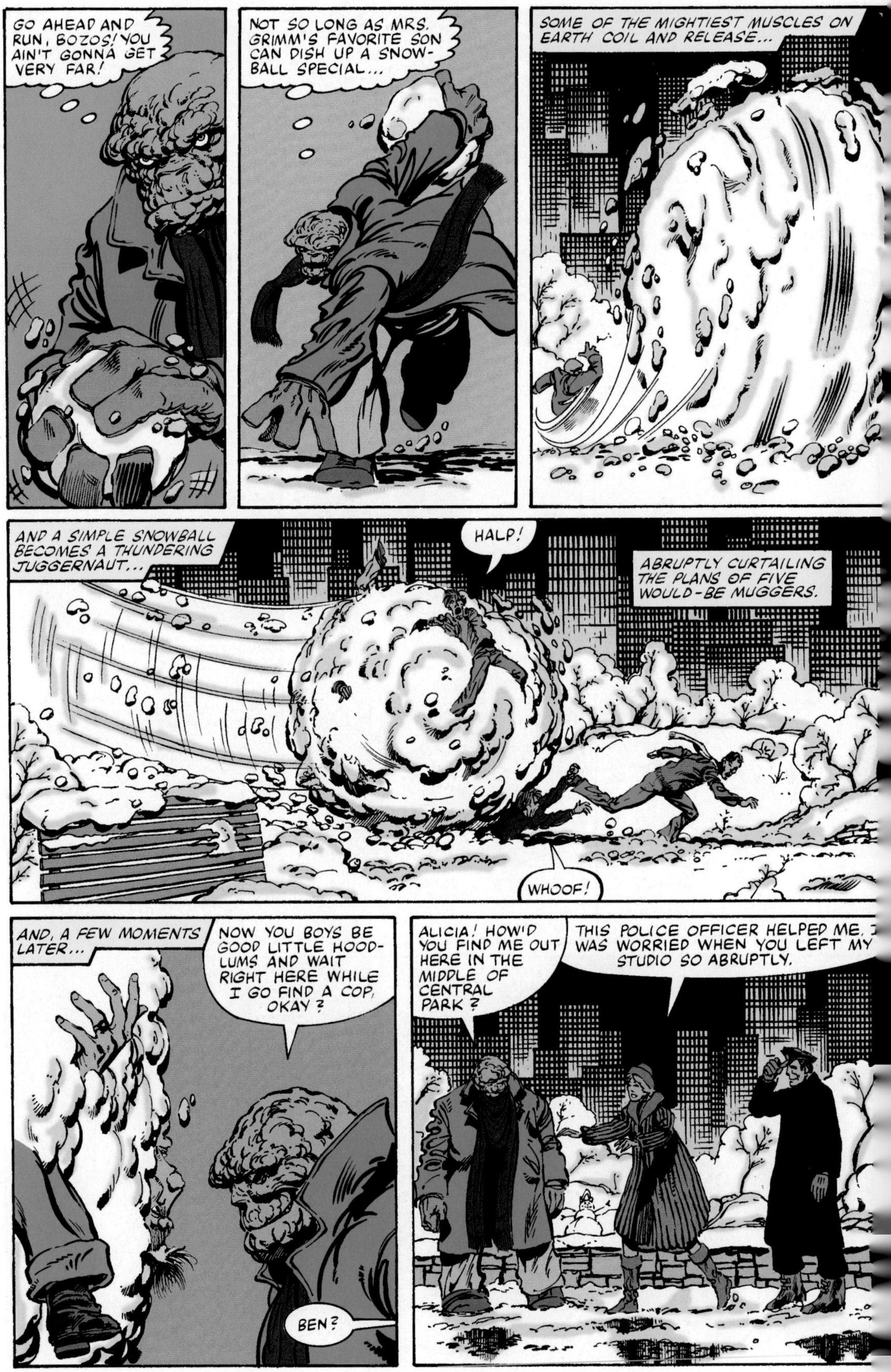
GO AHEAD AND RUN, BOZOS! YOU AIN'T GONNA GET VERY FAR!
NOT SO LONG AS MRS. GRIMM'S FAVORITE SON CAN DISH UP A SNOW-BALL SPECIAL...
SOME OF THE MIGHTIEST MUSCLES ON EARTH COIL AND RELEASE...
AND A SIMPLE SNOWBALL BECOMES A THUNDERING JUGGERNAUT...
HALP!
ABRUPTLY CURTAILING THE PLANS OF FIVE WOULD-BE MUGGERS.
WHOOF!
AND, A FEW MOMENTS LATER...
NOW YOU BOYS BE GOOD LITTLE HOOD-LUMS AND WAIT RIGHT HERE WHILE I GO FIND A COP, OKAY?
BEN?
ALICIA! HOW'D YOU FIND ME OUT HERE IN THE MIDDLE OF CENTRAL PARK?
THIS POLICE OFFICER HELPED ME. I WAS WORRIED WHEN YOU LEFT MY STUDIO SO ABRUPTLY.

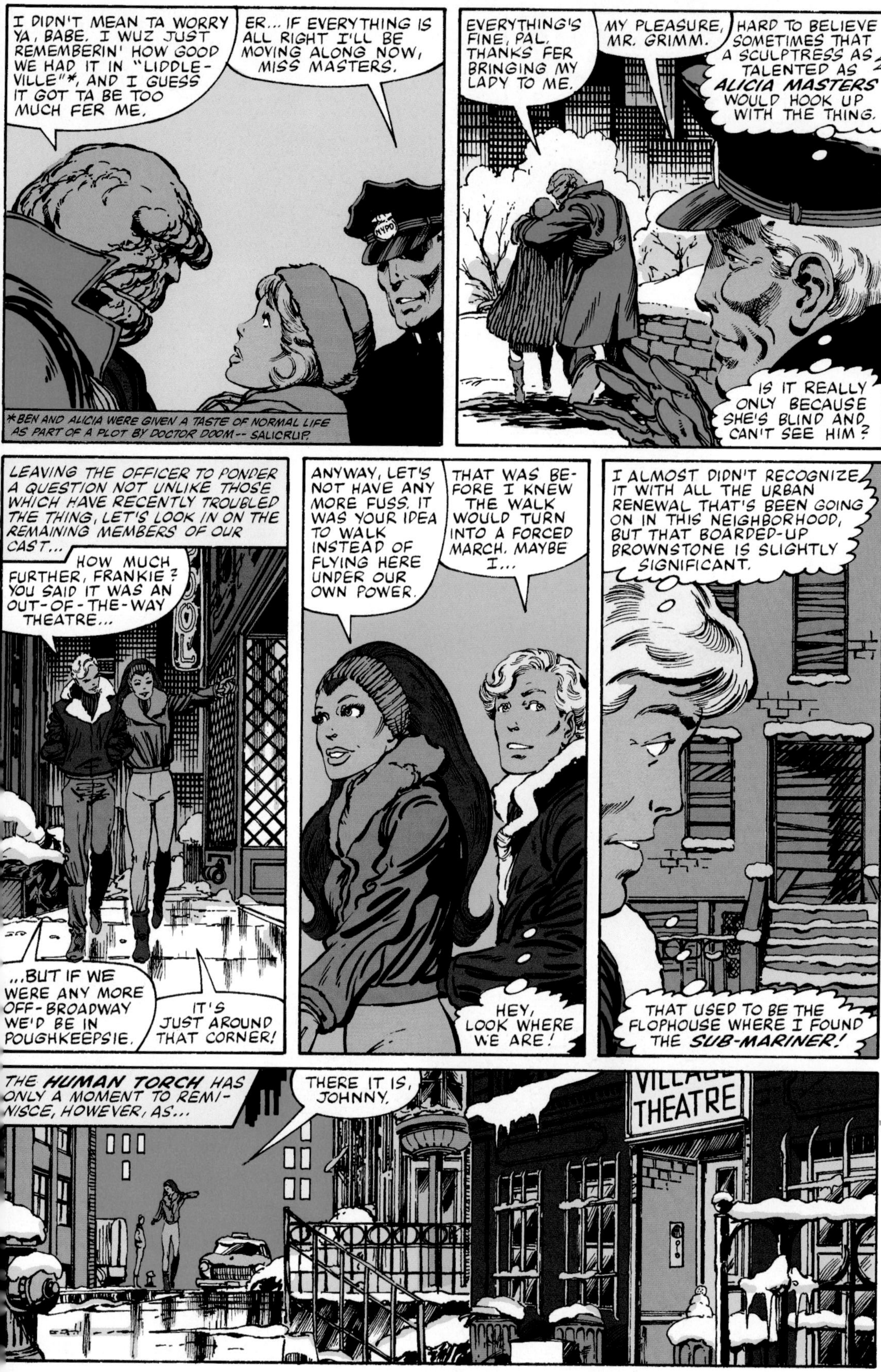
I DIDN'T MEAN TA WORRY YA, BABE. I WUZ JUST REMEMBERIN' HOW GOOD WE HAD IT IN "LIDDLE-VILLE"*, AND I GUESS IT GOT TA BE TOO MUCH FER ME.
ER... IF EVERYTHING IS ALL RIGHT I'LL BE MOVING ALONG NOW, MISS MASTERS.
*BEN AND ALICIA WERE GIVEN A TASTE OF NORMAL LIFE AS PART OF A PLOT BY DOCTOR DOOM-- SALICRUP.
EVERYTHING'S FINE, PAL. THANKS FER BRINGING MY LADY TO ME.
MY PLEASURE, MR. GRIMM.
HARD TO BELIEVE SOMETIMES THAT A SCULPTRESS AS TALENTED AS ALICIA MASTERS WOULD HOOK UP WITH THE THING.
IS IT REALLY ONLY BECAUSE SHE'S BLIND AND CAN'T SEE HIM?
LEAVING THE OFFICER TO PONDER A QUESTION NOT UNLIKE THOSE WHICH HAVE RECENTLY TROUBLED THE THING, LET'S LOOK IN ON THE REMAINING MEMBERS OF OUR CAST...
HOW MUCH FURTHER, FRANKIE? YOU SAID IT WAS AN OUT-OF-THE-WAY THEATRE...
...BUT IF WE WERE ANY MORE OFF-BROADWAY WE'D BE IN POUGHKEEPSIE.
IT'S JUST AROUND THAT CORNER!
ANYWAY, LET'S NOT HAVE ANY MORE FUSS. IT WAS YOUR IDEA TO WALK INSTEAD OF FLYING HERE UNDER OUR OWN POWER.
THAT WAS BEFORE I KNEW THE WALK WOULD TURN INTO A FORCED MARCH. MAYBE I...
HEY, LOOK WHERE WE ARE!
I ALMOST DIDN'T RECOGNIZE IT WITH ALL THE URBAN RENEWAL THAT'S BEEN GOING ON IN THIS NEIGHBORHOOD, BUT THAT BOARDED-UP BROWNSTONE IS SLIGHTLY SIGNIFICANT.
THAT USED TO BE THE FLOPHOUSE WHERE I FOUND THE SUB-MARINER!
THE HUMAN TORCH HAS ONLY A MOMENT TO REMINISCE, HOWEVER, AS...
THERE IT IS, JOHNNY.
THEATRE

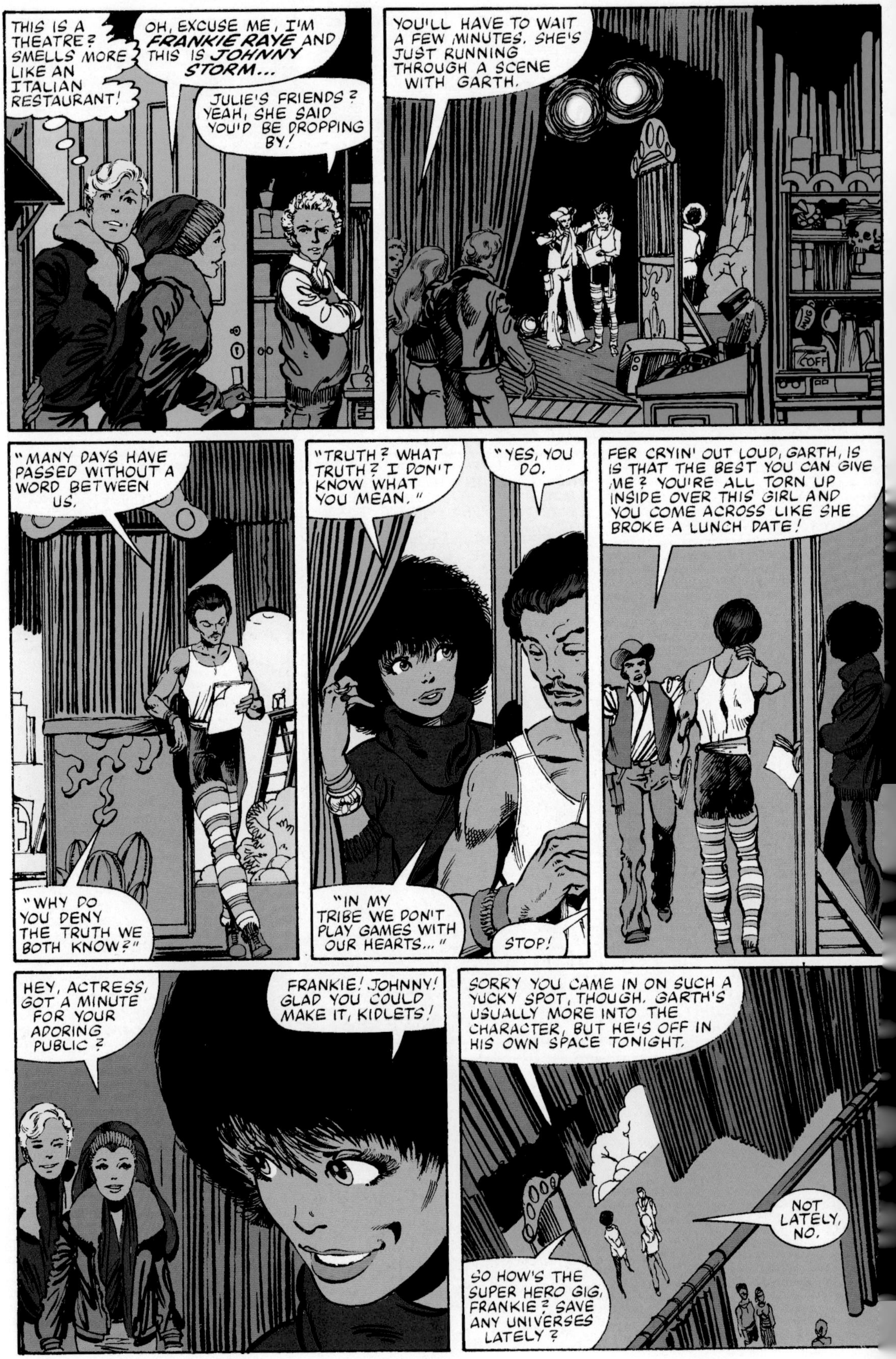
THIS IS A THEATRE? SMELLS MORE LIKE AN ITALIAN RESTAURANT!
OH, EXCUSE ME, I'M FRANKIE RAYE AND THIS IS JOHNNY STORM...
JULIE'S FRIENDS? YEAH, SHE SAID YOU'D BE DROPPING BY!
YOU'LL HAVE TO WAIT A FEW MINUTES. SHE'S JUST RUNNING THROUGH A SCENE WITH GARTH.
"MANY DAYS HAVE PASSED WITHOUT A WORD BETWEEN US.
"WHY DO YOU DENY THE TRUTH WE BOTH KNOW?"
"TRUTH? WHAT TRUTH? I DON'T KNOW WHAT YOU MEAN."
"YES, YOU DO.
"IN MY TRIBE WE DON'T PLAY GAMES WITH OUR HEARTS..."
STOP!
FER CRYIN' OUT LOUD, GARTH, IS IS THAT THE BEST YOU CAN GIVE ME? YOU'RE ALL TORN UP INSIDE OVER THIS GIRL AND YOU COME ACROSS LIKE SHE BROKE A LUNCH DATE!
HEY, ACTRESS, GOT A MINUTE FOR YOUR ADORING PUBLIC?
FRANKIE! JOHNNY! GLAD YOU COULD MAKE IT, KIDLETS!
SORRY YOU CAME IN ON SUCH A YUCKY SPOT, THOUGH. GARTH'S USUALLY MORE INTO THE CHARACTER, BUT HE'S OFF IN HIS OWN SPACE TONIGHT.
SO HOW'S THE SUPER HERO GIG, FRANKIE? SAVE ANY UNIVERSES LATELY?
NOT LATELY, NO.

NOTHING, HUH? WELL, THERE GOES MY *READER'S DIGEST* ARTICLE ON THE MOST FASCINATING PERSON I KNOW. I THOUGHT YOU SUPER-FOLK WERE ALWAYS OUT WORLD-SAVING.

SO DID I, BUT NO SUCH LUCK SO FAR.

JULIE, I HATE TO INTERRUPT, BUT WHY DOES THIS PLACE SMELL LIKE ABOUT FIVE TONS OF LASAGNA?

OH, THAT'S "MAMA LEON'S" NEXT DOOR. THEIR KITCHEN VENTS THROUGH HERE. WE'RE USED TO IT, BUT WE'VE HAD TO GIVE FREE TICKETS TO THEIR WHOLE STAFF TO BE SURE THEY'RE CLOSED OPENING NIGHT.

HEY YOU GUYS, LOOK AT THE SKY!

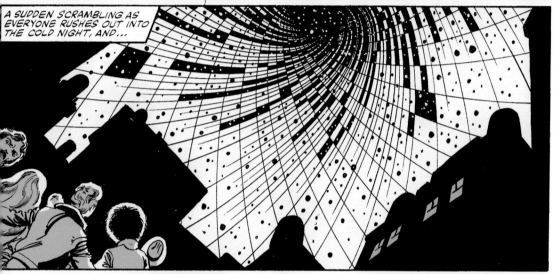

A SUDDEN SCRAMBLING AS EVERYONE RUSHES OUT INTO THE COLD NIGHT, AND...

JOHNNY, WHAT IS IT? I'VE NEVER SEEN ANYTHING LIKE IT!

ME NEITHER, BABE, BUT WHATEVER IT IS...

IT'S WORTH INVESTIGATING! **FLAME ON!**

HEY, WAIT FOR ME!

A BLINDING FLASH OF COMBUSTION AND TWO HUMAN TORCHES STREAK SKYWARD.

WHILE BACK AT THE BAXTER BUILDING...

REED, WHAT'S HAPPENING? ALL THE ALARMS SOUNDING AT ONCE...

THAT'S THE AUTOMATED MONITORS, DARLING. THE DEFENSE SCANNERS ARE REGISTERING AN ENORMOUS POWER-NEXUS OVER THE CITY. IT'S ALMOST AS IF THE LEADING EDGE OF A *SPACE WARP* WERE OPENING ABOVE NEW YORK.

OH, NO!

HEY, STRETCHO, IZZAT YOU MAKING ALL THEM CRAZY LIGHTS IN THE SKY, OR HAVE WE GOT OURSELVES ANOTHER MESS OF TROUBLE?

IT'S NOT MY DOING, BEN. STAND BY WHILST I FINISH CORRELATING THE DATA.

I'M AFRAID THIS MAY SIGNAL DIRE CONSE-QUENCES. THE INITIAL READINGS INDICATE THIS ENERGY IS NOT UNFAMILIAR...

BUT BEFORE MISTER FANTASTIC CAN CONTINUE...

EVERYBODY! *DUCK!*

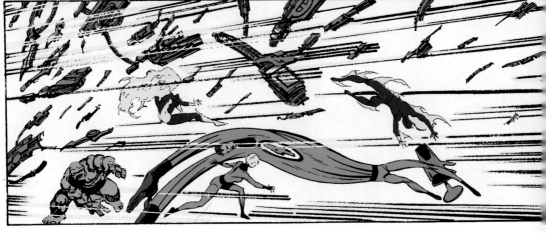

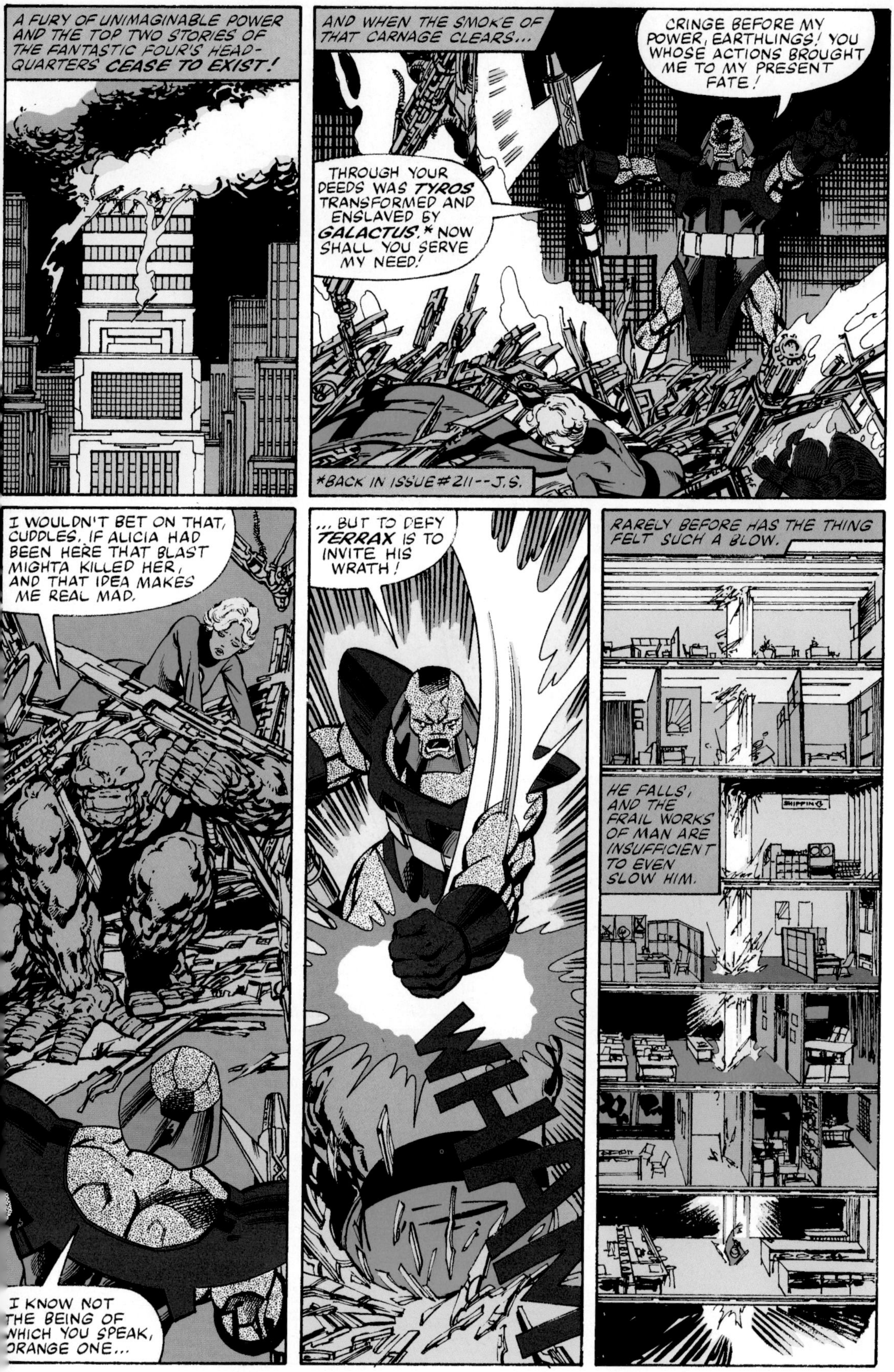
A FURY OF UNIMAGINABLE POWER AND THE TOP TWO STORIES OF THE FANTASTIC FOUR'S HEAD-QUARTERS CEASE TO EXIST!
AND WHEN THE SMOKE OF THAT CARNAGE CLEARS...
CRINGE BEFORE MY POWER, EARTHLINGS! YOU WHOSE ACTIONS BROUGHT ME TO MY PRESENT FATE!
THROUGH YOUR DEEDS WAS TYROS TRANSFORMED AND ENSLAVED BY GALACTUS!* NOW SHALL YOU SERVE MY NEED!
*BACK IN ISSUE #211--J.S.
I WOULDN'T BET ON THAT, CUDDLES. IF ALICIA HAD BEEN HERE THAT BLAST MIGHTA KILLED HER, AND THAT IDEA MAKES ME REAL MAD.
I KNOW NOT THE BEING OF WHICH YOU SPEAK, ORANGE ONE...
...BUT TO DEFY TERRAX IS TO INVITE HIS WRATH!
WHHAM
RARELY BEFORE HAS THE THING FELT SUCH A BLOW.
HE FALLS, AND THE FRAIL WORKS OF MAN ARE INSUFFICIENT TO EVEN SLOW HIM.
SHIPPING

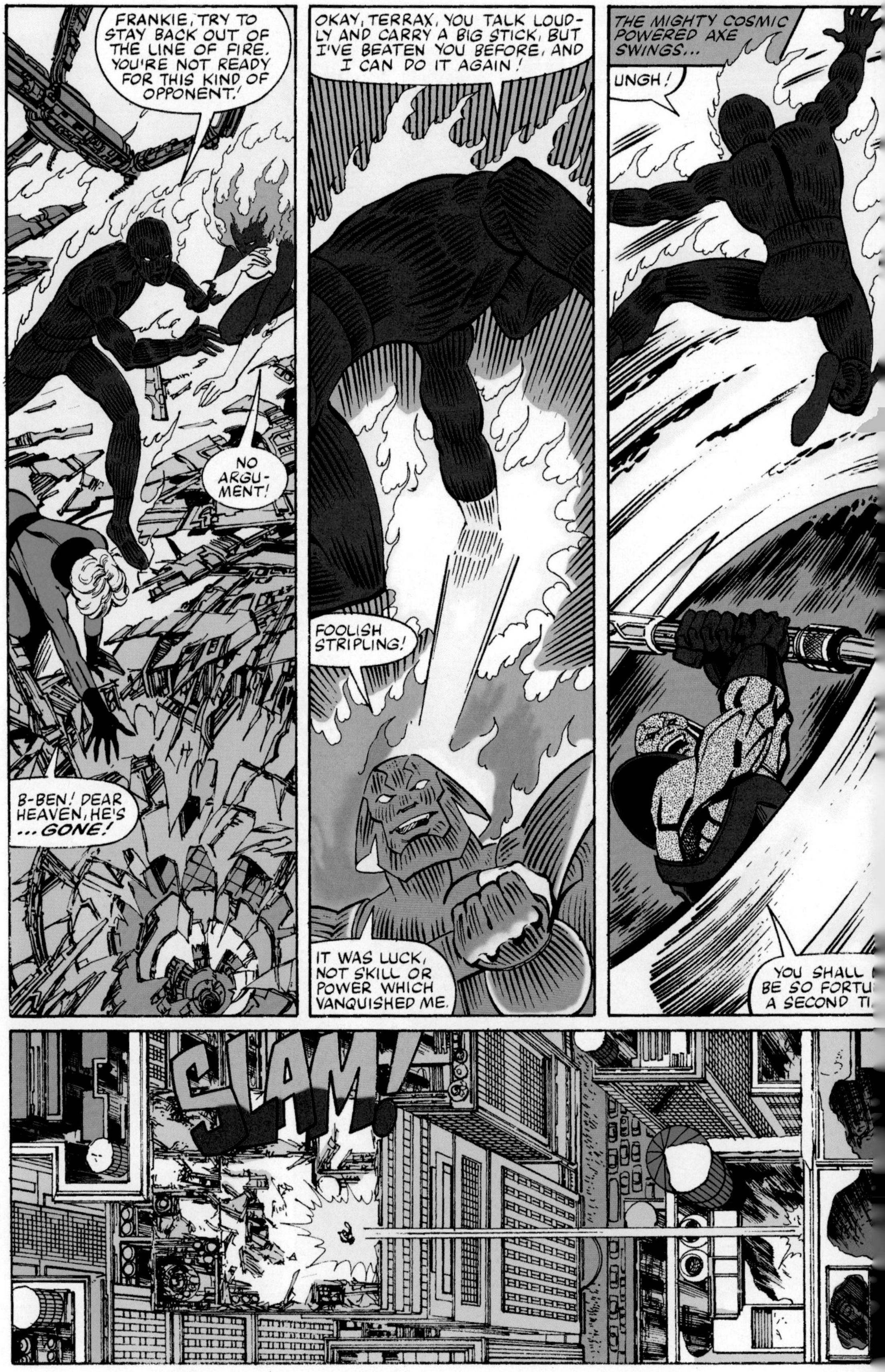
FRANKIE, TRY TO STAY BACK OUT OF THE LINE OF FIRE. YOU'RE NOT READY FOR THIS KIND OF OPPONENT!
NO ARGUMENT!
B-BEN! DEAR HEAVEN, HE'S ...GONE!
OKAY, TERRAX, YOU TALK LOUDLY AND CARRY A BIG STICK, BUT I'VE BEATEN YOU BEFORE, AND I CAN DO IT AGAIN!
FOOLISH STRIPLING!
IT WAS LUCK, NOT SKILL OR POWER WHICH VANQUISHED ME.
THE MIGHTY COSMIC POWERED AXE SWINGS...
UNGH!
YOU SHALL BE SO FORTU A SECOND TI
SLAM!

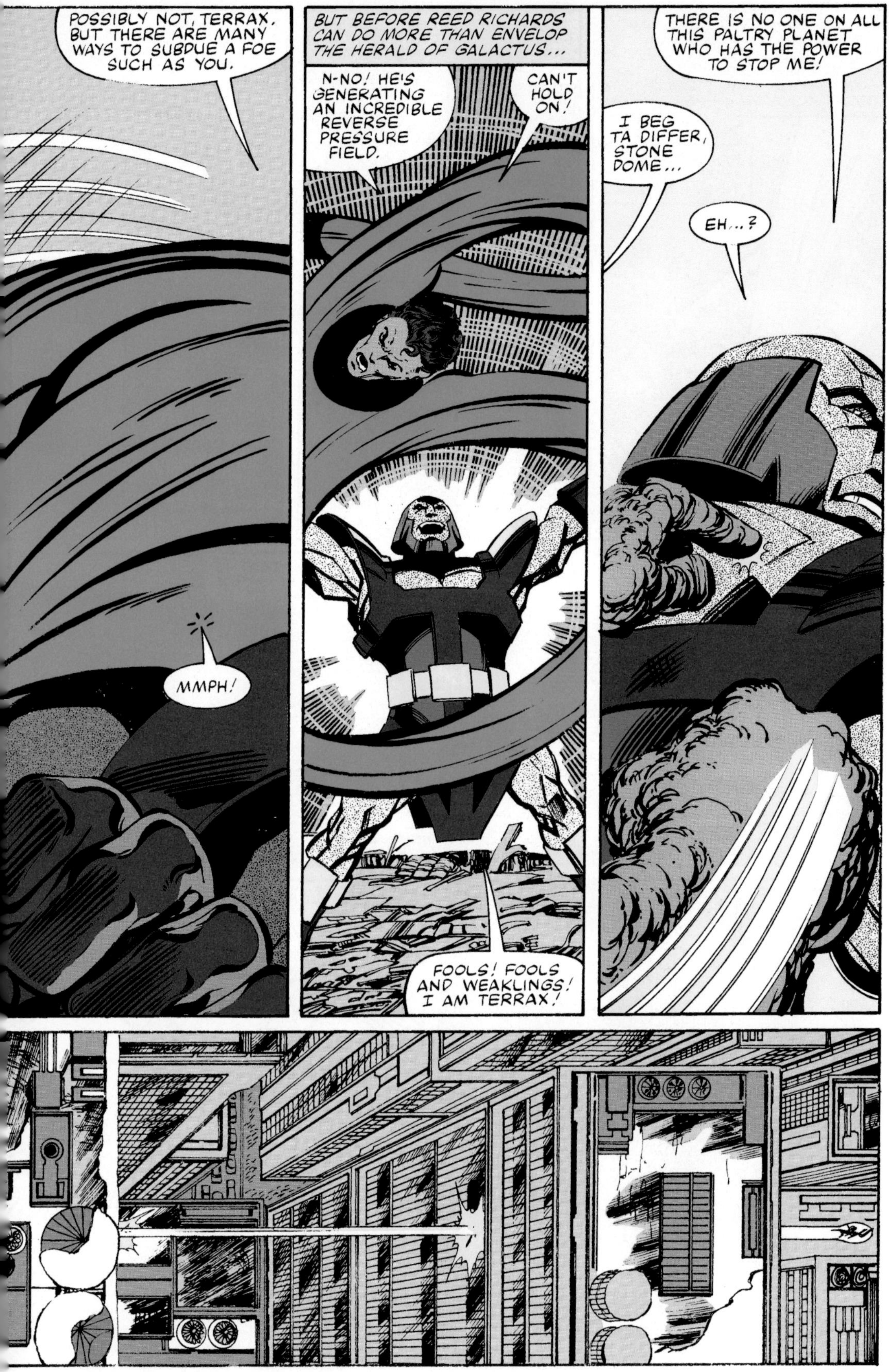
POSSIBLY NOT, TERRAX. BUT THERE ARE MANY WAYS TO SUBDUE A FOE SUCH AS YOU.
MMPH!
BUT BEFORE REED RICHARDS CAN DO MORE THAN ENVELOP THE HERALD OF GALACTUS...
N-NO! HE'S GENERATING AN INCREDIBLE REVERSE PRESSURE FIELD.
CAN'T HOLD ON!
FOOLS! FOOLS AND WEAKLINGS! I AM TERRAX!
THERE IS NO ONE ON ALL THIS PALTRY PLANET WHO HAS THE POWER TO STOP ME!
I BEG TA DIFFER, STONE DOME...
EH...?

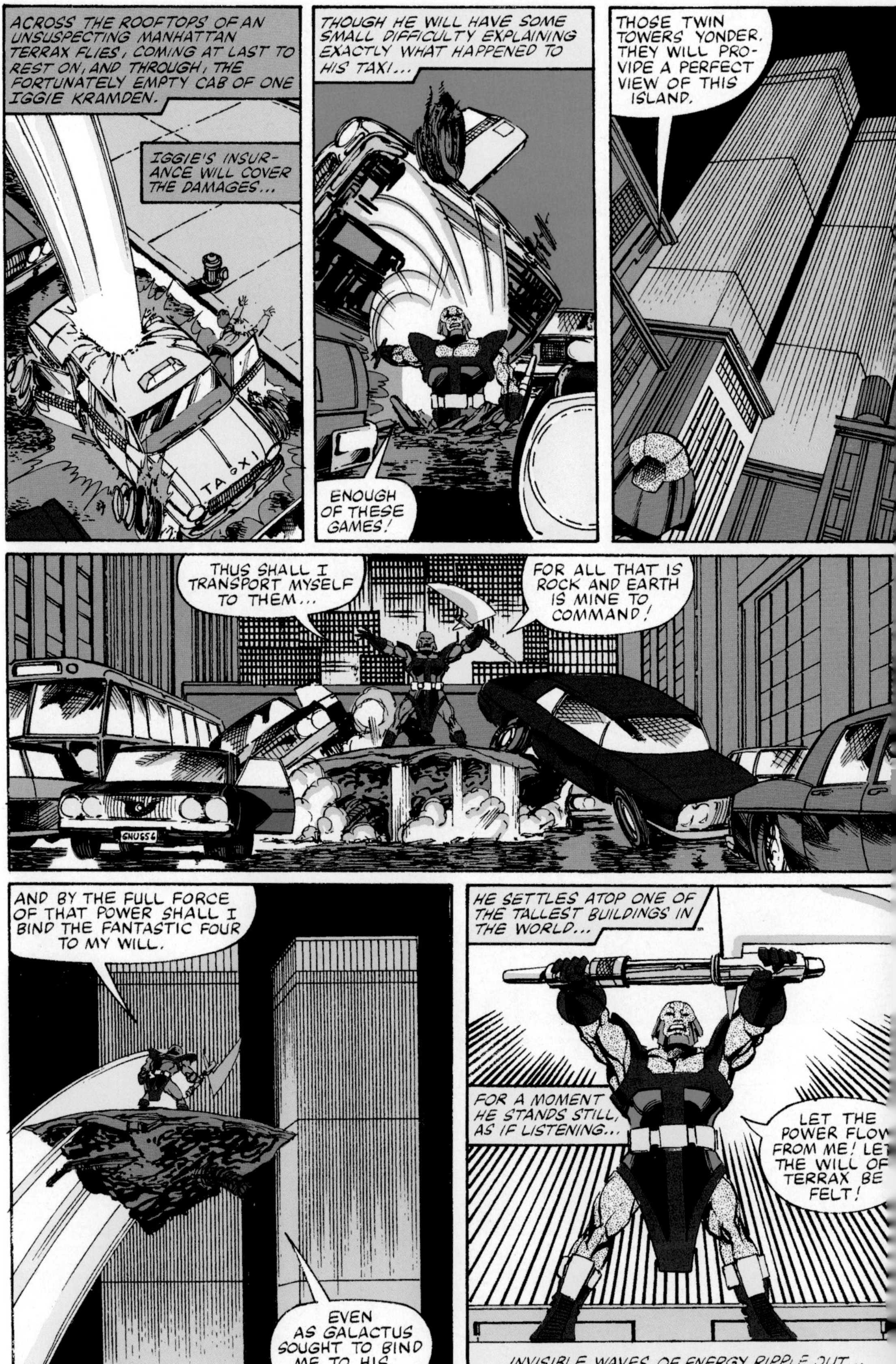
ACROSS THE ROOFTOPS OF AN UNSUSPECTING MANHATTAN TERRAX FLIES, COMING AT LAST TO REST ON, AND THROUGH, THE FORTUNATELY EMPTY CAB OF ONE IGGIE KRAMDEN.
IGGIE'S INSURANCE WILL COVER THE DAMAGES...
TAXI
THOUGH HE WILL HAVE SOME SMALL DIFFICULTY EXPLAINING EXACTLY WHAT HAPPENED TO HIS TAXI...
ENOUGH OF THESE GAMES!
THOSE TWIN TOWERS YONDER. THEY WILL PROVIDE A PERFECT VIEW OF THIS ISLAND.
THUS SHALL I TRANSPORT MYSELF TO THEM...
FOR ALL THAT IS ROCK AND EARTH IS MINE TO COMMAND!
GNU656
AND BY THE FULL FORCE OF THAT POWER SHALL I BIND THE FANTASTIC FOUR TO MY WILL.
EVEN AS GALACTUS SOUGHT TO BIND ME TO HIS.
HE SETTLES ATOP ONE OF THE TALLEST BUILDINGS IN THE WORLD...
FOR A MOMENT HE STANDS STILL, AS IF LISTENING...
LET THE POWER FLOW FROM ME! LET THE WILL OF TERRAX BE FELT!
INVISIBLE WAVES OF ENERGY RIPPLE OUT...

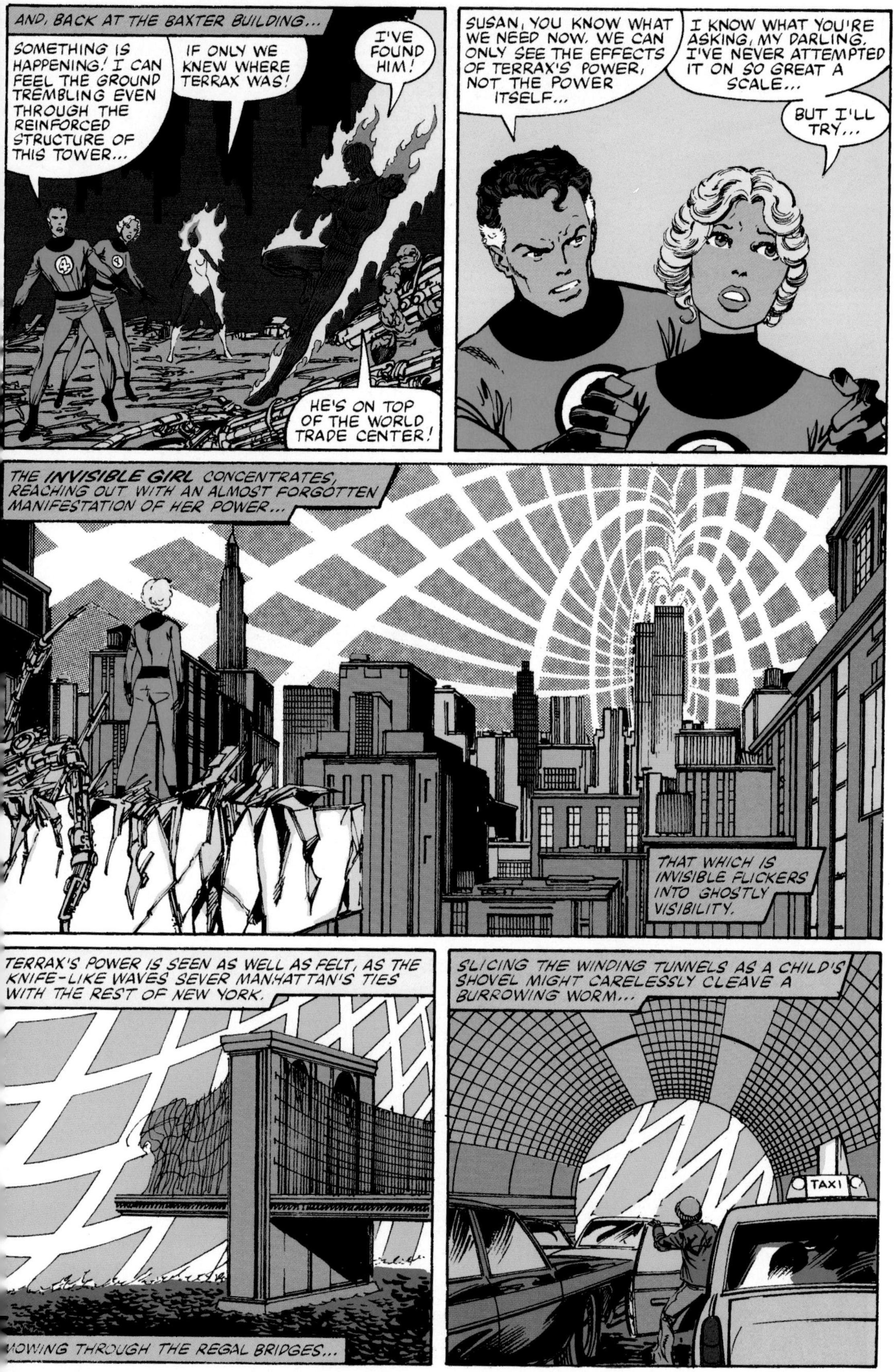
AND, BACK AT THE BAXTER BUILDING...
SOMETHING IS HAPPENING! I CAN FEEL THE GROUND TREMBLING EVEN THROUGH THE REINFORCED STRUCTURE OF THIS TOWER...
IF ONLY WE KNEW WHERE TERRAX WAS!
I'VE FOUND HIM!
HE'S ON TOP OF THE WORLD TRADE CENTER!
SUSAN, YOU KNOW WHAT WE NEED NOW. WE CAN ONLY SEE THE EFFECTS OF TERRAX'S POWER, NOT THE POWER ITSELF...
I KNOW WHAT YOU'RE ASKING, MY DARLING. I'VE NEVER ATTEMPTED IT ON SO GREAT A SCALE...
BUT I'LL TRY...
THE INVISIBLE GIRL CONCENTRATES, REACHING OUT WITH AN ALMOST FORGOTTEN MANIFESTATION OF HER POWER...
THAT WHICH IS INVISIBLE FLICKERS INTO GHOSTLY VISIBILITY.
TERRAX'S POWER IS SEEN AS WELL AS FELT, AS THE KNIFE-LIKE WAVES SEVER MANHATTAN'S TIES WITH THE REST OF NEW YORK.
MOWING THROUGH THE REGAL BRIDGES...
SLICING THE WINDING TUNNELS AS A CHILD'S SHOVEL MIGHT CARELESSLY CLEAVE A BURROWING WORM...
TAXI

AND TERRIBLE AS THE DAMAGE IS TO THE BRIDGES...

...IMAGINE, IF YOU WILL, THE CONDITION IN TUNNELS SUDDENLY OPENED TO THE RIVERS ABOVE!

ELSEWHERE...

SOME MILES AWAY IN THIS UNASSUMING HOUSE IN QUEENS...

MAY PARKER IS SPENDING A QUIET AFTERNOON WITH HER FAVORITE NEPHEW...

THAT WAS A LOT OF FUN, PETER. WE REALLY MUST DO IT MORE OFTEN.

I DON'T KNOW IF I'M UP TO IT, AUNT MAY. IT'S BEEN A LONG TIME SINCE I BUILT A SNOWMAN THAT BIG.

LET'S HOPE HE LASTS AT LEAST UNTIL...

ARGH!

MY SPIDER-SENSE... SUCH A PAINFUL SIGNAL!

PETER! WHAT ON EARTH...? ARE YOU ALL RIGHT?

I-I'M FINE, FINE, TOO ...TOO MUCH FRUITCAKE, NEED... AIR...

GOTTA GET OUTSIDE, MUST BE SOME HORRENDOUS MENACE ATTACKING.

CAN'T IMAGINE HOW IT COULD HAVE TRACKED ME HERE, BUT I CAN'T RISK ENDANGERING AUNT MAY... OR HAVING HER FIND OUT I'M SPIDER-MAN.

BUT AS PETER PARKER STAGGERS ONTO THE PORCH...

HE DISCOVERS THE REASON FOR HIS SUDDEN DANGER-ALERT IS NOT A DIRECT THREAT TO HIM...

HOLY...!! THE WHOLE ISLAND OF MANHATTAN HAS BEEN COVERED BY A GLOWING COCOON!

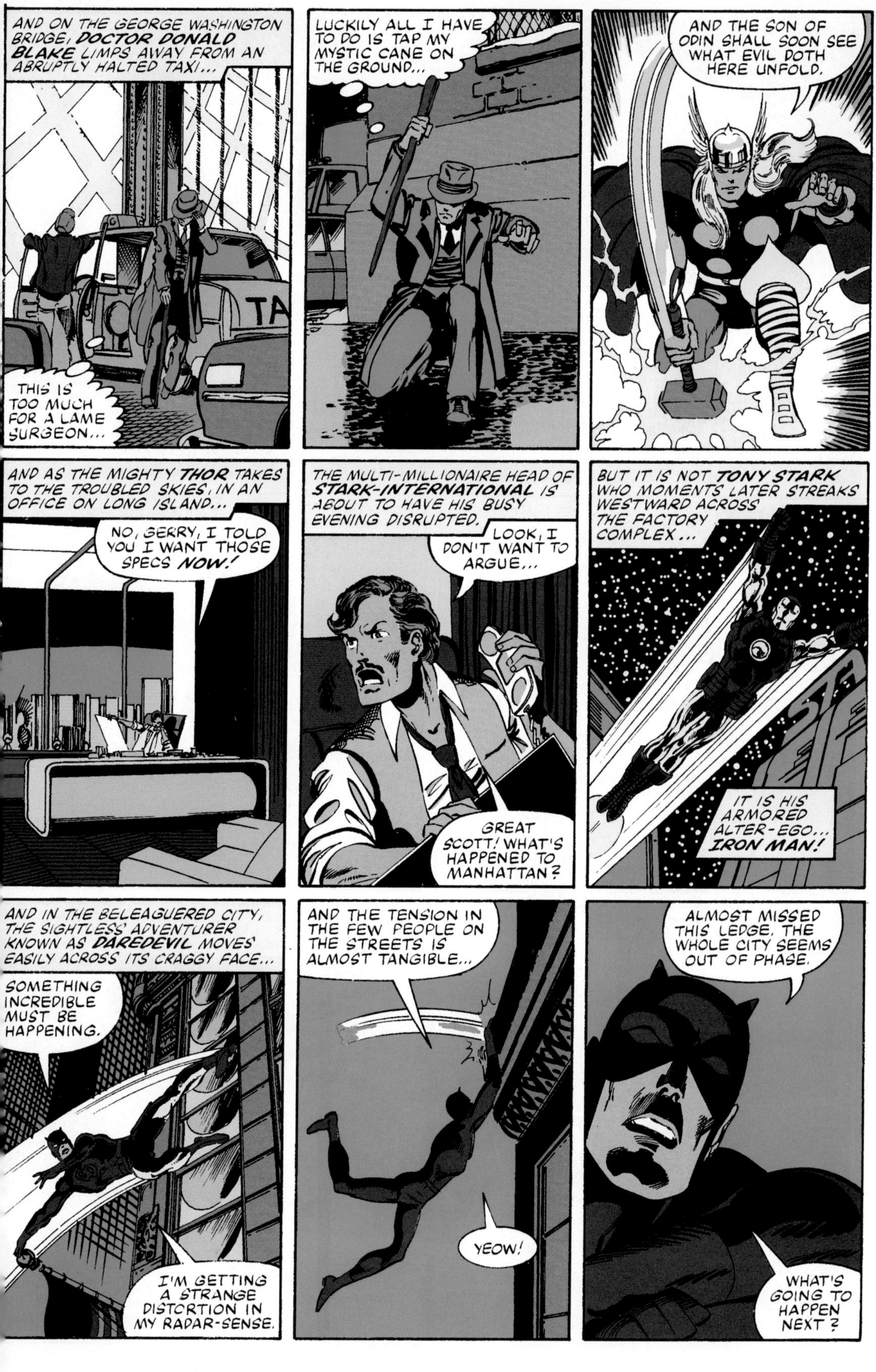

AND ON THE GEORGE WASHINGTON BRIDGE, DOCTOR DONALD BLAKE LIMPS AWAY FROM AN ABRUPTLY HALTED TAXI...
THIS IS TOO MUCH FOR A LAME SURGEON...
TA
LUCKILY ALL I HAVE TO DO IS TAP MY MYSTIC CANE ON THE GROUND...
AND THE SON OF ODIN SHALL SOON SEE WHAT EVIL DOTH HERE UNFOLD.
AND AS THE MIGHTY THOR TAKES TO THE TROUBLED SKIES, IN AN OFFICE ON LONG ISLAND...
NO, GERRY, I TOLD YOU I WANT THOSE SPECS NOW!
THE MULTI-MILLIONAIRE HEAD OF STARK-INTERNATIONAL IS ABOUT TO HAVE HIS BUSY EVENING DISRUPTED.
LOOK, I DON'T WANT TO ARGUE...
GREAT SCOTT! WHAT'S HAPPENED TO MANHATTAN?
BUT IT IS NOT TONY STARK WHO MOMENTS LATER STREAKS WESTWARD ACROSS THE FACTORY COMPLEX...
IT IS HIS ARMORED ALTER-EGO... IRON MAN!
AND IN THE BELEAGUERED CITY, THE SIGHTLESS ADVENTURER KNOWN AS DAREDEVIL MOVES EASILY ACROSS ITS CRAGGY FACE...
SOMETHING INCREDIBLE MUST BE HAPPENING.
I'M GETTING A STRANGE DISTORTION IN MY RADAR-SENSE.
AND THE TENSION IN THE FEW PEOPLE ON THE STREETS IS ALMOST TANGIBLE...
YEOW!
ALMOST MISSED THIS LEDGE. THE WHOLE CITY SEEMS OUT OF PHASE.
WHAT'S GOING TO HAPPEN NEXT?

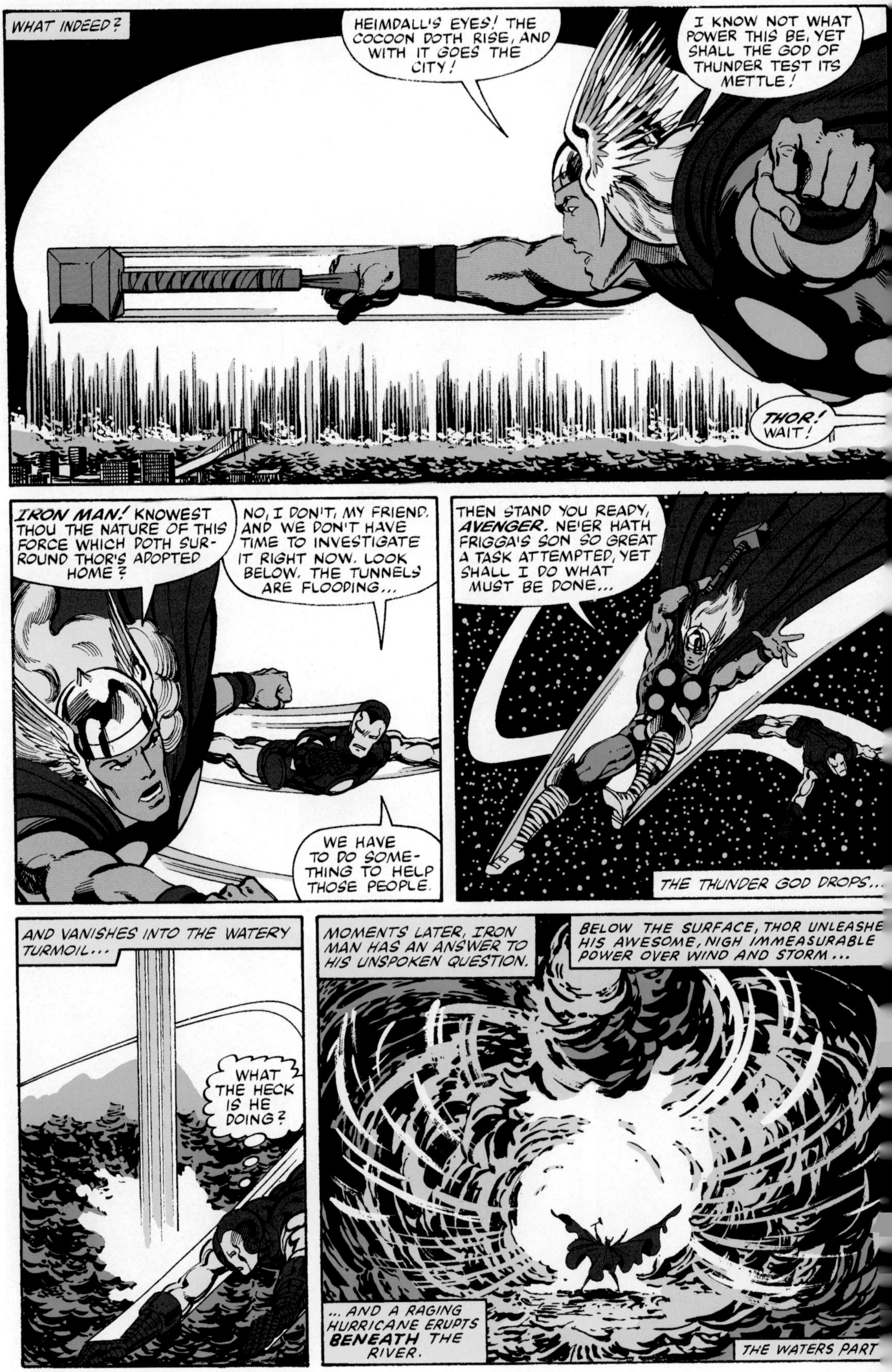
WHAT INDEED?
HEIMDALL'S EYES! THE COCOON DOTH RISE, AND WITH IT GOES THE CITY!
I KNOW NOT WHAT POWER THIS BE, YET SHALL THE GOD OF THUNDER TEST ITS METTLE!
THOR! WAIT!
IRON MAN! KNOWEST THOU THE NATURE OF THIS FORCE WHICH DOTH SURROUND THOR'S ADOPTED HOME?
NO, I DON'T, MY FRIEND. AND WE DON'T HAVE TIME TO INVESTIGATE IT RIGHT NOW. LOOK BELOW. THE TUNNELS ARE FLOODING...
WE HAVE TO DO SOMETHING TO HELP THOSE PEOPLE.
THEN STAND YOU READY, AVENGER. NE'ER HATH FRIGGA'S SON SO GREAT A TASK ATTEMPTED, YET SHALL I DO WHAT MUST BE DONE...
THE THUNDER GOD DROPS...
AND VANISHES INTO THE WATERY TURMOIL...
WHAT THE HECK IS HE DOING?
MOMENTS LATER, IRON MAN HAS AN ANSWER TO HIS UNSPOKEN QUESTION.
BELOW THE SURFACE, THOR UNLEASHE HIS AWESOME, NIGH IMMEASURABLE POWER OVER WIND AND STORM...
...AND A RAGING HURRICANE ERUPTS BENEATH THE RIVER.
THE WATERS PART

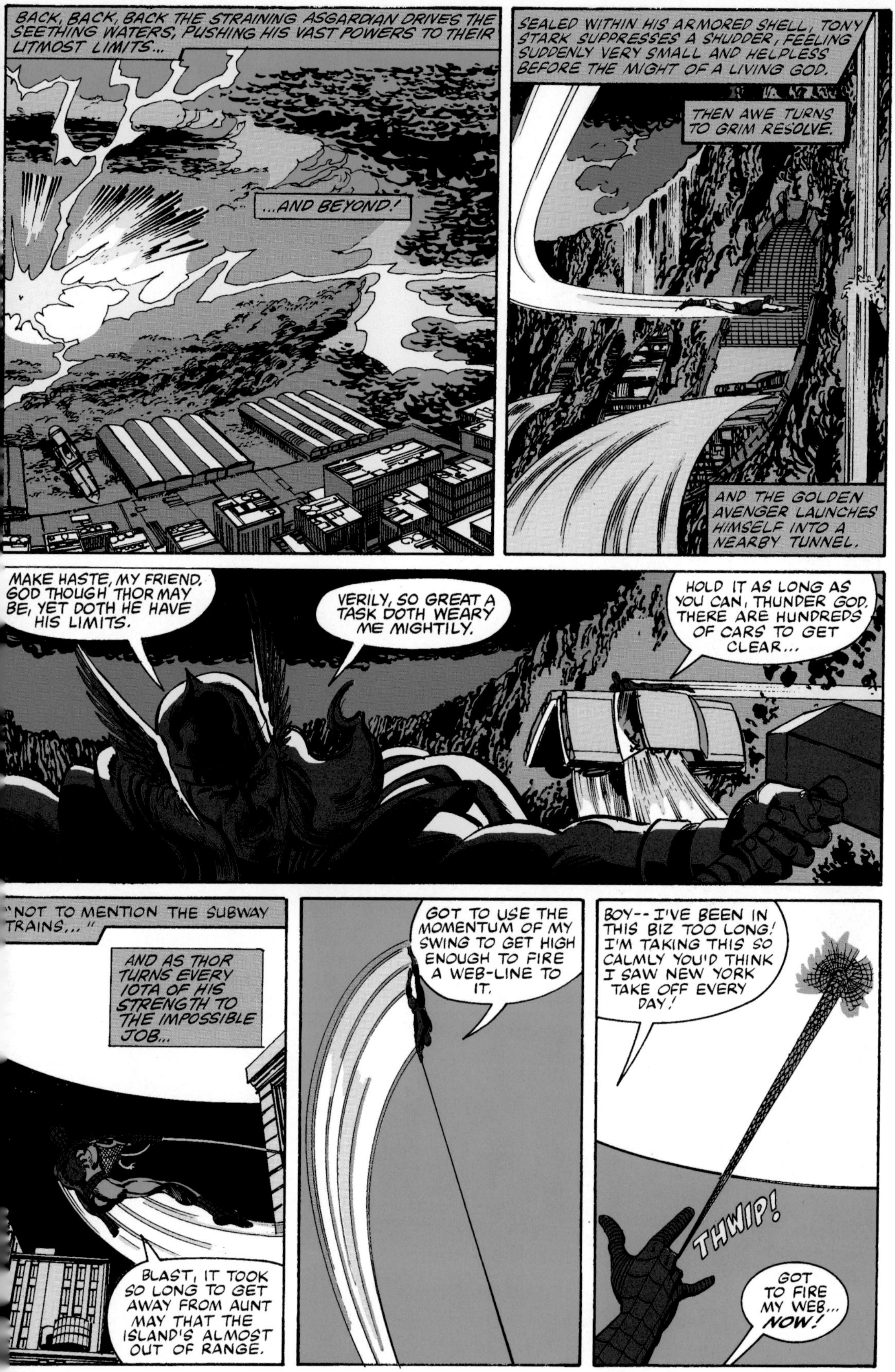
BACK, BACK, BACK THE STRAINING ASGARDIAN DRIVES THE SEETHING WATERS, PUSHING HIS VAST POWERS TO THEIR UTMOST LIMITS...
...AND BEYOND!
SEALED WITHIN HIS ARMORED SHELL, TONY STARK SUPPRESSES A SHUDDER, FEELING SUDDENLY VERY SMALL AND HELPLESS BEFORE THE MIGHT OF A LIVING GOD.
THEN AWE TURNS TO GRIM RESOLVE.
AND THE GOLDEN AVENGER LAUNCHES HIMSELF INTO A NEARBY TUNNEL.
MAKE HASTE, MY FRIEND, GOD THOUGH THOR MAY BE, YET DOTH HE HAVE HIS LIMITS.
VERILY, SO GREAT A TASK DOTH WEARY ME MIGHTILY.
HOLD IT AS LONG AS YOU CAN, THUNDER GOD. THERE ARE HUNDREDS OF CARS TO GET CLEAR...
"NOT TO MENTION THE SUBWAY TRAINS..."
AND AS THOR TURNS EVERY IOTA OF HIS STRENGTH TO THE IMPOSSIBLE JOB...
BLAST, IT TOOK SO LONG TO GET AWAY FROM AUNT MAY THAT THE ISLAND'S ALMOST OUT OF RANGE.
GOT TO USE THE MOMENTUM OF MY SWING TO GET HIGH ENOUGH TO FIRE A WEB-LINE TO IT.
BOY-- I'VE BEEN IN THIS BIZ TOO LONG! I'M TAKING THIS SO CALMLY YOU'D THINK I SAW NEW YORK TAKE OFF EVERY DAY!
THWIP!
GOT TO FIRE MY WEB... NOW!

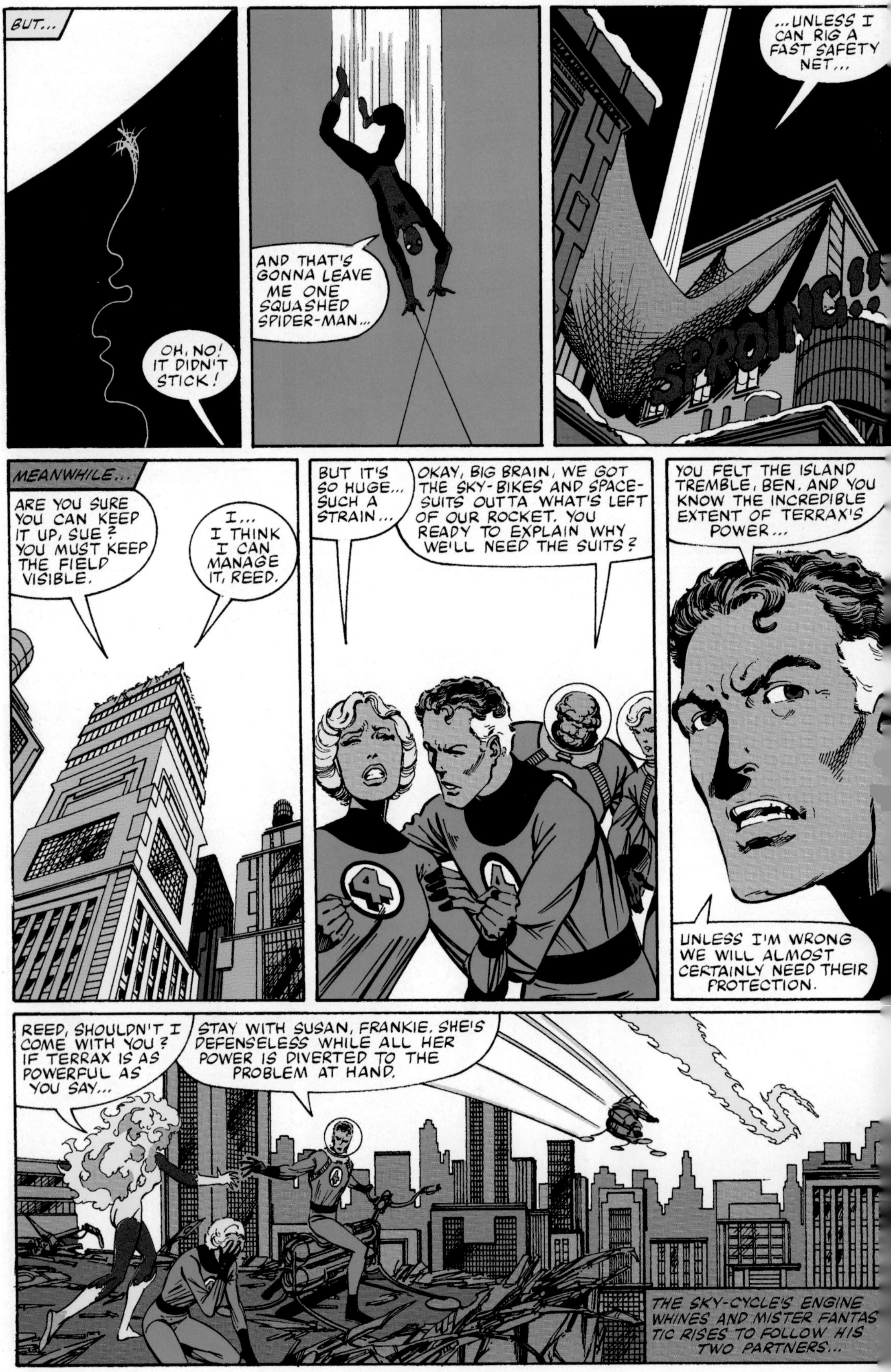
BUT...
OH, NO! IT DIDN'T STICK!
AND THAT'S GONNA LEAVE ME ONE SQUASHED SPIDER-MAN...
...UNLESS I CAN RIG A FAST SAFETY NET...
SPROING!!
MEANWHILE...
ARE YOU SURE YOU CAN KEEP IT UP, SUE? YOU MUST KEEP THE FIELD VISIBLE.
I... I THINK I CAN MANAGE IT, REED.
BUT IT'S SO HUGE... SUCH A STRAIN...
OKAY, BIG BRAIN, WE GOT THE SKY-BIKES AND SPACE-SUITS OUTTA WHAT'S LEFT OF OUR ROCKET. YOU READY TO EXPLAIN WHY WE'LL NEED THE SUITS?
YOU FELT THE ISLAND TREMBLE, BEN, AND YOU KNOW THE INCREDIBLE EXTENT OF TERRAX'S POWER...
UNLESS I'M WRONG WE WILL ALMOST CERTAINLY NEED THEIR PROTECTION.
REED, SHOULDN'T I COME WITH YOU? IF TERRAX IS AS POWERFUL AS YOU SAY...
STAY WITH SUSAN, FRANKIE. SHE'S DEFENSELESS WHILE ALL HER POWER IS DIVERTED TO THE PROBLEM AT HAND.
THE SKY-CYCLE'S ENGINE WHINES AND MISTER FANTASTIC RISES TO FOLLOW HIS TWO PARTNERS...

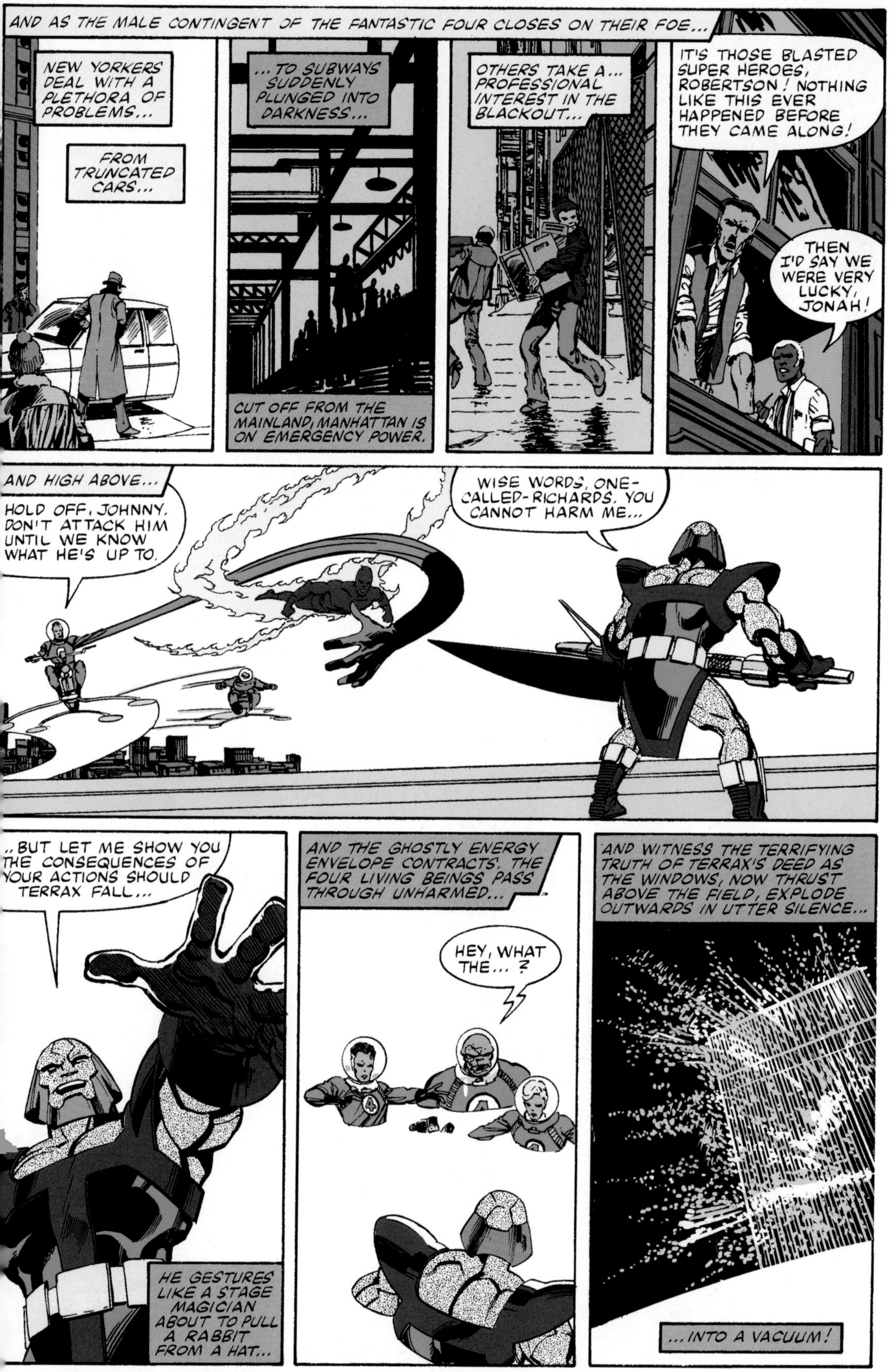
AND AS THE MALE CONTINGENT OF THE FANTASTIC FOUR CLOSES ON THEIR FOE...
NEW YORKERS DEAL WITH A PLETHORA OF PROBLEMS...
FROM TRUNCATED CARS...
...TO SUBWAYS SUDDENLY PLUNGED INTO DARKNESS...
CUT OFF FROM THE MAINLAND, MANHATTAN IS ON EMERGENCY POWER.
OTHERS TAKE A... PROFESSIONAL INTEREST IN THE BLACKOUT...
IT'S THOSE BLASTED SUPER HEROES, ROBERTSON! NOTHING LIKE THIS EVER HAPPENED BEFORE THEY CAME ALONG!
THEN I'D SAY WE WERE VERY LUCKY, JONAH!
AND HIGH ABOVE...
HOLD OFF, JOHNNY. DON'T ATTACK HIM UNTIL WE KNOW WHAT HE'S UP TO.
WISE WORDS, ONE-CALLED-RICHARDS. YOU CANNOT HARM ME...
...BUT LET ME SHOW YOU THE CONSEQUENCES OF YOUR ACTIONS SHOULD TERRAX FALL...
HE GESTURES LIKE A STAGE MAGICIAN ABOUT TO PULL A RABBIT FROM A HAT...
AND THE GHOSTLY ENERGY ENVELOPE CONTRACTS. THE FOUR LIVING BEINGS PASS THROUGH UNHARMED...
HEY, WHAT THE... ?
AND WITNESS THE TERRIFYING TRUTH OF TERRAX'S DEED AS THE WINDOWS, NOW THRUST ABOVE THE FIELD, EXPLODE OUTWARDS IN UTTER SILENCE...
...INTO A VACUUM!

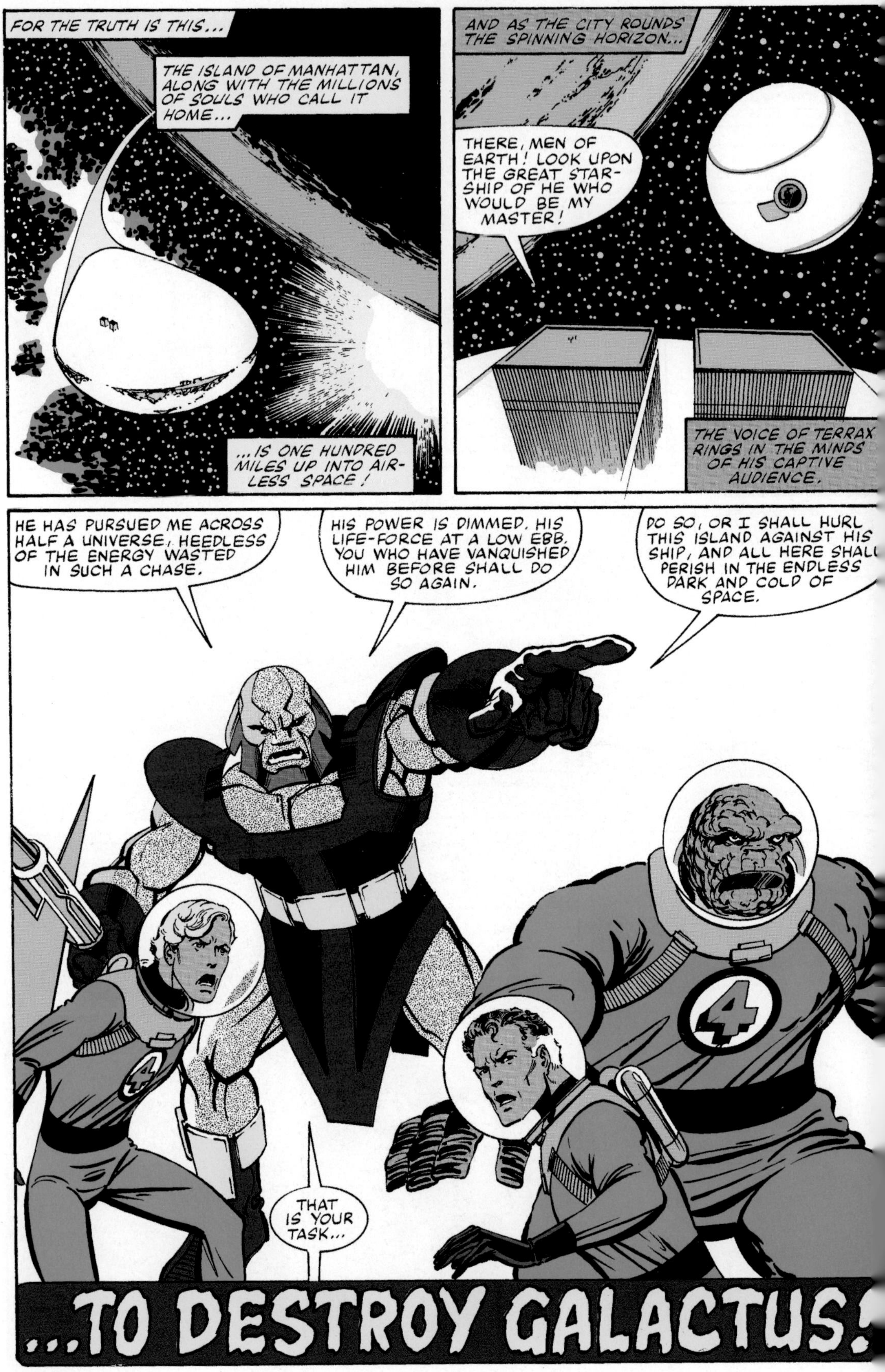

FOR THE TRUTH IS THIS...
THE ISLAND OF MANHATTAN, ALONG WITH THE MILLIONS OF SOULS WHO CALL IT HOME...
...IS ONE HUNDRED MILES UP INTO AIR-LESS SPACE!
AND AS THE CITY ROUNDS THE SPINNING HORIZON...
THERE, MEN OF EARTH! LOOK UPON THE GREAT STAR-SHIP OF HE WHO WOULD BE MY MASTER!
THE VOICE OF TERRAX RINGS IN THE MINDS OF HIS CAPTIVE AUDIENCE.
HE HAS PURSUED ME ACROSS HALF A UNIVERSE, HEEDLESS OF THE ENERGY WASTED IN SUCH A CHASE.
HIS POWER IS DIMMED, HIS LIFE-FORCE AT A LOW EBB. YOU WHO HAVE VANQUISHED HIM BEFORE SHALL DO SO AGAIN.
DO SO, OR I SHALL HURL THIS ISLAND AGAINST HIS SHIP, AND ALL HERE SHALL PERISH IN THE ENDLESS DARK AND COLD OF SPACE.
THAT IS YOUR TASK...
...TO DESTROY GALACTUS!

fantastic four # 243

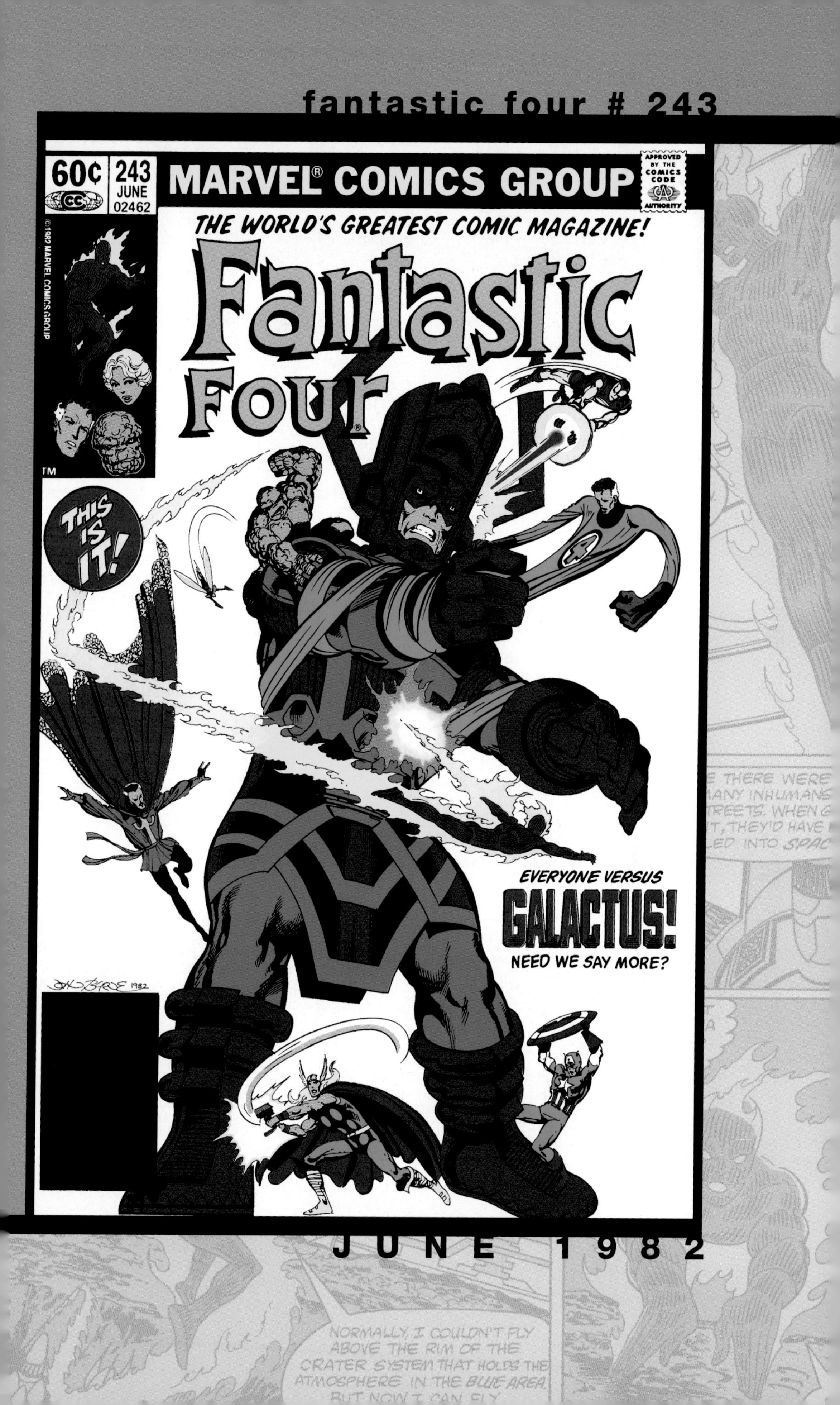
60¢
243
JUNE
02462
MARVEL® COMICS GROUP
APPROVED BY THE COMICS CODE AUTHORITY
THE WORLD'S GREATEST COMIC MAGAZINE!
Fantastic Four®
©1982 MARVEL COMICS GROUP
TM
THIS IS IT!
EVERYONE VERSUS
GALACTUS!
NEED WE SAY MORE?

JUNE 1982

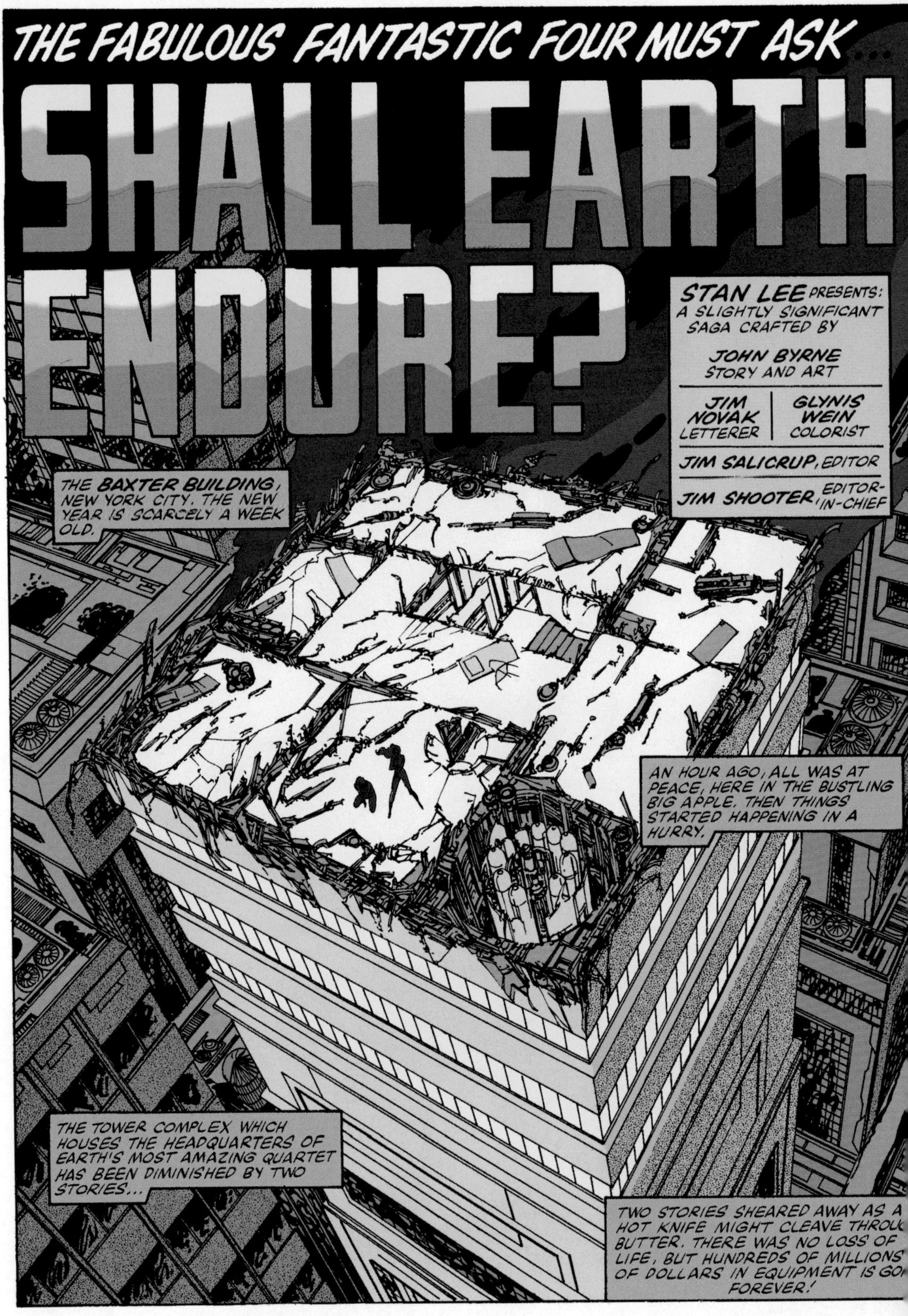
THE FABULOUS FANTASTIC FOUR MUST ASK...
SHALL EARTH ENDURE?
STAN LEE PRESENTS: A SLIGHTLY SIGNIFICANT SAGA CRAFTED BY
JOHN BYRNE STORY AND ART
JIM NOVAK LETTERER
GLYNIS WEIN COLORIST
JIM SALICRUP, EDITOR
JIM SHOOTER, EDITOR-IN-CHIEF
THE BAXTER BUILDING, NEW YORK CITY. THE NEW YEAR IS SCARCELY A WEEK OLD.
AN HOUR AGO, ALL WAS AT PEACE, HERE IN THE BUSTLING BIG APPLE. THEN THINGS STARTED HAPPENING IN A HURRY.
THE TOWER COMPLEX WHICH HOUSES THE HEADQUARTERS OF EARTH'S MOST AMAZING QUARTET HAS BEEN DIMINISHED BY TWO STORIES...
TWO STORIES SHEARED AWAY AS A HOT KNIFE MIGHT CLEAVE THROU BUTTER. THERE WAS NO LOSS OF LIFE, BUT HUNDREDS OF MILLIONS OF DOLLARS IN EQUIPMENT IS GO FOREVER!

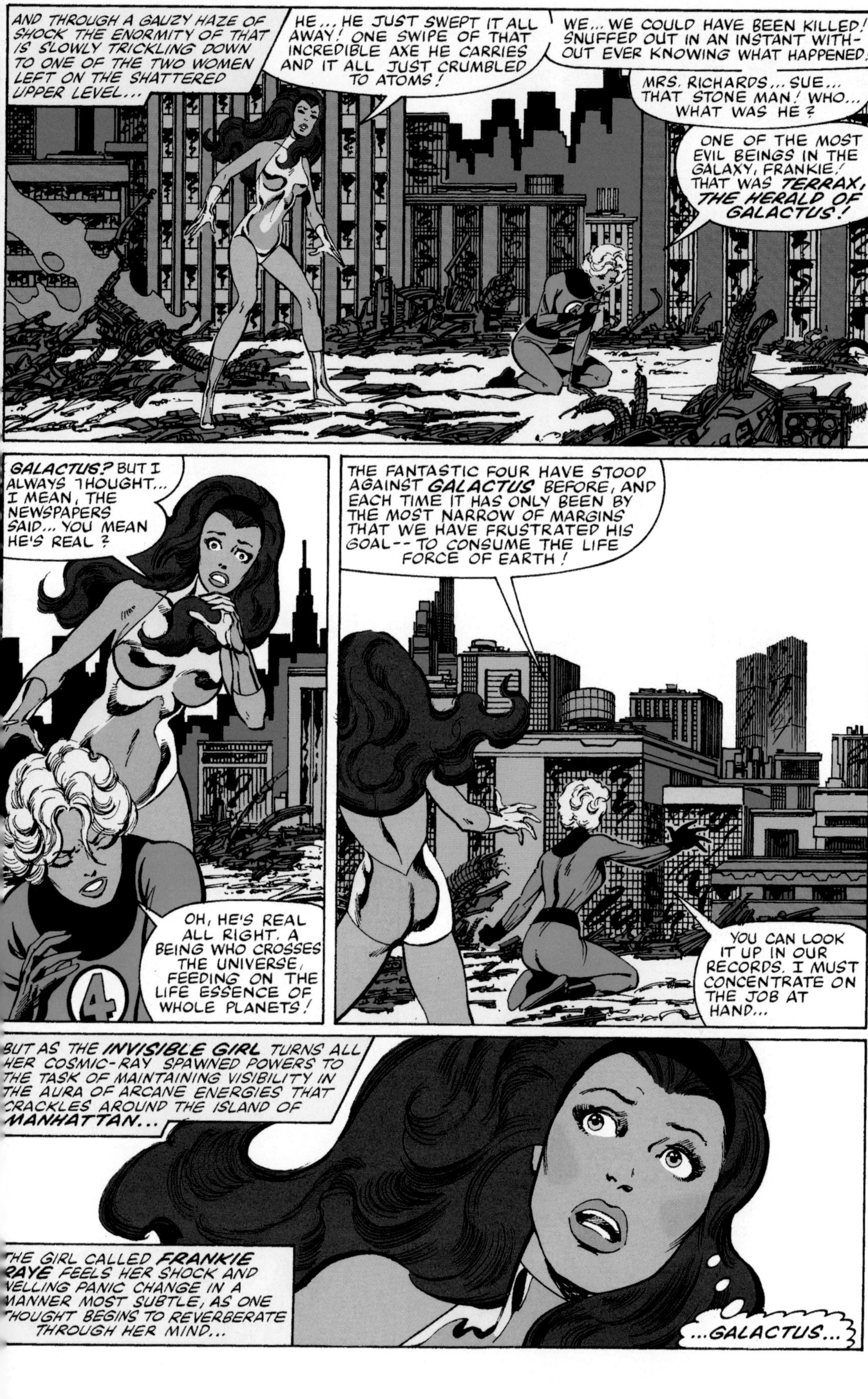
AND THROUGH A GAUZY HAZE OF SHOCK THE ENORMITY OF THAT IS SLOWLY TRICKLING DOWN TO ONE OF THE TWO WOMEN LEFT ON THE SHATTERED UPPER LEVEL...
HE... HE JUST SWEPT IT ALL AWAY! ONE SWIPE OF THAT INCREDIBLE AXE HE CARRIES AND IT ALL JUST CRUMBLED TO ATOMS!
WE... WE COULD HAVE BEEN KILLED! SNUFFED OUT IN AN INSTANT WITHOUT EVER KNOWING WHAT HAPPENED!
MRS. RICHARDS... SUE... THAT STONE MAN! WHO... WHAT WAS HE?
ONE OF THE MOST EVIL BEINGS IN THE GALAXY, FRANKIE! THAT WAS TERRAX, THE HERALD OF GALACTUS!
GALACTUS? BUT I ALWAYS THOUGHT... I MEAN, THE NEWSPAPERS SAID... YOU MEAN HE'S REAL?
OH, HE'S REAL ALL RIGHT. A BEING WHO CROSSES THE UNIVERSE, FEEDING ON THE LIFE ESSENCE OF WHOLE PLANETS!
4
THE FANTASTIC FOUR HAVE STOOD AGAINST GALACTUS BEFORE, AND EACH TIME IT HAS ONLY BEEN BY THE MOST NARROW OF MARGINS THAT WE HAVE FRUSTRATED HIS GOAL-- TO CONSUME THE LIFE FORCE OF EARTH!
YOU CAN LOOK IT UP IN OUR RECORDS. I MUST CONCENTRATE ON THE JOB AT HAND...
BUT AS THE INVISIBLE GIRL TURNS ALL HER COSMIC-RAY SPAWNED POWERS TO THE TASK OF MAINTAINING VISIBILITY IN THE AURA OF ARCANE ENERGIES THAT CRACKLES AROUND THE ISLAND OF MANHATTAN...
THE GIRL CALLED FRANKIE RAYE FEELS HER SHOCK AND WELLING PANIC CHANGE IN A MANNER MOST SUBTLE, AS ONE THOUGHT BEGINS TO REVERBERATE THROUGH HER MIND...
...GALACTUS...

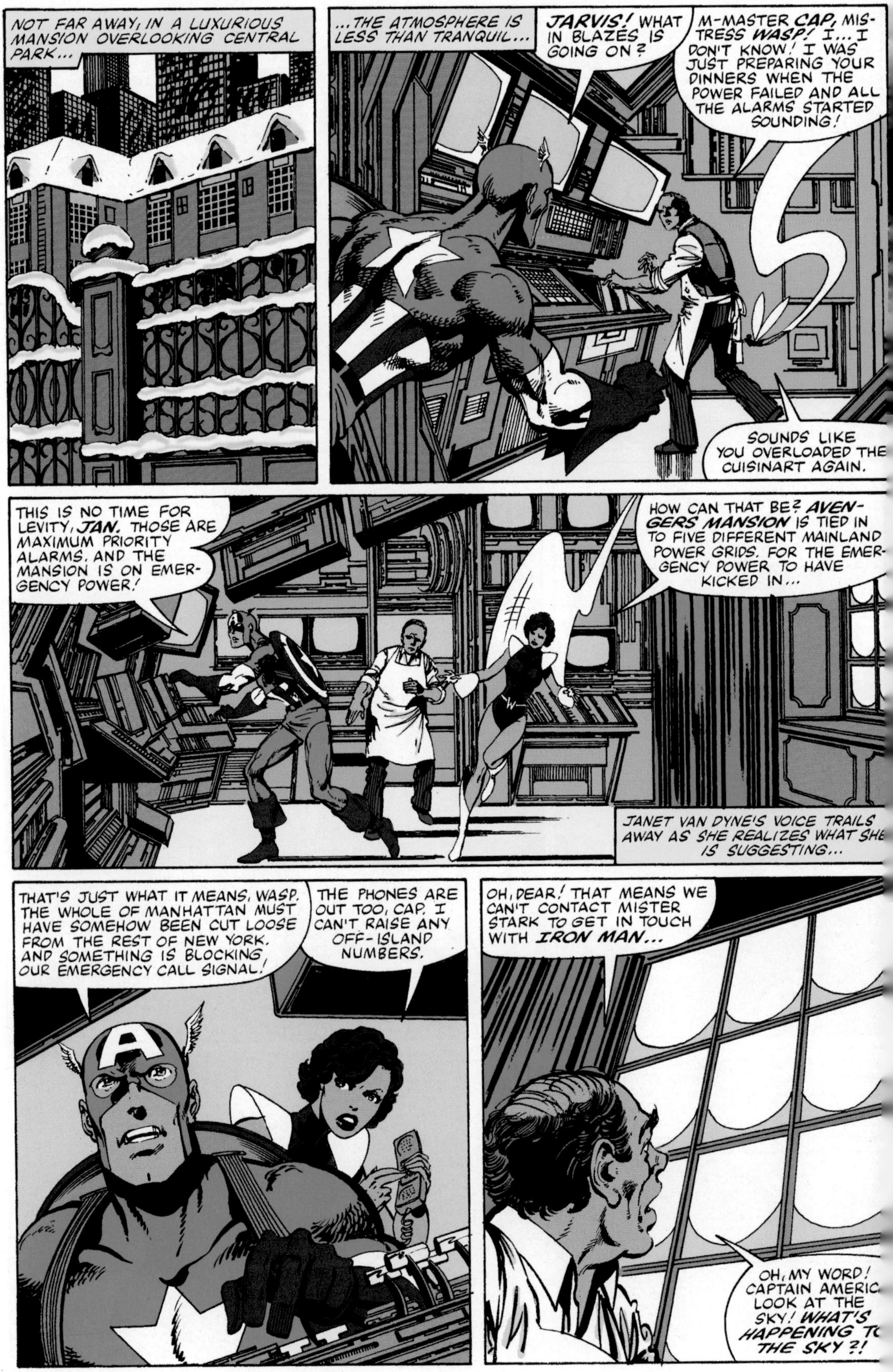
NOT FAR AWAY, IN A LUXURIOUS MANSION OVERLOOKING CENTRAL PARK...
...THE ATMOSPHERE IS LESS THAN TRANQUIL...
JARVIS! WHAT IN BLAZES IS GOING ON?
M-MASTER CAP, MISTRESS WASP! I...I DON'T KNOW! I WAS JUST PREPARING YOUR DINNERS WHEN THE POWER FAILED AND ALL THE ALARMS STARTED SOUNDING!
SOUNDS LIKE YOU OVERLOADED THE CUISINART AGAIN.
THIS IS NO TIME FOR LEVITY, JAN. THOSE ARE MAXIMUM PRIORITY ALARMS, AND THE MANSION IS ON EMERGENCY POWER!
HOW CAN THAT BE? AVENGERS MANSION IS TIED IN TO FIVE DIFFERENT MAINLAND POWER GRIDS. FOR THE EMERGENCY POWER TO HAVE KICKED IN...
JANET VAN DYNE'S VOICE TRAILS AWAY AS SHE REALIZES WHAT SHE IS SUGGESTING...
THAT'S JUST WHAT IT MEANS, WASP. THE WHOLE OF MANHATTAN MUST HAVE SOMEHOW BEEN CUT LOOSE FROM THE REST OF NEW YORK, AND SOMETHING IS BLOCKING OUR EMERGENCY CALL SIGNAL!
THE PHONES ARE OUT TOO, CAP. I CAN'T RAISE ANY OFF-ISLAND NUMBERS.
OH, DEAR! THAT MEANS WE CAN'T CONTACT MISTER STARK TO GET IN TOUCH WITH IRON MAN...
OH, MY WORD! CAPTAIN AMERIC LOOK AT THE SKY! WHAT'S HAPPENING T THE SKY?!

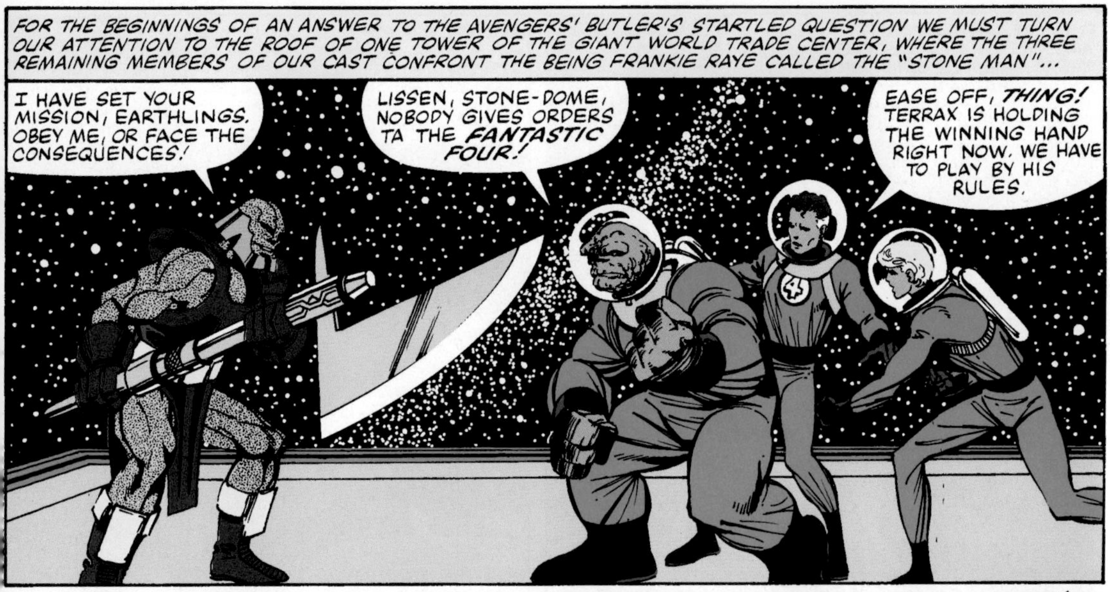
FOR THE BEGINNINGS OF AN ANSWER TO THE AVENGERS' BUTLER'S STARTLED QUESTION WE MUST TURN OUR ATTENTION TO THE ROOF OF ONE TOWER OF THE GIANT WORLD TRADE CENTER, WHERE THE THREE REMAINING MEMBERS OF OUR CAST CONFRONT THE BEING FRANKIE RAYE CALLED THE "STONE MAN"...
I HAVE SET YOUR MISSION, EARTHLINGS. OBEY ME, OR FACE THE CONSEQUENCES!
LISSEN, STONE-DOME, NOBODY GIVES ORDERS TA THE FANTASTIC FOUR!
EASE OFF, THING! TERRAX IS HOLDING THE WINNING HAND RIGHT NOW. WE HAVE TO PLAY BY HIS RULES.

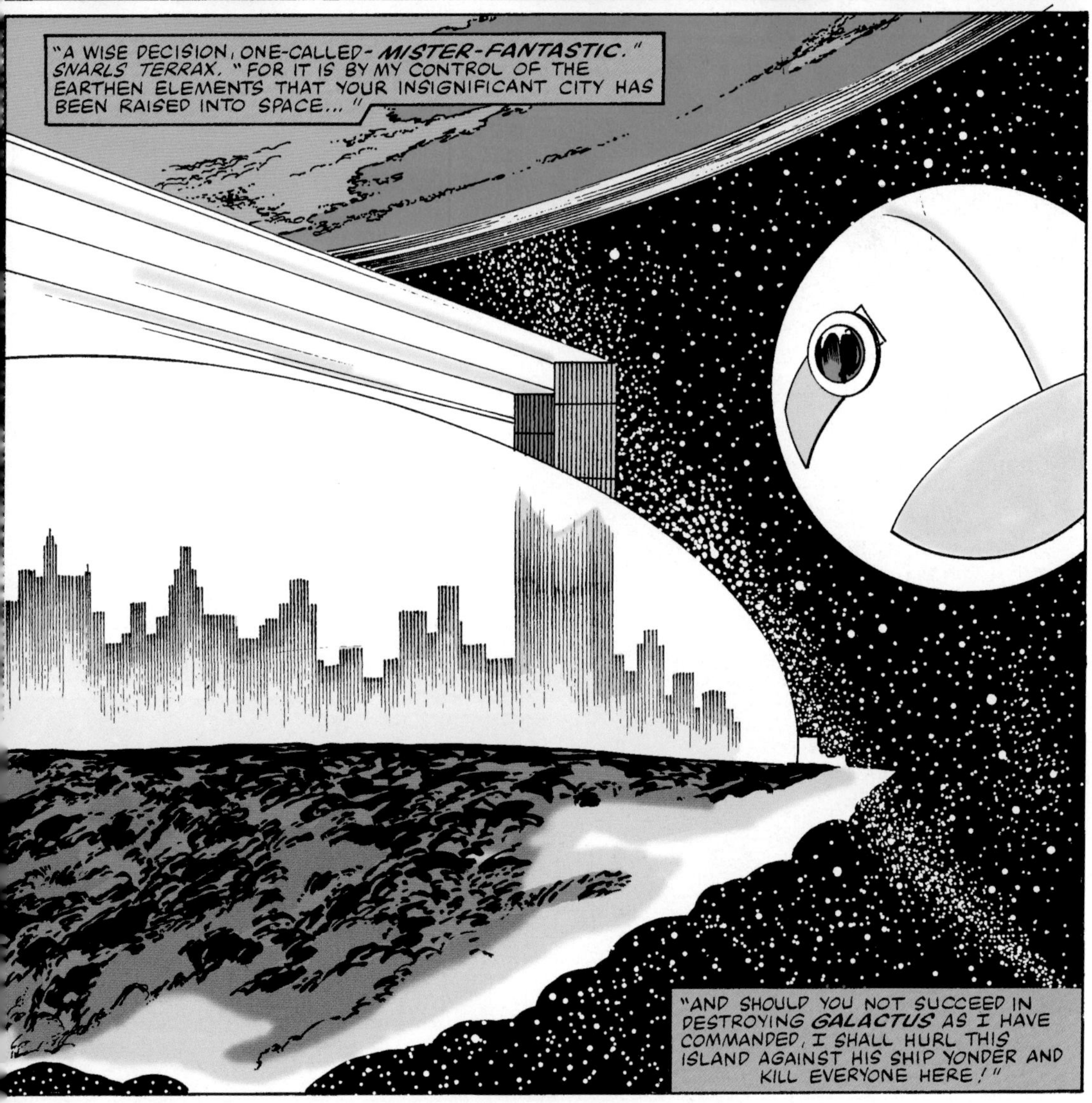
"A WISE DECISION, ONE-CALLED-MISTER-FANTASTIC," SNARLS TERRAX. "FOR IT IS BY MY CONTROL OF THE EARTHEN ELEMENTS THAT YOUR INSIGNIFICANT CITY HAS BEEN RAISED INTO SPACE..."
"AND SHOULD YOU NOT SUCCEED IN DESTROYING GALACTUS AS I HAVE COMMANDED, I SHALL HURL THIS ISLAND AGAINST HIS SHIP YONDER AND KILL EVERYONE HERE!"

BUT YOU CAN'T MEAN IT! THERE ARE MILLIONS OF PEOPLE DOWN THERE! PEOPLE WHO DON'T EVEN KNOW WHAT'S HAPPENED BECAUSE MY SISTER IS KEEPING YOUR FORCE-FIELD OPAQUE.

YOU CAN'T JUST CASUALLY MURDER ALL OF THEM!

HA HA HA HA! IGNORANT WHELP! HAVE YOUR YEARS AS THE HUMAN TORCH TAUGHT YOU NOTHING? I WAS THE HERALD OF GALACTUS. IT WAS MY TASK TO FIND WORLDS THAT HE MIGHT CONSUME!

WHAT CARE I FOR THE PUNY LIVES OF A SINGLE CITY?

THAT DOES IT! MAYBE IF I CRAM THAT FANCY SWIZZLE STICK DOWN YER MISERABLE THROAT YOU'LL LEARN A LITTLE COMPASSION!

BEN, IN HEAVEN'S NAME, STOP! HE'LL DO IT! YOU KNOW HE WILL!

THE EDGE OF FEAR IN REED RICHARDS' VOICE FREEZES BEN GRIMM.

YA... YA MEAN WE'RE GIVIN' UP? SAY IT AIN'T SO, STRETCHO!

ONLY A FOOL FIGHTS IN A BURNING HOUSE, BEN. WE MUST DO WHAT TERRAX WANTS.

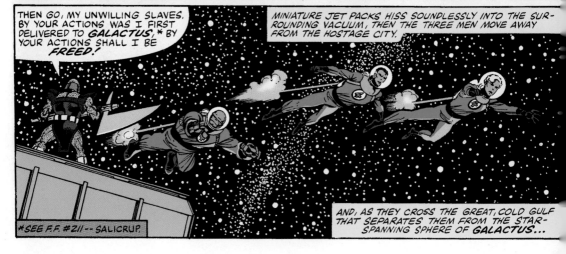

THEN GO, MY UNWILLING SLAVES. BY YOUR ACTIONS WAS I FIRST DELIVERED TO GALACTUS,* BY YOUR ACTIONS SHALL I BE FREED!

MINIATURE JET PACKS HISS SOUNDLESSLY INTO THE SURROUNDING VACUUM, THEN THE THREE MEN MOVE AWAY FROM THE HOSTAGE CITY.

AND, AS THEY CROSS THE GREAT, COLD GULF THAT SEPARATES THEM FROM THE STAR-SPANNING SPHERE OF GALACTUS...

*SEE F.F. #211 -- SALICRUP.

EYES NOT REMOTELY HUMAN MARK THEIR PROGRESS, AND GROW TIRED...

ENOUGH!

AGAIN MUST I CONTEND WITH THE CREATURES OF THIS TINY WORLD. THEY WHO, ALONE IN ALL *CREATION*, HAVE STYMIED MY WILL.*

YET DOES *GALACTUS* WEARY OF THIS ENDLESS CONFLICT, FOR WHAT MORE DO I DO THAN THAT WHICH ANY LIVING CREATURE MUST?

*MOST RECENTLY IN DAZZLER # 10-11 AND ROM #26,27. -- STAR-SPANNING SALICRUP.

HE MOVES THROUGH THE VAST CHAMBERS OF HIS SHIP, AND A WEIGHT BEYOND MEASURE SEEMS TO PRESS UPON HIM.

GALACTUS DOES WHAT *GALACTUS* MUST TO SURVIVE.

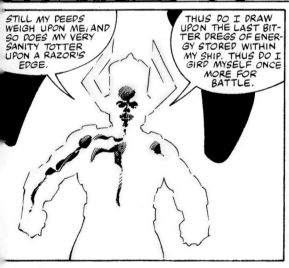

STILL MY DEEDS WEIGH UPON ME, AND SO DOES MY VERY SANITY TOTTER UPON A RAZOR'S EDGE.

THUS DO I DRAW UPON THE LAST BITTER DREGS OF ENERGY STORED WITHIN MY SHIP. THUS DO I GIRD MYSELF ONCE MORE FOR BATTLE.

GALACTUS IS REPLENISHED. MY LIMBS GROW STRONG AGAIN. BUT MY RESOURCES ARE SPENT. VICTORY MUST NOW BE MINE...

OR *GALACTUS* SHALL NOT FIGHT AGAIN.

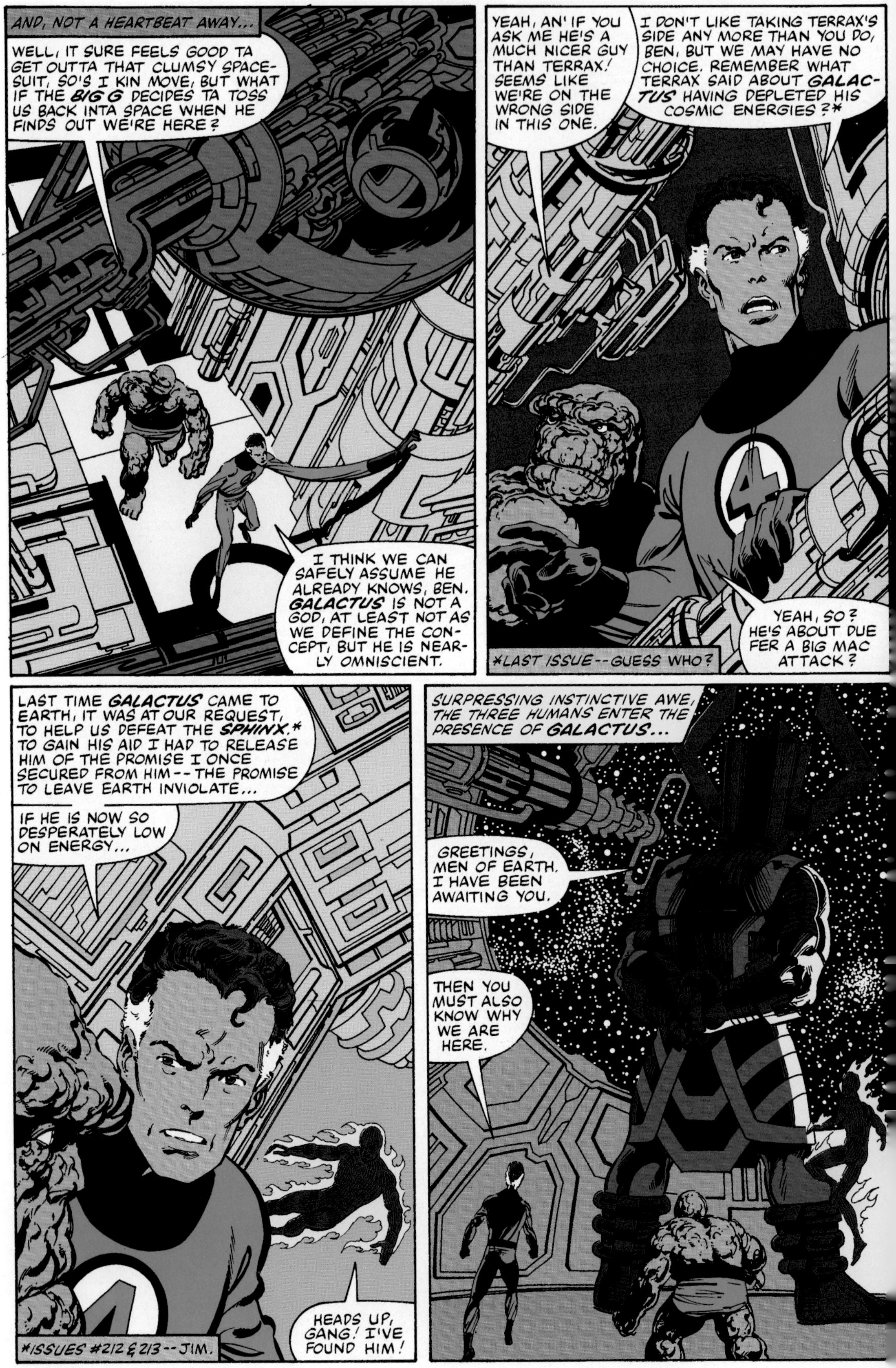

AND, NOT A HEARTBEAT AWAY...
WELL, IT SURE FEELS GOOD TA GET OUTTA THAT CLUMSY SPACE-SUIT, SO'S I KIN MOVE, BUT WHAT IF THE BIG G DECIDES TA TOSS US BACK INTA SPACE WHEN HE FINDS OUT WE'RE HERE?
I THINK WE CAN SAFELY ASSUME HE ALREADY KNOWS, BEN. GALACTUS IS NOT A GOD, AT LEAST NOT AS WE DEFINE THE CONCEPT, BUT HE IS NEARLY OMNISCIENT.
YEAH, AN' IF YOU ASK ME HE'S A MUCH NICER GUY THAN TERRAX! SEEMS LIKE WE'RE ON THE WRONG SIDE IN THIS ONE.
I DON'T LIKE TAKING TERRAX'S SIDE ANY MORE THAN YOU DO, BEN, BUT WE MAY HAVE NO CHOICE. REMEMBER WHAT TERRAX SAID ABOUT GALACTUS HAVING DEPLETED HIS COSMIC ENERGIES?*
*LAST ISSUE--GUESS WHO?
YEAH, SO? HE'S ABOUT DUE FER A BIG MAC ATTACK?
LAST TIME GALACTUS CAME TO EARTH, IT WAS AT OUR REQUEST, TO HELP US DEFEAT THE SPHINX.* TO GAIN HIS AID I HAD TO RELEASE HIM OF THE PROMISE I ONCE SECURED FROM HIM--THE PROMISE TO LEAVE EARTH INVIOLATE...
IF HE IS NOW SO DESPERATELY LOW ON ENERGY...
*ISSUES #212 & 213--JIM.
HEADS UP, GANG! I'VE FOUND HIM!
SURPRESSING INSTINCTIVE AWE, THE THREE HUMANS ENTER THE PRESENCE OF GALACTUS...
GREETINGS, MEN OF EARTH. I HAVE BEEN AWAITING YOU.
THEN YOU MUST ALSO KNOW WHY WE ARE HERE.

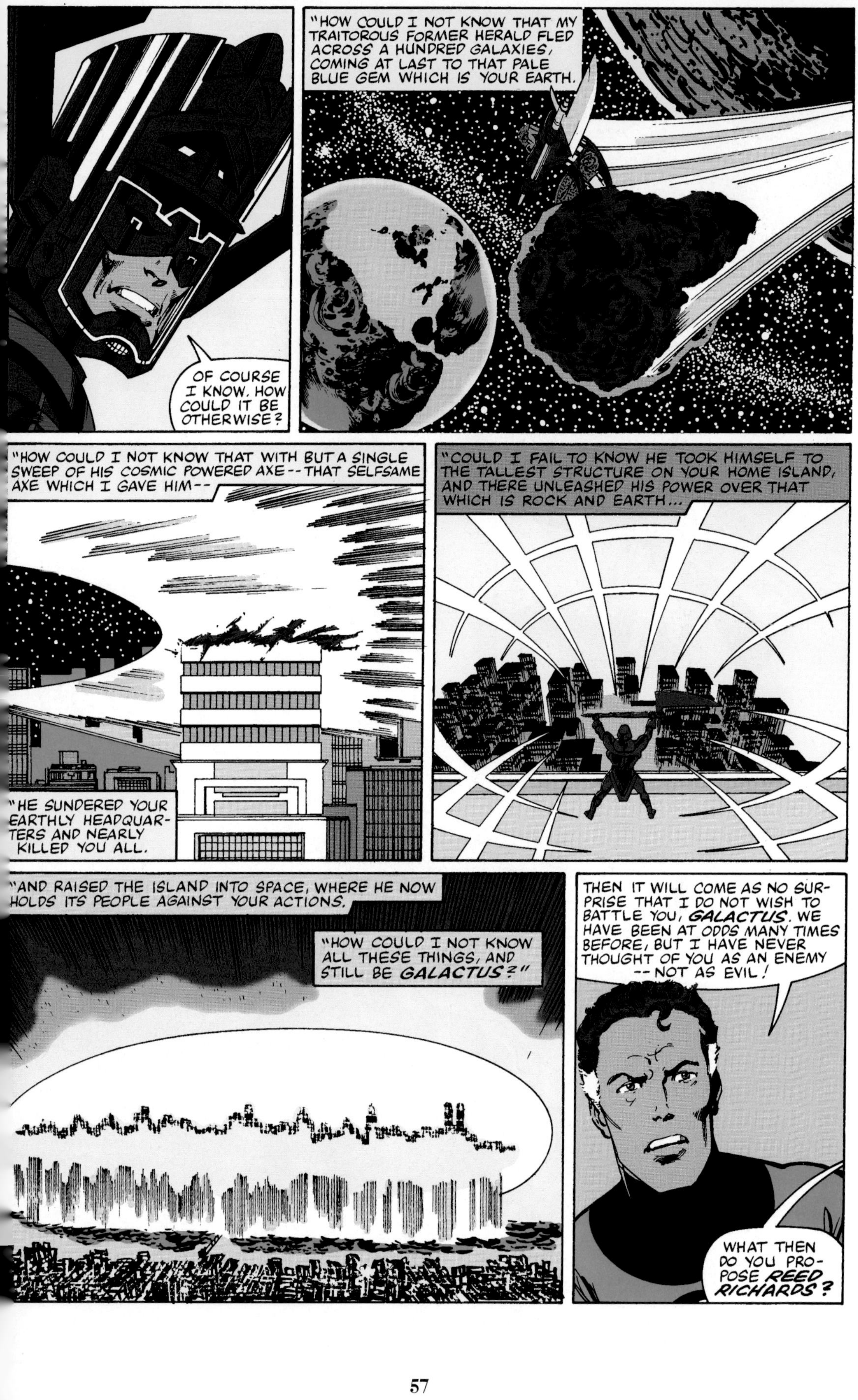
OF COURSE I KNOW. HOW COULD IT BE OTHERWISE?
"HOW COULD I NOT KNOW THAT MY TRAITOROUS FORMER HERALD FLED ACROSS A HUNDRED GALAXIES, COMING AT LAST TO THAT PALE BLUE GEM WHICH IS YOUR EARTH.
"HOW COULD I NOT KNOW THAT WITH BUT A SINGLE SWEEP OF HIS COSMIC POWERED AXE--THAT SELFSAME AXE WHICH I GAVE HIM--
"HE SUNDERED YOUR EARTHLY HEADQUARTERS AND NEARLY KILLED YOU ALL.
"COULD I FAIL TO KNOW HE TOOK HIMSELF TO THE TALLEST STRUCTURE ON YOUR HOME ISLAND, AND THERE UNLEASHED HIS POWER OVER THAT WHICH IS ROCK AND EARTH...
"AND RAISED THE ISLAND INTO SPACE, WHERE HE NOW HOLDS ITS PEOPLE AGAINST YOUR ACTIONS.
"HOW COULD I NOT KNOW ALL THESE THINGS, AND STILL BE GALACTUS?"
THEN IT WILL COME AS NO SURPRISE THAT I DO NOT WISH TO BATTLE YOU, GALACTUS. WE HAVE BEEN AT ODDS MANY TIMES BEFORE, BUT I HAVE NEVER THOUGHT OF YOU AS AN ENEMY --NOT AS EVIL!
WHAT THEN DO YOU PROPOSE REED RICHARDS?

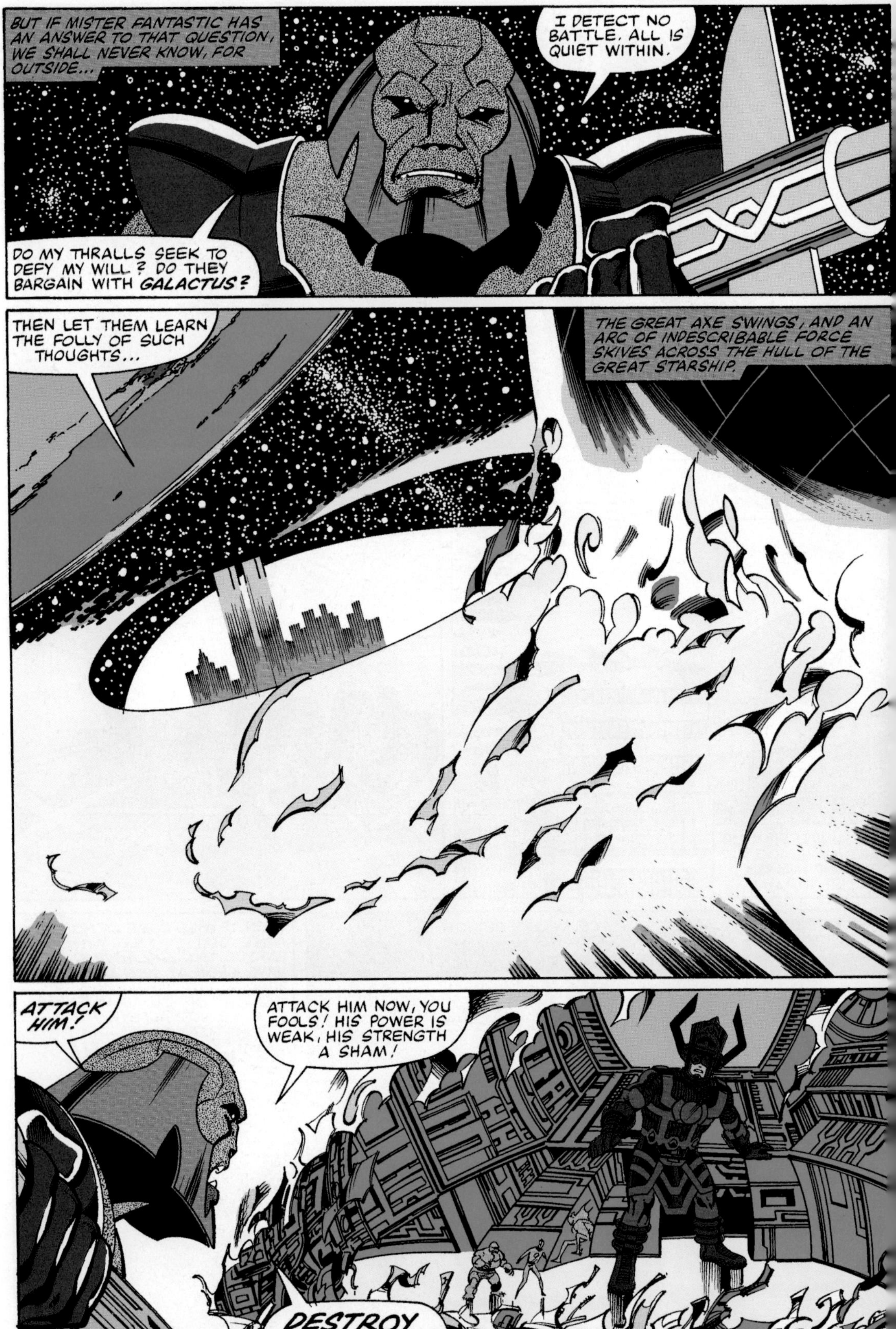
BUT IF MISTER FANTASTIC HAS AN ANSWER TO THAT QUESTION, WE SHALL NEVER KNOW, FOR OUTSIDE...
I DETECT NO BATTLE. ALL IS QUIET WITHIN.
DO MY THRALLS SEEK TO DEFY MY WILL? DO THEY BARGAIN WITH GALACTUS?
THEN LET THEM LEARN THE FOLLY OF SUCH THOUGHTS...
THE GREAT AXE SWINGS, AND AN ARC OF INDESCRIBABLE FORCE SKIVES ACROSS THE HULL OF THE GREAT STARSHIP.
ATTACK HIM!
ATTACK HIM NOW, YOU FOOLS! HIS POWER IS WEAK, HIS STRENGTH A SHAM!
DESTROY GALACTUS!

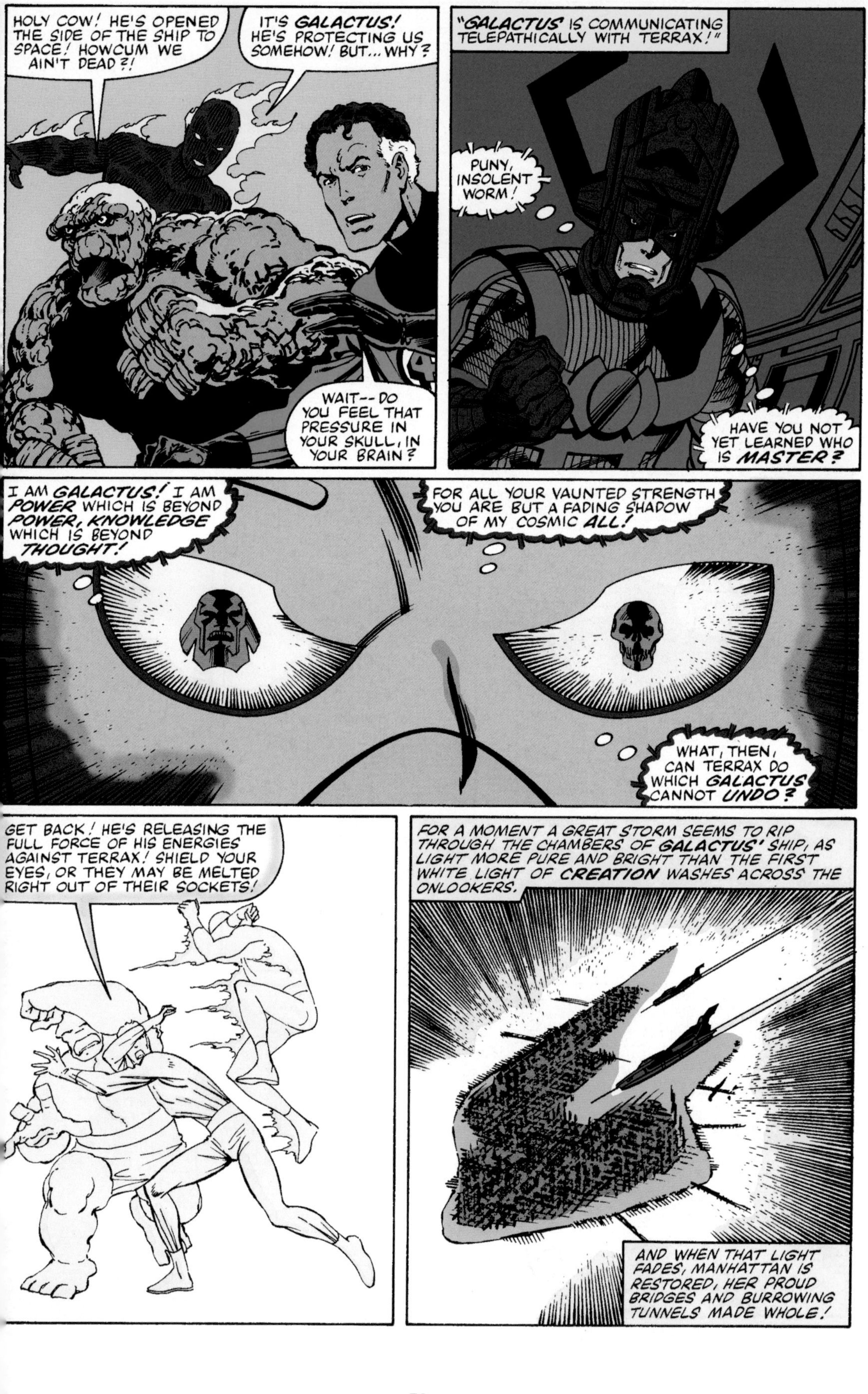

HOLY COW! HE'S OPENED THE SIDE OF THE SHIP TO SPACE! HOWCUM WE AIN'T DEAD?!
IT'S GALACTUS! HE'S PROTECTING US SOMEHOW! BUT... WHY?
WAIT-- DO YOU FEEL THAT PRESSURE IN YOUR SKULL, IN YOUR BRAIN?
"GALACTUS IS COMMUNICATING TELEPATHICALLY WITH TERRAX!"
PUNY, INSOLENT WORM!
HAVE YOU NOT YET LEARNED WHO IS MASTER?
I AM GALACTUS! I AM POWER WHICH IS BEYOND POWER, KNOWLEDGE WHICH IS BEYOND THOUGHT!
FOR ALL YOUR VAUNTED STRENGTH YOU ARE BUT A FADING SHADOW OF MY COSMIC ALL!
WHAT, THEN, CAN TERRAX DO WHICH GALACTUS CANNOT UNDO?
GET BACK! HE'S RELEASING THE FULL FORCE OF HIS ENERGIES AGAINST TERRAX! SHIELD YOUR EYES, OR THEY MAY BE MELTED RIGHT OUT OF THEIR SOCKETS!
FOR A MOMENT A GREAT STORM SEEMS TO RIP THROUGH THE CHAMBERS OF GALACTUS' SHIP, AS LIGHT MORE PURE AND BRIGHT THAN THE FIRST WHITE LIGHT OF CREATION WASHES ACROSS THE ONLOOKERS.
AND WHEN THAT LIGHT FADES, MANHATTAN IS RESTORED, HER PROUD BRIDGES AND BURROWING TUNNELS MADE WHOLE!

AND ACROSS THE ISLAND NEW YORKERS RETURN TO THEIR EVERYDAY LIVES, UNAWARE THAT THEY HAVE BEEN VICTIMS OF ANYTHING MORE THAN AN ALL-TOO FAMILIAR BLACKOUT.

BENEATH THE SNOWY STREETS THE SUBWAYS HUM TO LIFE...

IN MIDTOWN OFFICE BLOCKS, CAPTIVE BUSINESS-FOLK ARE FREED FROM ONCE-MORE FUNCTIONAL ELEVATORS...

THROUGHOUT MANHATTAN TELEPHONES JANGLE WITH NEWS OF THE EVENT FROM OFF-ISLAND CALLERS...

SHELDON, ARE YOU NERTZ?

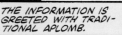
THE INFORMATION IS GREETED WITH TRADITIONAL APLOMB.

FIND OUT WHAT HAPPENED, ROBERTSON. IF *SPIDER-MAN* WAS INVOLVED, WE'LL HAVE HIM ROASTED IN TIMES SQUARE!

≥SIGH≥

AND, ATOP THE SHATTERED BAXTER BUILDING...

UHNH! THE FORCE-FIELD... TERRAX'S FORCE-FIELD... IT'S GONE. I CAN **STOP!**

BUT... THE STRAIN... TIRED. SO... TIRED...

SUE!

SHE'S PASSED OUT! AND WHAT'S THAT GLOW APPEARING ON TOP OF THE WORLD TRADE CENTER?

LIVING FLAME CRACKLES ABOUT FRANKIE RAYE...

THEN, HER RESOLVE SEEMS SOMEHOW TO SHIFT, AND THE FIRE DWINDLES...

I SHOULD GO... SHOULD INVESTIGATE... BUT... BUT...

ALMOST ROBOTLIKE SHE TURNS BACK TOWARDS THE BUILDING'S CORE, MOVING QUICKLY AWAY FROM THE UNCONSCIOUS INVISIBLE GIRL.

AS AGAIN A SINGLE CONSUMING THOUGHT POSSESSES HER...

...GALACTUS...

ELSEWHERE, WHAT OF THE GLOW FRANKIE RAYE NOTICED ATOP THE TWIN TOWERS OF THE WORLD TRADE CENTER?

AS THE GHOSTLY NIMBUS FADES, ACROSS THE 110 STORY GAP THAT SEPARATES THE TWO BUILDINGS, OPPOSING FORCES FACE EACH OTHER.

TO EVEN AN UNTRAINED EYE IT WOULD SEEM OBVIOUS THAT A GULF GREATER THAN MERE DISTANCE SEPARATES THE TWO SIDES IN THIS CONFRONTATION.

N...NO!

IT CANNOT BE! MY POWER IS GREATER THAN YOURS! YOU ARE DRAINED, WEAK! YOU SUBSIST ON THE ARTIFICIAL ENERGIES GENERATED WITHIN YOUR SHIP.

YOU CANNOT DO THIS! YOU HAVE NOT THE POWER!

"ARTIFICIAL ENERGIES?"

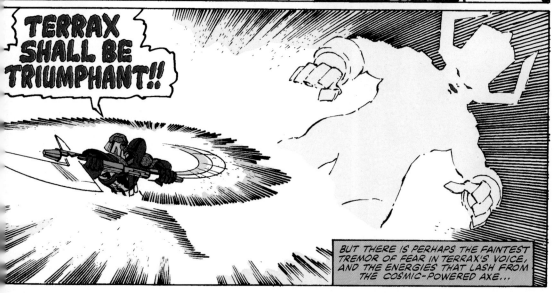

TERRAX SHALL BE TRIUMPHANT!!

BUT THERE IS PERHAPS THE FAINTEST TREMOR OF FEAR IN TERRAX'S VOICE, AND THE ENERGIES THAT LASH FROM THE COSMIC-POWERED AXE...

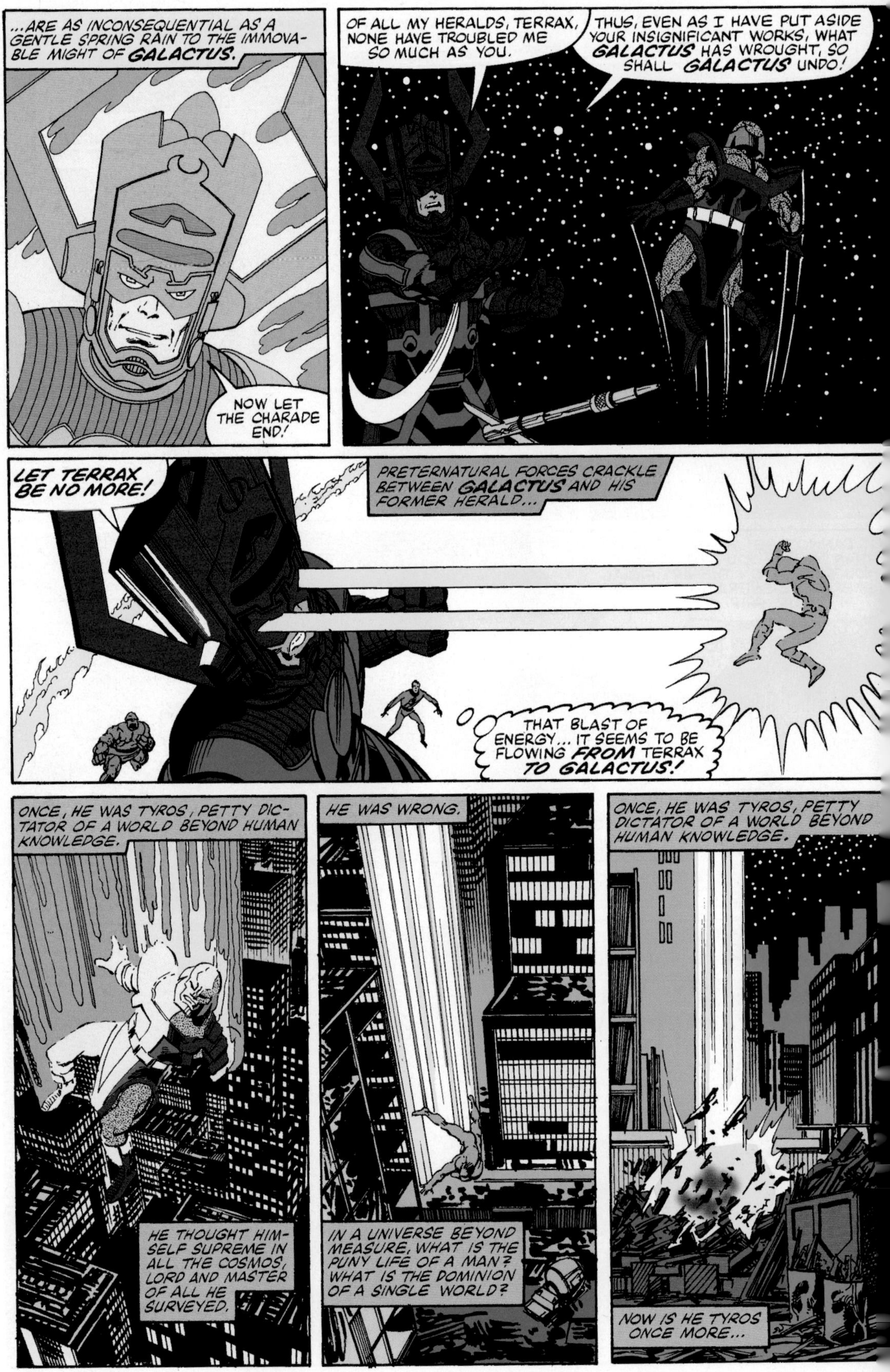
...ARE AS INCONSEQUENTIAL AS A GENTLE SPRING RAIN TO THE IMMOVABLE MIGHT OF GALACTUS.
NOW LET THE CHARADE END!
OF ALL MY HERALDS, TERRAX, NONE HAVE TROUBLED ME SO MUCH AS YOU.
THUS, EVEN AS I HAVE PUT ASIDE YOUR INSIGNIFICANT WORKS, WHAT GALACTUS HAS WROUGHT, SO SHALL GALACTUS UNDO!
LET TERRAX BE NO MORE!
PRETERNATURAL FORCES CRACKLE BETWEEN GALACTUS AND HIS FORMER HERALD...
THAT BLAST OF ENERGY... IT SEEMS TO BE FLOWING FROM TERRAX TO GALACTUS!
ONCE, HE WAS TYROS, PETTY DICTATOR OF A WORLD BEYOND HUMAN KNOWLEDGE.
HE THOUGHT HIMSELF SUPREME IN ALL THE COSMOS, LORD AND MASTER OF ALL HE SURVEYED.
HE WAS WRONG.
IN A UNIVERSE BEYOND MEASURE, WHAT IS THE PUNY LIFE OF A MAN? WHAT IS THE DOMINION OF A SINGLE WORLD?
ONCE, HE WAS TYROS, PETTY DICTATOR OF A WORLD BEYOND HUMAN KNOWLEDGE.
NOW IS HE TYROS ONCE MORE...

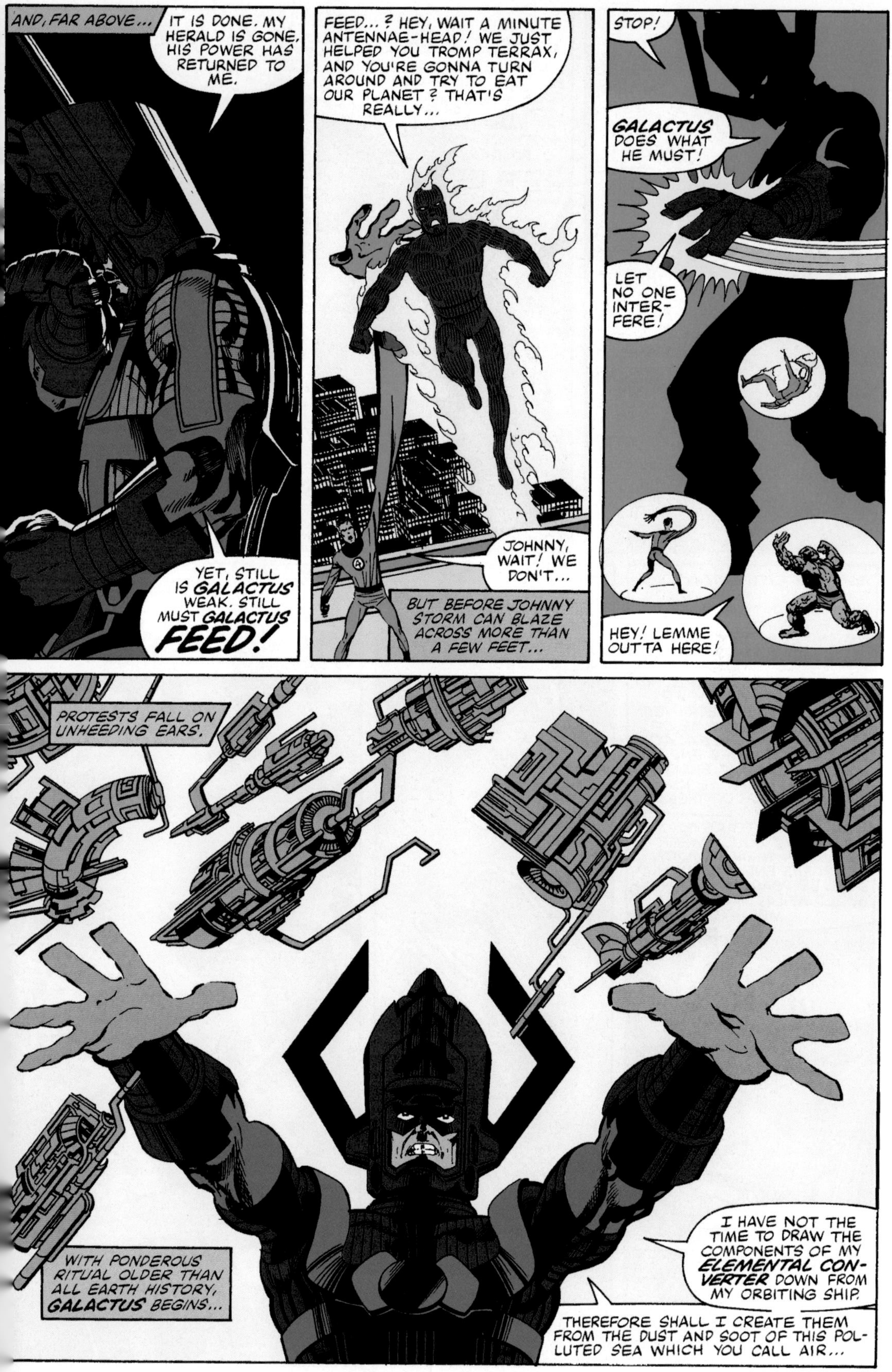

AND, FAR ABOVE...
IT IS DONE. MY HERALD IS GONE. HIS POWER HAS RETURNED TO ME.
YET, STILL IS GALACTUS WEAK. STILL MUST GALACTUS FEED!
FEED...? HEY, WAIT A MINUTE ANTENNAE-HEAD! WE JUST HELPED YOU TROMP TERRAX, AND YOU'RE GONNA TURN AROUND AND TRY TO EAT OUR PLANET? THAT'S REALLY...
JOHNNY, WAIT! WE DON'T...
BUT BEFORE JOHNNY STORM CAN BLAZE ACROSS MORE THAN A FEW FEET...
STOP!
GALACTUS DOES WHAT HE MUST!
LET NO ONE INTERFERE!
HEY! LEMME OUTTA HERE!
PROTESTS FALL ON UNHEEDING EARS.
WITH PONDEROUS RITUAL OLDER THAN ALL EARTH HISTORY, GALACTUS BEGINS...
I HAVE NOT THE TIME TO DRAW THE COMPONENTS OF MY ELEMENTAL CONVERTER DOWN FROM MY ORBITING SHIP.
THEREFORE SHALL I CREATE THEM FROM THE DUST AND SOOT OF THIS POLLUTED SEA WHICH YOU CALL AIR...

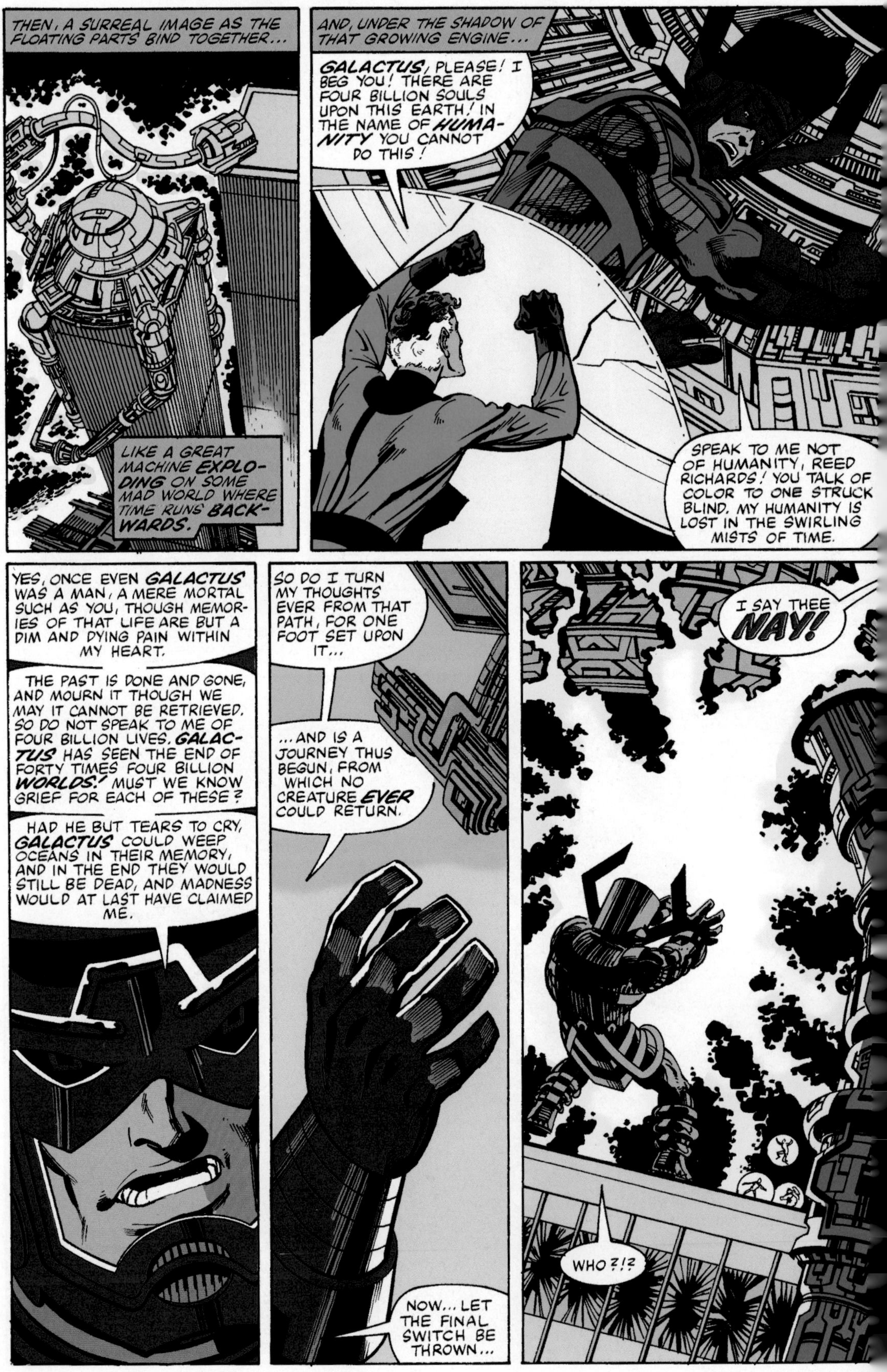
THEN, A SURREAL IMAGE AS THE FLOATING PARTS BIND TOGETHER...
LIKE A GREAT MACHINE EXPLODING ON SOME MAD WORLD WHERE TIME RUNS BACKWARDS.
AND, UNDER THE SHADOW OF THAT GROWING ENGINE...
GALACTUS, PLEASE! I BEG YOU! THERE ARE FOUR BILLION SOULS UPON THIS EARTH! IN THE NAME OF HUMANITY YOU CANNOT DO THIS!
SPEAK TO ME NOT OF HUMANITY, REED RICHARDS! YOU TALK OF COLOR TO ONE STRUCK BLIND. MY HUMANITY IS LOST IN THE SWIRLING MISTS OF TIME.
YES, ONCE EVEN GALACTUS WAS A MAN, A MERE MORTAL SUCH AS YOU, THOUGH MEMORIES OF THAT LIFE ARE BUT A DIM AND DYING PAIN WITHIN MY HEART.
THE PAST IS DONE AND GONE, AND MOURN IT THOUGH WE MAY IT CANNOT BE RETRIEVED. SO DO NOT SPEAK TO ME OF FOUR BILLION LIVES. GALACTUS HAS SEEN THE END OF FORTY TIMES FOUR BILLION WORLDS! MUST WE KNOW GRIEF FOR EACH OF THESE?
HAD HE BUT TEARS TO CRY, GALACTUS COULD WEEP OCEANS IN THEIR MEMORY, AND IN THE END THEY WOULD STILL BE DEAD, AND MADNESS WOULD AT LAST HAVE CLAIMED ME.
SO DO I TURN MY THOUGHTS EVER FROM THAT PATH, FOR ONE FOOT SET UPON IT...
...AND IS A JOURNEY THUS BEGUN, FROM WHICH NO CREATURE EVER COULD RETURN.
NOW... LET THE FINAL SWITCH BE THROWN...
I SAY THEE NAY!
WHO?!?

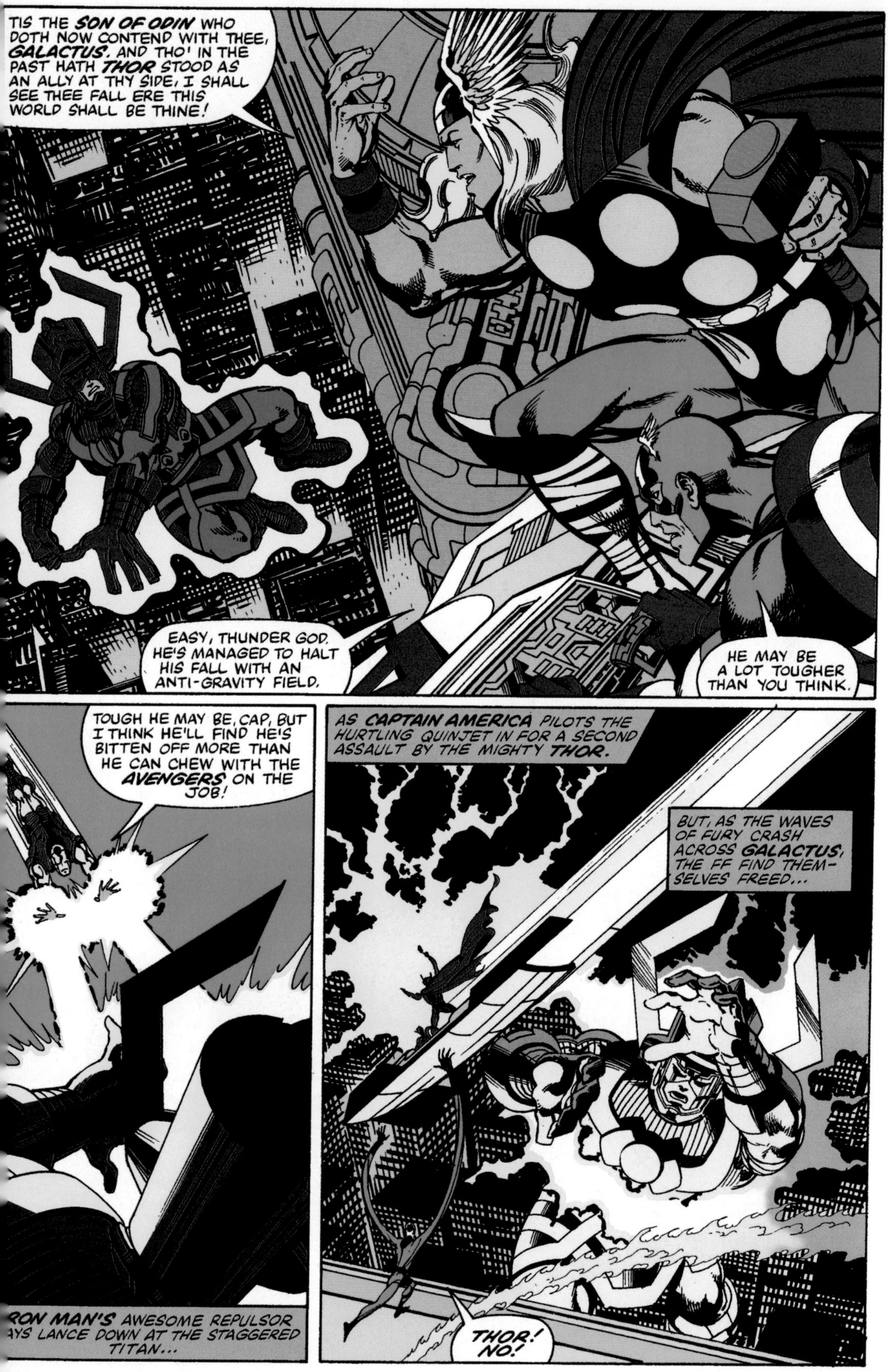
TIS THE SON OF ODIN WHO DOTH NOW CONTEND WITH THEE, GALACTUS. AND THO' IN THE PAST HATH THOR STOOD AS AN ALLY AT THY SIDE, I SHALL SEE THEE FALL ERE THIS WORLD SHALL BE THINE!
EASY, THUNDER GOD. HE'S MANAGED TO HALT HIS FALL WITH AN ANTI-GRAVITY FIELD.
HE MAY BE A LOT TOUGHER THAN YOU THINK.
TOUGH HE MAY BE, CAP, BUT I THINK HE'LL FIND HE'S BITTEN OFF MORE THAN HE CAN CHEW WITH THE AVENGERS ON THE JOB!
RON MAN'S AWESOME REPULSOR AYS LANCE DOWN AT THE STAGGERED TITAN...
AS CAPTAIN AMERICA PILOTS THE HURTLING QUINJET IN FOR A SECOND ASSAULT BY THE MIGHTY THOR.
BUT, AS THE WAVES OF FURY CRASH ACROSS GALACTUS, THE FF FIND THEMSELVES FREED...
THOR! NO!

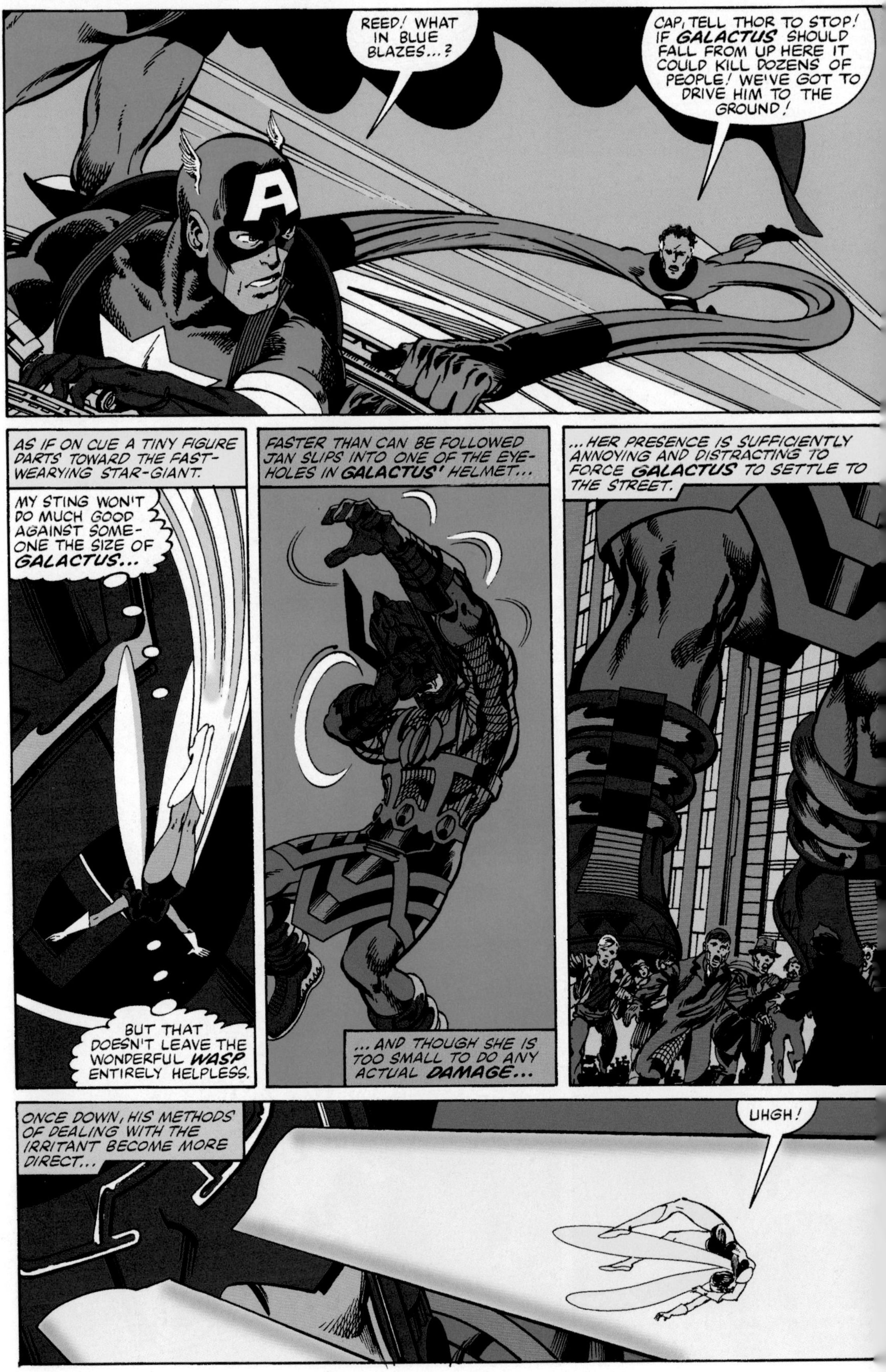

REED! WHAT IN BLUE BLAZES...?
CAP, TELL THOR TO STOP! IF GALACTUS SHOULD FALL FROM UP HERE IT COULD KILL DOZENS OF PEOPLE! WE'VE GOT TO DRIVE HIM TO THE GROUND!
AS IF ON CUE A TINY FIGURE DARTS TOWARD THE FAST-WEARYING STAR-GIANT.
MY STING WON'T DO MUCH GOOD AGAINST SOMEONE THE SIZE OF GALACTUS...
BUT THAT DOESN'T LEAVE THE WONDERFUL WASP ENTIRELY HELPLESS.
FASTER THAN CAN BE FOLLOWED JAN SLIPS INTO ONE OF THE EYE-HOLES IN GALACTUS' HELMET...
...AND THOUGH SHE IS TOO SMALL TO DO ANY ACTUAL DAMAGE...
...HER PRESENCE IS SUFFICIENTLY ANNOYING AND DISTRACTING TO FORCE GALACTUS TO SETTLE TO THE STREET.
ONCE DOWN, HIS METHODS OF DEALING WITH THE IRRITANT BECOME MORE DIRECT...
UHGH!

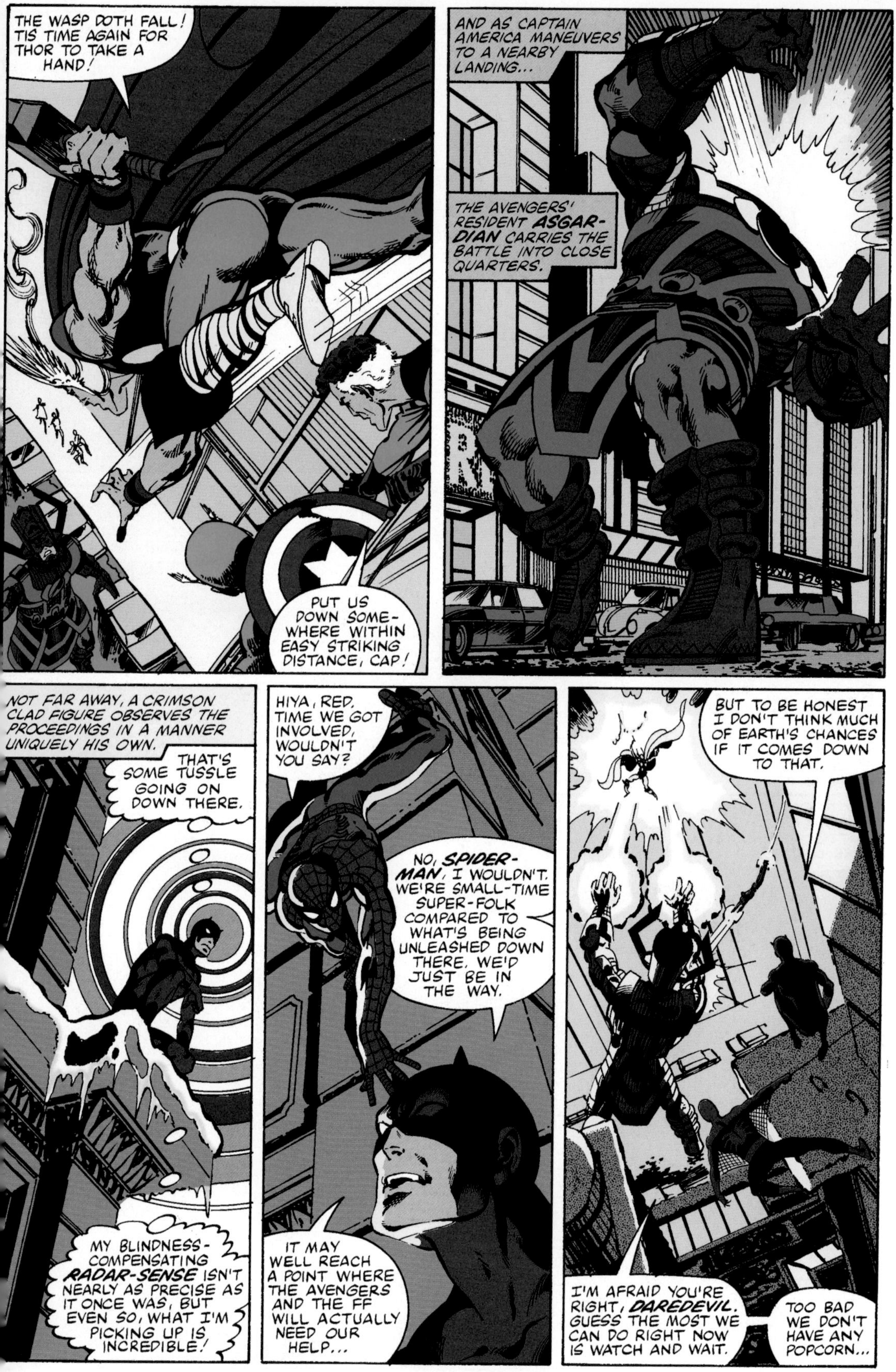
THE WASP DOTH FALL! 'TIS TIME AGAIN FOR THOR TO TAKE A HAND!
PUT US DOWN SOMEWHERE WITHIN EASY STRIKING DISTANCE, CAP!
AND AS CAPTAIN AMERICA MANEUVERS TO A NEARBY LANDING...
THE AVENGERS' RESIDENT ASGARDIAN CARRIES THE BATTLE INTO CLOSE QUARTERS.
NOT FAR AWAY, A CRIMSON CLAD FIGURE OBSERVES THE PROCEEDINGS IN A MANNER UNIQUELY HIS OWN.
THAT'S SOME TUSSLE GOING ON DOWN THERE.
MY BLINDNESS-COMPENSATING RADAR-SENSE ISN'T NEARLY AS PRECISE AS IT ONCE WAS, BUT EVEN SO, WHAT I'M PICKING UP IS INCREDIBLE!
HIYA, RED, TIME WE GOT INVOLVED, WOULDN'T YOU SAY?
NO, SPIDER-MAN, I WOULDN'T. WE'RE SMALL-TIME SUPER-FOLK COMPARED TO WHAT'S BEING UNLEASHED DOWN THERE. WE'D JUST BE IN THE WAY.
IT MAY WELL REACH A POINT WHERE THE AVENGERS AND THE FF WILL ACTUALLY NEED OUR HELP...
BUT TO BE HONEST I DON'T THINK MUCH OF EARTH'S CHANCES IF IT COMES DOWN TO THAT.
I'M AFRAID YOU'RE RIGHT, DAREDEVIL. GUESS THE MOST WE CAN DO RIGHT NOW IS WATCH AND WAIT.
TOO BAD WE DON'T HAVE ANY POPCORN...

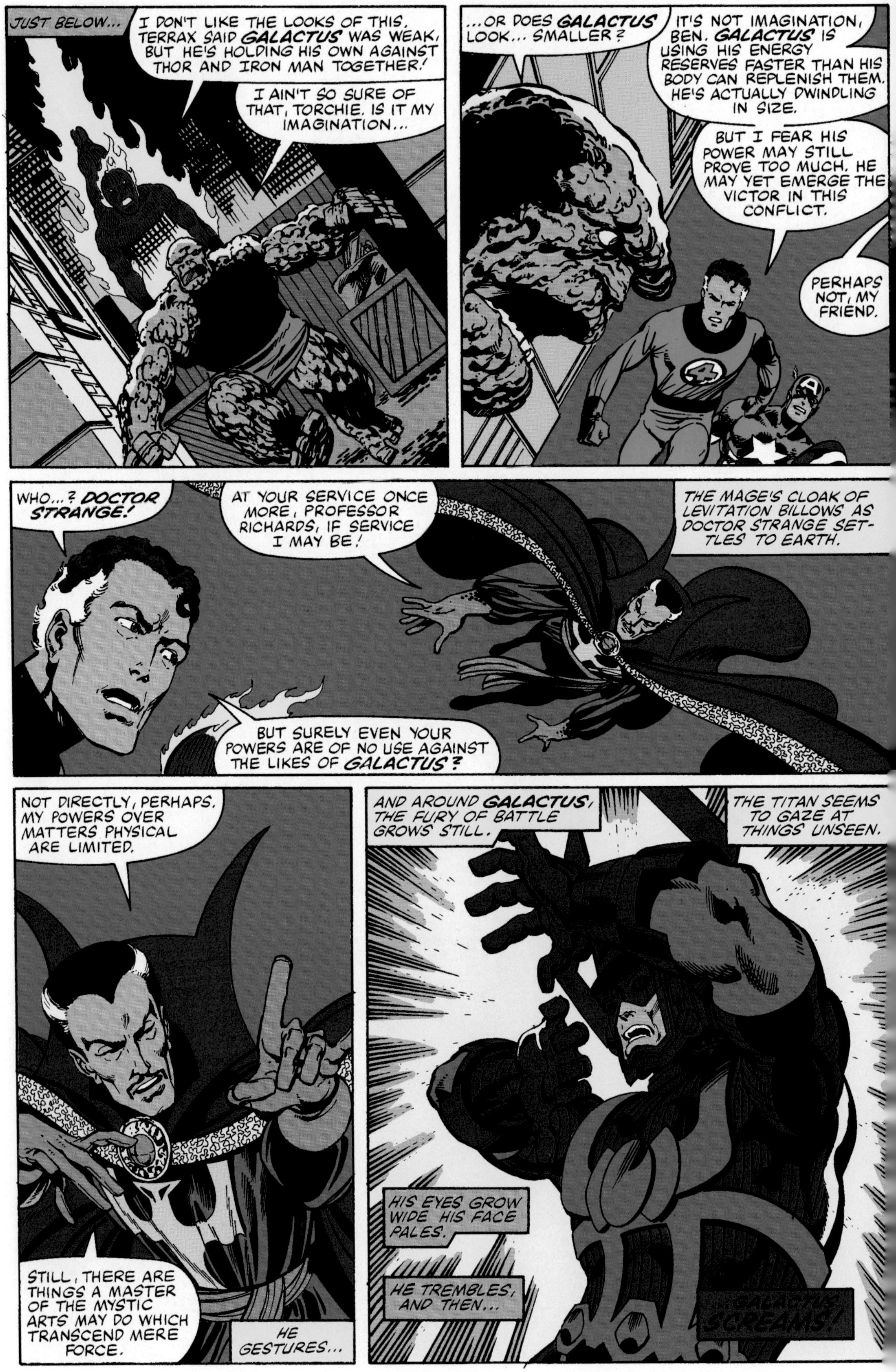
JUST BELOW...
I DON'T LIKE THE LOOKS OF THIS. TERRAX SAID GALACTUS WAS WEAK, BUT HE'S HOLDING HIS OWN AGAINST THOR AND IRON MAN TOGETHER!
I AIN'T SO SURE OF THAT, TORCHIE. IS IT MY IMAGINATION...
...OR DOES GALACTUS LOOK... SMALLER?
IT'S NOT IMAGINATION, BEN. GALACTUS IS USING HIS ENERGY RESERVES FASTER THAN HIS BODY CAN REPLENISH THEM. HE'S ACTUALLY DWINDLING IN SIZE.
BUT I FEAR HIS POWER MAY STILL PROVE TOO MUCH. HE MAY YET EMERGE THE VICTOR IN THIS CONFLICT.
PERHAPS NOT, MY FRIEND.
WHO...? DOCTOR STRANGE!
AT YOUR SERVICE ONCE MORE, PROFESSOR RICHARDS, IF SERVICE I MAY BE!
THE MAGE'S CLOAK OF LEVITATION BILLOWS AS DOCTOR STRANGE SETTLES TO EARTH.
BUT SURELY EVEN YOUR POWERS ARE OF NO USE AGAINST THE LIKES OF GALACTUS?
NOT DIRECTLY, PERHAPS. MY POWERS OVER MATTERS PHYSICAL ARE LIMITED.
STILL, THERE ARE THINGS A MASTER OF THE MYSTIC ARTS MAY DO WHICH TRANSCEND MERE FORCE.
HE GESTURES...
AND AROUND GALACTUS, THE FURY OF BATTLE GROWS STILL.
THE TITAN SEEMS TO GAZE AT THINGS UNSEEN.
HIS EYES GROW WIDE HIS FACE PALES.
HE TREMBLES, AND THEN...
...GALACTUS SCREAMS!

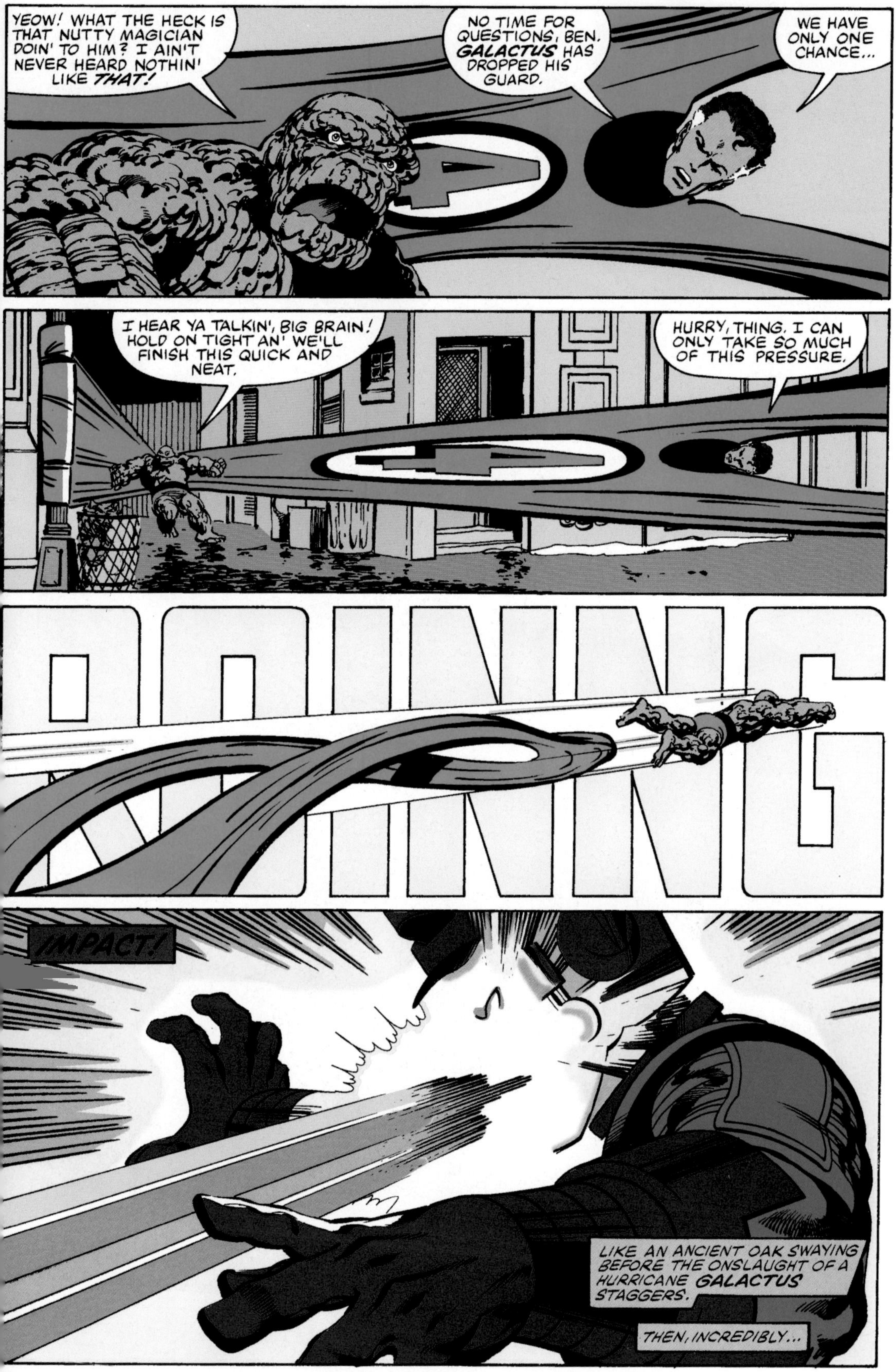
YEOW! WHAT THE HECK IS THAT NUTTY MAGICIAN DOIN' TO HIM? I AIN'T NEVER HEARD NOTHIN' LIKE *THAT!*
NO TIME FOR QUESTIONS, BEN. *GALACTUS* HAS DROPPED HIS GUARD.
WE HAVE ONLY ONE CHANCE...
I HEAR YA TALKIN', BIG BRAIN! HOLD ON TIGHT AN' WE'LL FINISH THIS QUICK AND NEAT.
HURRY, THING. I CAN ONLY TAKE SO MUCH OF THIS PRESSURE.
BOING
IMPACT!
LIKE AN ANCIENT OAK SWAYING BEFORE THE ONSLAUGHT OF A HURRICANE *GALACTUS* STAGGERS.
THEN, INCREDIBLY...

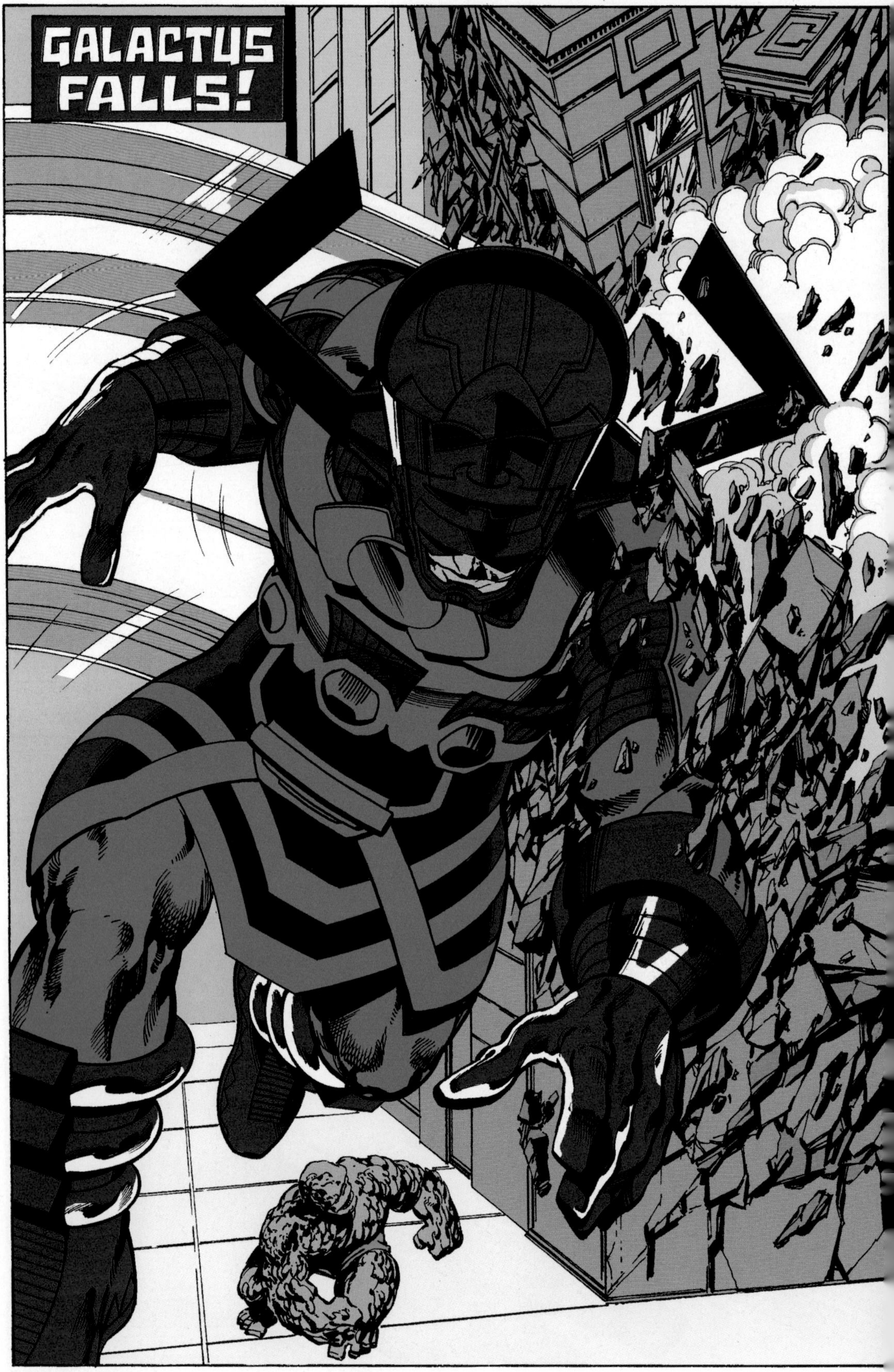
GALACTUS FALLS!

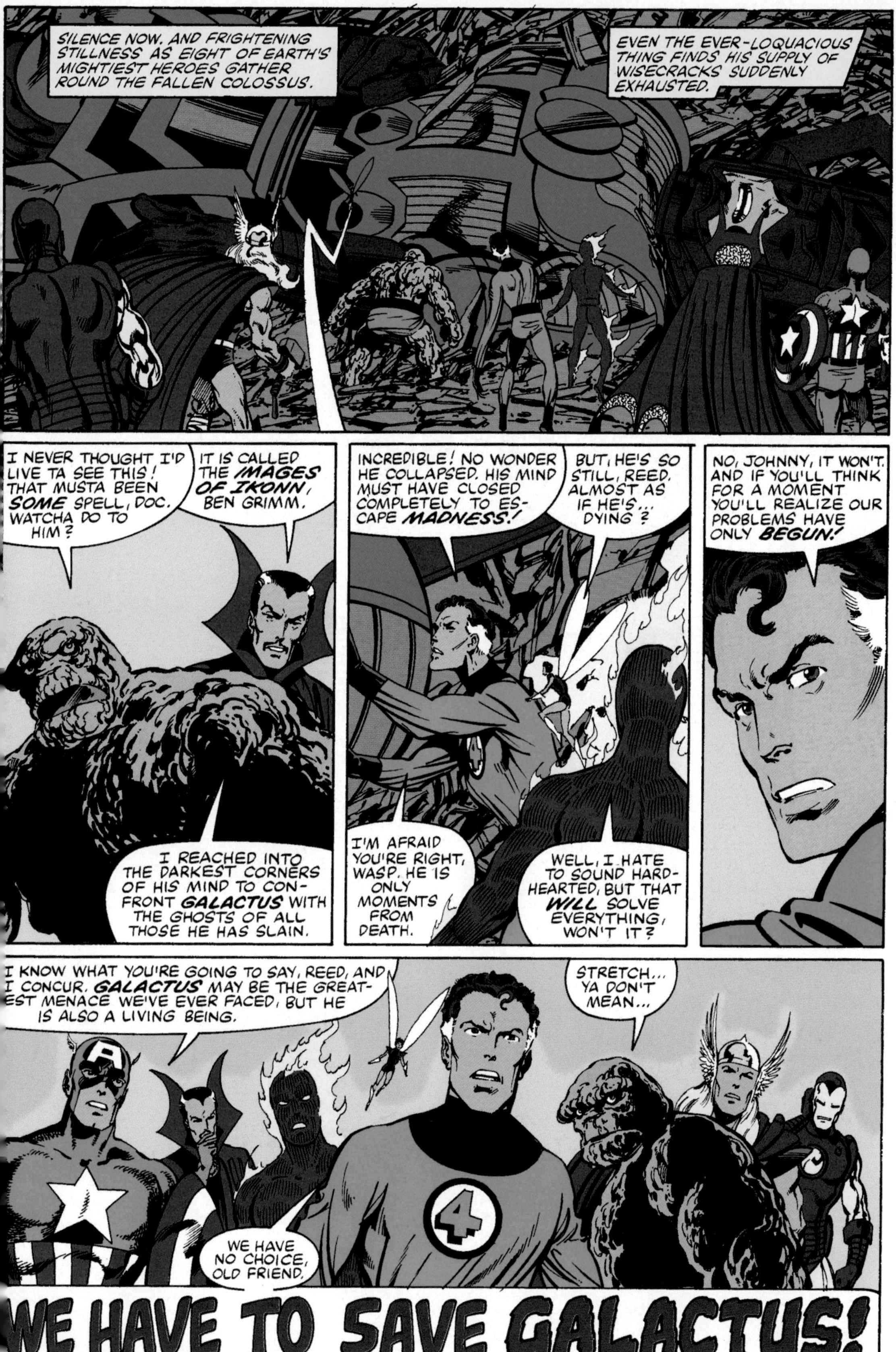
SILENCE NOW. AND FRIGHTENING STILLNESS AS EIGHT OF EARTH'S MIGHTIEST HEROES GATHER ROUND THE FALLEN COLOSSUS.
EVEN THE EVER-LOQUACIOUS THING FINDS HIS SUPPLY OF WISECRACKS SUDDENLY EXHAUSTED.
I NEVER THOUGHT I'D LIVE TA SEE THIS! THAT MUSTA BEEN SOME SPELL, DOC. WATCHA DO TO HIM?
IT IS CALLED THE IMAGES OF IKONN, BEN GRIMM.
I REACHED INTO THE DARKEST CORNERS OF HIS MIND TO CONFRONT GALACTUS WITH THE GHOSTS OF ALL THOSE HE HAS SLAIN.
INCREDIBLE! NO WONDER HE COLLAPSED. HIS MIND MUST HAVE CLOSED COMPLETELY TO ESCAPE MADNESS!
BUT, HE'S SO STILL, REED. ALMOST AS IF HE'S... DYING?
I'M AFRAID YOU'RE RIGHT, WASP. HE IS ONLY MOMENTS FROM DEATH.
WELL, I HATE TO SOUND HARD-HEARTED, BUT THAT WILL SOLVE EVERYTHING, WON'T IT?
NO, JOHNNY, IT WON'T. AND IF YOU'LL THINK FOR A MOMENT YOU'LL REALIZE OUR PROBLEMS HAVE ONLY BEGUN!
I KNOW WHAT YOU'RE GOING TO SAY, REED, AND I CONCUR. GALACTUS MAY BE THE GREATEST MENACE WE'VE EVER FACED, BUT HE IS ALSO A LIVING BEING.
STRETCH... YA DON'T MEAN...
WE HAVE NO CHOICE, OLD FRIEND.
WE HAVE TO SAVE GALACTUS!

fantastic four # 244

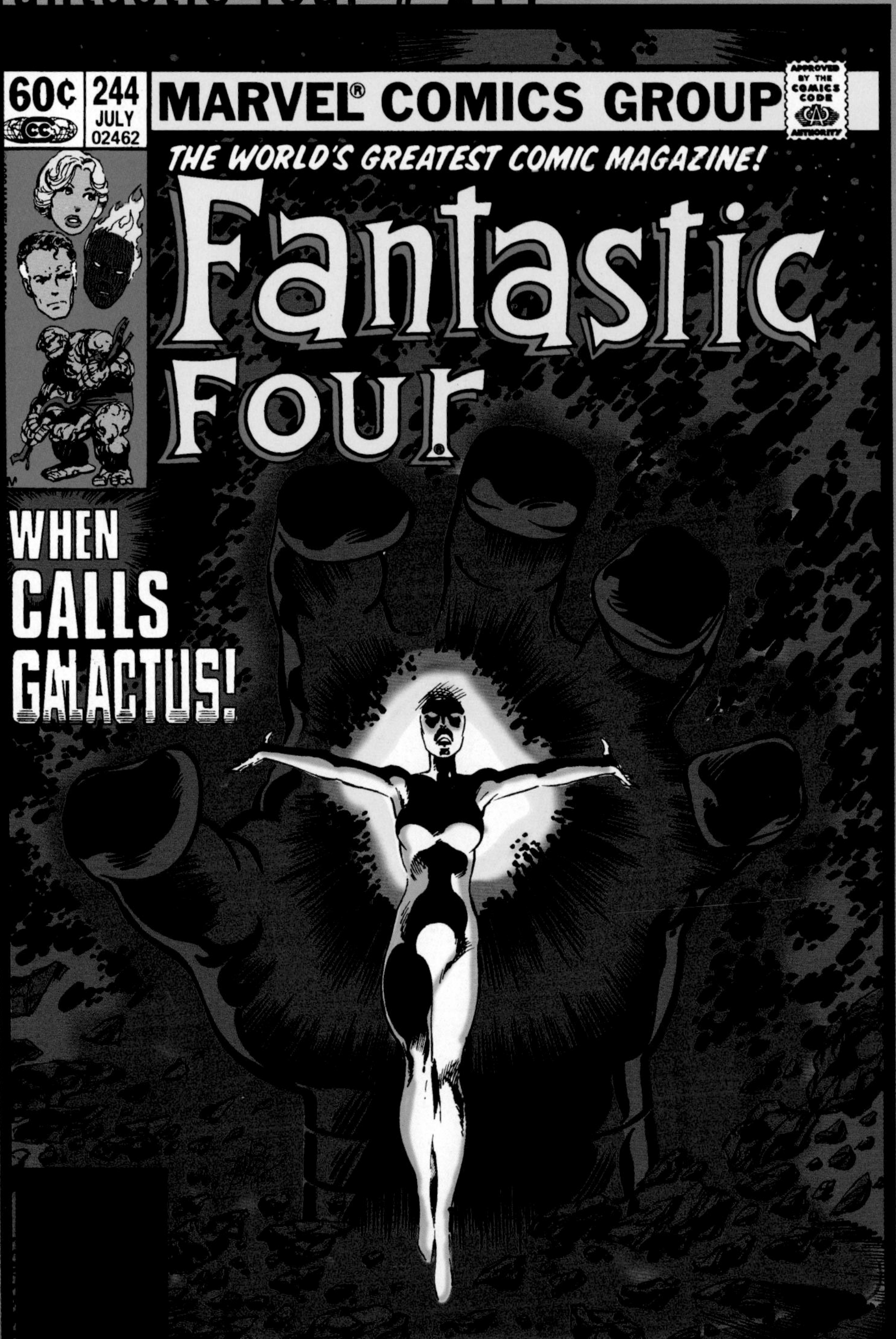
60¢
244
JULY
02462
MARVEL® COMICS GROUP
APPROVED BY THE COMICS CODE AUTHORITY
THE WORLD'S GREATEST COMIC MAGAZINE!
Fantastic Four
WHEN
CALLS
GALACTUS!

JULY 1982

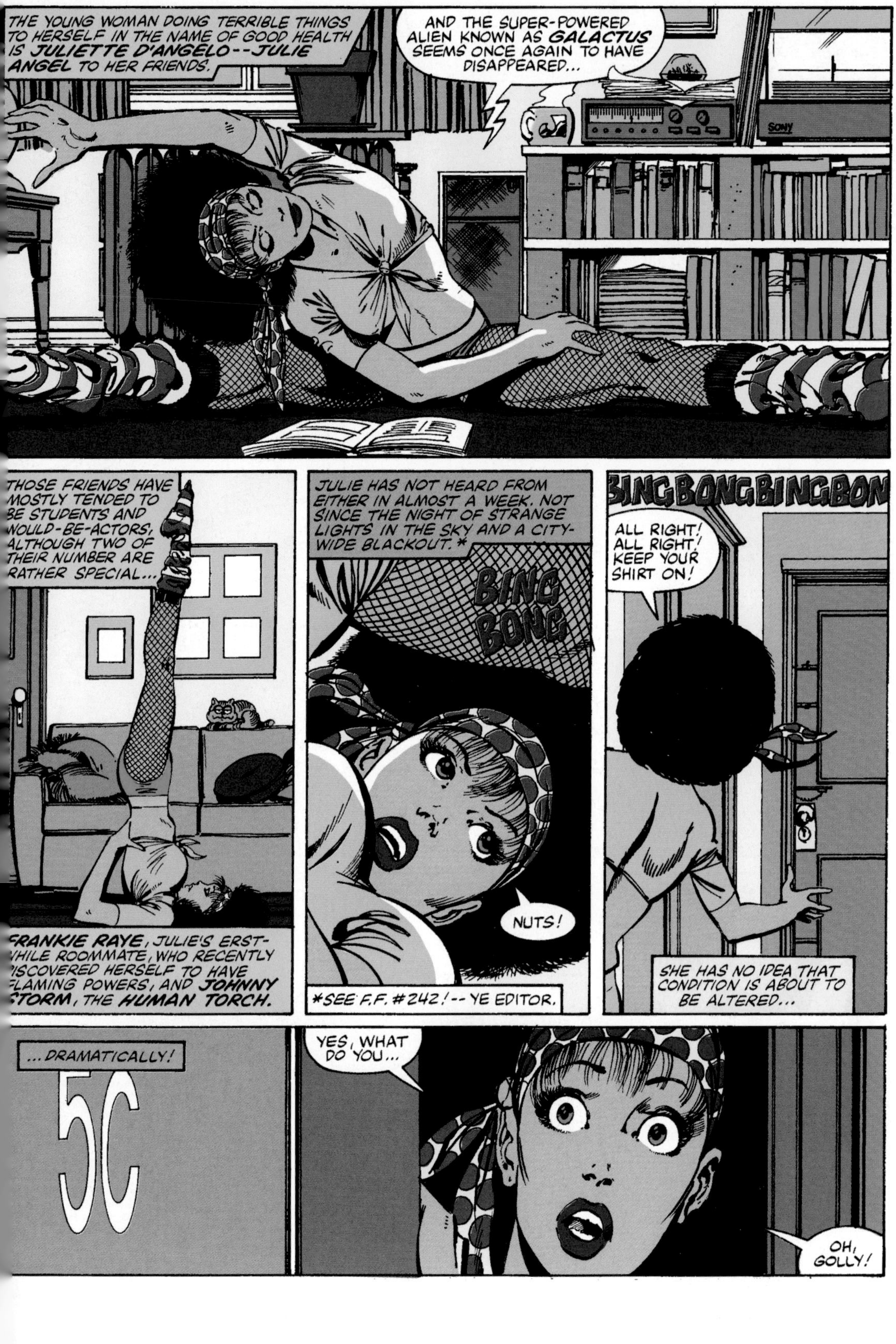
THE YOUNG WOMAN DOING TERRIBLE THINGS TO HERSELF IN THE NAME OF GOOD HEALTH IS JULIETTE D'ANGELO--JULIE ANGEL TO HER FRIENDS!
AND THE SUPER-POWERED ALIEN KNOWN AS GALACTUS SEEMS ONCE AGAIN TO HAVE DISAPPEARED...
SONY
THOSE FRIENDS HAVE MOSTLY TENDED TO BE STUDENTS AND WOULD-BE-ACTORS, ALTHOUGH TWO OF THEIR NUMBER ARE RATHER SPECIAL...
FRANKIE RAYE, JULIE'S ERST-WHILE ROOMMATE, WHO RECENTLY DISCOVERED HERSELF TO HAVE FLAMING POWERS, AND JOHNNY STORM, THE HUMAN TORCH.
JULIE HAS NOT HEARD FROM EITHER IN ALMOST A WEEK. NOT SINCE THE NIGHT OF STRANGE LIGHTS IN THE SKY AND A CITY-WIDE BLACKOUT.*
BING BONG
NUTS!
*SEE F.F. #242! -- YE EDITOR.
BINGBONGBINGBON
ALL RIGHT! ALL RIGHT! KEEP YOUR SHIRT ON!
SHE HAS NO IDEA THAT CONDITION IS ABOUT TO BE ALTERED...
...DRAMATICALLY!
5C
YES, WHAT DO YOU...
OH, GOLLY!

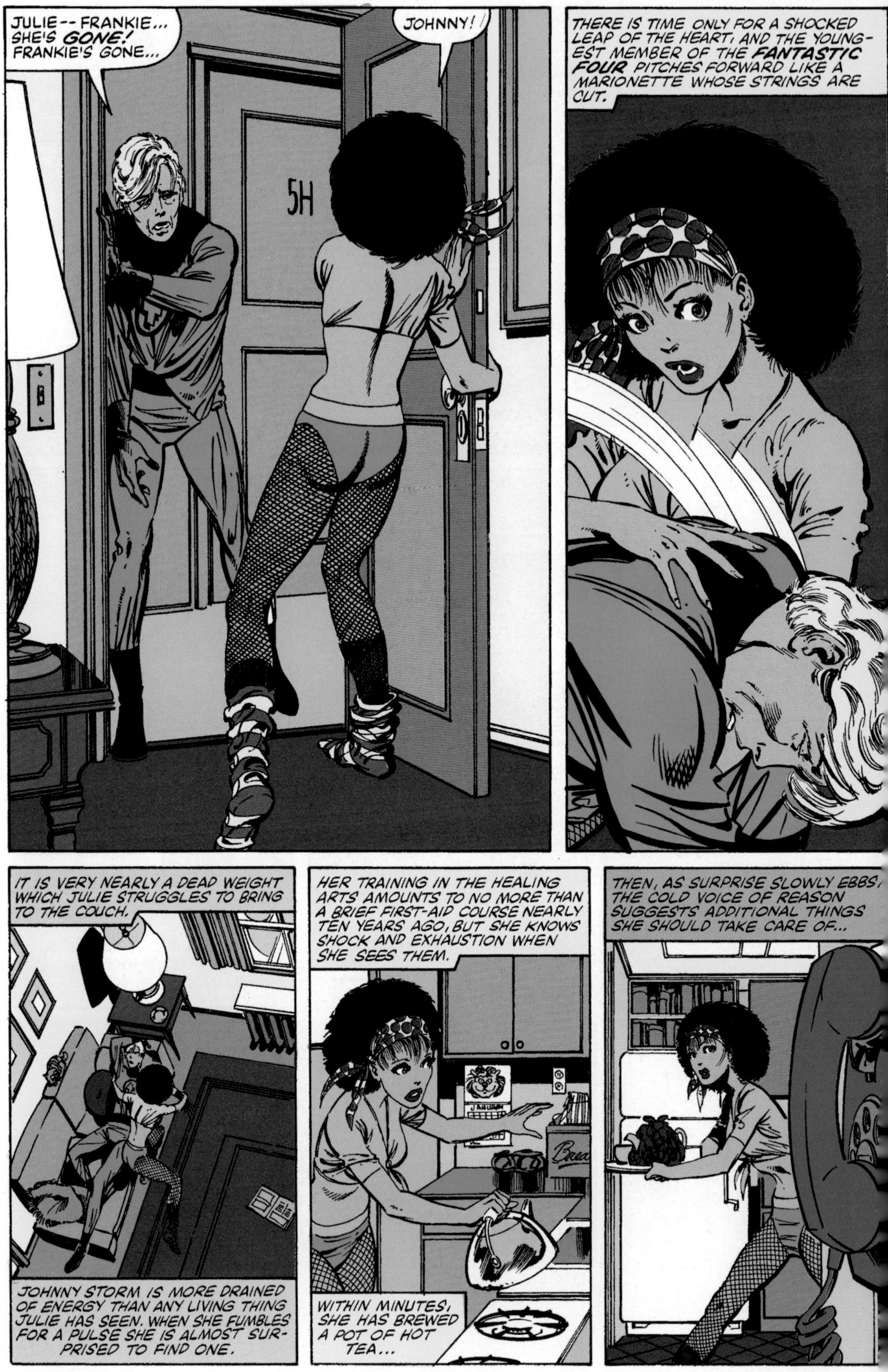
JULIE--FRANKIE... SHE'S GONE! FRANKIE'S GONE...
JOHNNY!
5H
THERE IS TIME ONLY FOR A SHOCKED LEAP OF THE HEART, AND THE YOUNGEST MEMBER OF THE FANTASTIC FOUR PITCHES FORWARD LIKE A MARIONETTE WHOSE STRINGS ARE CUT.
IT IS VERY NEARLY A DEAD WEIGHT WHICH JULIE STRUGGLES TO BRING TO THE COUCH.
JOHNNY STORM IS MORE DRAINED OF ENERGY THAN ANY LIVING THING JULIE HAS SEEN. WHEN SHE FUMBLES FOR A PULSE SHE IS ALMOST SURPRISED TO FIND ONE.
HER TRAINING IN THE HEALING ARTS AMOUNTS TO NO MORE THAN A BRIEF FIRST-AID COURSE NEARLY TEN YEARS AGO, BUT SHE KNOWS SHOCK AND EXHAUSTION WHEN SHE SEES THEM.
WITHIN MINUTES, SHE HAS BREWED A POT OF HOT TEA...
THEN, AS SURPRISE SLOWLY EBBS, THE COLD VOICE OF REASON SUGGESTS ADDITIONAL THINGS SHE SHOULD TAKE CARE OF...

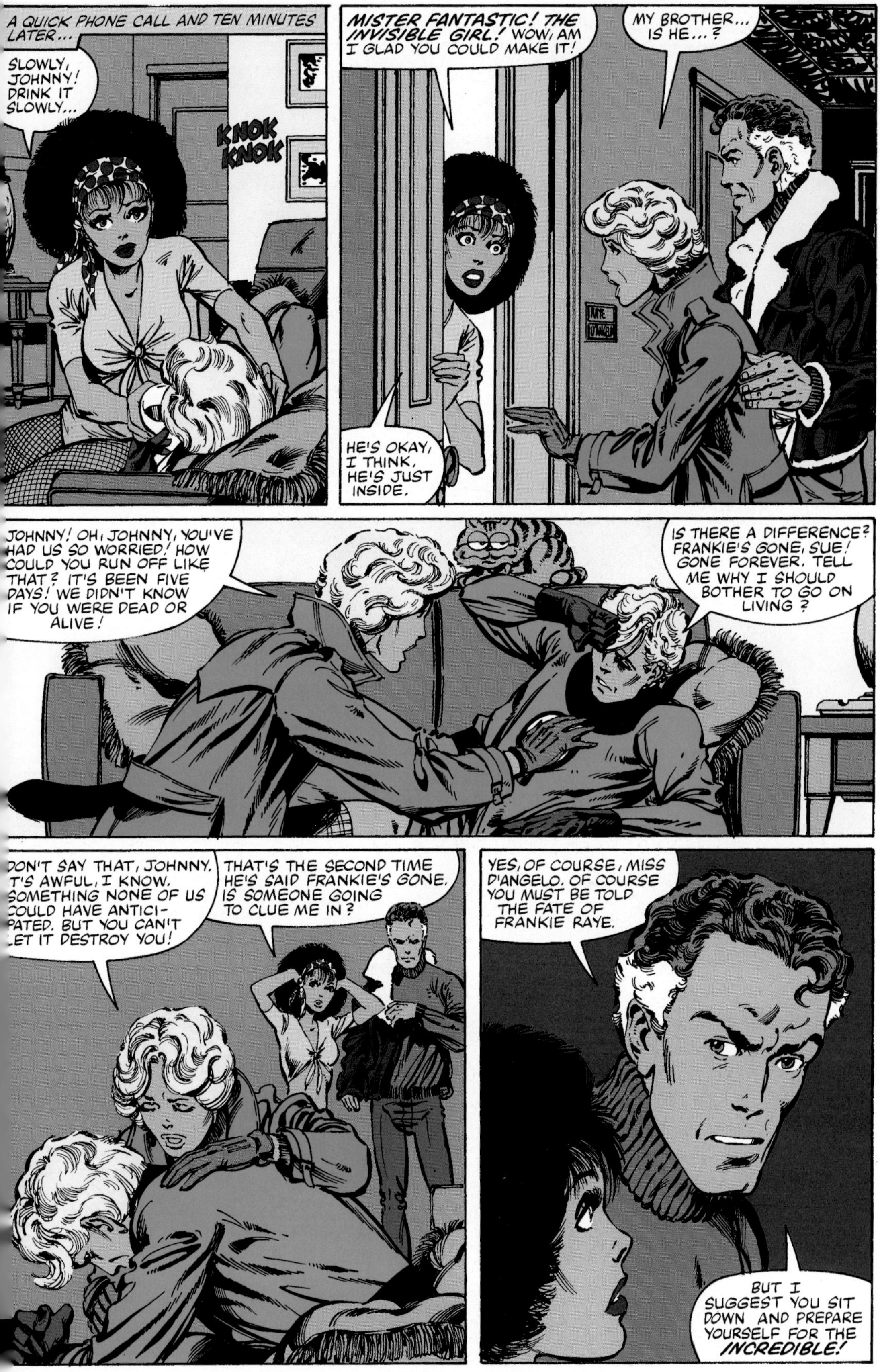

A QUICK PHONE CALL AND TEN MINUTES LATER...
SLOWLY, JOHNNY! DRINK IT SLOWLY...
KNOK KNOK
MISTER FANTASTIC! THE INVISIBLE GIRL! WOW, AM I GLAD YOU COULD MAKE IT!
MY BROTHER... IS HE...?
HE'S OKAY, I THINK. HE'S JUST INSIDE.
JOHNNY! OH, JOHNNY, YOU'VE HAD US SO WORRIED! HOW COULD YOU RUN OFF LIKE THAT? IT'S BEEN FIVE DAYS! WE DIDN'T KNOW IF YOU WERE DEAD OR ALIVE!
IS THERE A DIFFERENCE? FRANKIE'S GONE, SUE! GONE FOREVER. TELL ME WHY I SHOULD BOTHER TO GO ON LIVING?
DON'T SAY THAT, JOHNNY. IT'S AWFUL, I KNOW. SOMETHING NONE OF US COULD HAVE ANTICIPATED. BUT YOU CAN'T LET IT DESTROY YOU!
THAT'S THE SECOND TIME HE'S SAID FRANKIE'S GONE. IS SOMEONE GOING TO CLUE ME IN?
YES, OF COURSE, MISS D'ANGELO. OF COURSE YOU MUST BE TOLD THE FATE OF FRANKIE RAYE.
BUT I SUGGEST YOU SIT DOWN AND PREPARE YOURSELF FOR THE INCREDIBLE!

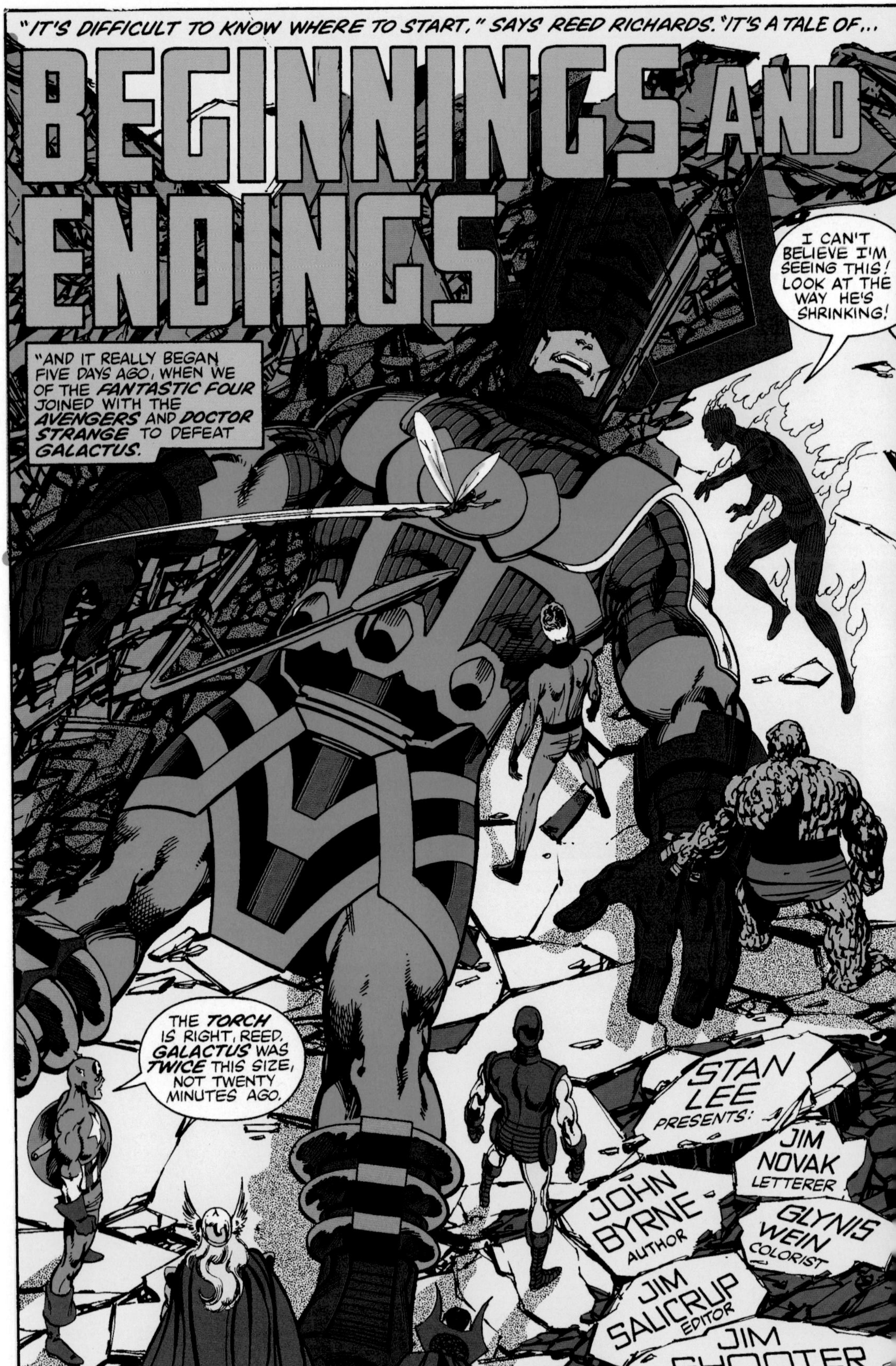
"IT'S DIFFICULT TO KNOW WHERE TO START," SAYS REED RICHARDS. "IT'S A TALE OF...
BEGINNINGS AND ENDINGS
I CAN'T BELIEVE I'M SEEING THIS! LOOK AT THE WAY HE'S SHRINKING!
"AND IT REALLY BEGAN FIVE DAYS AGO, WHEN WE OF THE FANTASTIC FOUR JOINED WITH THE AVENGERS AND DOCTOR STRANGE TO DEFEAT GALACTUS.
THE TORCH IS RIGHT, REED. GALACTUS WAS TWICE THIS SIZE, NOT TWENTY MINUTES AGO.
STAN LEE PRESENTS:
JIM NOVAK LETTERER
JOHN BYRNE AUTHOR
GLYNIS WEIN COLORIST
JIM SALICRUP EDITOR
JIM SHOOTER ALPHA/OMEGA

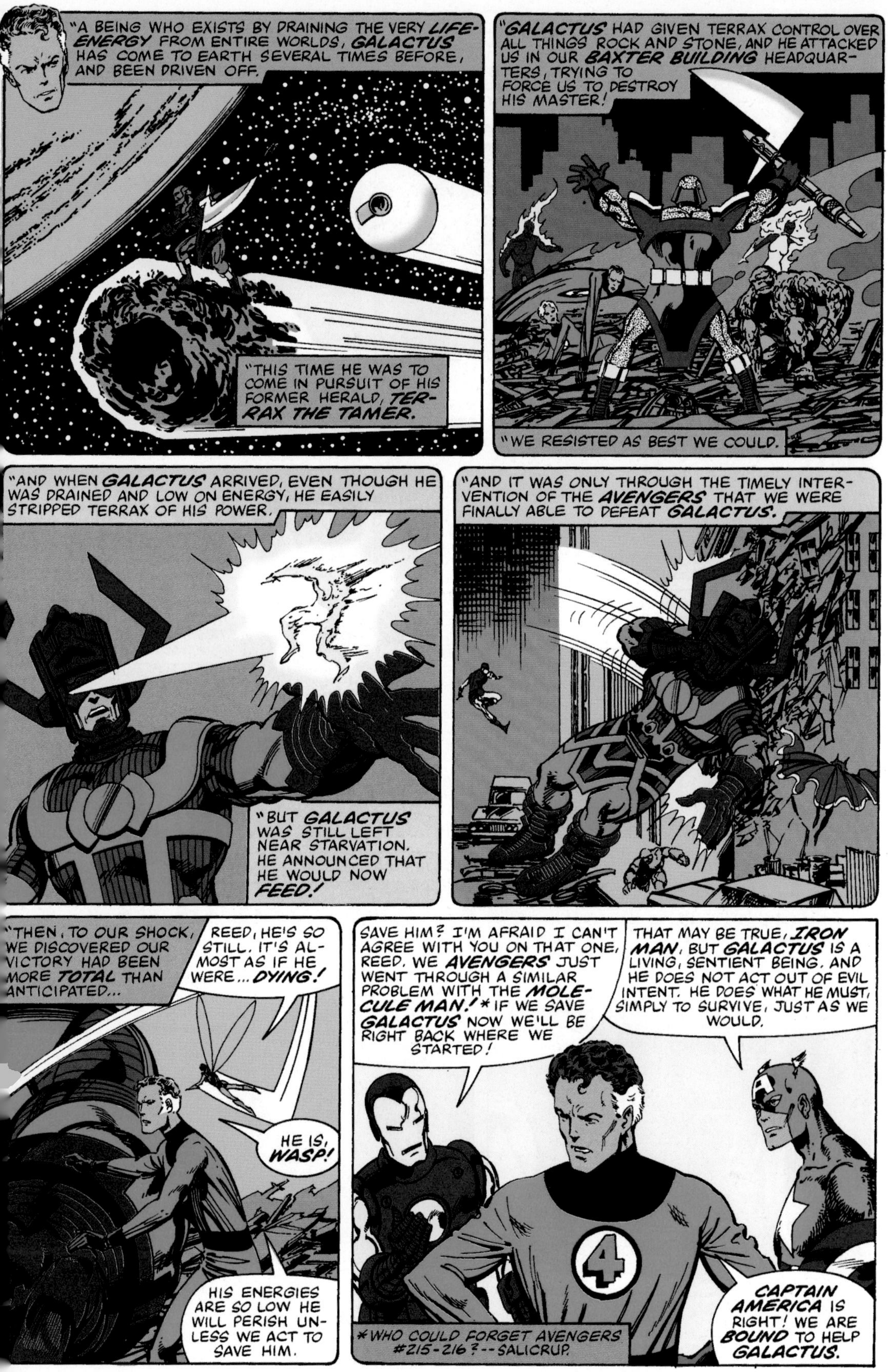
"A BEING WHO EXISTS BY DRAINING THE VERY LIFE-ENERGY FROM ENTIRE WORLDS, GALACTUS HAS COME TO EARTH SEVERAL TIMES BEFORE, AND BEEN DRIVEN OFF.
"THIS TIME HE WAS TO COME IN PURSUIT OF HIS FORMER HERALD, TERRAX THE TAMER.
"GALACTUS HAD GIVEN TERRAX CONTROL OVER ALL THINGS ROCK AND STONE, AND HE ATTACKED US IN OUR BAXTER BUILDING HEADQUARTERS, TRYING TO FORCE US TO DESTROY HIS MASTER!
"WE RESISTED AS BEST WE COULD.
"AND WHEN GALACTUS ARRIVED, EVEN THOUGH HE WAS DRAINED AND LOW ON ENERGY, HE EASILY STRIPPED TERRAX OF HIS POWER.
"BUT GALACTUS WAS STILL LEFT NEAR STARVATION. HE ANNOUNCED THAT HE WOULD NOW FEED!
"AND IT WAS ONLY THROUGH THE TIMELY INTERVENTION OF THE AVENGERS THAT WE WERE FINALLY ABLE TO DEFEAT GALACTUS.
"THEN, TO OUR SHOCK, WE DISCOVERED OUR VICTORY HAD BEEN MORE TOTAL THAN ANTICIPATED...
REED, HE'S SO STILL. IT'S ALMOST AS IF HE WERE... DYING!
HE IS, WASP!
HIS ENERGIES ARE SO LOW HE WILL PERISH UNLESS WE ACT TO SAVE HIM.
SAVE HIM? I'M AFRAID I CAN'T AGREE WITH YOU ON THAT ONE, REED. WE AVENGERS JUST WENT THROUGH A SIMILAR PROBLEM WITH THE MOLECULE MAN! * IF WE SAVE GALACTUS NOW WE'LL BE RIGHT BACK WHERE WE STARTED!
THAT MAY BE TRUE, IRON MAN, BUT GALACTUS IS A LIVING, SENTIENT BEING, AND HE DOES NOT ACT OUT OF EVIL INTENT. HE DOES WHAT HE MUST, SIMPLY TO SURVIVE, JUST AS WE WOULD.
CAPTAIN AMERICA IS RIGHT! WE ARE BOUND TO HELP GALACTUS.
* WHO COULD FORGET AVENGERS #215-216? --SALICRUP.

WE BETTER MOVE FAST THEN, STRETCH! THE WAY HE'S SHRINKIN' THERE'LL BE NOTHIN' LEFT OF HIM TA SAVE INSIDE A COUPLA HOURS.

BUT, WHAT IS THERE TO DO? I AM TRAINED IN BOTH THE *MYSTIC* AND THE *MEDICINAL* ARTS, YET SUCH A TASK AS THIS IS BEYOND EITHER SKILL.

DOCTOR STRANGE DOTH SPEAK TRULY, AS THE MORTAL DON BLAKE, *THOR* IS ALSO TRAINED AS A PHYSICIAN, BUT TO DOCTOR *GALACTUS...?!*

THE *THING* IS RIGHT. *GALACTUS* IS DWINDLING RAPIDLY. HIS ALIEN METABOLISM IS DRAWING ON HIS BODY'S OWN ENERGIES IN LIEU OF THE LIFE-ESSENCE OF THIS PLANET.

BUT, THERE WAS SOMETHING TERRAX SAID ABOUT *GALACTUS* SUBSISTING ON "ARTIFICIAL ENERGIES..."

IRON MAN, DO YOU THINK YOUR EMPLOYER WOULD SEE FIT TO LEND US SOME EQUIPMENT...?

"I DON'T CARE FOR THIS MUCH," REPLIED THE ARMORED AVENGER, "BUT I SEEM TO BE OUTVOTED. I'LL DO WHAT I CAN..."

SO IT IS THAT A FEW MINUTES LATER A FAMILIAR FIGURE STREAKS OVER A LONG ISLAND INDUSTRIAL SITE...

Stark

MOMENTS LATER, THE NIGHT SHIFT SHIPPING CLERK HAS A SURPRISING VISITOR.

THIS IS MIGHTY EXPENSIVE STUFF YOU'RE ASKIN' ME TA HAND OVER, BODYGUARD, BUT I GUESS IT'S OKAY, SEEIN' AS IT'S SIGNED BY MISTER STARK HIMSELF!

NATURALLY I HAD NO DIFFICULTY GAINING PERMISSION FROM MY "BOSS", SINCE I *AM* TONY STARK.

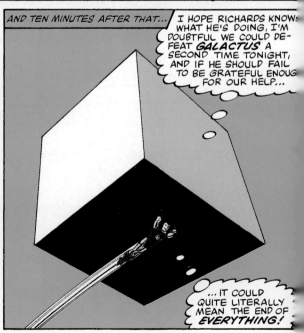

AND TEN MINUTES AFTER THAT...

I HOPE RICHARDS KNOWS WHAT HE'S DOING, I'M DOUBTFUL WE COULD DEFEAT *GALACTUS* A SECOND TIME TONIGHT, AND IF HE SHOULD FAIL TO BE GRATEFUL ENOUGH FOR OUR HELP...

...IT COULD QUITE LITERALLY MEAN THE END OF *EVERYTHING!*

WITHIN THE HOUR... OKAY, BIG BRAIN, WHERE DO I PLUG IN THIS POWER-ADAPTOR DOOHICKEY?

POLICE

RIGHT IN FRONT OF YOU, *BEN.* JUST GIVE ME A MOMENT TO MAKE FINAL ADJUSTMENTS.

A MOMENT IS ALL WE HAVE, REED RICHARDS. *GALACTUS* DOTH WASTE AWAY!

AND YOU STILL HAVE A LOT OF QUESTIONS TO ANSWER BEFORE I'LL LET YOU FIRE UP THAT CONTRAPTION IN THE MIDDLE OF THE STREET, RICHARDS.

YOU HAVE MY COMPLETE ASSURANCE NO DANGER WILL ARISE DIRECTLY FROM THIS MACHINE CHIEF. JUST HAVE YOUR MEN CONTINUE TO HOLD BACK THE PUBLIC.

AS SOON AS YOU WISH, THUNDER GOD. THIS MACHINE WILL FUNCTION SOMEWHAT IN THE NATURE OF A KIDNEY MACHINE, DRAWING OUT THE ENERGY WITHIN *GALACTUS*, ACCELERATING THE PARTICLES, AND RETURNING THEM AT A BOOSTED LEVEL TO HIS BODY.

THOR DOTH STAND READY. WHEN THIS ACTION TO COMMENCE?

AND ALL THOU DOST REQUIRE IS A SOURCE OF POWER FOR THIS PROCESS TO BEGIN, POWER SUCH AS IS CONTAINED WITHIN MY MIGHTY *URU HAMMER!*

79

FROM DEEP WITHIN THE SACRED MALLET, THE ELEMENTAL FORCES FLOW. ENERGY BEGINS TO CRACKLE ABOUT GALACTUS.

GHOSTLY LIGHTS FLICKER ACROSS HIM, SOME FROM THE MECHANISM...

SOME FROM THE VERY CORE OF THE STAR-BEING HIMSELF. A PROCESS MUCH AKIN TO HEALING BEGINS...

GALACTUS STIRS...

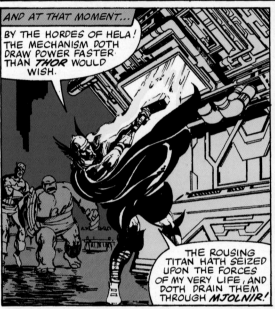

AND AT THAT MOMENT...

BY THE HORDES OF HELA! THE MECHANISM DOTH DRAW POWER FASTER THAN THOR WOULD WISH.

THE ROUSING TITAN HATH SEIZED UPON THE FORCES OF MY VERY LIFE, AND DOTH DRAIN THEM THROUGH MJOLNIR!

BUT BEFORE EVEN THOR HIMSELF HAS FULLY REALIZED HIS PREDICAMENT, THE STAR-SPANGLED VETERAN OF A THOUSAND BATTLES HAS MOVED INSTINCTIVELY.

DON'T WORRY, ASGARDIAN. STARK INTERNATIONAL'S OVER-GROWN TINKERTOY'S ARE TOUGH...

RRANG

...BUT MY SHIELD IS TOUGHER!

UHNNN! CAPTAIN AMERICA! THOU HAST SURELY SAVED ME!

THERE IS LITTLE TIME FOR GRATITUDE HOWEVER...

BOOM

HOLY CATS! THE WHOLE BLAMED THING'S EXPLODED.! MEBBE I CAN HAUL GALACTUS OUTTA THERE BEFORE...

NO, BEN, WAIT! ALL OF YOU STAND BACK THERE ARE FORCES AT WORK HERE BEYOND HUMAN COMPREHENSION!

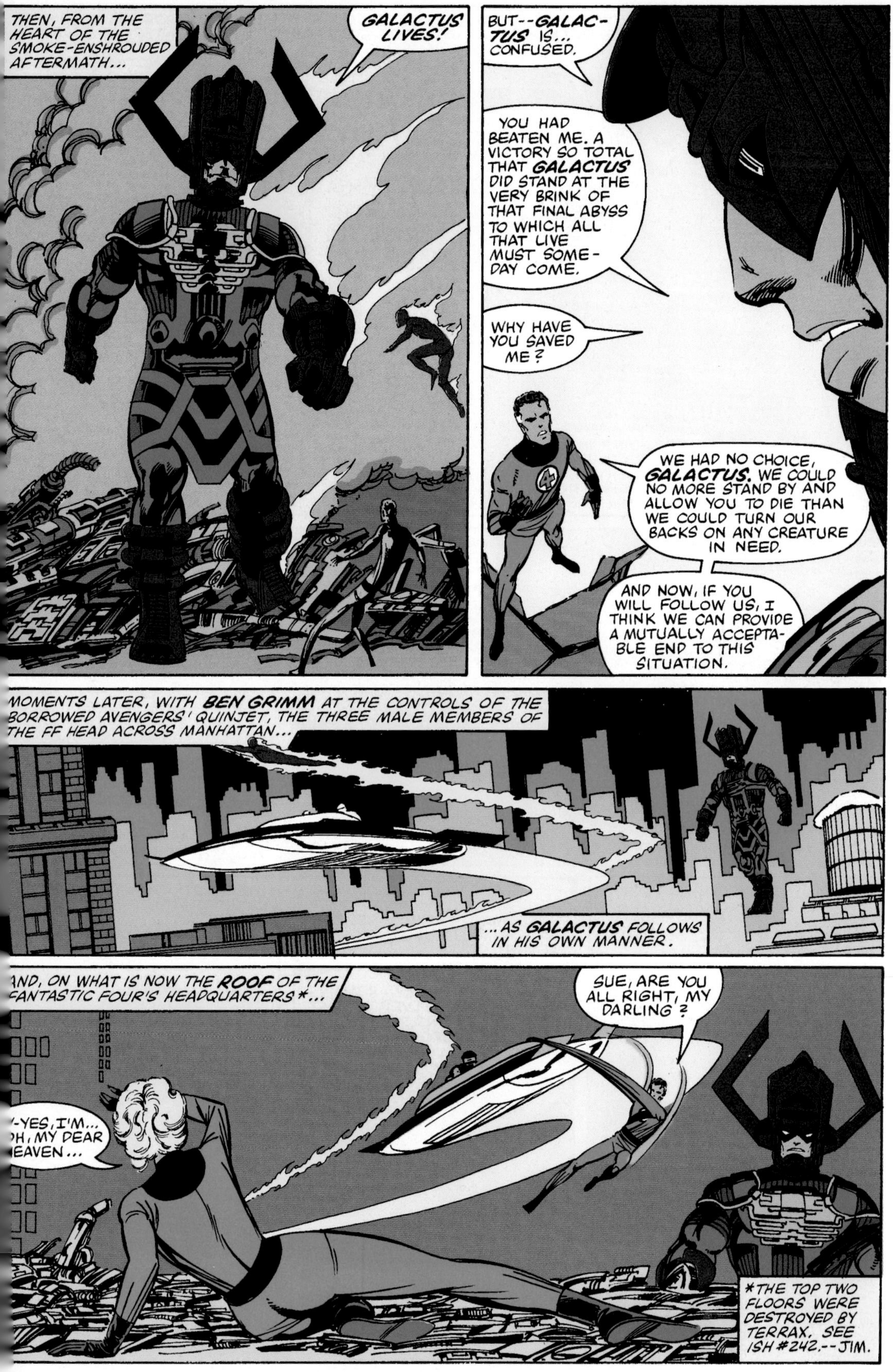
THEN, FROM THE HEART OF THE SMOKE-ENSHROUDED AFTERMATH...
GALACTUS LIVES!
BUT--GALACTUS IS... CONFUSED.
YOU HAD BEATEN ME. A VICTORY SO TOTAL THAT GALACTUS DID STAND AT THE VERY BRINK OF THAT FINAL ABYSS TO WHICH ALL THAT LIVE MUST SOMEDAY COME.
WHY HAVE YOU SAVED ME?
WE HAD NO CHOICE, GALACTUS. WE COULD NO MORE STAND BY AND ALLOW YOU TO DIE THAN WE COULD TURN OUR BACKS ON ANY CREATURE IN NEED.
AND NOW, IF YOU WILL FOLLOW US, I THINK WE CAN PROVIDE A MUTUALLY ACCEPTABLE END TO THIS SITUATION.
MOMENTS LATER, WITH BEN GRIMM AT THE CONTROLS OF THE BORROWED AVENGERS' QUINJET, THE THREE MALE MEMBERS OF THE FF HEAD ACROSS MANHATTAN...
...AS GALACTUS FOLLOWS IN HIS OWN MANNER.
AND, ON WHAT IS NOW THE ROOF OF THE FANTASTIC FOUR'S HEADQUARTERS*...
SUE, ARE YOU ALL RIGHT, MY DARLING?
-YES, I'M... OH, MY DEAR HEAVEN...
*THE TOP TWO FLOORS WERE DESTROYED BY TERRAX. SEE ISH #242.--JIM.

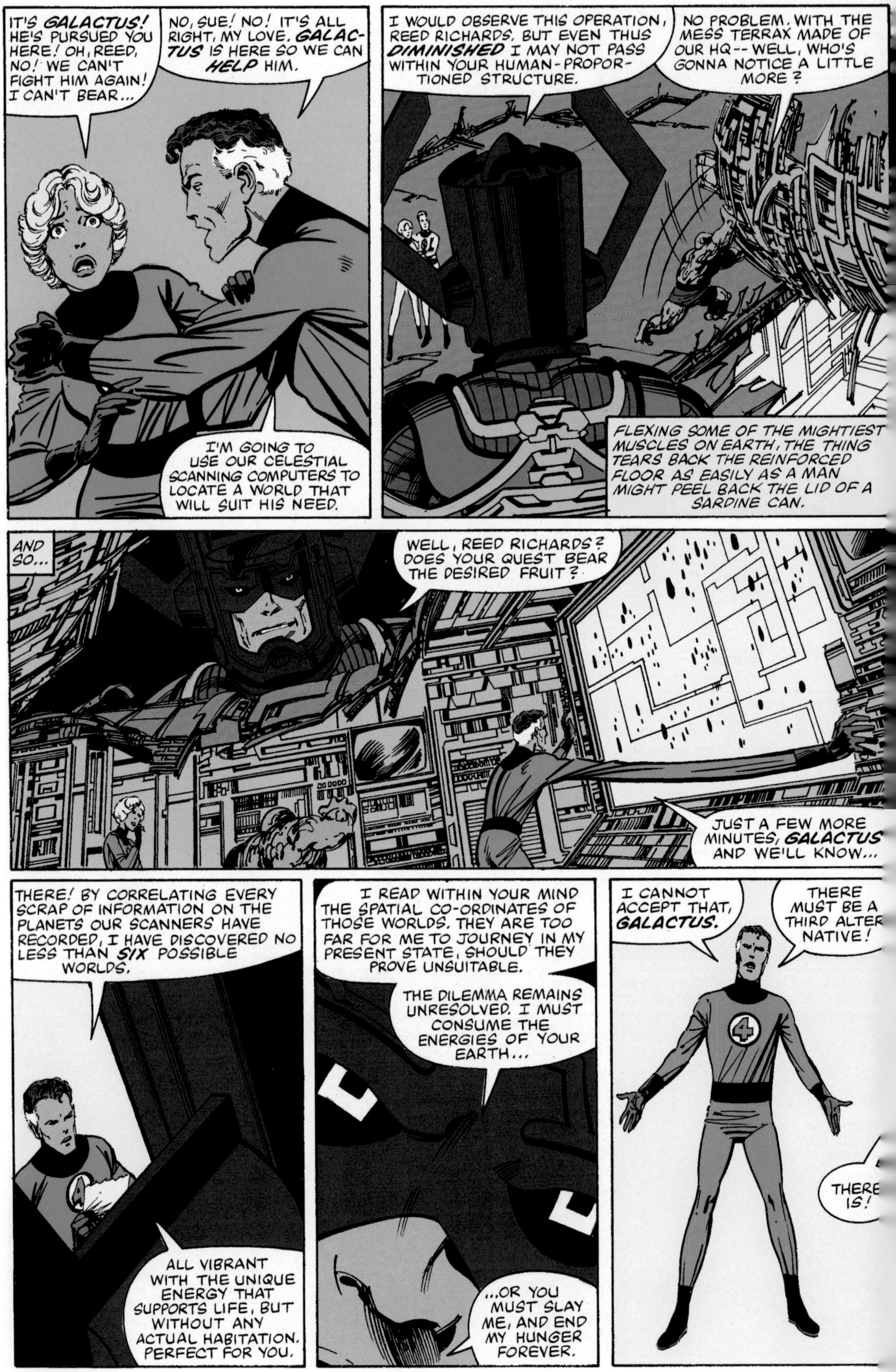
IT'S GALACTUS! HE'S PURSUED YOU HERE! OH, REED, NO! WE CAN'T FIGHT HIM AGAIN! I CAN'T BEAR...
NO, SUE! NO! IT'S ALL RIGHT, MY LOVE. GALACTUS IS HERE SO WE CAN HELP HIM.
I'M GOING TO USE OUR CELESTIAL SCANNING COMPUTERS TO LOCATE A WORLD THAT WILL SUIT HIS NEED.
I WOULD OBSERVE THIS OPERATION, REED RICHARDS, BUT EVEN THUS DIMINISHED I MAY NOT PASS WITHIN YOUR HUMAN-PROPORTIONED STRUCTURE.
NO PROBLEM. WITH THE MESS TERRAX MADE OF OUR HQ--WELL, WHO'S GONNA NOTICE A LITTLE MORE?
FLEXING SOME OF THE MIGHTIEST MUSCLES ON EARTH, THE THING TEARS BACK THE REINFORCED FLOOR AS EASILY AS A MAN MIGHT PEEL BACK THE LID OF A SARDINE CAN.
AND SO...
WELL, REED RICHARDS? DOES YOUR QUEST BEAR THE DESIRED FRUIT?
JUST A FEW MORE MINUTES, GALACTUS AND WE'LL KNOW...
THERE! BY CORRELATING EVERY SCRAP OF INFORMATION ON THE PLANETS OUR SCANNERS HAVE RECORDED, I HAVE DISCOVERED NO LESS THAN SIX POSSIBLE WORLDS.
ALL VIBRANT WITH THE UNIQUE ENERGY THAT SUPPORTS LIFE, BUT WITHOUT ANY ACTUAL HABITATION. PERFECT FOR YOU.
I READ WITHIN YOUR MIND THE SPATIAL CO-ORDINATES OF THOSE WORLDS. THEY ARE TOO FAR FOR ME TO JOURNEY IN MY PRESENT STATE, SHOULD THEY PROVE UNSUITABLE.
THE DILEMMA REMAINS UNRESOLVED. I MUST CONSUME THE ENERGIES OF YOUR EARTH...
...OR YOU MUST SLAY ME, AND END MY HUNGER FOREVER.
I CANNOT ACCEPT THAT, GALACTUS.
THERE MUST BE A THIRD ALTER NATIVE!
THERE IS!

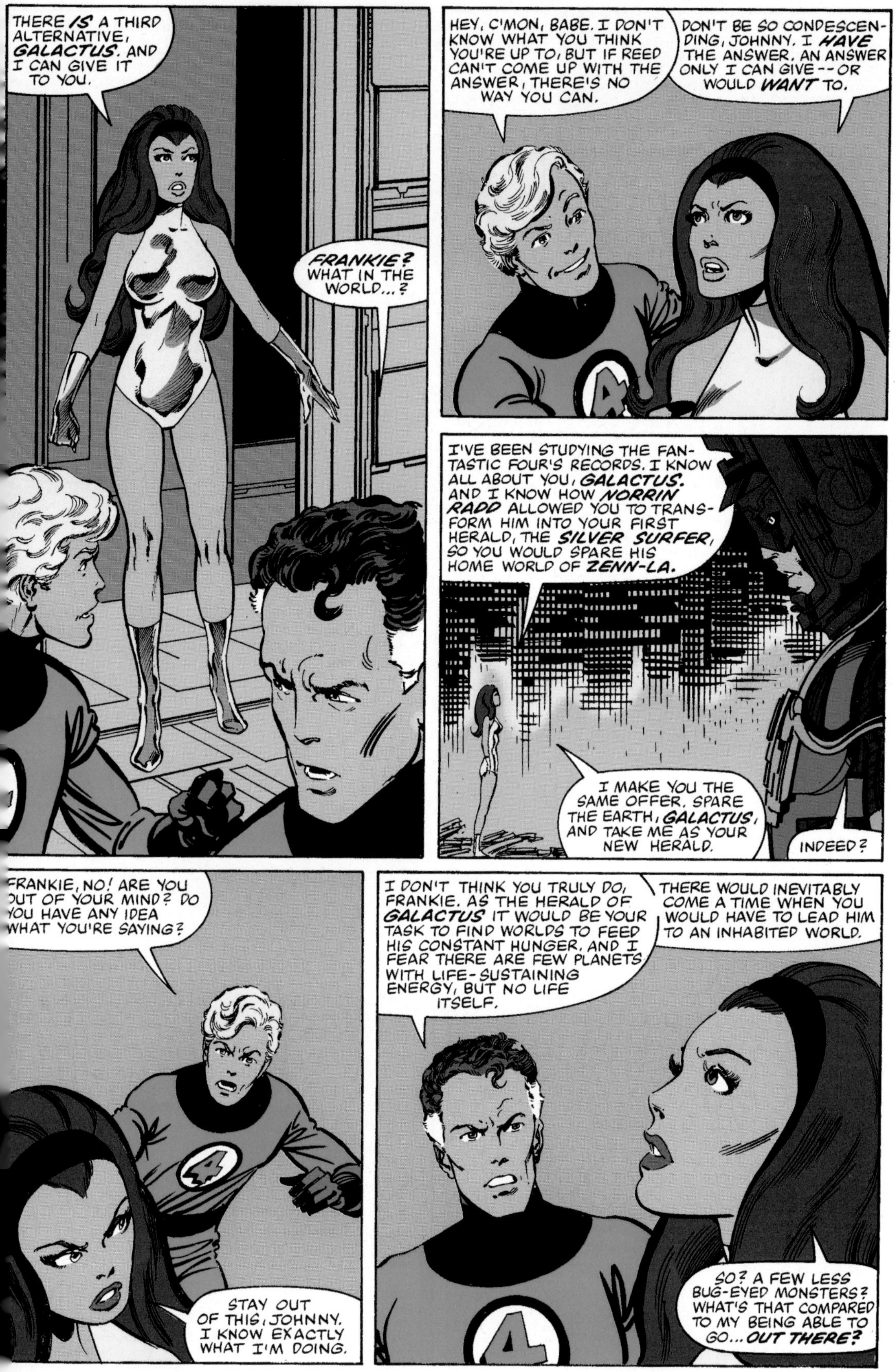
THERE IS A THIRD ALTERNATIVE, GALACTUS. AND I CAN GIVE IT TO YOU.
FRANKIE? WHAT IN THE WORLD...?
HEY, C'MON, BABE. I DON'T KNOW WHAT YOU THINK YOU'RE UP TO, BUT IF REED CAN'T COME UP WITH THE ANSWER, THERE'S NO WAY YOU CAN.
DON'T BE SO CONDESCENDING, JOHNNY. I HAVE THE ANSWER. AN ANSWER ONLY I CAN GIVE--OR WOULD WANT TO.
I'VE BEEN STUDYING THE FANTASTIC FOUR'S RECORDS. I KNOW ALL ABOUT YOU, GALACTUS. AND I KNOW HOW NORRIN RADD ALLOWED YOU TO TRANSFORM HIM INTO YOUR FIRST HERALD, THE SILVER SURFER, SO YOU WOULD SPARE HIS HOME WORLD OF ZENN-LA.
I MAKE YOU THE SAME OFFER. SPARE THE EARTH, GALACTUS, AND TAKE ME AS YOUR NEW HERALD.
INDEED?
FRANKIE, NO! ARE YOU OUT OF YOUR MIND? DO YOU HAVE ANY IDEA WHAT YOU'RE SAYING?
STAY OUT OF THIS, JOHNNY. I KNOW EXACTLY WHAT I'M DOING.
I DON'T THINK YOU TRULY DO, FRANKIE. AS THE HERALD OF GALACTUS IT WOULD BE YOUR TASK TO FIND WORLDS TO FEED HIS CONSTANT HUNGER. AND I FEAR THERE ARE FEW PLANETS WITH LIFE-SUSTAINING ENERGY, BUT NO LIFE ITSELF.
THERE WOULD INEVITABLY COME A TIME WHEN YOU WOULD HAVE TO LEAD HIM TO AN INHABITED WORLD.
SO? A FEW LESS BUG-EYED MONSTERS? WHAT'S THAT COMPARED TO MY BEING ABLE TO GO... OUT THERE?

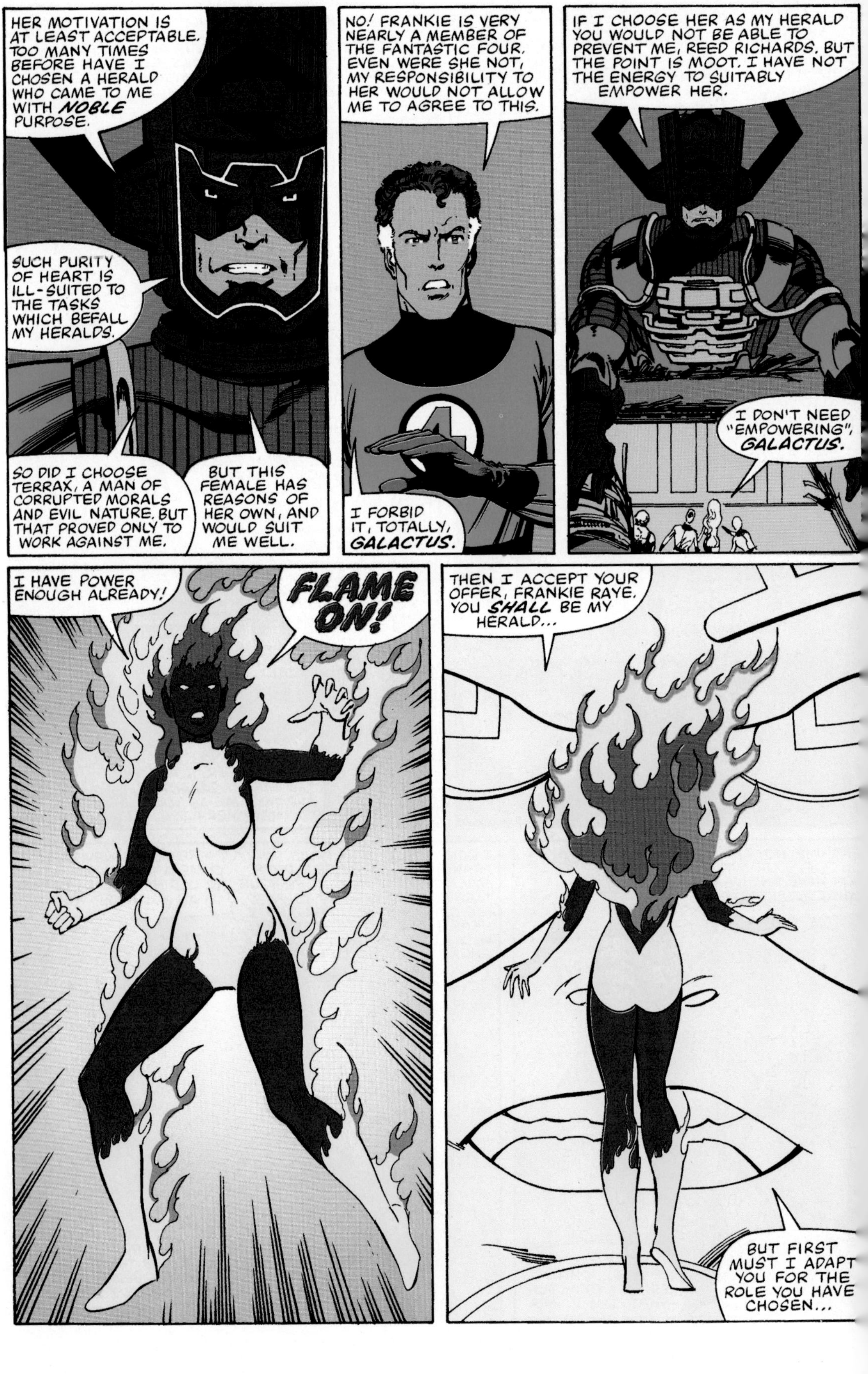
HER MOTIVATION IS AT LEAST ACCEPTABLE. TOO MANY TIMES BEFORE HAVE I CHOSEN A HERALD WHO CAME TO ME WITH NOBLE PURPOSE.
SUCH PURITY OF HEART IS ILL-SUITED TO THE TASKS WHICH BEFALL MY HERALDS.
SO DID I CHOOSE TERRAX, A MAN OF CORRUPTED MORALS AND EVIL NATURE. BUT THAT PROVED ONLY TO WORK AGAINST ME.
BUT THIS FEMALE HAS REASONS OF HER OWN, AND WOULD SUIT ME WELL.
NO! FRANKIE IS VERY NEARLY A MEMBER OF THE FANTASTIC FOUR. EVEN WERE SHE NOT, MY RESPONSIBILITY TO HER WOULD NOT ALLOW ME TO AGREE TO THIS.
I FORBID IT, TOTALLY, GALACTUS.
IF I CHOOSE HER AS MY HERALD YOU WOULD NOT BE ABLE TO PREVENT ME, REED RICHARDS. BUT THE POINT IS MOOT. I HAVE NOT THE ENERGY TO SUITABLY EMPOWER HER.
I DON'T NEED "EMPOWERING", GALACTUS.
I HAVE POWER ENOUGH ALREADY!
FLAME ON!
THEN I ACCEPT YOUR OFFER, FRANKIE RAYE. YOU SHALL BE MY HERALD...
BUT FIRST MUST I ADAPT YOU FOR THE ROLE YOU HAVE CHOSEN...

THEN, AS THE INDESCRIBABLE ENERGIES BEGIN TO FLOW BETWEEN THE GIRL AND THE STAR-GOD...

FRANKIE! NO! DON'T DO THIS TO US! PLEEEASE!

JOHNNY, KEEP BACK! THOSE FORCES MAY BE HARMFUL TO ANY-ONE NOT DIRECTLY INVOLVED.

I'LL THROW OUT AN INVISIBLE FORCE FIELD BUBBLE. I DON'T KNOW IF IT WILL BLOCK THE POWER OF GALACTUS, BUT...

YEOW! LOOKIT HIM! HE'S ALL LIT UP LIKE SOME-THIN' OUT OF A C.B. DEMILLE MOVIE! THERE'S GOTTA BE SOMETHING WE CAN DO, REED.

THERE ...IS NOT.

'THE CHOICE WAS NEVER WITH US, IT BELONGS SOLELY TO FRANKIE...

"AND SHE HAS MADE IT."

HEAR ME, MORTAL WOMAN! FEEL THE TOUCH OF GALAC-TUS IN YOUR MIND. DO NOT FLEE FROM MY PRESENCE.

ONLY GALACTUS CAN GUIDE YOU SAFELY THROUGH THE CORRI-DORS OF MADNESS AS YOUR HUMANITY SLIPS AWAY-- SLIPS AWAY TO BE REPLACED BY SOME-THING GREATER!

THE WOMAN THAT YOU WERE IS NO MORE. THE MUNDANE ASPECTS OF YOUR EXISTENCE ARE INCONSEQUENTIAL.

THE CREATURE WHO ONCE CALLED HER-SELF FRANKIE RAYE IS REBORN...

NOW AND FOR-EVERMORE SHALL YOU BE THE HERALD OF GALACTUS!

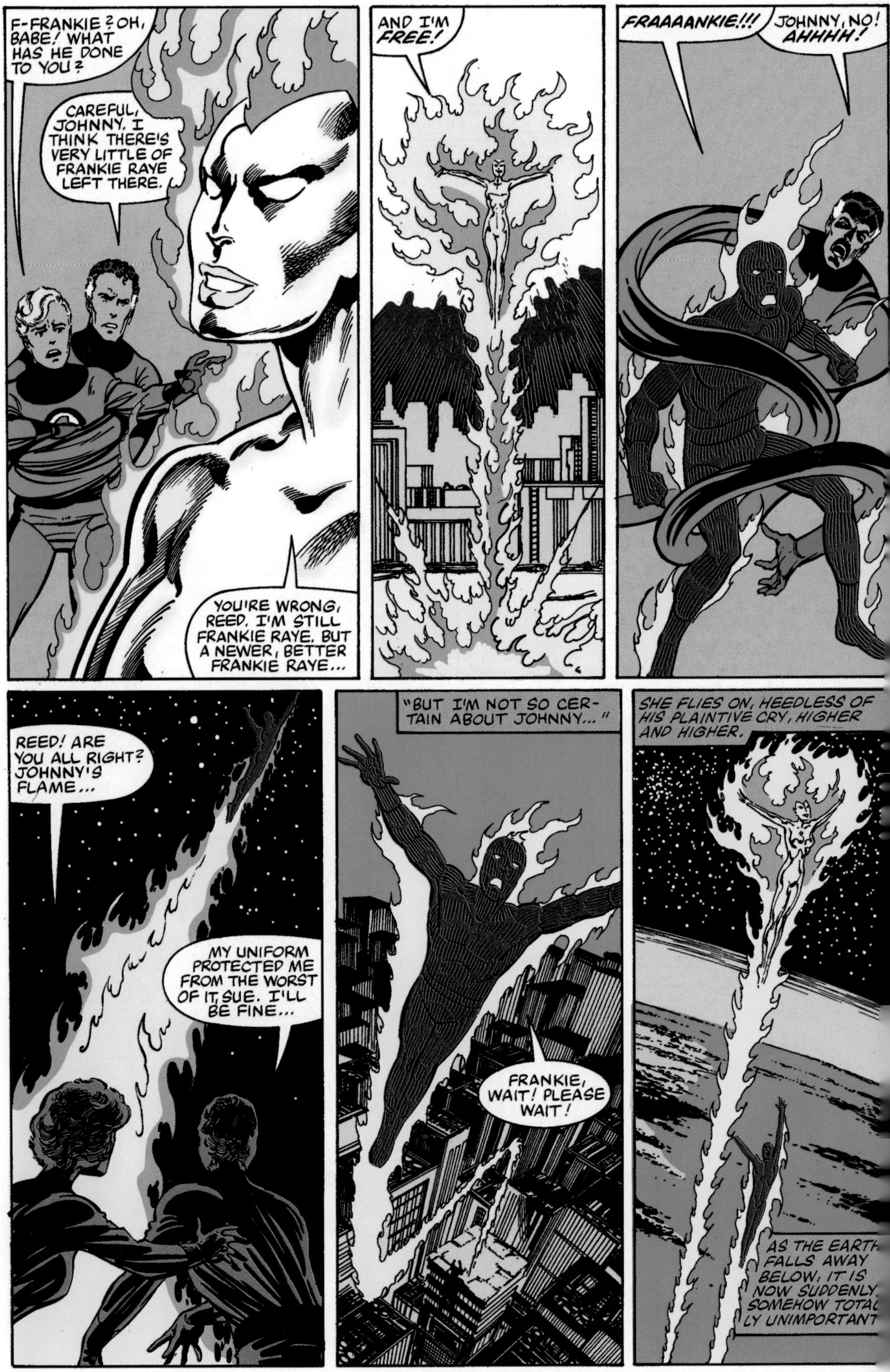

F-FRANKIE? OH, BABE! WHAT HAS HE DONE TO YOU?
CAREFUL, JOHNNY. I THINK THERE'S VERY LITTLE OF FRANKIE RAYE LEFT THERE.
YOU'RE WRONG, REED. I'M STILL FRANKIE RAYE. BUT A NEWER, BETTER FRANKIE RAYE...
AND I'M FREE!
FRAAAANKIE!!!
JOHNNY, NO! AHHHH!
REED! ARE YOU ALL RIGHT? JOHNNY'S FLAME...
MY UNIFORM PROTECTED ME FROM THE WORST OF IT, SUE. I'LL BE FINE...
"BUT I'M NOT SO CERTAIN ABOUT JOHNNY..."
FRANKIE, WAIT! PLEASE WAIT!
SHE FLIES ON, HEEDLESS OF HIS PLAINTIVE CRY, HIGHER AND HIGHER.
AS THE EARTH FALLS AWAY BELOW, IT IS NOW SUDDENLY, SOMEHOW TOTALLY UNIMPORTANT

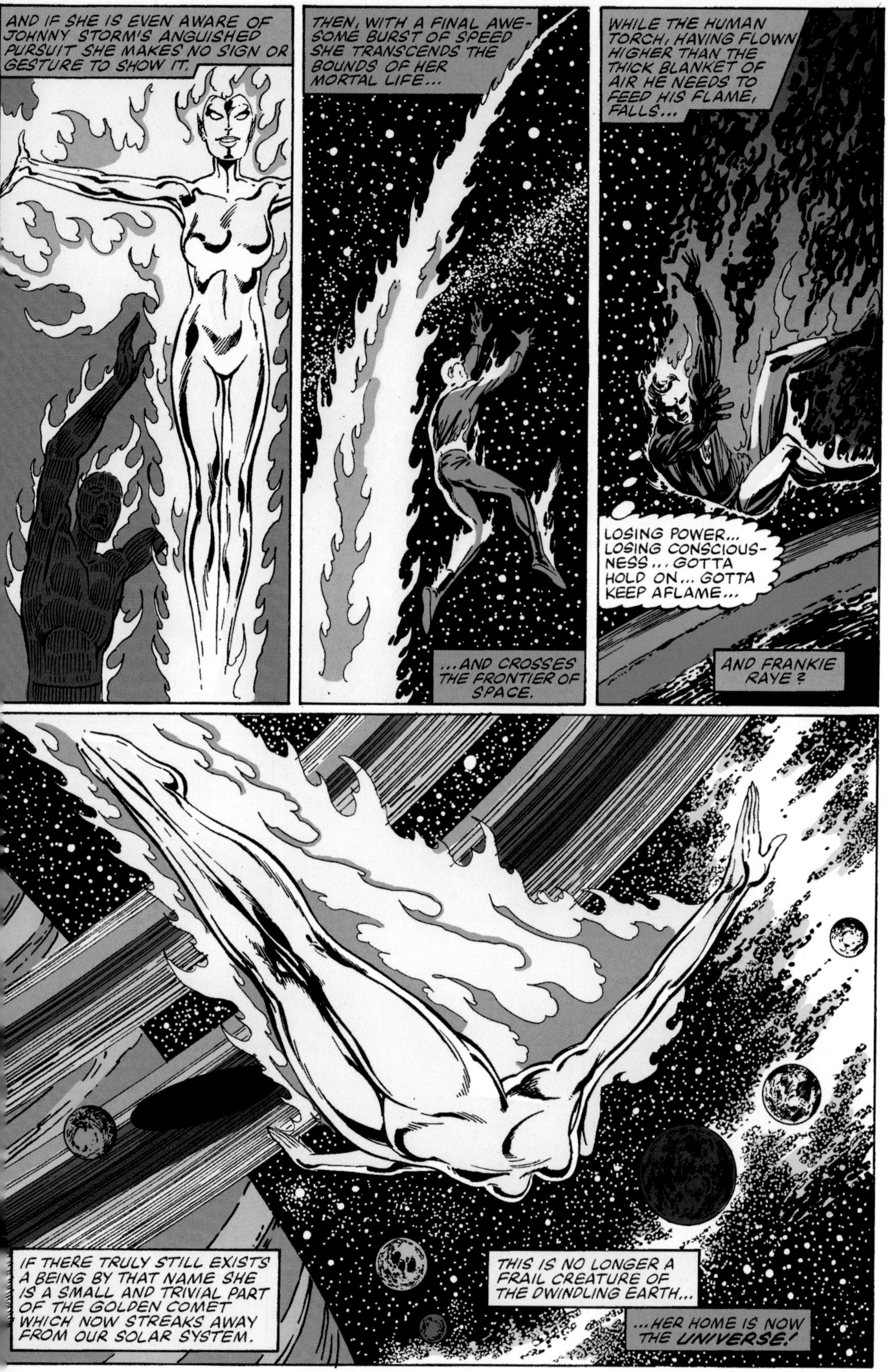
AND IF SHE IS EVEN AWARE OF JOHNNY STORM'S ANGUISHED PURSUIT SHE MAKES NO SIGN OR GESTURE TO SHOW IT.
THEN, WITH A FINAL AWESOME BURST OF SPEED SHE TRANSCENDS THE BOUNDS OF HER MORTAL LIFE...
...AND CROSSES THE FRONTIER OF SPACE.
WHILE THE HUMAN TORCH, HAVING FLOWN HIGHER THAN THE THICK BLANKET OF AIR HE NEEDS TO FEED HIS FLAME, FALLS...
LOSING POWER... LOSING CONSCIOUSNESS... GOTTA HOLD ON... GOTTA KEEP AFLAME...
AND FRANKIE RAYE?
IF THERE TRULY STILL EXISTS A BEING BY THAT NAME SHE IS A SMALL AND TRIVIAL PART OF THE GOLDEN COMET WHICH NOW STREAKS AWAY FROM OUR SOLAR SYSTEM.
THIS IS NO LONGER A FRAIL CREATURE OF THE DWINDLING EARTH...
...HER HOME IS NOW THE UNIVERSE!

BACK ON EARTH...

WELL, *GALACTUS*, YOU HAVE YOUR HERALD. I DON'T THINK WE WILL EVER KNOW IF THIS WAS THE RIGHT THING TO DO, OR IF WE SHOULD HAVE TRIED SOMETHING, *ANY-THING*, TO STOP YOU FROM TAKING HER.

I DID NOT "TAKE HER", REED RICHARDS. SHE CHOSE A PATH SHE HAS LONG HUNGERED TO TRED. I TOUCHED HER MIND. I KNOW THIS TO BE TRUE.

AND TRUE ALSO WAS MY VOW, MY PACT WITH HER. THE WOMAN IS MY HERALD AND SO SHALL EARTH REMAIN INVIOLATE.

YET, PERHAPS THERE IS ANOTHER REASON I STAY MY HAND. A DEEPER, TRUER REASON.

PERHAPS IT IS BECAUSE YOU RISKED ALL TO SAVE ME, WHEN IT WOULD HAVE BEEN EASY TO DO OTHERWISE.

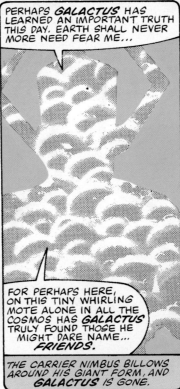

PERHAPS *GALACTUS* HAS LEARNED AN IMPORTANT TRUTH THIS DAY. EARTH SHALL NEVER MORE NEED FEAR ME...

FOR PERHAPS HERE, ON THIS TINY WHIRLING MOTE ALONE IN ALL THE COSMOS HAS *GALACTUS* TRULY FOUND THOSE HE MIGHT DARE NAME... *FRIENDS.*

THE CARRIER NIMBUS BILLOWS AROUND HIS GIANT FORM, AND GALACTUS IS GONE.

IT'S OVER! *GALACTUS* WILL NOT TROUBLE US AGAIN! PERHAPS HIS HUMANITY IS NOT SO LOST AS HE MIGHT THINK, IF HE CAN STILL BE TOUCHED BY SIMPLE HUMAN COMPASSION.

I THINK I'M IMPRESSED.

BUT... BUT, REED, WHERE'S THE TORCH? WHERE IS JOHNNY?

88

AND THAT QUESTION REMAINED UNANSWERED, UNTIL YOUR CALL, JUST HALF AN HOUR AGO.

WOW!

JOHNNY, COME BACK WITH US. YOU'VE SUFFERED A TERRIBLE LOSS, YOU SHOULDN'T BE ALONE.

WHY NOT? I MEAN, I MIGHT AS WELL GET USED TO IT, RIGHT? I'M GONNA BE ALONE FOR THE REST OF MY LIFE, AREN'T I?

HOW CAN YOU SAY THAT? THE FANTASTIC FOUR IS MORE THAN JUST A SUPER HERO GROUP, WE'RE A FAMILY. AND YOU'D BE PART OF THAT FAMILY EVEN IF YOU WEREN'T MY BROTHER.

DON'T TRY TO SIDE-STEP THE OBVIOUS, SIS. YOU KNOW WHAT I MEAN. EVERY WOMAN I'VE EVER LOVED HAS BEEN TAKEN FROM ME, SOMEHOW.

I DUNNO. MAYBE IT'S ME. MAYBE I *AM* THE JERK SOME PEOPLE THINK.

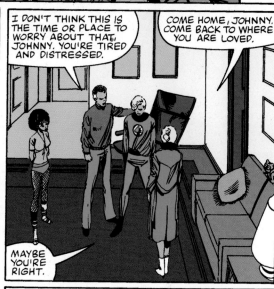

I DON'T THINK THIS IS THE TIME OR PLACE TO WORRY ABOUT THAT, JOHNNY. YOU'RE TIRED AND DISTRESSED.

COME HOME, JOHNNY. COME BACK TO WHERE YOU ARE LOVED.

MAYBE YOU'RE RIGHT.

OKAY. BACK TO THE BAXTER BUILDING. BACK TO PLAYING HERO. THANKS FOR THE TEA, JULIE. THANKS FOR... FOR...

HEY, NO PROBLEM, YOU KNOW? I MEAN, IF YOU EVER, WELL, NEED A SHOULDER TO CRY ON -- YOU KNOW THE NUMBER.

YEAH. YEAH, KNOW. THANKS.

THEY GO, AND SILENCE ROLLS ACROSS THIS SMALL, MID-MANHATTAN APARTMENT. JULIETTE D'ANGELO SAGS ONTO THE COUCH, REED RICHARDS' WORDS FLOWING OVER HER AGAIN AND AGAIN.

SUDDENLY HER EXERCISES SEEM VERY TRIVIAL THINGS INDEED...

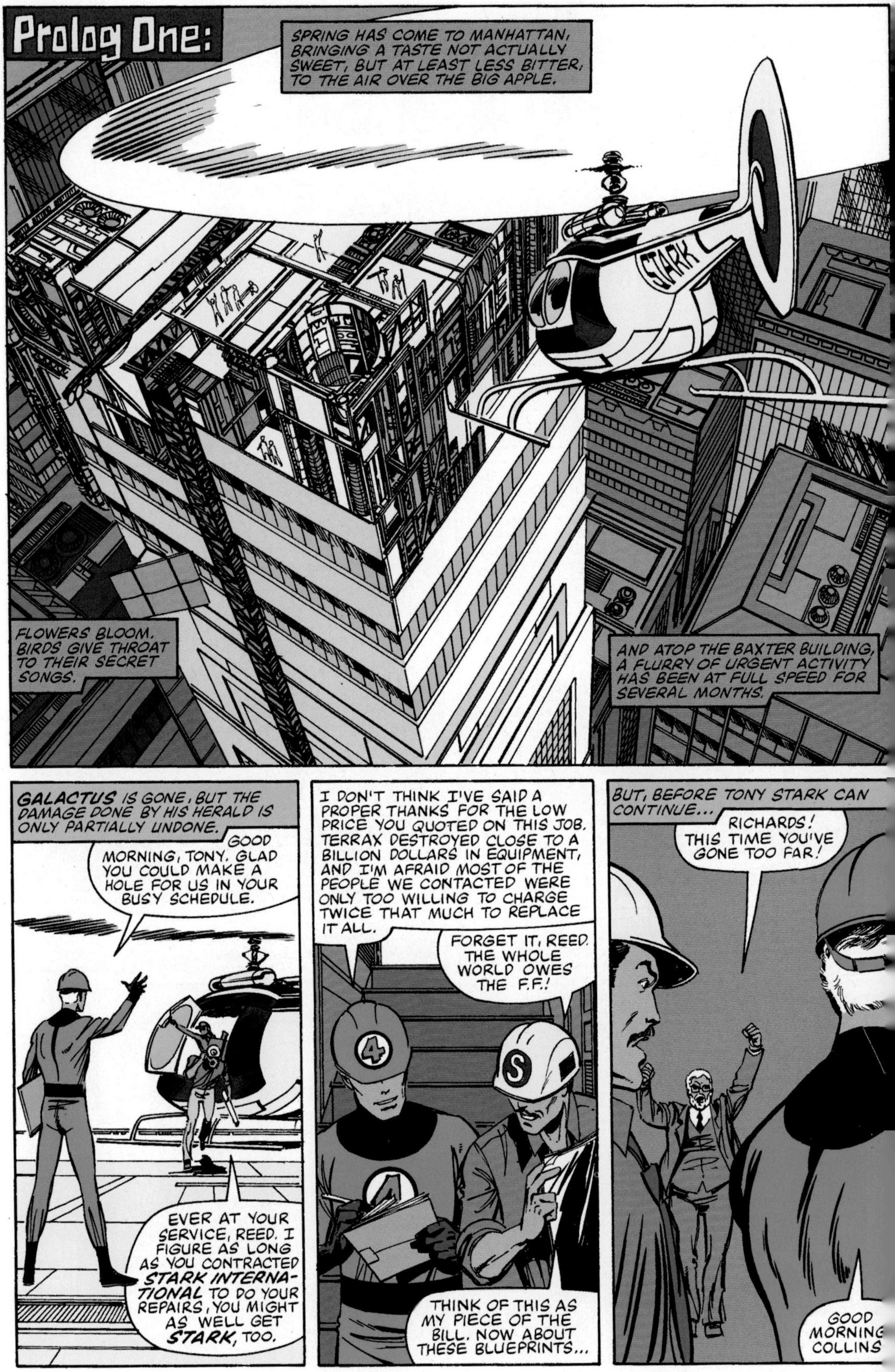
Prolog One:
SPRING HAS COME TO MANHATTAN, BRINGING A TASTE NOT ACTUALLY SWEET, BUT AT LEAST LESS BITTER, TO THE AIR OVER THE BIG APPLE.
STARK
FLOWERS BLOOM. BIRDS GIVE THROAT TO THEIR SECRET SONGS.
AND ATOP THE BAXTER BUILDING, A FLURRY OF URGENT ACTIVITY HAS BEEN AT FULL SPEED FOR SEVERAL MONTHS.
GALACTUS IS GONE, BUT THE DAMAGE DONE BY HIS HERALD IS ONLY PARTIALLY UNDONE.
GOOD MORNING, TONY. GLAD YOU COULD MAKE A HOLE FOR US IN YOUR BUSY SCHEDULE.
EVER AT YOUR SERVICE, REED. I FIGURE AS LONG AS YOU CONTRACTED STARK INTERNATIONAL TO DO YOUR REPAIRS, YOU MIGHT AS WELL GET STARK, TOO.
I DON'T THINK I'VE SAID A PROPER THANKS FOR THE LOW PRICE YOU QUOTED ON THIS JOB. TERRAX DESTROYED CLOSE TO A BILLION DOLLARS IN EQUIPMENT, AND I'M AFRAID MOST OF THE PEOPLE WE CONTACTED WERE ONLY TOO WILLING TO CHARGE TWICE THAT MUCH TO REPLACE IT ALL.
FORGET IT, REED. THE WHOLE WORLD OWES THE F.F.!
THINK OF THIS AS MY PIECE OF THE BILL. NOW ABOUT THESE BLUEPRINTS...
BUT, BEFORE TONY STARK CAN CONTINUE...
RICHARDS! THIS TIME YOU'VE GONE TOO FAR!
GOOD MORNING COLLINS

THAT'S *MISTER* COLLINS TO YOU! AND DON'T YOU "GOOD MORNING" ME! I COME BACK FROM THREE MONTHS IN EUROPE, AND WHAT DO I FIND? YOU LUNATICS HAVE *DESTROYED* MY BUILDING! WELL, I'M NOT GOING TO STAND FOR THIS ANY MORE, IS THAT CLEAR?

≡SIGH≡

HEY, WHERE DO YOU THINK YOU'RE GOING? DON'T YOU WALK AWAY FROM ME! I'M NOT FINISHED WITH YOU, YET!

I THINK THIS HAS GONE ON QUITE LONG ENOUGH.

I WANT YOU PEOPLE *OUT*, DO YOU UNDERSTAND? OUT! OUT! OUT! I WON'T HAVE YOU DESTROYING MY PROPERTY VALUES -- ER... AND ENDANGER-ING MY OTHER TENANTS. YOU'VE GOT TWENTY-FOUR HOURS TO CLEAR OUT! OUT!

MISTER COLLINS...

I THINK THIS CHECK SHOULD TAKE CARE OF THIS MATTER...

AND WE WON'T BE HEARING FROM YOU AGAIN, WILL WE?

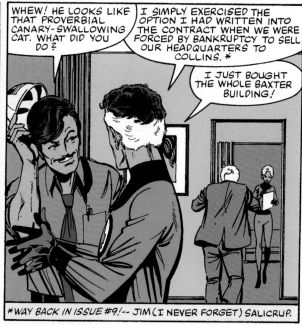

WHEW! HE LOOKS LIKE THAT PROVERBIAL CANARY-SWALLOWING CAT. WHAT DID YOU DO?

I SIMPLY EXERCISED THE OPTION I HAD WRITTEN INTO THE CONTRACT WHEN WE WERE FORCED BY BANKRUPTCY TO SELL OUR HEADQUARTERS TO COLLINS. *

I JUST BOUGHT THE WHOLE BAXTER BUILDING!

*WAY BACK IN ISSUE #9! -- JIM (I NEVER FORGET) SALICRUP.

REED, I'VE COMPLETED THE CHECKS OF THE REST OF THE... OH, GOOD MORNING, MR. COLLINS... MISTER COLLINS?

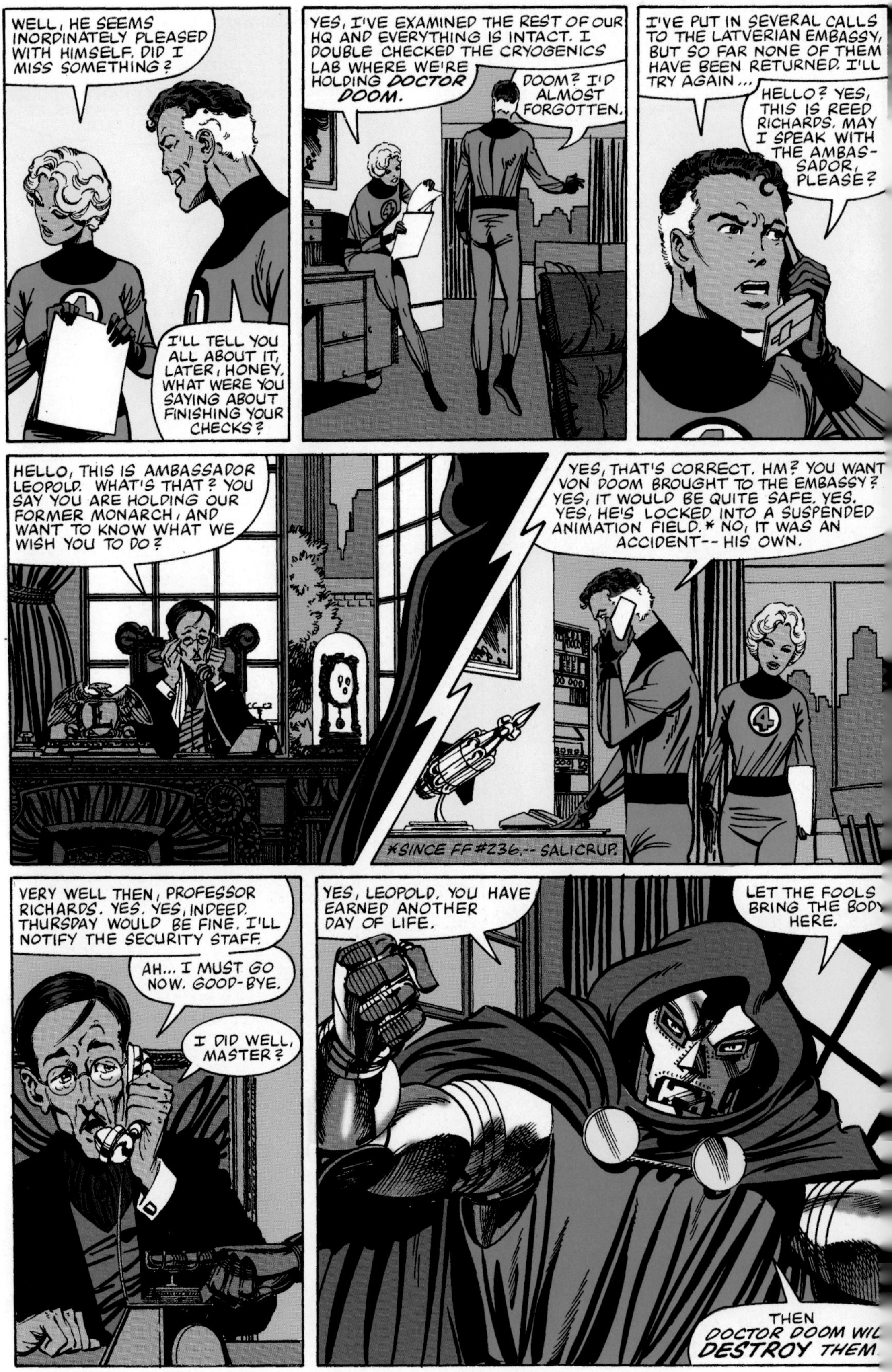

WELL, HE SEEMS INORDINATELY PLEASED WITH HIMSELF. DID I MISS SOMETHING?
I'LL TELL YOU ALL ABOUT IT, LATER, HONEY. WHAT WERE YOU SAYING ABOUT FINISHING YOUR CHECKS?
YES, I'VE EXAMINED THE REST OF OUR HQ AND EVERYTHING IS INTACT. I DOUBLE CHECKED THE CRYOGENICS LAB WHERE WE'RE HOLDING DOCTOR DOOM.
DOOM? I'D ALMOST FORGOTTEN.
I'VE PUT IN SEVERAL CALLS TO THE LATVERIAN EMBASSY, BUT SO FAR NONE OF THEM HAVE BEEN RETURNED. I'LL TRY AGAIN...
HELLO? YES, THIS IS REED RICHARDS. MAY I SPEAK WITH THE AMBASSADOR, PLEASE?
HELLO, THIS IS AMBASSADOR LEOPOLD. WHAT'S THAT? YOU SAY YOU ARE HOLDING OUR FORMER MONARCH, AND WANT TO KNOW WHAT WE WISH YOU TO DO?
YES, THAT'S CORRECT. HM? YOU WANT VON DOOM BROUGHT TO THE EMBASSY? YES, IT WOULD BE QUITE SAFE. YES. YES, HE'S LOCKED INTO A SUSPENDED ANIMATION FIELD.* NO, IT WAS AN ACCIDENT-- HIS OWN.
*SINCE FF #236.-- SALICRUP.
VERY WELL THEN, PROFESSOR RICHARDS. YES. YES, INDEED. THURSDAY WOULD BE FINE. I'LL NOTIFY THE SECURITY STAFF.
AH... I MUST GO NOW. GOOD-BYE.
I DID WELL, MASTER?
YES, LEOPOLD. YOU HAVE EARNED ANOTHER DAY OF LIFE.
LET THE FOOLS BRING THE BODY HERE.
THEN DOCTOR DOOM WIL DESTROY THEM

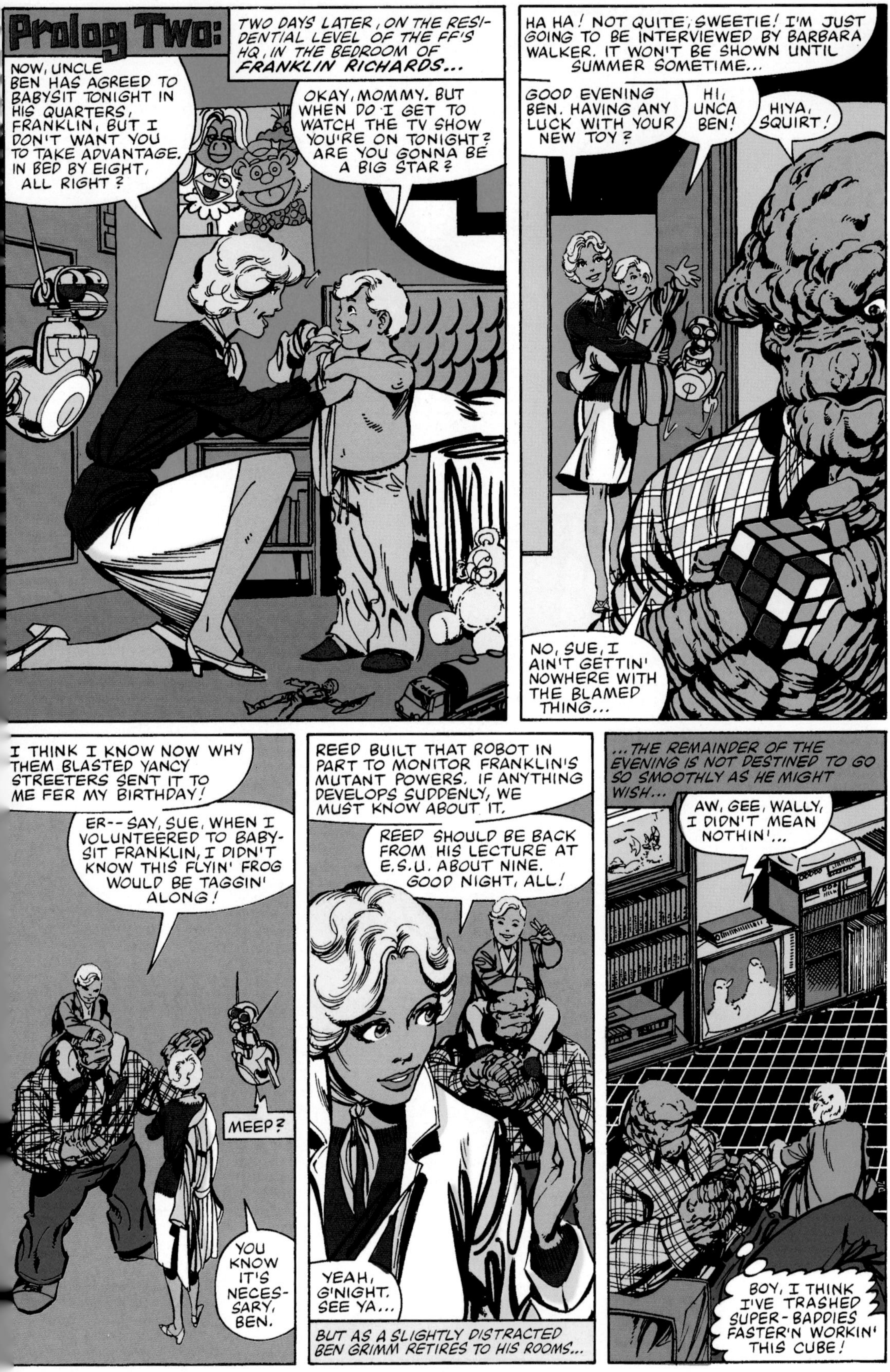
Prolog Two:
TWO DAYS LATER, ON THE RESIDENTIAL LEVEL OF THE FF'S HQ, IN THE BEDROOM OF FRANKLIN RICHARDS...
NOW, UNCLE BEN HAS AGREED TO BABYSIT TONIGHT IN HIS QUARTERS, FRANKLIN, BUT I DON'T WANT YOU TO TAKE ADVANTAGE. IN BED BY EIGHT, ALL RIGHT?
OKAY, MOMMY. BUT WHEN DO I GET TO WATCH THE TV SHOW YOU'RE ON TONIGHT? ARE YOU GONNA BE A BIG STAR?
HA HA! NOT QUITE, SWEETIE! I'M JUST GOING TO BE INTERVIEWED BY BARBARA WALKER. IT WON'T BE SHOWN UNTIL SUMMER SOMETIME...
GOOD EVENING BEN. HAVING ANY LUCK WITH YOUR NEW TOY?
HI, UNCA BEN!
HIYA, SQUIRT!
NO, SUE, I AIN'T GETTIN' NOWHERE WITH THE BLAMED THING...
I THINK I KNOW NOW WHY THEM BLASTED YANCY STREETERS SENT IT TO ME FER MY BIRTHDAY!
ER-- SAY, SUE, WHEN I VOLUNTEERED TO BABY-SIT FRANKLIN, I DIDN'T KNOW THIS FLYIN' FROG WOULD BE TAGGIN' ALONG!
MEEP?
YOU KNOW IT'S NECES-SARY, BEN.
REED BUILT THAT ROBOT IN PART TO MONITOR FRANKLIN'S MUTANT POWERS. IF ANYTHING DEVELOPS SUDDENLY, WE MUST KNOW ABOUT IT.
REED SHOULD BE BACK FROM HIS LECTURE AT E.S.U. ABOUT NINE. GOOD NIGHT, ALL!
YEAH, G'NIGHT. SEE YA...
BUT AS A SLIGHTLY DISTRACTED BEN GRIMM RETIRES TO HIS ROOMS...
...THE REMAINDER OF THE EVENING IS NOT DESTINED TO GO SO SMOOTHLY AS HE MIGHT WISH...
AW, GEE, WALLY, I DIDN'T MEAN NOTHIN'...
BOY, I THINK I'VE TRASHED SUPER-BADDIES FASTER'N WORKIN' THIS CUBE!

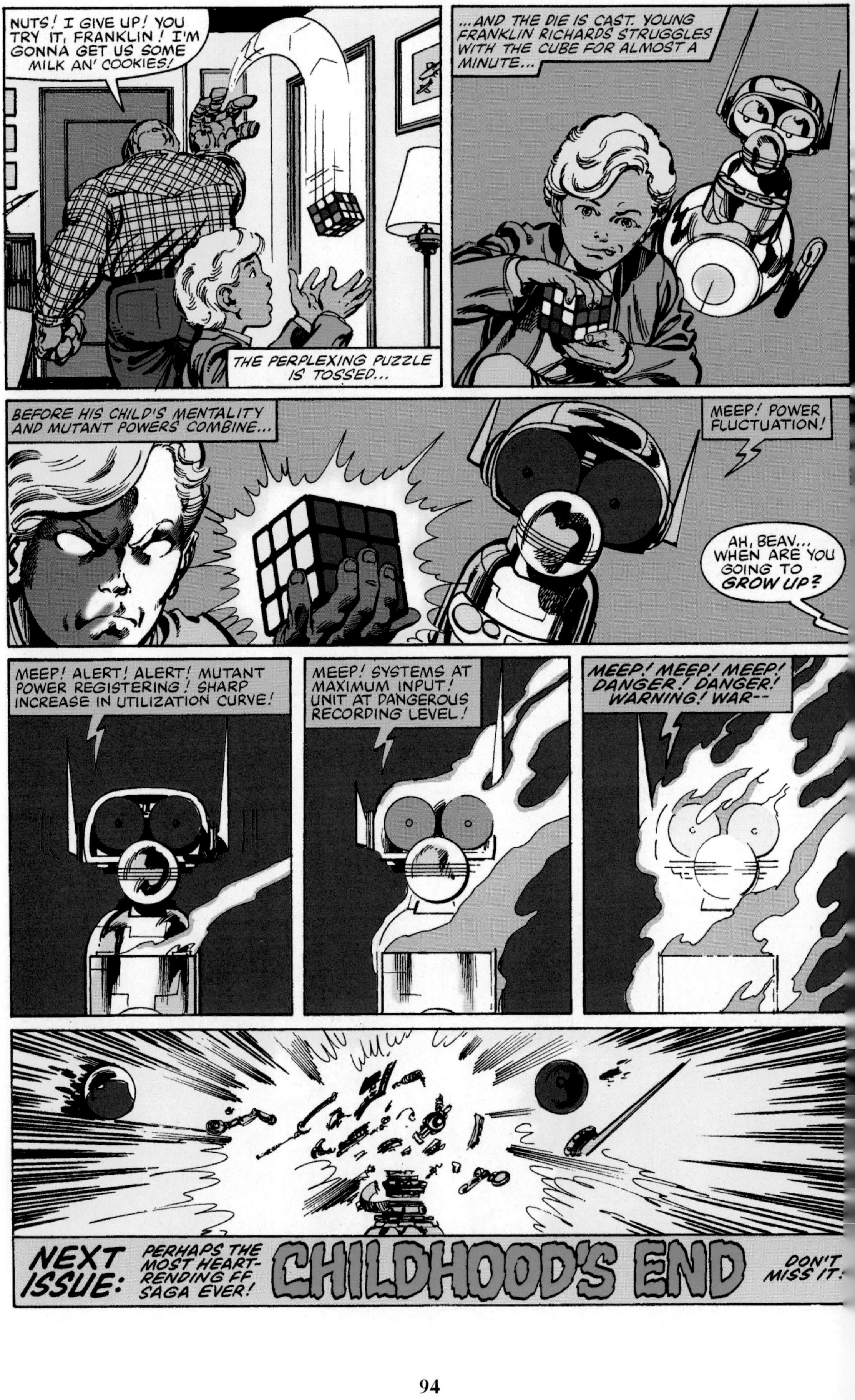
NUTS! I GIVE UP! YOU TRY IT, FRANKLIN! I'M GONNA GET US SOME MILK AN' COOKIES!
THE PERPLEXING PUZZLE IS TOSSED...
...AND THE DIE IS CAST. YOUNG FRANKLIN RICHARDS STRUGGLES WITH THE CUBE FOR ALMOST A MINUTE...
BEFORE HIS CHILD'S MENTALITY AND MUTANT POWERS COMBINE...
MEEP! POWER FLUCTUATION!
AH, BEAV... WHEN ARE YOU GOING TO GROW UP?
MEEP! ALERT! ALERT! MUTANT POWER REGISTERING! SHARP INCREASE IN UTILIZATION CURVE!
MEEP! SYSTEMS AT MAXIMUM INPUT! UNIT AT DANGEROUS RECORDING LEVEL!
MEEP! MEEP! MEEP! DANGER! DANGER! WARNING! WAR--
NEXT ISSUE:
PERHAPS THE MOST HEART-RENDING FF SAGA EVER!
CHILDHOOD'S END
DON'T MISS IT!

fantastic four # 245

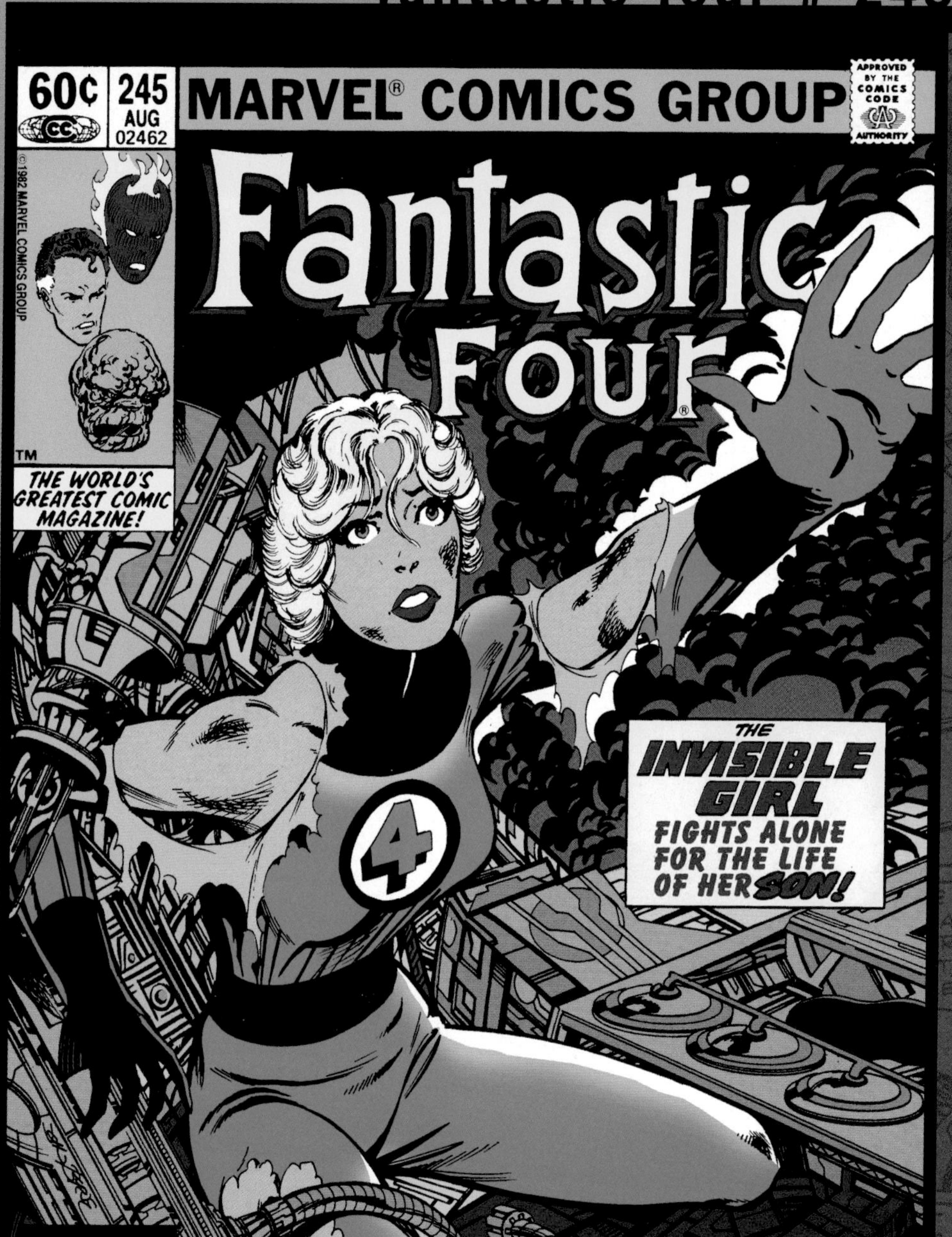

60¢
245
AUG
02462
MARVEL® COMICS GROUP
APPROVED BY THE COMICS CODE AUTHORITY
© 1982 MARVEL COMICS GROUP
Fantastic Four®
THE WORLD'S GREATEST COMIC MAGAZINE!
THE INVISIBLE GIRL FIGHTS ALONE FOR THE LIFE OF HER SON!
CHILDHOOD'S END!

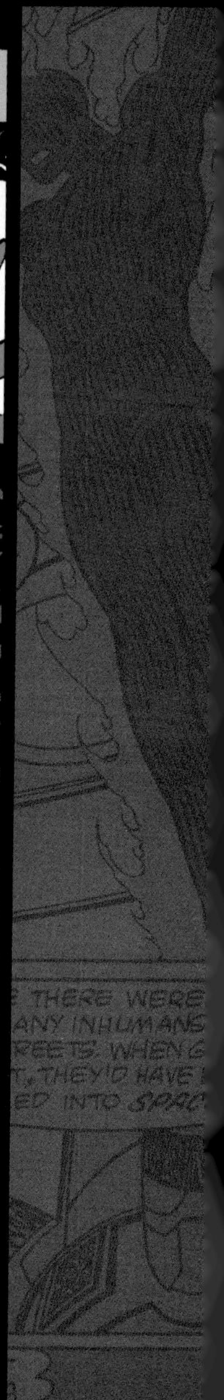

AUGUST 1982

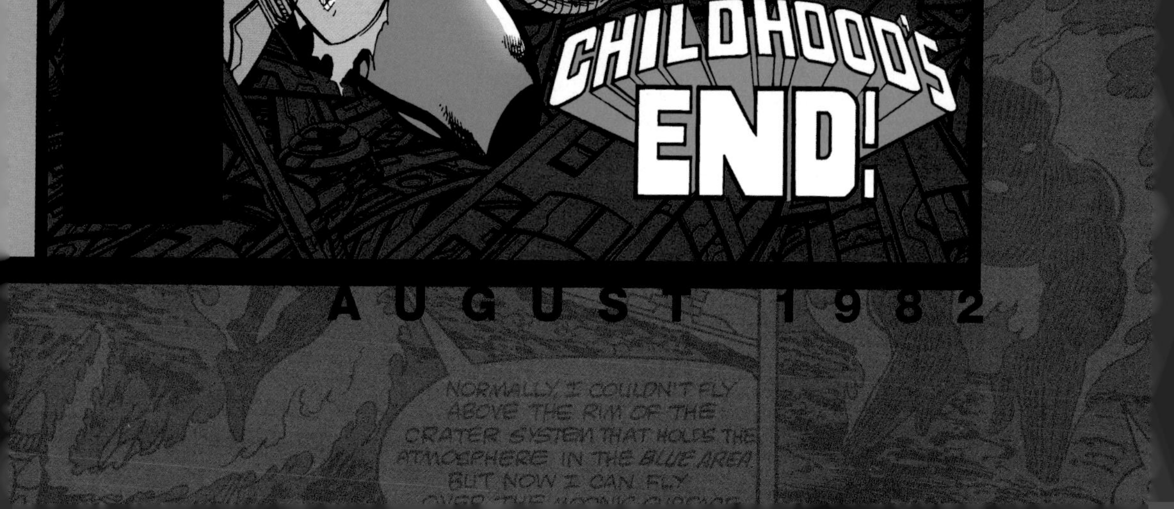

NORMALLY I COULDN'T FLY ABOVE THE RIM OF THE CRATER SYSTEM THAT HOLDS THE ATMOSPHERE IN THE BLUE AREA BUT NOW I CAN FLY

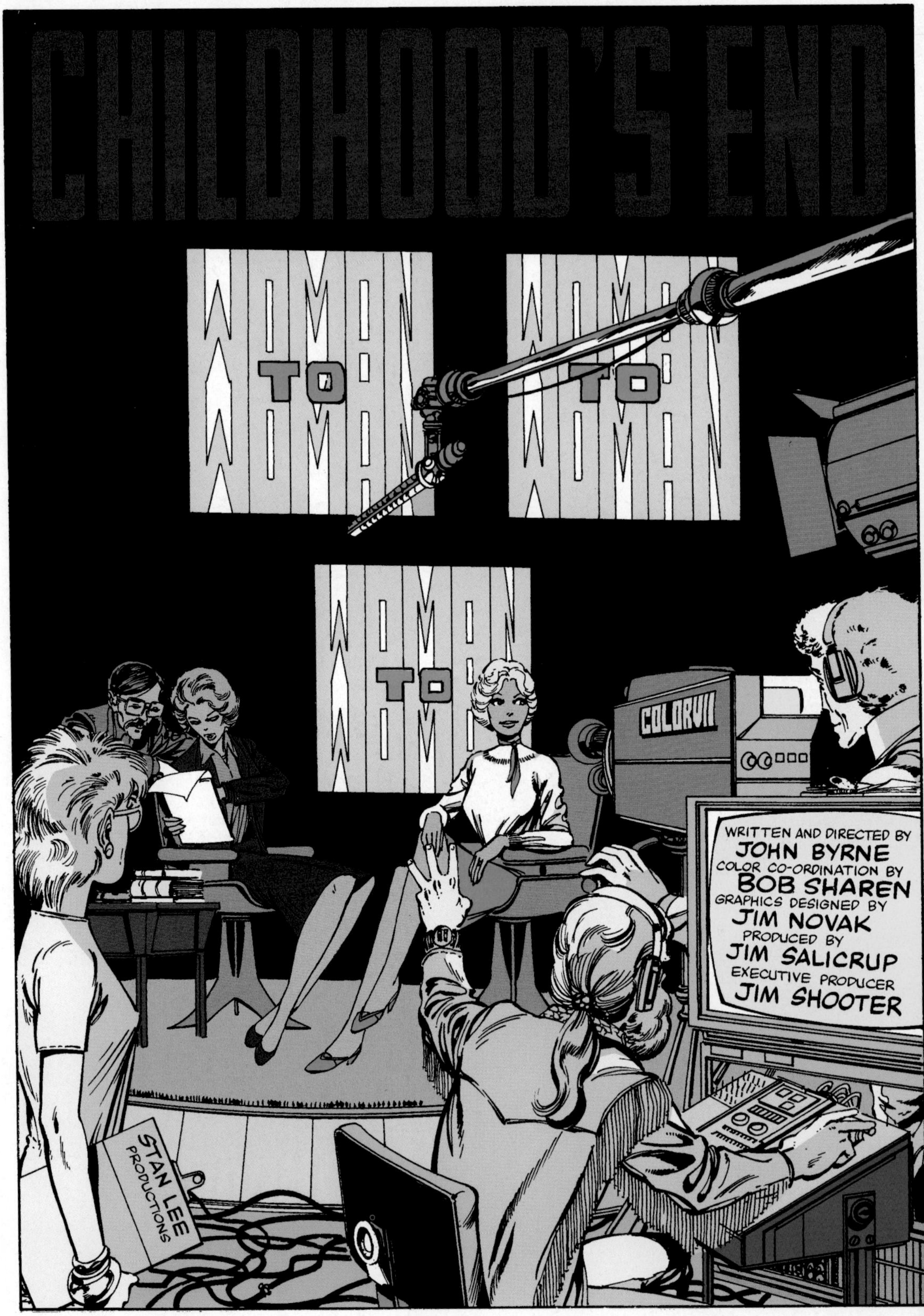
CHILDHOOD'S END
WOMAN TO WOMAN
COLORVII
WRITTEN AND DIRECTED BY
JOHN BYRNE
COLOR CO-ORDINATION BY
BOB SHAREN
GRAPHICS DESIGNED BY
JIM NOVAK
PRODUCED BY
JIM SALICRUP
EXECUTIVE PRODUCER
JIM SHOOTER
STAN LEE
PRODUCTIONS

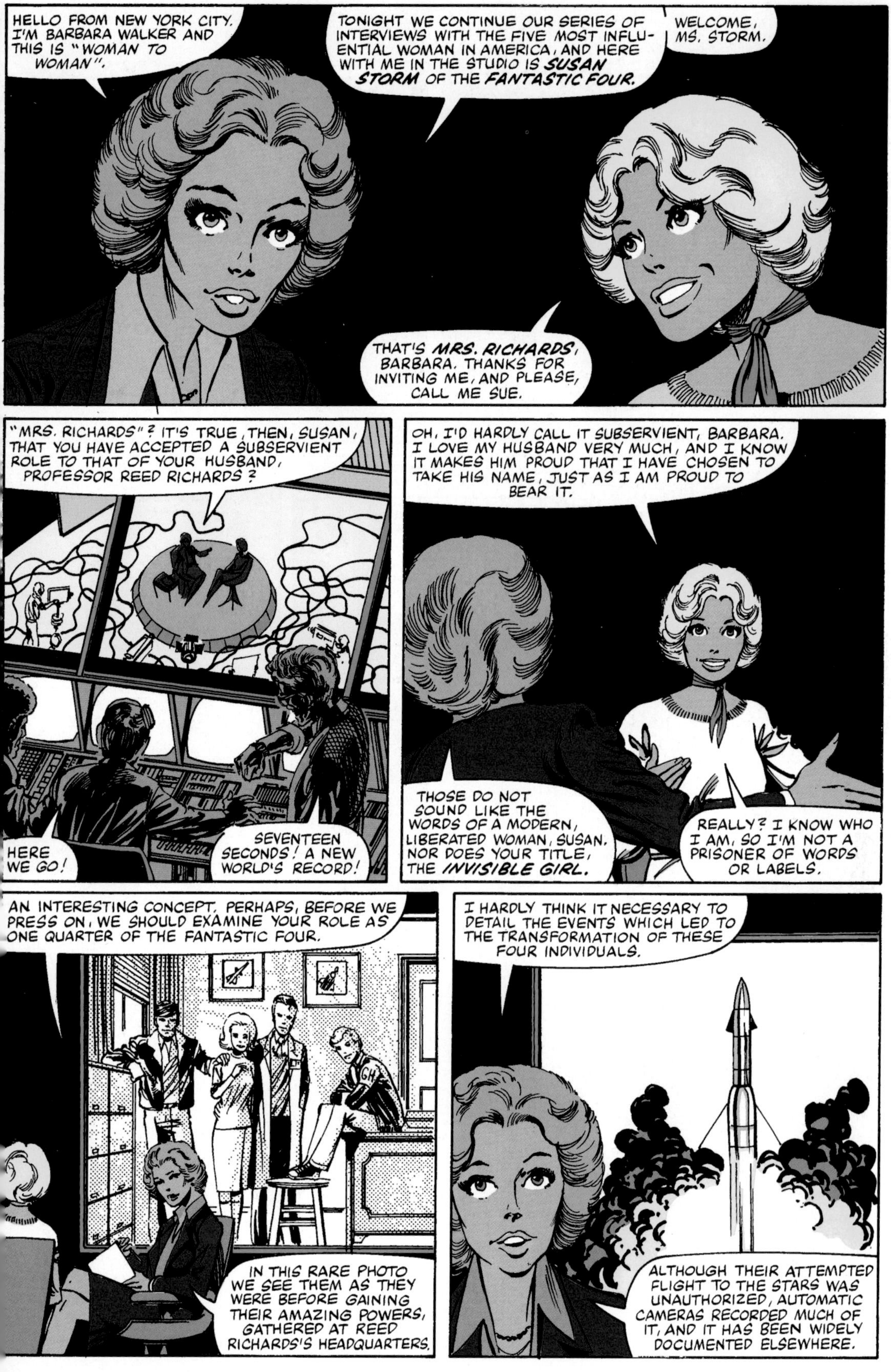

HELLO FROM NEW YORK CITY. I'M BARBARA WALKER AND THIS IS "WOMAN TO WOMAN".
TONIGHT WE CONTINUE OUR SERIES OF INTERVIEWS WITH THE FIVE MOST INFLUENTIAL WOMAN IN AMERICA, AND HERE WITH ME IN THE STUDIO IS SUSAN STORM OF THE FANTASTIC FOUR.
WELCOME, MS. STORM.
THAT'S MRS. RICHARDS, BARBARA. THANKS FOR INVITING ME, AND PLEASE, CALL ME SUE.
"MRS. RICHARDS"? IT'S TRUE, THEN, SUSAN, THAT YOU HAVE ACCEPTED A SUBSERVIENT ROLE TO THAT OF YOUR HUSBAND, PROFESSOR REED RICHARDS?
HERE WE GO!
SEVENTEEN SECONDS! A NEW WORLD'S RECORD!
OH, I'D HARDLY CALL IT SUBSERVIENT, BARBARA. I LOVE MY HUSBAND VERY MUCH, AND I KNOW IT MAKES HIM PROUD THAT I HAVE CHOSEN TO TAKE HIS NAME, JUST AS I AM PROUD TO BEAR IT.
THOSE DO NOT SOUND LIKE THE WORDS OF A MODERN, LIBERATED WOMAN, SUSAN. NOR DOES YOUR TITLE, THE INVISIBLE GIRL.
REALLY? I KNOW WHO I AM, SO I'M NOT A PRISONER OF WORDS OR LABELS.
AN INTERESTING CONCEPT. PERHAPS, BEFORE WE PRESS ON, WE SHOULD EXAMINE YOUR ROLE AS ONE QUARTER OF THE FANTASTIC FOUR.
IN THIS RARE PHOTO WE SEE THEM AS THEY WERE BEFORE GAINING THEIR AMAZING POWERS, GATHERED AT REED RICHARDS'S HEADQUARTERS.
I HARDLY THINK IT NECESSARY TO DETAIL THE EVENTS WHICH LED TO THE TRANSFORMATION OF THESE FOUR INDIVIDUALS.
ALTHOUGH THEIR ATTEMPTED FLIGHT TO THE STARS WAS UNAUTHORIZED, AUTOMATIC CAMERAS RECORDED MUCH OF IT, AND IT HAS BEEN WIDELY DOCUMENTED ELSEWHERE.

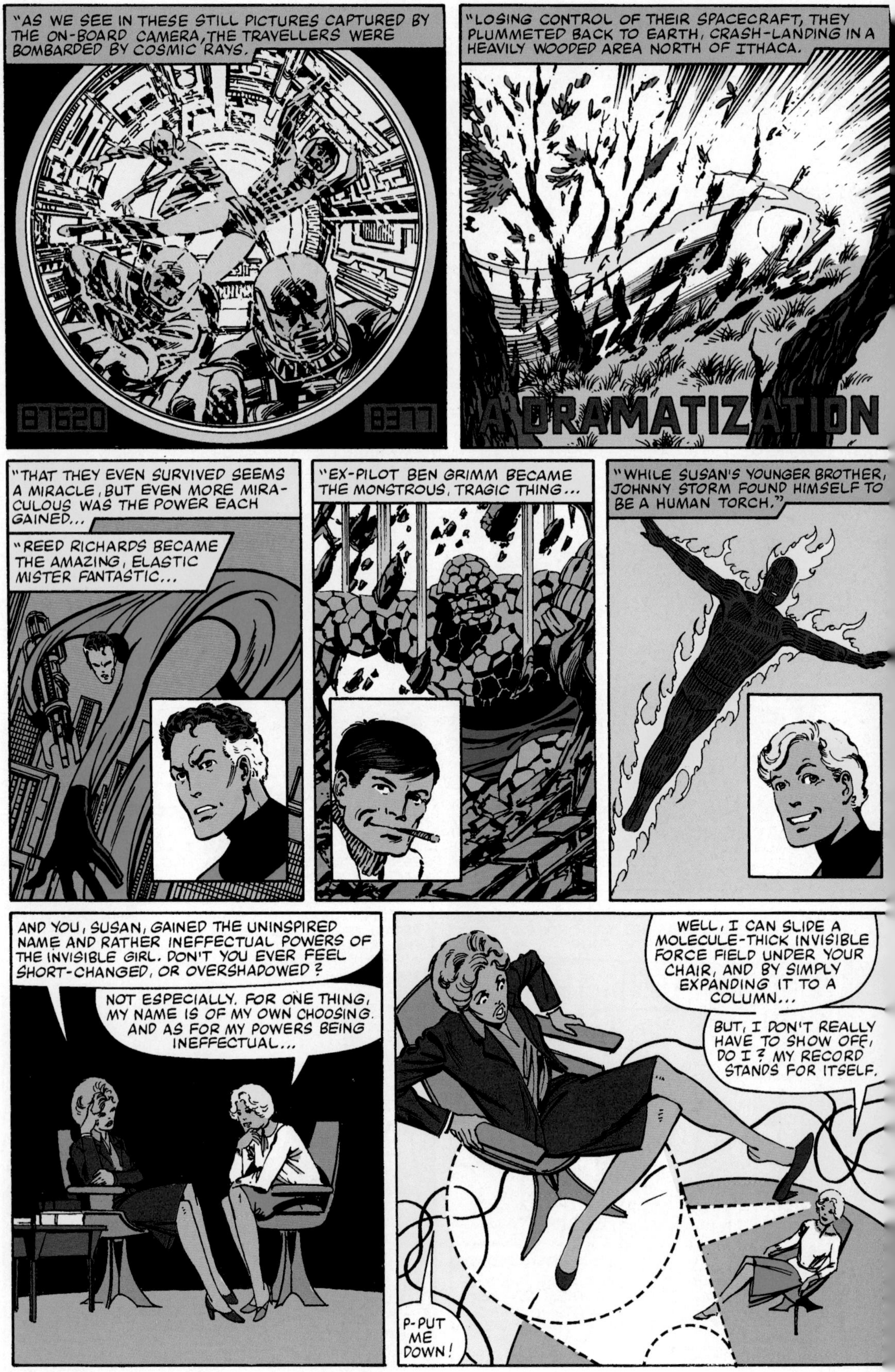
"AS WE SEE IN THESE STILL PICTURES CAPTURED BY THE ON-BOARD CAMERA, THE TRAVELLERS WERE BOMBARDED BY COSMIC RAYS.
"LOSING CONTROL OF THEIR SPACECRAFT, THEY PLUMMETED BACK TO EARTH, CRASH-LANDING IN A HEAVILY WOODED AREA NORTH OF ITHACA.
A DRAMATIZATION
"THAT THEY EVEN SURVIVED SEEMS A MIRACLE, BUT EVEN MORE MIRACULOUS WAS THE POWER EACH GAINED...
"REED RICHARDS BECAME THE AMAZING, ELASTIC MISTER FANTASTIC...
"EX-PILOT BEN GRIMM BECAME THE MONSTROUS, TRAGIC THING...
"WHILE SUSAN'S YOUNGER BROTHER, JOHNNY STORM FOUND HIMSELF TO BE A HUMAN TORCH."
AND YOU, SUSAN, GAINED THE UNINSPIRED NAME AND RATHER INEFFECTUAL POWERS OF THE INVISIBLE GIRL. DON'T YOU EVER FEEL SHORT-CHANGED, OR OVERSHADOWED?
NOT ESPECIALLY. FOR ONE THING, MY NAME IS OF MY OWN CHOOSING. AND AS FOR MY POWERS BEING INEFFECTUAL...
WELL, I CAN SLIDE A MOLECULE-THICK INVISIBLE FORCE FIELD UNDER YOUR CHAIR, AND BY SIMPLY EXPANDING IT TO A COLUMN...
BUT, I DON'T REALLY HAVE TO SHOW OFF, DO I? MY RECORD STANDS FOR ITSELF.
P-PUT ME DOWN!

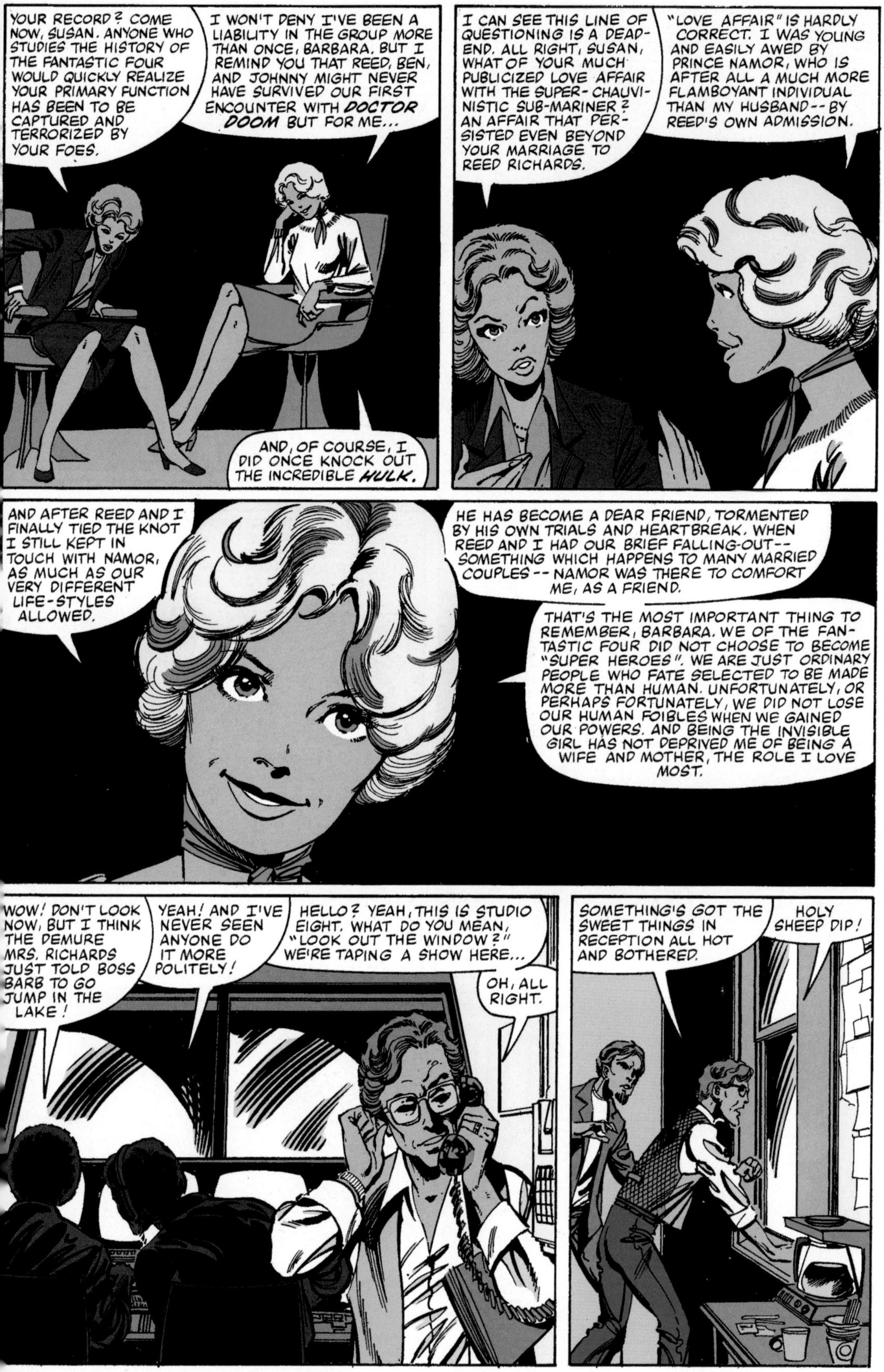

YOUR RECORD? COME NOW, SUSAN. ANYONE WHO STUDIES THE HISTORY OF THE FANTASTIC FOUR WOULD QUICKLY REALIZE YOUR PRIMARY FUNCTION HAS BEEN TO BE CAPTURED AND TERRORIZED BY YOUR FOES.
I WON'T DENY I'VE BEEN A LIABILITY IN THE GROUP MORE THAN ONCE, BARBARA. BUT I REMIND YOU THAT REED, BEN, AND JOHNNY MIGHT NEVER HAVE SURVIVED OUR FIRST ENCOUNTER WITH DOCTOR DOOM BUT FOR ME...
AND, OF COURSE, I DID ONCE KNOCK OUT THE INCREDIBLE HULK.
I CAN SEE THIS LINE OF QUESTIONING IS A DEAD-END. ALL RIGHT, SUSAN, WHAT OF YOUR MUCH PUBLICIZED LOVE AFFAIR WITH THE SUPER-CHAUVINISTIC SUB-MARINER? AN AFFAIR THAT PERSISTED EVEN BEYOND YOUR MARRIAGE TO REED RICHARDS.
"LOVE AFFAIR" IS HARDLY CORRECT. I WAS YOUNG AND EASILY AWED BY PRINCE NAMOR, WHO IS AFTER ALL A MUCH MORE FLAMBOYANT INDIVIDUAL THAN MY HUSBAND--BY REED'S OWN ADMISSION.
AND AFTER REED AND I FINALLY TIED THE KNOT I STILL KEPT IN TOUCH WITH NAMOR, AS MUCH AS OUR VERY DIFFERENT LIFE-STYLES ALLOWED.
HE HAS BECOME A DEAR FRIEND, TORMENTED BY HIS OWN TRIALS AND HEARTBREAK. WHEN REED AND I HAD OUR BRIEF FALLING-OUT-- SOMETHING WHICH HAPPENS TO MANY MARRIED COUPLES -- NAMOR WAS THERE TO COMFORT ME, AS A FRIEND.
THAT'S THE MOST IMPORTANT THING TO REMEMBER, BARBARA. WE OF THE FANTASTIC FOUR DID NOT CHOOSE TO BECOME "SUPER HEROES". WE ARE JUST ORDINARY PEOPLE WHO FATE SELECTED TO BE MADE MORE THAN HUMAN. UNFORTUNATELY, OR PERHAPS FORTUNATELY, WE DID NOT LOSE OUR HUMAN FOIBLES WHEN WE GAINED OUR POWERS. AND BEING THE INVISIBLE GIRL HAS NOT DEPRIVED ME OF BEING A WIFE AND MOTHER, THE ROLE I LOVE MOST.
WOW! DON'T LOOK NOW, BUT I THINK THE DEMURE MRS. RICHARDS JUST TOLD BOSS BARB TO GO JUMP IN THE LAKE!
YEAH! AND I'VE NEVER SEEN ANYONE DO IT MORE POLITELY!
HELLO? YEAH, THIS IS STUDIO EIGHT. WHAT DO YOU MEAN, "LOOK OUT THE WINDOW?" WE'RE TAPING A SHOW HERE...
OH, ALL RIGHT.
SOMETHING'S GOT THE SWEET THINGS IN RECEPTION ALL HOT AND BOTHERED.
HOLY SHEEP DIP!

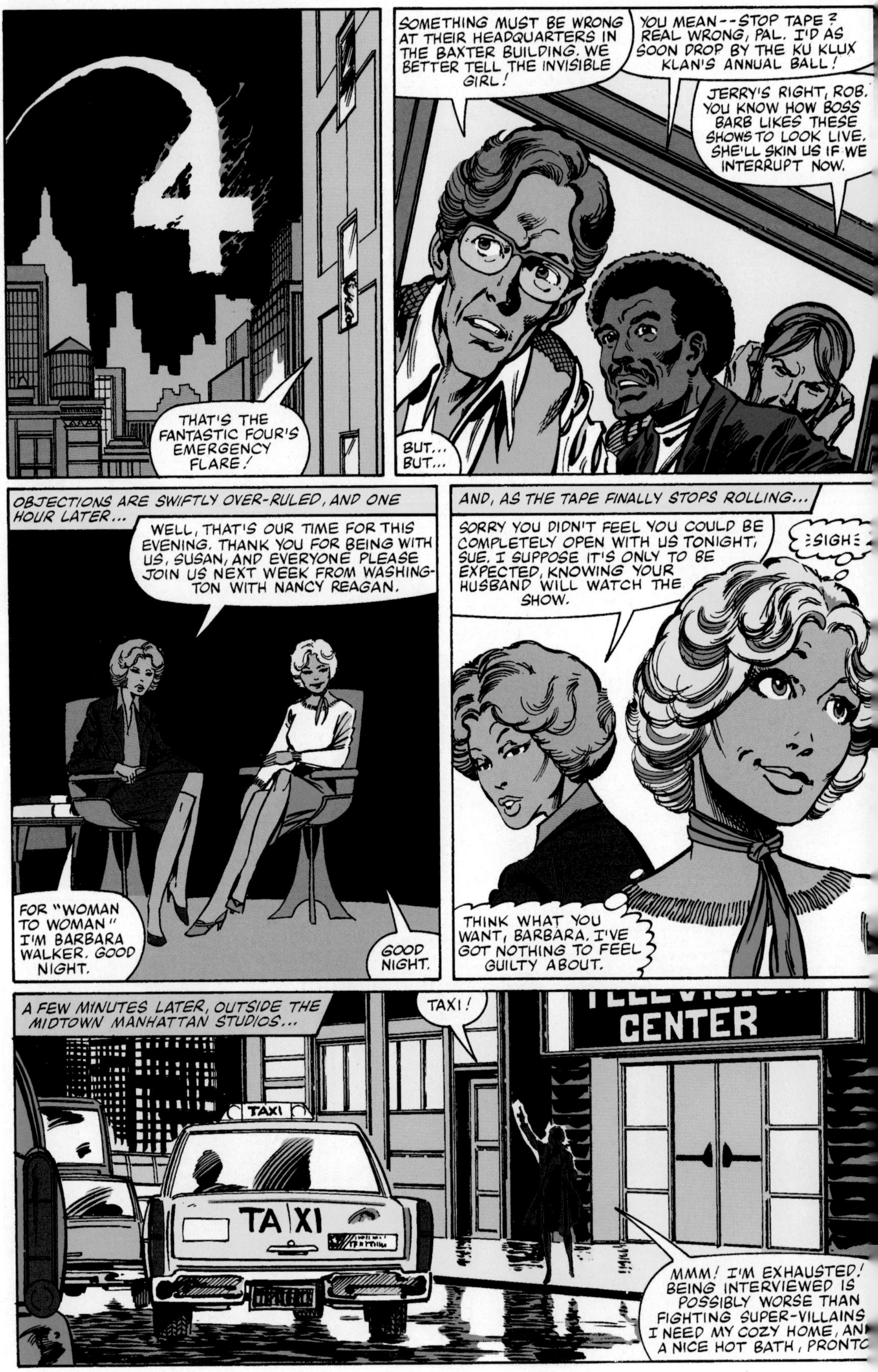
THAT'S THE FANTASTIC FOUR'S EMERGENCY FLARE!
SOMETHING MUST BE WRONG AT THEIR HEADQUARTERS IN THE BAXTER BUILDING. WE BETTER TELL THE INVISIBLE GIRL!
YOU MEAN--STOP TAPE? REAL WRONG, PAL. I'D AS SOON DROP BY THE KU KLUX KLAN'S ANNUAL BALL!
JERRY'S RIGHT, ROB. YOU KNOW HOW BOSS BARB LIKES THESE SHOWS TO LOOK LIVE. SHE'LL SKIN US IF WE INTERRUPT NOW.
BUT... BUT...
OBJECTIONS ARE SWIFTLY OVER-RULED, AND ONE HOUR LATER...
WELL, THAT'S OUR TIME FOR THIS EVENING. THANK YOU FOR BEING WITH US, SUSAN, AND EVERYONE PLEASE JOIN US NEXT WEEK FROM WASHINGTON WITH NANCY REAGAN.
FOR "WOMAN TO WOMAN" I'M BARBARA WALKER. GOOD NIGHT.
GOOD NIGHT.
AND, AS THE TAPE FINALLY STOPS ROLLING...
SORRY YOU DIDN'T FEEL YOU COULD BE COMPLETELY OPEN WITH US TONIGHT, SUE. I SUPPOSE IT'S ONLY TO BE EXPECTED, KNOWING YOUR HUSBAND WILL WATCH THE SHOW.
SIGH
THINK WHAT YOU WANT, BARBARA. I'VE GOT NOTHING TO FEEL GUILTY ABOUT.
A FEW MINUTES LATER, OUTSIDE THE MIDTOWN MANHATTAN STUDIOS...
TAXI!
CENTER
TAXI
TAXI
MMM! I'M EXHAUSTED! BEING INTERVIEWED IS POSSIBLY WORSE THAN FIGHTING SUPER-VILLAINS. I NEED MY COZY HOME, AN A NICE HOT BATH, PRONTO

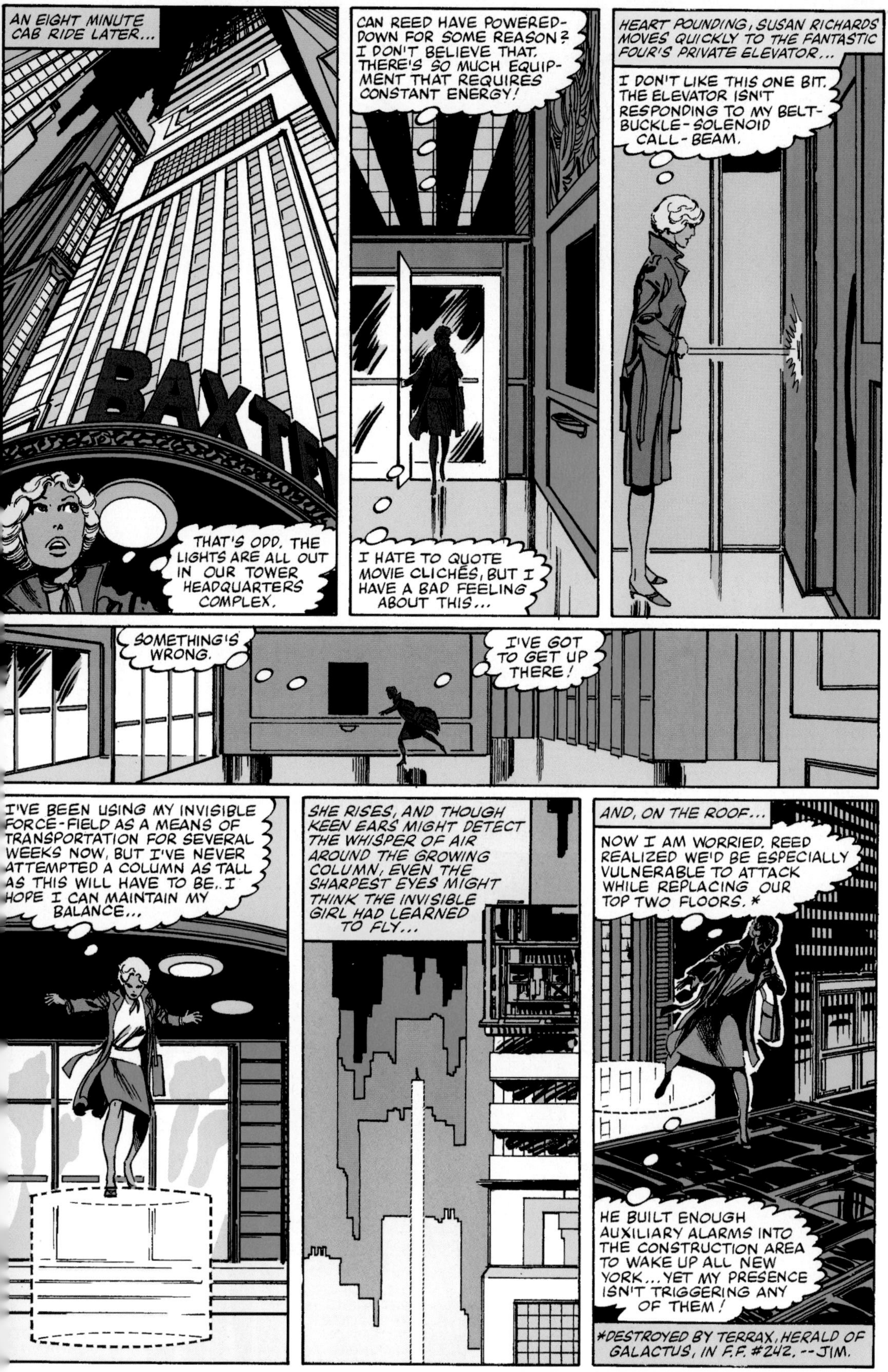

AN EIGHT MINUTE CAB RIDE LATER...
BAXTER
THAT'S ODD. THE LIGHTS ARE ALL OUT IN OUR TOWER HEADQUARTERS COMPLEX.
CAN REED HAVE POWERED-DOWN FOR SOME REASON? I DON'T BELIEVE THAT. THERE'S SO MUCH EQUIPMENT THAT REQUIRES CONSTANT ENERGY!
I HATE TO QUOTE MOVIE CLICHÉS, BUT I HAVE A BAD FEELING ABOUT THIS...
HEART POUNDING, SUSAN RICHARDS MOVES QUICKLY TO THE FANTASTIC FOUR'S PRIVATE ELEVATOR...
I DON'T LIKE THIS ONE BIT. THE ELEVATOR ISN'T RESPONDING TO MY BELT-BUCKLE-SOLENOID CALL-BEAM.
SOMETHING'S WRONG.
I'VE GOT TO GET UP THERE!
I'VE BEEN USING MY INVISIBLE FORCE-FIELD AS A MEANS OF TRANSPORTATION FOR SEVERAL WEEKS NOW, BUT I'VE NEVER ATTEMPTED A COLUMN AS TALL AS THIS WILL HAVE TO BE.. I HOPE I CAN MAINTAIN MY BALANCE...
SHE RISES, AND THOUGH KEEN EARS MIGHT DETECT THE WHISPER OF AIR AROUND THE GROWING COLUMN, EVEN THE SHARPEST EYES MIGHT THINK THE INVISIBLE GIRL HAD LEARNED TO FLY...
AND, ON THE ROOF...
NOW I AM WORRIED. REED REALIZED WE'D BE ESPECIALLY VULNERABLE TO ATTACK WHILE REPLACING OUR TOP TWO FLOORS. *
HE BUILT ENOUGH AUXILIARY ALARMS INTO THE CONSTRUCTION AREA TO WAKE UP ALL NEW YORK... YET MY PRESENCE ISN'T TRIGGERING ANY OF THEM!
*DESTROYED BY TERRAX, HERALD OF GALACTUS, IN F.F. #242. --JIM.

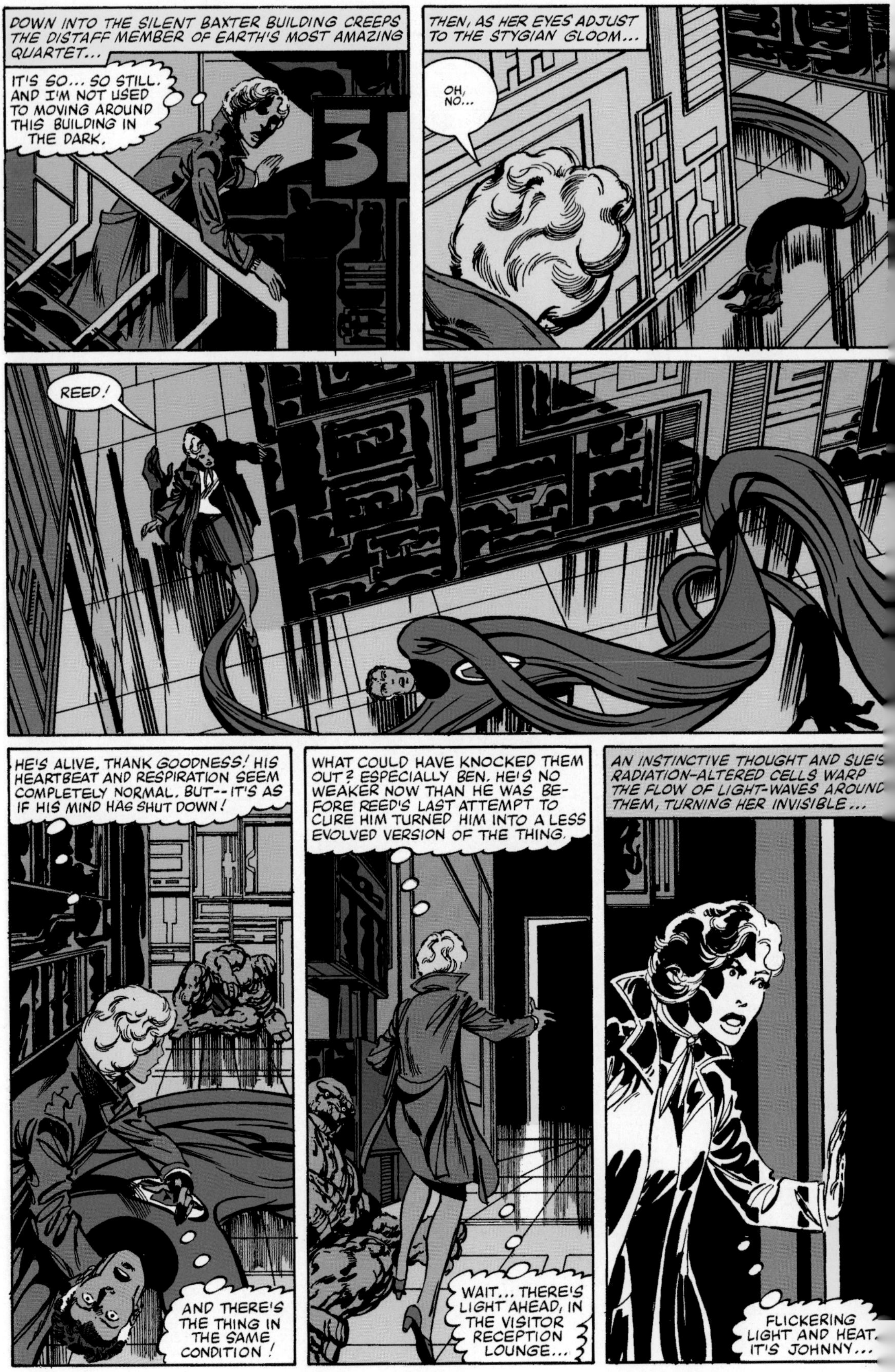
DOWN INTO THE SILENT BAXTER BUILDING CREEPS THE DISTAFF MEMBER OF EARTH'S MOST AMAZING QUARTET...
IT'S SO... SO STILL. AND I'M NOT USED TO MOVING AROUND THIS BUILDING IN THE DARK.
THEN, AS HER EYES ADJUST TO THE STYGIAN GLOOM...
OH, NO...
REED!
HE'S ALIVE, THANK GOODNESS! HIS HEARTBEAT AND RESPIRATION SEEM COMPLETELY NORMAL. BUT--IT'S AS IF HIS MIND HAS SHUT DOWN!
AND THERE'S THE THING IN THE SAME CONDITION!
WHAT COULD HAVE KNOCKED THEM OUT? ESPECIALLY BEN. HE'S NO WEAKER NOW THAN HE WAS BEFORE REED'S LAST ATTEMPT TO CURE HIM TURNED HIM INTO A LESS EVOLVED VERSION OF THE THING.
WAIT... THERE'S LIGHT AHEAD, IN THE VISITOR RECEPTION LOUNGE...
AN INSTINCTIVE THOUGHT AND SUE'S RADIATION-ALTERED CELLS WARP THE FLOW OF LIGHT-WAVES AROUND THEM, TURNING HER INVISIBLE...
FLICKERING LIGHT AND HEAT. IT'S JOHNNY...

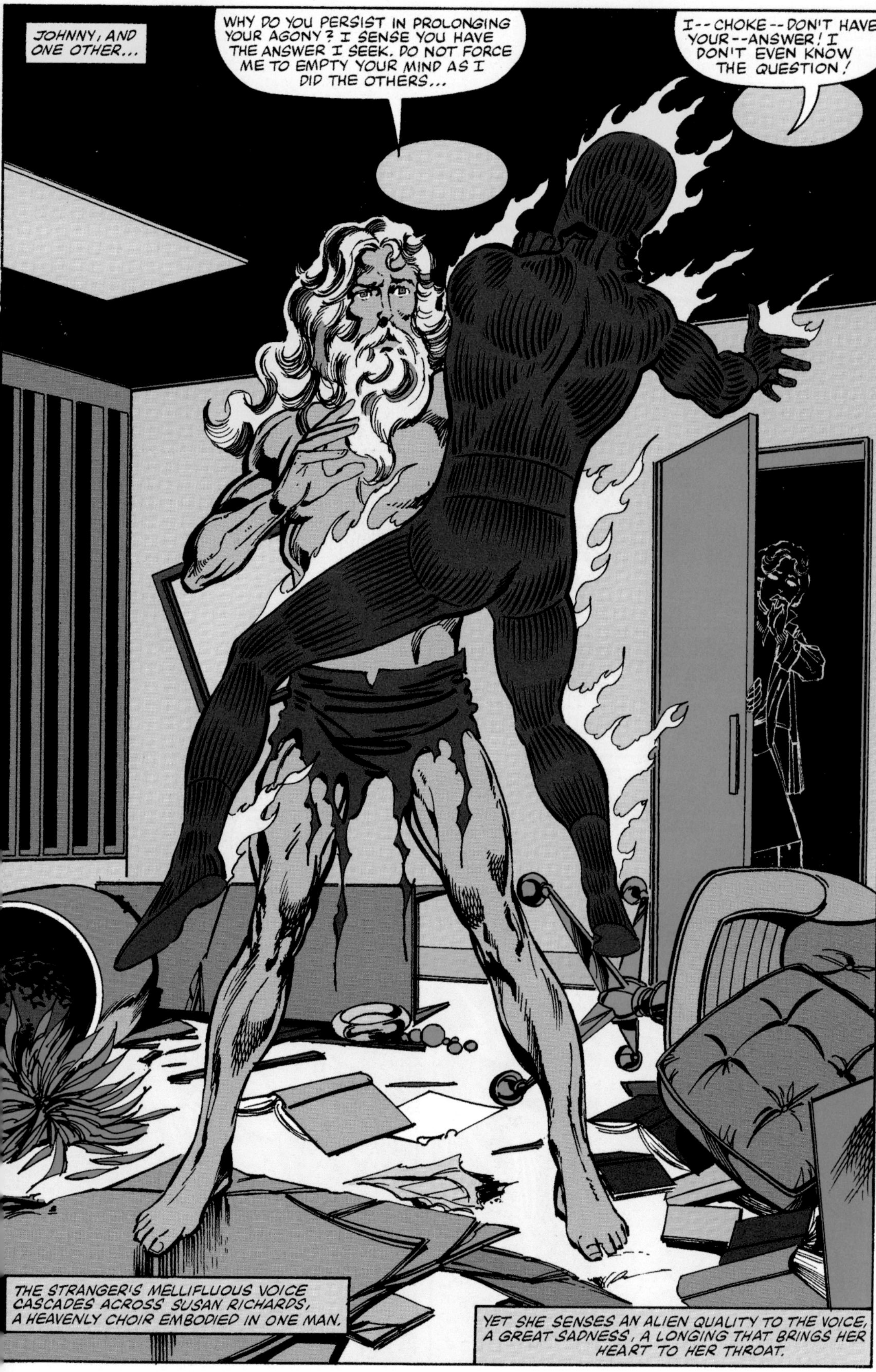
JOHNNY, AND ONE OTHER...
WHY DO YOU PERSIST IN PROLONGING YOUR AGONY? I SENSE YOU HAVE THE ANSWER I SEEK. DO NOT FORCE ME TO EMPTY YOUR MIND AS I DID THE OTHERS...
I--CHOKE--DON'T HAVE YOUR--ANSWER! I DON'T EVEN KNOW THE QUESTION!
THE STRANGER'S MELLIFLUOUS VOICE CASCADES ACROSS SUSAN RICHARDS, A HEAVENLY CHOIR EMBODIED IN ONE MAN.
YET SHE SENSES AN ALIEN QUALITY TO THE VOICE, A GREAT SADNESS, A LONGING THAT BRINGS HER HEART TO HER THROAT.

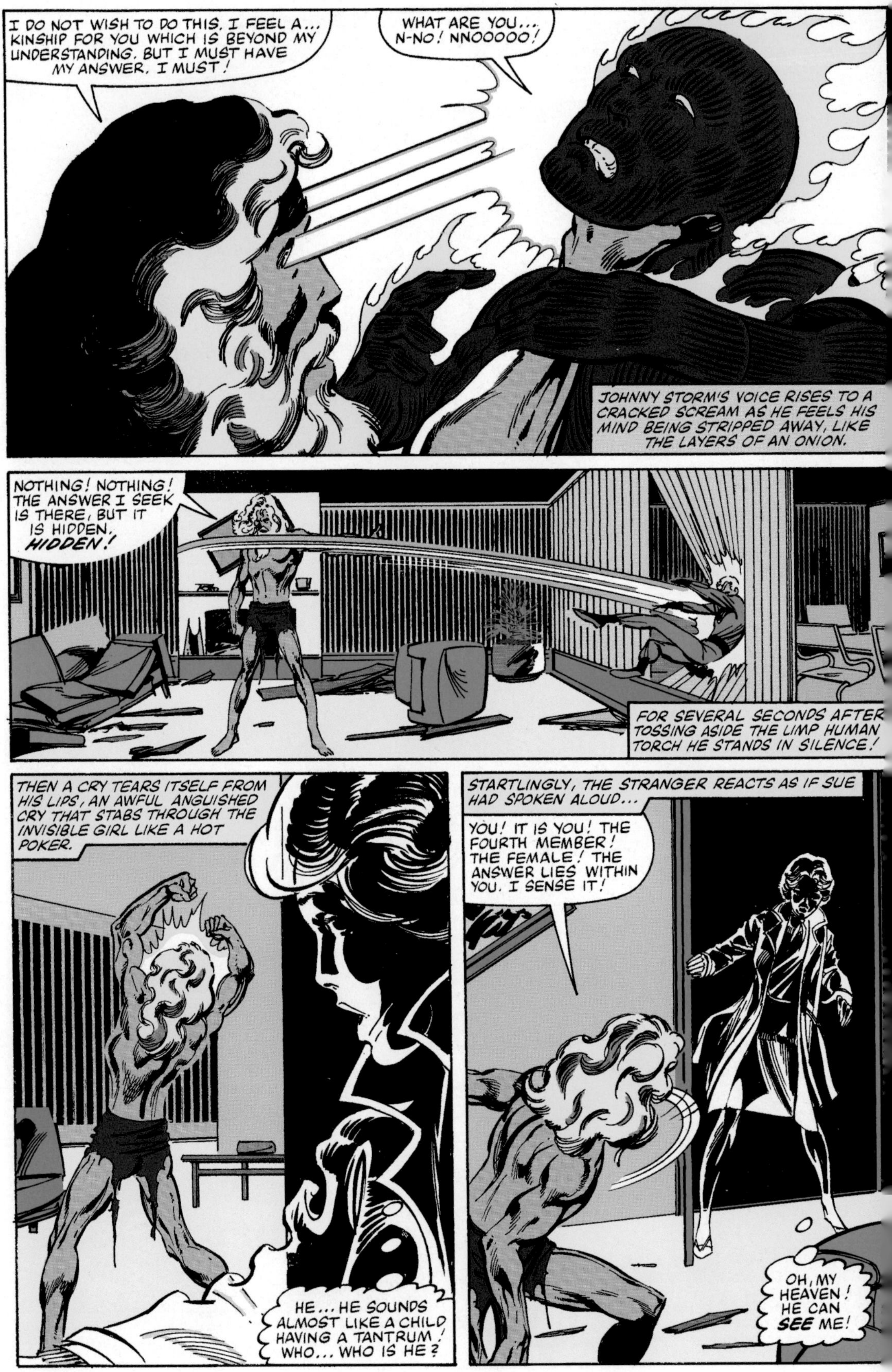
I DO NOT WISH TO DO THIS. I FEEL A... KINSHIP FOR YOU WHICH IS BEYOND MY UNDERSTANDING. BUT I MUST HAVE MY ANSWER. I MUST!
WHAT ARE YOU... N-NO! NNOOOOO!
JOHNNY STORM'S VOICE RISES TO A CRACKED SCREAM AS HE FEELS HIS MIND BEING STRIPPED AWAY, LIKE THE LAYERS OF AN ONION.
NOTHING! NOTHING! THE ANSWER I SEEK IS THERE, BUT IT IS HIDDEN. HIDDEN!
FOR SEVERAL SECONDS AFTER TOSSING ASIDE THE LIMP HUMAN TORCH HE STANDS IN SILENCE!
THEN A CRY TEARS ITSELF FROM HIS LIPS, AN AWFUL ANGUISHED CRY THAT STABS THROUGH THE INVISIBLE GIRL LIKE A HOT POKER.
HE... HE SOUNDS ALMOST LIKE A CHILD HAVING A TANTRUM! WHO... WHO IS HE?
STARTLINGLY, THE STRANGER REACTS AS IF SUE HAD SPOKEN ALOUD...
YOU! IT IS YOU! THE FOURTH MEMBER! THE FEMALE! THE ANSWER LIES WITHIN YOU. I SENSE IT!
OH, MY HEAVEN! HE CAN SEE ME!

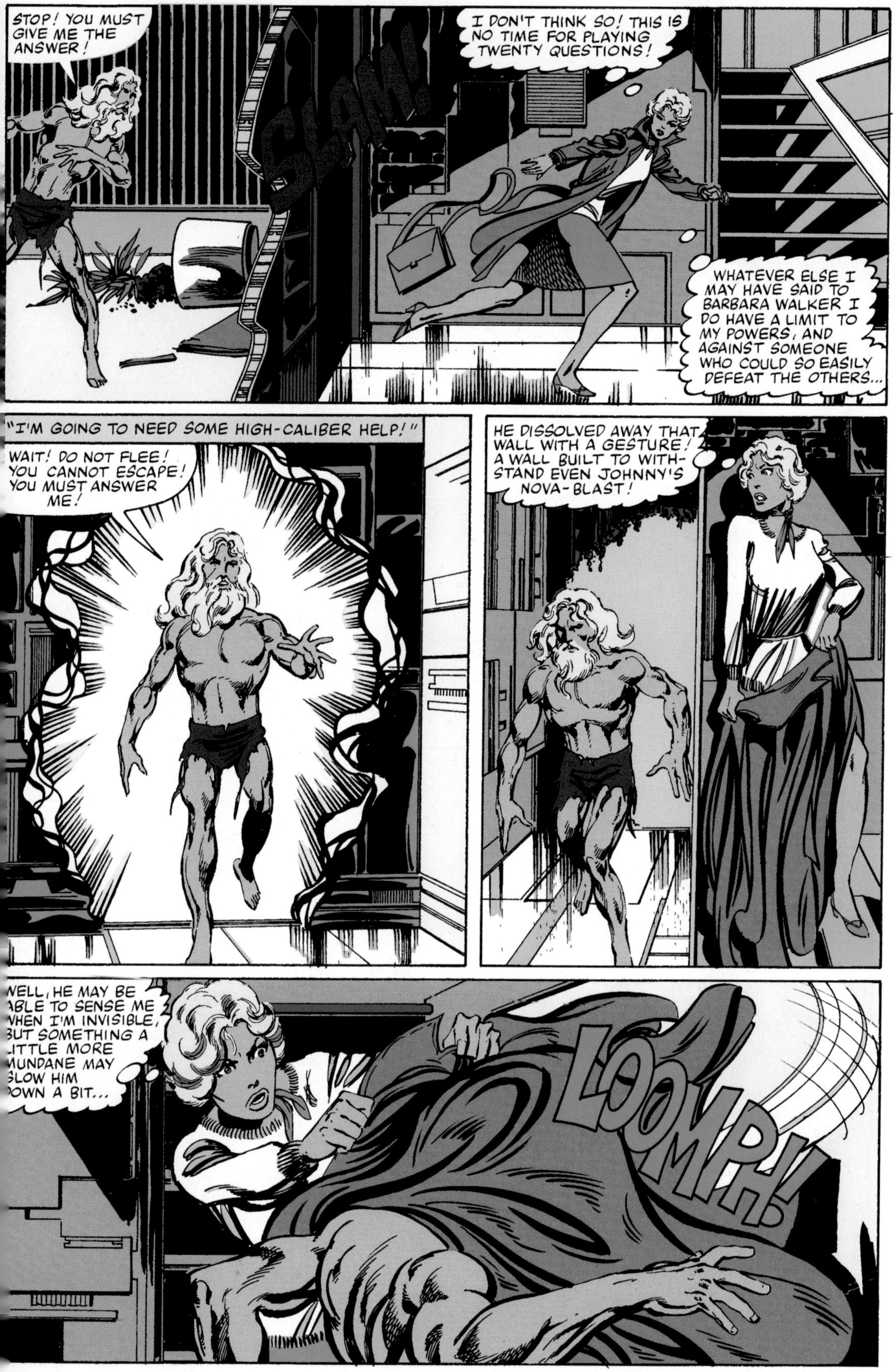
STOP! YOU MUST GIVE ME THE ANSWER!
SLAM!!
I DON'T THINK SO! THIS IS NO TIME FOR PLAYING TWENTY QUESTIONS!
WHATEVER ELSE I MAY HAVE SAID TO BARBARA WALKER I DO HAVE A LIMIT TO MY POWERS, AND AGAINST SOMEONE WHO COULD SO EASILY DEFEAT THE OTHERS...
"I'M GOING TO NEED SOME HIGH-CALIBER HELP!"
WAIT! DO NOT FLEE! YOU CANNOT ESCAPE! YOU MUST ANSWER ME!
HE DISSOLVED AWAY THAT WALL WITH A GESTURE! A WALL BUILT TO WITHSTAND EVEN JOHNNY'S NOVA-BLAST!
WELL, HE MAY BE ABLE TO SENSE ME WHEN I'M INVISIBLE, BUT SOMETHING A LITTLE MORE MUNDANE MAY SLOW HIM DOWN A BIT...
LOOMPH!

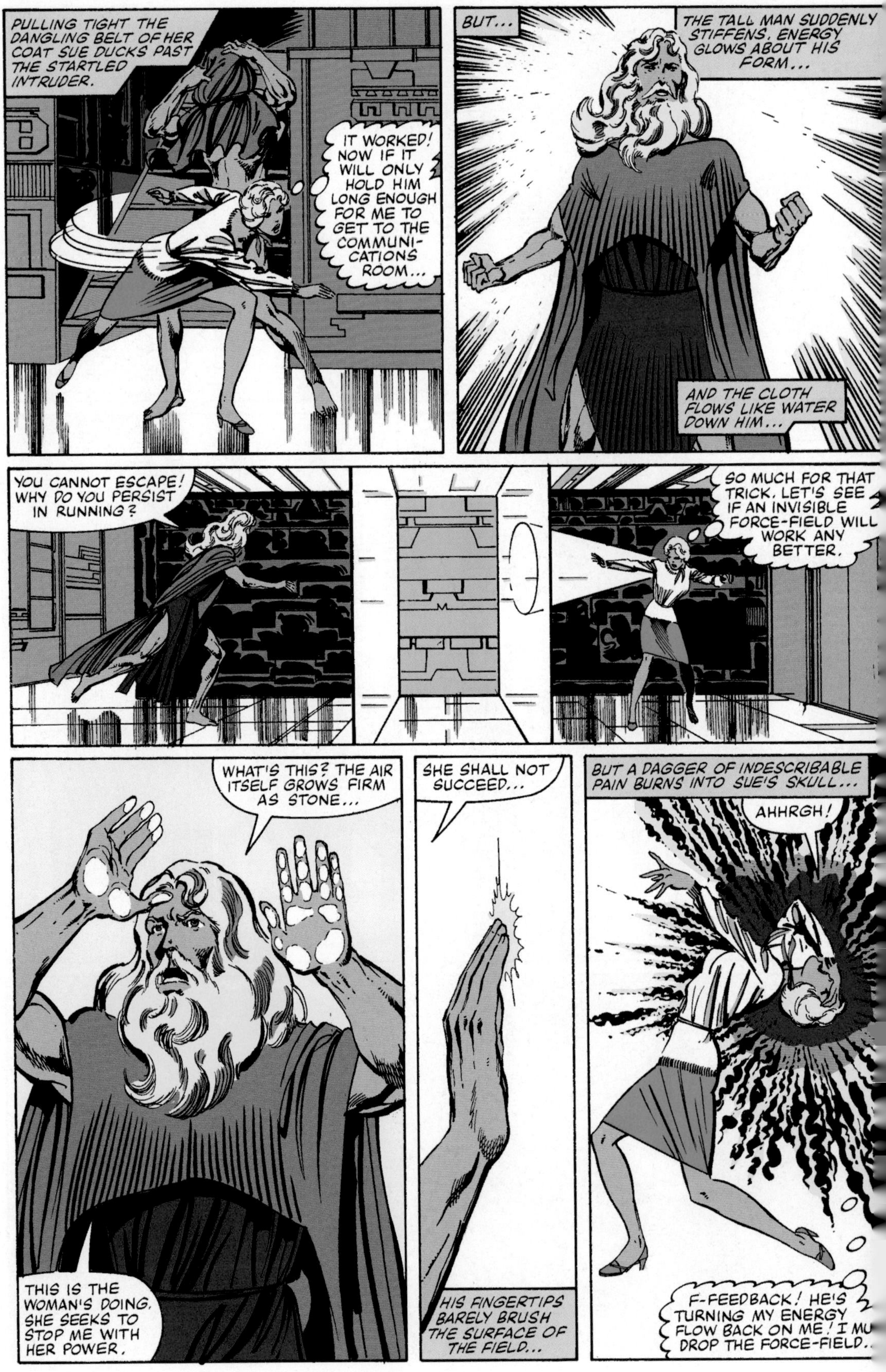
PULLING TIGHT THE DANGLING BELT OF HER COAT SUE DUCKS PAST THE STARTLED INTRUDER.
IT WORKED! NOW IF IT WILL ONLY HOLD HIM LONG ENOUGH FOR ME TO GET TO THE COMMUNICATIONS ROOM...
BUT...
THE TALL MAN SUDDENLY STIFFENS. ENERGY GLOWS ABOUT HIS FORM...
AND THE CLOTH FLOWS LIKE WATER DOWN HIM...
YOU CANNOT ESCAPE! WHY DO YOU PERSIST IN RUNNING?
SO MUCH FOR THAT TRICK. LET'S SEE IF AN INVISIBLE FORCE-FIELD WILL WORK ANY BETTER.
WHAT'S THIS? THE AIR ITSELF GROWS FIRM AS STONE...
THIS IS THE WOMAN'S DOING. SHE SEEKS TO STOP ME WITH HER POWER.
SHE SHALL NOT SUCCEED...
HIS FINGERTIPS BARELY BRUSH THE SURFACE OF THE FIELD...
BUT A DAGGER OF INDESCRIBABLE PAIN BURNS INTO SUE'S SKULL...
AHHRGH!
F-FEEDBACK! HE'S TURNING MY ENERGY FLOW BACK ON ME! I MU DROP THE FORCE-FIELD...

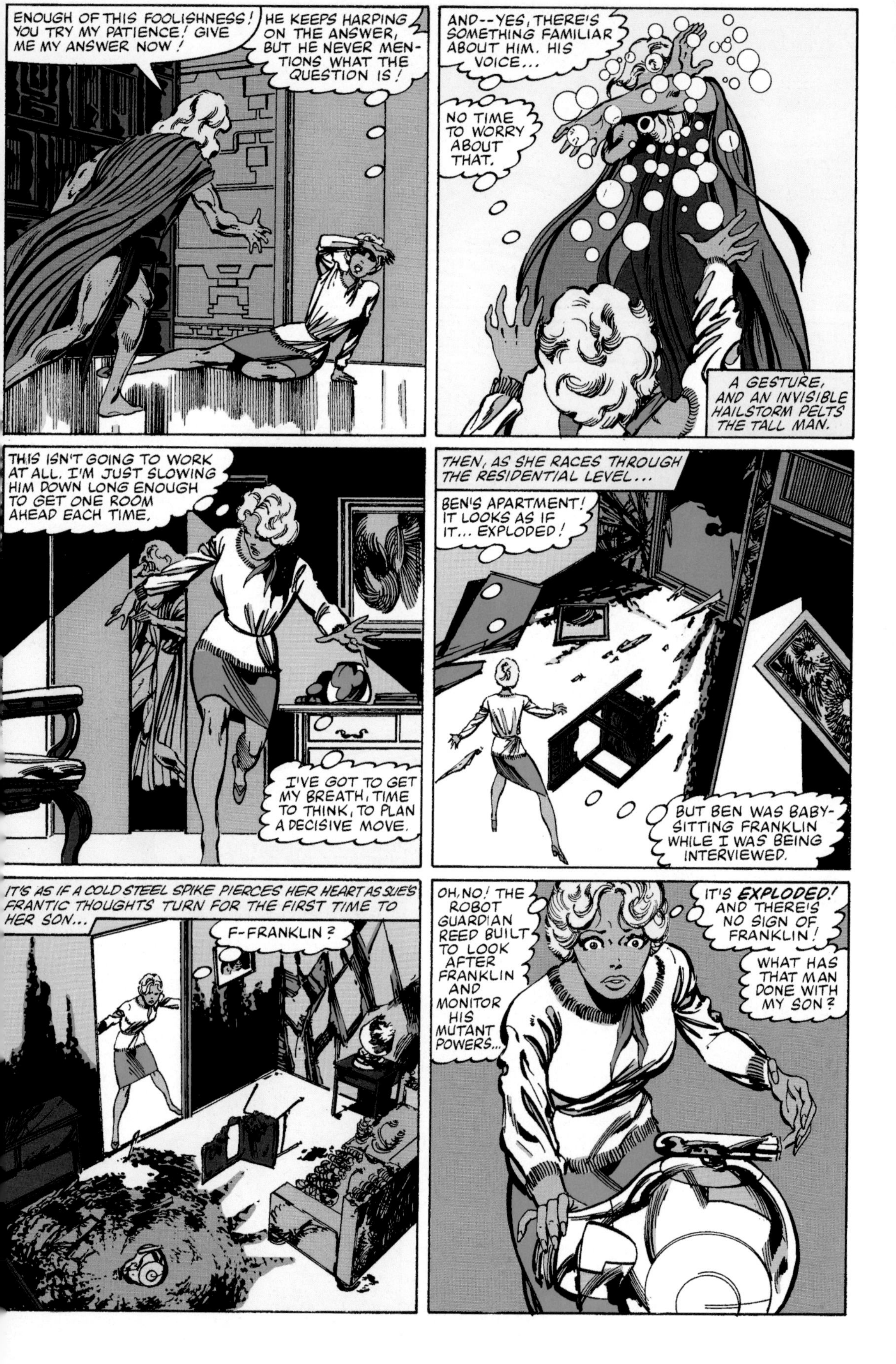
ENOUGH OF THIS FOOLISHNESS! YOU TRY MY PATIENCE! GIVE ME MY ANSWER NOW!
HE KEEPS HARPING ON THE ANSWER, BUT HE NEVER MENTIONS WHAT THE QUESTION IS!
AND--YES, THERE'S SOMETHING FAMILIAR ABOUT HIM. HIS VOICE...
NO TIME TO WORRY ABOUT THAT.
A GESTURE, AND AN INVISIBLE HAILSTORM PELTS THE TALL MAN.
THIS ISN'T GOING TO WORK AT ALL. I'M JUST SLOWING HIM DOWN LONG ENOUGH TO GET ONE ROOM AHEAD EACH TIME.
I'VE GOT TO GET MY BREATH, TIME TO THINK, TO PLAN A DECISIVE MOVE.
THEN, AS SHE RACES THROUGH THE RESIDENTIAL LEVEL...
BEN'S APARTMENT! IT LOOKS AS IF IT... EXPLODED!
BUT BEN WAS BABY-SITTING FRANKLIN WHILE I WAS BEING INTERVIEWED.
IT'S AS IF A COLD STEEL SPIKE PIERCES HER HEART AS SUE'S FRANTIC THOUGHTS TURN FOR THE FIRST TIME TO HER SON...
F-FRANKLIN?
OH, NO! THE ROBOT GUARDIAN REED BUILT TO LOOK AFTER FRANKLIN AND MONITOR HIS MUTANT POWERS...
IT'S EXPLODED! AND THERE'S NO SIGN OF FRANKLIN!
WHAT HAS THAT MAN DONE WITH MY SON?

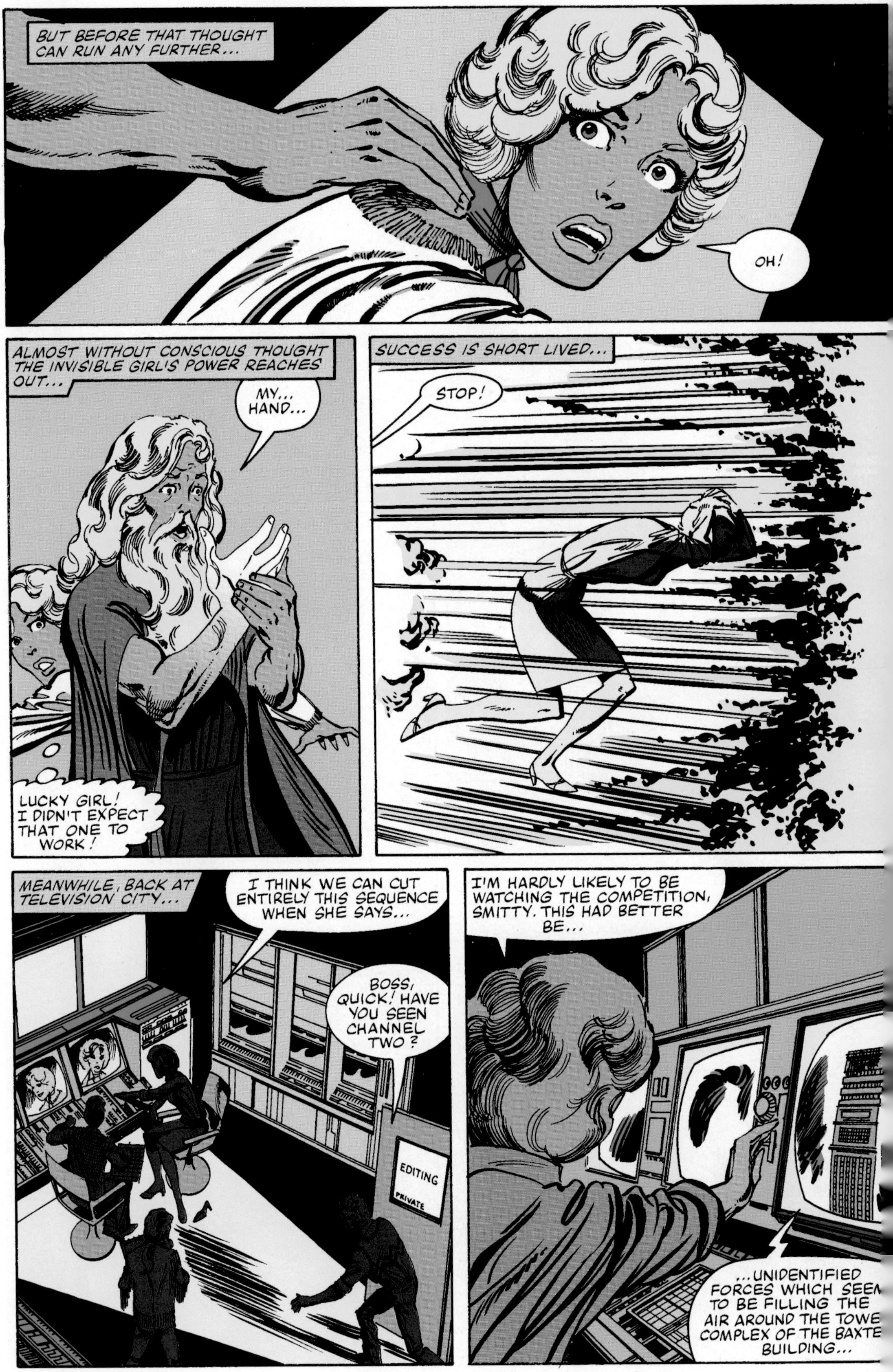
BUT BEFORE THAT THOUGHT CAN RUN ANY FURTHER...
OH!
ALMOST WITHOUT CONSCIOUS THOUGHT THE INVISIBLE GIRL'S POWER REACHES OUT...
MY... HAND...
LUCKY GIRL! I DIDN'T EXPECT THAT ONE TO WORK!
SUCCESS IS SHORT LIVED...
STOP!
MEANWHILE, BACK AT TELEVISION CITY...
I THINK WE CAN CUT ENTIRELY THIS SEQUENCE WHEN SHE SAYS...
BOSS, QUICK! HAVE YOU SEEN CHANNEL TWO?
EDITING
PRIVATE
I'M HARDLY LIKELY TO BE WATCHING THE COMPETITION, SMITTY. THIS HAD BETTER BE...
...UNIDENTIFIED FORCES WHICH SEEM TO BE FILLING THE AIR AROUND THE TOWE COMPLEX OF THE BAXTE BUILDING...

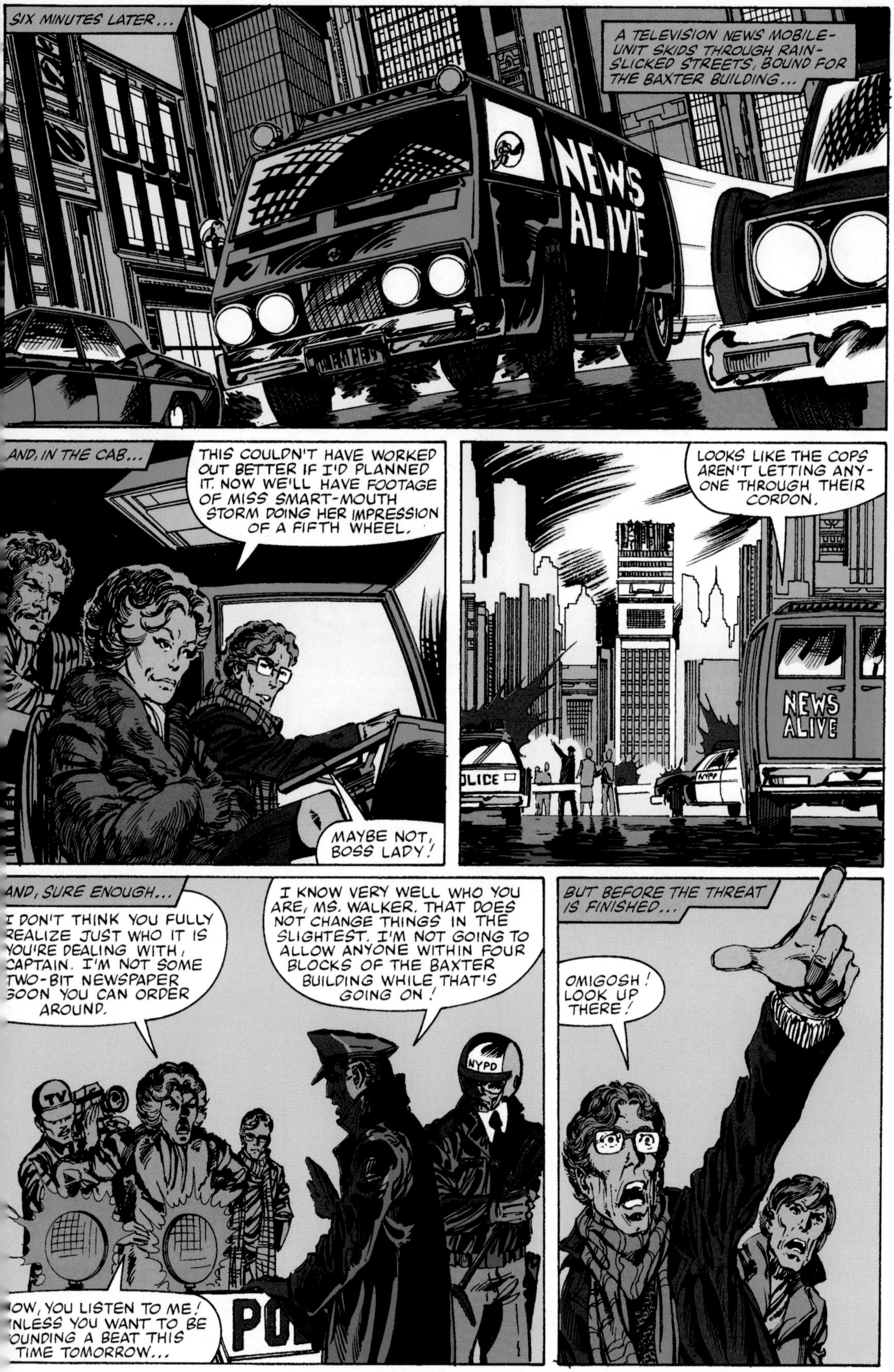
SIX MINUTES LATER...
A TELEVISION NEWS MOBILE-UNIT SKIDS THROUGH RAIN-SLICKED STREETS, BOUND FOR THE BAXTER BUILDING...
NEWS ALIVE
AND, IN THE CAB...
THIS COULDN'T HAVE WORKED OUT BETTER IF I'D PLANNED IT. NOW WE'LL HAVE FOOTAGE OF MISS SMART-MOUTH STORM DOING HER IMPRESSION OF A FIFTH WHEEL.
MAYBE NOT, BOSS LADY!
LOOKS LIKE THE COPS AREN'T LETTING ANY-ONE THROUGH THEIR CORDON.
NEWS ALIVE
AND, SURE ENOUGH...
I DON'T THINK YOU FULLY REALIZE JUST WHO IT IS YOU'RE DEALING WITH, CAPTAIN. I'M NOT SOME TWO-BIT NEWSPAPER GOON YOU CAN ORDER AROUND.
I KNOW VERY WELL WHO YOU ARE, MS. WALKER. THAT DOES NOT CHANGE THINGS IN THE SLIGHTEST. I'M NOT GOING TO ALLOW ANYONE WITHIN FOUR BLOCKS OF THE BAXTER BUILDING WHILE THAT'S GOING ON!
TV
NYPD
OW, YOU LISTEN TO ME! NLESS YOU WANT TO BE OUNDING A BEAT THIS TIME TOMORROW...
BUT BEFORE THE THREAT IS FINISHED...
OMIGOSH! LOOK UP THERE!

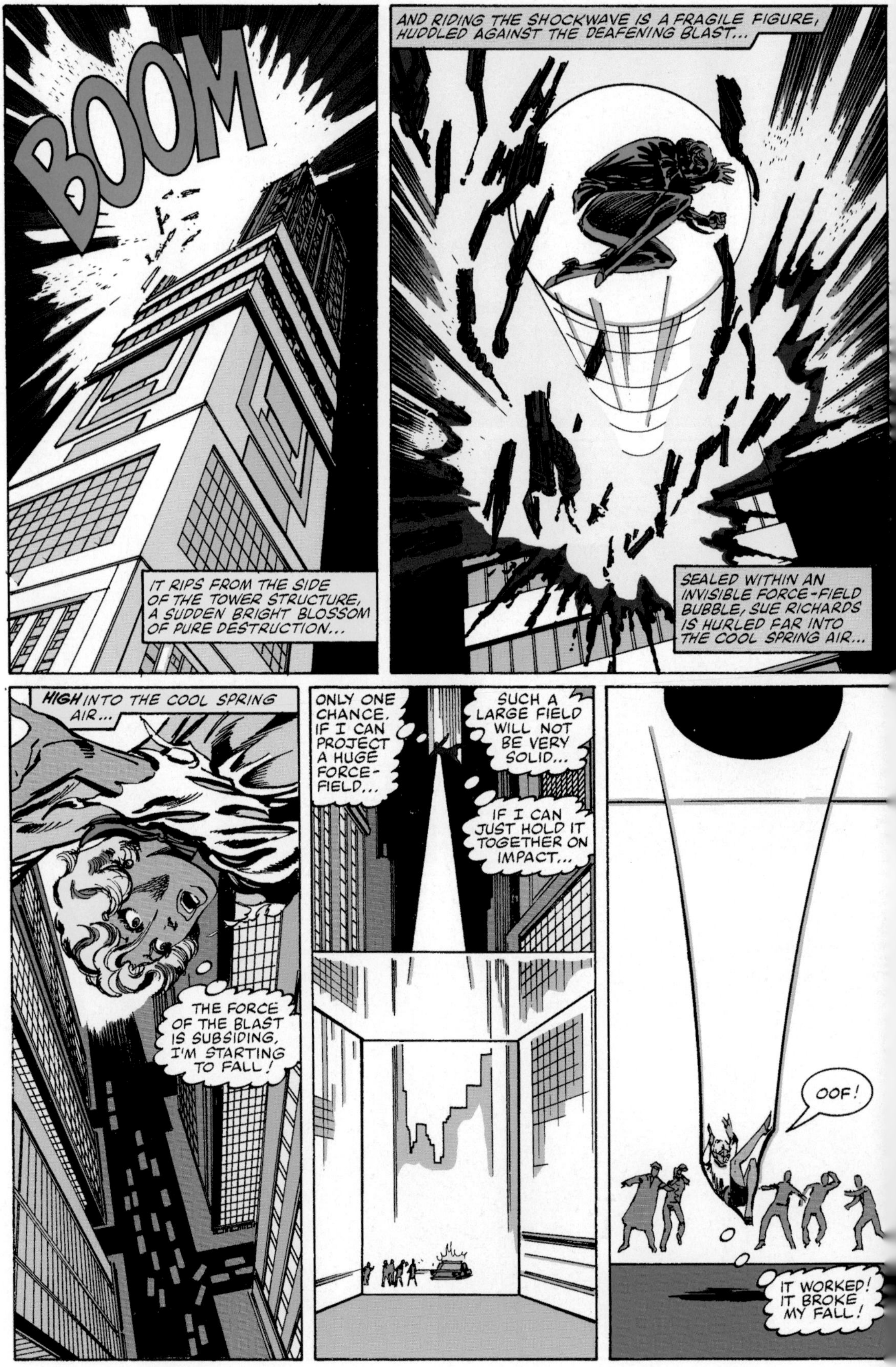
BOOM
AND RIDING THE SHOCKWAVE IS A FRAGILE FIGURE, HUDDLED AGAINST THE DEAFENING BLAST...
IT RIPS FROM THE SIDE OF THE TOWER STRUCTURE, A SUDDEN BRIGHT BLOSSOM OF PURE DESTRUCTION...
SEALED WITHIN AN INVISIBLE FORCE-FIELD BUBBLE, SUE RICHARDS IS HURLED FAR INTO THE COOL SPRING AIR...
HIGH INTO THE COOL SPRING AIR...
THE FORCE OF THE BLAST IS SUBSIDING, I'M STARTING TO FALL!
ONLY ONE CHANCE. IF I CAN PROJECT A HUGE FORCE-FIELD...
SUCH A LARGE FIELD WILL NOT BE VERY SOLID...
IF I CAN JUST HOLD IT TOGETHER ON IMPACT...
OOF!
IT WORKED! IT BROKE MY FALL!

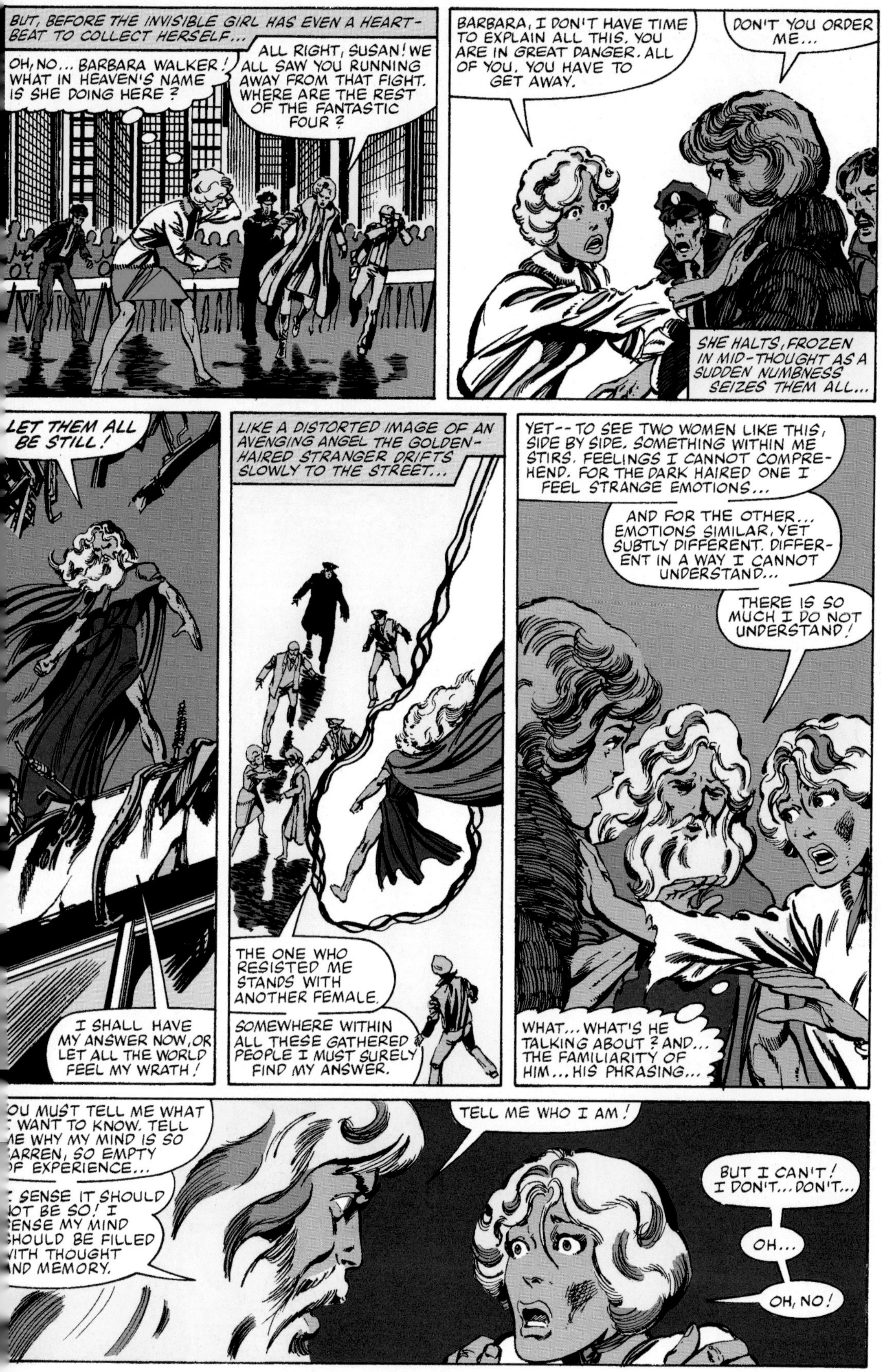
BUT, BEFORE THE INVISIBLE GIRL HAS EVEN A HEART-BEAT TO COLLECT HERSELF...
OH, NO... BARBARA WALKER! WHAT IN HEAVEN'S NAME IS SHE DOING HERE?
ALL RIGHT, SUSAN! WE ALL SAW YOU RUNNING AWAY FROM THAT FIGHT. WHERE ARE THE REST OF THE FANTASTIC FOUR?
BARBARA, I DON'T HAVE TIME TO EXPLAIN ALL THIS. YOU ARE IN GREAT DANGER. ALL OF YOU. YOU HAVE TO GET AWAY.
DON'T YOU ORDER ME...
SHE HALTS, FROZEN IN MID-THOUGHT AS A SUDDEN NUMBNESS SEIZES THEM ALL...
LET THEM ALL BE STILL!
I SHALL HAVE MY ANSWER NOW, OR LET ALL THE WORLD FEEL MY WRATH!
LIKE A DISTORTED IMAGE OF AN AVENGING ANGEL THE GOLDEN-HAIRED STRANGER DRIFTS SLOWLY TO THE STREET...
THE ONE WHO RESISTED ME STANDS WITH ANOTHER FEMALE.
SOMEWHERE WITHIN ALL THESE GATHERED PEOPLE I MUST SURELY FIND MY ANSWER.
YET-- TO SEE TWO WOMEN LIKE THIS, SIDE BY SIDE, SOMETHING WITHIN ME STIRS. FEELINGS I CANNOT COMPRE-HEND. FOR THE DARK HAIRED ONE I FEEL STRANGE EMOTIONS...
AND FOR THE OTHER... EMOTIONS SIMILAR, YET SUBTLY DIFFERENT. DIFFER-ENT IN A WAY I CANNOT UNDERSTAND...
THERE IS SO MUCH I DO NOT UNDERSTAND!
WHAT... WHAT'S HE TALKING ABOUT? AND... THE FAMILIARITY OF HIM... HIS PHRASING...
OU MUST TELL ME WHAT WANT TO KNOW. TELL ME WHY MY MIND IS SO ARREN, SO EMPTY OF EXPERIENCE...
SENSE IT SHOULD NOT BE SO! I ENSE MY MIND HOULD BE FILLED WITH THOUGHT ND MEMORY.
TELL ME WHO I AM!
BUT I CAN'T! I DON'T... DON'T...
OH...
OH, NO!

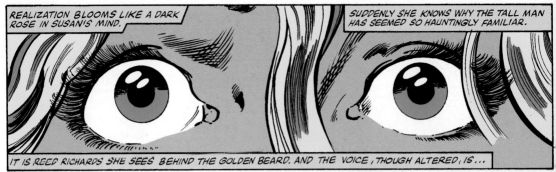

REALIZATION BLOOMS LIKE A DARK ROSE IN SUSAN'S MIND.

SUDDENLY SHE KNOWS WHY THE TALL MAN HAS SEEMED SO HAUNTINGLY FAMILIAR.

IT IS REED RICHARDS SHE SEES BEHIND THE GOLDEN BEARD. AND THE VOICE, THOUGH ALTERED, IS...

F-FRANKLIN?

OH-- OH, FRANKLIN! IT IS *YOU!* DEAR HEAVEN, IT IS YOU!

HE STAGGERS BACK AS IF PHYSICALLY ASSAULTED. MEMORY EXPLODES ACROSS THE EMPTINESS WITHIN HIS SKULL, SWEEPING HIM AWAY, DROWNING HIM.

FRANKLIN! YES! I AM FRANKLIN BENJAMIN RICHARDS! BUT I AM INCOMPLETE! I AM NOT WHOLE!

WHY AM I SO EMPTY? WHERE IS MY LIFE?

HE COLLAPSES, GREAT TEARING SOBS WRACKING HIS BODY...

DON'T BE AFRAID, FRANKLIN. I'M HERE. M-MOMMY'S HERE.

MOMMY? MOMMY? WHAT'S HAPPENED TO ME, MOMMY?

THE VOICE IS SUDDENLY THAT OF A LITTLE BOY, LOST.

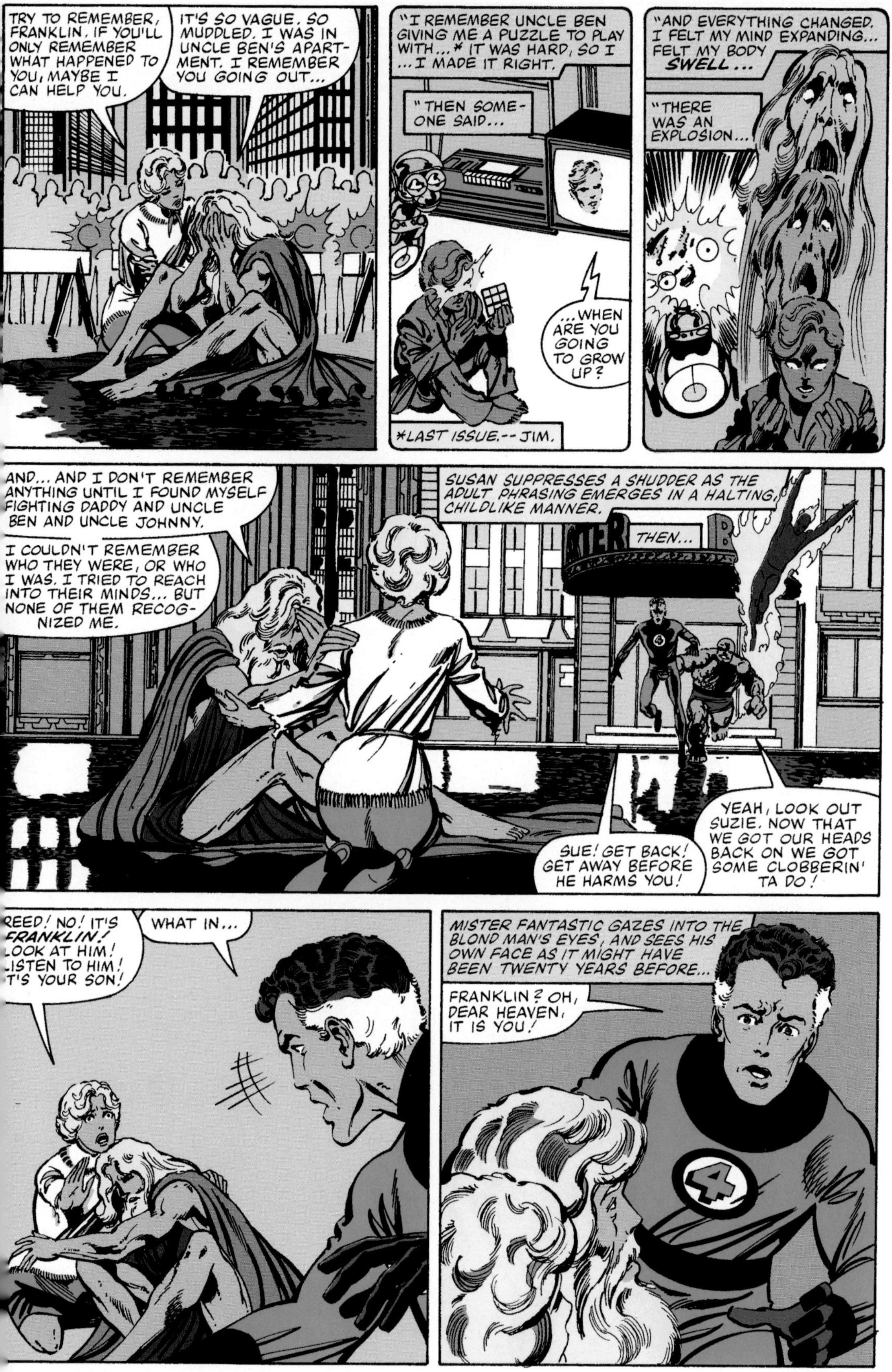

TRY TO REMEMBER, FRANKLIN. IF YOU'LL ONLY REMEMBER WHAT HAPPENED TO YOU, MAYBE I CAN HELP YOU.
IT'S SO VAGUE. SO MUDDLED. I WAS IN UNCLE BEN'S APARTMENT. I REMEMBER YOU GOING OUT...
"I REMEMBER UNCLE BEN GIVING ME A PUZZLE TO PLAY WITH...* IT WAS HARD, SO I ...I MADE IT RIGHT.
"THEN SOMEONE SAID...
...WHEN ARE YOU GOING TO GROW UP?
*LAST ISSUE.-- JIM.
"AND EVERYTHING CHANGED. I FELT MY MIND EXPANDING... FELT MY BODY SWELL...
"THERE WAS AN EXPLOSION...
AND... AND I DON'T REMEMBER ANYTHING UNTIL I FOUND MYSELF FIGHTING DADDY AND UNCLE BEN AND UNCLE JOHNNY.
I COULDN'T REMEMBER WHO THEY WERE, OR WHO I WAS. I TRIED TO REACH INTO THEIR MINDS... BUT NONE OF THEM RECOGNIZED ME.
SUSAN SUPPRESSES A SHUDDER AS THE ADULT PHRASING EMERGES IN A HALTING, CHILDLIKE MANNER.
THEN...
SUE! GET BACK! GET AWAY BEFORE HE HARMS YOU!
YEAH, LOOK OUT SUZIE. NOW THAT WE GOT OUR HEADS BACK ON WE GOT SOME CLOBBERIN' TA DO!
REED! NO! IT'S FRANKLIN! LOOK AT HIM! LISTEN TO HIM! IT'S YOUR SON!
WHAT IN...
MISTER FANTASTIC GAZES INTO THE BLOND MAN'S EYES, AND SEES HIS OWN FACE AS IT MIGHT HAVE BEEN TWENTY YEARS BEFORE...
FRANKLIN? OH, DEAR HEAVEN, IT IS YOU!

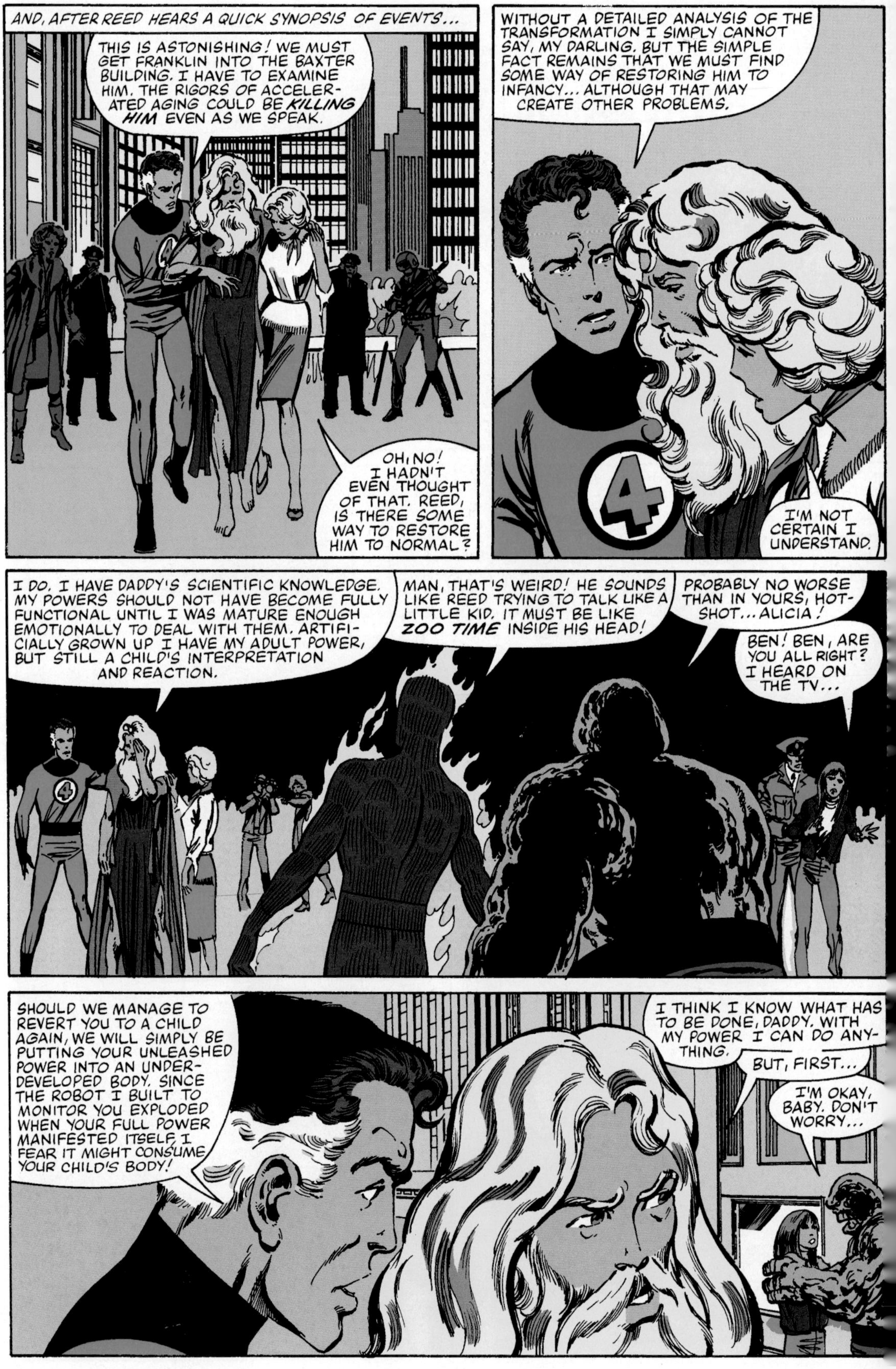
AND, AFTER REED HEARS A QUICK SYNOPSIS OF EVENTS...
THIS IS ASTONISHING! WE MUST GET FRANKLIN INTO THE BAXTER BUILDING. I HAVE TO EXAMINE HIM. THE RIGORS OF ACCELERATED AGING COULD BE *KILLING HIM* EVEN AS WE SPEAK.
OH, NO! I HADN'T EVEN THOUGHT OF THAT. REED, IS THERE SOME WAY TO RESTORE HIM TO NORMAL?
WITHOUT A DETAILED ANALYSIS OF THE TRANSFORMATION I SIMPLY CANNOT SAY, MY DARLING. BUT THE SIMPLE FACT REMAINS THAT WE MUST FIND SOME WAY OF RESTORING HIM TO INFANCY... ALTHOUGH THAT MAY CREATE OTHER PROBLEMS.
I'M NOT CERTAIN I UNDERSTAND.
I DO. I HAVE DADDY'S SCIENTIFIC KNOWLEDGE. MY POWERS SHOULD NOT HAVE BECOME FULLY FUNCTIONAL UNTIL I WAS MATURE ENOUGH EMOTIONALLY TO DEAL WITH THEM. ARTIFICIALLY GROWN UP I HAVE MY ADULT POWER, BUT STILL A CHILD'S INTERPRETATION AND REACTION.
MAN, THAT'S WEIRD! HE SOUNDS LIKE REED TRYING TO TALK LIKE A LITTLE KID. IT MUST BE LIKE *ZOO TIME* INSIDE HIS HEAD!
PROBABLY NO WORSE THAN IN YOURS, HOT-SHOT... ALICIA!
BEN! BEN, ARE YOU ALL RIGHT? I HEARD ON THE TV...
SHOULD WE MANAGE TO REVERT YOU TO A CHILD AGAIN, WE WILL SIMPLY BE PUTTING YOUR UNLEASHED POWER INTO AN UNDER-DEVELOPED BODY. SINCE THE ROBOT I BUILT TO MONITOR YOU EXPLODED WHEN YOUR FULL POWER MANIFESTED ITSELF, I FEAR IT MIGHT CONSUME YOUR CHILD'S BODY!
I THINK I KNOW WHAT HAS TO BE DONE, DADDY. WITH MY POWER I CAN DO ANYTHING.
BUT, FIRST...
I'M OKAY, BABY. DON'T WORRY...

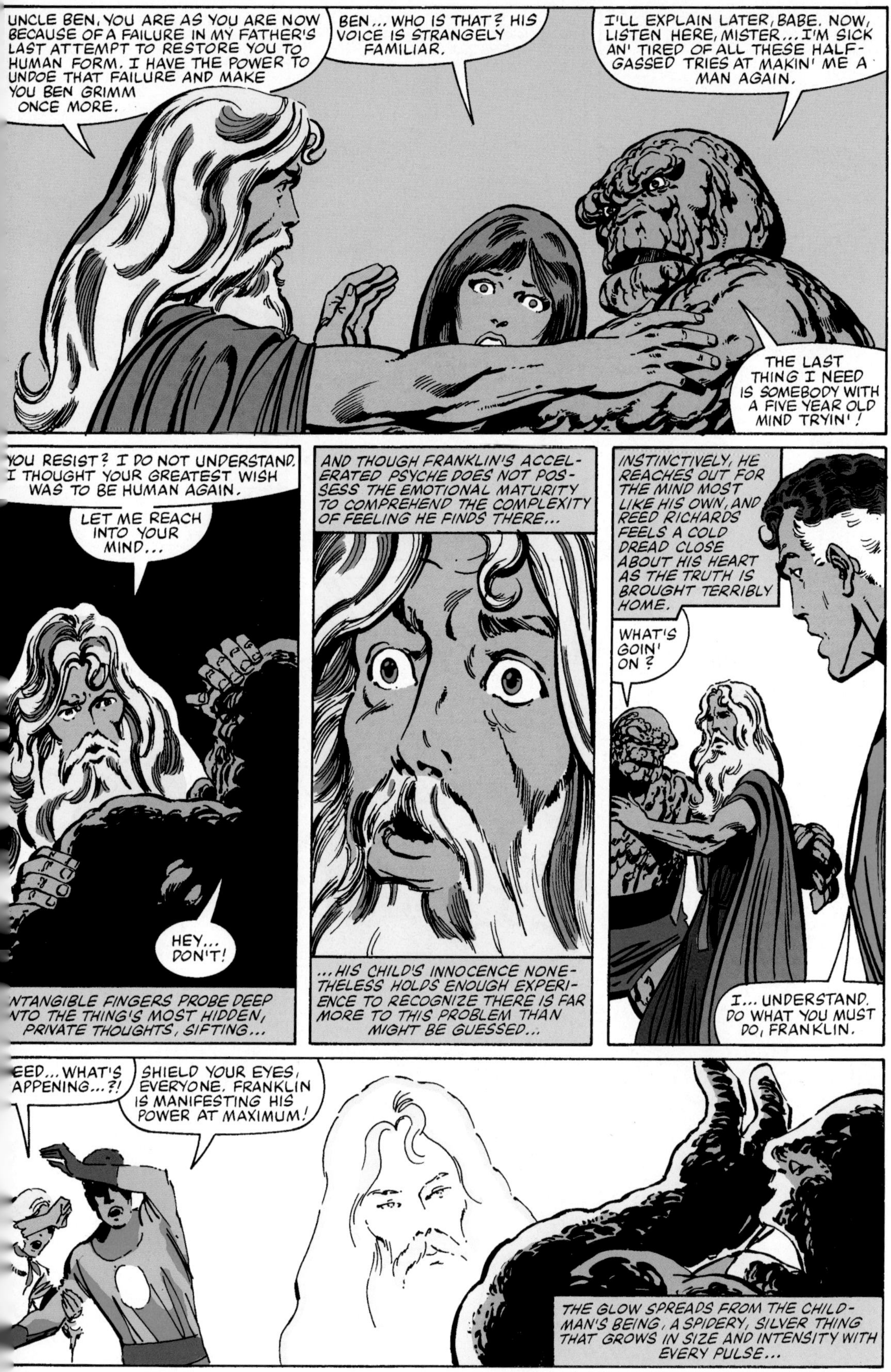
UNCLE BEN, YOU ARE AS YOU ARE NOW BECAUSE OF A FAILURE IN MY FATHER'S LAST ATTEMPT TO RESTORE YOU TO HUMAN FORM. I HAVE THE POWER TO UNDOE THAT FAILURE AND MAKE YOU BEN GRIMM ONCE MORE.
BEN... WHO IS THAT? HIS VOICE IS STRANGELY FAMILIAR.
I'LL EXPLAIN LATER, BABE. NOW, LISTEN HERE, MISTER... I'M SICK AN' TIRED OF ALL THESE HALF-GASSED TRIES AT MAKIN' ME A MAN AGAIN.
THE LAST THING I NEED IS SOMEBODY WITH A FIVE YEAR OLD MIND TRYIN'!
YOU RESIST? I DO NOT UNDERSTAND. I THOUGHT YOUR GREATEST WISH WAS TO BE HUMAN AGAIN.
LET ME REACH INTO YOUR MIND...
HEY... DON'T!
NTANGIBLE FINGERS PROBE DEEP NTO THE THING'S MOST HIDDEN, PRIVATE THOUGHTS, SIFTING...
AND THOUGH FRANKLIN'S ACCELERATED PSYCHE DOES NOT POSSESS THE EMOTIONAL MATURITY TO COMPREHEND THE COMPLEXITY OF FEELING HE FINDS THERE...
...HIS CHILD'S INNOCENCE NONETHELESS HOLDS ENOUGH EXPERIENCE TO RECOGNIZE THERE IS FAR MORE TO THIS PROBLEM THAN MIGHT BE GUESSED...
INSTINCTIVELY, HE REACHES OUT FOR THE MIND MOST LIKE HIS OWN, AND REED RICHARDS FEELS A COLD DREAD CLOSE ABOUT HIS HEART AS THE TRUTH IS BROUGHT TERRIBLY HOME.
WHAT'S GOIN' ON?
I... UNDERSTAND. DO WHAT YOU MUST DO, FRANKLIN.
EED... WHAT'S APPENING...?!
SHIELD YOUR EYES, EVERYONE. FRANKLIN IS MANIFESTING HIS POWER AT MAXIMUM!
THE GLOW SPREADS FROM THE CHILD-MAN'S BEING, A SPIDERY, SILVER THING THAT GROWS IN SIZE AND INTENSITY WITH EVERY PULSE...

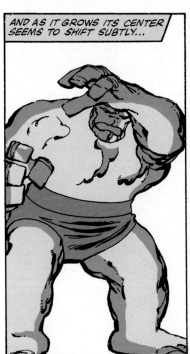

AND AS IT GROWS ITS CENTER SEEMS TO SHIFT SUBTLY...

UNTIL THE HEART OF THE SHIMMERING NIMBUS SWIRLS AROUND THE CONFUSED THING...

AND, AS THE LIGHT BECOMES ALMOST TOO INTENSE TO WATCH...

FROM DEEP WITHIN COMES A GRUMBLING, CRACKLING SOUND, LIKE ICE BREAKING BEFORE THE PROW OF A GREAT SHIP...

AND, WHEN THE LUMINESCENCE SUDDENLY WINKS OUT...

A STARTLED AND TRANSFORMED BEN GRIMM FACES HIS FRIENDS...

HOLY CATS! HE'S MADE ME ALL ROCKY AGAIN!

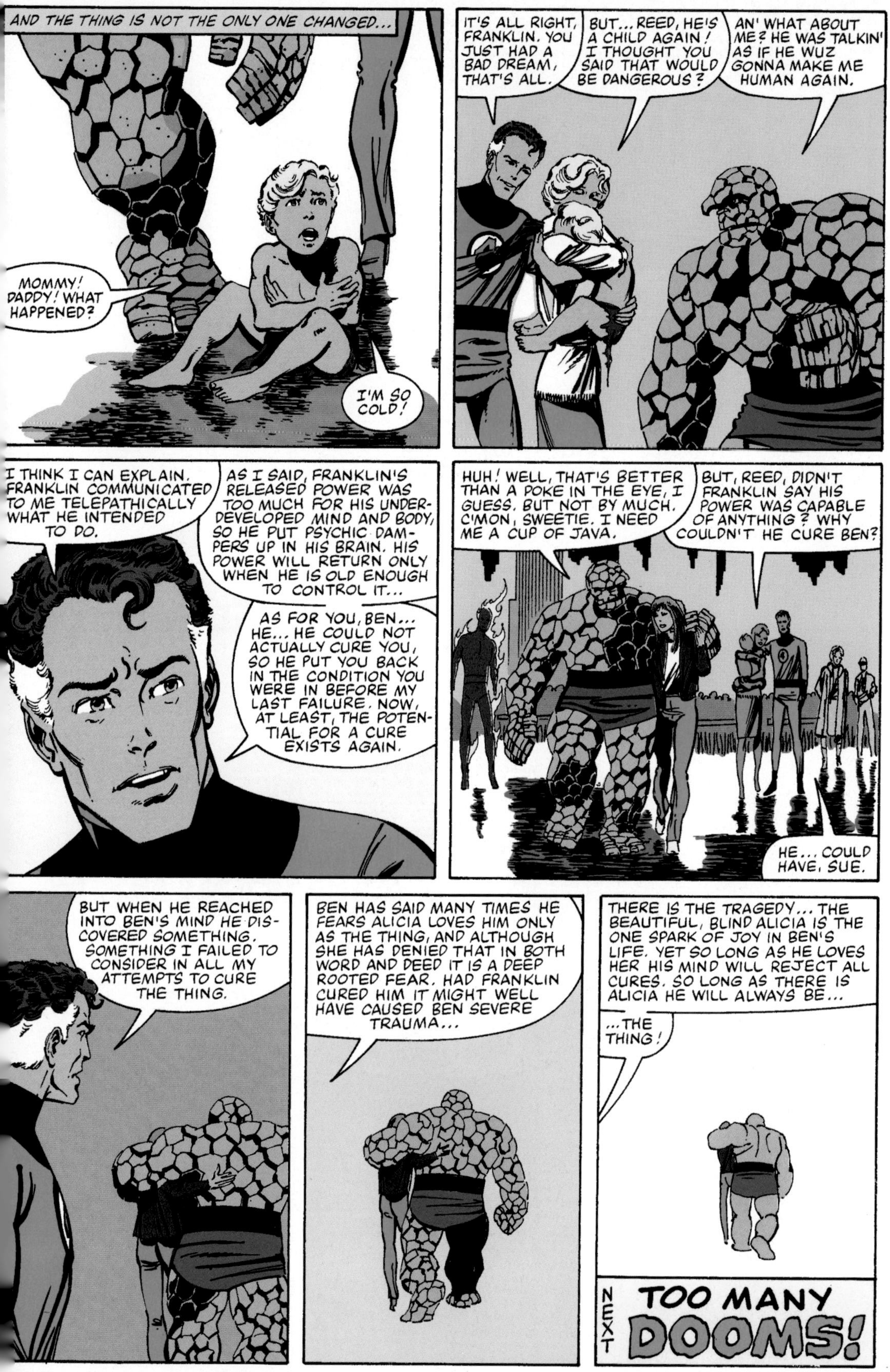
AND THE THING IS NOT THE ONLY ONE CHANGED...
MOMMY! DADDY! WHAT HAPPENED?
I'M SO COLD!
IT'S ALL RIGHT, FRANKLIN. YOU JUST HAD A BAD DREAM, THAT'S ALL.
BUT... REED, HE'S A CHILD AGAIN! I THOUGHT YOU SAID THAT WOULD BE DANGEROUS?
AN' WHAT ABOUT ME? HE WAS TALKIN' AS IF HE WUZ GONNA MAKE ME HUMAN AGAIN.
I THINK I CAN EXPLAIN. FRANKLIN COMMUNICATED TO ME TELEPATHICALLY WHAT HE INTENDED TO DO.
AS I SAID, FRANKLIN'S RELEASED POWER WAS TOO MUCH FOR HIS UNDER-DEVELOPED MIND AND BODY, SO HE PUT PSYCHIC DAMPERS UP IN HIS BRAIN. HIS POWER WILL RETURN ONLY WHEN HE IS OLD ENOUGH TO CONTROL IT...
AS FOR YOU, BEN... HE... HE COULD NOT ACTUALLY CURE YOU, SO HE PUT YOU BACK IN THE CONDITION YOU WERE IN BEFORE MY LAST FAILURE. NOW, AT LEAST, THE POTENTIAL FOR A CURE EXISTS AGAIN.
HUH! WELL, THAT'S BETTER THAN A POKE IN THE EYE, I GUESS. BUT NOT BY MUCH. C'MON, SWEETIE. I NEED ME A CUP OF JAVA.
BUT, REED, DIDN'T FRANKLIN SAY HIS POWER WAS CAPABLE OF ANYTHING? WHY COULDN'T HE CURE BEN?
HE... COULD HAVE, SUE.
BUT WHEN HE REACHED INTO BEN'S MIND HE DISCOVERED SOMETHING. SOMETHING I FAILED TO CONSIDER IN ALL MY ATTEMPTS TO CURE THE THING.
BEN HAS SAID MANY TIMES HE FEARS ALICIA LOVES HIM ONLY AS THE THING, AND ALTHOUGH SHE HAS DENIED THAT IN BOTH WORD AND DEED IT IS A DEEP ROOTED FEAR. HAD FRANKLIN CURED HIM IT MIGHT WELL HAVE CAUSED BEN SEVERE TRAUMA...
THERE IS THE TRAGEDY... THE BEAUTIFUL, BLIND ALICIA IS THE ONE SPARK OF JOY IN BEN'S LIFE. YET SO LONG AS HE LOVES HER HIS MIND WILL REJECT ALL CURES. SO LONG AS THERE IS ALICIA HE WILL ALWAYS BE...
...THE THING!
NEXT
TOO MANY DOOMS!

fantastic four # 246

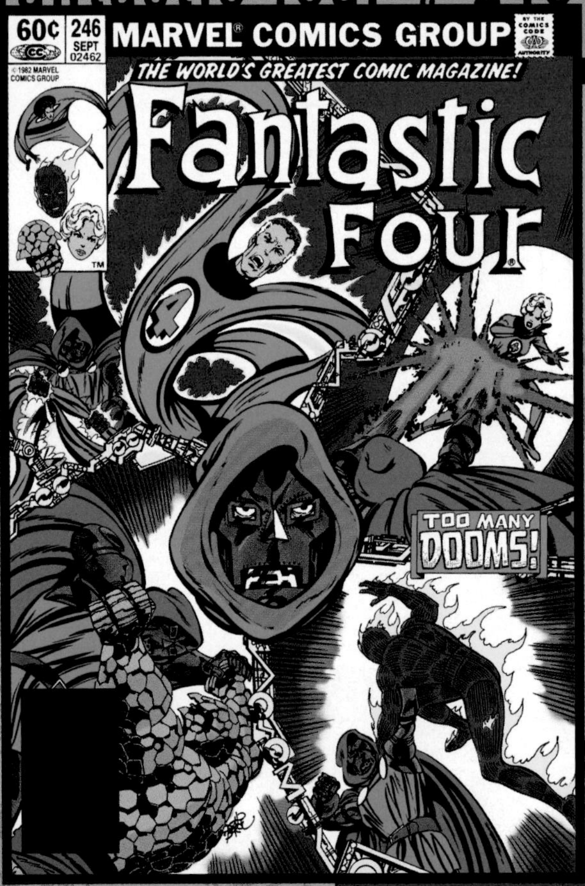
60¢
246
SEPT
02462
MARVEL COMICS GROUP
©1982 MARVEL COMICS GROUP
THE WORLD'S GREATEST COMIC MAGAZINE!
Fantastic Four
TOO MANY DOOMS!

SEPTEMBER
1982

fantastic four # 247

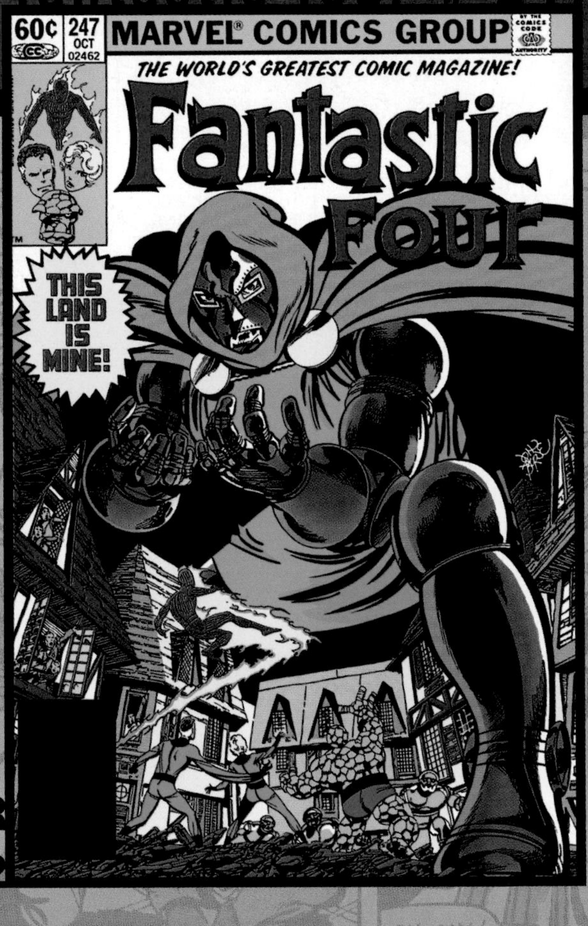
60¢
247
OCT
02462
MARVEL COMICS GROUP
THE WORLD'S GREATEST COMIC MAGAZINE!
Fantastic Four
THIS LAND IS MINE!

OCTOBER
1982

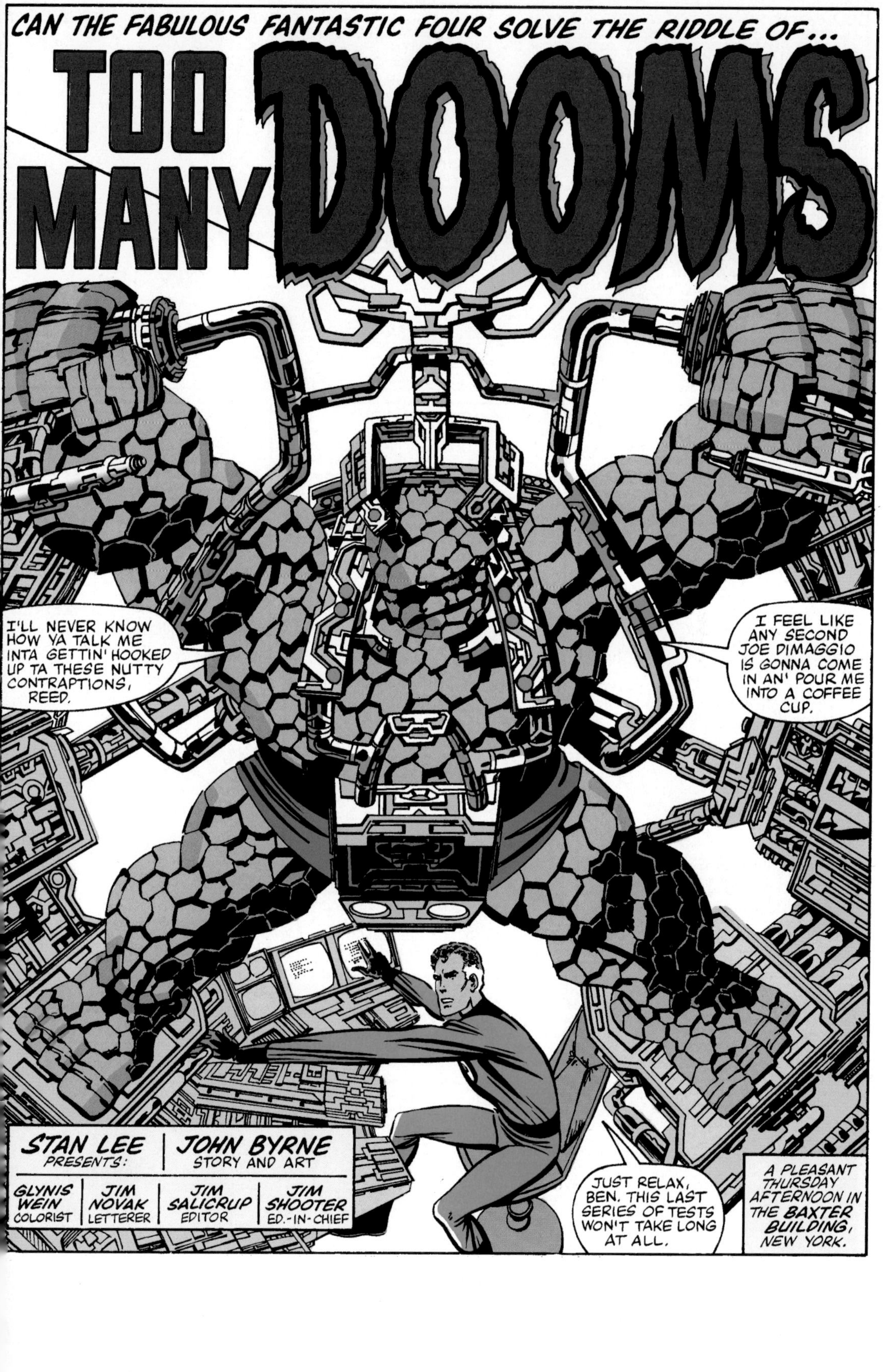
CAN THE FABULOUS FANTASTIC FOUR SOLVE THE RIDDLE OF...
TOO MANY DOOMS
I'LL NEVER KNOW HOW YA TALK ME INTA GETTIN' HOOKED UP TA THESE NUTTY CONTRAPTIONS, REED.
I FEEL LIKE ANY SECOND JOE DIMAGGIO IS GONNA COME IN AN' POUR ME INTO A COFFEE CUP.
STAN LEE PRESENTS: JOHN BYRNE STORY AND ART
GLYNIS WEIN COLORIST JIM NOVAK LETTERER JIM SALICRUP EDITOR JIM SHOOTER ED.-IN-CHIEF
JUST RELAX, BEN. THIS LAST SERIES OF TESTS WON'T TAKE LONG AT ALL.
A PLEASANT THURSDAY AFTERNOON IN THE BAXTER BUILDING, NEW YORK.

AS *REED RICHARDS'* FACILE FINGERS SKIM ACROSS THE CONTROL CONSOLES BEFORE HIM, COAXING EVER MORE COMPLEX DATA FROM THE MECHANISMS WHICH SCAN HIS LONG-TIME FRIEND AND PARTNER, HIS UNMATCHED INTELLECT TURNS ELSEWHERE...

HOW HOLLOW THIS ALL SEEMS. HOW MEANINGLESS TO CONTINUE WITH THESE TESTS OF BEN'S CONDITION.

YET, I MUST CONTINUE WITH THE CHARADE. I MUST AT LEAST *PRETEND* TO STILL SEEK A CURE.

"HOW MUCH SIMPLER IT WOULD HAVE BEEN HAD THE LAST DEVICE I CONSTRUCTED TO UNDO THE EFFECTS OF BEN'S BOMBARDMENT BY *COSMIC RAYS* HAD SUCCEEDED IN TRANSFORMING HIM.

"BUT I COULD NOT THEN KNOW THERE WERE FORCES OTHER THAN RADIATION AT WORK IN HIS BODY...

"FORCES WHICH CAUSED THE MACHINE TO EXPLODE, LEAVING HIM STILL TRAPPED IN THE GROTESQUE BODY OF THE *THING*.

"ALBEIT A VERSION OF HIMSELF CLOSER TO HIS ORIGINAL METAMORPHOSIS.

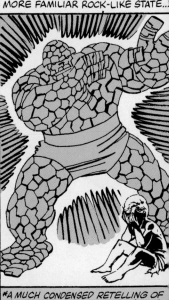

"AND SO HE REMAINED, UNTIL MY YOUNG SON *FRANKLIN'S* MUTANT POWER -- POWER NOW INOPERATIVE -- CHANGED BEN BACK TO HIS MORE FAMILIAR ROCK-LIKE STATE...*

*A MUCH CONDENSED RETELLING OF ISSUES #238 THROUGH 245. -- SALICRU

BEFORE LOSING HIS INCREDIBLE POWERS FRANKLIN LINKED MY MIND WITH BEN'S, ALLOWING ME TO LEARN WHY ALL MY ATTEMPTS TO RESTORE HIM TO HUMAN FORM HAVE MET WITH AT BEST LIMITED SUCCESS...

THE ONLY JOY IN BEN'S LIFE IS THE LOVE OF THE BEAUTIFUL, BLIND *ALICIA MASTERS.* YET BEN HAS SAID HE FEARS ALICIA LOVES ONLY THE THING, NOT *BEN GRIMM,* THE MAN.

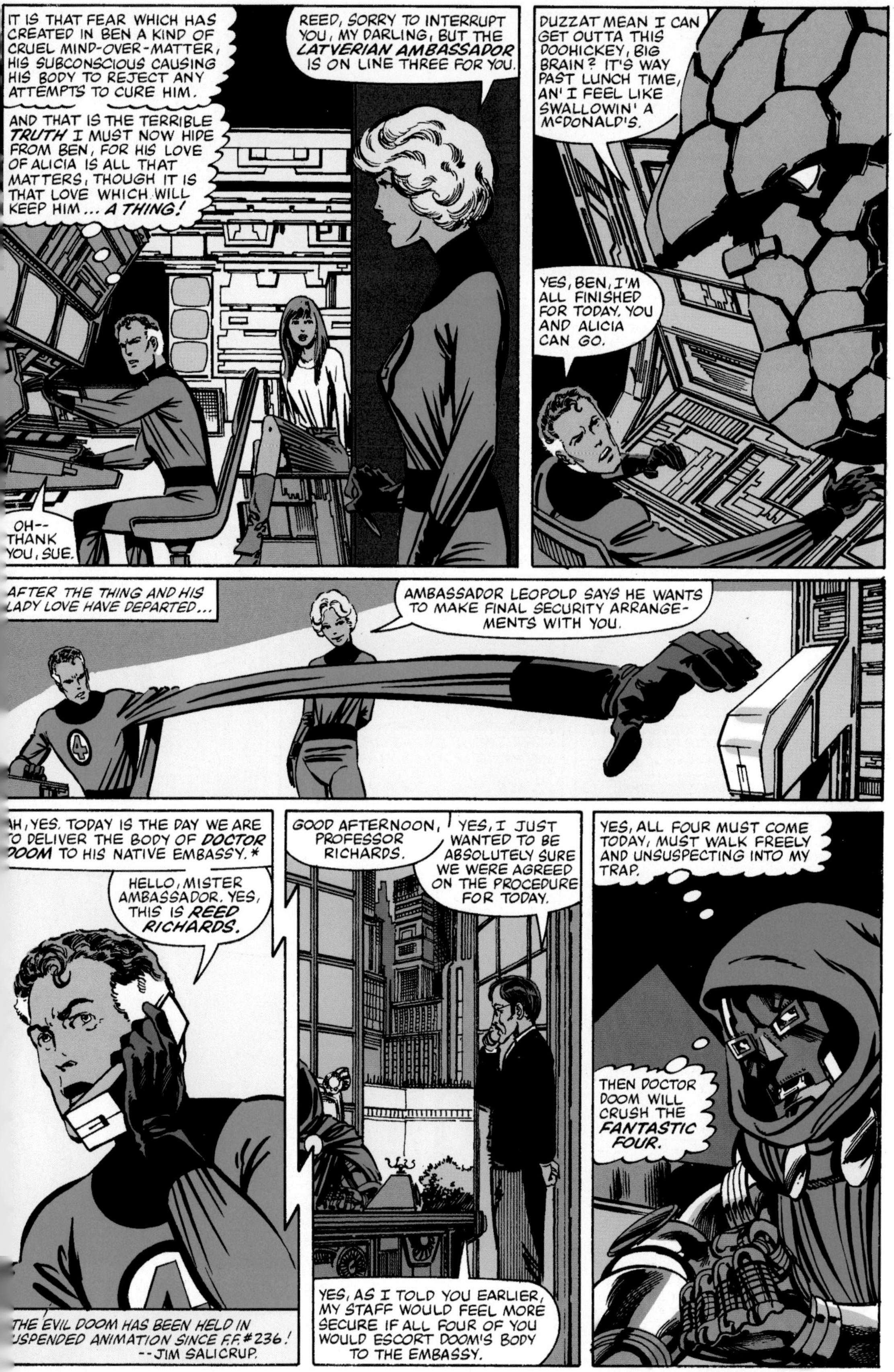
IT IS THAT FEAR WHICH HAS CREATED IN BEN A KIND OF CRUEL MIND-OVER-MATTER, HIS SUBCONSCIOUS CAUSING HIS BODY TO REJECT ANY ATTEMPTS TO CURE HIM.
AND THAT IS THE TERRIBLE TRUTH I MUST NOW HIDE FROM BEN, FOR HIS LOVE OF ALICIA IS ALL THAT MATTERS, THOUGH IT IS THAT LOVE WHICH WILL KEEP HIM... A THING!
REED, SORRY TO INTERRUPT YOU, MY DARLING, BUT THE LATVERIAN AMBASSADOR IS ON LINE THREE FOR YOU.
OH-- THANK YOU, SUE.
DUZZAT MEAN I CAN GET OUTTA THIS DOOHICKEY, BIG BRAIN? IT'S WAY PAST LUNCH TIME, AN' I FEEL LIKE SWALLOWIN' A McDONALD'S.
YES, BEN, I'M ALL FINISHED FOR TODAY. YOU AND ALICIA CAN GO.
AFTER THE THING AND HIS LADY LOVE HAVE DEPARTED...
AMBASSADOR LEOPOLD SAYS HE WANTS TO MAKE FINAL SECURITY ARRANGEMENTS WITH YOU.
AH, YES. TODAY IS THE DAY WE ARE TO DELIVER THE BODY OF DOCTOR DOOM TO HIS NATIVE EMBASSY.*
HELLO, MISTER AMBASSADOR. YES, THIS IS REED RICHARDS.
*THE EVIL DOOM HAS BEEN HELD IN SUSPENDED ANIMATION SINCE F.F. #236! --JIM SALICRUP.
GOOD AFTERNOON, PROFESSOR RICHARDS.
YES, I JUST WANTED TO BE ABSOLUTELY SURE WE WERE AGREED ON THE PROCEDURE FOR TODAY.
YES, AS I TOLD YOU EARLIER, MY STAFF WOULD FEEL MORE SECURE IF ALL FOUR OF YOU WOULD ESCORT DOOM'S BODY TO THE EMBASSY.
YES, ALL FOUR MUST COME TODAY, MUST WALK FREELY AND UNSUSPECTING INTO MY TRAP.
THEN DOCTOR DOOM WILL CRUSH THE FANTASTIC FOUR.

AND, AS A FIENDISH MASTER PLAN SWINGS INCH BY INCH TOWARDS DEVASTATING FRUITION...

TO THE NORTH AND WEST A CURIOUS ANACHRONISM RISES FROM THE PLEASANT ROLLING HILLS OF THE ADIRONDACS...

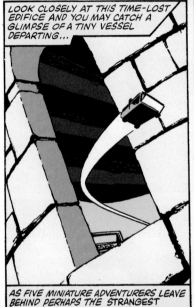

LOOK CLOSELY AT THIS TIME-LOST EDIFICE AND YOU MAY CATCH A GLIMPSE OF A TINY VESSEL DEPARTING...

AS FIVE MINIATURE ADVENTURERS LEAVE BEHIND PERHAPS THE STRANGEST EXPLOIT OF THEIR CAREERS:..*

*FOR FULL DETAILS SEE MICRONAUTS #41.--J.S.

FOR WITHIN THE CHAMBER LIES A STRANGELY CHILLING ARTIFACT...

SURROUNDED BY THE ARCANE MECHANISMS WHICH MAINTAIN IT, A TYPICAL MIDWESTERN TOWN STANDS ON A TABLETOP!

AND ON THE OUTSKIRTS OF THAT HAMLET, A SECOND CASTLE, MIRRORING THE LARGER STRUCTURE WITHIN WHICH IT STANDS, LOOMS OVER "LIDDLEVILLE,"

IN THE RUINED THRONE-ROOM THE AFTERMATH OF FURIOUS BATTLE BELIES THE PEACEFUL EXTERIOR, AS TWO FORMER PARTNERS FACE EACH OTHER AS BITTER ENEMIES.

PUPPET MASTER, I SWEAR TO YOU. BE IT A YEAR OR A LIFETIME, I WILL DESTROY YOU FOR THIS.

THE SMALLER MAN LAUGHS.

BOLD WORDS, VON DOOM, FROM ONE WHOSE MIND IS TRAPPED WITHIN A MELTING ROBOT BODY. YOUR TREACHERY HAS DESTROYED THE DREAMS OF HAPPINESS I BUILT HERE FOR MY STEP-DAUGHTER ALICIA, AND I AM TRAPPED IN THIS ROBOTIC VERSION OF MY TRUE SELF...

...BUT YOUR OWN MONSTROUS EGO WAS YOUR UNDOING.

YOU WERE NOT CONTENT TO SIMPLY RENDER THE *FANTASTIC FOUR* HELPLESS, THEIR IDENTITIES TRANSFERRED LIKE MINE INTO DUPLICATES OF THEMSELVES. YOU CHOSE TO USE MY LIDDLEVILLE TO TORMENT YOUR OLD NEMESIS, REED RICHARDS. SO YOU SOWED THE SEEDS OF YOUR OWN DEFEAT... *

*TOLD FULLY IN F.F. #236.-- SALICRUP.

AND YOU UNDERESTIMATED ME. YOU NEVER GUESSED I HAD SECRETED HERE A SMALL AMOUNT OF MY MIND-CONTROLLING *RADIOACTIVE CLAY.*

ENOUGH TO CREATE A STATUE OF YOU, AND THUS TO CONTROL YOU...

YOU ARE A FOOL, PHILIP MASTERS!

WHAT? THAT VOICE!

BUT IT CAN'T BE!

BUT IT IS, PUPPET MASTER! IT IS!

THIS IS IMPOSSIBLE! YOUR MIND IS TRAPPED IN THE IMMOBILIZED BODY!

YOU CANNOT BE FREE! YOU CANNOT DESTROY MY PLANS OF REVENGE!

YOUR PALTRY PLANS DO NOT INTEREST ME, PUPPET MASTER!

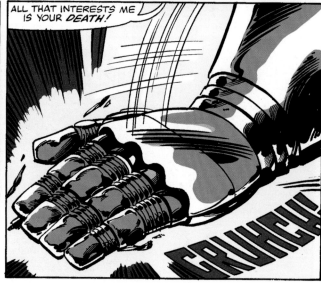

ALL THAT INTERESTS ME IS YOUR *DEATH!*

CRUNCH!

123

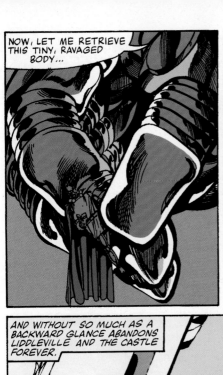

NOW, LET ME RETRIEVE THIS TINY, RAVAGED BODY...

FOR WITHOUT IT THE PLAN WOULD BE AN EMPTY GAME, WITHOUT ANY HOPE OF TRUE VICTORY FOR DOCTOR DOOM.

WITH SURPRISING TENDERNESS THE IRON-CLAD FIGURE TUCKS THE TINY ROBOT INTO A SPECIAL CASE PREPARED FOR JUST THAT PURPOSE...

AND WITHOUT SO MUCH AS A BACKWARD GLANCE ABANDONS LIDDLEVILLE AND THE CASTLE FOREVER.

PHASE ONE IS FINISHED. PHASE TWO MUST EVEN NOW BE DRAWING TO ITS FATEFUL CONCLUSION.

MEANWHILE, IN MANHATTAN...

IT WAS A GOOD IDEA TO USE THE NEW FANTASTICAR TO DELIVER DOOM'S BODY TO THE EMBASSY.

WE HAVEN'T HAD THE OPPORTUNITY TO GIVE HER A REAL SHAKE-DOWN SINCE TONY STARK DELIVERED HER!*

*STARK INTERNATIONAL IS REBUILDING THE EQUIPMENT DESTROYED BY TERRAX THE UNTAMED IN ISH #242!-- GUESS WHO

SKIMMING ALMOST SOUNDLESSLY OVER THE ROOFTOPS THE AMAZING MACHINE COMES QUICKLY TO THE GREEN ENCLOSURE BEHIND THE EMBASSY.

THERE'S THE SECURITY GUARD WAITING JUST WHERE LEOPOLD SAID-- BUT I DON'T SEE THE AMBASSADOR.

AND, ABOVE...

THEY HAVE ARRIVED, LEOPOLD. PHASE TWO IS NOW COMPLETE. PREPARE FOR PHASE THREE.

BUT, MASTER... TO BRING THEM INTO THE EMBASSY...

IF YOUR PLAN SHOULD FAIL...

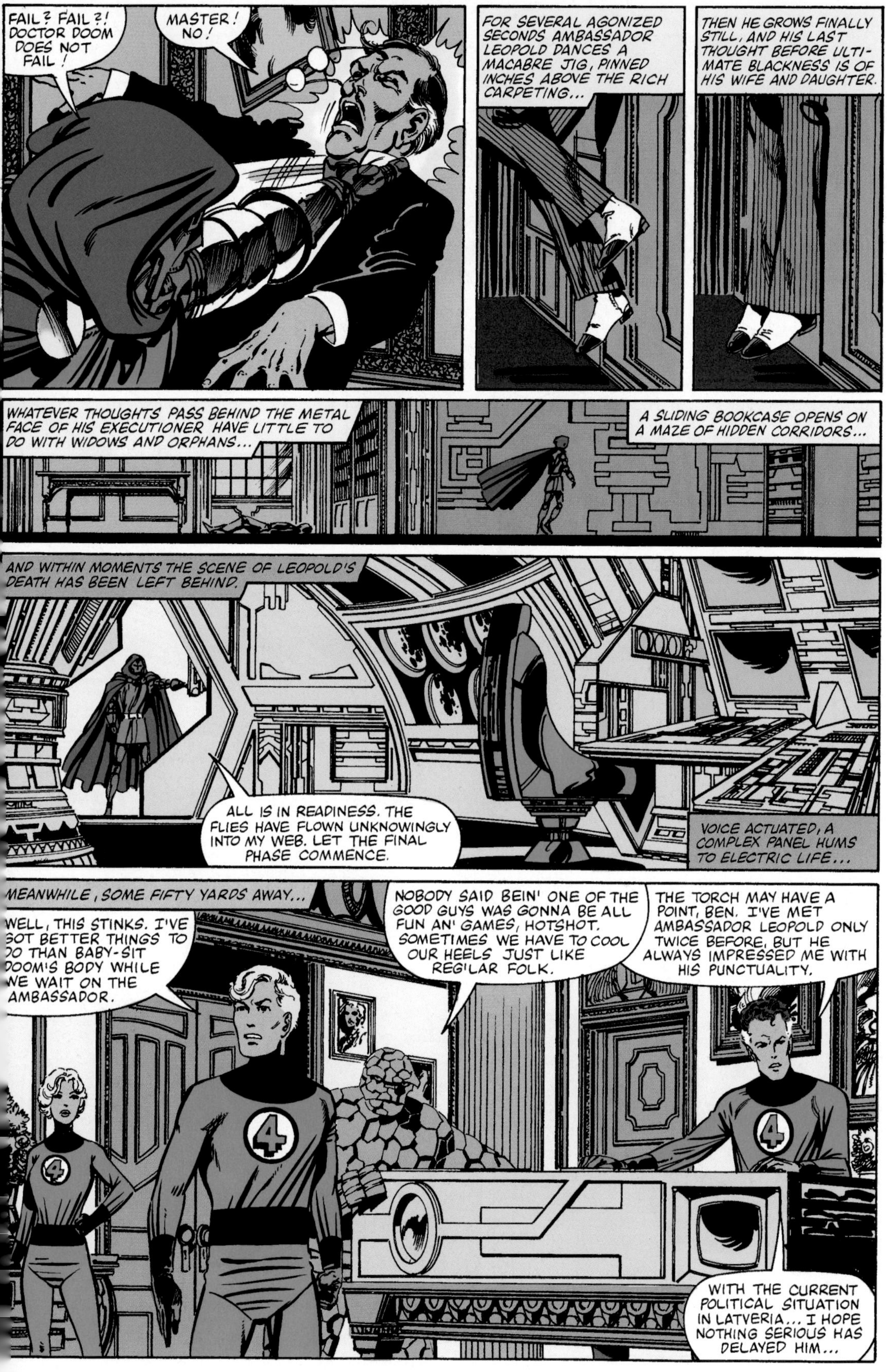
FAIL? FAIL?! DOCTOR DOOM DOES NOT FAIL!
MASTER! NO!
FOR SEVERAL AGONIZED SECONDS AMBASSADOR LEOPOLD DANCES A MACABRE JIG, PINNED INCHES ABOVE THE RICH CARPETING...
THEN HE GROWS FINALLY STILL, AND HIS LAST THOUGHT BEFORE ULTIMATE BLACKNESS IS OF HIS WIFE AND DAUGHTER.
WHATEVER THOUGHTS PASS BEHIND THE METAL FACE OF HIS EXECUTIONER HAVE LITTLE TO DO WITH WIDOWS AND ORPHANS...
A SLIDING BOOKCASE OPENS ON A MAZE OF HIDDEN CORRIDORS...
AND WITHIN MOMENTS THE SCENE OF LEOPOLD'S DEATH HAS BEEN LEFT BEHIND.
ALL IS IN READINESS. THE FLIES HAVE FLOWN UNKNOWINGLY INTO MY WEB. LET THE FINAL PHASE COMMENCE.
VOICE ACTUATED, A COMPLEX PANEL HUMS TO ELECTRIC LIFE...
MEANWHILE, SOME FIFTY YARDS AWAY...
WELL, THIS STINKS. I'VE GOT BETTER THINGS TO DO THAN BABY-SIT DOOM'S BODY WHILE WE WAIT ON THE AMBASSADOR.
NOBODY SAID BEIN' ONE OF THE GOOD GUYS WAS GONNA BE ALL FUN AN' GAMES, HOTSHOT. SOMETIMES WE HAVE TO COOL OUR HEELS JUST LIKE REG'LAR FOLK.
THE TORCH MAY HAVE A POINT, BEN. I'VE MET AMBASSADOR LEOPOLD ONLY TWICE BEFORE, BUT HE ALWAYS IMPRESSED ME WITH HIS PUNCTUALITY.
WITH THE CURRENT POLITICAL SITUATION IN LATVERIA... I HOPE NOTHING SERIOUS HAS DELAYED HIM...

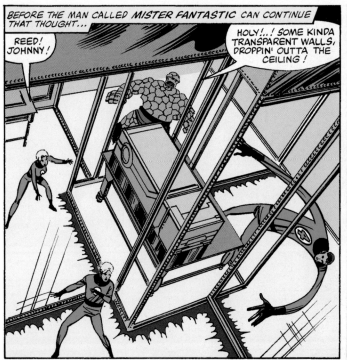

BEFORE THE MAN CALLED *MISTER FANTASTIC* CAN CONTINUE THAT THOUGHT...

REED! JOHNNY!

HOLY!..! SOME KINDA TRANSPARENT WALLS, DROPPIN' OUTTA THE CEILING!

AND, NO SOONER HAS THAT HAPPENED...

THE FLOOR'S OPENING! THERE'S A PIT BELOW!

WELL, WHOEVER DREAMED UP THIS LITTLE TRAP HAS SLIPPED A GROOVE IF HE THINKS IT'LL STOP THE *HUMAN TORCH!*

FLAME ON!

BUT, AS LIVING FLAME BLOSSOMS ABOUT *JOHNNY STORM...*

NO!

STREAMS OF FIRE-PROOF GLOP--CAN'T DODGE IN TIME...

HIS FLAME SUDDENLY DOUSED, THE YOUNGEST MEMBER OF THE FANTASTIC FOUR TUMBLES HEADLONG INTO DARKNESS...

WHAT THE HECK IS GOING ON? THE KING OF LATVERIA ISN'T OUR ENEMY, AND WITH DOOM SAFELY UNDER LOCK AND KEY...

WHO'S BEHIND THIS ATTACK?!

THE ANSWER FREEZES JOHNNY'S BLOOD IN HIS VEINS...

WELCOME, JOHNNY STORM, TO THE MOMENT OF YOUR ANNIHILATION!

DOOM!

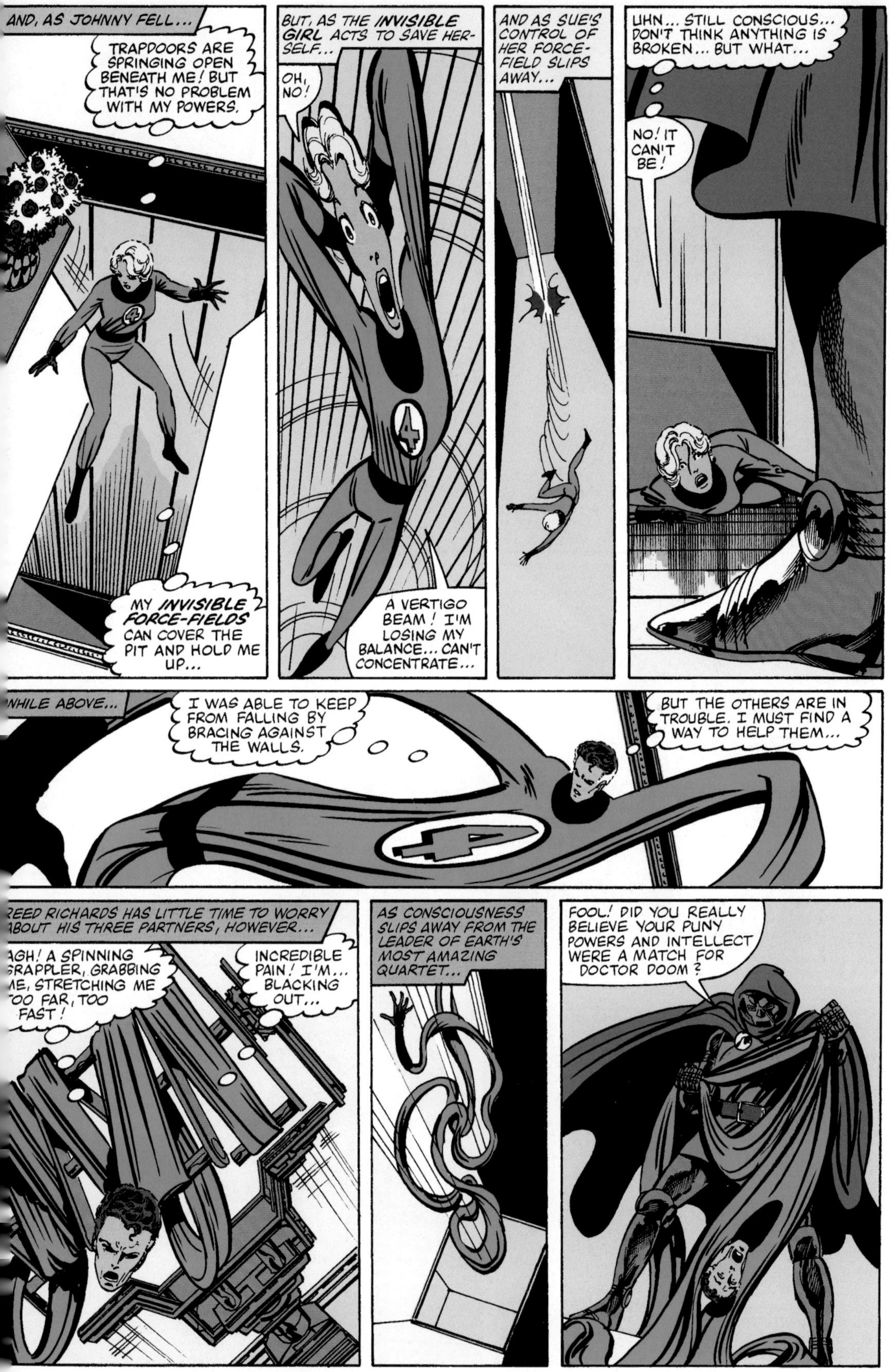

AND, AS JOHNNY FELL...
TRAPDOORS ARE SPRINGING OPEN BENEATH ME! BUT THAT'S NO PROBLEM WITH MY POWERS.
MY *INVISIBLE FORCE-FIELDS* CAN COVER THE PIT AND HOLD ME UP...
BUT, AS THE *INVISIBLE GIRL* ACTS TO SAVE HERSELF...
OH, NO!
A VERTIGO BEAM! I'M LOSING MY BALANCE... CAN'T CONCENTRATE...
AND AS SUE'S CONTROL OF HER FORCE-FIELD SLIPS AWAY...
UHN... STILL CONSCIOUS... DON'T THINK ANYTHING IS BROKEN... BUT WHAT...
NO! IT CAN'T BE!
WHILE ABOVE...
I WAS ABLE TO KEEP FROM FALLING BY BRACING AGAINST THE WALLS.
BUT THE OTHERS ARE IN TROUBLE. I MUST FIND A WAY TO HELP THEM...
REED RICHARDS HAS LITTLE TIME TO WORRY ABOUT HIS THREE PARTNERS, HOWEVER...
AGH! A SPINNING GRAPPLER, GRABBING ME, STRETCHING ME TOO FAR, TOO FAST!
INCREDIBLE PAIN! I'M... BLACKING OUT...
AS CONSCIOUSNESS SLIPS AWAY FROM THE LEADER OF EARTH'S MOST AMAZING QUARTET...
FOOL! DID YOU REALLY BELIEVE YOUR PUNY POWERS AND INTELLECT WERE A MATCH FOR DOCTOR DOOM?

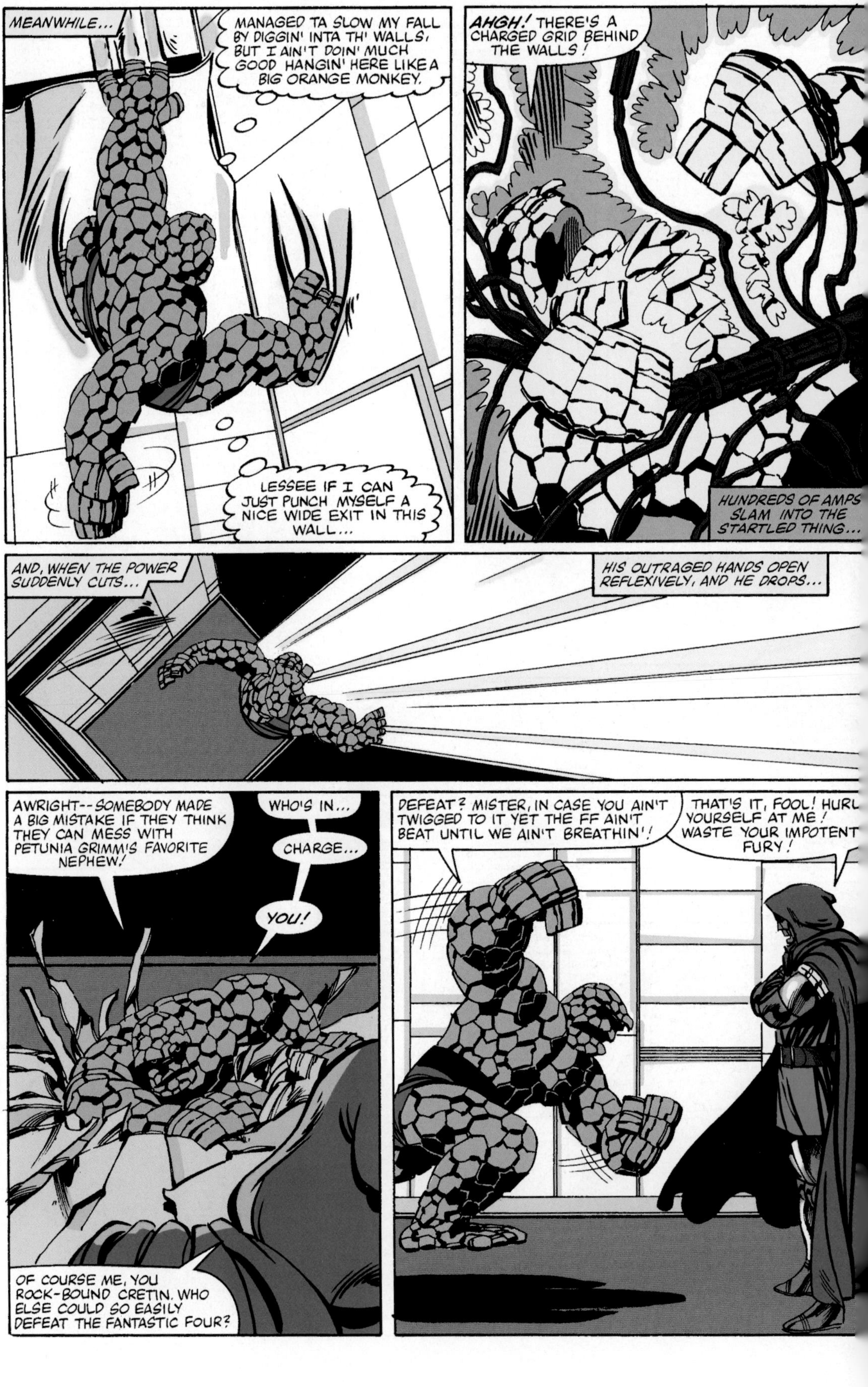
MEANWHILE...
MANAGED TA SLOW MY FALL BY DIGGIN' INTA TH' WALLS, BUT I AIN'T DOIN' MUCH GOOD HANGIN' HERE LIKE A BIG ORANGE MONKEY.
LESSEE IF I CAN JUST PUNCH MYSELF A NICE WIDE EXIT IN THIS WALL...
AHGH! THERE'S A CHARGED GRID BEHIND THE WALLS!
HUNDREDS OF AMPS SLAM INTO THE STARTLED THING...
AND, WHEN THE POWER SUDDENLY CUTS...
HIS OUTRAGED HANDS OPEN REFLEXIVELY, AND HE DROPS...
AWRIGHT--SOMEBODY MADE A BIG MISTAKE IF THEY THINK THEY CAN MESS WITH PETUNIA GRIMM'S FAVORITE NEPHEW!
WHO'S IN...
CHARGE...
YOU!
OF COURSE ME, YOU ROCK-BOUND CRETIN. WHO ELSE COULD SO EASILY DEFEAT THE FANTASTIC FOUR?
DEFEAT? MISTER, IN CASE YOU AIN'T TWIGGED TO IT YET THE FF AIN'T BEAT UNTIL WE AIN'T BREATHIN'!
THAT'S IT, FOOL! HURL YOURSELF AT ME! WASTE YOUR IMPOTENT FURY!

WAM

EXCELLENT, THING, AS EVER YOUR BRUTISH REACTIONS ARE AS PREDICTABLE AS THEY ARE STUPID.

ANOTHER DOOM...IS THIS THE REAL ONE, OR ANOTHER ILLUSION?

OKAY, DOOM, I DON'T KNOW HOW HOW YA GOT OUTTA SUSPENDED ANIMATION AND INTO ACTION SO FAST, BUT IF YOU THINK I'M GONNA FALL FER TH' SAME GAG TWICE...

THEN YOU AIN'T EXACTLY OVER-BOOKED IN THE SMARTS DEPARTMENT EITHER...

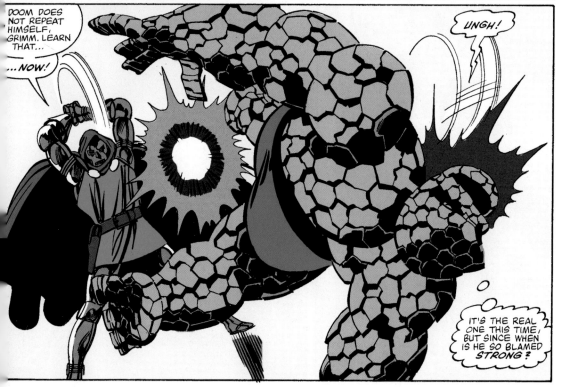

DOOM DOES NOT REPEAT HIMSELF, GRIMM. LEARN THAT...

...NOW!

UNGH!

IT'S THE REAL ONE THIS TIME, BUT SINCE WHEN IS HE SO BLAMED STRONG?

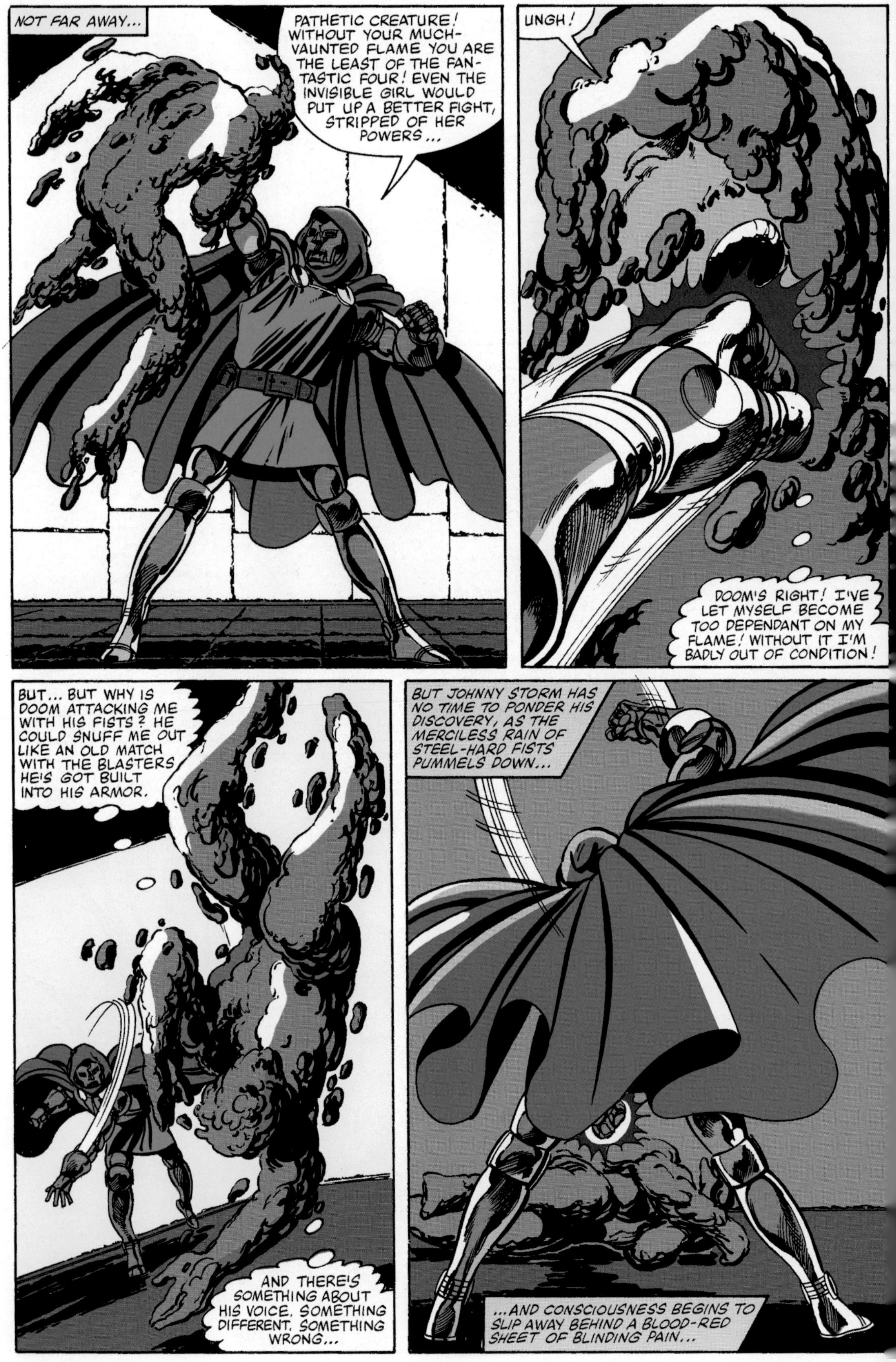
NOT FAR AWAY...
PATHETIC CREATURE! WITHOUT YOUR MUCH-VAUNTED FLAME YOU ARE THE LEAST OF THE FANTASTIC FOUR! EVEN THE INVISIBLE GIRL WOULD PUT UP A BETTER FIGHT, STRIPPED OF HER POWERS...
UNGH!
DOOM'S RIGHT! I'VE LET MYSELF BECOME TOO DEPENDANT ON MY FLAME! WITHOUT IT I'M BADLY OUT OF CONDITION!
BUT... BUT WHY IS DOOM ATTACKING ME WITH HIS FISTS? HE COULD SNUFF ME OUT LIKE AN OLD MATCH WITH THE BLASTERS HE'S GOT BUILT INTO HIS ARMOR.
AND THERE'S SOMETHING ABOUT HIS VOICE, SOMETHING DIFFERENT, SOMETHING WRONG...
BUT JOHNNY STORM HAS NO TIME TO PONDER HIS DISCOVERY, AS THE MERCILESS RAIN OF STEEL-HARD FISTS PUMMELS DOWN...
...AND CONSCIOUSNESS BEGINS TO SLIP AWAY BEHIND A BLOOD-RED SHEET OF BLINDING PAIN...

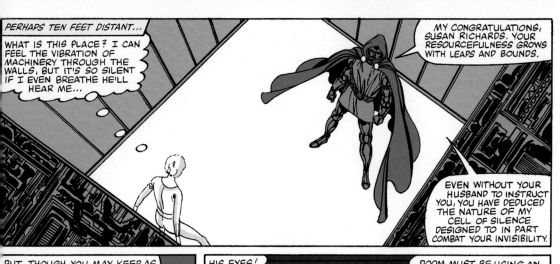

PERHAPS TEN FEET DISTANT...

WHAT IS THIS PLACE? I CAN FEEL THE VIBRATION OF MACHINERY THROUGH THE WALLS, BUT IT'S SO SILENT IF I EVEN BREATHE HE'LL HEAR ME...

MY CONGRATULATIONS, SUSAN RICHARDS. YOUR RESOURCEFULNESS GROWS WITH LEAPS AND BOUNDS.

EVEN WITHOUT YOUR HUSBAND TO INSTRUCT YOU, YOU HAVE DEDUCED THE NATURE OF MY CELL OF SILENCE DESIGNED TO IN PART COMBAT YOUR INVISIBILITY.

BUT, THOUGH YOU MAY KEEP AS QUIET AND MOTIONLESS AS HUMANLY POSSIBLE, DOCTOR DOOM HAS OTHER WAYS TO FIND YOU...

HIS EYES!

DOOM MUST BE USING AN INFRA-RED SCANNER. NOW I UNDERSTAND WHY THIS ROOM IS SO SMALL.

IT CUTS MY MANEUVERING SPACE ALMOST TO NOTHING, AND HE ONLY HAS TO STAY CLOSE TO A COR-NER TO KEEP ME ALWAYS IN THE LINE OF...

..FIRE!

SURRENDER! YIELD TO DOCTOR DOOM AND I PROMISE YOU A SWIFT, PAINLESS DEATH!

I KNOW YOU'RE A MAN OF YOUR WORD, ON DOOM...

BUT SOMEHOW THAT OFFER IS LESS THAN APPEALING...

I WISH I FELT AS CONFIDENT AS I SOUND. THE WAY HE'S HAMMER-ING AT MY FORCE-FIELD...

IT WON'T LAST MORE THAN A FEW MINUTES...

MEANWHILE, ALMOST CLOSE ENOUGH TO TOUCH...

YOU'LL HAVE TO DO BETTER THAN THAT, DOOM. YOU'LL FIND MISTER FANTASTIC MORE THAN A MATCH FOR YOU EVERY TIME!

INCREDIBLE! I MISCALCULATED THE TIME IT WOULD TAKE YOU TO RECOVER FROM THE GRAPPLER.

NO MATTER. DOOM IS READY FOR EVERY CONTINGENCY.

I AM STILL IN CONTACT WITH YOUR PLIABLE FORM, AND SO LONG AS I AM, I CAN DO...

...THIS!

INCREDIBLE FORCE RIPS THROUGH REED RICHARDS' RADIATION ALTERED CELLS...

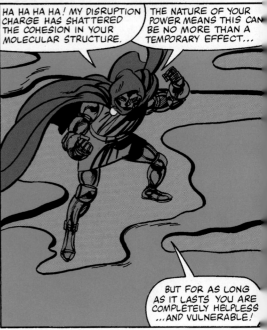

HA HA HA HA! MY DISRUPTION CHARGE HAS SHATTERED THE COHESION IN YOUR MOLECULAR STRUCTURE.

THE NATURE OF YOUR POWER MEANS THIS CAN BE NO MORE THAN A TEMPORARY EFFECT...

BUT FOR AS LONG AS IT LASTS YOU ARE COMPLETELY HELPLESS ...AND VULNERABLE!

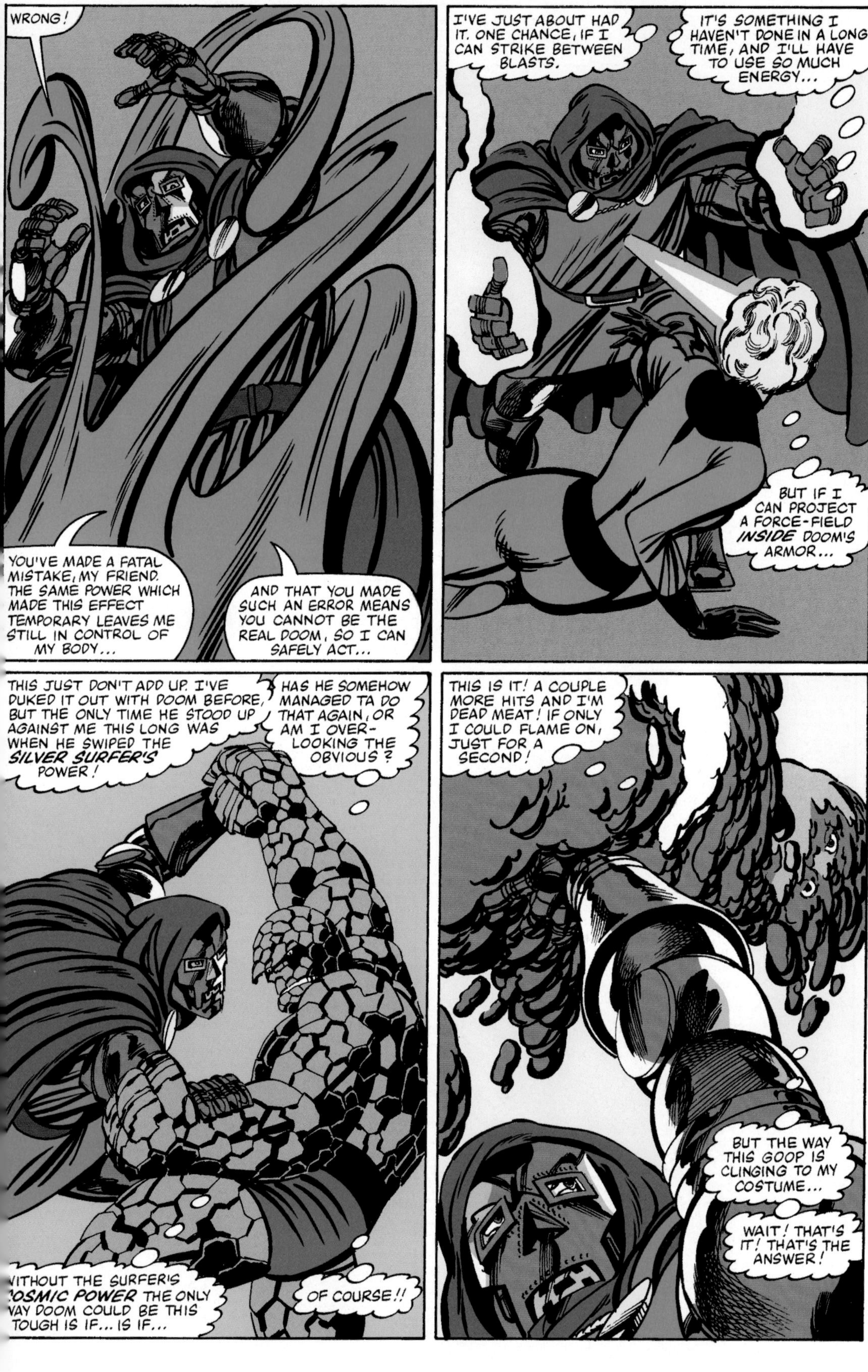
WRONG!
YOU'VE MADE A FATAL MISTAKE, MY FRIEND. THE SAME POWER WHICH MADE THIS EFFECT TEMPORARY LEAVES ME STILL IN CONTROL OF MY BODY...
AND THAT YOU MADE SUCH AN ERROR MEANS YOU CANNOT BE THE REAL DOOM, SO I CAN SAFELY ACT...
I'VE JUST ABOUT HAD IT. ONE CHANCE, IF I CAN STRIKE BETWEEN BLASTS.
IT'S SOMETHING I HAVEN'T DONE IN A LONG TIME, AND I'LL HAVE TO USE SO MUCH ENERGY...
BUT IF I CAN PROJECT A FORCE-FIELD INSIDE DOOM'S ARMOR...
THIS JUST DON'T ADD UP. I'VE DUKED IT OUT WITH DOOM BEFORE, BUT THE ONLY TIME HE STOOD UP AGAINST ME THIS LONG WAS WHEN HE SWIPED THE SILVER SURFER'S POWER!
HAS HE SOMEHOW MANAGED TA DO THAT AGAIN, OR AM I OVER-LOOKING THE OBVIOUS?
WITHOUT THE SURFER'S COSMIC POWER THE ONLY WAY DOOM COULD BE THIS TOUGH IS IF... IS IF...
OF COURSE!!
THIS IS IT! A COUPLE MORE HITS AND I'M DEAD MEAT! IF ONLY I COULD FLAME ON, JUST FOR A SECOND!
BUT THE WAY THIS GOOP IS CLINGING TO MY COSTUME...
WAIT! THAT'S IT! THAT'S THE ANSWER!

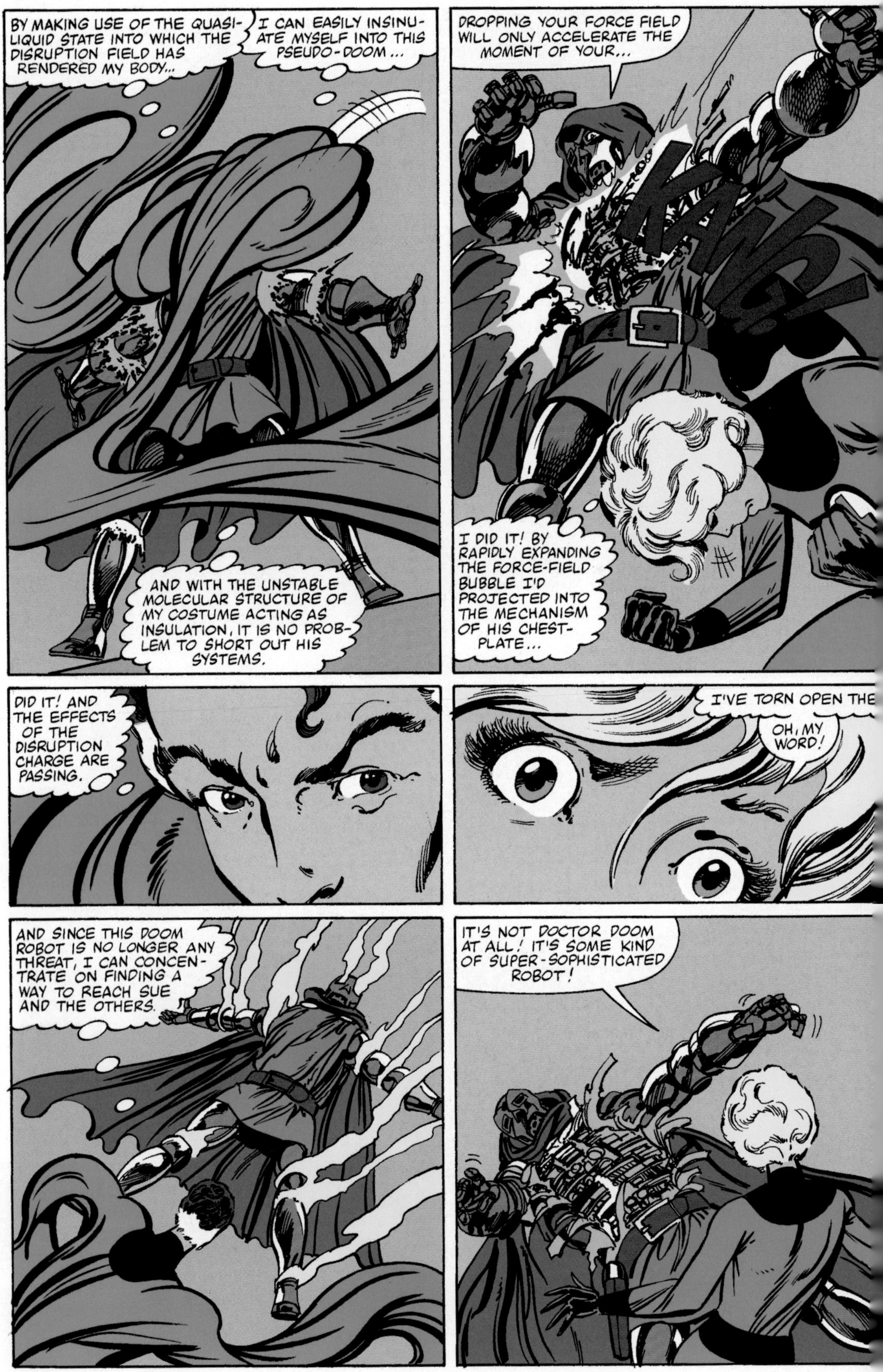
BY MAKING USE OF THE QUASI-LIQUID STATE INTO WHICH THE DISRUPTION FIELD HAS RENDERED MY BODY...
I CAN EASILY INSINUATE MYSELF INTO THIS PSEUDO-DOOM...
AND WITH THE UNSTABLE MOLECULAR STRUCTURE OF MY COSTUME ACTING AS INSULATION, IT IS NO PROBLEM TO SHORT OUT HIS SYSTEMS.
DROPPING YOUR FORCE FIELD WILL ONLY ACCELERATE THE MOMENT OF YOUR...
KANG!
I DID IT! BY RAPIDLY EXPANDING THE FORCE-FIELD BUBBLE I'D PROJECTED INTO THE MECHANISM OF HIS CHEST-PLATE...
DID IT! AND THE EFFECTS OF THE DISRUPTION CHARGE ARE PASSING.
I'VE TORN OPEN THE
OH, MY WORD!
AND SINCE THIS DOOM ROBOT IS NO LONGER ANY THREAT, I CAN CONCENTRATE ON FINDING A WAY TO REACH SUE AND THE OTHERS.
IT'S NOT DOCTOR DOOM AT ALL! IT'S SOME KIND OF SUPER-SOPHISTICATED ROBOT!

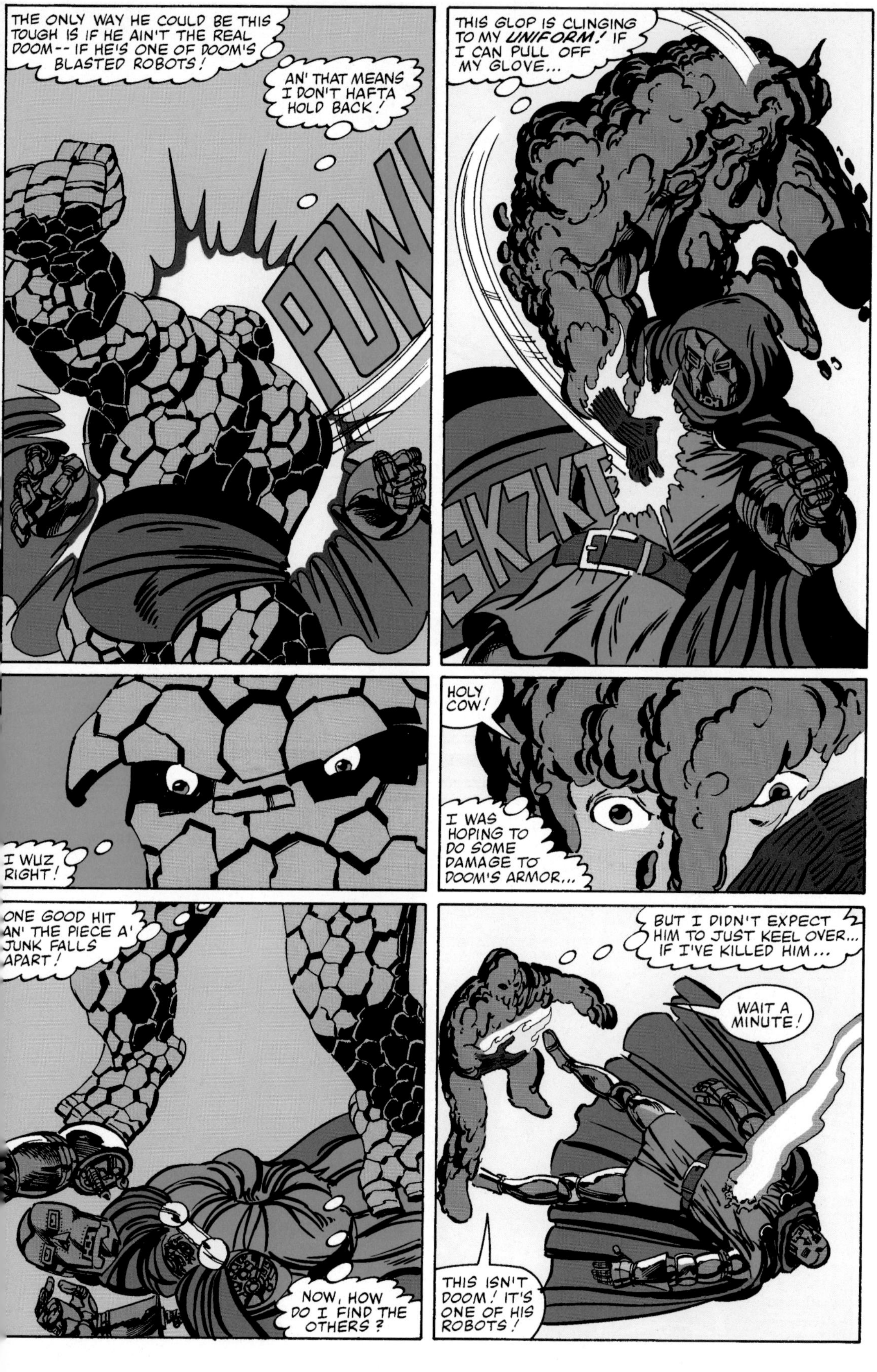
THE ONLY WAY HE COULD BE THIS TOUGH IS IF HE AIN'T THE REAL DOOM-- IF HE'S ONE OF DOOM'S BLASTED ROBOTS!
AN' THAT MEANS I DON'T HAFTA HOLD BACK!
POW
THIS GLOP IS CLINGING TO MY UNIFORM! IF I CAN PULL OFF MY GLOVE...
SKZKT
I WUZ RIGHT!
HOLY COW!
I WAS HOPING TO DO SOME DAMAGE TO DOOM'S ARMOR...
ONE GOOD HIT AN' THE PIECE A' JUNK FALLS APART!
NOW, HOW DO I FIND THE OTHERS?
BUT I DIDN'T EXPECT HIM TO JUST KEEL OVER... IF I'VE KILLED HIM...
WAIT A MINUTE!
THIS ISN'T DOOM! IT'S ONE OF HIS ROBOTS!

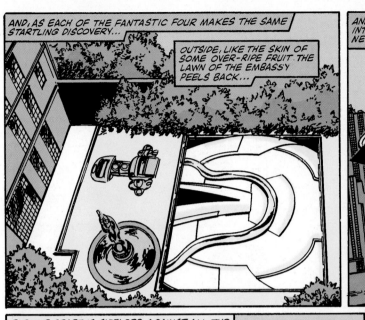

AND, AS EACH OF THE FANTASTIC FOUR MAKES THE SAME STARTLING DISCOVERY...

OUTSIDE, LIKE THE SKIN OF SOME OVER-RIPE FRUIT, THE LAWN OF THE EMBASSY PEELS BACK...

AND A STRANGE, GLEAMING SHIP RISES INTO THE LATE AFTERNOON SKIES ABOVE NEW YORK.

YET, NOT A HEAD TURNS TO MARK ITS PASSAGE.

FOR THE CRAFT IS SHIELDED AGAINST ALL THE EYES OF MAN--BOTH REAL AND MECHANICAL...

SAVE FOR ONE PAIR OF UNHUMAN EYES WHICH DIRECT THEIR OWNER TO AN INTERCEPT COURSE...

A HATCH HUMS OPEN...

AND WITHIN MOMENTS THE FLYING FIGURE ENTERS THE MASTER CONTROL ROOM.

REPORT!

ALL GOES AS PLANNED, BROTHER. AS ANTICIPATED, OUR BROTHERS HAVE FAILED TO DESTROY THE FANTASTIC FOUR, BUT THEY CREATED SUFFICIENT DISTRACTION...

THE CONTINGENCY PLAN WAS ENACTED FLAWLESSLY. NOW THE TRUE BODY OF OUR MASTER REQUIRES ONLY THE RESTORATION OF HIS MIND.

AS GOOD AS DONE. I RETRIEVED WITH NO DIFFICULTY THE BODY INTO WHICH IT HAD BEEN TRANSFERRED.

THEN PLACE IT WITHIN THE PREPARED MECHANISM, AND LET US PROCEED.

ROBOTIC HANDS MOVE WITH SWIFT PRECISION...

IF THEIR COMPUTER BRAINS HAVE ANY CONCEPT OF A SUPREME DEITY, PERHAPS A BRIEF PRAYER IS OFFERED UP...

BEFORE AN IRON-GAUNTLETED FIST CLOSES ABOUT A SWITCH...

AND THE AWESOME ENERGIES OF AN UNLEASHED HUMAN MIND LEAP ACROSS THE GULF BETWEEN THE TINY REPLICA...

...AND THE TRUE BODY OF THE ERSTWHILE MONARCH OF LATVERIA.

DOOM'S BODY CONVULSES AS IF A BILLION AMPS WERE SHATTERING HIS NERVOUS SYSTEM.

BEHIND THE MASK HIS MOUTH STRETCHES IN A SOUNDLESS SCREAM.

AND IT IS DONE!

WITH THE SUDDENNESS OF A SUMMER STORM THE PROCESS IS ENDED...

...AND IT IS THE TRUE VICTOR VON DOOM WHO RISES TO SURVEY HIS SURROUNDINGS...

ALL HAIL DOOM, TRUE LORD OF LATVERIA! MASTER OF THE WORLD!

SILENCE! DOOM HAS NO NEED OF SUCH PETTY MOUTHINGS!

REPORT TO ME WHAT IS HAPPENING. WHICH PLAN HAS RETURNED ME TO MY TRUE FORM?

PLAN EPSILON, MY LIEGE. EVEN NOW THE FANTASTIC FOUR ARE PRISONERS IN THE HOLDING SPACE BELOW US, AS OUR CRAFT MAKES ITS COURSE FOR THE LATVERIAN CAPITOL.

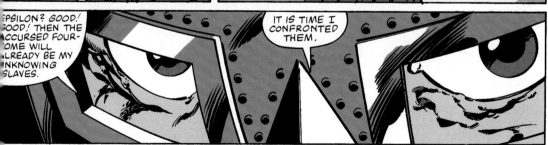

EPSILON? GOOD! GOOD! THEN THE ACCURSED FOURSOME WILL ALREADY BE MY UNKNOWING SLAVES.

IT IS TIME I CONFRONTED THEM.

MOMENTS LATER, POWERFUL MOTORS GRUMBLE TO LIFE DEEP WITHIN THE SAUCER-SHIP.

REED!

SUE! JOHNNY! BEN! YOU'VE ALL DEFEATED YOUR ROBOTIC OPPONENTS!

MAYBE. YOU SURE LOOK AN' SOUND LIKE REED RICHARDS, BUT IF DOOM COULD BUILD ROBOTS OF HIMSELF... HOW DO I KNOW YOU'RE ALL TH' REAL McCOYS?

OH, BEN, DON'T EVEN THINK SUCH A THING! THIS IS THE REAL REED!

IT HAS TO BE!

EASY, HONEY. IT'S ME ALL RIGHT. BUT WE'RE NOT OUT OF THIS YET...

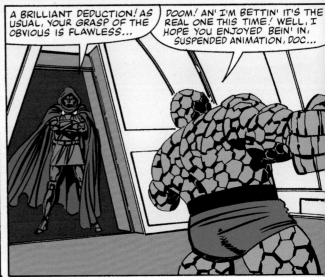

A BRILLIANT DEDUCTION! AS USUAL, YOUR GRASP OF THE OBVIOUS IS FLAWLESS...

DOOM! AN' I'M BETTIN' IT'S THE REAL ONE THIS TIME! WELL, I HOPE YOU ENJOYED BEIN' IN' SUSPENDED ANIMATION, DOC...

'CAUSE I'M GONNA PUT YA RIGHT BACK TO SLEEPY-BYES BEFORE... BEFORE...

HEY... WHAT GIVES? I CAN'T HIT THE CREEP?

OF COURSE NOT, YOU DOLT.

WHILE YOU BATTLED MY ROBOT DUPLICATES YOU WERE BEING SUBTLY AFFECTED.

THE POWER OF MY INHIBITOR RAY HAS MADE IT IMPOSSIBLE FO YOU TO DIRECT ANY ATTA AGAINST MY PERSO

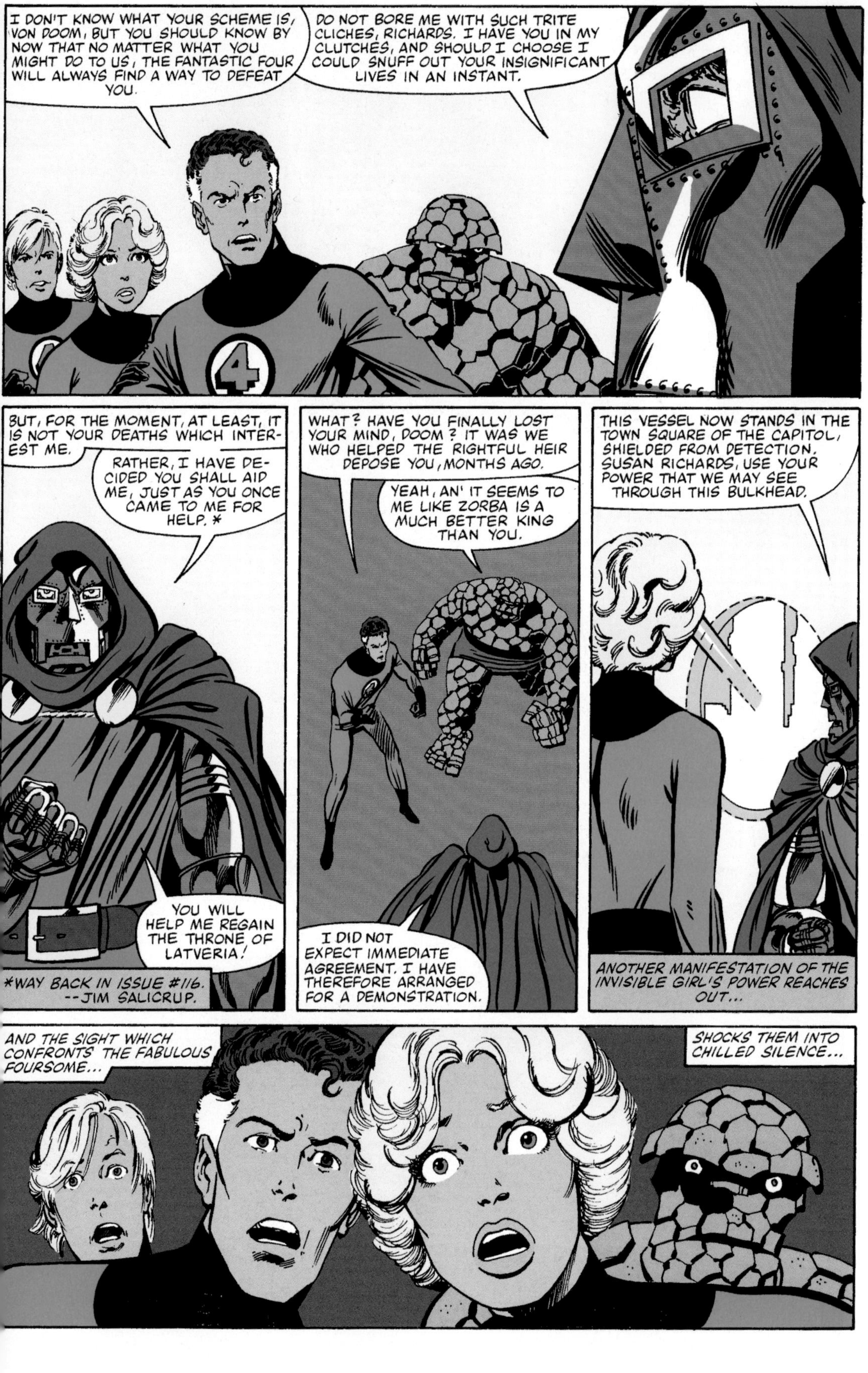

I DON'T KNOW WHAT YOUR SCHEME IS, VON DOOM, BUT YOU SHOULD KNOW BY NOW THAT NO MATTER WHAT YOU MIGHT DO TO US, THE FANTASTIC FOUR WILL ALWAYS FIND A WAY TO DEFEAT YOU.
DO NOT BORE ME WITH SUCH TRITE CLICHES, RICHARDS. I HAVE YOU IN MY CLUTCHES, AND SHOULD I CHOOSE I COULD SNUFF OUT YOUR INSIGNIFICANT LIVES IN AN INSTANT.
BUT, FOR THE MOMENT, AT LEAST, IT IS NOT YOUR DEATHS WHICH INTEREST ME.
RATHER, I HAVE DECIDED YOU SHALL AID ME, JUST AS YOU ONCE CAME TO ME FOR HELP. *
YOU WILL HELP ME REGAIN THE THRONE OF LATVERIA!
*WAY BACK IN ISSUE #116. --JIM SALICRUP.
WHAT? HAVE YOU FINALLY LOST YOUR MIND, DOOM? IT WAS WE WHO HELPED THE RIGHTFUL HEIR DEPOSE YOU, MONTHS AGO.
YEAH, AN' IT SEEMS TO ME LIKE ZORBA IS A MUCH BETTER KING THAN YOU.
I DID NOT EXPECT IMMEDIATE AGREEMENT. I HAVE THEREFORE ARRANGED FOR A DEMONSTRATION.
THIS VESSEL NOW STANDS IN THE TOWN SQUARE OF THE CAPITOL, SHIELDED FROM DETECTION. SUSAN RICHARDS, USE YOUR POWER THAT WE MAY SEE THROUGH THIS BULKHEAD.
ANOTHER MANIFESTATION OF THE INVISIBLE GIRL'S POWER REACHES OUT...
AND THE SIGHT WHICH CONFRONTS THE FABULOUS FOURSOME...
SHOCKS THEM INTO CHILLED SILENCE...

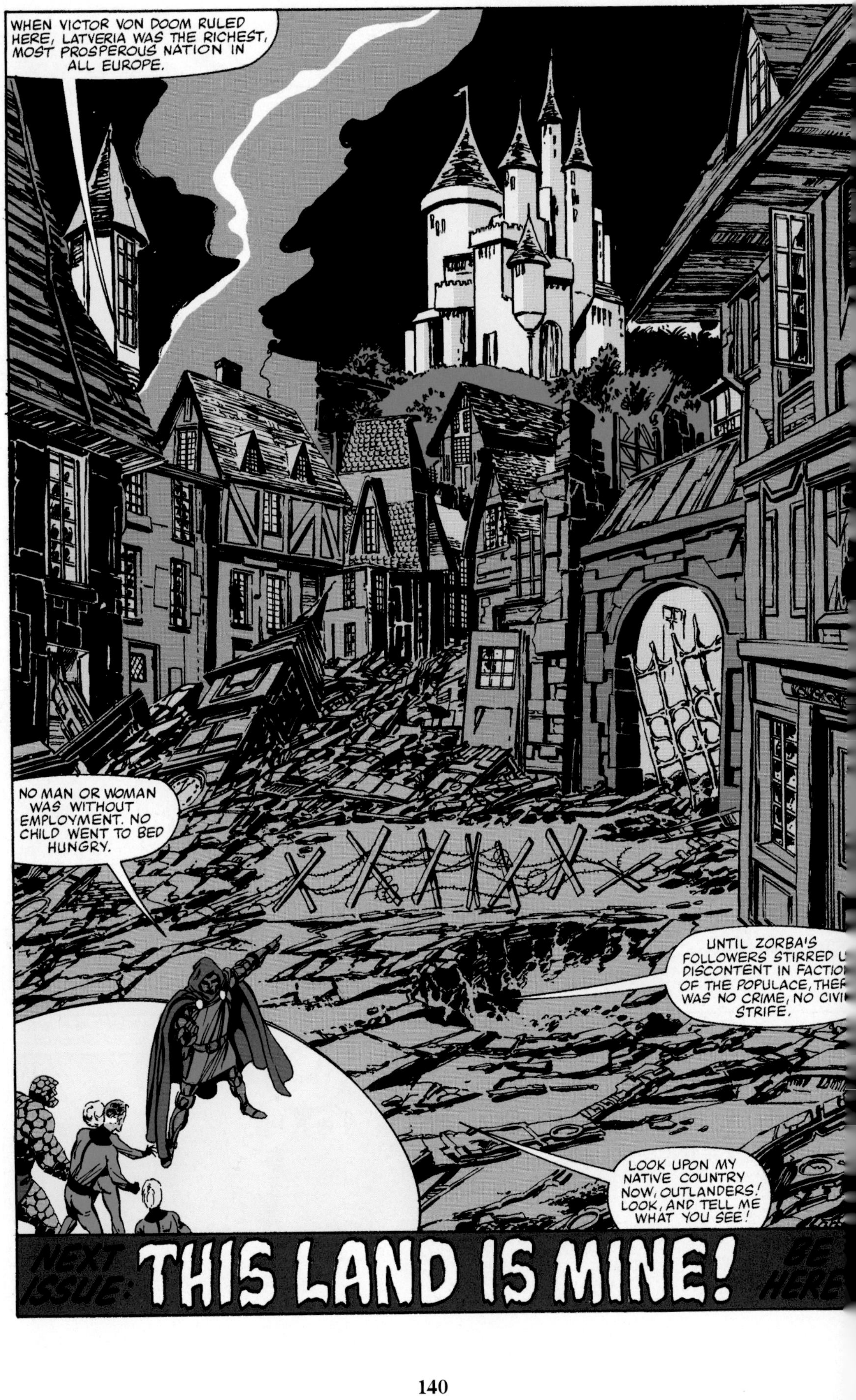
WHEN VICTOR VON DOOM RULED HERE, LATVERIA WAS THE RICHEST, MOST PROSPEROUS NATION IN ALL EUROPE.
NO MAN OR WOMAN WAS WITHOUT EMPLOYMENT. NO CHILD WENT TO BED HUNGRY.
UNTIL ZORBA'S FOLLOWERS STIRRED U DISCONTENT IN FACTIO OF THE POPULACE, THER WAS NO CRIME, NO CIVI STRIFE.
LOOK UPON MY NATIVE COUNTRY NOW, OUTLANDERS! LOOK, AND TELL ME WHAT YOU SEE!
NEXT ISSUE: THIS LAND IS MINE!

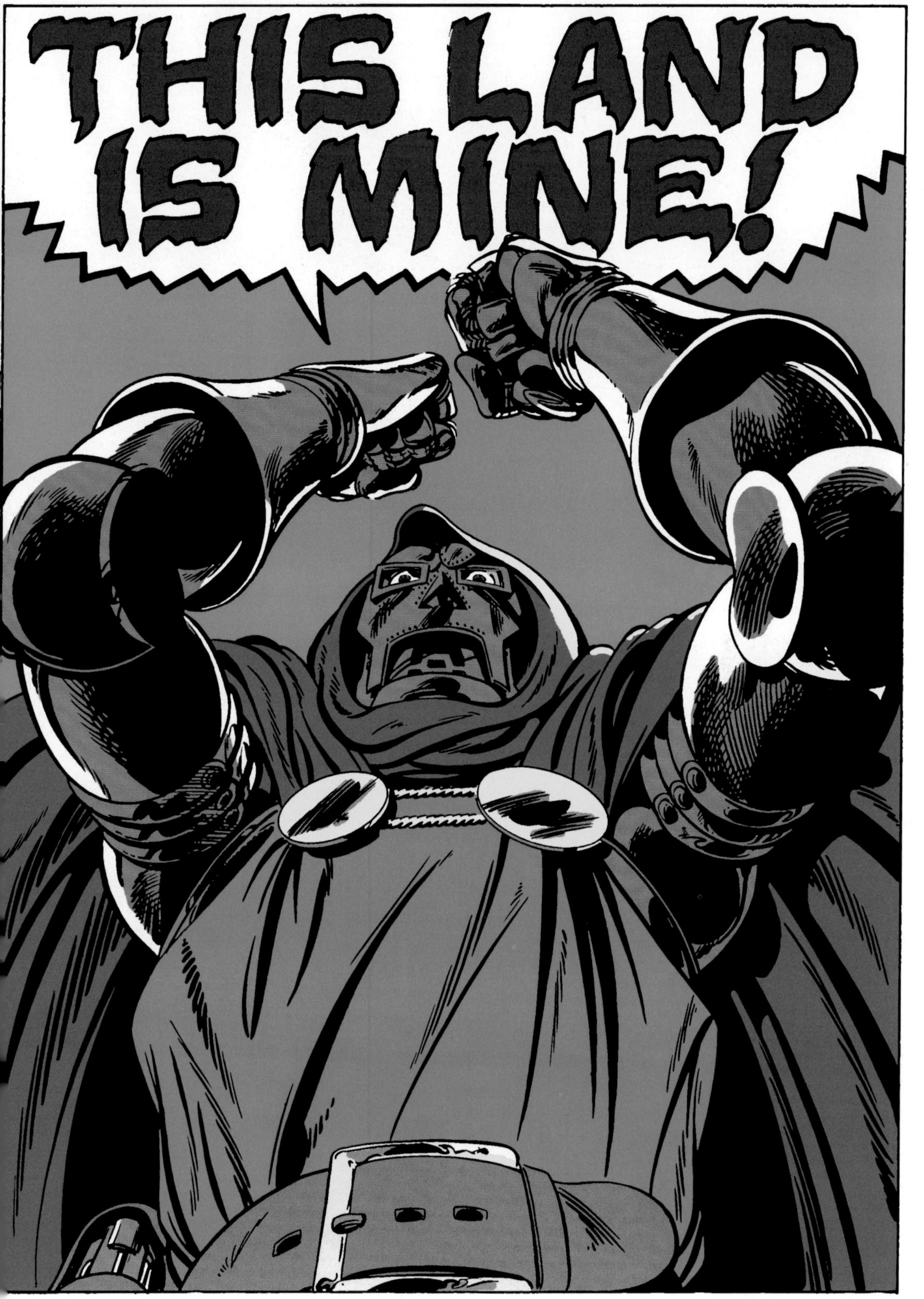
THIS LAND IS MINE!

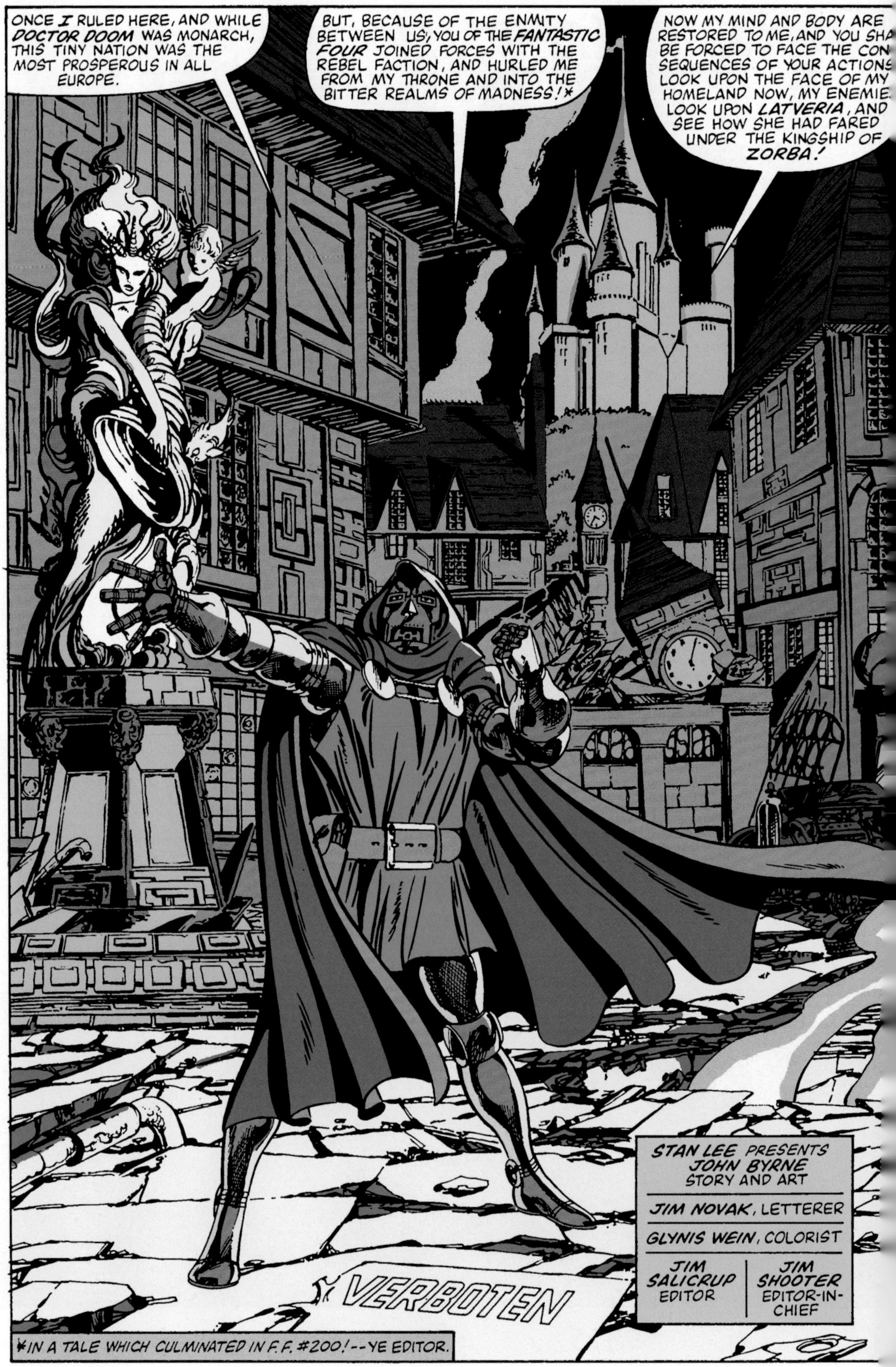
ONCE I RULED HERE, AND WHILE DOCTOR DOOM WAS MONARCH, THIS TINY NATION WAS THE MOST PROSPEROUS IN ALL EUROPE.
BUT, BECAUSE OF THE ENMITY BETWEEN US, YOU OF THE FANTASTIC FOUR JOINED FORCES WITH THE REBEL FACTION, AND HURLED ME FROM MY THRONE AND INTO THE BITTER REALMS OF MADNESS!*
NOW MY MIND AND BODY ARE RESTORED TO ME, AND YOU SHA BE FORCED TO FACE THE CON SEQUENCES OF YOUR ACTIONS LOOK UPON THE FACE OF MY HOMELAND NOW, MY ENEMIE LOOK UPON LATVERIA, AND SEE HOW SHE HAD FARED UNDER THE KINGSHIP OF ZORBA!
STAN LEE PRESENTS JOHN BYRNE STORY AND ART
JIM NOVAK, LETTERER
GLYNIS WEIN, COLORIST
JIM SALICRUP EDITOR
JIM SHOOTER EDITOR-IN-CHIEF
VERBOTEN
*IN A TALE WHICH CULMINATED IN F.F. #200! -- YE EDITOR.

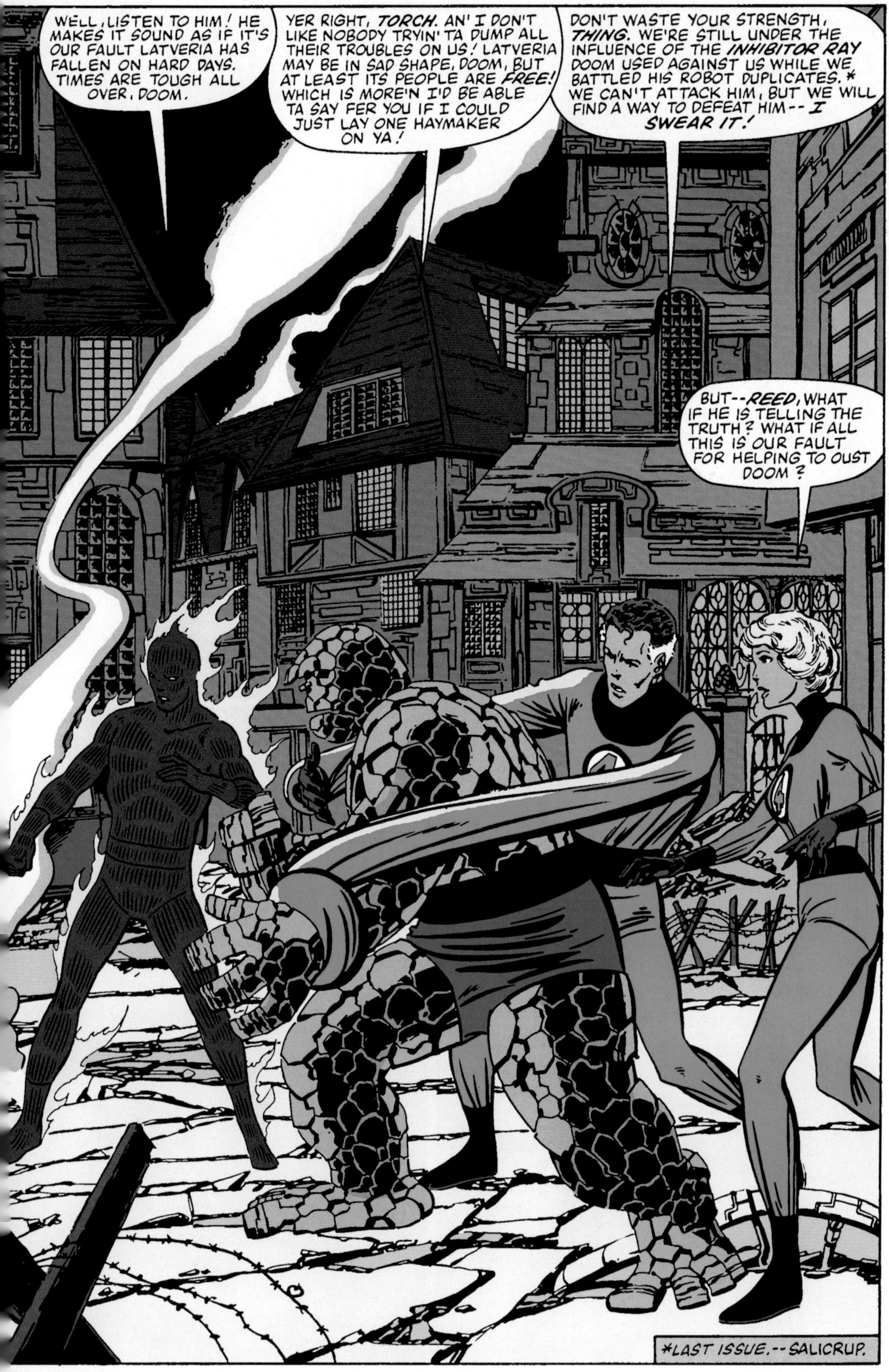
WELL, LISTEN TO HIM! HE MAKES IT SOUND AS IF IT'S OUR FAULT LATVERIA HAS FALLEN ON HARD DAYS. TIMES ARE TOUGH ALL OVER, DOOM.
YER RIGHT, TORCH. AN' I DON'T LIKE NOBODY TRYIN' TA DUMP ALL THEIR TROUBLES ON US! LATVERIA MAY BE IN SAD SHAPE, DOOM, BUT AT LEAST ITS PEOPLE ARE FREE! WHICH IS MORE'N I'D BE ABLE TA SAY FER YOU IF I COULD JUST LAY ONE HAYMAKER ON YA!
DON'T WASTE YOUR STRENGTH, THING. WE'RE STILL UNDER THE INFLUENCE OF THE INHIBITOR RAY DOOM USED AGAINST US WHILE WE BATTLED HIS ROBOT DUPLICATES.* WE CAN'T ATTACK HIM, BUT WE WILL FIND A WAY TO DEFEAT HIM-- I SWEAR IT!
BUT--REED, WHAT IF HE IS TELLING THE TRUTH? WHAT IF ALL THIS IS OUR FAULT FOR HELPING TO OUST DOOM?
*LAST ISSUE.--SALICRUP.

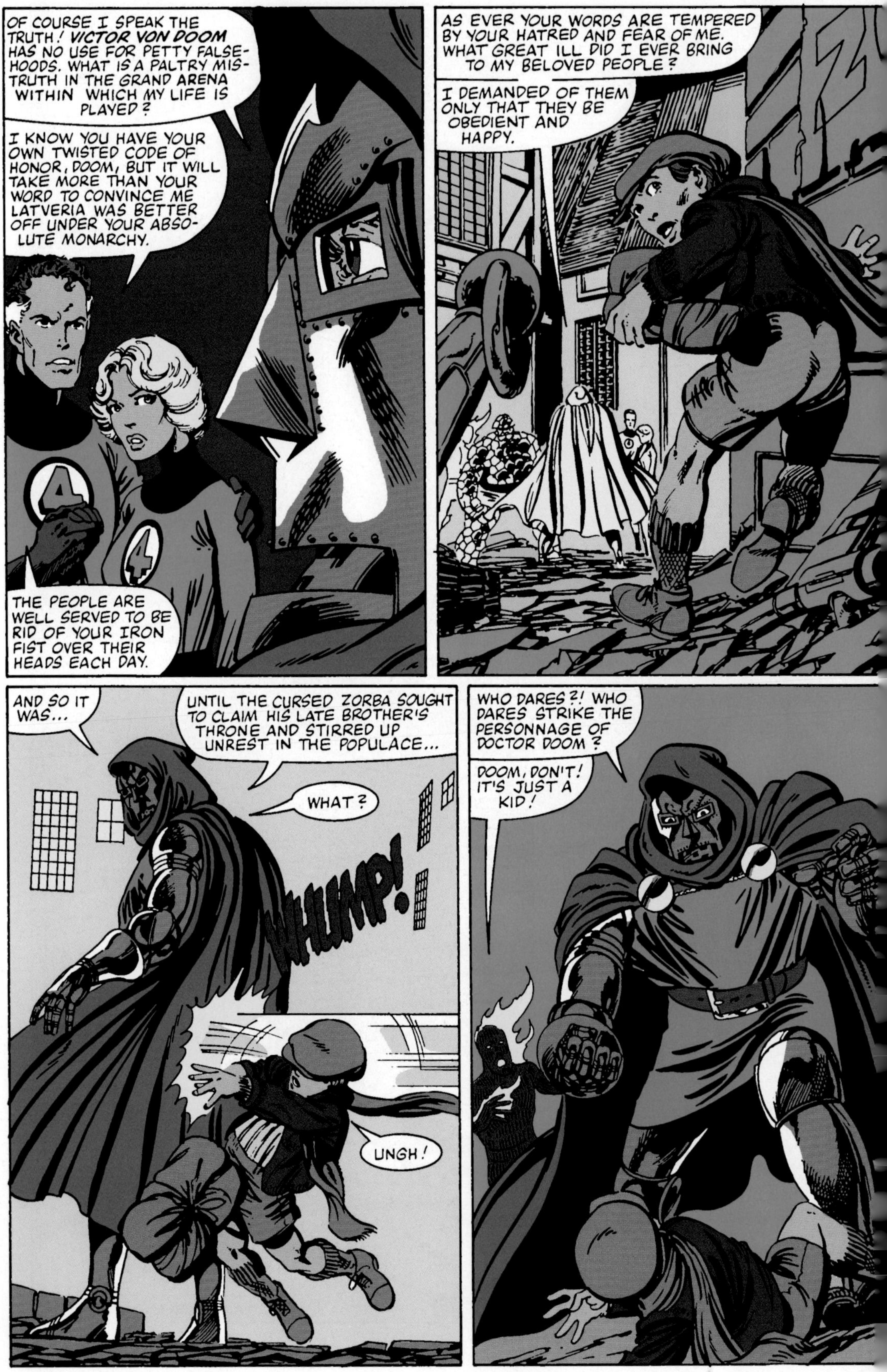
OF COURSE I SPEAK THE TRUTH! VICTOR VON DOOM HAS NO USE FOR PETTY FALSEHOODS. WHAT IS A PALTRY MIS-TRUTH IN THE GRAND ARENA WITHIN WHICH MY LIFE IS PLAYED?
I KNOW YOU HAVE YOUR OWN TWISTED CODE OF HONOR, DOOM, BUT IT WILL TAKE MORE THAN YOUR WORD TO CONVINCE ME LATVERIA WAS BETTER OFF UNDER YOUR ABSOLUTE MONARCHY.
THE PEOPLE ARE WELL SERVED TO BE RID OF YOUR IRON FIST OVER THEIR HEADS EACH DAY.
AS EVER YOUR WORDS ARE TEMPERED BY YOUR HATRED AND FEAR OF ME. WHAT GREAT ILL DID I EVER BRING TO MY BELOVED PEOPLE?
I DEMANDED OF THEM ONLY THAT THEY BE OBEDIENT AND HAPPY.
AND SO IT WAS...
UNTIL THE CURSED ZORBA SOUGHT TO CLAIM HIS LATE BROTHER'S THRONE AND STIRRED UP UNREST IN THE POPULACE...
WHAT?
WHUMP!
UNGH!
WHO DARES?! WHO DARES STRIKE THE PERSONNAGE OF DOCTOR DOOM?
DOOM, DON'T! IT'S JUST A KID!

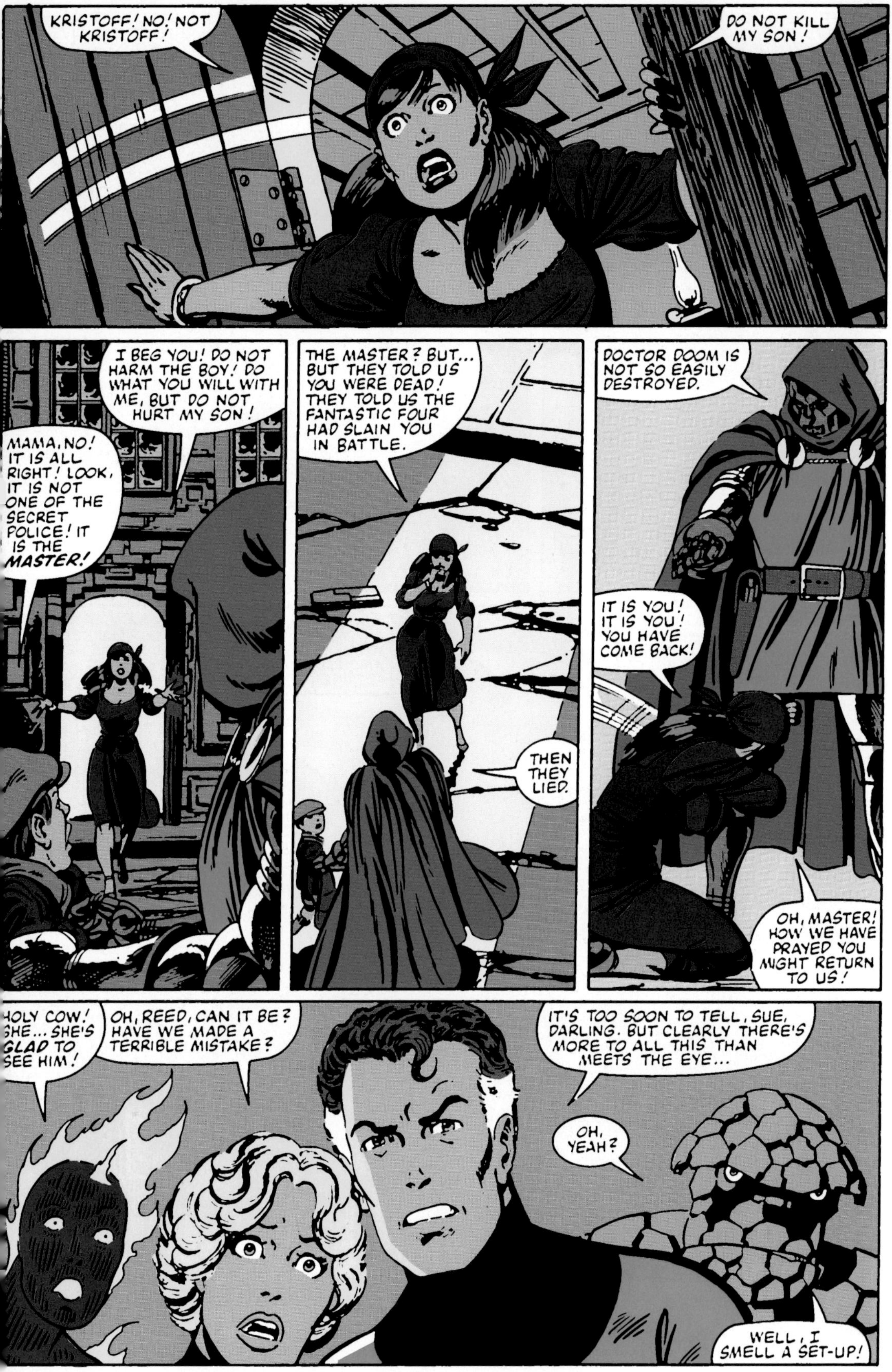
KRISTOFF! NO! NOT KRISTOFF!
DO NOT KILL MY SON!
I BEG YOU! DO NOT HARM THE BOY! DO WHAT YOU WILL WITH ME, BUT DO NOT HURT MY SON!
MAMA, NO! IT IS ALL RIGHT! LOOK, IT IS NOT ONE OF THE SECRET POLICE! IT IS THE MASTER!
THE MASTER? BUT... BUT THEY TOLD US YOU WERE DEAD! THEY TOLD US THE FANTASTIC FOUR HAD SLAIN YOU IN BATTLE.
THEN THEY LIED.
DOCTOR DOOM IS NOT SO EASILY DESTROYED.
IT IS YOU! IT IS YOU! YOU HAVE COME BACK!
OH, MASTER! HOW WE HAVE PRAYED YOU MIGHT RETURN TO US!
HOLY COW! SHE... SHE'S GLAD TO SEE HIM!
OH, REED, CAN IT BE? HAVE WE MADE A TERRIBLE MISTAKE?
IT'S TOO SOON TO TELL, SUE, DARLING. BUT CLEARLY THERE'S MORE TO ALL THIS THAN MEETS THE EYE...
OH, YEAH?
WELL, I SMELL A SET-UP!

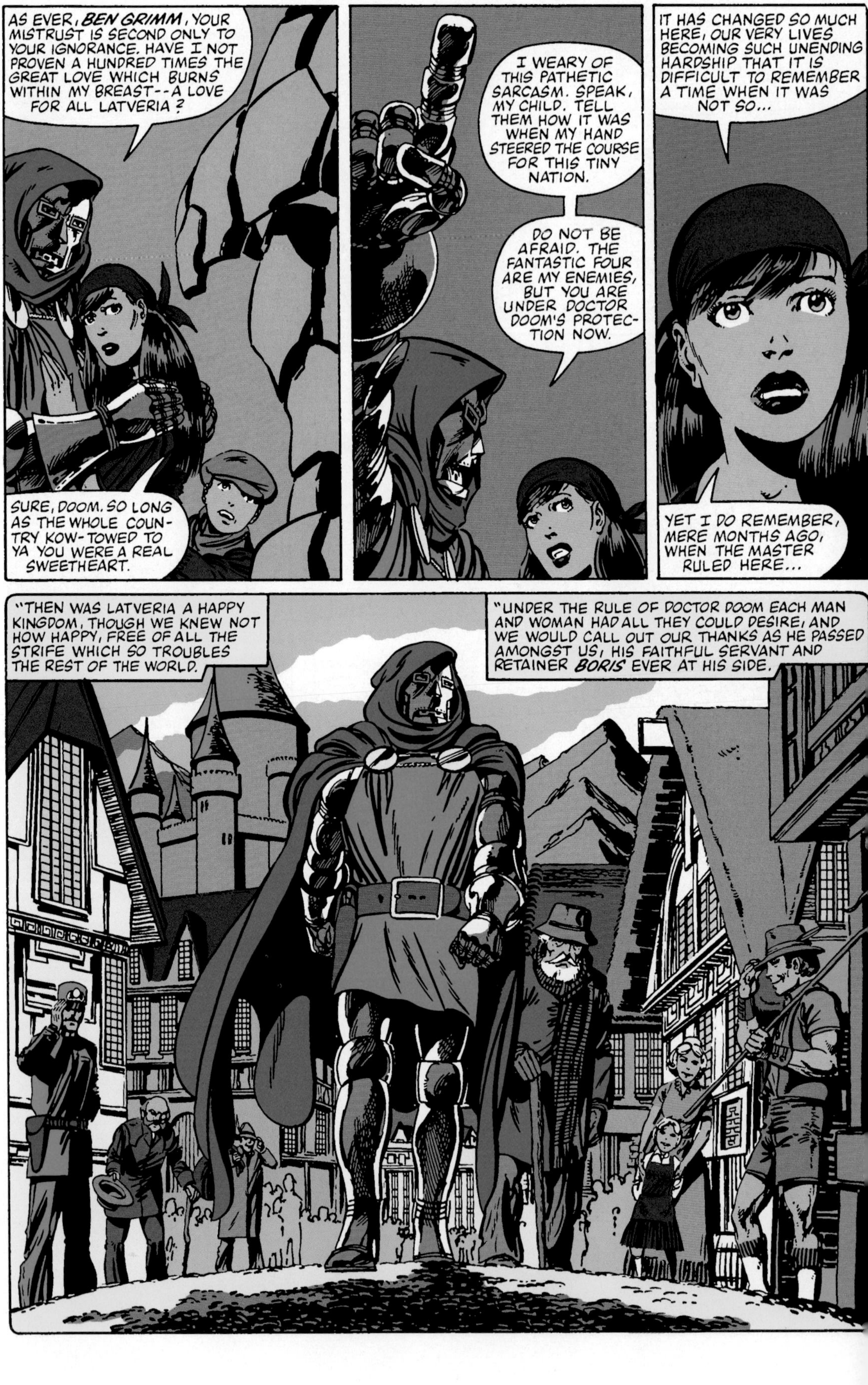
AS EVER, BEN GRIMM, YOUR MISTRUST IS SECOND ONLY TO YOUR IGNORANCE. HAVE I NOT PROVEN A HUNDRED TIMES THE GREAT LOVE WHICH BURNS WITHIN MY BREAST--A LOVE FOR ALL LATVERIA?
SURE, DOOM. SO LONG AS THE WHOLE COUNTRY KOW-TOWED TO YA YOU WERE A REAL SWEETHEART.
I WEARY OF THIS PATHETIC SARCASM. SPEAK, MY CHILD. TELL THEM HOW IT WAS WHEN MY HAND STEERED THE COURSE FOR THIS TINY NATION.
DO NOT BE AFRAID. THE FANTASTIC FOUR ARE MY ENEMIES, BUT YOU ARE UNDER DOCTOR DOOM'S PROTECTION NOW.
IT HAS CHANGED SO MUCH HERE, OUR VERY LIVES BECOMING SUCH UNENDING HARDSHIP THAT IT IS DIFFICULT TO REMEMBER A TIME WHEN IT WAS NOT SO...
YET I DO REMEMBER, MERE MONTHS AGO, WHEN THE MASTER RULED HERE...
"THEN WAS LATVERIA A HAPPY KINGDOM, THOUGH WE KNEW NOT HOW HAPPY, FREE OF ALL THE STRIFE WHICH SO TROUBLES THE REST OF THE WORLD.
"UNDER THE RULE OF DOCTOR DOOM EACH MAN AND WOMAN HAD ALL THEY COULD DESIRE, AND WE WOULD CALL OUT OUR THANKS AS HE PASSED AMONGST US, HIS FAITHFUL SERVANT AND RETAINER BORIS EVER AT HIS SIDE.

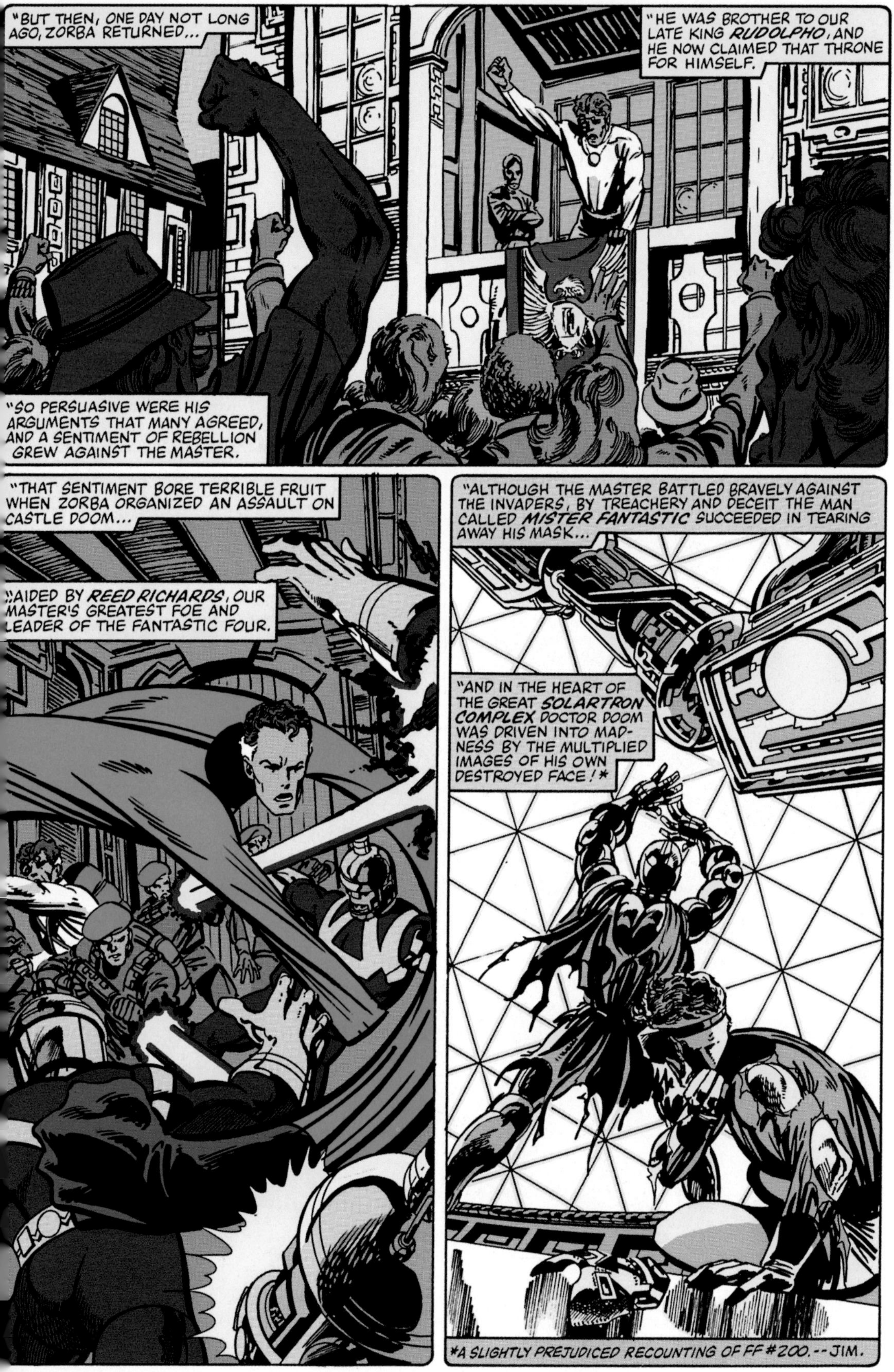
"BUT THEN, ONE DAY NOT LONG AGO, ZORBA RETURNED...
"HE WAS BROTHER TO OUR LATE KING RUDOLPHO, AND HE NOW CLAIMED THAT THRONE FOR HIMSELF.
"SO PERSUASIVE WERE HIS ARGUMENTS THAT MANY AGREED, AND A SENTIMENT OF REBELLION GREW AGAINST THE MASTER.
"THAT SENTIMENT BORE TERRIBLE FRUIT WHEN ZORBA ORGANIZED AN ASSAULT ON CASTLE DOOM...
"AIDED BY REED RICHARDS, OUR MASTER'S GREATEST FOE AND LEADER OF THE FANTASTIC FOUR.
"ALTHOUGH THE MASTER BATTLED BRAVELY AGAINST THE INVADERS, BY TREACHERY AND DECEIT THE MAN CALLED MISTER FANTASTIC SUCCEEDED IN TEARING AWAY HIS MASK...
"AND IN THE HEART OF THE GREAT SOLARTRON COMPLEX DOCTOR DOOM WAS DRIVEN INTO MADNESS BY THE MULTIPLIED IMAGES OF HIS OWN DESTROYED FACE! *
*A SLIGHTLY PREJUDICED RECOUNTING OF FF #200.--JIM.

"FOR A MOMENT IT SEEMED A NEW GOLDEN AGE HAD COME TO LATVERIA. AS HAPPY AS WE HAD BEEN UNDER THE MASTER...

"ZORBA PROMISED THAT, AFTER FREE ELECTIONS, WE WOULD BE EVEN HAPPIER.

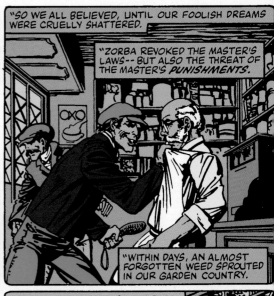

"SO WE ALL BELIEVED, UNTIL OUR FOOLISH DREAMS WERE CRUELLY SHATTERED.

"ZORBA REVOKED THE MASTER'S LAWS-- BUT ALSO THE THREAT OF THE MASTER'S *PUNISHMENTS*.

"WITHIN DAYS, AN ALMOST FORGOTTEN WEED SPROUTED IN OUR GARDEN COUNTRY.

"WHERE ONCE WE HAD KNOW SAFETY IN OUR HOMES, AND PEACE IN THE SOOTHING DARKNESS OF THE EVENING, NOW WE KNEW FEAR, AND THE NAMELESS HORRORS WHICH STALK THE NIGHT.

"LATVERIA WAS RE-LEARNING *CRIME.*

"AND, WORSE AND WORSE, WE BEGAN TO KNOW POVERTY AND HUNGER.

"PRICES ROSE WITHOUT REASON-- AND STOCKS WERE DEPLETED WITH-OUT REPLACEMENT.

"THEN, THE DAY BEFORE WE WERE TO HAVE OUR FIRST FREE ELECTIONS, ZORBA DECLARED *MARTIAL LAW...*

"UNTIL THE 'PRESENT SITUA-TION' WAS CORRECTED, HE WOULD REMAIN AS KING.

"TEN DAYS AGO WE LEARNED OF THE FINAL INJUSTICE. THE MASTER'S *GUARDIAN ROBOTS* HAD BEEN REPROGRAMMED.

"LATVERIA NOW HAS A RUTHLESS, MECHANICAL *SECRET POLICE.*"

148

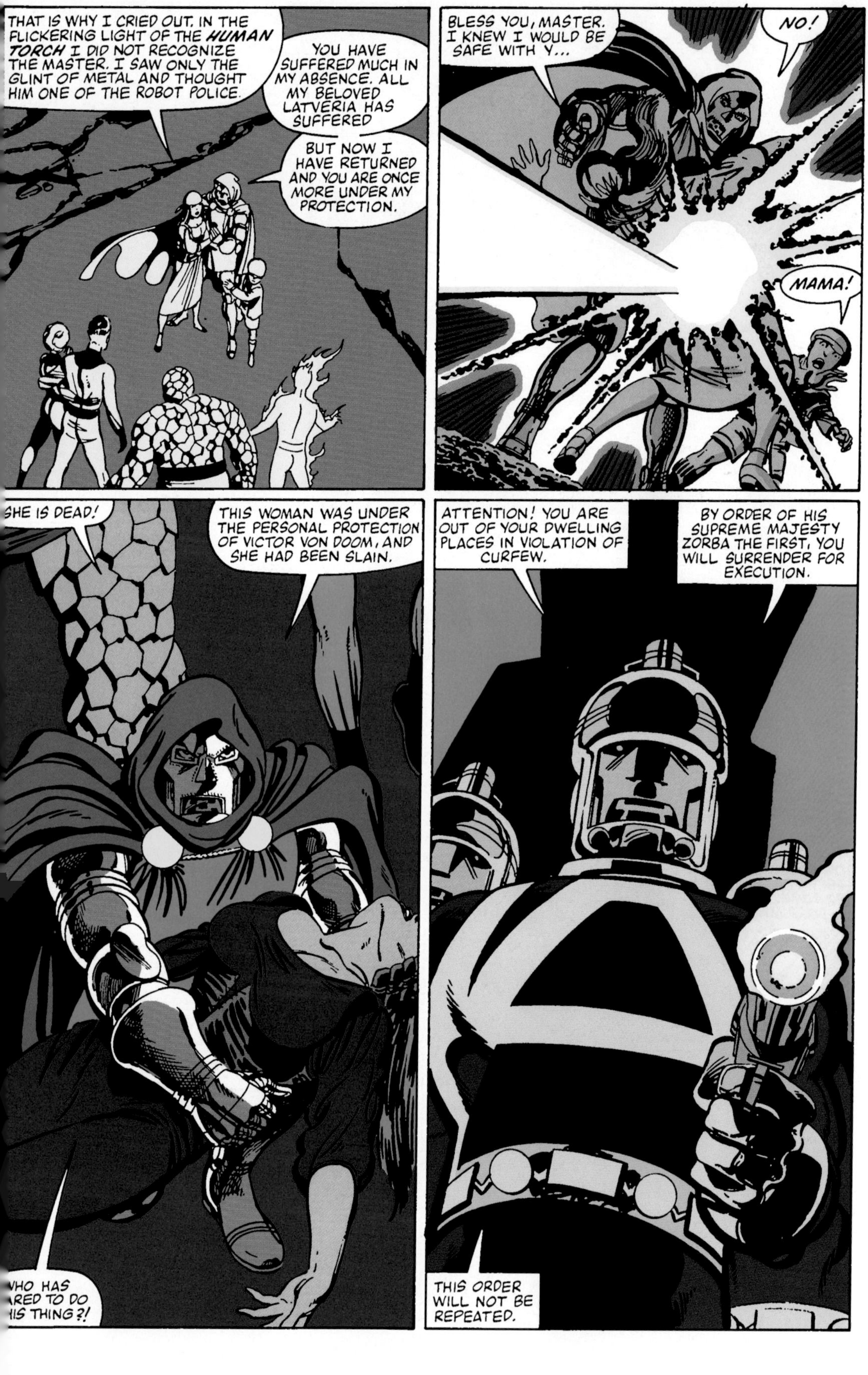
THAT IS WHY I CRIED OUT. IN THE FLICKERING LIGHT OF THE *HUMAN TORCH* I DID NOT RECOGNIZE THE MASTER. I SAW ONLY THE GLINT OF METAL AND THOUGHT HIM ONE OF THE ROBOT POLICE.
YOU HAVE SUFFERED MUCH IN MY ABSENCE. ALL MY BELOVED LATVERIA HAS SUFFERED
BUT NOW I HAVE RETURNED AND YOU ARE ONCE MORE UNDER MY PROTECTION.
BLESS YOU, MASTER. I KNEW I WOULD BE SAFE WITH Y...
NO!
MAMA!
SHE IS DEAD!
THIS WOMAN WAS UNDER THE PERSONAL PROTECTION OF VICTOR VON DOOM, AND SHE HAD BEEN SLAIN.
WHO HAS
ARED TO DO
HIS THING?!
ATTENTION! YOU ARE OUT OF YOUR DWELLING PLACES IN VIOLATION OF CURFEW.
BY ORDER OF HIS SUPREME MAJESTY ZORBA THE FIRST, YOU WILL SURRENDER FOR EXECUTION.
THIS ORDER WILL NOT BE REPEATED.

UNLIVING, UNHUMAN DOGS! YOU DARE GIVE ORDERS TO YOUR CREATOR?

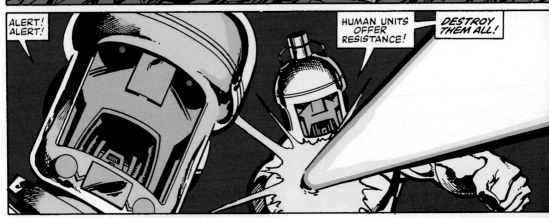

ALERT! ALERT!

HUMAN UNITS OFFER RESISTANCE!

DESTROY THEM ALL!

OWW! HEY, I ALMOST FELT THAT! WE BETTER DO SOMETHIN' FAST, BOSS MAN!

I CAN SHIELD US FROM THEIR BLASTS WITH AN INVISIBLE FORCE FIELD, BUT ARE WE GOING TO STRIKE BACK?

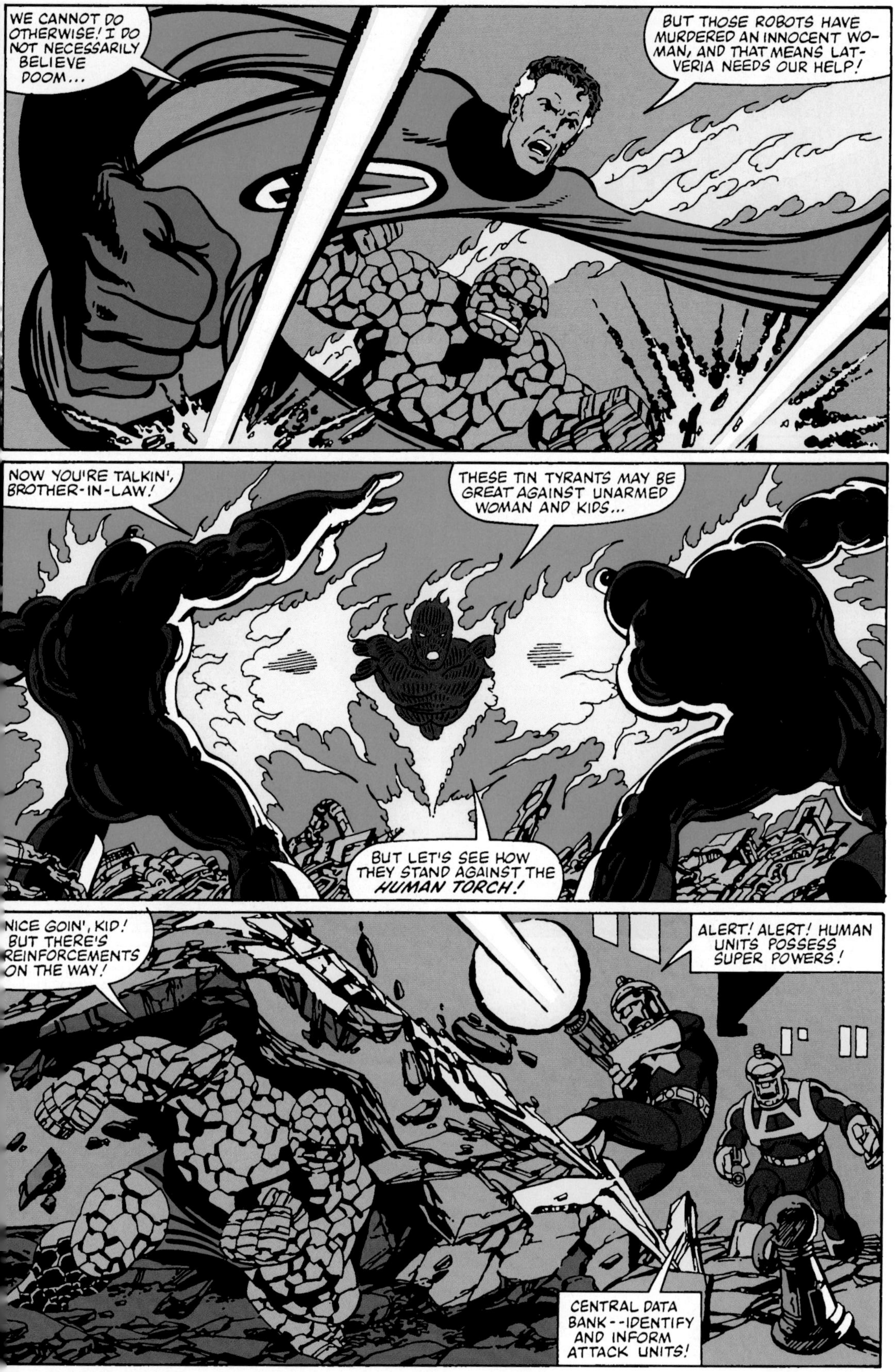
WE CANNOT DO OTHERWISE! I DO NOT NECESSARILY BELIEVE DOOM...
BUT THOSE ROBOTS HAVE MURDERED AN INNOCENT WOMAN, AND THAT MEANS LATVERIA NEEDS OUR HELP!
NOW YOU'RE TALKIN', BROTHER-IN-LAW!
THESE TIN TYRANTS MAY BE GREAT AGAINST UNARMED WOMAN AND KIDS...
BUT LET'S SEE HOW THEY STAND AGAINST THE HUMAN TORCH!
NICE GOIN', KID! BUT THERE'S REINFORCEMENTS ON THE WAY!
ALERT! ALERT! HUMAN UNITS POSSESS SUPER POWERS!
CENTRAL DATA BANK--IDENTIFY AND INFORM ATTACK UNITS!

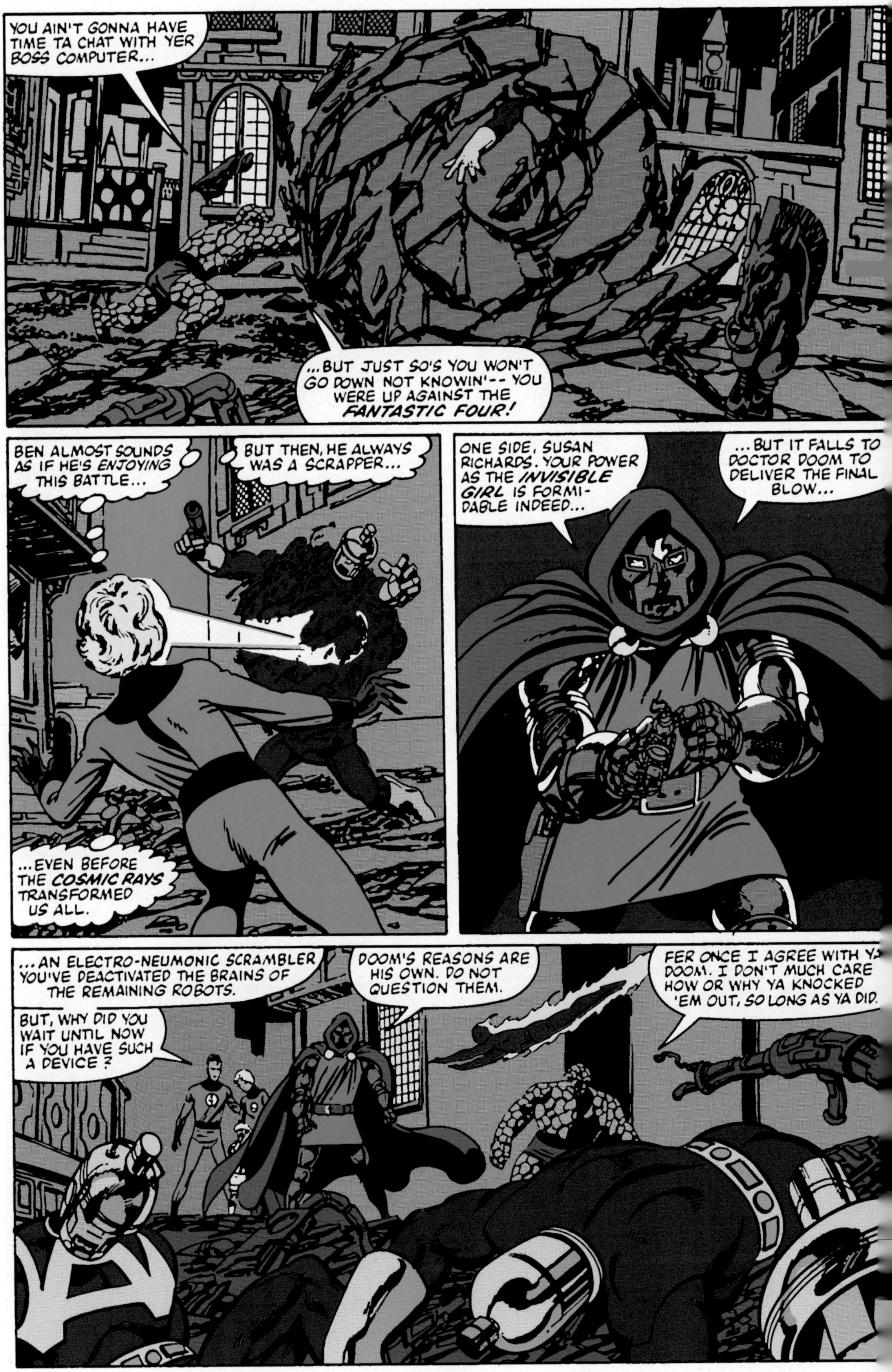
YOU AIN'T GONNA HAVE TIME TA CHAT WITH YER BOSS COMPUTER...
...BUT JUST SO'S YOU WON'T GO DOWN NOT KNOWIN'-- YOU WERE UP AGAINST THE FANTASTIC FOUR!
BEN ALMOST SOUNDS AS IF HE'S ENJOYING THIS BATTLE...
BUT THEN, HE ALWAYS WAS A SCRAPPER...
...EVEN BEFORE THE COSMIC RAYS TRANSFORMED US ALL.
ONE SIDE, SUSAN RICHARDS. YOUR POWER AS THE INVISIBLE GIRL IS FORMIDABLE INDEED...
...BUT IT FALLS TO DOCTOR DOOM TO DELIVER THE FINAL BLOW...
...AN ELECTRO-NEUMONIC SCRAMBLER YOU'VE DEACTIVATED THE BRAINS OF THE REMAINING ROBOTS.
BUT, WHY DID YOU WAIT UNTIL NOW IF YOU HAVE SUCH A DEVICE?
DOOM'S REASONS ARE HIS OWN. DO NOT QUESTION THEM.
FER ONCE I AGREE WITH YA DOOM. I DON'T MUCH CARE HOW OR WHY YA KNOCKED 'EM OUT, SO LONG AS YA DID.

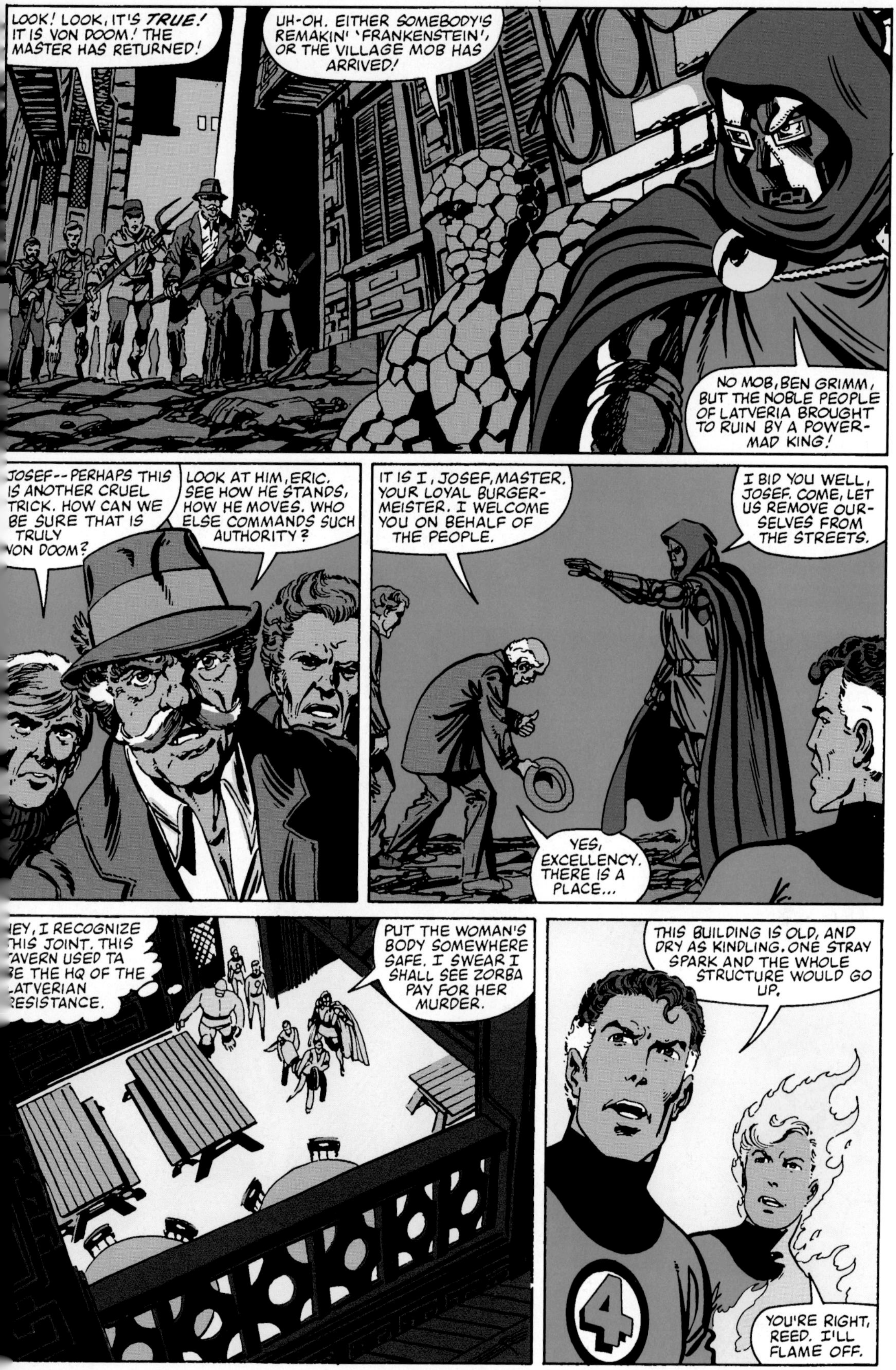
LOOK! LOOK, IT'S TRUE! IT IS VON DOOM! THE MASTER HAS RETURNED!
UH-OH. EITHER SOMEBODY'S REMAKIN' 'FRANKENSTEIN', OR THE VILLAGE MOB HAS ARRIVED!
NO MOB, BEN GRIMM, BUT THE NOBLE PEOPLE OF LATVERIA BROUGHT TO RUIN BY A POWER-MAD KING!
JOSEF--PERHAPS THIS IS ANOTHER CRUEL TRICK. HOW CAN WE BE SURE THAT IS TRULY VON DOOM?
LOOK AT HIM, ERIC. SEE HOW HE STANDS, HOW HE MOVES. WHO ELSE COMMANDS SUCH AUTHORITY?
IT IS I, JOSEF, MASTER. YOUR LOYAL BURGER-MEISTER. I WELCOME YOU ON BEHALF OF THE PEOPLE.
I BID YOU WELL, JOSEF. COME, LET US REMOVE OUR-SELVES FROM THE STREETS.
YES, EXCELLENCY. THERE IS A PLACE...
HEY, I RECOGNIZE THIS JOINT. THIS TAVERN USED TA BE THE HQ OF THE LATVERIAN RESISTANCE.
PUT THE WOMAN'S BODY SOMEWHERE SAFE. I SWEAR I SHALL SEE ZORBA PAY FOR HER MURDER.
THIS BUILDING IS OLD, AND DRY AS KINDLING. ONE STRAY SPARK AND THE WHOLE STRUCTURE WOULD GO UP.
YOU'RE RIGHT, REED. I'LL FLAME OFF.

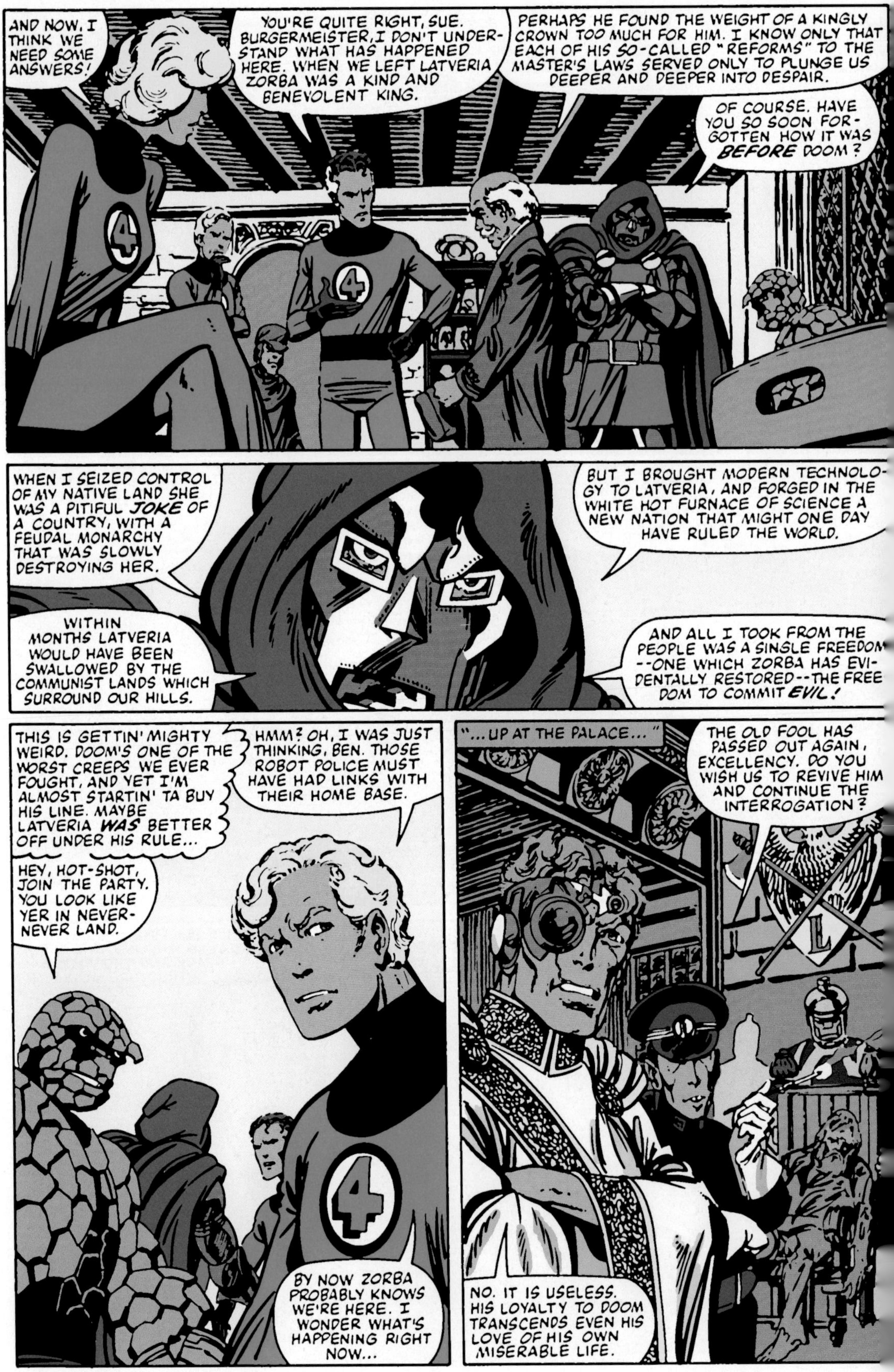
AND NOW, I THINK WE NEED SOME ANSWERS!
YOU'RE QUITE RIGHT, SUE. BURGERMEISTER, I DON'T UNDERSTAND WHAT HAS HAPPENED HERE. WHEN WE LEFT LATVERIA ZORBA WAS A KIND AND BENEVOLENT KING.
PERHAPS HE FOUND THE WEIGHT OF A KINGLY CROWN TOO MUCH FOR HIM. I KNOW ONLY THAT EACH OF HIS SO-CALLED "REFORMS" TO THE MASTER'S LAWS SERVED ONLY TO PLUNGE US DEEPER AND DEEPER INTO DESPAIR.
OF COURSE. HAVE YOU SO SOON FORGOTTEN HOW IT WAS BEFORE DOOM?
WHEN I SEIZED CONTROL OF MY NATIVE LAND SHE WAS A PITIFUL JOKE OF A COUNTRY, WITH A FEUDAL MONARCHY THAT WAS SLOWLY DESTROYING HER.
BUT I BROUGHT MODERN TECHNOLOGY TO LATVERIA, AND FORGED IN THE WHITE HOT FURNACE OF SCIENCE A NEW NATION THAT MIGHT ONE DAY HAVE RULED THE WORLD.
WITHIN MONTHS LATVERIA WOULD HAVE BEEN SWALLOWED BY THE COMMUNIST LANDS WHICH SURROUND OUR HILLS.
AND ALL I TOOK FROM THE PEOPLE WAS A SINGLE FREEDOM --ONE WHICH ZORBA HAS EVIDENTALLY RESTORED--THE FREEDOM TO COMMIT EVIL!
THIS IS GETTIN' MIGHTY WEIRD. DOOM'S ONE OF THE WORST CREEPS WE EVER FOUGHT, AND YET I'M ALMOST STARTIN' TA BUY HIS LINE. MAYBE LATVERIA WAS BETTER OFF UNDER HIS RULE...
HEY, HOT-SHOT, JOIN THE PARTY. YOU LOOK LIKE YER IN NEVER-NEVER LAND.
HMM? OH, I WAS JUST THINKING, BEN. THOSE ROBOT POLICE MUST HAVE HAD LINKS WITH THEIR HOME BASE.
BY NOW ZORBA PROBABLY KNOWS WE'RE HERE. I WONDER WHAT'S HAPPENING RIGHT NOW...
"...UP AT THE PALACE..."
THE OLD FOOL HAS PASSED OUT AGAIN, EXCELLENCY. DO YOU WISH US TO REVIVE HIM AND CONTINUE THE INTERROGATION?
NO. IT IS USELESS. HIS LOYALTY TO DOOM TRANSCENDS EVEN HIS LOVE OF HIS OWN MISERABLE LIFE.

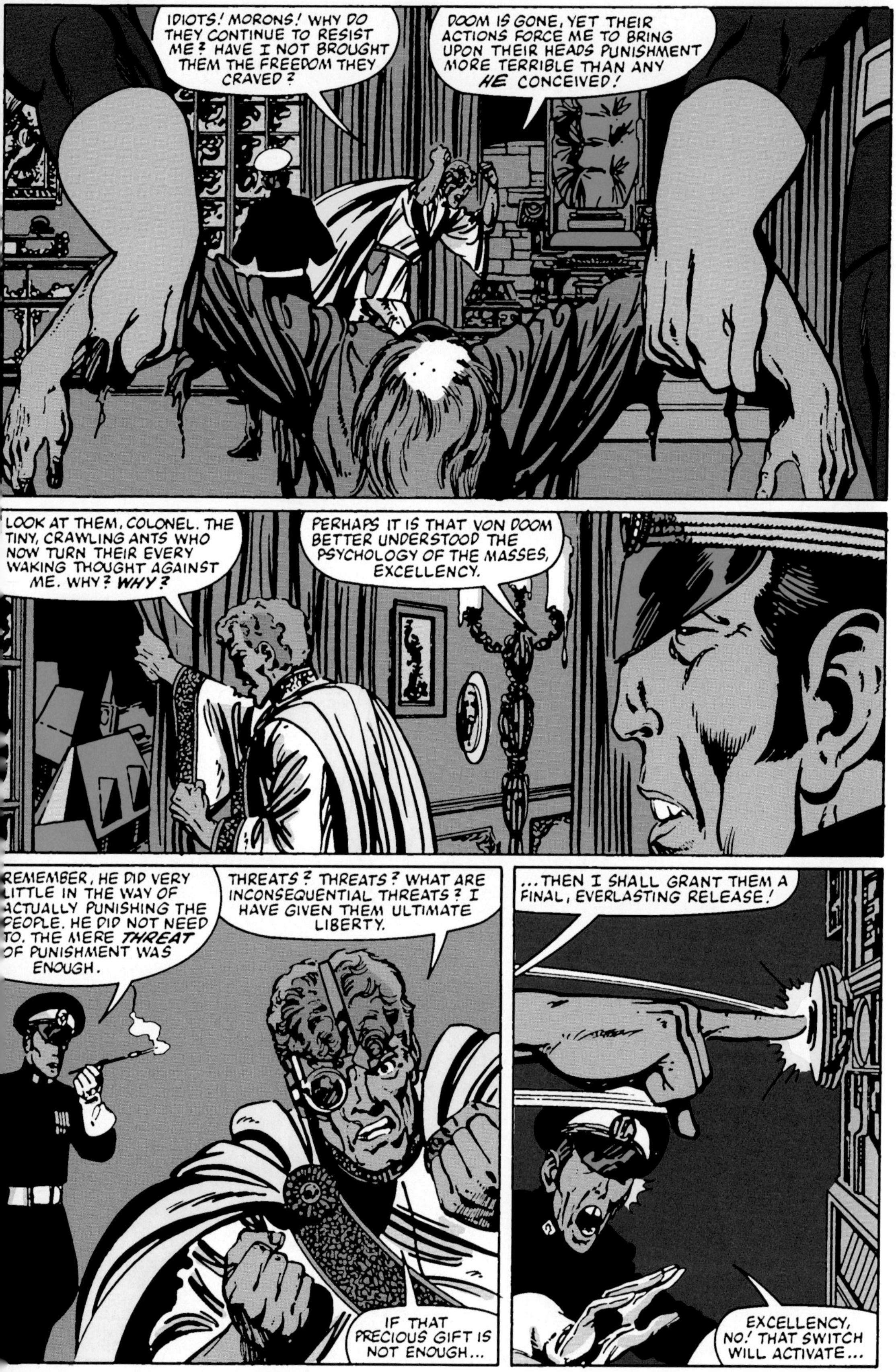
IDIOTS! MORONS! WHY DO THEY CONTINUE TO RESIST ME? HAVE I NOT BROUGHT THEM THE FREEDOM THEY CRAVED?
DOOM IS GONE, YET THEIR ACTIONS FORCE ME TO BRING UPON THEIR HEADS PUNISHMENT MORE TERRIBLE THAN ANY *HE* CONCEIVED!
LOOK AT THEM, COLONEL. THE TINY, CRAWLING ANTS WHO NOW TURN THEIR EVERY WAKING THOUGHT AGAINST ME. WHY? *WHY?*
PERHAPS IT IS THAT VON DOOM BETTER UNDERSTOOD THE PSYCHOLOGY OF THE MASSES, EXCELLENCY.
REMEMBER, HE DID VERY LITTLE IN THE WAY OF ACTUALLY PUNISHING THE PEOPLE. HE DID NOT NEED TO. THE MERE *THREAT* OF PUNISHMENT WAS ENOUGH.
THREATS? THREATS? WHAT ARE INCONSEQUENTIAL THREATS? I HAVE GIVEN THEM ULTIMATE LIBERTY.
IF THAT PRECIOUS GIFT IS NOT ENOUGH...
...THEN I SHALL GRANT THEM A FINAL, EVERLASTING RELEASE!
EXCELLENCY, NO! THAT SWITCH WILL ACTIVATE...

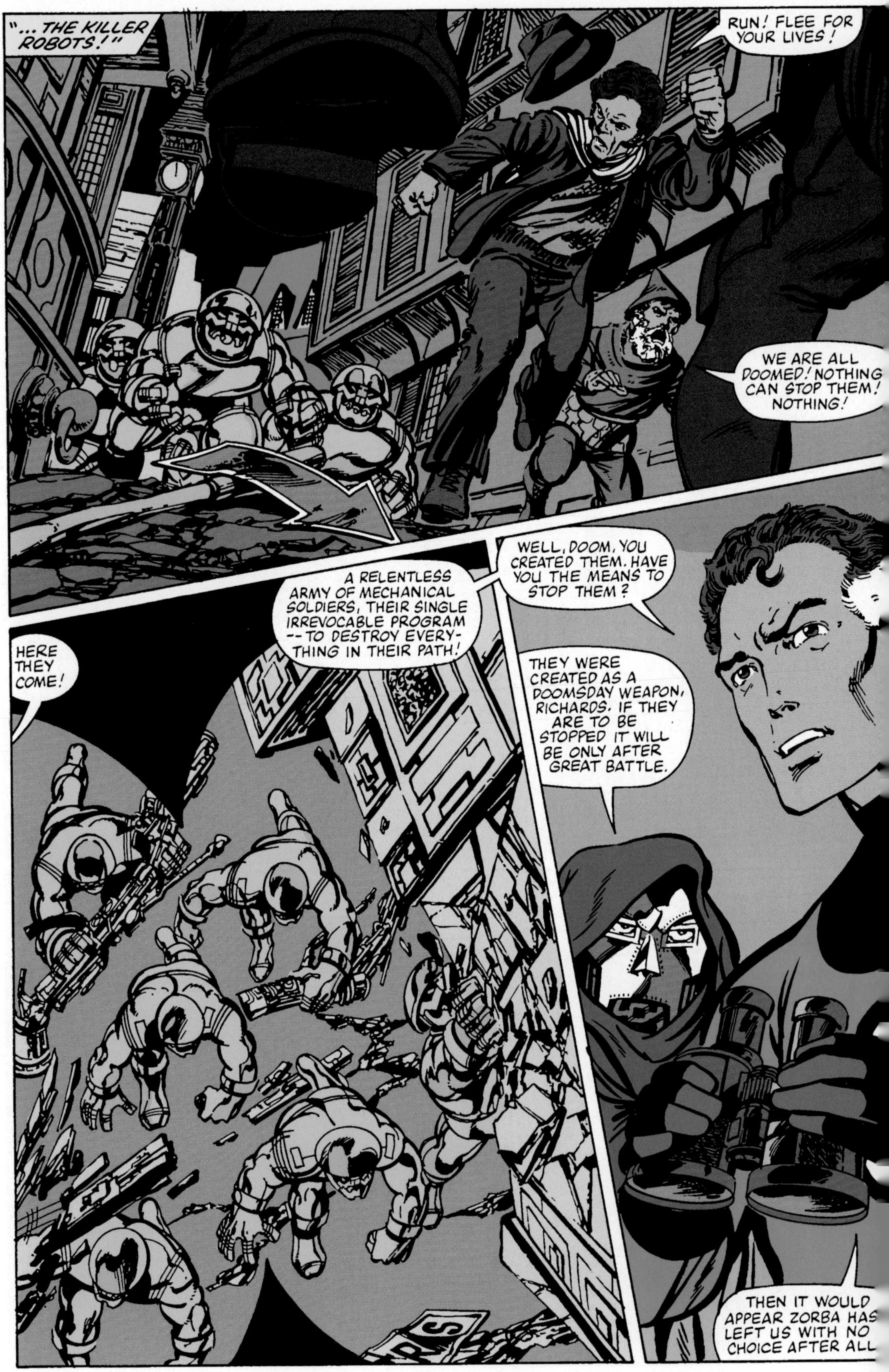
"...THE KILLER ROBOTS!"
RUN! FLEE FOR YOUR LIVES!
WE ARE ALL DOOMED! NOTHING CAN STOP THEM! NOTHING!
HERE THEY COME!
A RELENTLESS ARMY OF MECHANICAL SOLDIERS, THEIR SINGLE IRREVOCABLE PROGRAM --TO DESTROY EVERYTHING IN THEIR PATH!
WELL, DOOM, YOU CREATED THEM. HAVE YOU THE MEANS TO STOP THEM?
THEY WERE CREATED AS A DOOMSDAY WEAPON, RICHARDS. IF THEY ARE TO BE STOPPED IT WILL BE ONLY AFTER GREAT BATTLE.
THEN IT WOULD APPEAR ZORBA HAS LEFT US WITH NO CHOICE AFTER ALL

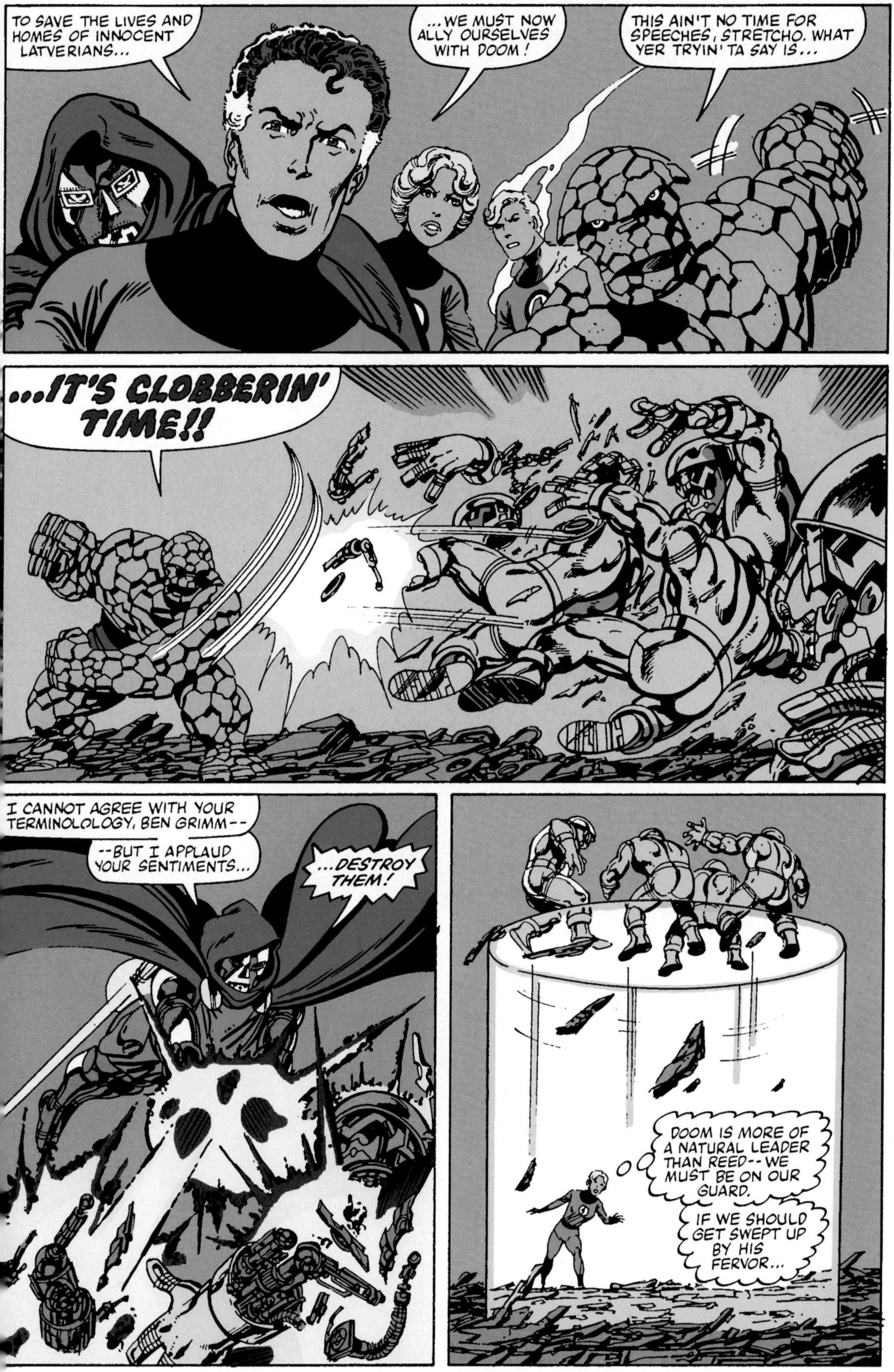
TO SAVE THE LIVES AND HOMES OF INNOCENT LATVERIANS...
...WE MUST NOW ALLY OURSELVES WITH DOOM!
THIS AIN'T NO TIME FOR SPEECHES, STRETCHO. WHAT YER TRYIN' TA SAY IS...
...IT'S CLOBBERIN' TIME!!
I CANNOT AGREE WITH YOUR TERMINOLOLOGY, BEN GRIMM--
--BUT I APPLAUD YOUR SENTIMENTS...
...DESTROY THEM!
DOOM IS MORE OF A NATURAL LEADER THAN REED--WE MUST BE ON OUR GUARD.
IF WE SHOULD GET SWEPT UP BY HIS FERVOR...

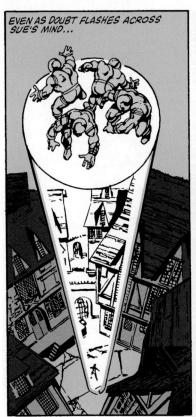

EVEN AS DOUBT FLASHES ACROSS SUE'S MIND...

AND WHEN THE INVISIBLE ALSO BECOMES INTANGIBLE...

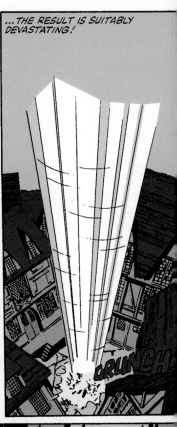

...THE RESULT IS SUITABLY DEVASTATING!

CRUNCH

YAY, TEAM! WE'RE HITTIN' 'EM SO HARD, THEY CAN'T THINK STRAIGHT!

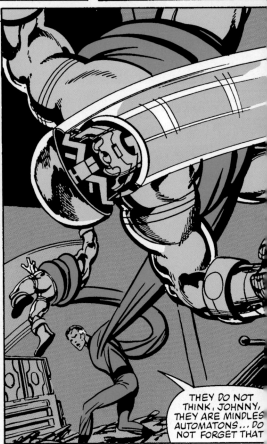

THEY DO NOT THINK, JOHNNY, THEY ARE MINDLES AUTOMATONS... DO NOT FORGET THAT

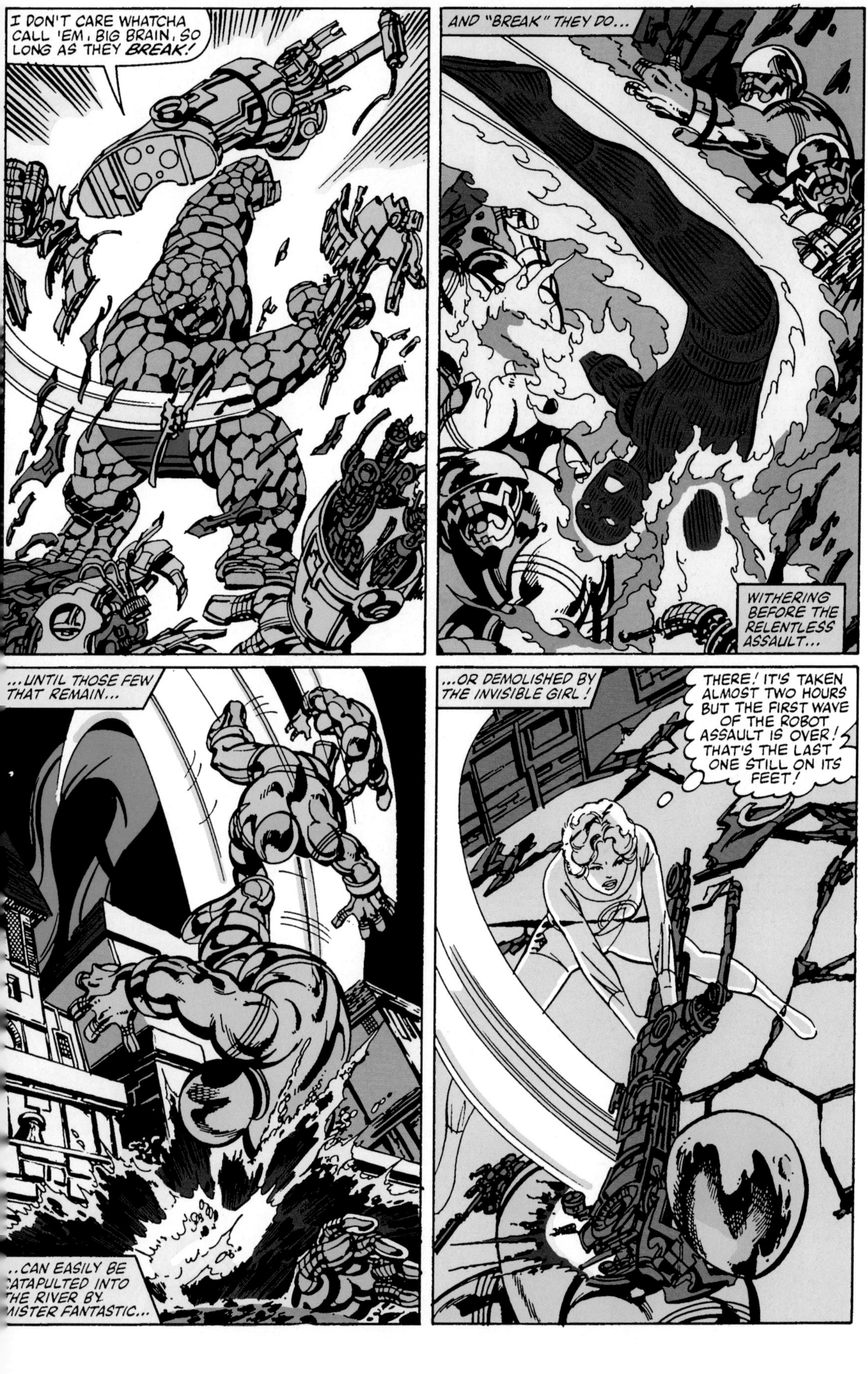
I DON'T CARE WHATCHA CALL 'EM, BIG BRAIN, SO LONG AS THEY BREAK!
AND "BREAK" THEY DO...
WITHERING BEFORE THE RELENTLESS ASSAULT...
...UNTIL THOSE FEW THAT REMAIN...
...CAN EASILY BE CATAPULTED INTO THE RIVER BY MISTER FANTASTIC...
...OR DEMOLISHED BY THE INVISIBLE GIRL!
THERE! IT'S TAKEN ALMOST TWO HOURS BUT THE FIRST WAVE OF THE ROBOT ASSAULT IS OVER! THAT'S THE LAST ONE STILL ON ITS FEET!

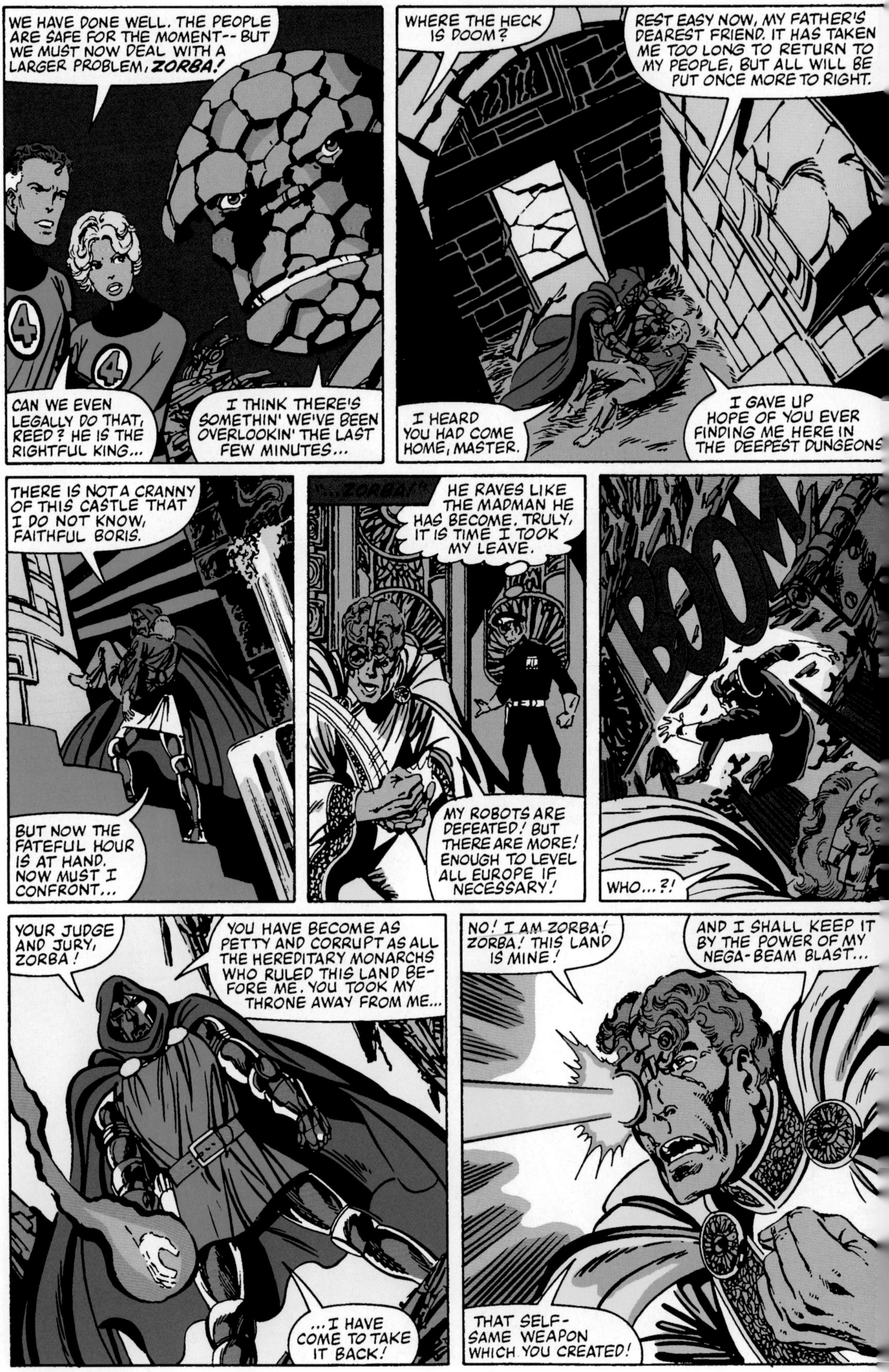
WE HAVE DONE WELL. THE PEOPLE ARE SAFE FOR THE MOMENT-- BUT WE MUST NOW DEAL WITH A LARGER PROBLEM, ZORBA!
CAN WE EVEN LEGALLY DO THAT, REED? HE IS THE RIGHTFUL KING...
I THINK THERE'S SOMETHIN' WE'VE BEEN OVERLOOKIN' THE LAST FEW MINUTES...
WHERE THE HECK IS DOOM?
REST EASY NOW, MY FATHER'S DEAREST FRIEND. IT HAS TAKEN ME TOO LONG TO RETURN TO MY PEOPLE, BUT ALL WILL BE PUT ONCE MORE TO RIGHT.
I HEARD YOU HAD COME HOME, MASTER.
I GAVE UP HOPE OF YOU EVER FINDING ME HERE IN THE DEEPEST DUNGEONS
THERE IS NOT A CRANNY OF THIS CASTLE THAT I DO NOT KNOW, FAITHFUL BORIS.
BUT NOW THE FATEFUL HOUR IS AT HAND. NOW MUST I CONFRONT...
"...ZORBA!"
HE RAVES LIKE THE MADMAN HE HAS BECOME. TRULY, IT IS TIME I TOOK MY LEAVE.
MY ROBOTS ARE DEFEATED! BUT THERE ARE MORE! ENOUGH TO LEVEL ALL EUROPE IF NECESSARY!
BOOM
WHO...?!
YOUR JUDGE AND JURY, ZORBA!
YOU HAVE BECOME AS PETTY AND CORRUPT AS ALL THE HEREDITARY MONARCHS WHO RULED THIS LAND BEFORE ME. YOU TOOK MY THRONE AWAY FROM ME...
...I HAVE COME TO TAKE IT BACK!
NO! I AM ZORBA! ZORBA! THIS LAND IS MINE!
AND I SHALL KEEP IT BY THE POWER OF MY NEGA-BEAM BLAST...
THAT SELF-SAME WEAPON WHICH YOU CREATED!

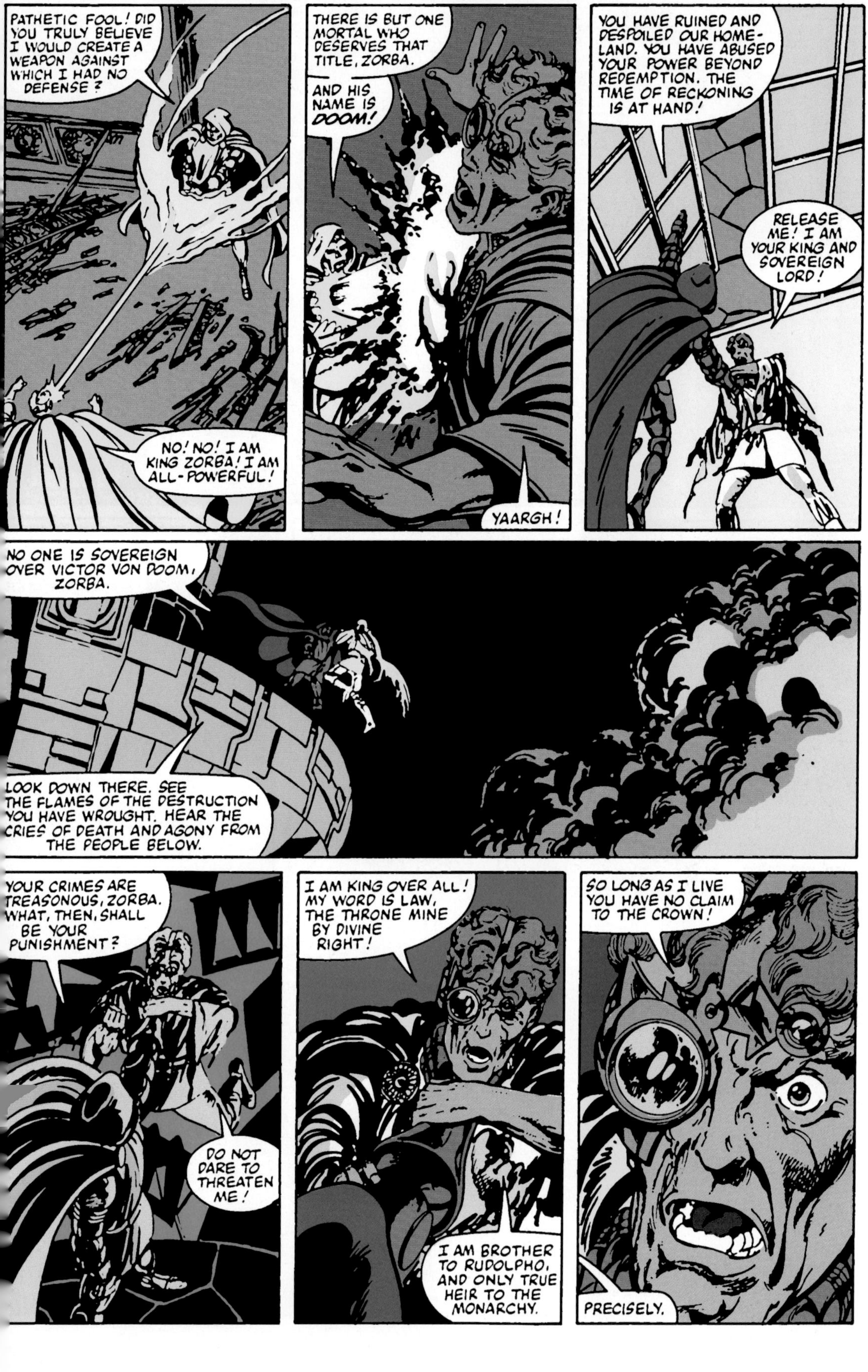
PATHETIC FOOL! DID YOU TRULY BELIEVE I WOULD CREATE A WEAPON AGAINST WHICH I HAD NO DEFENSE?
NO! NO! I AM KING ZORBA! I AM ALL-POWERFUL!
THERE IS BUT ONE MORTAL WHO DESERVES THAT TITLE, ZORBA.
AND HIS NAME IS DOOM!
YAARGH!
YOU HAVE RUINED AND DESPOILED OUR HOME-LAND. YOU HAVE ABUSED YOUR POWER BEYOND REDEMPTION. THE TIME OF RECKONING IS AT HAND!
RELEASE ME! I AM YOUR KING AND SOVEREIGN LORD!
NO ONE IS SOVEREIGN OVER VICTOR VON DOOM, ZORBA.
LOOK DOWN THERE. SEE THE FLAMES OF THE DESTRUCTION YOU HAVE WROUGHT. HEAR THE CRIES OF DEATH AND AGONY FROM THE PEOPLE BELOW.
YOUR CRIMES ARE TREASONOUS, ZORBA. WHAT, THEN, SHALL BE YOUR PUNISHMENT?
DO NOT DARE TO THREATEN ME!
I AM KING OVER ALL! MY WORD IS LAW, THE THRONE MINE BY DIVINE RIGHT!
I AM BROTHER TO RUDOLPHO, AND ONLY TRUE HEIR TO THE MONARCHY.
SO LONG AS I LIVE YOU HAVE NO CLAIM TO THE CROWN!
PRECISELY.

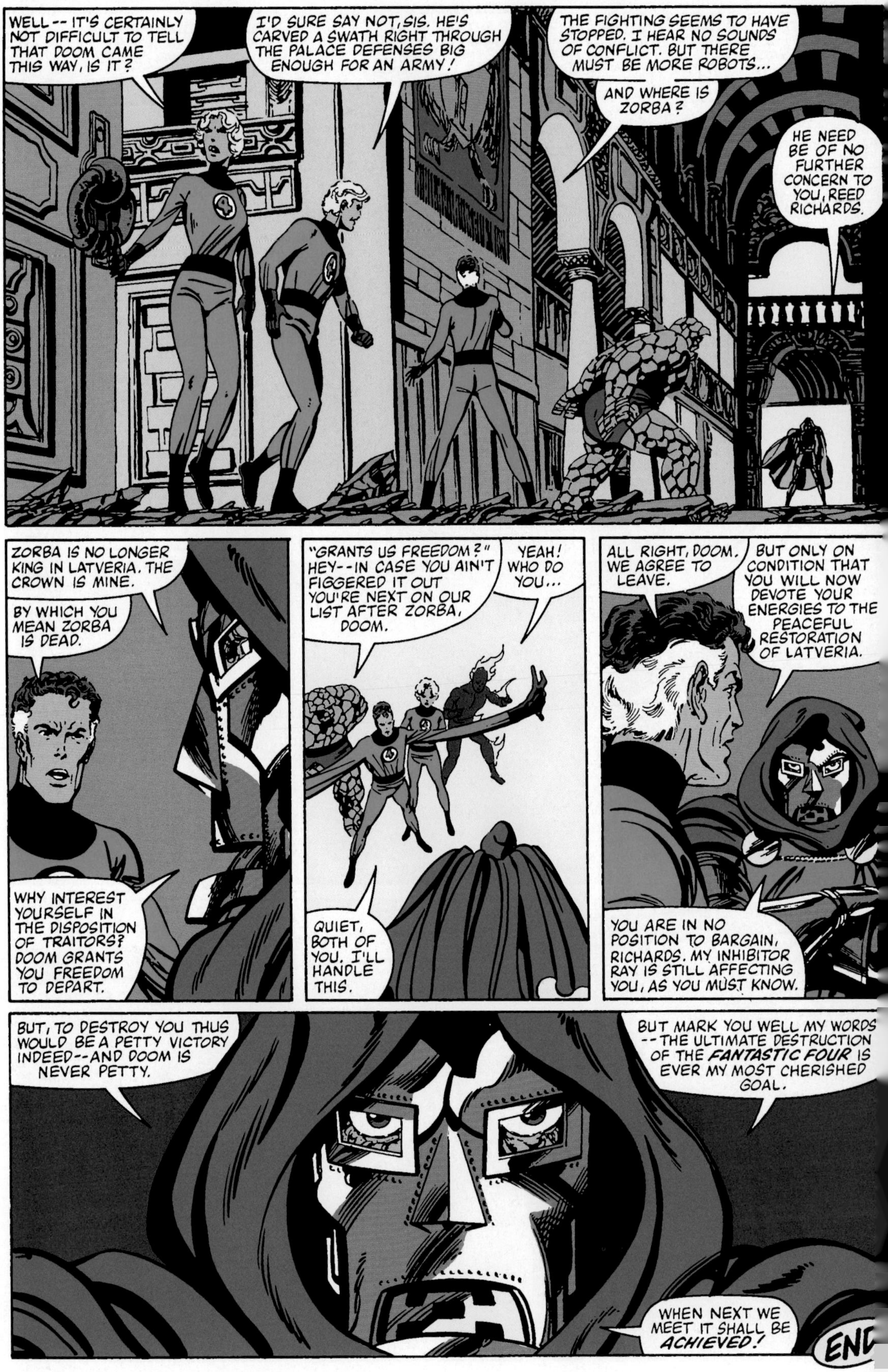
WELL -- IT'S CERTAINLY NOT DIFFICULT TO TELL THAT DOOM CAME THIS WAY, IS IT?
I'D SURE SAY NOT, SIS. HE'S CARVED A SWATH RIGHT THROUGH THE PALACE DEFENSES BIG ENOUGH FOR AN ARMY!
THE FIGHTING SEEMS TO HAVE STOPPED. I HEAR NO SOUNDS OF CONFLICT. BUT THERE MUST BE MORE ROBOTS...
AND WHERE IS ZORBA?
HE NEED BE OF NO FURTHER CONCERN TO YOU, REED RICHARDS.
ZORBA IS NO LONGER KING IN LATVERIA. THE CROWN IS MINE.
BY WHICH YOU MEAN ZORBA IS DEAD.
WHY INTEREST YOURSELF IN THE DISPOSITION OF TRAITORS? DOOM GRANTS YOU FREEDOM TO DEPART.
"GRANTS US FREEDOM?" HEY--IN CASE YOU AIN'T FIGGERED IT OUT YOU'RE NEXT ON OUR LIST AFTER ZORBA, DOOM.
YEAH! WHO DO YOU...
QUIET, BOTH OF YOU. I'LL HANDLE THIS.
ALL RIGHT, DOOM. WE AGREE TO LEAVE.
BUT ONLY ON CONDITION THAT YOU WILL NOW DEVOTE YOUR ENERGIES TO THE PEACEFUL RESTORATION OF LATVERIA.
YOU ARE IN NO POSITION TO BARGAIN, RICHARDS. MY INHIBITOR RAY IS STILL AFFECTING YOU, AS YOU MUST KNOW.
BUT, TO DESTROY YOU THUS WOULD BE A PETTY VICTORY INDEED--AND DOOM IS NEVER PETTY.
BUT MARK YOU WELL MY WORDS --THE ULTIMATE DESTRUCTION OF THE FANTASTIC FOUR IS EVER MY MOST CHERISHED GOAL.
WHEN NEXT WE MEET IT SHALL BE ACHIEVED!
END

fantastic four # 248

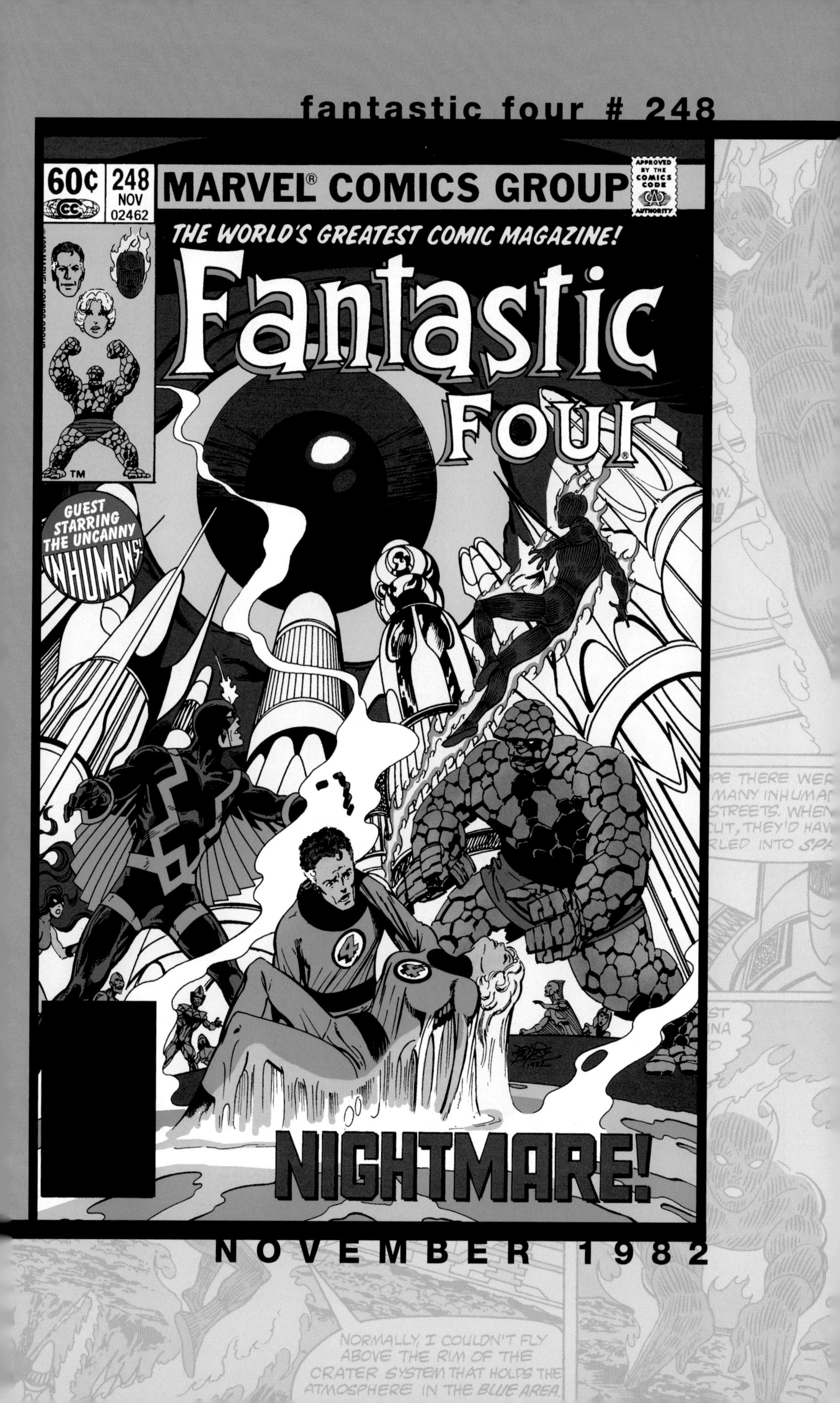
60¢
248
NOV
02462
MARVEL COMICS GROUP
APPROVED BY THE COMICS CODE AUTHORITY
THE WORLD'S GREATEST COMIC MAGAZINE!
Fantastic Four
GUEST STARRING THE UNCANNY INHUMANS!
NIGHTMARE!

NOVEMBER 1982

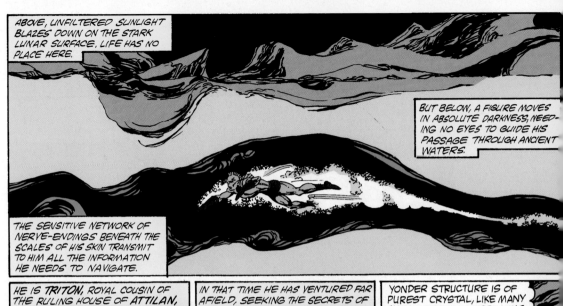

ABOVE, UNFILTERED SUNLIGHT BLAZES DOWN ON THE STARK LUNAR SURFACE, LIFE HAS NO PLACE HERE.

BUT BELOW, A FIGURE MOVES IN ABSOLUTE DARKNESS, NEEDING NO EYES TO GUIDE HIS PASSAGE THROUGH ANCIENT WATERS.

THE SENSITIVE NETWORK OF NERVE-ENDINGS BENEATH THE SCALES OF HIS SKIN TRANSMIT TO HIM ALL THE INFORMATION HE NEEDS TO NAVIGATE.

HE IS *TRITON*, ROYAL COUSIN OF THE RULING HOUSE OF *ATTILAN*, AND HE IS EXPLORING.

IT HAS BEEN MORE THAN A MONTH SINCE HE DISCOVERED THESE SUB-LUNAR CHANNELS...

IN THAT TIME HE HAS VENTURED FAR AFIELD, SEEKING THE SECRETS OF HIS NEW WORLD.

BUT NEVER QUITE SO FAR AS THIS...

BY THE AWE-SOME GENES OF *ARGON!*

YONDER STRUCTURE IS OF PUREST CRYSTAL, LIKE MANY SUCH NATURAL OUTGROWTHS WE HAVE FOUND HERE ON THE *MOON*...

YET... THIS ONE IS SOMEHOW *DIFFERENT!*

I SENSE AN INTELLIGENT HAND IN THE SUBTLE SHAPINGS.

IS IT POSSIBLE I HAVE DISCOVERED SOME UNGUESSED ARTIFACT OF A FORGOTTEN LUNAR CIVILIZATION? OR COULD IT BE...

ARRGH!

THE LIGHT WHICH BURSTS ACROSS THIS TIME-LOST CAVERN IS LIKE NONE EVER SEEN BY HUMAN EYES...

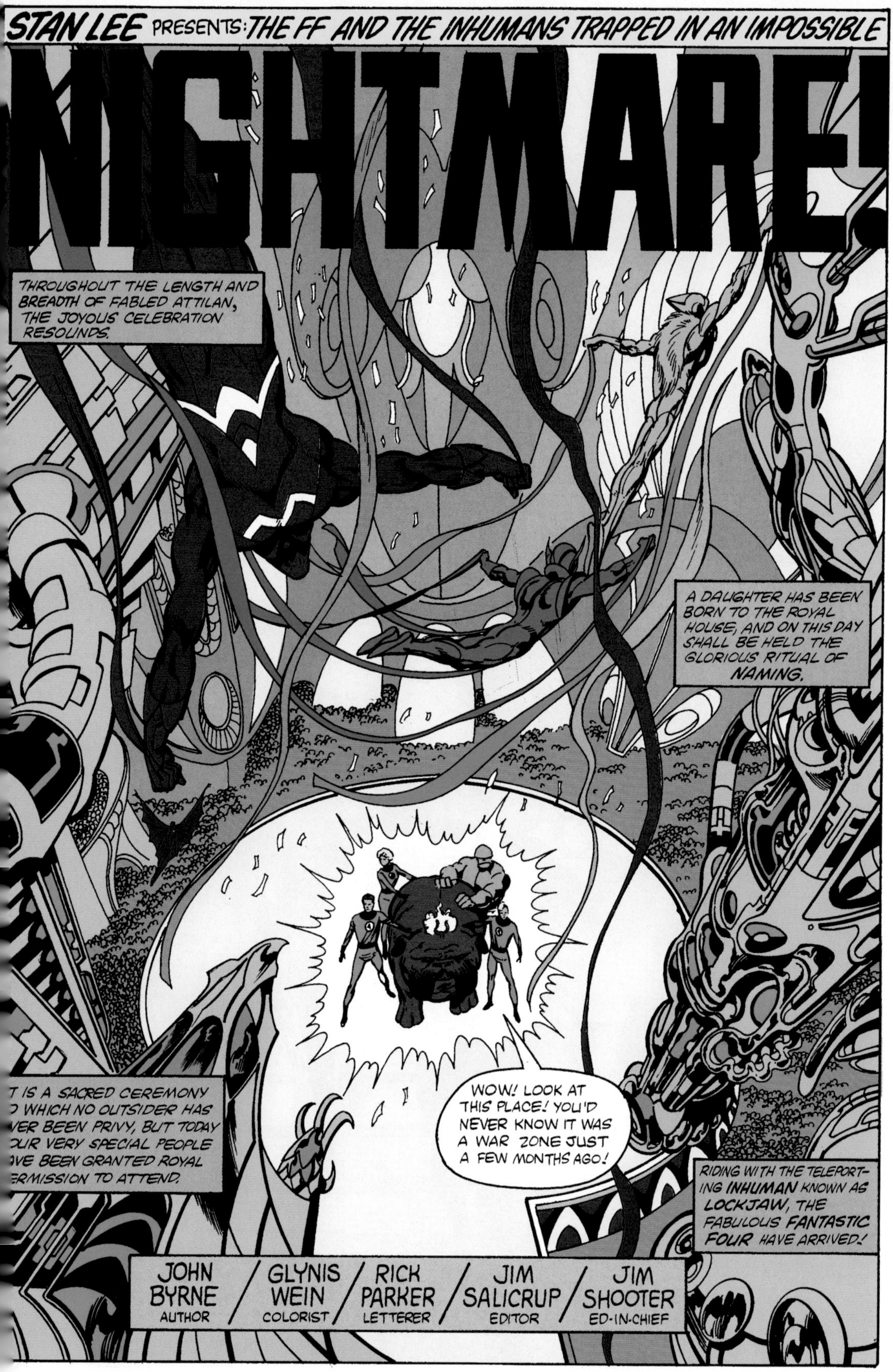
STAN LEE PRESENTS: THE FF AND THE INHUMANS TRAPPED IN AN IMPOSSIBLE
NIGHTMARE!
THROUGHOUT THE LENGTH AND BREADTH OF FABLED ATTILAN, THE JOYOUS CELEBRATION RESOUNDS.
A DAUGHTER HAS BEEN BORN TO THE ROYAL HOUSE, AND ON THIS DAY SHALL BE HELD THE GLORIOUS RITUAL OF NAMING.
T IS A SACRED CEREMONY O WHICH NO OUTSIDER HAS VER BEEN PRIVY, BUT TODAY OUR VERY SPECIAL PEOPLE AVE BEEN GRANTED ROYAL ERMISSION TO ATTEND.
WOW! LOOK AT THIS PLACE! YOU'D NEVER KNOW IT WAS A WAR ZONE JUST A FEW MONTHS AGO!
RIDING WITH THE TELEPORTING INHUMAN KNOWN AS LOCKJAW, THE FABULOUS FANTASTIC FOUR HAVE ARRIVED!
JOHN BYRNE AUTHOR / GLYNIS WEIN COLORIST / RICK PARKER LETTERER / JIM SALICRUP EDITOR / JIM SHOOTER ED-IN-CHIEF

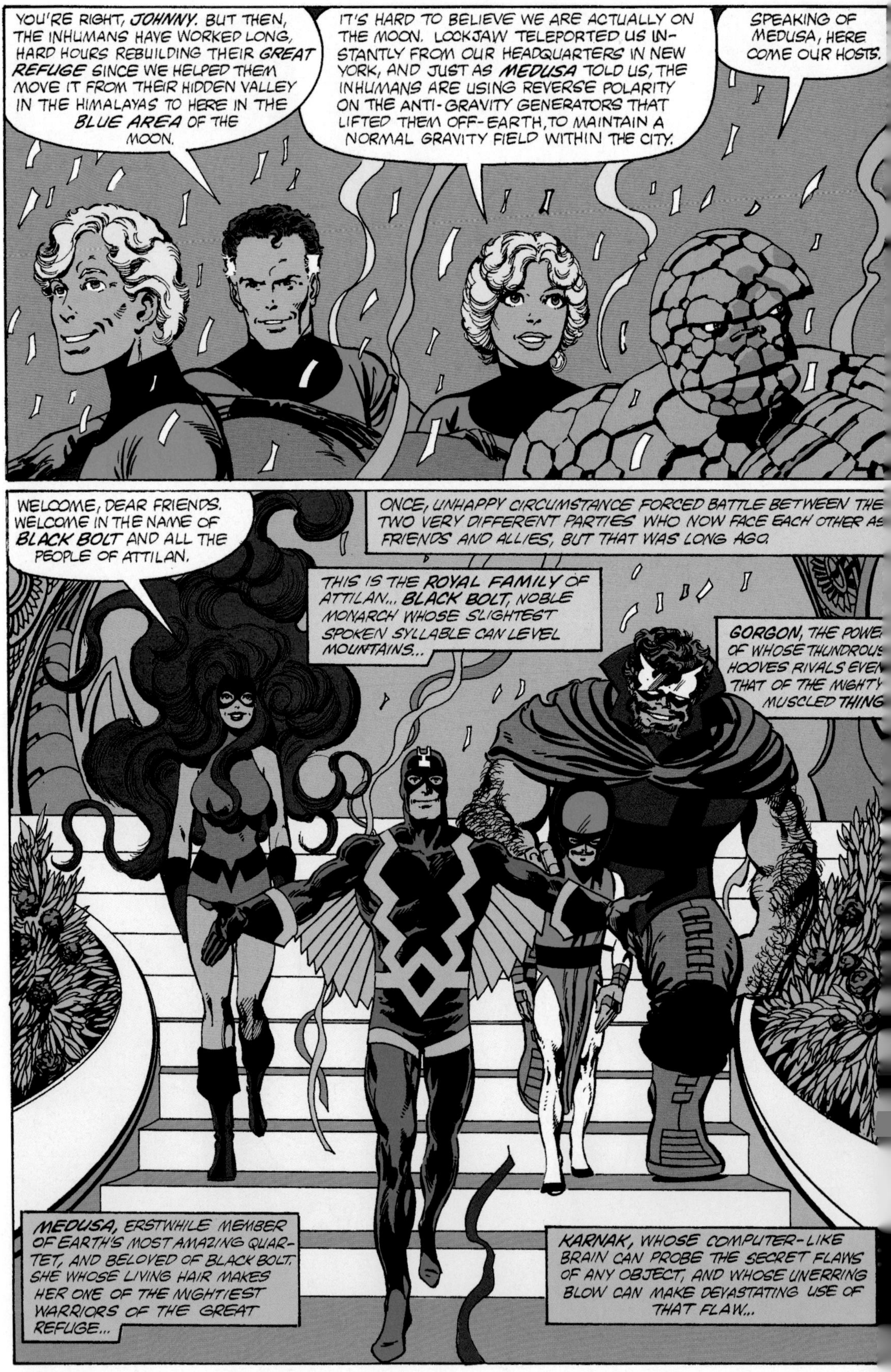

YOU'RE RIGHT, JOHNNY. BUT THEN, THE INHUMANS HAVE WORKED LONG, HARD HOURS REBUILDING THEIR GREAT REFUGE SINCE WE HELPED THEM MOVE IT FROM THEIR HIDDEN VALLEY IN THE HIMALAYAS TO HERE IN THE BLUE AREA OF THE MOON.
IT'S HARD TO BELIEVE WE ARE ACTUALLY ON THE MOON. LOCKJAW TELEPORTED US INSTANTLY FROM OUR HEADQUARTERS IN NEW YORK, AND JUST AS MEDUSA TOLD US, THE INHUMANS ARE USING REVERSE POLARITY ON THE ANTI-GRAVITY GENERATORS THAT LIFTED THEM OFF-EARTH, TO MAINTAIN A NORMAL GRAVITY FIELD WITHIN THE CITY.
SPEAKING OF MEDUSA, HERE COME OUR HOSTS.
WELCOME, DEAR FRIENDS. WELCOME IN THE NAME OF BLACK BOLT AND ALL THE PEOPLE OF ATTILAN.
ONCE, UNHAPPY CIRCUMSTANCE FORCED BATTLE BETWEEN THE TWO VERY DIFFERENT PARTIES WHO NOW FACE EACH OTHER AS FRIENDS AND ALLIES, BUT THAT WAS LONG AGO.
THIS IS THE ROYAL FAMILY OF ATTILAN... BLACK BOLT, NOBLE MONARCH WHOSE SLIGHTEST SPOKEN SYLLABLE CAN LEVEL MOUNTAINS...
GORGON, THE POWE OF WHOSE THUNDROUS HOOVES RIVALS EVEN THAT OF THE MIGHTY MUSCLED THING
MEDUSA, ERSTWHILE MEMBER OF EARTH'S MOST AMAZING QUARTET, AND BELOVED OF BLACK BOLT. SHE WHOSE LIVING HAIR MAKES HER ONE OF THE MIGHTIEST WARRIORS OF THE GREAT REFUGE...
KARNAK, WHOSE COMPUTER-LIKE BRAIN CAN PROBE THE SECRET FLAWS OF ANY OBJECT, AND WHOSE UNERRING BLOW CAN MAKE DEVASTATING USE OF THAT FLAW...

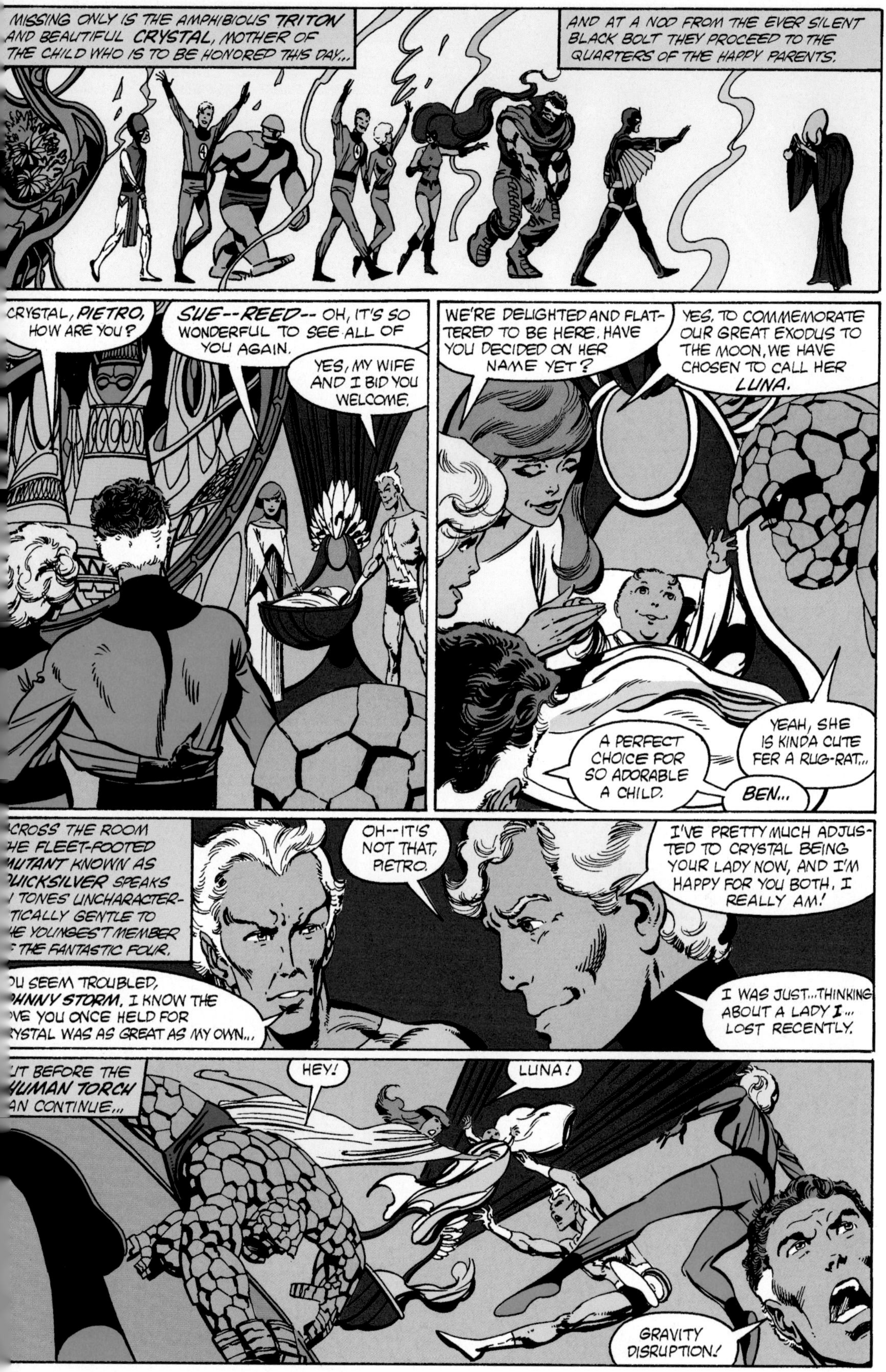

MISSING ONLY IS THE AMPHIBIOUS TRITON AND BEAUTIFUL CRYSTAL, MOTHER OF THE CHILD WHO IS TO BE HONORED THIS DAY...
AND AT A NOD FROM THE EVER SILENT BLACK BOLT THEY PROCEED TO THE QUARTERS OF THE HAPPY PARENTS.
CRYSTAL, PIETRO, HOW ARE YOU?
SUE--REED-- OH, IT'S SO WONDERFUL TO SEE ALL OF YOU AGAIN.
YES, MY WIFE AND I BID YOU WELCOME.
WE'RE DELIGHTED AND FLATTERED TO BE HERE. HAVE YOU DECIDED ON HER NAME YET?
YES, TO COMMEMORATE OUR GREAT EXODUS TO THE MOON, WE HAVE CHOSEN TO CALL HER LUNA.
A PERFECT CHOICE FOR SO ADORABLE A CHILD.
YEAH, SHE IS KINDA CUTE FER A RUG-RAT...
BEN...
CROSS THE ROOM HE FLEET-FOOTED MUTANT KNOWN AS UICKSILVER SPEAKS TONES UNCHARACTERISTICALLY GENTLE TO HE YOUNGEST MEMBER F THE FANTASTIC FOUR.
OH--IT'S NOT THAT, PIETRO.
I'VE PRETTY MUCH ADJUSTED TO CRYSTAL BEING YOUR LADY NOW, AND I'M HAPPY FOR YOU BOTH. I REALLY AM!
OU SEEM TROUBLED, OHNNY STORM. I KNOW THE OVE YOU ONCE HELD FOR RYSTAL WAS AS GREAT AS MY OWN...
I WAS JUST...THINKING ABOUT A LADY I... LOST RECENTLY.
UT BEFORE THE HUMAN TORCH AN CONTINUE...
HEY!
LUNA!
GRAVITY DISRUPTION!

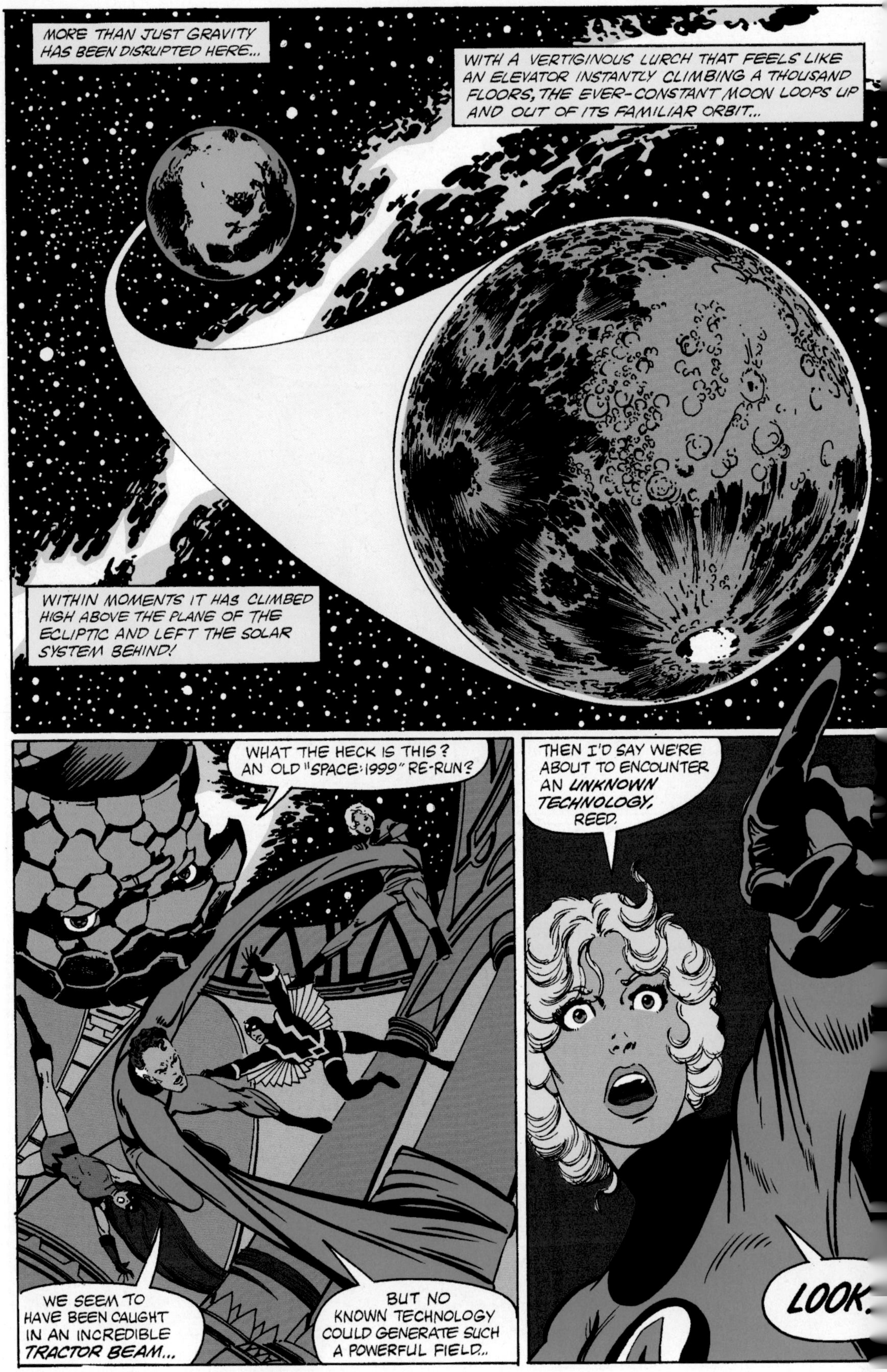

MORE THAN JUST GRAVITY HAS BEEN DISRUPTED HERE...
WITH A VERTIGINOUS LURCH THAT FEELS LIKE AN ELEVATOR INSTANTLY CLIMBING A THOUSAND FLOORS, THE EVER-CONSTANT MOON LOOPS UP AND OUT OF ITS FAMILIAR ORBIT...
WITHIN MOMENTS IT HAS CLIMBED HIGH ABOVE THE PLANE OF THE ECLIPTIC AND LEFT THE SOLAR SYSTEM BEHIND!
WHAT THE HECK IS THIS? AN OLD "SPACE:1999" RE-RUN?
WE SEEM TO HAVE BEEN CAUGHT IN AN INCREDIBLE TRACTOR BEAM...
BUT NO KNOWN TECHNOLOGY COULD GENERATE SUCH A POWERFUL FIELD...
THEN I'D SAY WE'RE ABOUT TO ENCOUNTER AN UNKNOWN TECHNOLOGY, REED.
LOOK!

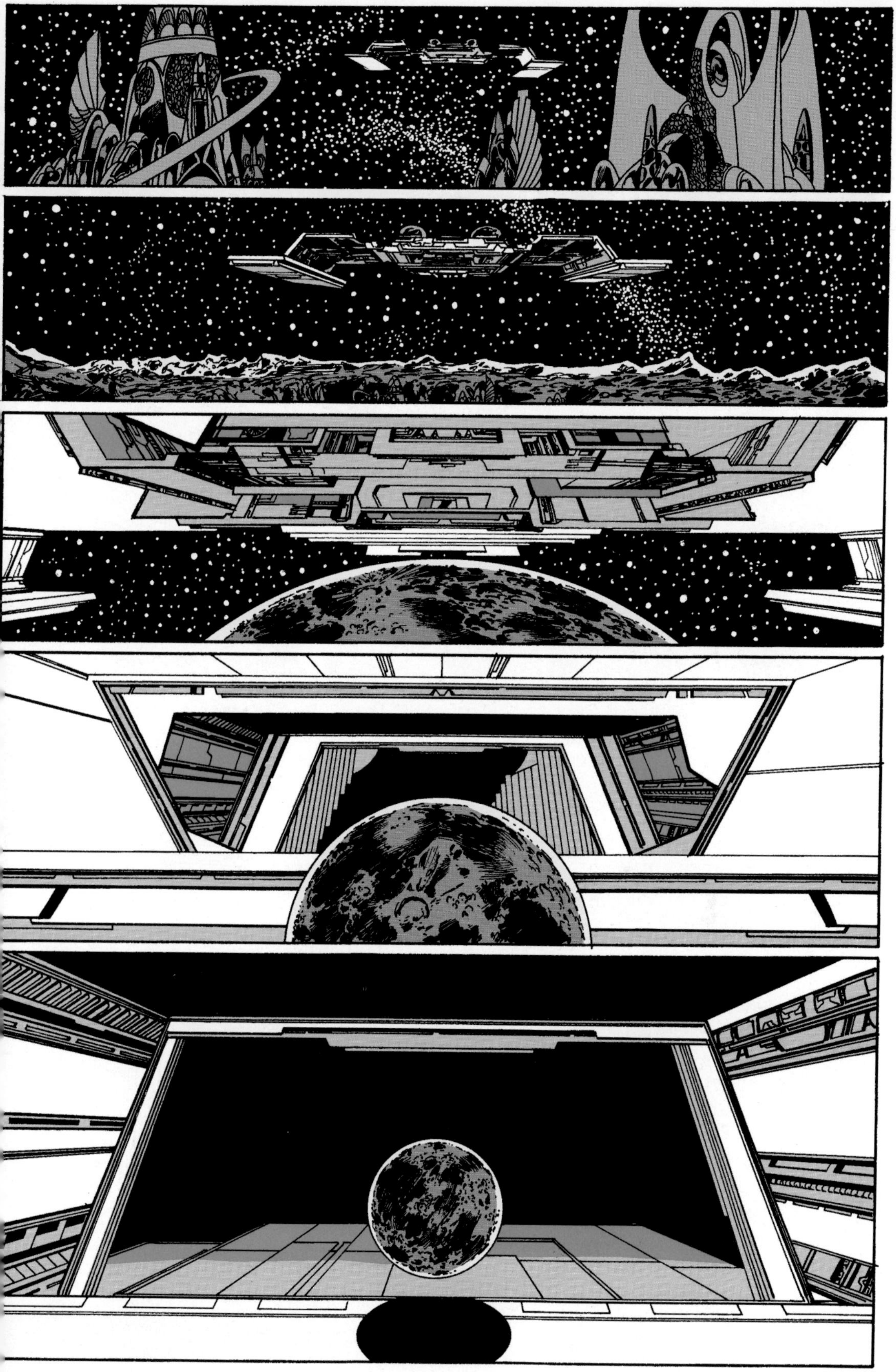

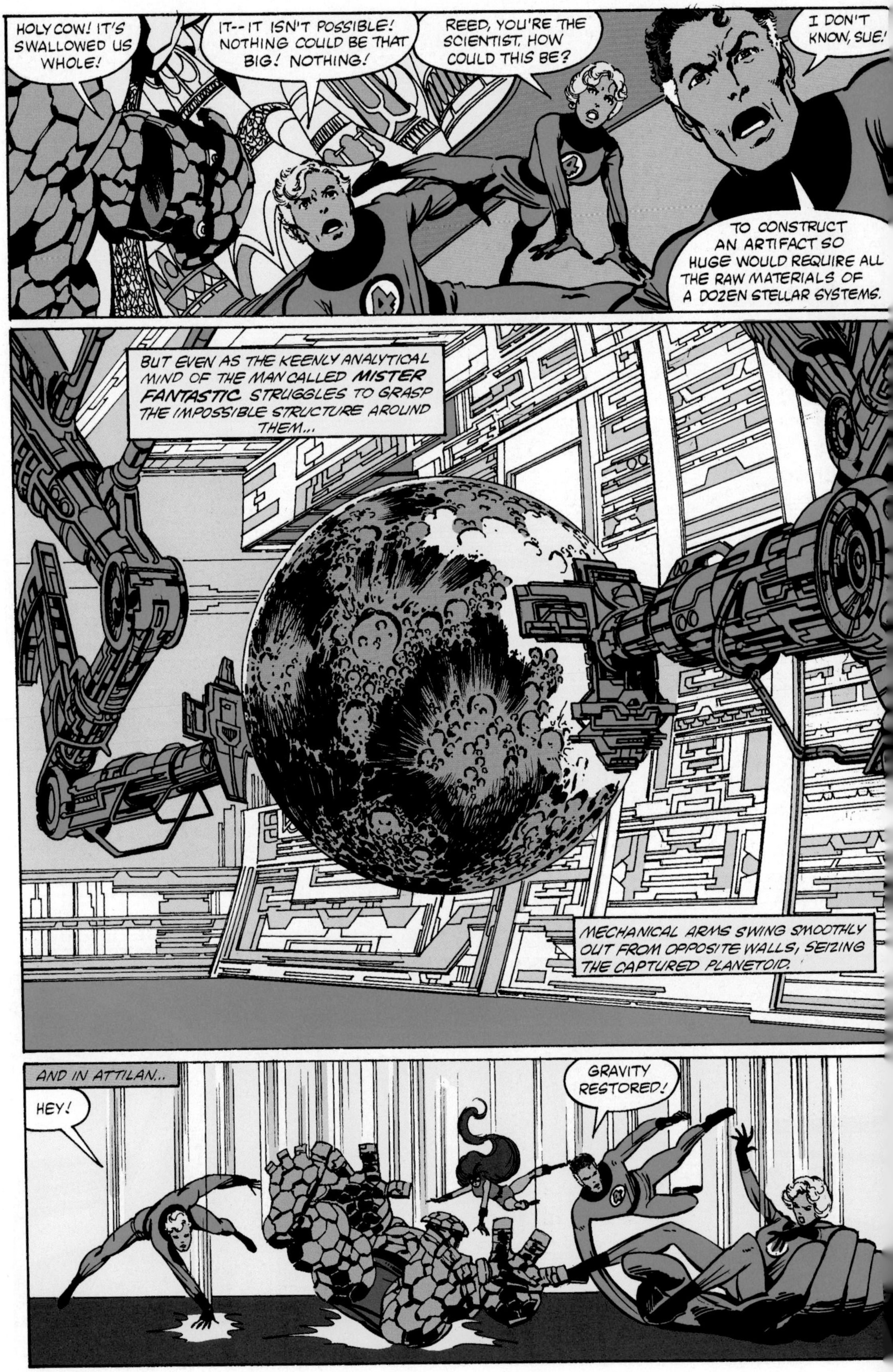
HOLY COW! IT'S SWALLOWED US WHOLE!
IT--IT ISN'T POSSIBLE! NOTHING COULD BE THAT BIG! NOTHING!
REED, YOU'RE THE SCIENTIST. HOW COULD THIS BE?
I DON'T KNOW, SUE!
TO CONSTRUCT AN ARTIFACT SO HUGE WOULD REQUIRE ALL THE RAW MATERIALS OF A DOZEN STELLAR SYSTEMS.
BUT EVEN AS THE KEENLY ANALYTICAL MIND OF THE MAN CALLED MISTER FANTASTIC STRUGGLES TO GRASP THE IMPOSSIBLE STRUCTURE AROUND THEM...
MECHANICAL ARMS SWING SMOOTHLY OUT FROM OPPOSITE WALLS, SEIZING THE CAPTURED PLANETOID.
AND IN ATTILAN...
HEY!
GRAVITY RESTORED!

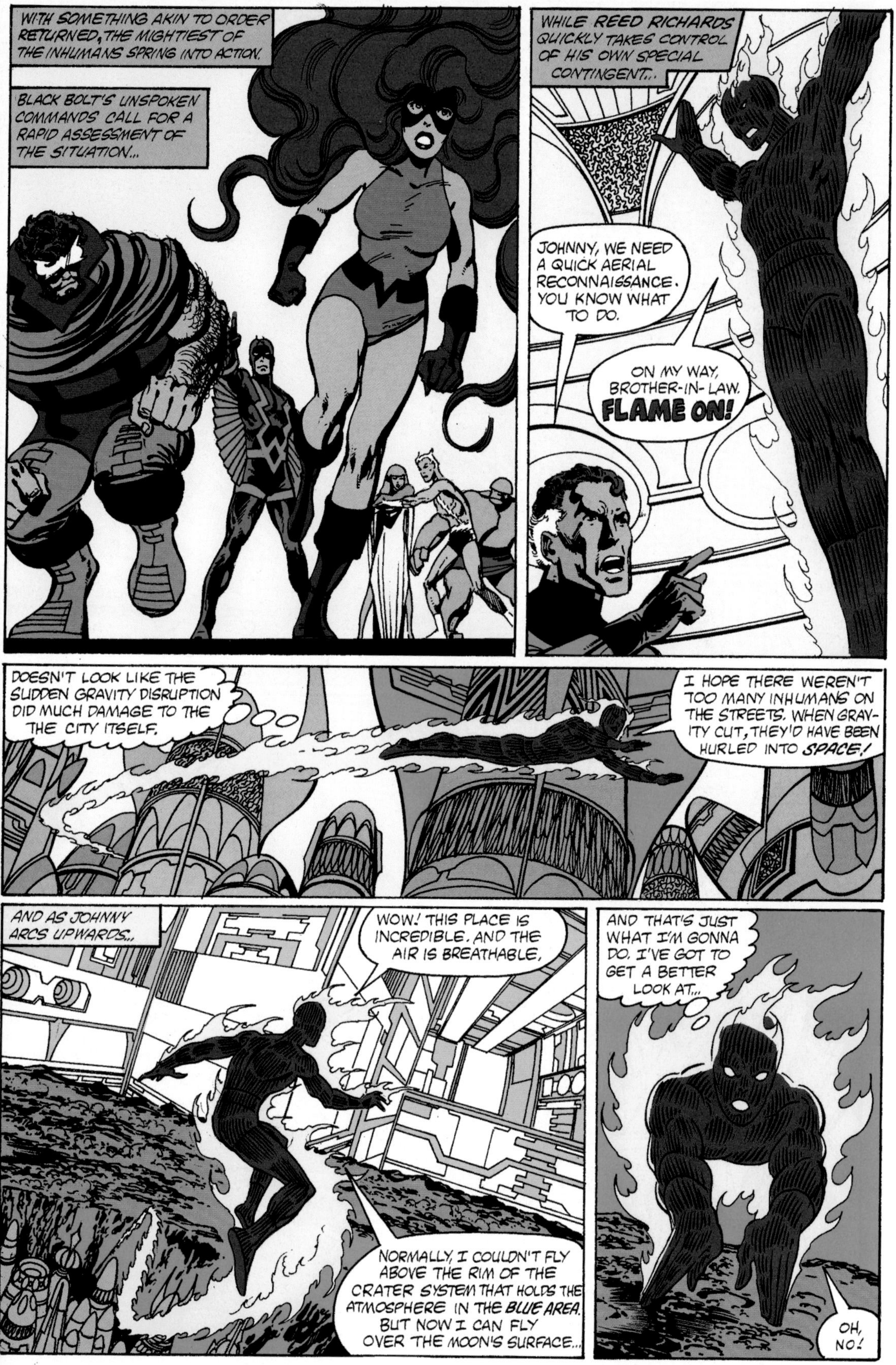
WITH SOMETHING AKIN TO ORDER RETURNED, THE MIGHTIEST OF THE INHUMANS SPRING INTO ACTION.
BLACK BOLT'S UNSPOKEN COMMANDS CALL FOR A RAPID ASSESSMENT OF THE SITUATION...
WHILE REED RICHARDS QUICKLY TAKES CONTROL OF HIS OWN SPECIAL CONTINGENT...
JOHNNY, WE NEED A QUICK AERIAL RECONNAISSANCE. YOU KNOW WHAT TO DO.
ON MY WAY, BROTHER-IN-LAW. FLAME ON!
DOESN'T LOOK LIKE THE SUDDEN GRAVITY DISRUPTION DID MUCH DAMAGE TO THE THE CITY ITSELF.
I HOPE THERE WEREN'T TOO MANY INHUMANS ON THE STREETS. WHEN GRAVITY CUT, THEY'D HAVE BEEN HURLED INTO SPACE!
AND AS JOHNNY ARCS UPWARDS...
WOW! THIS PLACE IS INCREDIBLE. AND THE AIR IS BREATHABLE.
NORMALLY, I COULDN'T FLY ABOVE THE RIM OF THE CRATER SYSTEM THAT HOLDS THE ATMOSPHERE IN THE BLUE AREA. BUT NOW I CAN FLY OVER THE MOON'S SURFACE...
AND THAT'S JUST WHAT I'M GONNA DO. I'VE GOT TO GET A BETTER LOOK AT...
OH, NO!

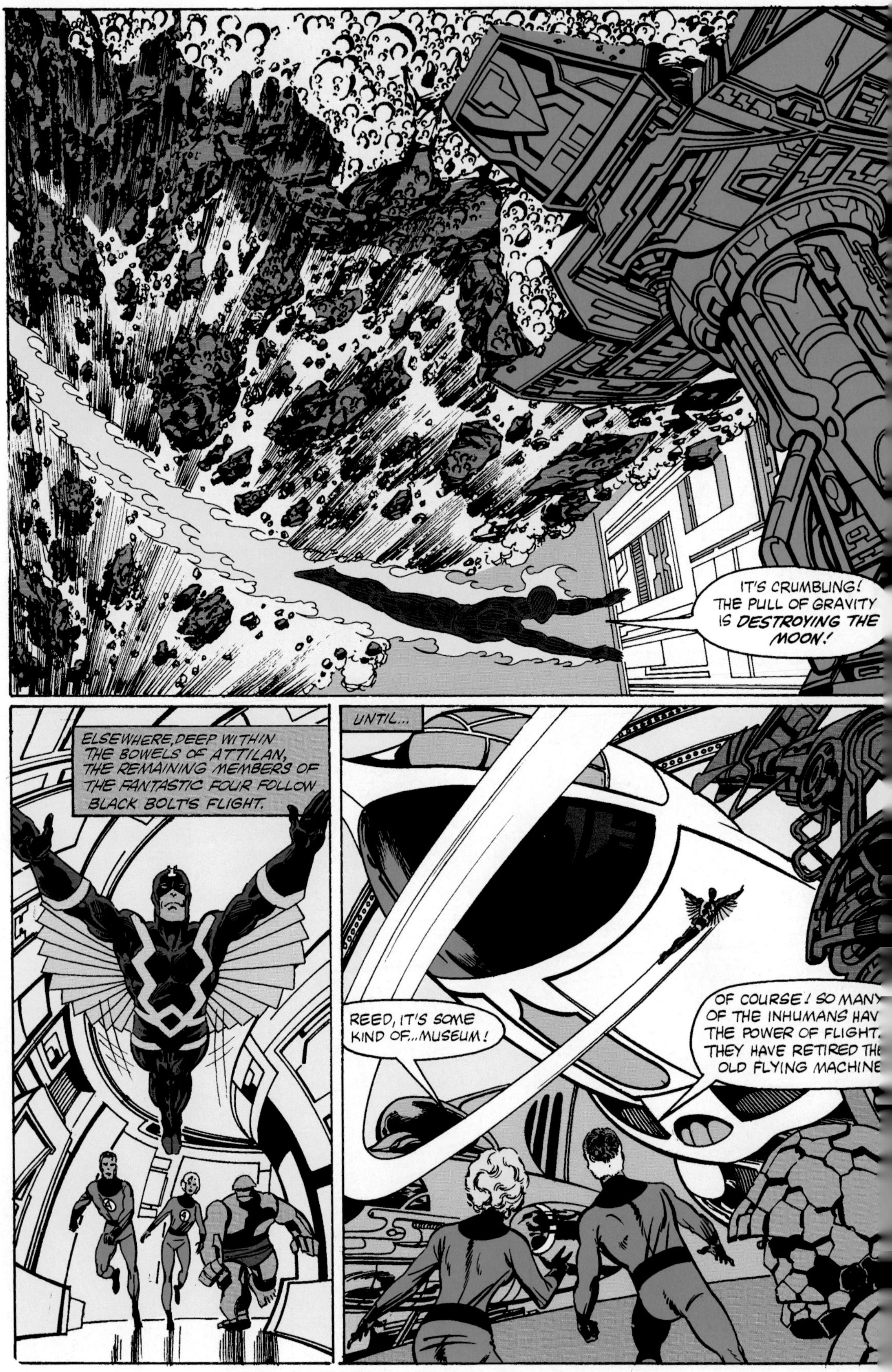
IT'S CRUMBLING! THE PULL OF GRAVITY IS DESTROYING THE MOON!
ELSEWHERE, DEEP WITHIN THE BOWELS OF ATTILAN, THE REMAINING MEMBERS OF THE FANTASTIC FOUR FOLLOW BLACK BOLT'S FLIGHT.
UNTIL...
REED, IT'S SOME KIND OF... MUSEUM!
OF COURSE! SO MANY OF THE INHUMANS HAV THE POWER OF FLIGHT. THEY HAVE RETIRED TH OLD FLYING MACHINE

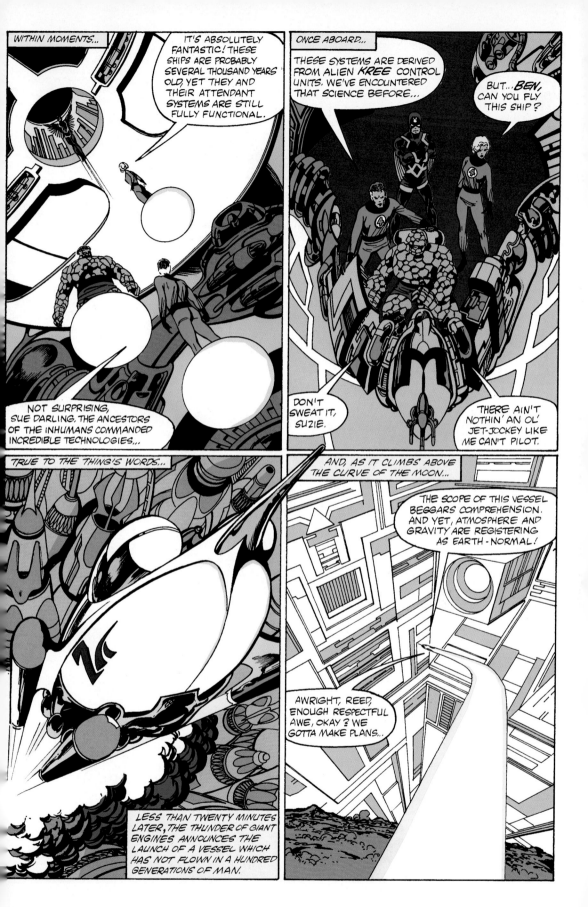

WITHIN MOMENTS...

IT'S ABSOLUTELY FANTASTIC! THESE SHIPS ARE PROBABLY SEVERAL THOUSAND YEARS OLD, YET THEY AND THEIR ATTENDANT SYSTEMS ARE STILL FULLY FUNCTIONAL.

NOT SURPRISING, SUE DARLING. THE ANCESTORS OF THE INHUMANS COMMANDED INCREDIBLE TECHNOLOGIES...

ONCE ABOARD...

THESE SYSTEMS ARE DERIVED FROM ALIEN KREE CONTROL UNITS. WE'VE ENCOUNTERED THAT SCIENCE BEFORE...

BUT... BEN, CAN YOU FLY THIS SHIP?

DON'T SWEAT IT, SUZIE.

THERE AIN'T NOTHIN' AN OL' JET-JOCKEY LIKE ME CAN'T PILOT.

TRUE TO THE THING'S WORDS...

LESS THAN TWENTY MINUTES LATER, THE THUNDER OF GIANT ENGINES ANNOUNCES THE LAUNCH OF A VESSEL WHICH HAS NOT FLOWN IN A HUNDRED GENERATIONS OF MAN.

AND, AS IT CLIMBS ABOVE THE CURVE OF THE MOON...

THE SCOPE OF THIS VESSEL BEGGARS COMPREHENSION. AND YET, ATMOSPHERE AND GRAVITY ARE REGISTERING AS EARTH-NORMAL!

AWRIGHT, REED, ENOUGH RESPECTFUL AWE, OKAY? WE GOTTA MAKE PLANS...

173

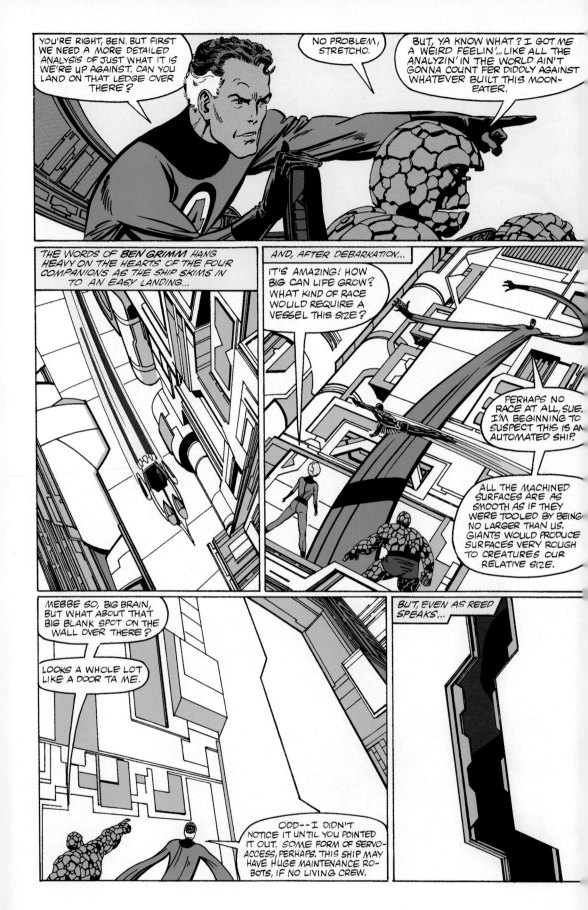

YOU'RE RIGHT, BEN, BUT FIRST WE NEED A MORE DETAILED ANALYSIS OF JUST WHAT IT IS WE'RE UP AGAINST. CAN YOU LAND ON THAT LEDGE OVER THERE?

NO PROBLEM, STRETCHO.

BUT, YA KNOW WHAT? I GOT ME A WEIRD FEELIN'...LIKE ALL THE ANALYZIN' IN THE WORLD AIN'T GONNA COUNT FER DIDDLY AGAINST WHATEVER BUILT THIS MOON-EATER.

THE WORDS OF *BEN GRIMM* HANG HEAVY ON THE HEARTS OF THE FOUR COMPANIONS AS THE SHIP SKIMS IN TO AN EASY LANDING...

AND, AFTER DEBARKATION...

IT'S AMAZING! HOW BIG CAN LIFE GROW? WHAT KIND OF RACE WOULD REQUIRE A VESSEL THIS SIZE?

PERHAPS NO RACE AT ALL, SUE. I'M BEGINNING TO SUSPECT THIS IS AN AUTOMATED SHIP.

ALL THE MACHINED SURFACES ARE AS SMOOTH AS IF THEY WERE TOOLED BY BEING NO LARGER THAN US. GIANTS WOULD PRODUCE SURFACES VERY ROUGH TO CREATURES OUR RELATIVE SIZE.

MEBBE SO, BIG BRAIN, BUT WHAT ABOUT THAT BIG BLANK SPOT ON THE WALL OVER THERE?

LOOKS A WHOLE LOT LIKE A DOOR TA ME.

ODD-- I DIDN'T NOTICE IT UNTIL YOU POINTED IT OUT. SOME FORM OF SERVO-ACCESS, PERHAPS. THIS SHIP MAY HAVE HUGE MAINTENANCE ROBOTS, IF NO LIVING CREW.

BUT, EVEN AS REED SPEAKS...

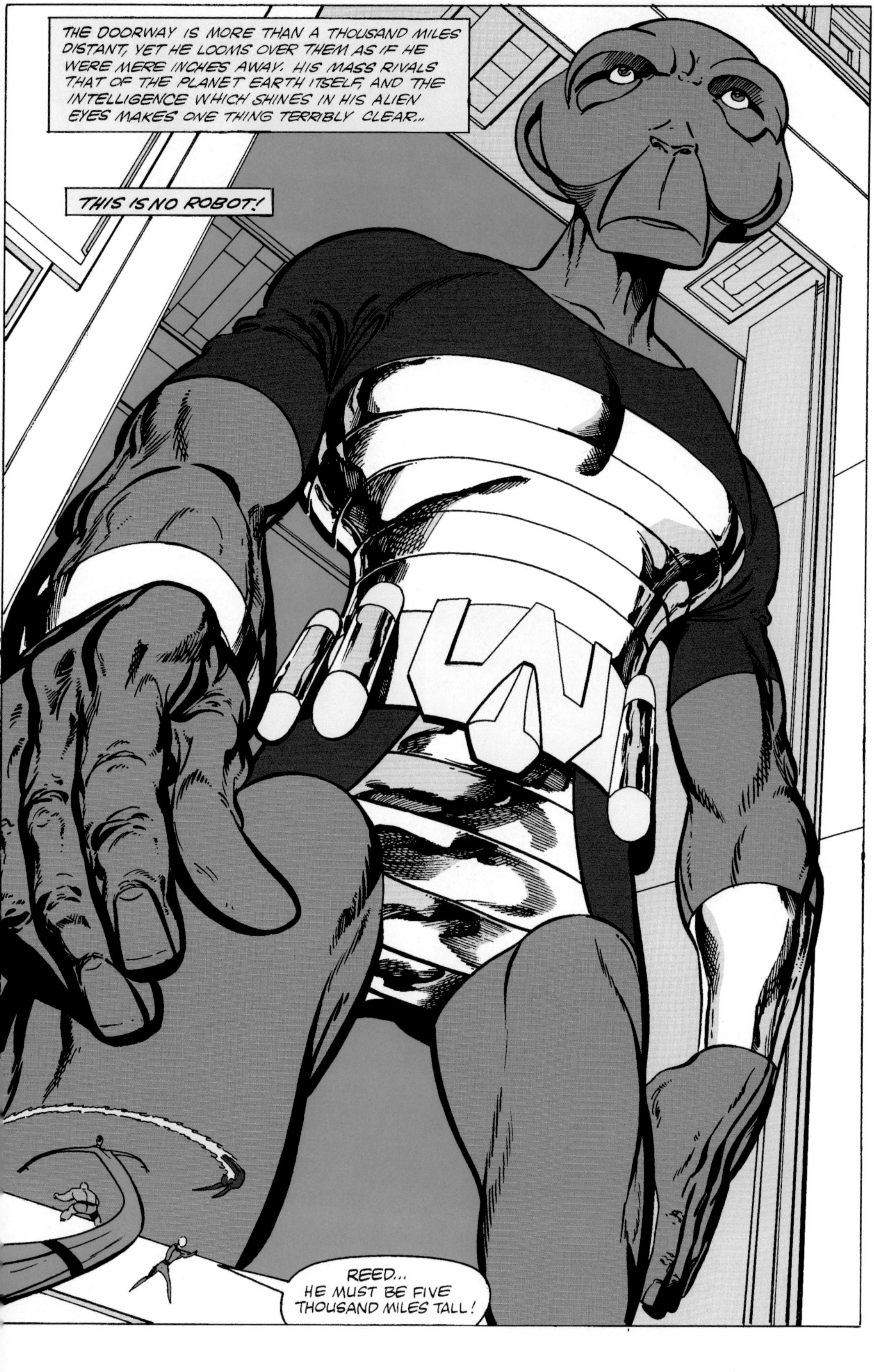
THE DOORWAY IS MORE THAN A THOUSAND MILES DISTANT, YET HE LOOMS OVER THEM AS IF HE WERE MERE INCHES AWAY. HIS MASS RIVALS THAT OF THE PLANET EARTH ITSELF, AND THE INTELLIGENCE WHICH SHINES IN HIS ALIEN EYES MAKES ONE THING TERRIBLY CLEAR...
THIS IS NO ROBOT!
REED... HE MUST BE FIVE THOUSAND MILES TALL!

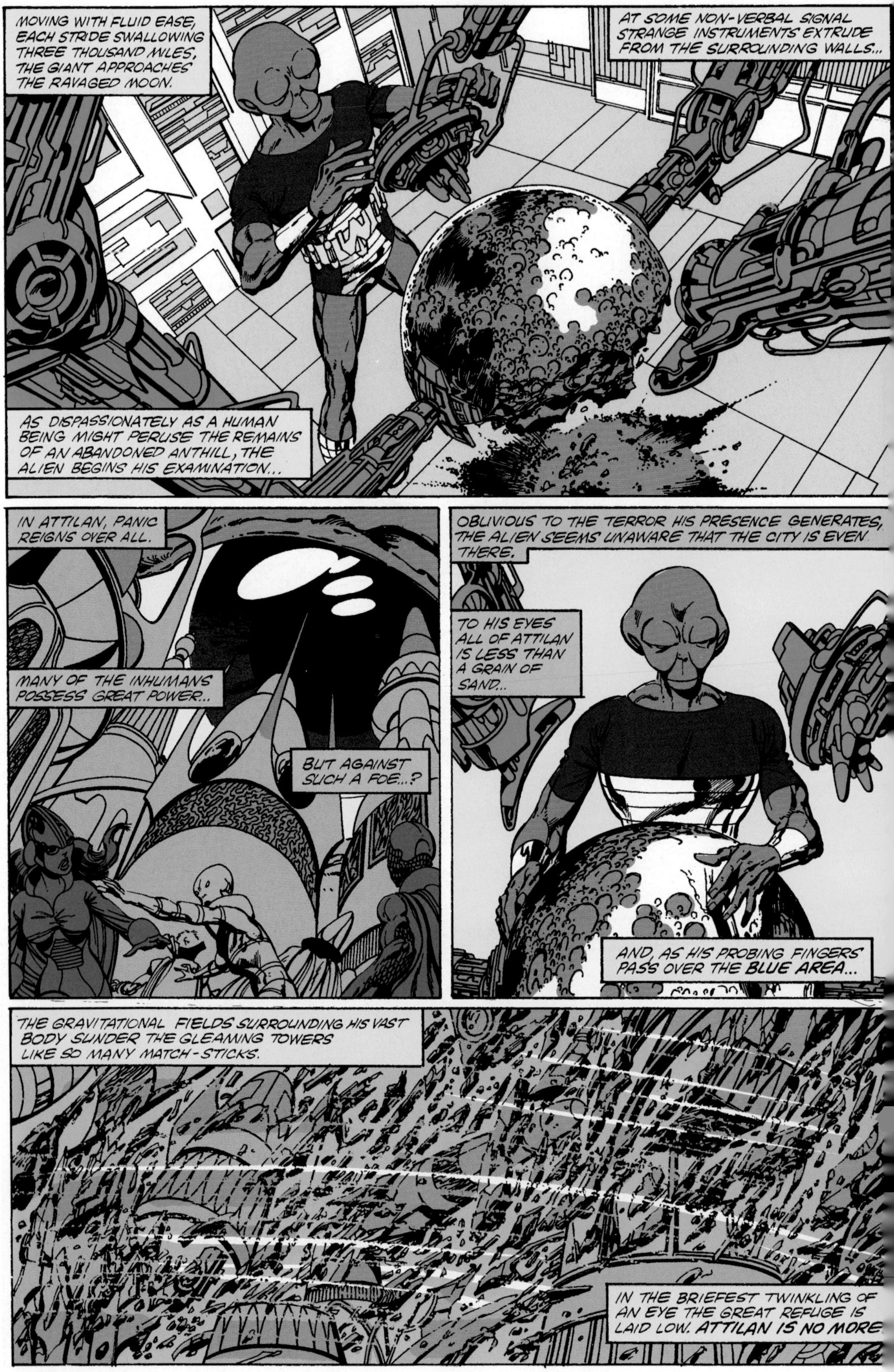
MOVING WITH FLUID EASE, EACH STRIDE SWALLOWING THREE THOUSAND MILES, THE GIANT APPROACHES THE RAVAGED MOON.
AT SOME NON-VERBAL SIGNAL STRANGE INSTRUMENTS EXTRUDE FROM THE SURROUNDING WALLS...
AS DISPASSIONATELY AS A HUMAN BEING MIGHT PERUSE THE REMAINS OF AN ABANDONED ANTHILL, THE ALIEN BEGINS HIS EXAMINATION...
IN ATTILAN, PANIC REIGNS OVER ALL.
MANY OF THE INHUMANS POSSESS GREAT POWER...
BUT AGAINST SUCH A FOE...?
OBLIVIOUS TO THE TERROR HIS PRESENCE GENERATES, THE ALIEN SEEMS UNAWARE THAT THE CITY IS EVEN THERE.
TO HIS EYES ALL OF ATTILAN IS LESS THAN A GRAIN OF SAND...
AND, AS HIS PROBING FINGERS PASS OVER THE BLUE AREA...
THE GRAVITATIONAL FIELDS SURROUNDING HIS VAST BODY SUNDER THE GLEAMING TOWERS LIKE SO MANY MATCH-STICKS.
IN THE BRIEFEST TWINKLING OF AN EYE THE GREAT REFUGE IS LAID LOW. ATTILAN IS NO MORE

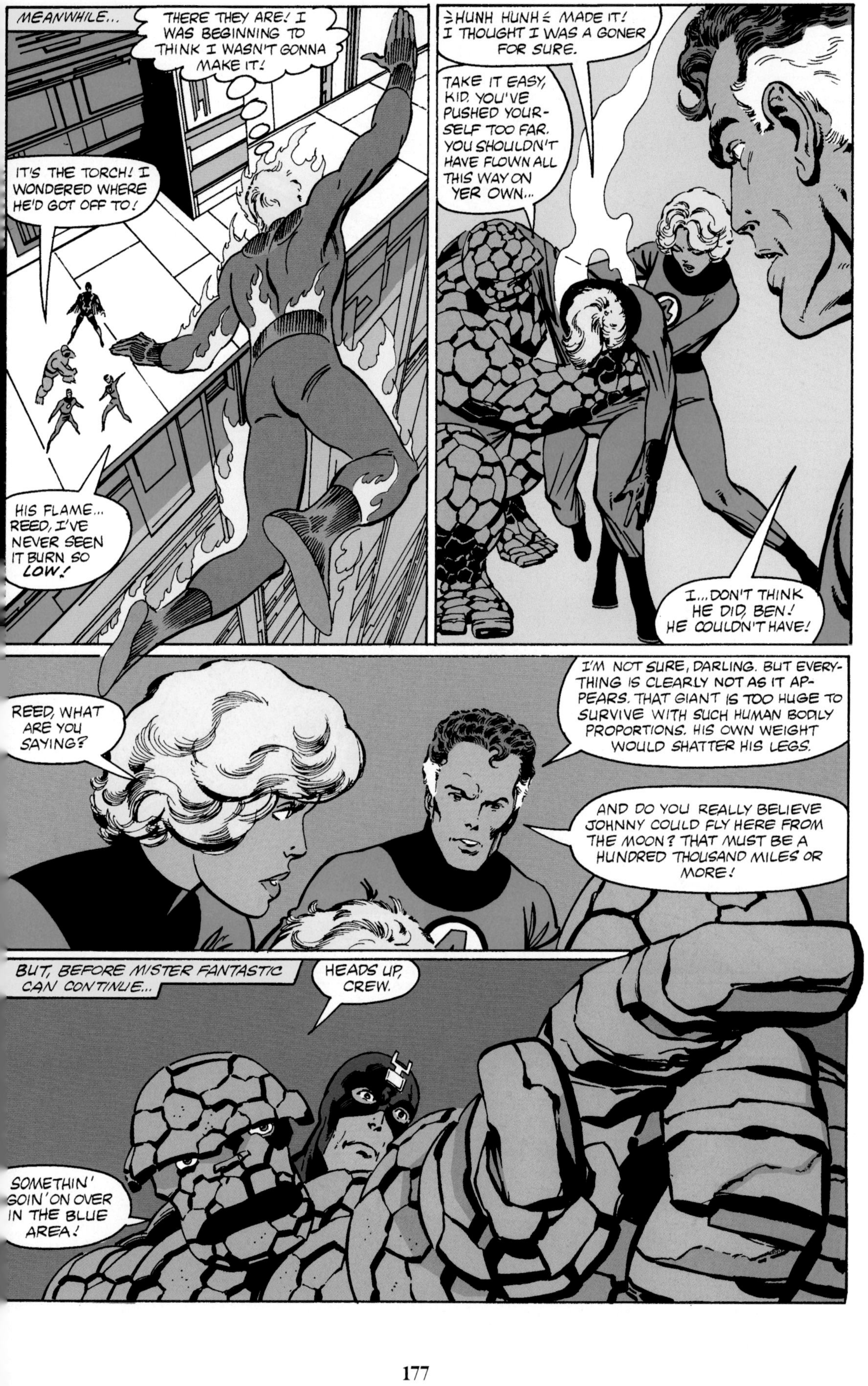
MEANWHILE...
THERE THEY ARE! I WAS BEGINNING TO THINK I WASN'T GONNA MAKE IT!
IT'S THE TORCH! I WONDERED WHERE HE'D GOT OFF TO!
HIS FLAME... REED, I'VE NEVER SEEN IT BURN SO LOW!
≥HUNH HUNH≤ MADE IT! I THOUGHT I WAS A GONER FOR SURE.
TAKE IT EASY, KID. YOU'VE PUSHED YOURSELF TOO FAR. YOU SHOULDN'T HAVE FLOWN ALL THIS WAY ON YER OWN...
I... DON'T THINK HE DID, BEN! HE COULDN'T HAVE!
REED, WHAT ARE YOU SAYING?
I'M NOT SURE, DARLING. BUT EVERYTHING IS CLEARLY NOT AS IT APPEARS. THAT GIANT IS TOO HUGE TO SURVIVE WITH SUCH HUMAN BODILY PROPORTIONS. HIS OWN WEIGHT WOULD SHATTER HIS LEGS.
AND DO YOU REALLY BELIEVE JOHNNY COULD FLY HERE FROM THE MOON? THAT MUST BE A HUNDRED THOUSAND MILES OR MORE!
BUT, BEFORE MISTER FANTASTIC CAN CONTINUE...
HEADS UP, CREW.
SOMETHIN' GOIN' ON OVER IN THE BLUE AREA!

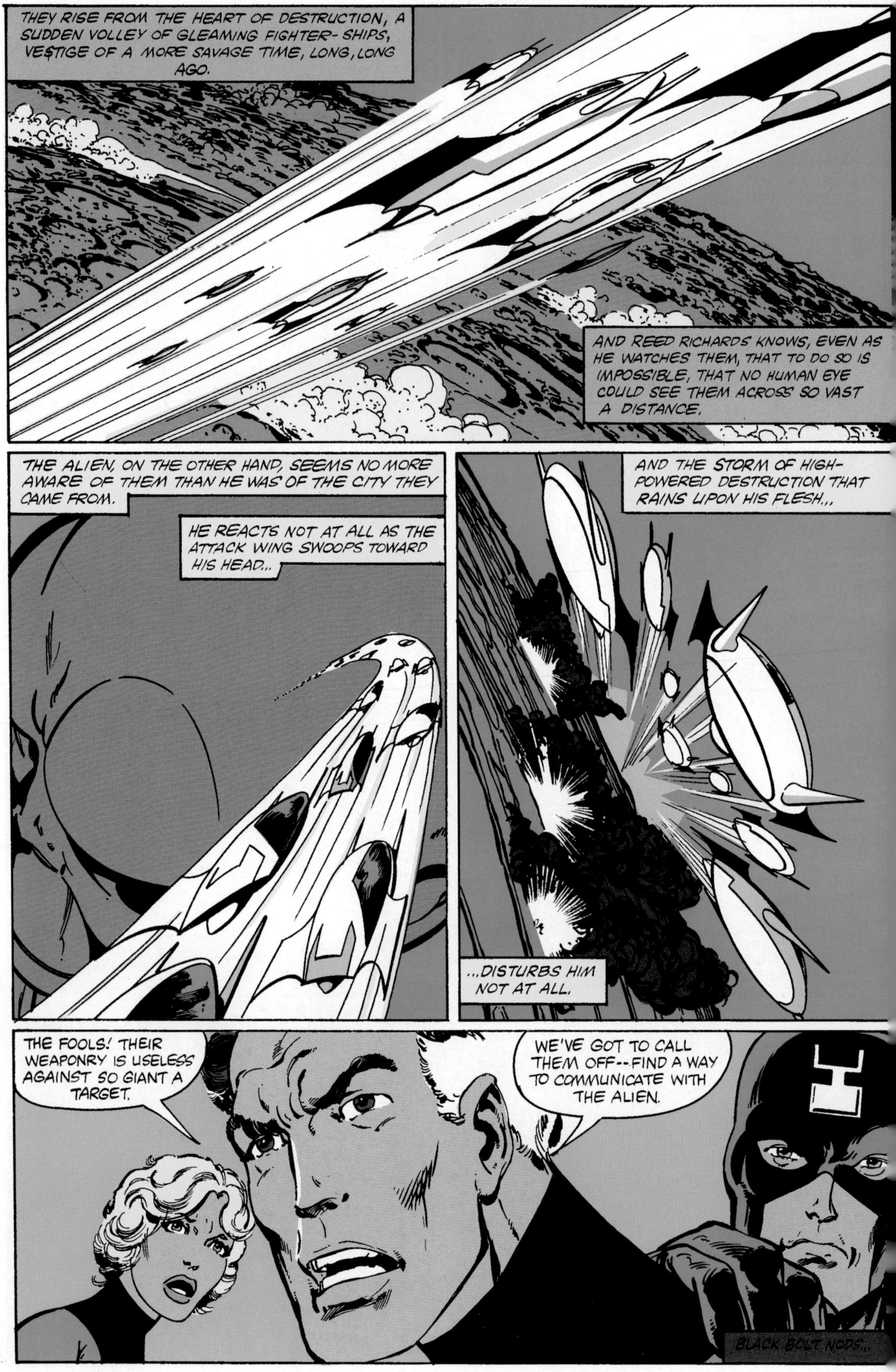
THEY RISE FROM THE HEART OF DESTRUCTION, A SUDDEN VOLLEY OF GLEAMING FIGHTER-SHIPS, VE$TIGE OF A MORE SAVAGE TIME, LONG, LONG AGO.
AND REED RICHARDS KNOWS, EVEN AS HE WATCHES THEM, THAT TO DO SO IS IMPOSSIBLE, THAT NO HUMAN EYE COULD SEE THEM ACROSS SO VAST A DISTANCE.
THE ALIEN, ON THE OTHER HAND, SEEMS NO MORE AWARE OF THEM THAN HE WAS OF THE CITY THEY CAME FROM.
HE REACTS NOT AT ALL AS THE ATTACK WING SWOOPS TOWARD HIS HEAD...
AND THE STORM OF HIGH-POWERED DESTRUCTION THAT RAINS UPON HIS FLESH...
...DISTURBS HIM NOT AT ALL.
THE FOOLS! THEIR WEAPONRY IS USELESS AGAINST SO GIANT A TARGET.
WE'VE GOT TO CALL THEM OFF--FIND A WAY TO COMMUNICATE WITH THE ALIEN.
BLACK BOLT NODS...

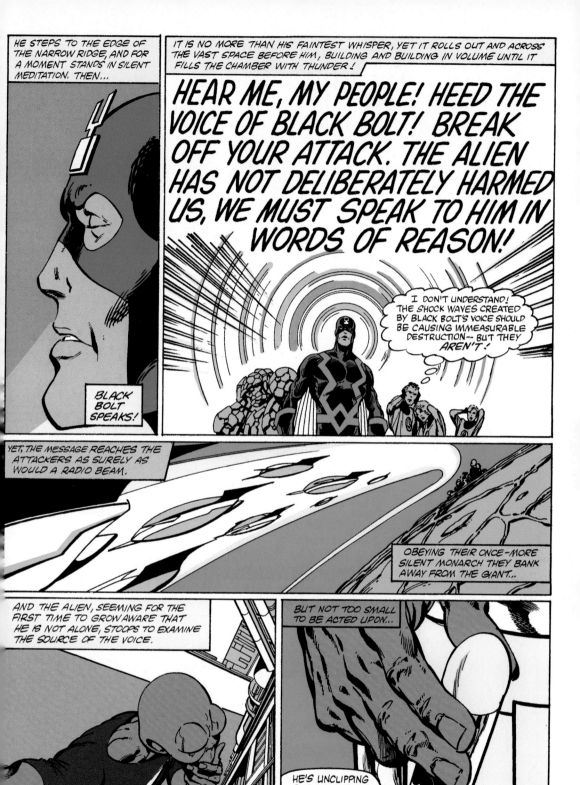

HE STEPS TO THE EDGE OF THE NARROW RIDGE, AND FOR A MOMENT STANDS IN SILENT MEDITATION. THEN...

IT IS NO MORE THAN HIS FAINTEST WHISPER, YET IT ROLLS OUT AND ACROSS THE VAST SPACE BEFORE HIM, BUILDING AND BUILDING IN VOLUME UNTIL IT FILLS THE CHAMBER WITH THUNDER!

HEAR ME, MY PEOPLE! HEED THE VOICE OF BLACK BOLT! BREAK OFF YOUR ATTACK. THE ALIEN HAS NOT DELIBERATELY HARMED US, WE MUST SPEAK TO HIM IN WORDS OF REASON!

I DON'T UNDERSTAND! THE SHOCK WAVES CREATED BY BLACK BOLT'S VOICE SHOULD BE CAUSING IMMEASURABLE DESTRUCTION-- BUT THEY AREN'T!

BLACK BOLT SPEAKS!

YET, THE MESSAGE REACHES THE ATTACKERS AS SURELY AS WOULD A RADIO BEAM.

OBEYING THEIR ONCE-MORE SILENT MONARCH THEY BANK AWAY FROM THE GIANT...

AND THE ALIEN, SEEMING FOR THE FIRST TIME TO GROW AWARE THAT HE IS NOT ALONE, STOOPS TO EXAMINE THE SOURCE OF THE VOICE.

THE TINY HUMANS ARE MICROSCOPIC TO HIM. FAR TOO SMALL TO BE SEEN.

BUT NOT TOO SMALL TO BE ACTED UPON...

HE'S UNCLIPPING ONE OF THE CAN-ISTERS ON HIS BELT...

I SURE HOPE IT'S A MICROSCOPE!

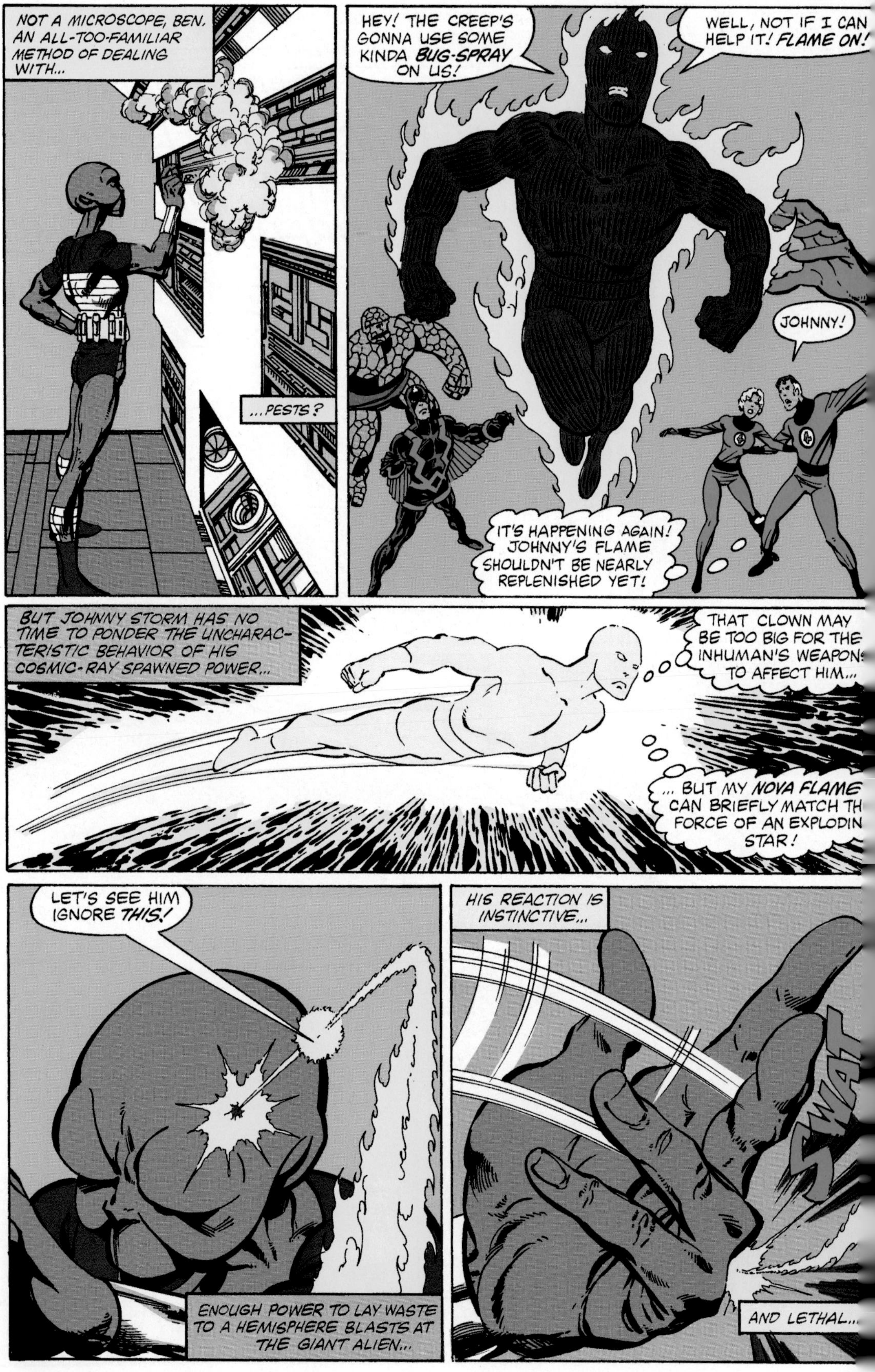

NOT A MICROSCOPE, BEN. AN ALL-TOO-FAMILIAR METHOD OF DEALING WITH...
...PESTS?
HEY! THE CREEP'S GONNA USE SOME KINDA BUG-SPRAY ON US!
WELL, NOT IF I CAN HELP IT! FLAME ON!
JOHNNY!
IT'S HAPPENING AGAIN! JOHNNY'S FLAME SHOULDN'T BE NEARLY REPLENISHED YET!
BUT JOHNNY STORM HAS NO TIME TO PONDER THE UNCHARACTERISTIC BEHAVIOR OF HIS COSMIC-RAY SPAWNED POWER...
THAT CLOWN MAY BE TOO BIG FOR THE INHUMAN'S WEAPONS TO AFFECT HIM...
... BUT MY NOVA FLAME CAN BRIEFLY MATCH TH FORCE OF AN EXPLODIN STAR!
LET'S SEE HIM IGNORE THIS!
ENOUGH POWER TO LAY WASTE TO A HEMISPHERE BLASTS AT THE GIANT ALIEN...
HIS REACTION IS INSTINCTIVE...
SWAT
AND LETHAL...

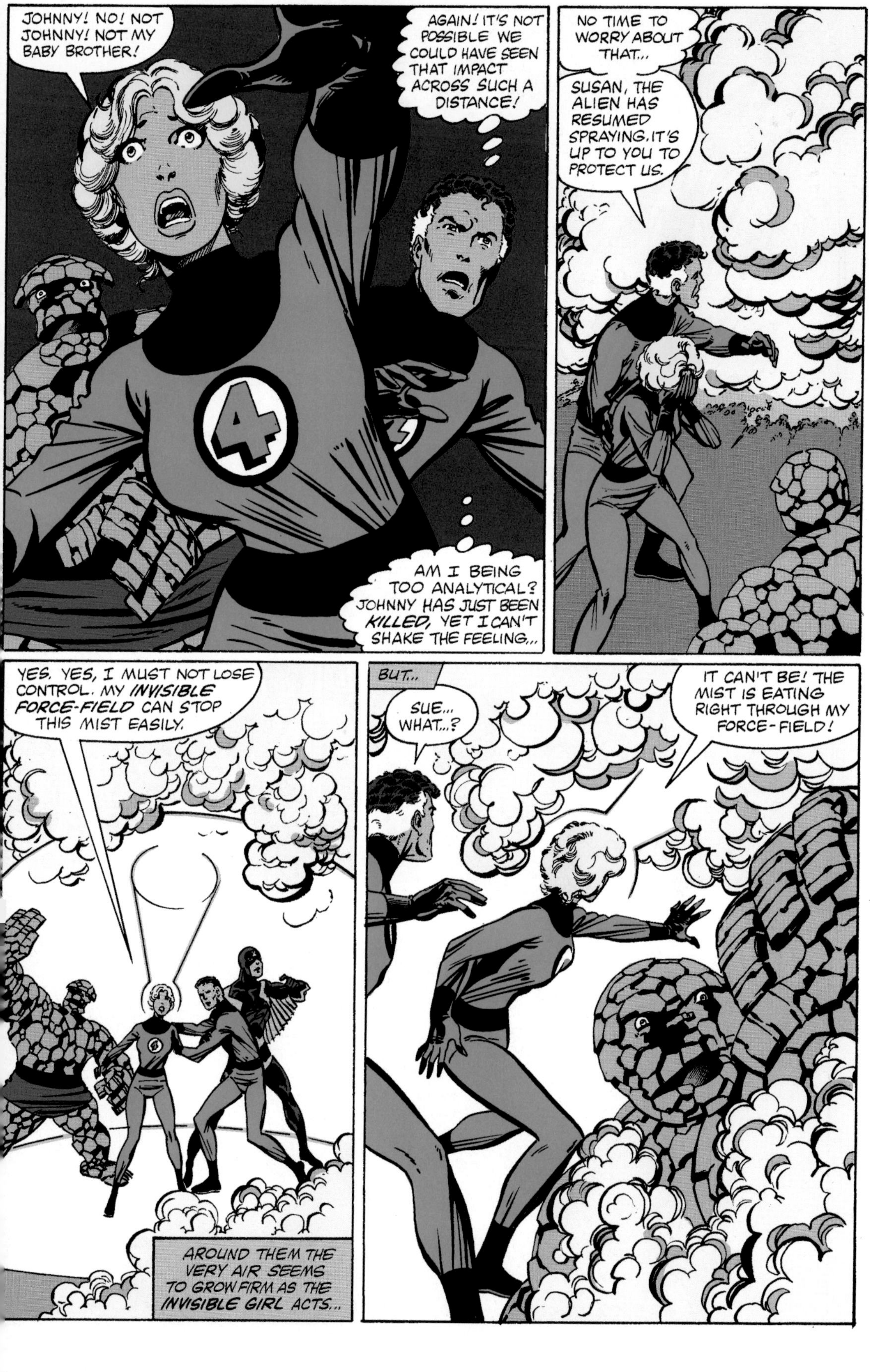
JOHNNY! NO! NOT JOHNNY! NOT MY BABY BROTHER!
AGAIN! IT'S NOT POSSIBLE WE COULD HAVE SEEN THAT IMPACT ACROSS SUCH A DISTANCE!
AM I BEING TOO ANALYTICAL? JOHNNY HAS JUST BEEN KILLED, YET I CAN'T SHAKE THE FEELING...
NO TIME TO WORRY ABOUT THAT...
SUSAN, THE ALIEN HAS RESUMED SPRAYING. IT'S UP TO YOU TO PROTECT US.
YES. YES, I MUST NOT LOSE CONTROL. MY INVISIBLE FORCE-FIELD CAN STOP THIS MIST EASILY.
AROUND THEM THE VERY AIR SEEMS TO GROW FIRM AS THE INVISIBLE GIRL ACTS...
BUT...
SUE... WHAT...?
IT CAN'T BE! THE MIST IS EATING RIGHT THROUGH MY FORCE-FIELD!

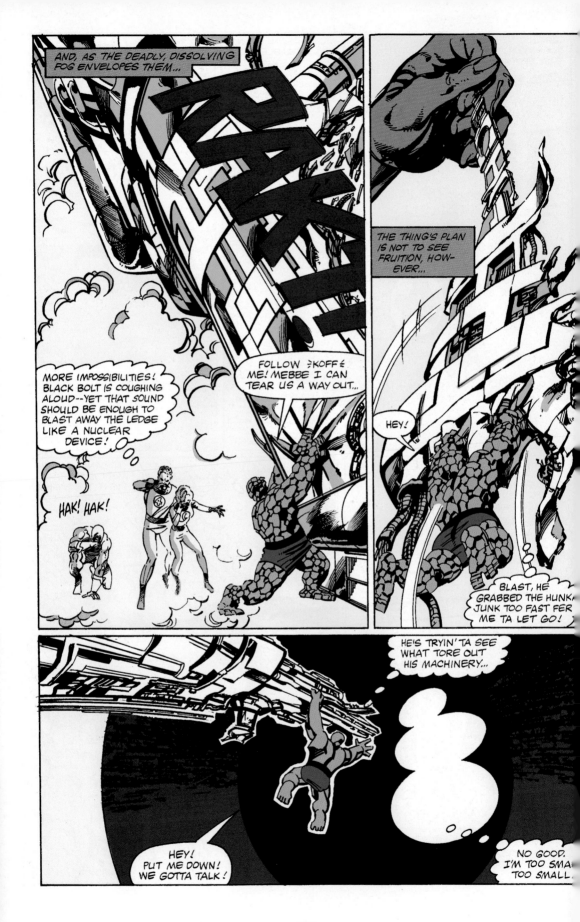

AND, AS THE DEADLY, DISSOLVING FOG ENVELOPES THEM...

RAK!!

THE THING'S PLAN IS NOT TO SEE FRUITION, HOW- EVER...

MORE IMPOSSIBILITIES! BLACK BOLT IS COUGHING ALOUD--YET THAT SOUND SHOULD BE ENOUGH TO BLAST AWAY THE LEDGE LIKE A NUCLEAR DEVICE!

FOLLOW ≶KOFF≶ ME! MEBBE I CAN TEAR US A WAY OUT...

HEY!

HAK! HAK!

BLAST, HE GRABBED THE HUNK JUNK TOO FAST FER ME TA LET GO!

HE'S TRYIN' TA SEE WHAT TORE OUT HIS MACHINERY...

HEY! PUT ME DOWN! WE GOTTA TALK!

NO GOOD. I'M TOO SMA TOO SMALL.

182

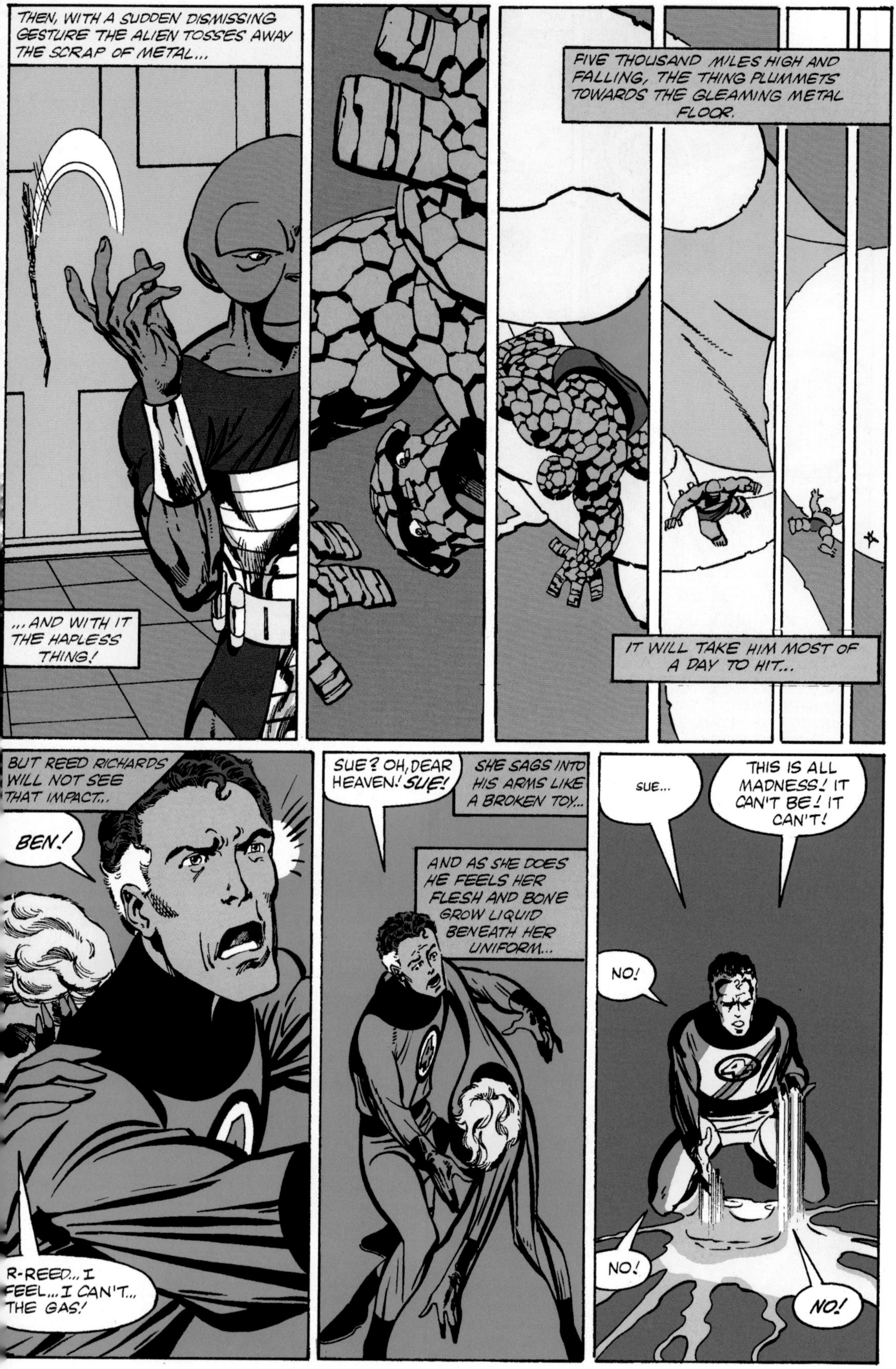
THEN, WITH A SUDDEN DISMISSING GESTURE THE ALIEN TOSSES AWAY THE SCRAP OF METAL...
...AND WITH IT THE HAPLESS THING!
FIVE THOUSAND MILES HIGH AND FALLING, THE THING PLUMMETS TOWARDS THE GLEAMING METAL FLOOR.
IT WILL TAKE HIM MOST OF A DAY TO HIT...
BUT REED RICHARDS WILL NOT SEE THAT IMPACT...
BEN!
R-REED... I FEEL... I CAN'T... THE GAS!
SUE? OH, DEAR HEAVEN! SUE!
SHE SAGS INTO HIS ARMS LIKE A BROKEN TOY...
AND AS SHE DOES HE FEELS HER FLESH AND BONE GROW LIQUID BENEATH HER UNIFORM...
SUE...
THIS IS ALL MADNESS! IT CAN'T BE! IT CAN'T!
NO!
NO!
NO!

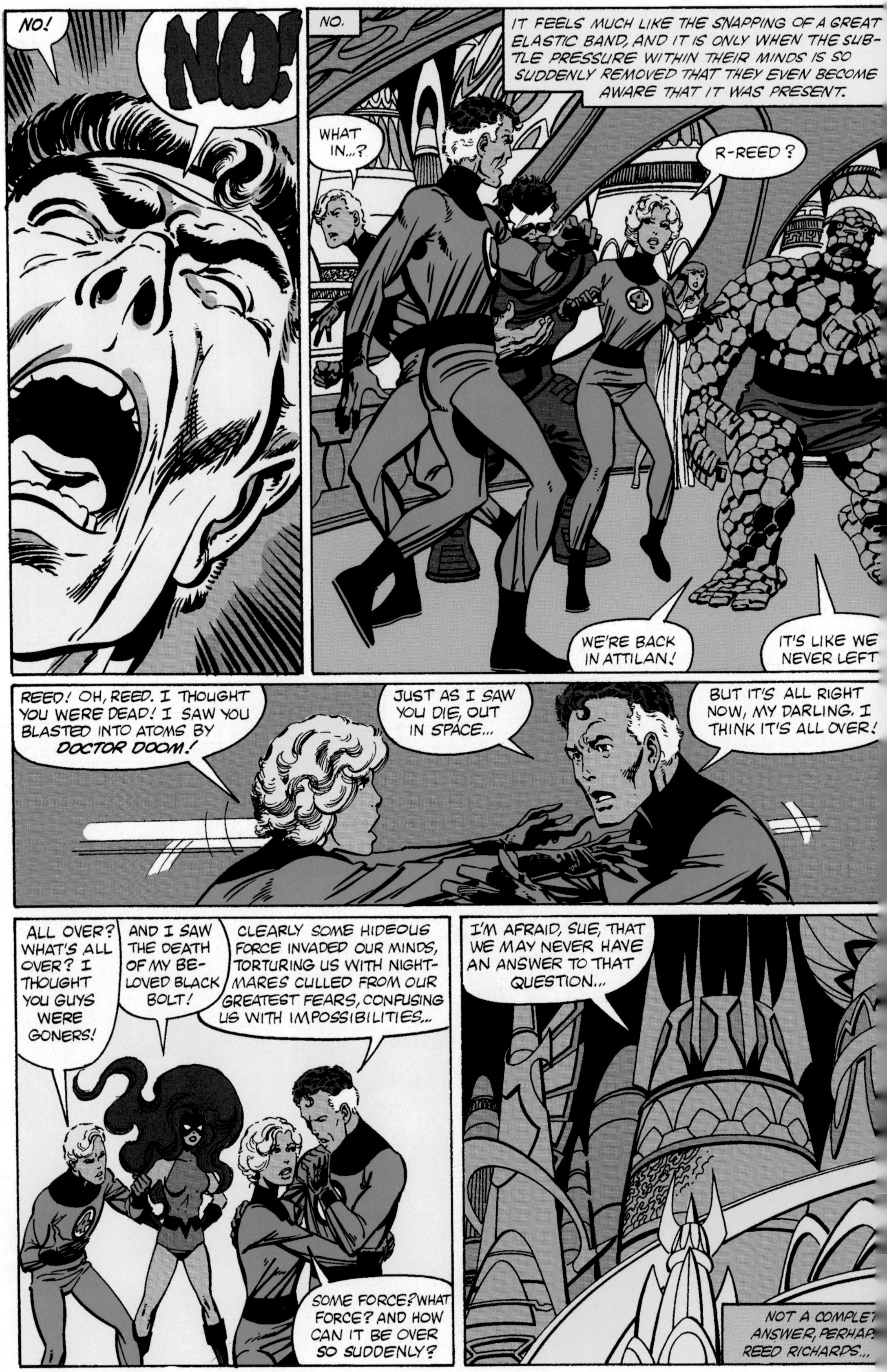
NO!
NO!
NO.
IT FEELS MUCH LIKE THE SNAPPING OF A GREAT ELASTIC BAND, AND IT IS ONLY WHEN THE SUBTLE PRESSURE WITHIN THEIR MINDS IS SO SUDDENLY REMOVED THAT THEY EVEN BECOME AWARE THAT IT WAS PRESENT.
WHAT IN...?
R-REED?
WE'RE BACK IN ATTILAN!
IT'S LIKE WE NEVER LEFT
REED! OH, REED. I THOUGHT YOU WERE DEAD! I SAW YOU BLASTED INTO ATOMS BY DOCTOR DOOM!
JUST AS I SAW YOU DIE, OUT IN SPACE...
BUT IT'S ALL RIGHT NOW, MY DARLING. I THINK IT'S ALL OVER!
ALL OVER? WHAT'S ALL OVER? I THOUGHT YOU GUYS WERE GONERS!
AND I SAW THE DEATH OF MY BELOVED BLACK BOLT!
CLEARLY SOME HIDEOUS FORCE INVADED OUR MINDS, TORTURING US WITH NIGHTMARES CULLED FROM OUR GREATEST FEARS, CONFUSING US WITH IMPOSSIBILITIES...
SOME FORCE? WHAT FORCE? AND HOW CAN IT BE OVER SO SUDDENLY?
I'M AFRAID, SUE, THAT WE MAY NEVER HAVE AN ANSWER TO THAT QUESTION...
NOT A COMPLET ANSWER, PERHAP REED RICHARDS...

BUT HERE, IN A HIDDEN GROTTO SOME TWENTY MILES FROM ATTILAN, ENDINGS AND BEGINNINGS MEET AS ONE.

IT IS OVER!

THE DEMON IS GONE FROM MY MIND. I HAVE *TRIUMPHED!*

YET I MUST RETURN SWIFTLY TO ATTILAN AND MY NOBLE COUSINS. THIS PLACE MAY NOT BE UNIQUE, AND SHOULD OTHERS OF ITS ILK EXIST, THEY MUST BE FOUND AND QUICKLY DESTROYED.

I DO NOT KNOW WHAT RACE CREATED THIS TEMPLE OF NIGHTMARES, BUT IT IS CLEAR THAT THEY HAD LITTLE LOVE FOR THINGS WHICH LIVE!

THEY CREATED A CRYSTAL LATTICE WHICH BORES INTO A LIVING MIND-- CREATING HORRIBLE NIGHTMARES!

...I AM LUCKY TO HAVE WON OVER ITS INFLUENCE, YET SOMEHOW I FEEL VICTORY WAS NOT MINE ALONE.

AS I WRITHED IN FINAL TORMENT I SENSED THE TOUCH OF... ANOTHER IN MY MIND...

HE SWIMS AWAY, BOUND FOR THE GREAT REFUGE, AND A WELL-DESERVED REST.

AND, PERHAPS, TRITON WILL NEVER TRULY KNOW THAT THERE *WAS* ANOTHER WITH HIM IN THE LAST MOMENT OF HIS STRUGGLE...

WAS REED RICHARDS' ANGUISHED DENIAL OF HIS WIFE'S DESTRUCTION THAT FOR A MOMENT BROKE THE EVIL SPELL, AND GAVE THE GREEN INHUMAN TIME ENOUGH TO STRIKE.

THE HAND THAT CRAFTED THIS CRYSTAL DREAM-WEAVER ACTED OUT OF HATE, CONSUMING HATE OF ALL THAT THINKS AND LIVES. YET WHAT DEFEATED IT? NO MORE THAN THAT SIMPLE, PURE EMOTION MEN CALL *LOVE*.

NEXT ISSUE: HE STRIKES FROM SPACE AND EVEN THE *FF* CANNOT STOP HIM.'

man and super-man!

fantastic four # 249

60¢
249
DEC
02462
MARVEL® COMICS GROUP
APPROVED BY THE COMICS CODE AUTHORITY
THE WORLD'S GREATEST COMIC MAGAZINE!
Fantastic Four®
"MAN AND SUPER-MAN!"

DECEMBER 1982

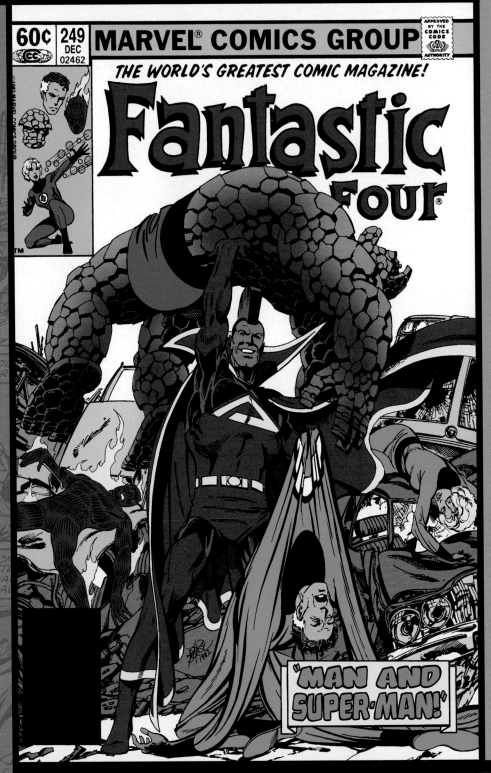

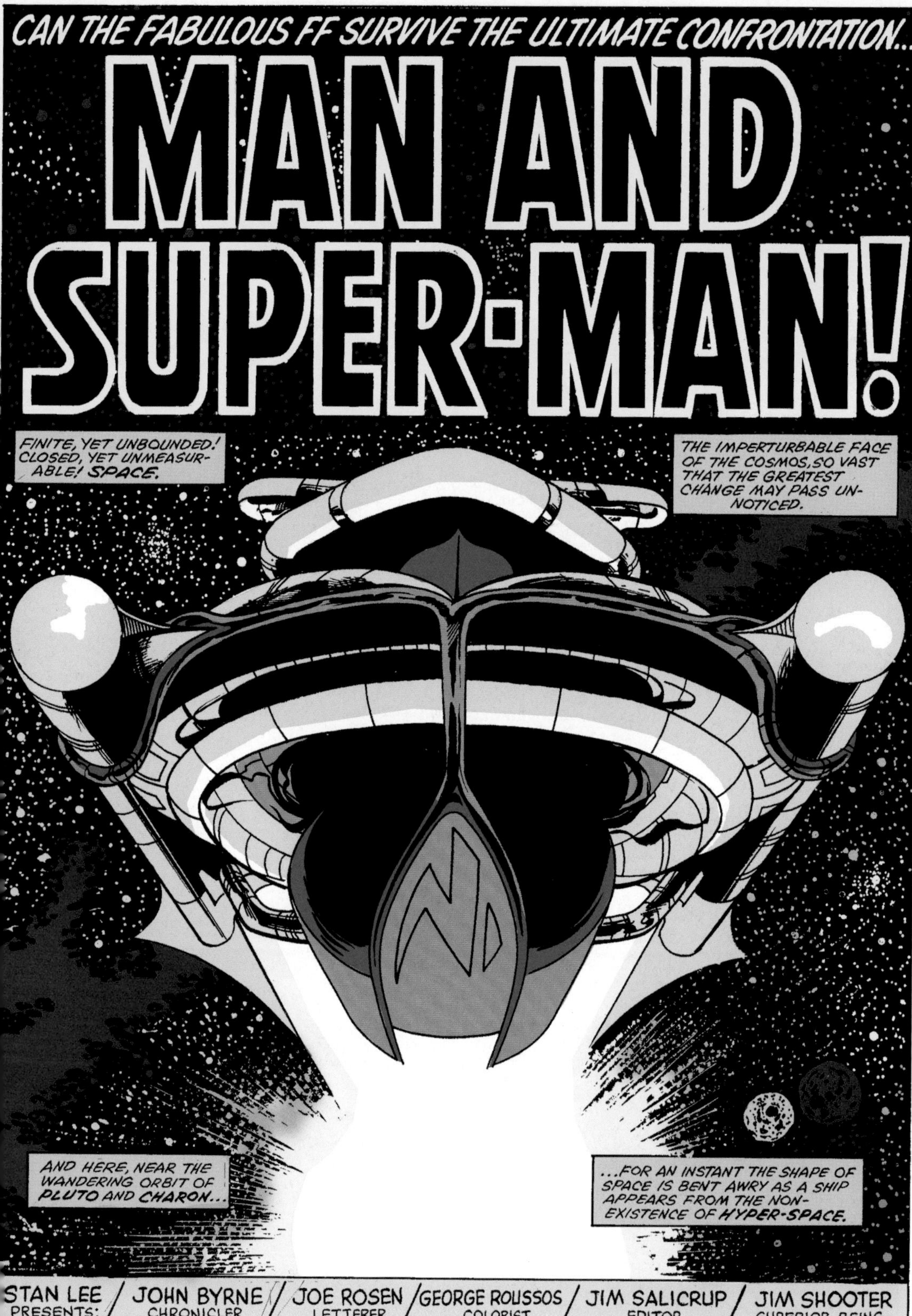

CAN THE FABULOUS FF SURVIVE THE ULTIMATE CONFRONTATION...
MAN AND SUPER-MAN!
FINITE, YET UNBOUNDED! CLOSED, YET UNMEASURABLE! SPACE.
THE IMPERTURBABLE FACE OF THE COSMOS, SO VAST THAT THE GREATEST CHANGE MAY PASS UNNOTICED.
AND HERE, NEAR THE WANDERING ORBIT OF PLUTO AND CHARON...
...FOR AN INSTANT THE SHAPE OF SPACE IS BENT AWRY AS A SHIP APPEARS FROM THE NON-EXISTENCE OF HYPER-SPACE.
STAN LEE PRESENTS: / JOHN BYRNE CHRONICLER / JOE ROSEN LETTERER / GEORGE ROUSSOS COLORIST / JIM SALICRUP EDITOR / JIM SHOOTER SUPERIOR BEING

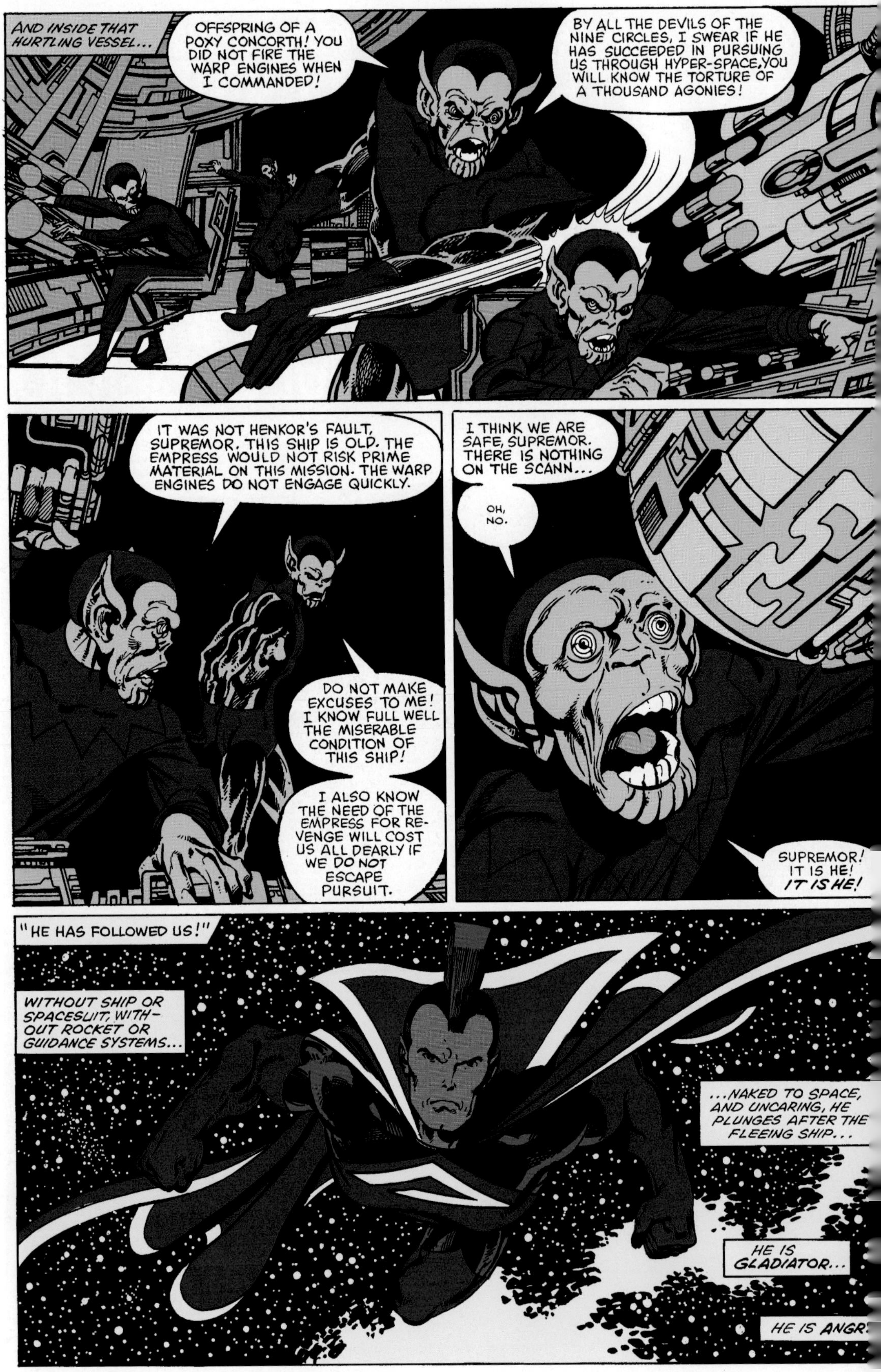
AND INSIDE THAT HURTLING VESSEL...
OFFSPRING OF A POXY CONCORTH! YOU DID NOT FIRE THE WARP ENGINES WHEN I COMMANDED!
BY ALL THE DEVILS OF THE NINE CIRCLES, I SWEAR IF HE HAS SUCCEEDED IN PURSUING US THROUGH HYPER-SPACE, YOU WILL KNOW THE TORTURE OF A THOUSAND AGONIES!
IT WAS NOT HENKOR'S FAULT, SUPREMOR. THIS SHIP IS OLD. THE EMPRESS WOULD NOT RISK PRIME MATERIAL ON THIS MISSION. THE WARP ENGINES DO NOT ENGAGE QUICKLY.
DO NOT MAKE EXCUSES TO ME! I KNOW FULL WELL THE MISERABLE CONDITION OF THIS SHIP!
I ALSO KNOW THE NEED OF THE EMPRESS FOR RE-VENGE WILL COST US ALL DEARLY IF WE DO NOT ESCAPE PURSUIT.
I THINK WE ARE SAFE, SUPREMOR. THERE IS NOTHING ON THE SCANN...
OH, NO.
SUPREMOR! IT IS HE! IT IS HE!
"HE HAS FOLLOWED US!"
WITHOUT SHIP OR SPACESUIT, WITH-OUT ROCKET OR GUIDANCE SYSTEMS...
...NAKED TO SPACE, AND UNCARING, HE PLUNGES AFTER THE FLEEING SHIP...
HE IS GLADIATOR...
HE IS ANGR

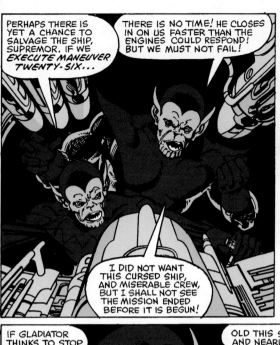

PERHAPS THERE IS YET A CHANCE TO SALVAGE THE SHIP, SUPREMOR, IF WE *EXECUTE MANEUVER TWENTY-SIX*...

THERE IS NO TIME! HE CLOSES IN ON US FASTER THAN THE ENGINES COULD RESPOND! BUT WE MUST NOT FAIL!

I DID NOT WANT THIS CURSED SHIP, AND MISERABLE CREW, BUT I SHALL NOT SEE THE MISSION ENDED BEFORE IT IS BEGUN!

THE EMPRESS HAS CHARGED US WITH THE DESTRUCTION OF THE *FANTASTIC FOUR.*

THAT IS THE MOST GLORIOUS GOAL ANY *SKRULL* WARRIOR COULD ATTAIN.

IF GLADIATOR THINKS TO STOP US, LET HIM BEWARE!

OLD THIS SHIP MAY BE, AND NEARLY USELESS...

...BUT THERE IS YET ONE PROCEDURE EVEN GLADIATOR MUST FEAR...

A SWITCH IS THROWN.

WITHIN THE ANCIENT MECHANISMS, CIRCUITS CLOSE IN READINESS...

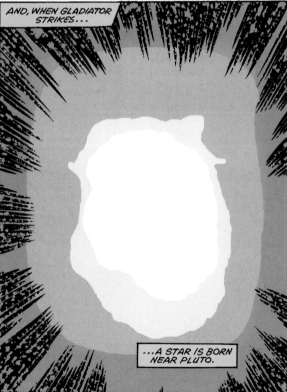

AND, WHEN GLADIATOR STRIKES...

...A STAR IS BORN NEAR PLUTO.

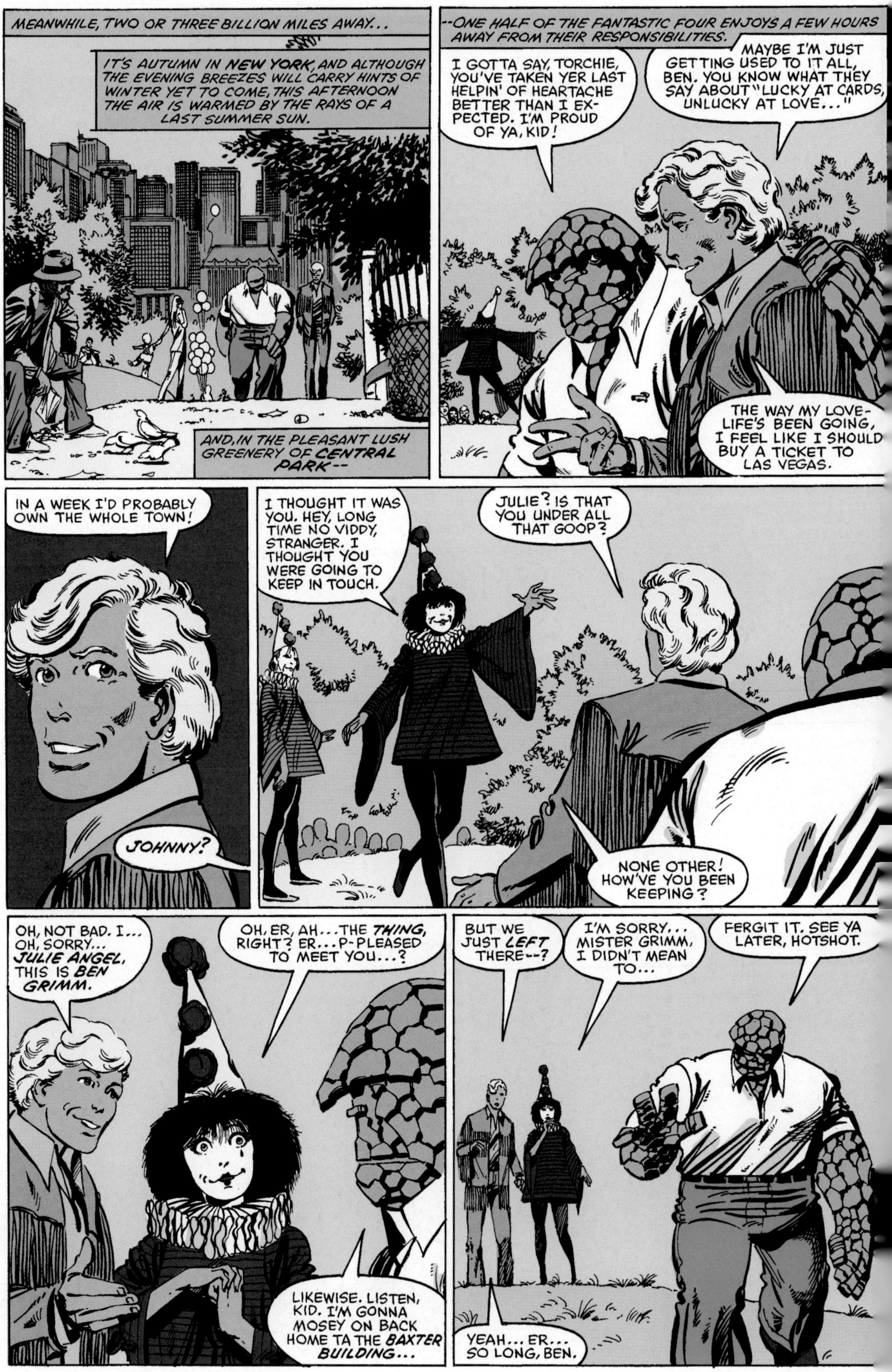
MEANWHILE, TWO OR THREE BILLION MILES AWAY...
IT'S AUTUMN IN NEW YORK, AND ALTHOUGH THE EVENING BREEZES WILL CARRY HINTS OF WINTER YET TO COME, THIS AFTERNOON THE AIR IS WARMED BY THE RAYS OF A LAST SUMMER SUN.
AND, IN THE PLEASANT LUSH GREENERY OF CENTRAL PARK--
--ONE HALF OF THE FANTASTIC FOUR ENJOYS A FEW HOURS AWAY FROM THEIR RESPONSIBILITIES.
I GOTTA SAY, TORCHIE, YOU'VE TAKEN YER LAST HELPIN' OF HEARTACHE BETTER THAN I EXPECTED. I'M PROUD OF YA, KID!
MAYBE I'M JUST GETTING USED TO IT ALL, BEN. YOU KNOW WHAT THEY SAY ABOUT "LUCKY AT CARDS, UNLUCKY AT LOVE..."
THE WAY MY LOVE-LIFE'S BEEN GOING, I FEEL LIKE I SHOULD BUY A TICKET TO LAS VEGAS.
IN A WEEK I'D PROBABLY OWN THE WHOLE TOWN!
JOHNNY?
I THOUGHT IT WAS YOU. HEY, LONG TIME NO VIDDY, STRANGER. I THOUGHT YOU WERE GOING TO KEEP IN TOUCH.
JULIE? IS THAT YOU UNDER ALL THAT GOOP?
NONE OTHER! HOW'VE YOU BEEN KEEPING?
OH, NOT BAD. I... OH, SORRY... JULIE ANGEL, THIS IS BEN GRIMM.
OH, ER, AH... THE THING, RIGHT? ER... P-PLEASED TO MEET YOU...?
LIKEWISE. LISTEN, KID. I'M GONNA MOSEY ON BACK HOME TA THE BAXTER BUILDING...
BUT WE JUST LEFT THERE--?
I'M SORRY... MISTER GRIMM, I DIDN'T MEAN TO...
FERGIT IT. SEE YA LATER, HOTSHOT.
YEAH... ER... SO LONG, BEN.

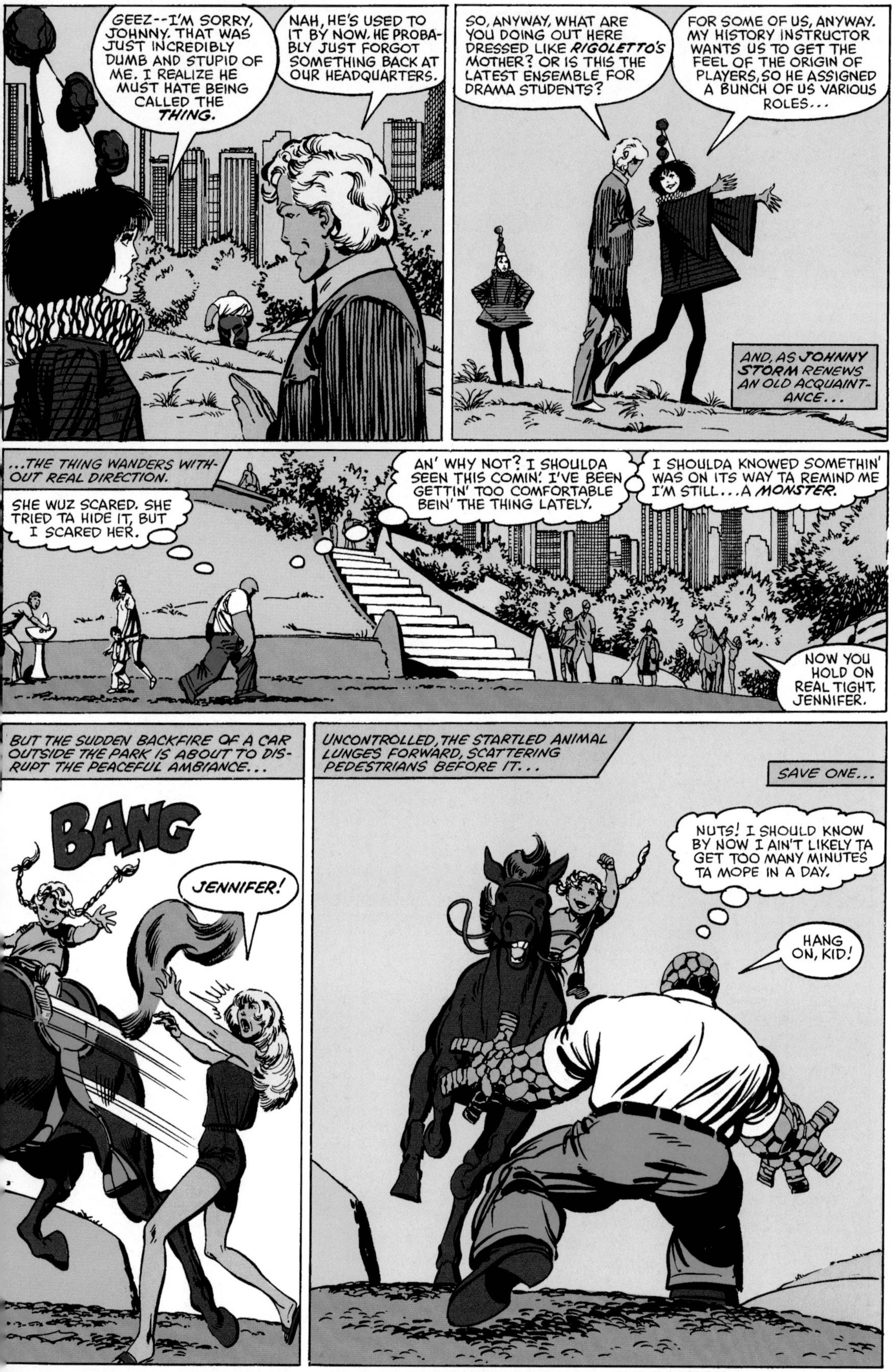
GEEZ--I'M SORRY, JOHNNY. THAT WAS JUST INCREDIBLY DUMB AND STUPID OF ME. I REALIZE HE MUST HATE BEING CALLED THE THING.
NAH, HE'S USED TO IT BY NOW. HE PROBABLY JUST FORGOT SOMETHING BACK AT OUR HEADQUARTERS.
AND, AS JOHNNY STORM RENEWS AN OLD ACQUAINTANCE...
SO, ANYWAY, WHAT ARE YOU DOING OUT HERE DRESSED LIKE RIGOLETTO'S MOTHER? OR IS THIS THE LATEST ENSEMBLE FOR DRAMA STUDENTS?
FOR SOME OF US, ANYWAY. MY HISTORY INSTRUCTOR WANTS US TO GET THE FEEL OF THE ORIGIN OF PLAYERS, SO HE ASSIGNED A BUNCH OF US VARIOUS ROLES...
...THE THING WANDERS WITHOUT REAL DIRECTION.
SHE WUZ SCARED. SHE TRIED TA HIDE IT, BUT I SCARED HER.
AN' WHY NOT? I SHOULDA SEEN THIS COMIN'. I'VE BEEN GETTIN' TOO COMFORTABLE BEIN' THE THING LATELY.
I SHOULDA KNOWED SOMETHIN' WAS ON ITS WAY TA REMIND ME I'M STILL...A MONSTER.
NOW YOU HOLD ON REAL TIGHT, JENNIFER.
BUT THE SUDDEN BACKFIRE OF A CAR OUTSIDE THE PARK IS ABOUT TO DISRUPT THE PEACEFUL AMBIANCE...
BANG
JENNIFER!
UNCONTROLLED, THE STARTLED ANIMAL LUNGES FORWARD, SCATTERING PEDESTRIANS BEFORE IT...
SAVE ONE...
NUTS! I SHOULD KNOW BY NOW I AIN'T LIKELY TA GET TOO MANY MINUTES TA MOPE IN A DAY.
HANG ON, KID!

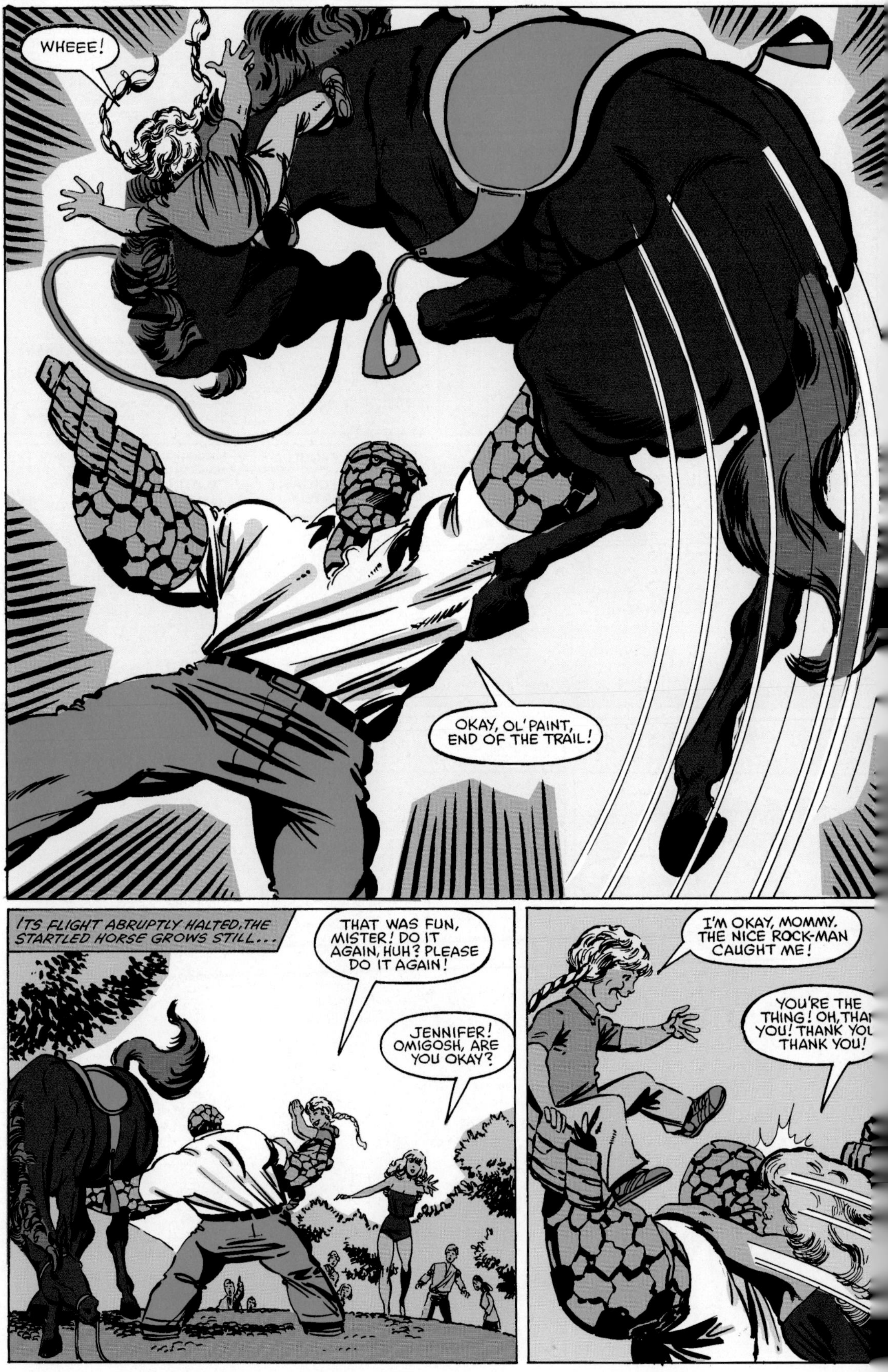
WHEEE!
OKAY, OL' PAINT, END OF THE TRAIL!
ITS FLIGHT ABRUPTLY HALTED, THE STARTLED HORSE GROWS STILL...
THAT WAS FUN, MISTER! DO IT AGAIN, HUH? PLEASE DO IT AGAIN!
JENNIFER! OMIGOSH, ARE YOU OKAY?
I'M OKAY, MOMMY. THE NICE ROCK-MAN CAUGHT ME!
YOU'RE THE THING! OH, THA
YOU! THANK YO
THANK YOU!

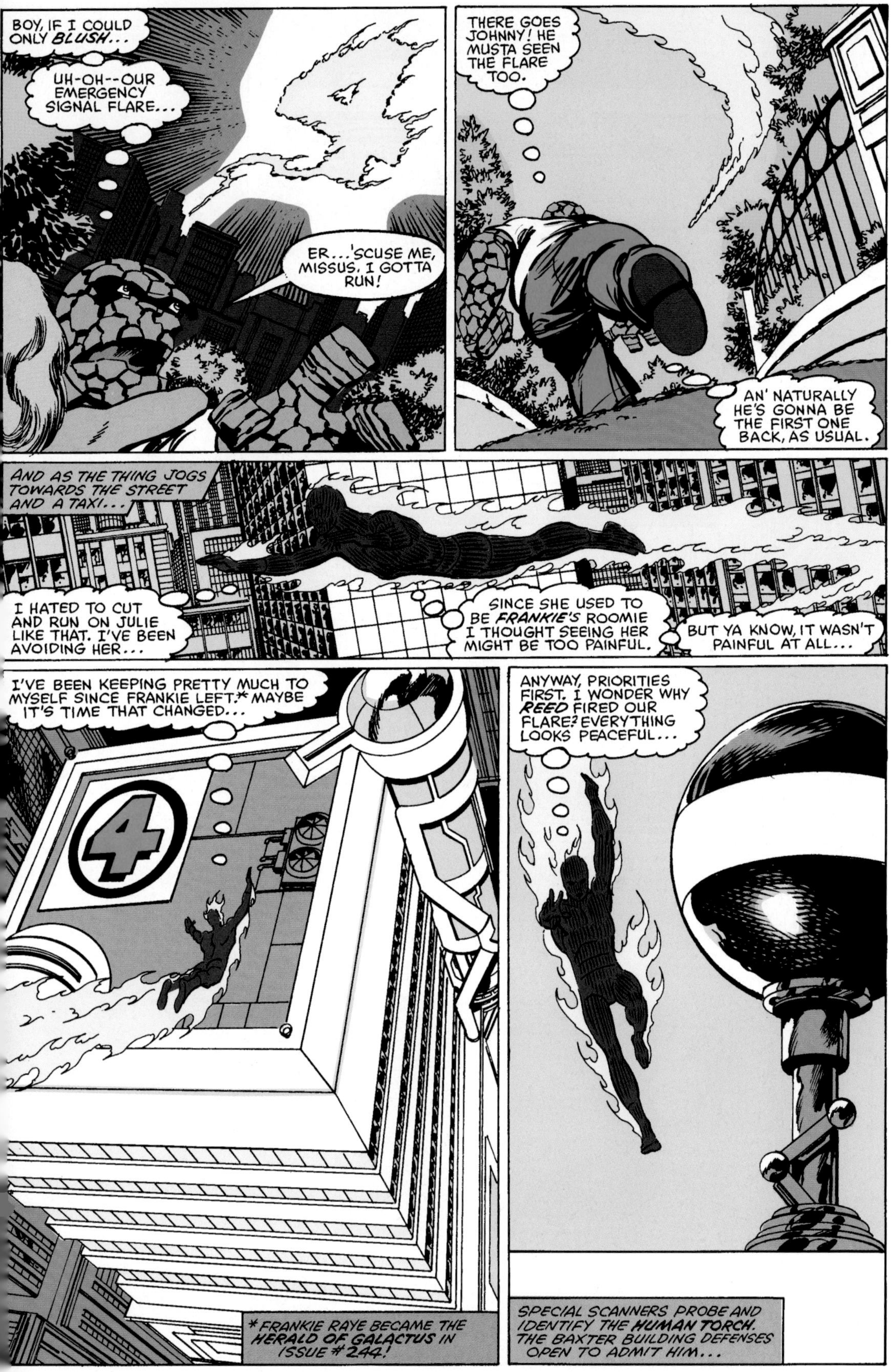

BOY, IF I COULD ONLY BLUSH...
UH-OH--OUR EMERGENCY SIGNAL FLARE...
ER...'SCUSE ME, MISSUS, I GOTTA RUN!
THERE GOES JOHNNY! HE MUSTA SEEN THE FLARE TOO.
AN' NATURALLY HE'S GONNA BE THE FIRST ONE BACK, AS USUAL.
AND AS THE THING JOGS TOWARDS THE STREET AND A TAXI...
I HATED TO CUT AND RUN ON JULIE LIKE THAT. I'VE BEEN AVOIDING HER...
SINCE SHE USED TO BE FRANKIE'S ROOMIE I THOUGHT SEEING HER MIGHT BE TOO PAINFUL.
BUT YA KNOW, IT WASN'T PAINFUL AT ALL...
I'VE BEEN KEEPING PRETTY MUCH TO MYSELF SINCE FRANKIE LEFT.* MAYBE IT'S TIME THAT CHANGED...
*FRANKIE RAYE BECAME THE HERALD OF GALACTUS IN ISSUE #244!
ANYWAY, PRIORITIES FIRST. I WONDER WHY REED FIRED OUR FLARE? EVERYTHING LOOKS PEACEFUL...
SPECIAL SCANNERS PROBE AND IDENTIFY THE HUMAN TORCH. THE BAXTER BUILDING DEFENSES OPEN TO ADMIT HIM...

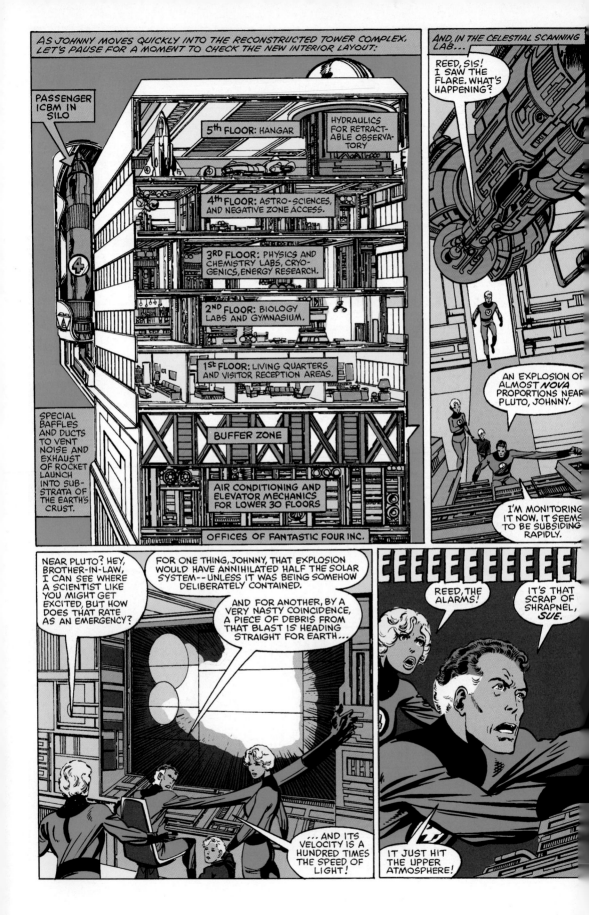

AS JOHNNY MOVES QUICKLY INTO THE RECONSTRUCTED TOWER COMPLEX, LET'S PAUSE FOR A MOMENT TO CHECK THE NEW INTERIOR LAYOUT:

PASSENGER ICBM IN SILO

5TH FLOOR: HANGAR

HYDRAULICS FOR RETRACTABLE OBSERVATORY

4TH FLOOR: ASTRO-SCIENCES, AND NEGATIVE ZONE ACCESS.

3RD FLOOR: PHYSICS AND CHEMISTRY LABS, CRYOGENICS, ENERGY RESEARCH.

2ND FLOOR: BIOLOGY LABS AND GYMNASIUM.

1ST FLOOR: LIVING QUARTERS AND VISITOR RECEPTION AREAS.

SPECIAL BAFFLES AND DUCTS TO VENT NOISE AND EXHAUST OF ROCKET LAUNCH INTO SUBSTRATA OF THE EARTH'S CRUST.

BUFFER ZONE

AIR CONDITIONING AND ELEVATOR MECHANICS FOR LOWER 30 FLOORS

OFFICES OF FANTASTIC FOUR INC.

AND, IN THE CELESTIAL SCANNING LAB...

REED, SIS! I SAW THE FLARE. WHAT'S HAPPENING?

AN EXPLOSION OF ALMOST *NOVA* PROPORTIONS NEAR PLUTO, JOHNNY.

I'M MONITORING IT NOW. IT SEEMS TO BE SUBSIDING RAPIDLY.

NEAR PLUTO? HEY, BROTHER-IN-LAW, I CAN SEE WHERE A SCIENTIST LIKE YOU MIGHT GET EXCITED, BUT HOW DOES THAT RATE AS AN EMERGENCY?

FOR ONE THING, JOHNNY, THAT EXPLOSION WOULD HAVE ANNIHILATED HALF THE SOLAR SYSTEM-- UNLESS IT WAS BEING SOMEHOW DELIBERATELY CONTAINED.

AND FOR ANOTHER, BY A VERY NASTY COINCIDENCE, A PIECE OF DEBRIS FROM THAT BLAST IS HEADING STRAIGHT FOR EARTH...

... AND ITS VELOCITY IS A HUNDRED TIMES THE SPEED OF LIGHT!

EEEEEEEEEEE

REED, THE ALARMS!

IT'S THAT SCRAP OF SHRAPNEL, SUE.

IT JUST HIT THE UPPER ATMOSPHERE!

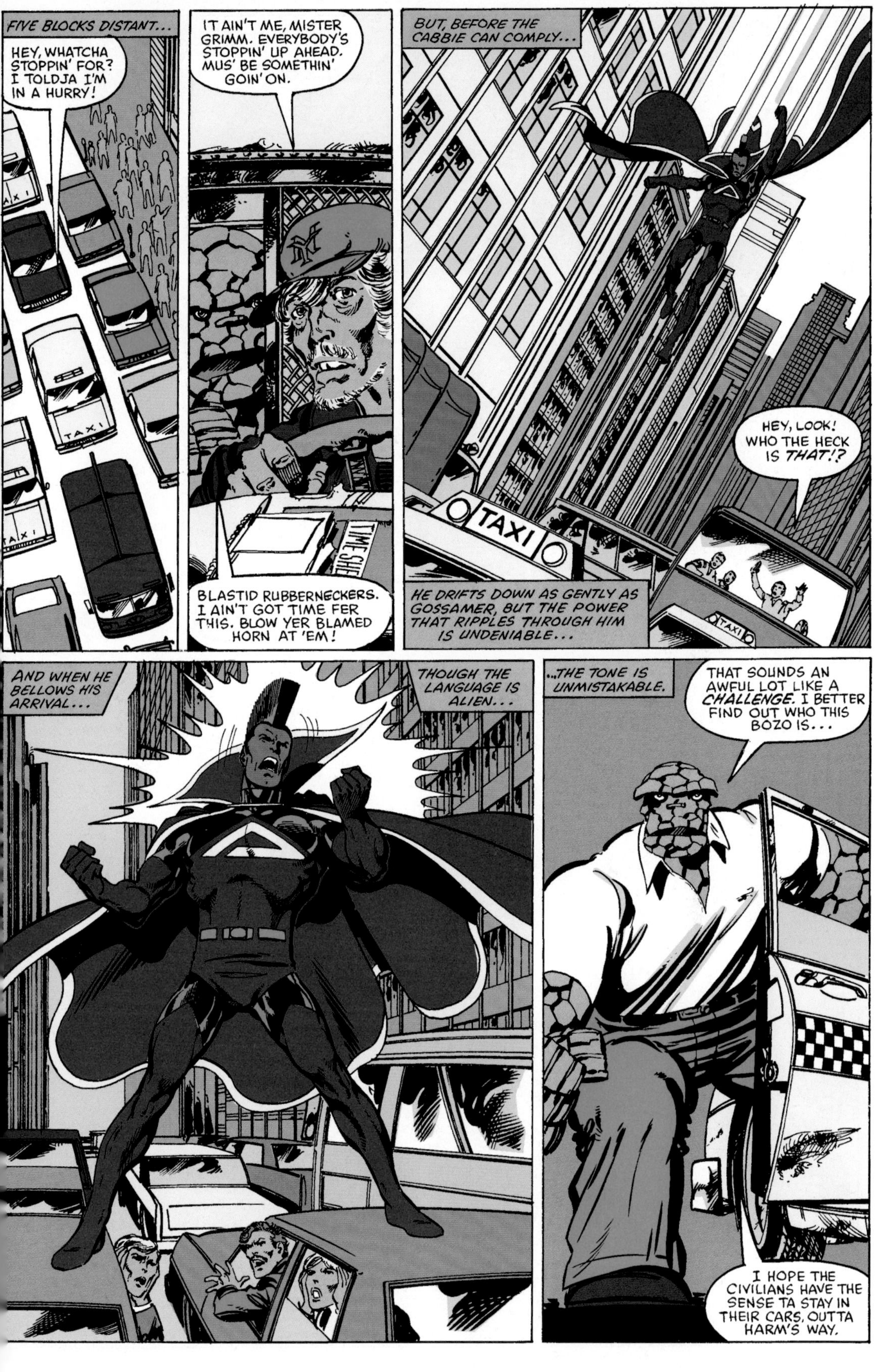
FIVE BLOCKS DISTANT...
HEY, WHATCHA STOPPIN' FOR? I TOLDJA I'M IN A HURRY!
IT AIN'T ME, MISTER GRIMM. EVERYBODY'S STOPPIN' UP AHEAD. MUS' BE SOMETHIN' GOIN' ON.
BLASTID RUBBERNECKERS. I AIN'T GOT TIME FER THIS. BLOW YER BLAMED HORN AT 'EM!
BUT, BEFORE THE CABBIE CAN COMPLY...
HEY, LOOK! WHO THE HECK IS THAT!?
HE DRIFTS DOWN AS GENTLY AS GOSSAMER, BUT THE POWER THAT RIPPLES THROUGH HIM IS UNDENIABLE...
AND WHEN HE BELLOWS HIS ARRIVAL...
THOUGH THE LANGUAGE IS ALIEN...
...THE TONE IS UNMISTAKABLE.
THAT SOUNDS AN AWFUL LOT LIKE A CHALLENGE. I BETTER FIND OUT WHO THIS BOZO IS...
I HOPE THE CIVILIANS HAVE THE SENSE TA STAY IN THEIR CARS, OUTTA HARM'S WAY.

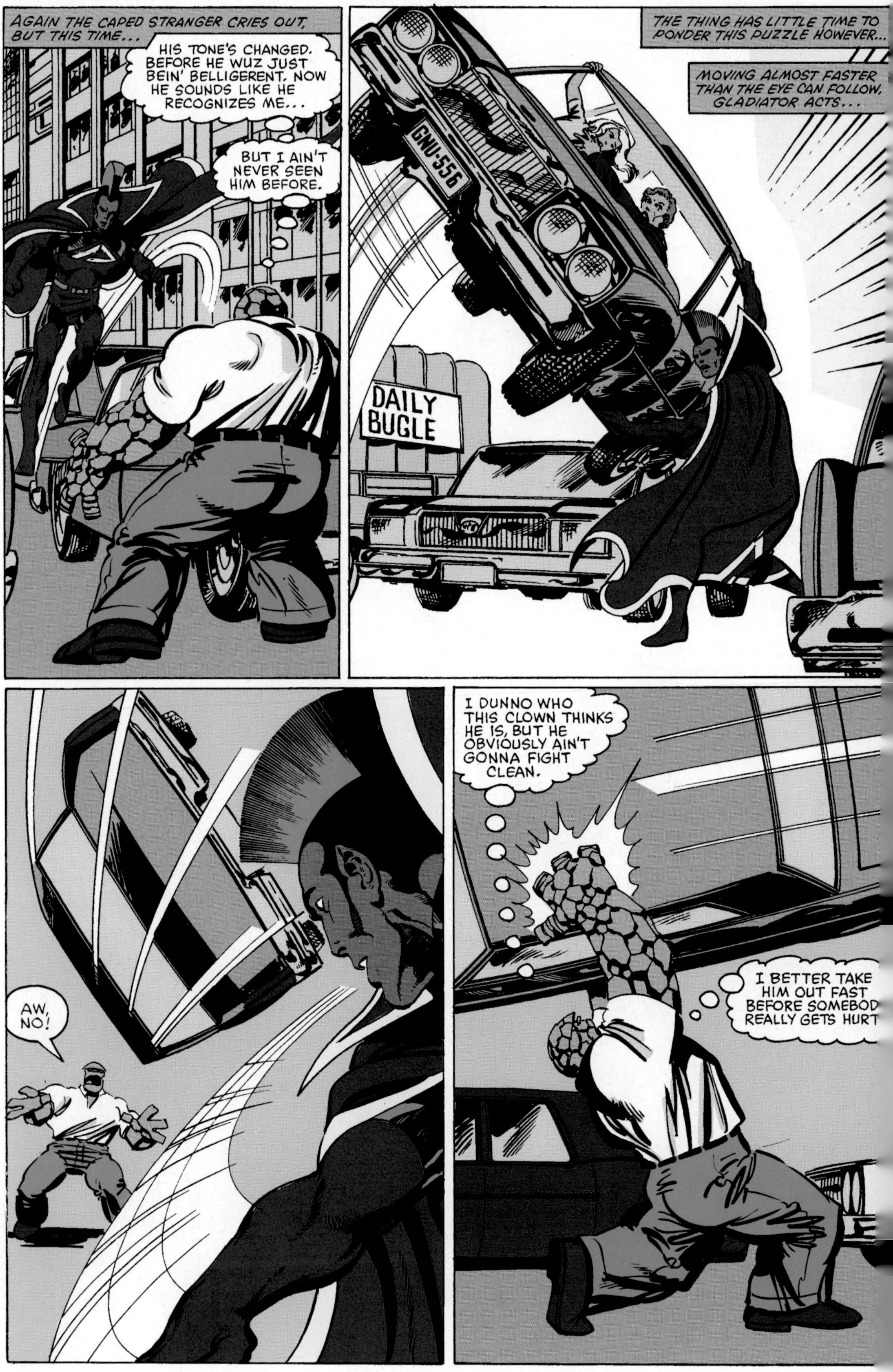
AGAIN THE CAPED STRANGER CRIES OUT, BUT THIS TIME...
HIS TONE'S CHANGED. BEFORE HE WUZ JUST BEIN' BELLIGERENT. NOW HE SOUNDS LIKE HE RECOGNIZES ME...
BUT I AIN'T NEVER SEEN HIM BEFORE.
THE THING HAS LITTLE TIME TO PONDER THIS PUZZLE HOWEVER...
MOVING ALMOST FASTER THAN THE EYE CAN FOLLOW, GLADIATOR ACTS...
GNU-556
DAILY BUGLE
AW, NO!
I DUNNO WHO THIS CLOWN THINKS HE IS, BUT HE OBVIOUSLY AIN'T GONNA FIGHT CLEAN.
I BETTER TAKE HIM OUT FAST BEFORE SOMEBOD REALLY GETS HURT

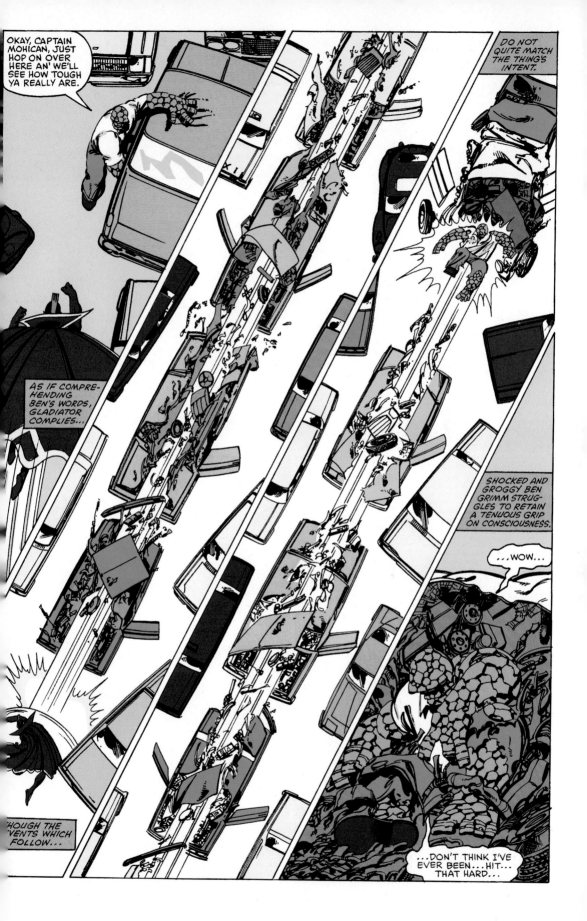

OKAY, CAPTAIN MOHICAN, JUST HOP ON OVER HERE AN' WE'LL SEE HOW TOUGH YA REALLY ARE.

DO NOT QUITE MATCH THE THING'S INTENT.

AS IF COMPRE-HENDING BEN'S WORDS, GLADIATOR COMPLIES...

SHOCKED AND GROGGY BEN GRIMM STRUG-GLES TO RETAIN A TENUOUS GRIP ON CONSCIOUSNESS.

...WOW...

HOUGH THE VENTS WHICH FOLLOW...

...DON'T THINK I'VE EVER BEEN...HIT... THAT HARD...

197

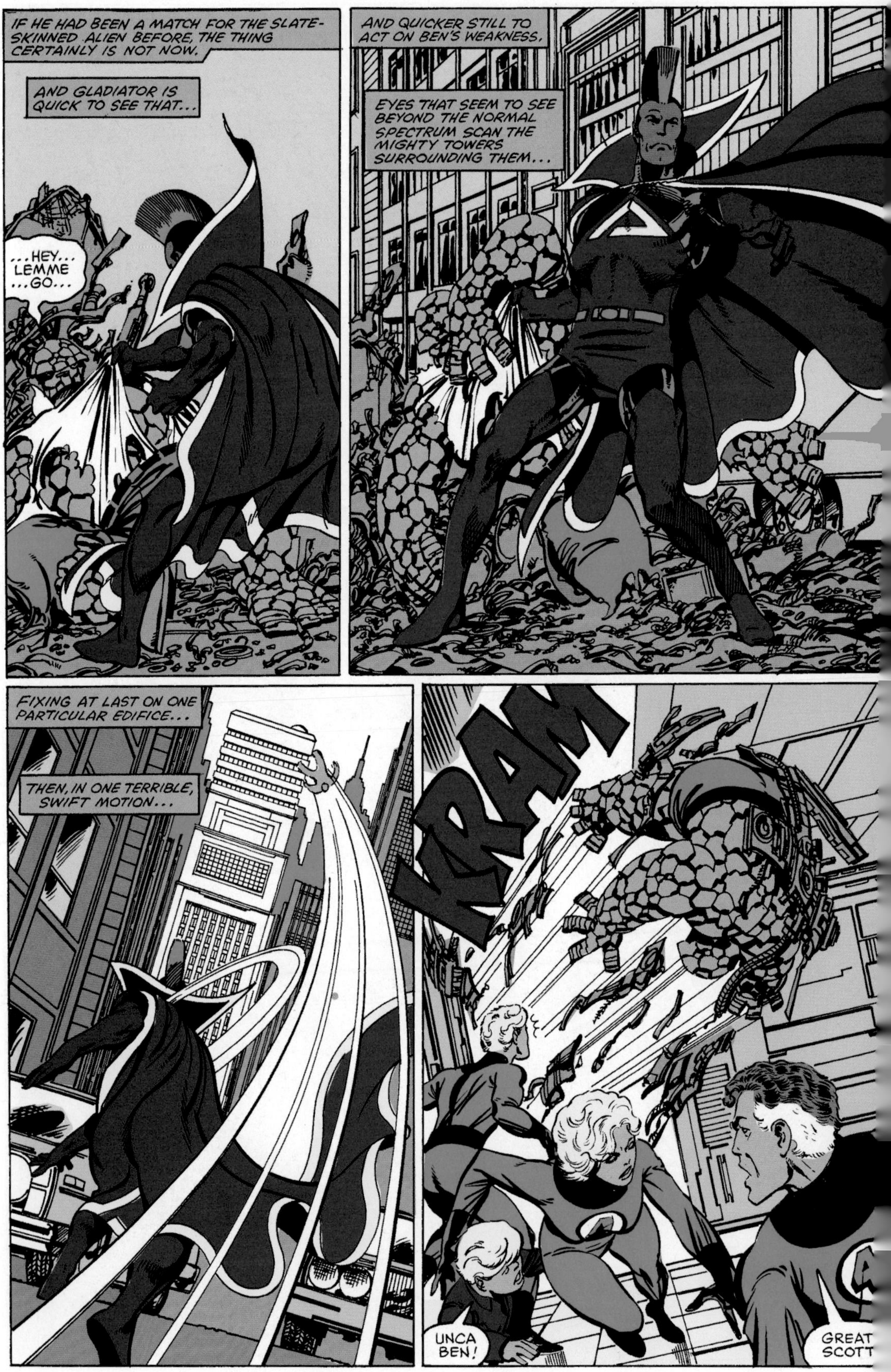
IF HE HAD BEEN A MATCH FOR THE SLATE-SKINNED ALIEN BEFORE, THE THING CERTAINLY IS NOT NOW.
AND GLADIATOR IS QUICK TO SEE THAT...
...HEY... LEMME ...GO...
AND QUICKER STILL TO ACT ON BEN'S WEAKNESS.
EYES THAT SEEM TO SEE BEYOND THE NORMAL SPECTRUM SCAN THE MIGHTY TOWERS SURROUNDING THEM...
FIXING AT LAST ON ONE PARTICULAR EDIFICE...
THEN, IN ONE TERRIBLE, SWIFT MOTION...
KRAM
UNCA BEN!
GREAT SCOTT

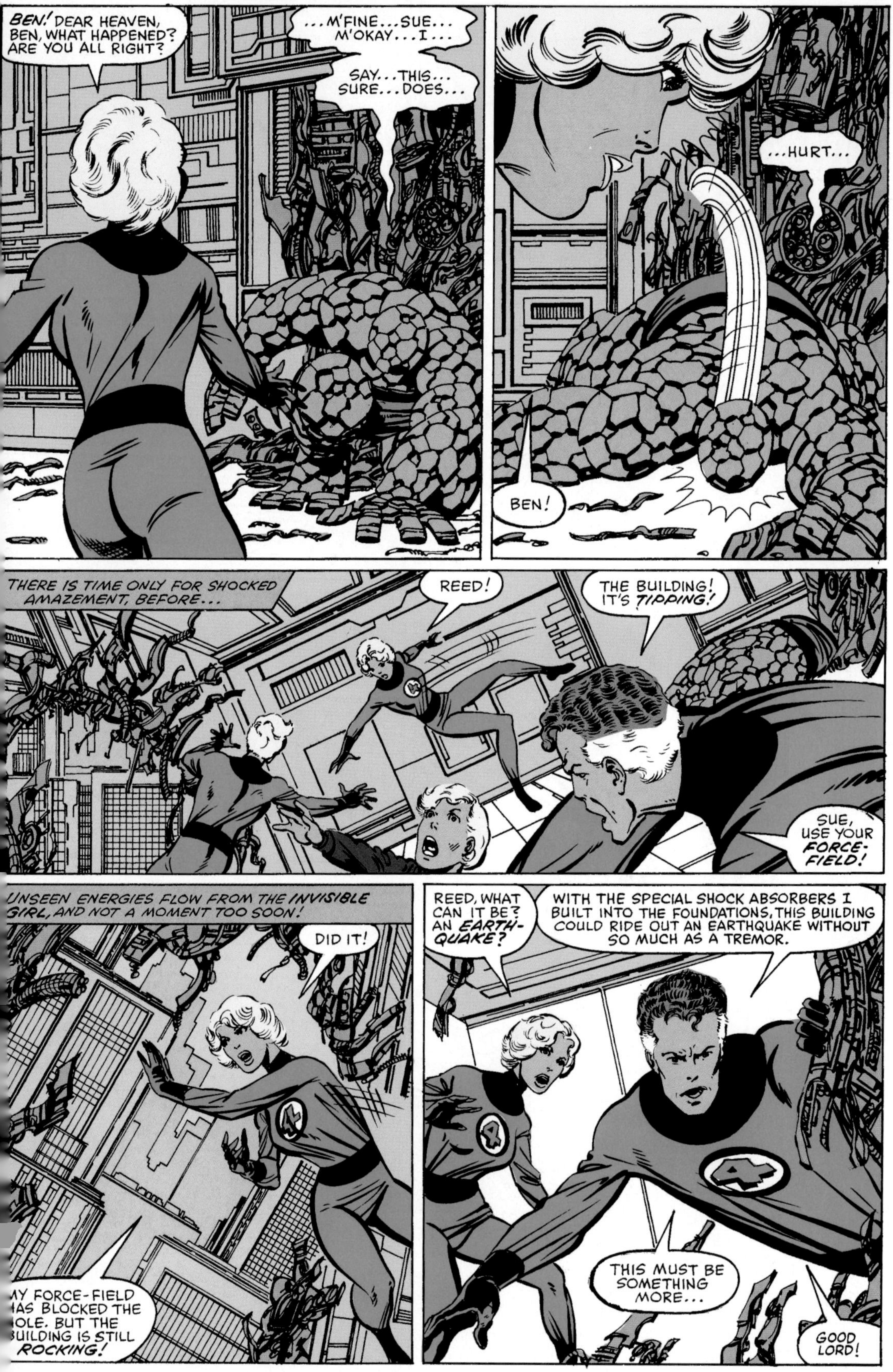
BEN! DEAR HEAVEN, BEN, WHAT HAPPENED? ARE YOU ALL RIGHT?
...M'FINE...SUE... M'OKAY...I...
SAY...THIS... SURE...DOES...
...HURT...
BEN!
THERE IS TIME ONLY FOR SHOCKED AMAZEMENT, BEFORE...
REED!
THE BUILDING! IT'S TIPPING!
SUE, USE YOUR FORCE-FIELD!
UNSEEN ENERGIES FLOW FROM THE INVISIBLE GIRL, AND NOT A MOMENT TOO SOON!
DID IT!
MY FORCE-FIELD HAS BLOCKED THE HOLE. BUT THE BUILDING IS STILL ROCKING!
REED, WHAT CAN IT BE? AN EARTHQUAKE?
WITH THE SPECIAL SHOCK ABSORBERS I BUILT INTO THE FOUNDATIONS, THIS BUILDING COULD RIDE OUT AN EARTHQUAKE WITHOUT SO MUCH AS A TREMOR.
THIS MUST BE SOMETHING MORE...
GOOD LORD!

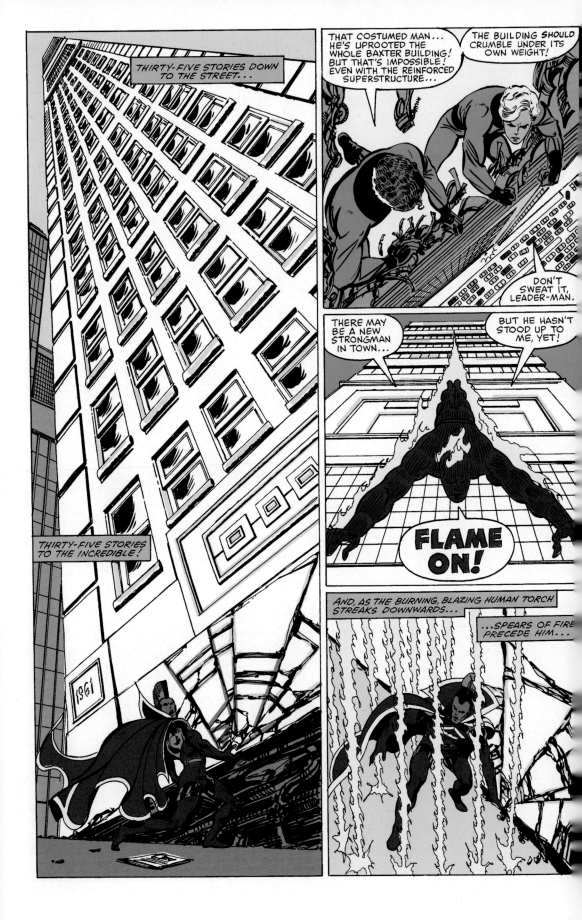

THIRTY-FIVE STORIES DOWN TO THE STREET...

THIRTY-FIVE STORIES TO THE INCREDIBLE!

1861

THAT COSTUMED MAN... HE'S UPROOTED THE WHOLE BAXTER BUILDING! BUT THAT'S IMPOSSIBLE! EVEN WITH THE REINFORCED SUPERSTRUCTURE...

THE BUILDING SHOULD CRUMBLE UNDER ITS OWN WEIGHT!

DON'T SWEAT IT, LEADER-MAN.

THERE MAY BE A NEW STRONGMAN IN TOWN...

BUT HE HASN'T STOOD UP TO ME, YET!

FLAME ON!

AND, AS THE BURNING, BLAZING HUMAN TORCH STREAKS DOWNWARDS...

...SPEARS OF FIRE PRECEDE HIM...

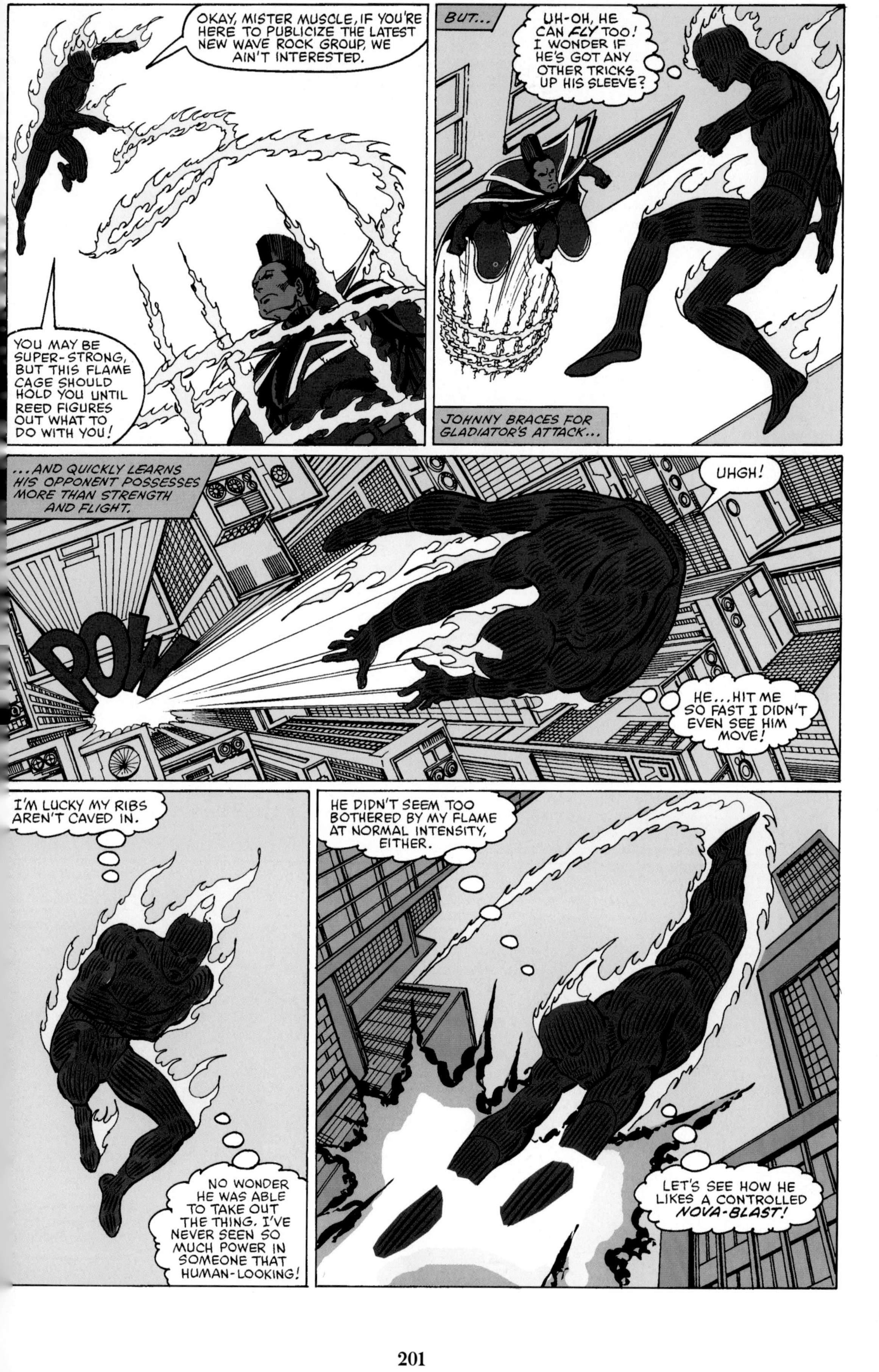
OKAY, MISTER MUSCLE, IF YOU'RE HERE TO PUBLICIZE THE LATEST NEW WAVE ROCK GROUP, WE AIN'T INTERESTED.
YOU MAY BE SUPER-STRONG, BUT THIS FLAME CAGE SHOULD HOLD YOU UNTIL REED FIGURES OUT WHAT TO DO WITH YOU!
BUT...
UH-OH, HE CAN FLY TOO! I WONDER IF HE'S GOT ANY OTHER TRICKS UP HIS SLEEVE?
JOHNNY BRACES FOR GLADIATOR'S ATTACK...
...AND QUICKLY LEARNS HIS OPPONENT POSSESSES MORE THAN STRENGTH AND FLIGHT.
UHGH!
POW
HE...HIT ME SO FAST I DIDN'T EVEN SEE HIM MOVE!
I'M LUCKY MY RIBS AREN'T CAVED IN.
NO WONDER HE WAS ABLE TO TAKE OUT THE THING. I'VE NEVER SEEN SO MUCH POWER IN SOMEONE THAT HUMAN-LOOKING!
HE DIDN'T SEEM TOO BOTHERED BY MY FLAME AT NORMAL INTENSITY, EITHER.
LET'S SEE HOW HE LIKES A CONTROLLED NOVA-BLAST!

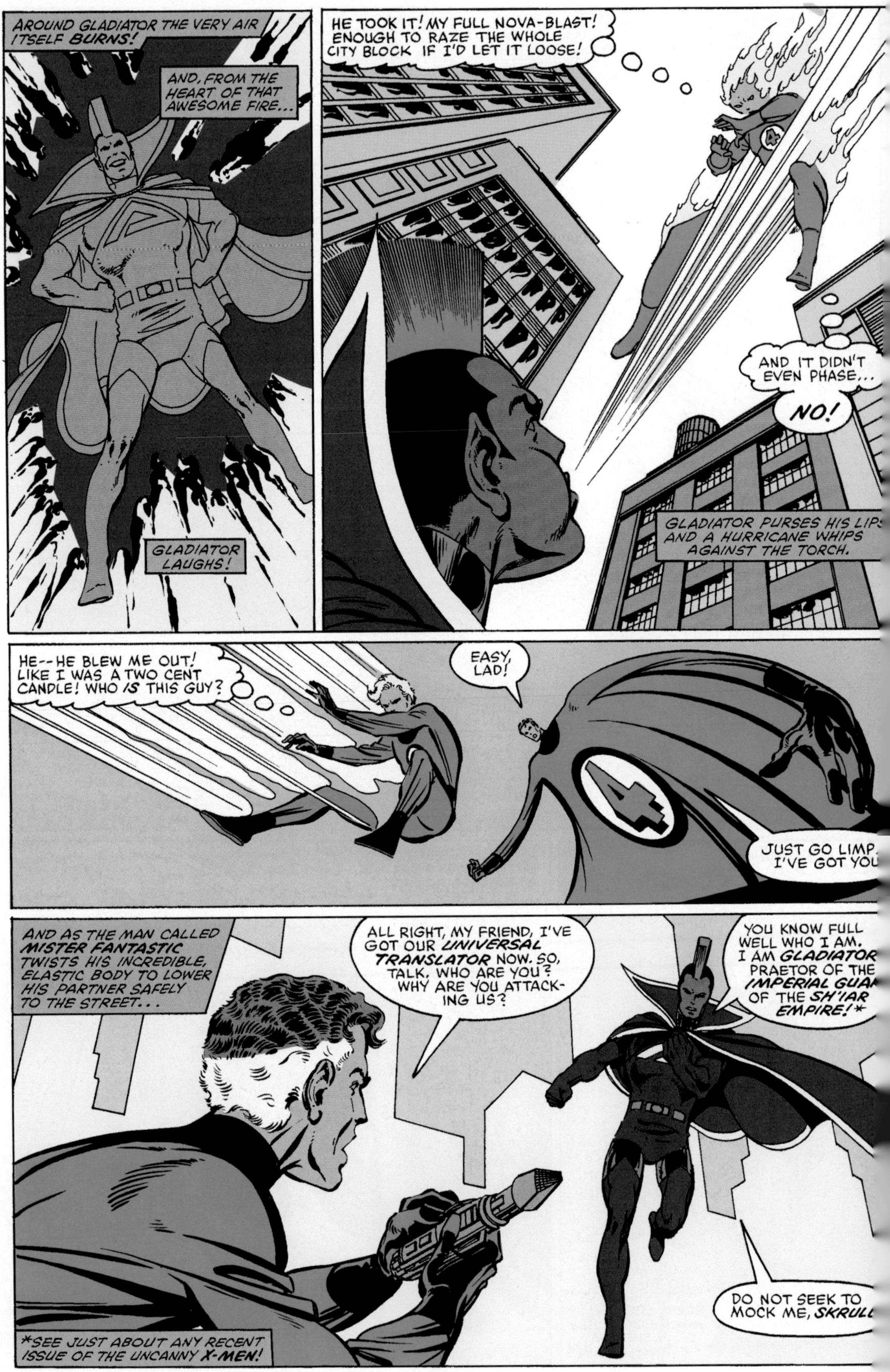

AROUND GLADIATOR THE VERY AIR ITSELF BURNS!
AND, FROM THE HEART OF THAT AWESOME FIRE...
GLADIATOR LAUGHS!
HE TOOK IT! MY FULL NOVA-BLAST! ENOUGH TO RAZE THE WHOLE CITY BLOCK IF I'D LET IT LOOSE!
AND IT DIDN'T EVEN PHASE...
NO!
GLADIATOR PURSES HIS LIPS AND A HURRICANE WHIPS AGAINST THE TORCH.
HE--HE BLEW ME OUT! LIKE I WAS A TWO CENT CANDLE! WHO IS THIS GUY?
EASY, LAD!
JUST GO LIMP. I'VE GOT YOU
AND AS THE MAN CALLED MISTER FANTASTIC TWISTS HIS INCREDIBLE, ELASTIC BODY TO LOWER HIS PARTNER SAFELY TO THE STREET...
ALL RIGHT, MY FRIEND, I'VE GOT OUR UNIVERSAL TRANSLATOR NOW. SO, TALK. WHO ARE YOU? WHY ARE YOU ATTACKING US?
YOU KNOW FULL WELL WHO I AM. I AM GLADIATOR PRAETOR OF THE IMPERIAL GUA OF THE SH'IAR EMPIRE!*
DO NOT SEEK TO MOCK ME, SKRUL
*SEE JUST ABOUT ANY RECENT ISSUE OF THE UNCANNY X-MEN!

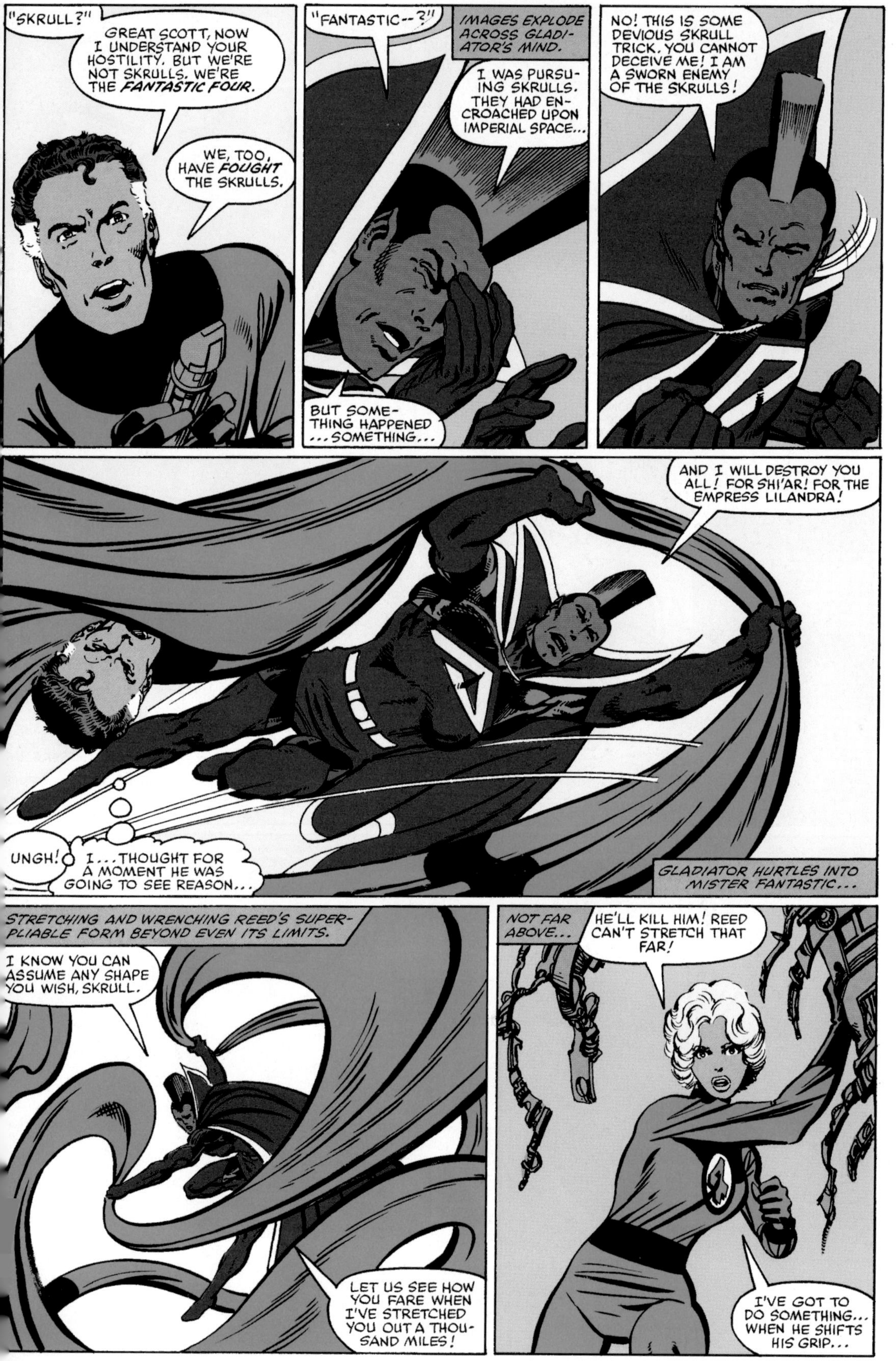
"SKRULL?"
GREAT SCOTT, NOW I UNDERSTAND YOUR HOSTILITY. BUT WE'RE NOT SKRULLS. WE'RE THE FANTASTIC FOUR.
WE, TOO, HAVE FOUGHT THE SKRULLS.
"FANTASTIC--?"
IMAGES EXPLODE ACROSS GLADIATOR'S MIND.
I WAS PURSUING SKRULLS. THEY HAD ENCROACHED UPON IMPERIAL SPACE...
BUT SOMETHING HAPPENED ...SOMETHING...
NO! THIS IS SOME DEVIOUS SKRULL TRICK. YOU CANNOT DECEIVE ME! I AM A SWORN ENEMY OF THE SKRULLS!
AND I WILL DESTROY YOU ALL! FOR SHI'AR! FOR THE EMPRESS LILANDRA!
UNGH!
I...THOUGHT FOR A MOMENT HE WAS GOING TO SEE REASON...
GLADIATOR HURTLES INTO MISTER FANTASTIC...
STRETCHING AND WRENCHING REED'S SUPER-PLIABLE FORM BEYOND EVEN ITS LIMITS.
I KNOW YOU CAN ASSUME ANY SHAPE YOU WISH, SKRULL.
LET US SEE HOW YOU FARE WHEN I'VE STRETCHED YOU OUT A THOUSAND MILES!
NOT FAR ABOVE...
HE'LL KILL HIM! REED CAN'T STRETCH THAT FAR!
I'VE GOT TO DO SOMETHING... WHEN HE SHIFTS HIS GRIP...

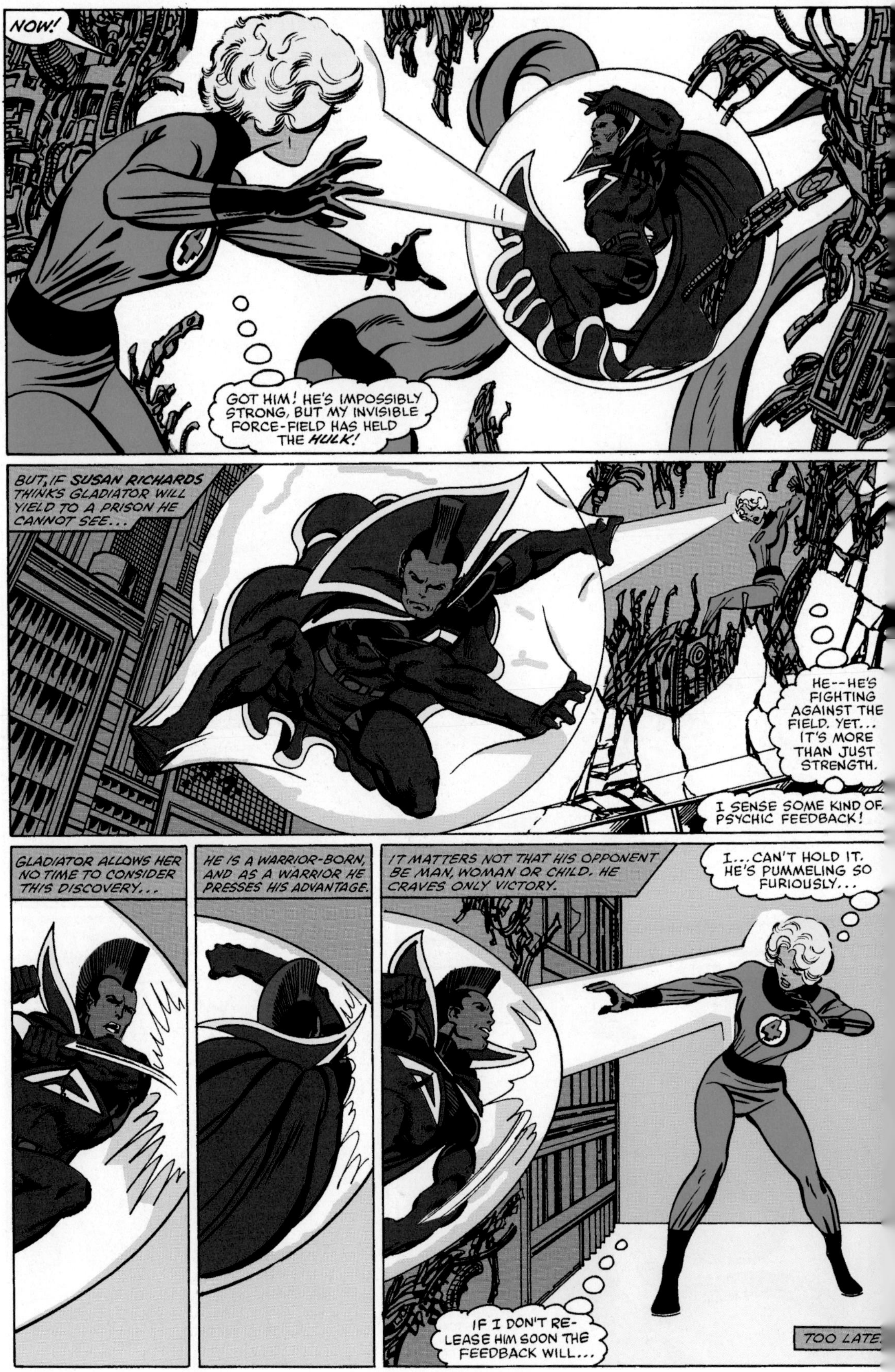
NOW!
GOT HIM! HE'S IMPOSSIBLY STRONG, BUT MY INVISIBLE FORCE-FIELD HAS HELD THE HULK!
BUT, IF SUSAN RICHARDS THINKS GLADIATOR WILL YIELD TO A PRISON HE CANNOT SEE...
HE--HE'S FIGHTING AGAINST THE FIELD. YET... IT'S MORE THAN JUST STRENGTH.
I SENSE SOME KIND OF PSYCHIC FEEDBACK!
GLADIATOR ALLOWS HER NO TIME TO CONSIDER THIS DISCOVERY...
HE IS A WARRIOR-BORN, AND AS A WARRIOR HE PRESSES HIS ADVANTAGE.
IT MATTERS NOT THAT HIS OPPONENT BE MAN, WOMAN OR CHILD. HE CRAVES ONLY VICTORY.
I... CAN'T HOLD IT. HE'S PUMMELING SO FURIOUSLY...
IF I DON'T RELEASE HIM SOON THE FEEDBACK WILL...
TOO LATE

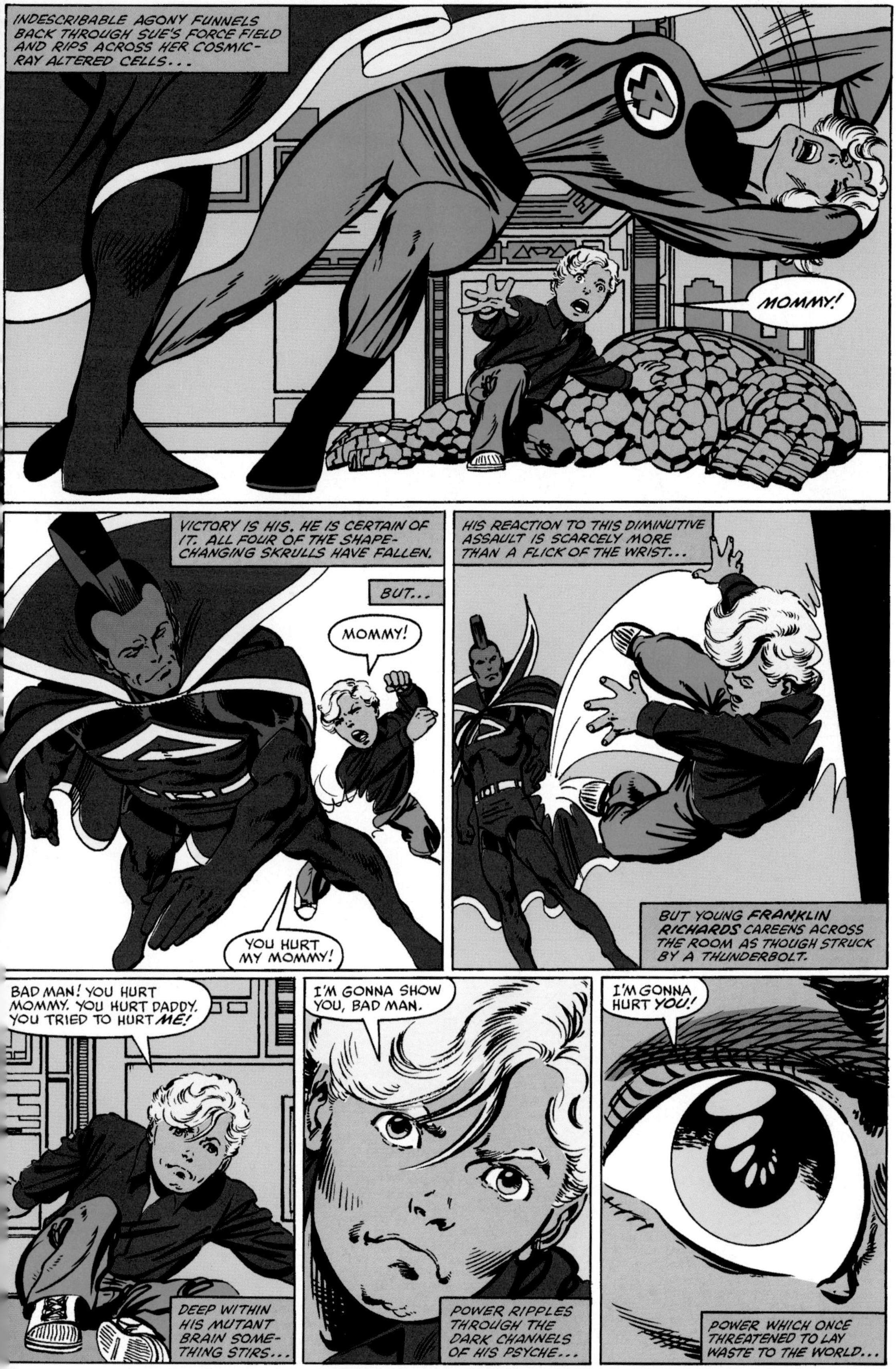
INDESCRIBABLE AGONY FUNNELS BACK THROUGH SUE'S FORCE FIELD AND RIPS ACROSS HER COSMIC-RAY ALTERED CELLS...
MOMMY!
VICTORY IS HIS. HE IS CERTAIN OF IT. ALL FOUR OF THE SHAPE-CHANGING SKRULLS HAVE FALLEN.
BUT...
MOMMY!
YOU HURT MY MOMMY!
HIS REACTION TO THIS DIMINUTIVE ASSAULT IS SCARCELY MORE THAN A FLICK OF THE WRIST...
BUT YOUNG FRANKLIN RICHARDS CAREENS ACROSS THE ROOM AS THOUGH STRUCK BY A THUNDERBOLT.
BAD MAN! YOU HURT MOMMY. YOU HURT DADDY. YOU TRIED TO HURT ME!
DEEP WITHIN HIS MUTANT BRAIN SOMETHING STIRS...
I'M GONNA SHOW YOU, BAD MAN.
POWER RIPPLES THROUGH THE DARK CHANNELS OF HIS PSYCHE...
I'M GONNA HURT YOU!
POWER WHICH ONCE THREATENED TO LAY WASTE TO THE WORLD...

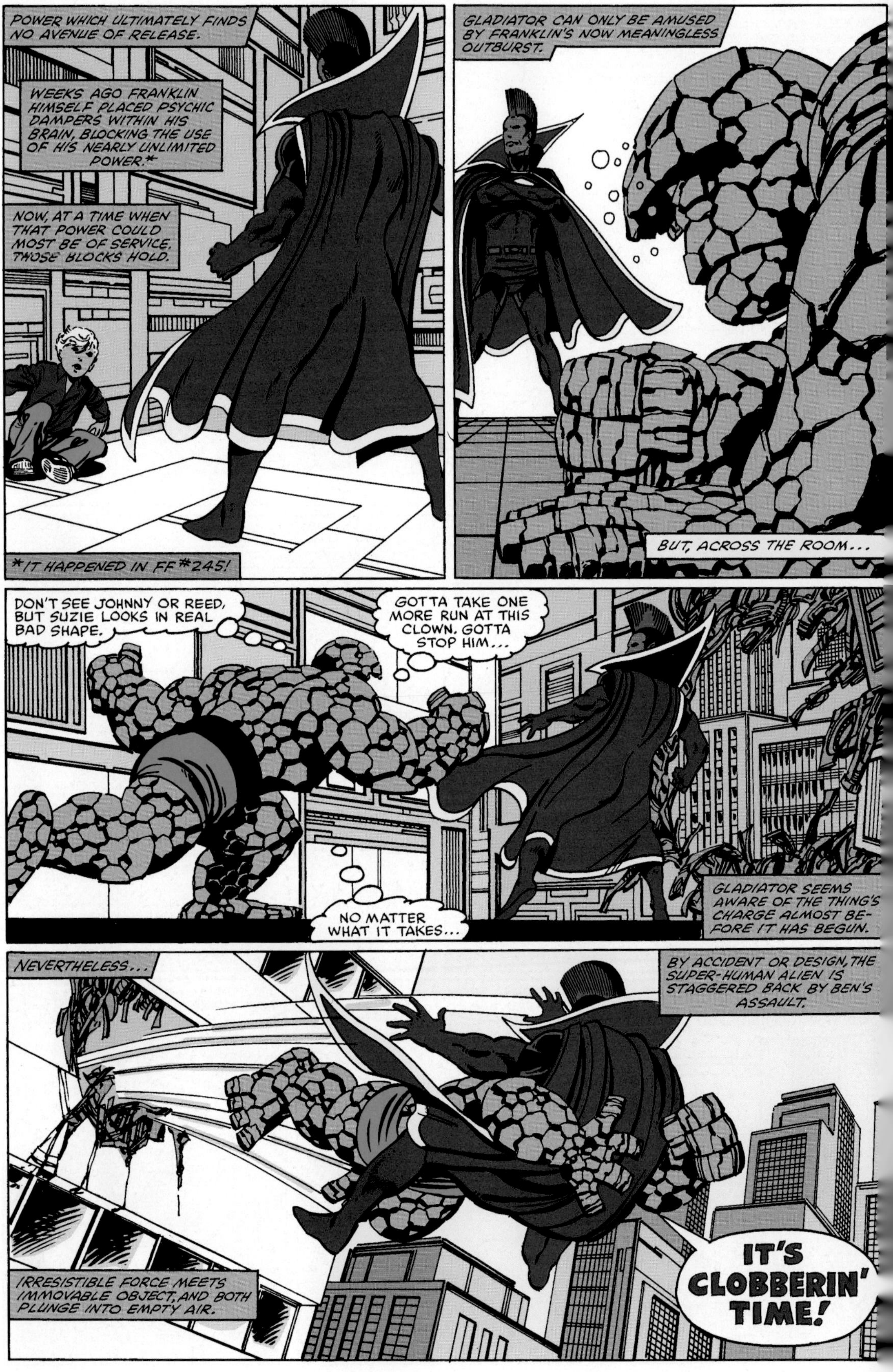
POWER WHICH ULTIMATELY FINDS NO AVENUE OF RELEASE.
WEEKS AGO FRANKLIN HIMSELF PLACED PSYCHIC DAMPERS WITHIN HIS BRAIN, BLOCKING THE USE OF HIS NEARLY UNLIMITED POWER.*
NOW, AT A TIME WHEN THAT POWER COULD MOST BE OF SERVICE, THOSE BLOCKS HOLD.
*IT HAPPENED IN FF #245!
GLADIATOR CAN ONLY BE AMUSED BY FRANKLIN'S NOW MEANINGLESS OUTBURST.
BUT, ACROSS THE ROOM...
DON'T SEE JOHNNY OR REED, BUT SUZIE LOOKS IN REAL BAD SHAPE.
GOTTA TAKE ONE MORE RUN AT THIS CLOWN. GOTTA STOP HIM...
NO MATTER WHAT IT TAKES...
GLADIATOR SEEMS AWARE OF THE THING'S CHARGE ALMOST BEFORE IT HAS BEGUN.
NEVERTHELESS...
BY ACCIDENT OR DESIGN, THE SUPER-HUMAN ALIEN IS STAGGERED BACK BY BEN'S ASSAULT.
IRRESISTIBLE FORCE MEETS IMMOVABLE OBJECT, AND BOTH PLUNGE INTO EMPTY AIR.
IT'S CLOBBERIN' TIME!

BUT THE THING'S FAMOUS BATTLE CRY IS BRAVADO AND NO MORE. STILL DAZED AND WEAK, HE IS NO MATCH FOR GLADIATOR...

THINGS GO BETTER WITH...

KRUNG!

GLADIATOR'S VICTORY CRY SHATTERS WINDOWS FOR BLOCKS AROUND.

HE IS WITHOUT DOUBT THAT NO ONE ON ALL THIS TINY WORLD IS A MATCH FOR HIM--

--TIL HE HEARS WORDS IN HIS OWN TONGUE!

YOU ARE NOT VICTOR YET, WARRIOR OF THE SHI'AR...

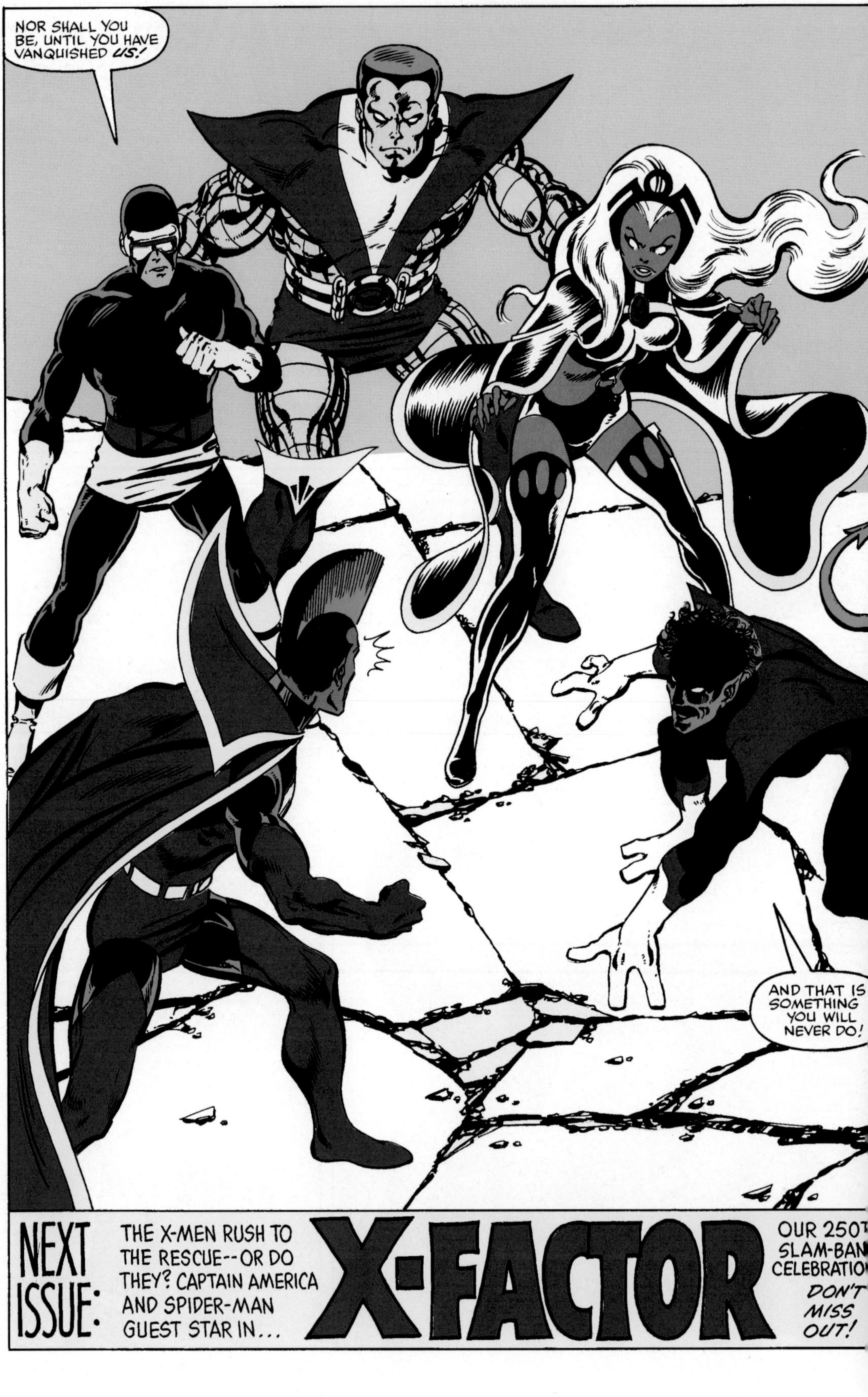
NOR SHALL YOU BE, UNTIL YOU HAVE VANQUISHED US!
AND THAT IS SOMETHING YOU WILL NEVER DO!
NEXT ISSUE:
THE X-MEN RUSH TO THE RESCUE--OR DO THEY? CAPTAIN AMERICA AND SPIDER-MAN GUEST STAR IN...
X-FACTOR
OUR 250T SLAM-BAN CELEBRATIO
DON'T MISS OUT!

fantastic four # 250

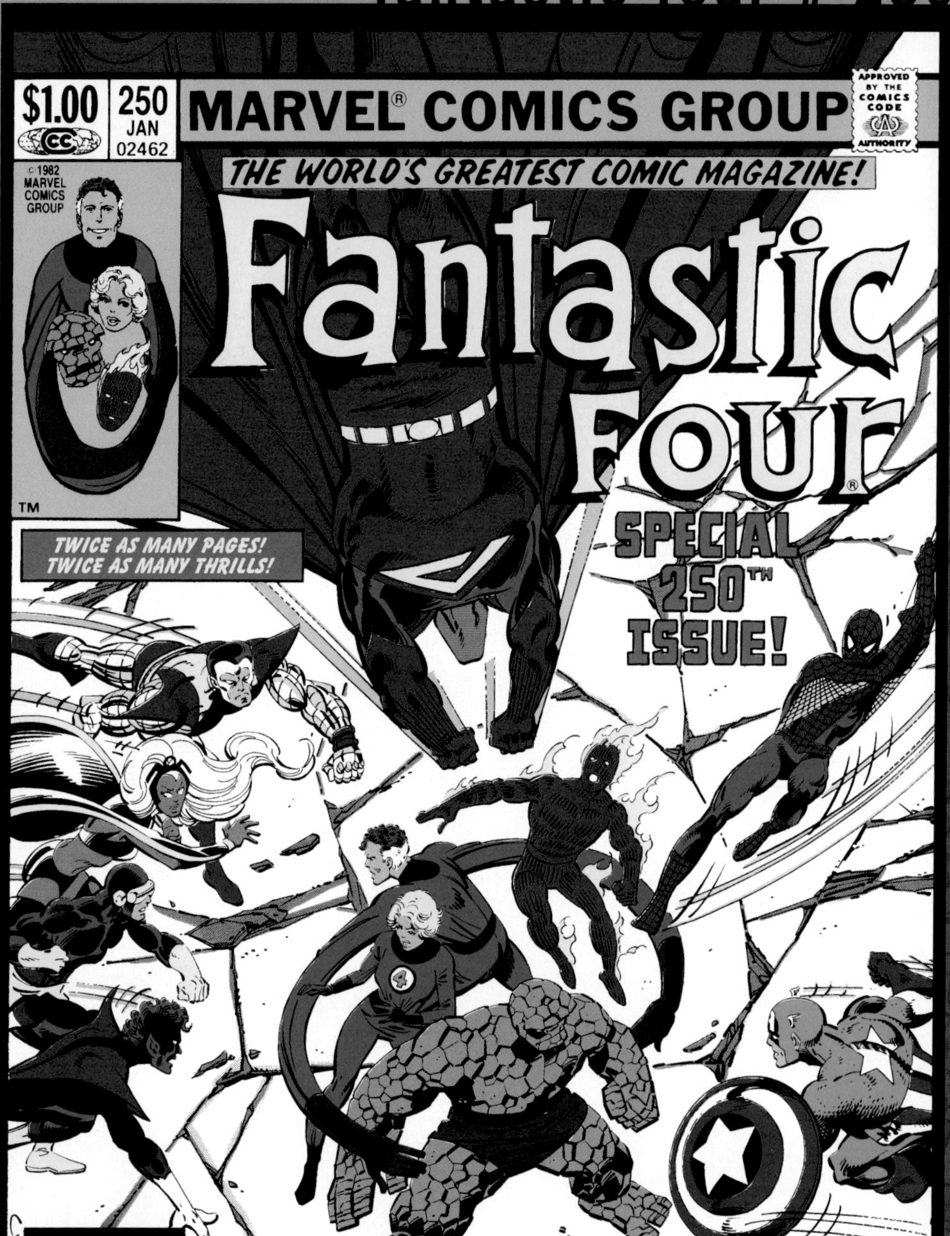

$1.00
250
JAN
02462
MARVEL® COMICS GROUP
APPROVED BY THE COMICS CODE AUTHORITY
©1982 MARVEL COMICS GROUP
THE WORLD'S GREATEST COMIC MAGAZINE!
Fantastic Four®
TM
TWICE AS MANY PAGES! TWICE AS MANY THRILLS!
SPECIAL 250TH ISSUE!
"X-FACTOR!"

JANUARY 1983

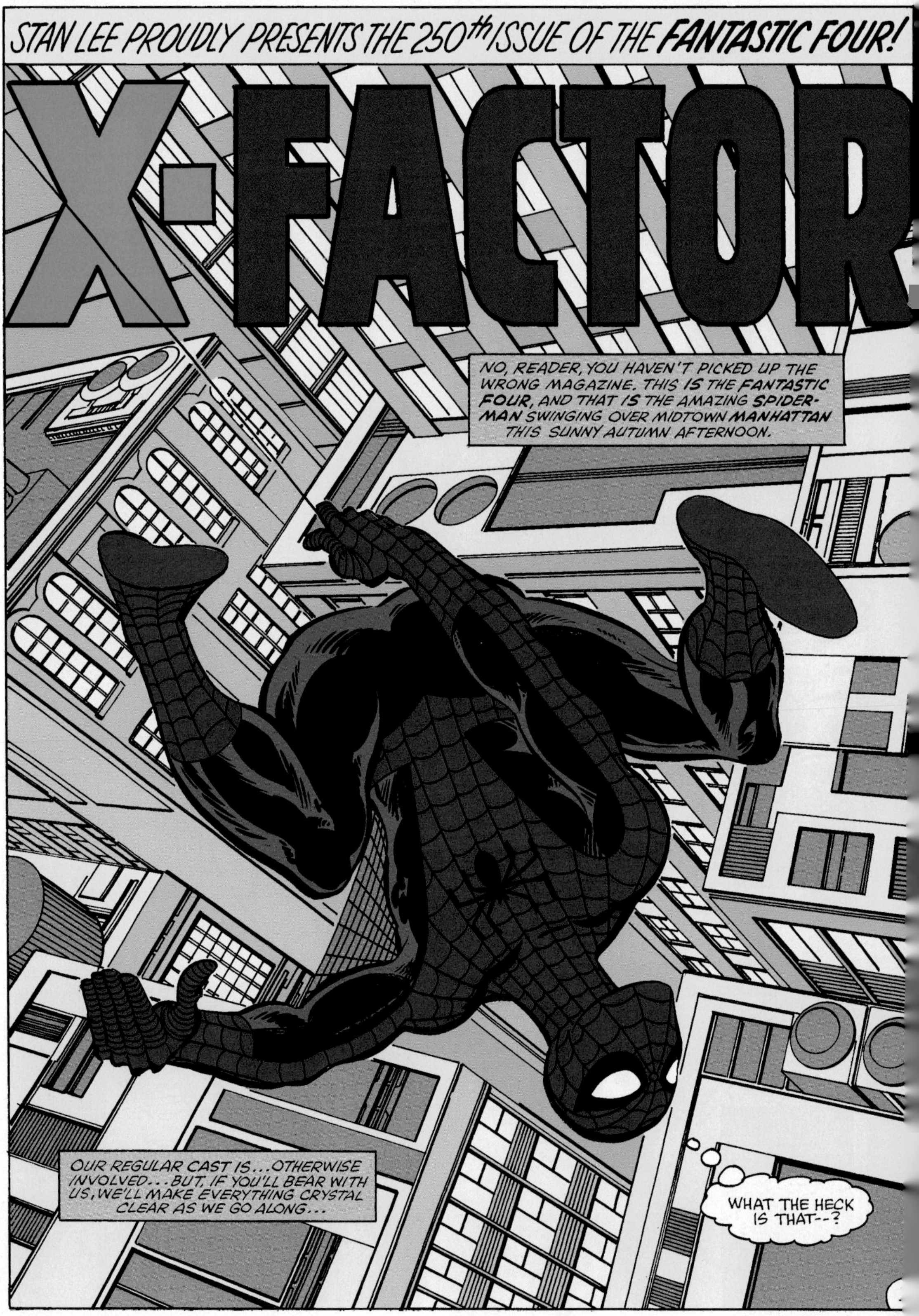
STAN LEE PROUDLY PRESENTS THE 250th ISSUE OF THE FANTASTIC FOUR!
X-FACTOR
NO, READER, YOU HAVEN'T PICKED UP THE WRONG MAGAZINE. THIS IS THE FANTASTIC FOUR, AND THAT IS THE AMAZING SPIDER-MAN SWINGING OVER MIDTOWN MANHATTAN THIS SUNNY AUTUMN AFTERNOON.
OUR REGULAR CAST IS...OTHERWISE INVOLVED...BUT, IF YOU'LL BEAR WITH US, WE'LL MAKE EVERYTHING CRYSTAL CLEAR AS WE GO ALONG...
WHAT THE HECK IS THAT--?

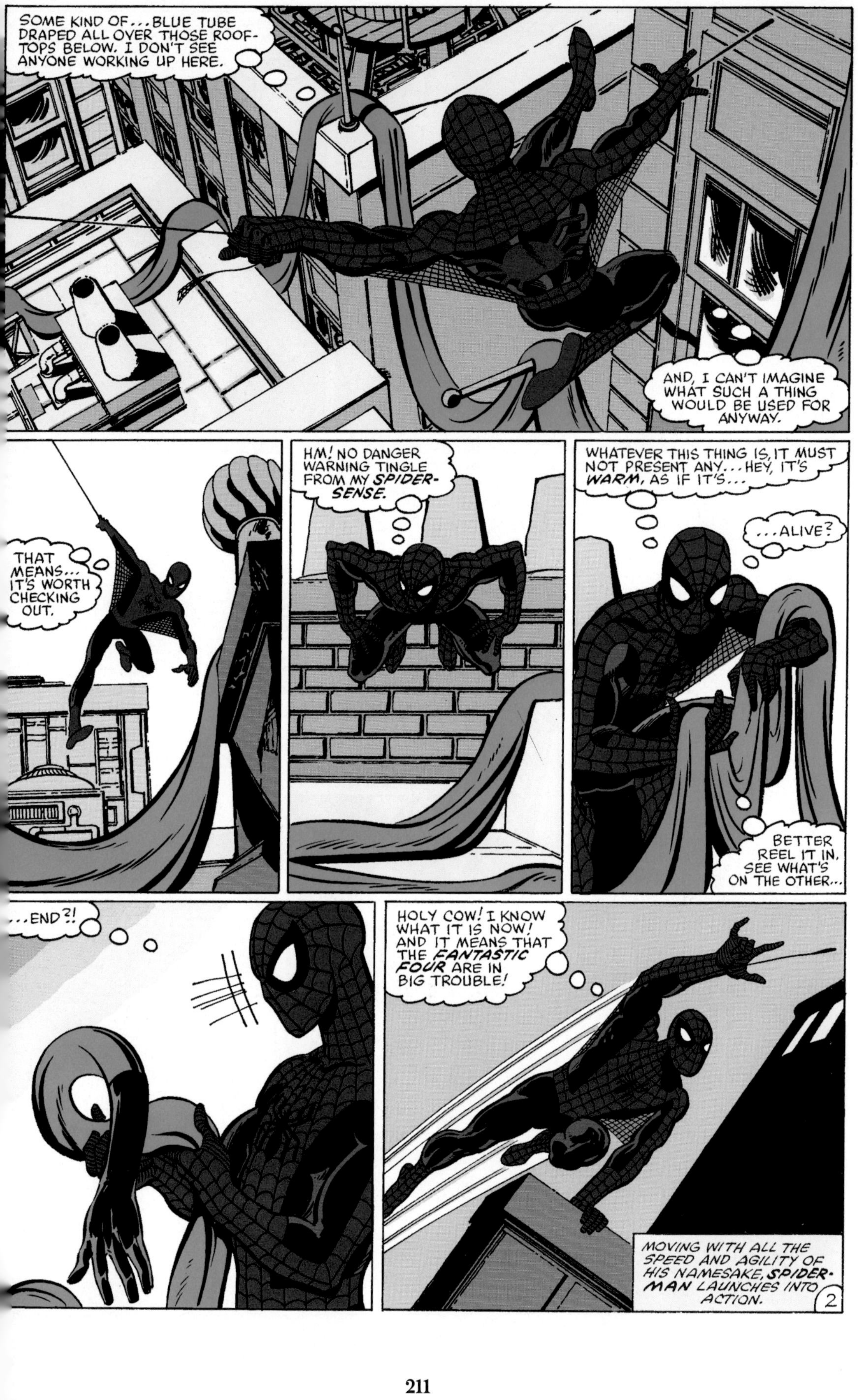
SOME KIND OF... BLUE TUBE DRAPED ALL OVER THOSE ROOF-TOPS BELOW. I DON'T SEE ANYONE WORKING UP HERE.
AND, I CAN'T IMAGINE WHAT SUCH A THING WOULD BE USED FOR ANYWAY.
THAT MEANS... IT'S WORTH CHECKING OUT.
HM! NO DANGER WARNING TINGLE FROM MY SPIDER-SENSE.
WHATEVER THIS THING IS, IT MUST NOT PRESENT ANY... HEY, IT'S WARM, AS IF IT'S...
...ALIVE?
BETTER REEL IT IN, SEE WHAT'S ON THE OTHER...
...END?!
HOLY COW! I KNOW WHAT IT IS NOW! AND IT MEANS THAT THE FANTASTIC FOUR ARE IN BIG TROUBLE!
MOVING WITH ALL THE SPEED AND AGILITY OF HIS NAMESAKE, SPIDER-MAN LAUNCHES INTO ACTION.
2

AND, WITHIN A HEARTBEAT...

THERE HE IS! *MISTER FANTASTIC,* THE *FF'S* HEAD HONCHO!

BOY, HE LOOKS IN MISERABLE SHAPE!

PROFESSOR *RICHARDS...* REED...ARE YOU OKAY?

WH-WHAT... S-SPIDER-MAN? WHAT ARE YOU DOING HERE? WHAT HAPPENED TO ME?

I THINK THAT'S MY QUESTION, FRIEND.

YES--YES, I REMEMBER. I WAS *ATTACKED*--ALL OF THE FANTASTIC FOUR WERE ATTACKED--BY AN INCREDIBLE BEING.

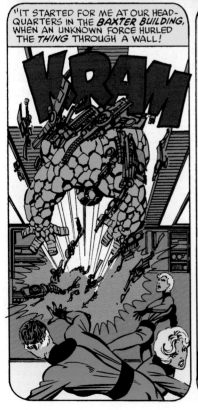

"IT STARTED FOR ME AT OUR HEAD-QUARTERS IN THE *BAXTER BUILDING,* WHEN AN UNKNOWN FORCE HURLED THE *THING* THROUGH A WALL!"

KRAM

"THAT FORCE DID NOT STAY UNKNOWN FOR LONG. SUDDENLY THE WHOLE BUILDING WAS ROCKING..."

"...BECAUSE A COSTUMED MAN HAD *PICKED IT UP* BY ONE CORNER!"

"THAT SHOULD HAVE BEEN IMPOSSIBLE--THE BUILDING SHOULD HAVE FALLEN APART--BUT BEFORE I COULD ANALYZE FURTHER..."

I AM *GLADIATOR,* PRAETOR OF THE IMPERIAL GUARD OF THE SH'IAR EMPIRE. I HAVE COME TO DESTROY YOU, *SKRULLS!**

**AS TRANSLATED LAST ISSUE BY REED'S UNIVERSAL TRANSLATOR!*

3

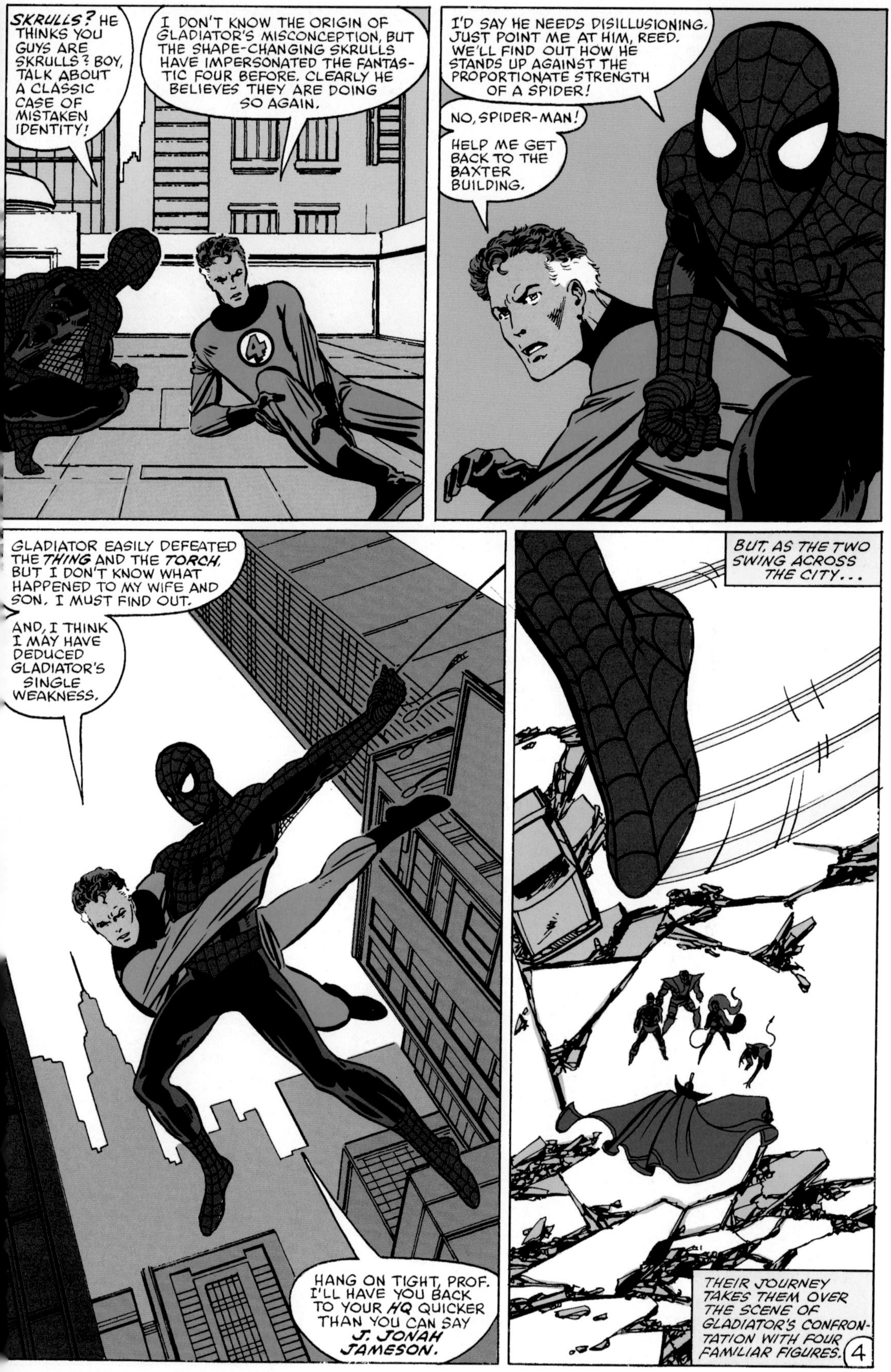
SKRULLS? HE THINKS YOU GUYS ARE SKRULLS? BOY, TALK ABOUT A CLASSIC CASE OF MISTAKEN IDENTITY!
I DON'T KNOW THE ORIGIN OF GLADIATOR'S MISCONCEPTION, BUT THE SHAPE-CHANGING SKRULLS HAVE IMPERSONATED THE FANTASTIC FOUR BEFORE. CLEARLY HE BELIEVES THEY ARE DOING SO AGAIN.
I'D SAY HE NEEDS DISILLUSIONING. JUST POINT ME AT HIM, REED. WE'LL FIND OUT HOW HE STANDS UP AGAINST THE PROPORTIONATE STRENGTH OF A SPIDER!
NO, SPIDER-MAN!
HELP ME GET BACK TO THE BAXTER BUILDING.
GLADIATOR EASILY DEFEATED THE THING AND THE TORCH, BUT I DON'T KNOW WHAT HAPPENED TO MY WIFE AND SON. I MUST FIND OUT.
AND, I THINK I MAY HAVE DEDUCED GLADIATOR'S SINGLE WEAKNESS.
HANG ON TIGHT, PROF. I'LL HAVE YOU BACK TO YOUR HQ QUICKER THAN YOU CAN SAY J. JONAH JAMESON.
BUT, AS THE TWO SWING ACROSS THE CITY...
THEIR JOURNEY TAKES THEM OVER THE SCENE OF GLADIATOR'S CONFRONTATION WITH FOUR FAMILIAR FIGURES.
4

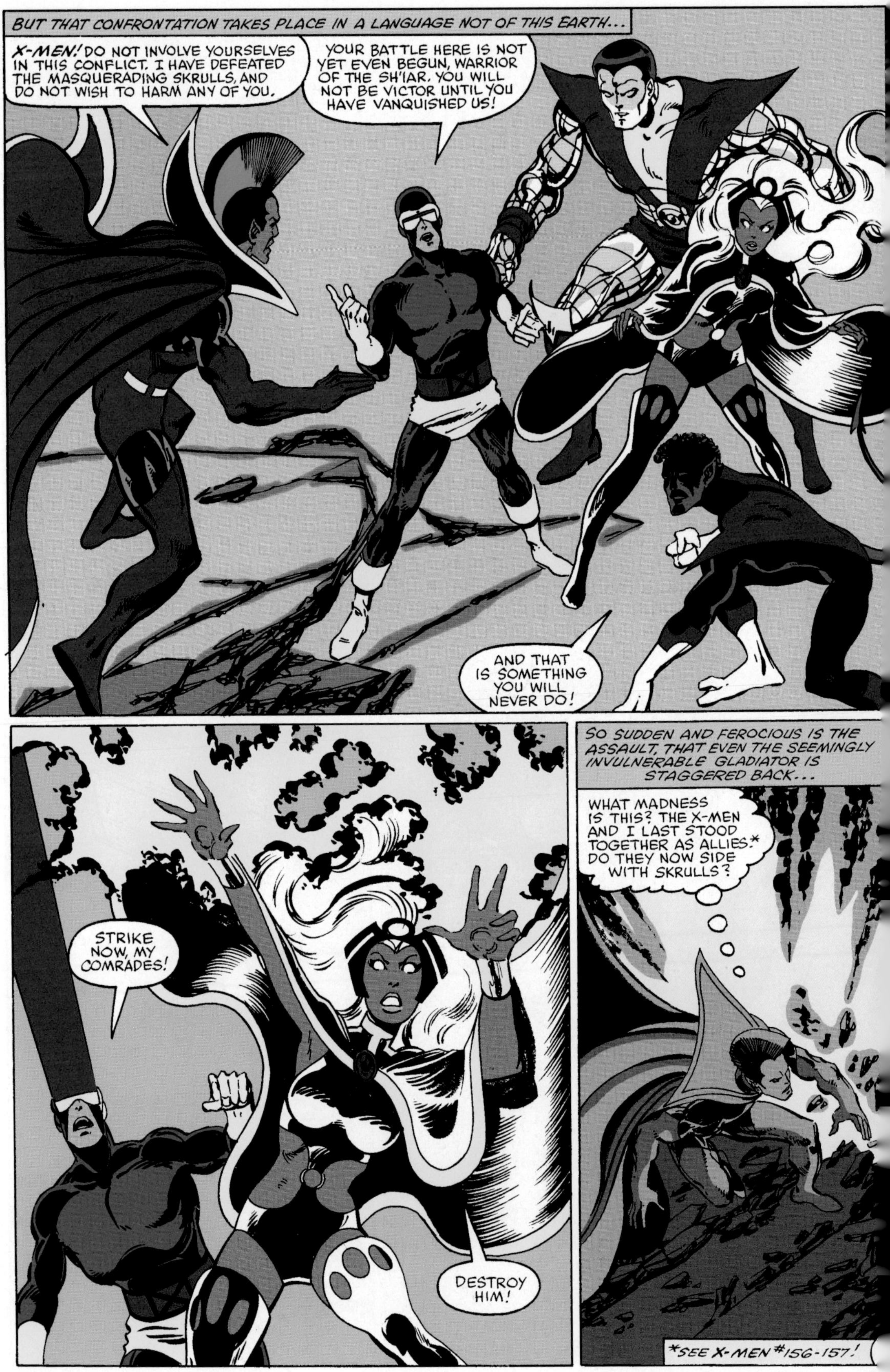
BUT THAT CONFRONTATION TAKES PLACE IN A LANGUAGE NOT OF THIS EARTH...
X-MEN! DO NOT INVOLVE YOURSELVES IN THIS CONFLICT. I HAVE DEFEATED THE MASQUERADING SKRULLS, AND DO NOT WISH TO HARM ANY OF YOU.
YOUR BATTLE HERE IS NOT YET EVEN BEGUN, WARRIOR OF THE SH'IAR. YOU WILL NOT BE VICTOR UNTIL YOU HAVE VANQUISHED US!
AND THAT IS SOMETHING YOU WILL NEVER DO!
STRIKE NOW, MY COMRADES!
DESTROY HIM!
SO SUDDEN AND FEROCIOUS IS THE ASSAULT, THAT EVEN THE SEEMINGLY INVULNERABLE GLADIATOR IS STAGGERED BACK...
WHAT MADNESS IS THIS? THE X-MEN AND I LAST STOOD TOGETHER AS ALLIES.* DO THEY NOW SIDE WITH SKRULLS?
*SEE X-MEN #156-157!

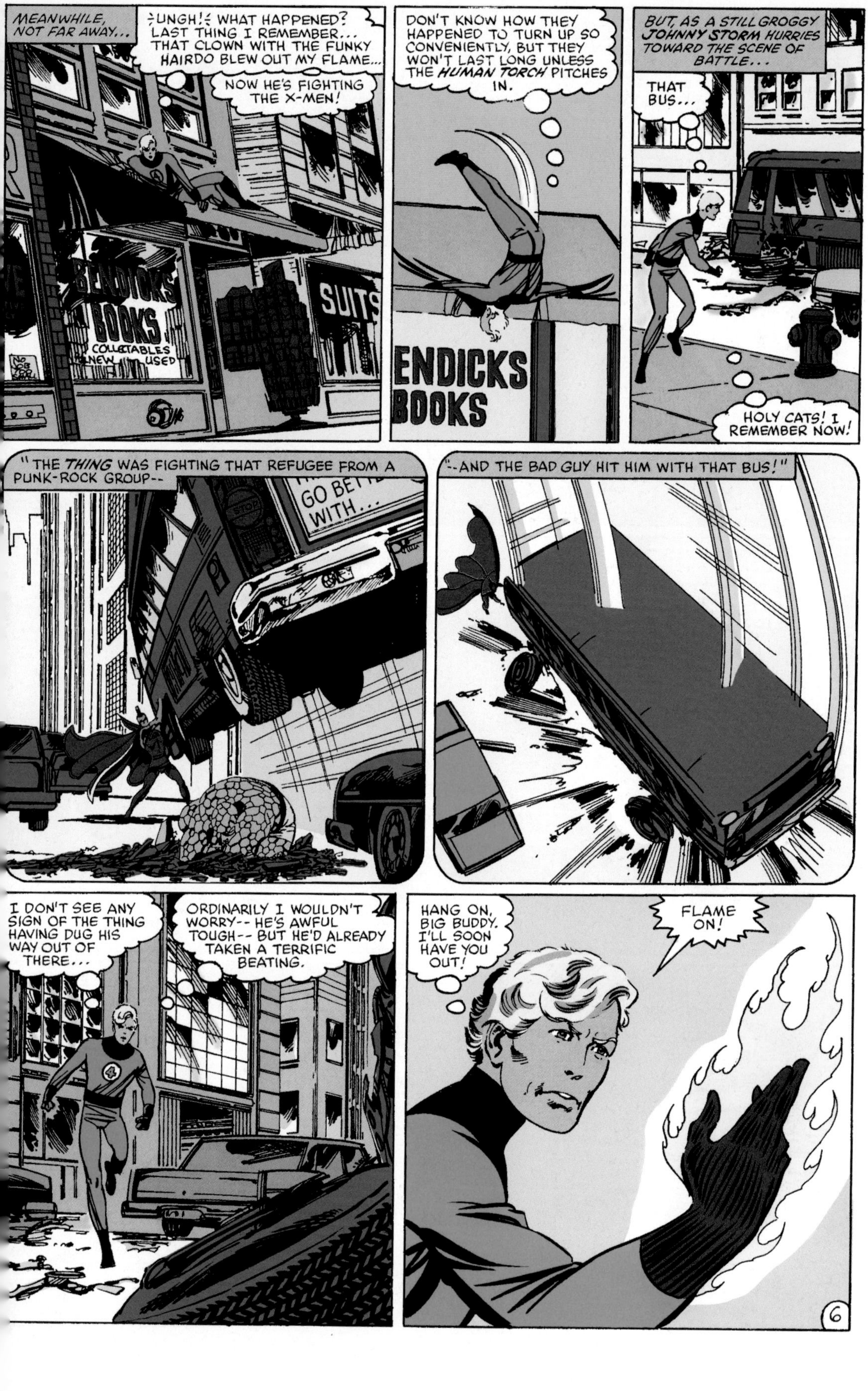
MEANWHILE, NOT FAR AWAY...
UNGH! WHAT HAPPENED? LAST THING I REMEMBER... THAT CLOWN WITH THE FUNKY HAIRDO BLEW OUT MY FLAME...
NOW HE'S FIGHTING THE X-MEN!
BENDICKS BOOKS
COLLECTABLES NEW USED
SUITS
DON'T KNOW HOW THEY HAPPENED TO TURN UP SO CONVENIENTLY, BUT THEY WON'T LAST LONG UNLESS THE HUMAN TORCH PITCHES IN.
ENDICKS BOOKS
BUT, AS A STILL GROGGY JOHNNY STORM HURRIES TOWARD THE SCENE OF BATTLE...
THAT BUS...
HOLY CATS! I REMEMBER NOW!
"THE THING WAS FIGHTING THAT REFUGEE FROM A PUNK-ROCK GROUP--
GO BETT WITH...
"--AND THE BAD GUY HIT HIM WITH THAT BUS!"
I DON'T SEE ANY SIGN OF THE THING HAVING DUG HIS WAY OUT OF THERE...
ORDINARILY I WOULDN'T WORRY-- HE'S AWFUL TOUGH-- BUT HE'D ALREADY TAKEN A TERRIFIC BEATING.
HANG ON, BIG BUDDY. I'LL SOON HAVE YOU OUT!
FLAME ON!
6

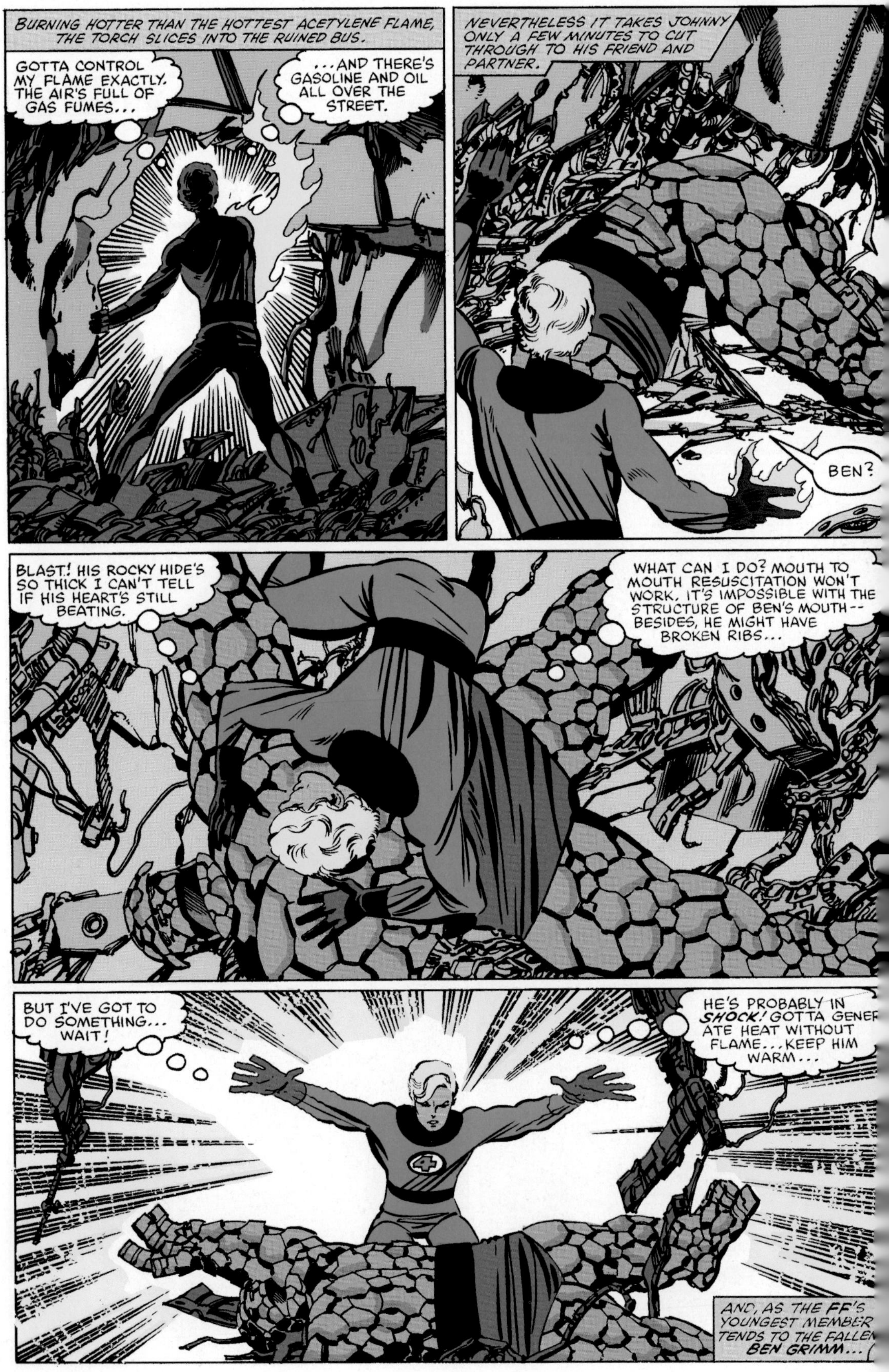

BURNING HOTTER THAN THE HOTTEST ACETYLENE FLAME, THE TORCH SLICES INTO THE RUINED BUS.
GOTTA CONTROL MY FLAME EXACTLY. THE AIR'S FULL OF GAS FUMES...
...AND THERE'S GASOLINE AND OIL ALL OVER THE STREET.
NEVERTHELESS IT TAKES JOHNNY ONLY A FEW MINUTES TO CUT THROUGH TO HIS FRIEND AND PARTNER.
BEN?
BLAST! HIS ROCKY HIDE'S SO THICK I CAN'T TELL IF HIS HEART'S STILL BEATING.
WHAT CAN I DO? MOUTH TO MOUTH RESUSCITATION WON'T WORK. IT'S IMPOSSIBLE WITH THE STRUCTURE OF BEN'S MOUTH-- BESIDES, HE MIGHT HAVE BROKEN RIBS...
BUT I'VE GOT TO DO SOMETHING... WAIT!
HE'S PROBABLY IN SHOCK! GOTTA GENER ATE HEAT WITHOUT FLAME... KEEP HIM WARM...
AND, AS THE FF'S YOUNGEST MEMBER TENDS TO THE FALLEN BEN GRIMM...

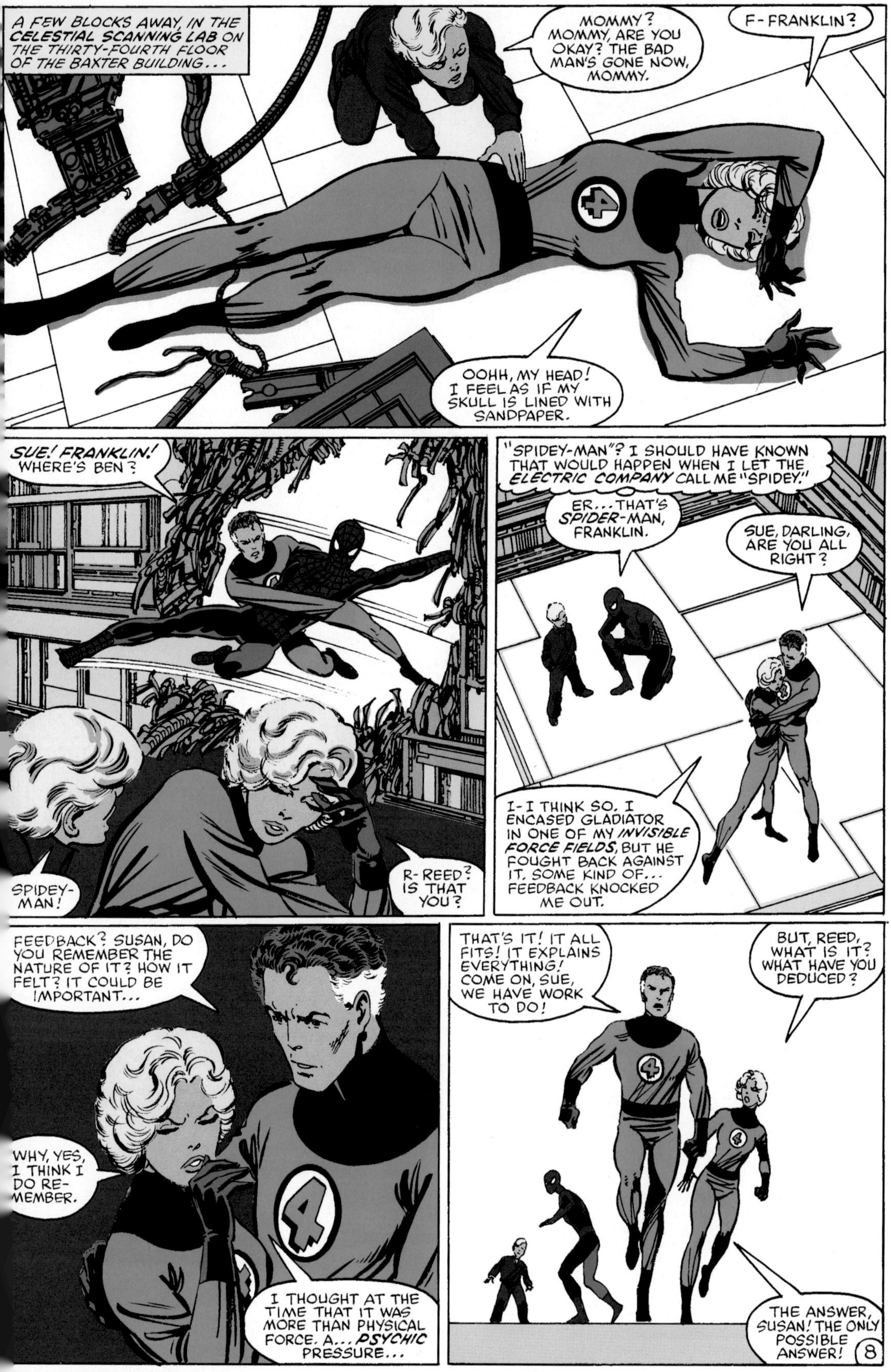

A FEW BLOCKS AWAY, IN THE CELESTIAL SCANNING LAB ON THE THIRTY-FOURTH FLOOR OF THE BAXTER BUILDING...
MOMMY? MOMMY, ARE YOU OKAY? THE BAD MAN'S GONE NOW, MOMMY.
F-FRANKLIN?
OOHH, MY HEAD! I FEEL AS IF MY SKULL IS LINED WITH SANDPAPER.
SUE! FRANKLIN! WHERE'S BEN?
SPIDEY-MAN!
R-REED? IS THAT YOU?
"SPIDEY-MAN"? I SHOULD HAVE KNOWN THAT WOULD HAPPEN WHEN I LET THE ELECTRIC COMPANY CALL ME "SPIDEY."
ER... THAT'S SPIDER-MAN, FRANKLIN.
SUE, DARLING, ARE YOU ALL RIGHT?
I-I THINK SO. I ENCASED GLADIATOR IN ONE OF MY INVISIBLE FORCE FIELDS, BUT HE FOUGHT BACK AGAINST IT. SOME KIND OF... FEEDBACK KNOCKED ME OUT.
FEEDBACK? SUSAN, DO YOU REMEMBER THE NATURE OF IT? HOW IT FELT? IT COULD BE IMPORTANT...
WHY, YES, I THINK I DO RE-MEMBER.
I THOUGHT AT THE TIME THAT IT WAS MORE THAN PHYSICAL FORCE. A... PSYCHIC PRESSURE...
THAT'S IT! IT ALL FITS! IT EXPLAINS EVERYTHING! COME ON, SUE, WE HAVE WORK TO DO!
BUT, REED, WHAT IS IT? WHAT HAVE YOU DEDUCED?
THE ANSWER, SUSAN! THE ONLY POSSIBLE ANSWER!
8

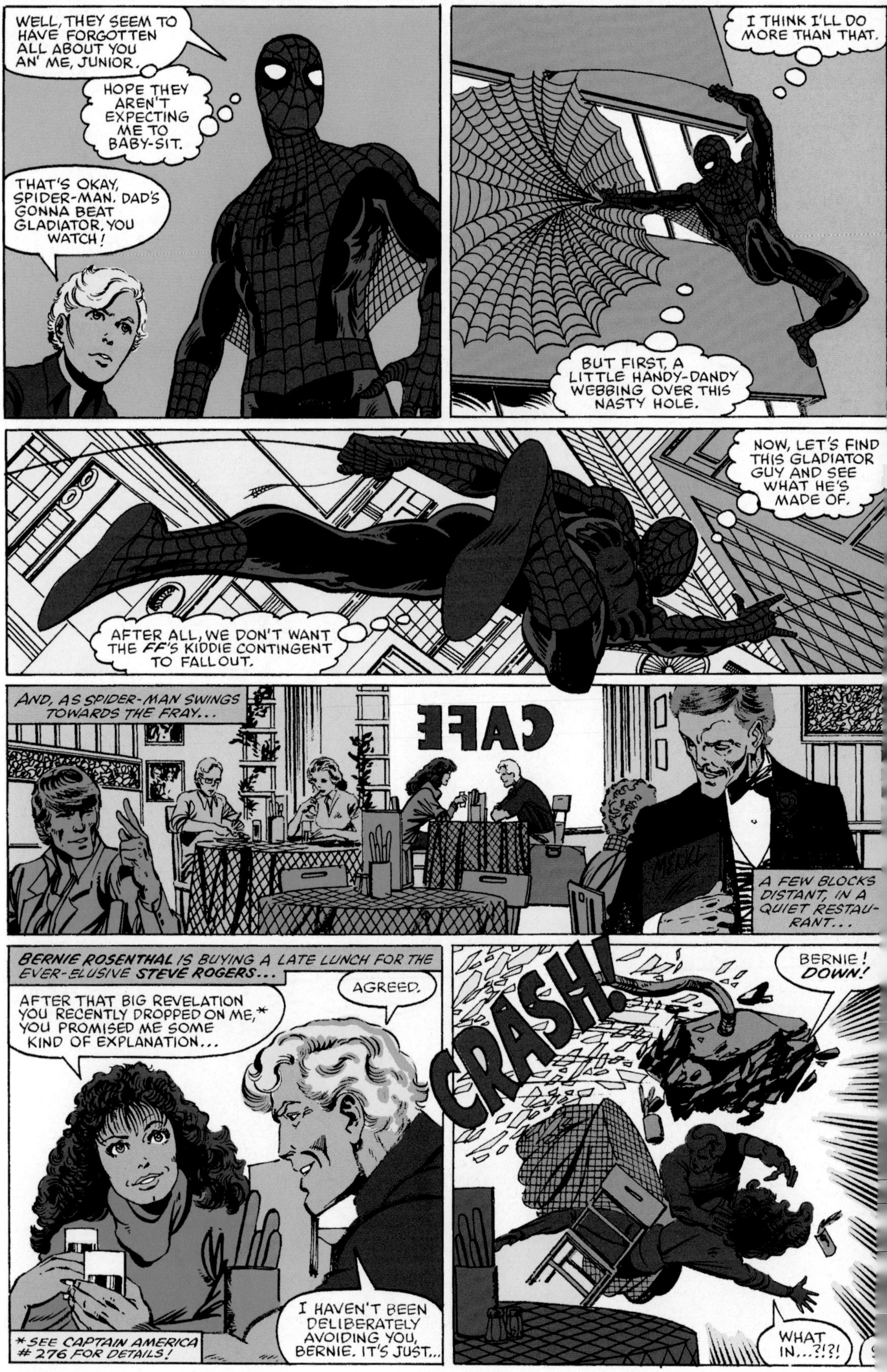
WELL, THEY SEEM TO HAVE FORGOTTEN ALL ABOUT YOU AN' ME, JUNIOR.
HOPE THEY AREN'T EXPECTING ME TO BABY-SIT.
THAT'S OKAY, SPIDER-MAN. DAD'S GONNA BEAT GLADIATOR, YOU WATCH!
I THINK I'LL DO MORE THAN THAT.
BUT FIRST, A LITTLE HANDY-DANDY WEBBING OVER THIS NASTY HOLE.
NOW, LET'S FIND THIS GLADIATOR GUY AND SEE WHAT HE'S MADE OF.
AFTER ALL, WE DON'T WANT THE FF'S KIDDIE CONTINGENT TO FALL OUT.
AND, AS SPIDER-MAN SWINGS TOWARDS THE FRAY...
CAFE
A FEW BLOCKS DISTANT, IN A QUIET RESTAU-RANT...
BERNIE ROSENTHAL IS BUYING A LATE LUNCH FOR THE EVER-ELUSIVE STEVE ROGERS...
AFTER THAT BIG REVELATION YOU RECENTLY DROPPED ON ME,* YOU PROMISED ME SOME KIND OF EXPLANATION...
AGREED.
I HAVEN'T BEEN DELIBERATELY AVOIDING YOU, BERNIE. IT'S JUST...
*SEE CAPTAIN AMERICA #276 FOR DETAILS!
CRASH!
BERNIE! DOWN!
WHAT IN...?!?!

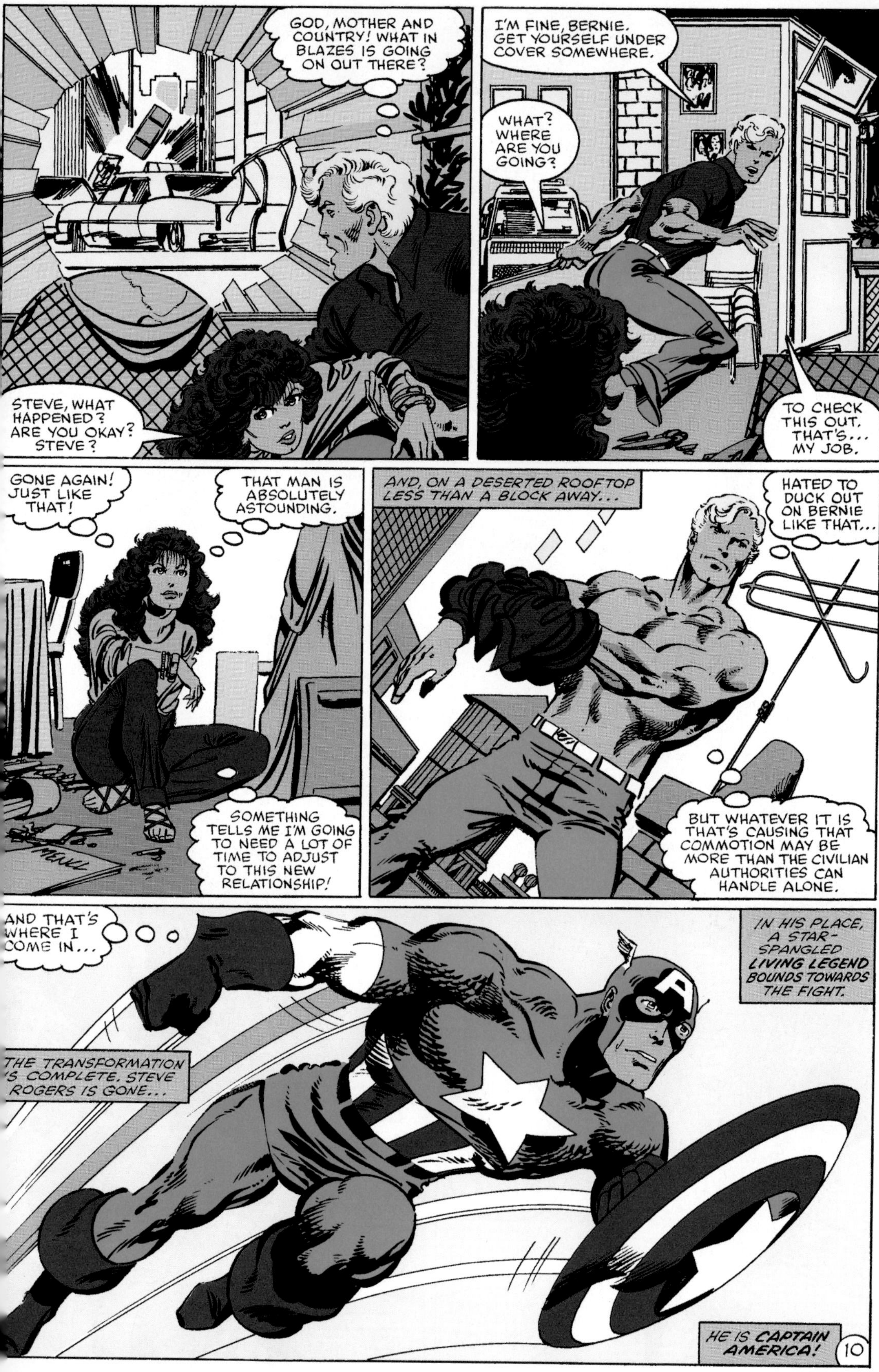
GOD, MOTHER AND COUNTRY! WHAT IN BLAZES IS GOING ON OUT THERE?
STEVE, WHAT HAPPENED? ARE YOU OKAY? STEVE?
I'M FINE, BERNIE. GET YOURSELF UNDER COVER SOMEWHERE.
WHAT? WHERE ARE YOU GOING?
TO CHECK THIS OUT. THAT'S... MY JOB.
GONE AGAIN! JUST LIKE THAT!
THAT MAN IS ABSOLUTELY ASTOUNDING.
SOMETHING TELLS ME I'M GOING TO NEED A LOT OF TIME TO ADJUST TO THIS NEW RELATIONSHIP!
AND, ON A DESERTED ROOFTOP LESS THAN A BLOCK AWAY...
HATED TO DUCK OUT ON BERNIE LIKE THAT...
BUT WHATEVER IT IS THAT'S CAUSING THAT COMMOTION MAY BE MORE THAN THE CIVILIAN AUTHORITIES CAN HANDLE ALONE.
AND THAT'S WHERE I COME IN...
THE TRANSFORMATION IS COMPLETE. STEVE ROGERS IS GONE...
IN HIS PLACE, A STAR-SPANGLED LIVING LEGEND BOUNDS TOWARDS THE FIGHT.
HE IS CAPTAIN AMERICA!
10

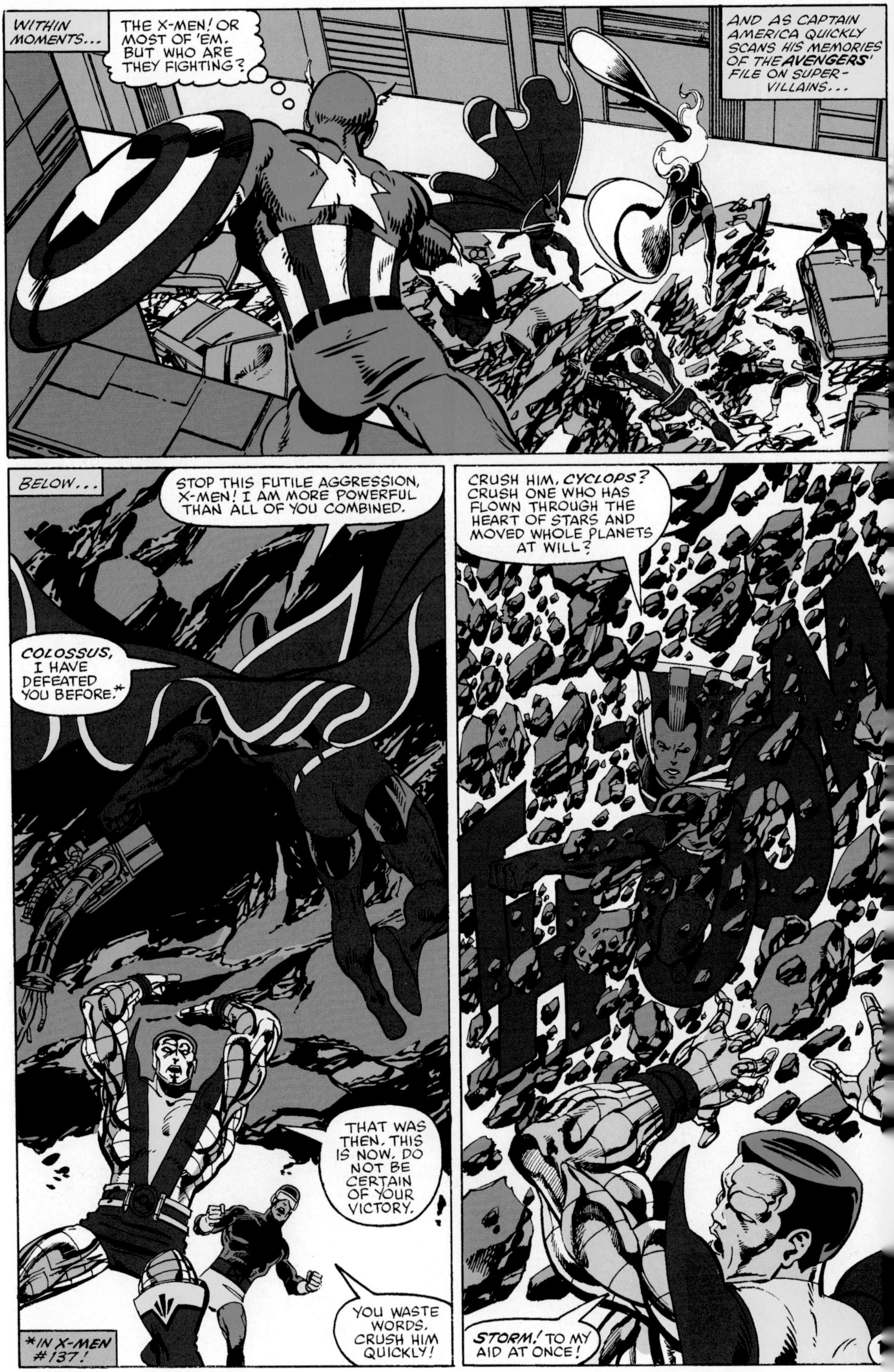

WITHIN MOMENTS...
THE X-MEN! OR MOST OF 'EM. BUT WHO ARE THEY FIGHTING?
AND AS CAPTAIN AMERICA QUICKLY SCANS HIS MEMORIES OF THE AVENGERS' FILE ON SUPER-VILLAINS...
BELOW...
STOP THIS FUTILE AGGRESSION, X-MEN! I AM MORE POWERFUL THAN ALL OF YOU COMBINED.
COLOSSUS, I HAVE DEFEATED YOU BEFORE.*
THAT WAS THEN. THIS IS NOW. DO NOT BE CERTAIN OF YOUR VICTORY.
YOU WASTE WORDS. CRUSH HIM QUICKLY!
*IN X-MEN #137!
CRUSH HIM, CYCLOPS? CRUSH ONE WHO HAS FLOWN THROUGH THE HEART OF STARS AND MOVED WHOLE PLANETS AT WILL?
THOOM
STORM! TO MY AID AT ONCE!

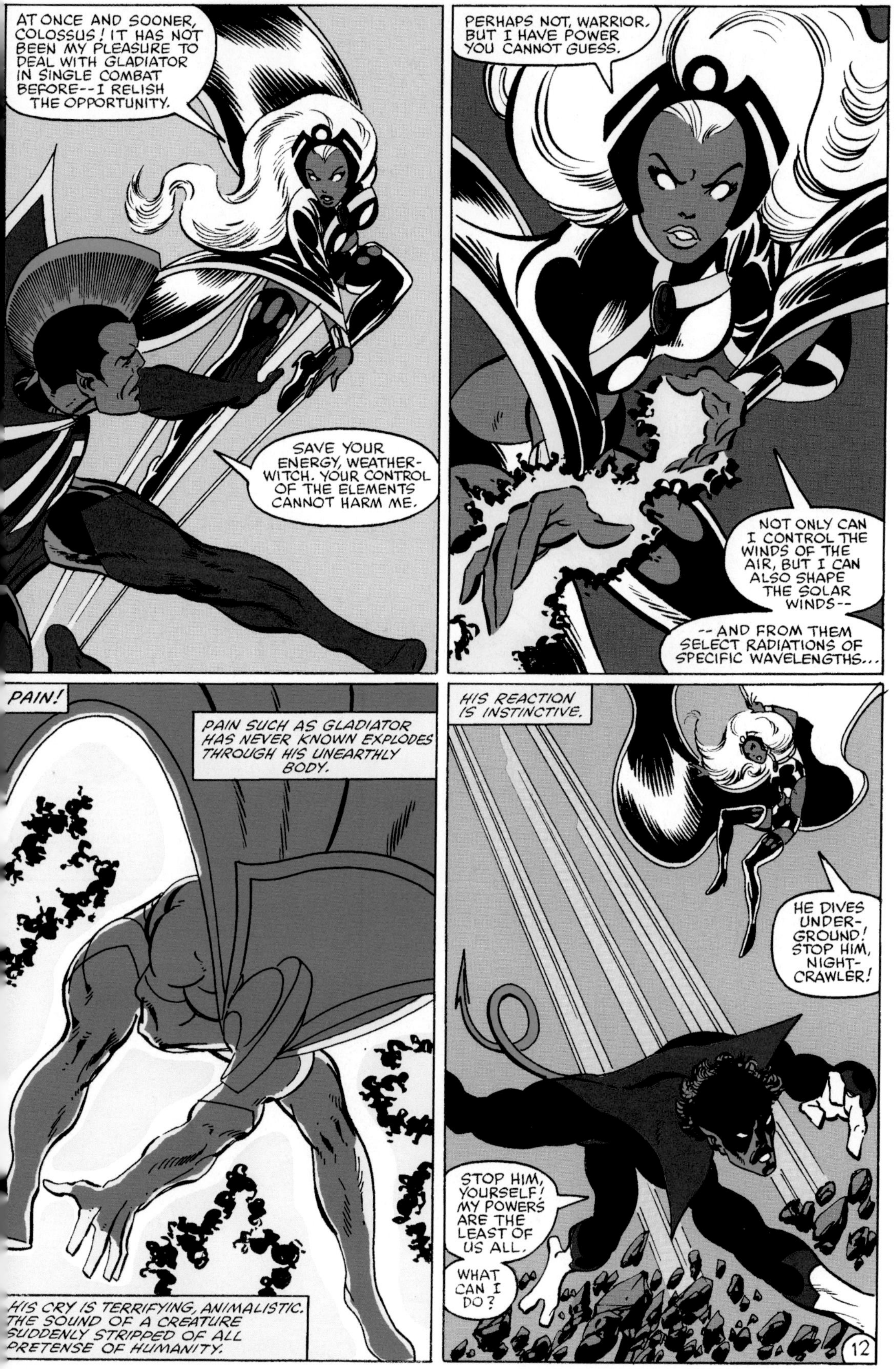

AT ONCE AND SOONER, COLOSSUS! IT HAS NOT BEEN MY PLEASURE TO DEAL WITH GLADIATOR IN SINGLE COMBAT BEFORE--I RELISH THE OPPORTUNITY.
SAVE YOUR ENERGY, WEATHER-WITCH. YOUR CONTROL OF THE ELEMENTS CANNOT HARM ME.
PERHAPS NOT, WARRIOR, BUT I HAVE POWER YOU CANNOT GUESS.
NOT ONLY CAN I CONTROL THE WINDS OF THE AIR, BUT I CAN ALSO SHAPE THE SOLAR WINDS--
--AND FROM THEM SELECT RADIATIONS OF SPECIFIC WAVELENGTHS...
PAIN!
PAIN SUCH AS GLADIATOR HAS NEVER KNOWN EXPLODES THROUGH HIS UNEARTHLY BODY.
HIS CRY IS TERRIFYING, ANIMALISTIC. THE SOUND OF A CREATURE SUDDENLY STRIPPED OF ALL PRETENSE OF HUMANITY.
HIS REACTION IS INSTINCTIVE.
HE DIVES UNDER-GROUND! STOP HIM, NIGHT-CRAWLER!
STOP HIM, YOURSELF! MY POWERS ARE THE LEAST OF US ALL.
WHAT CAN I DO?
12

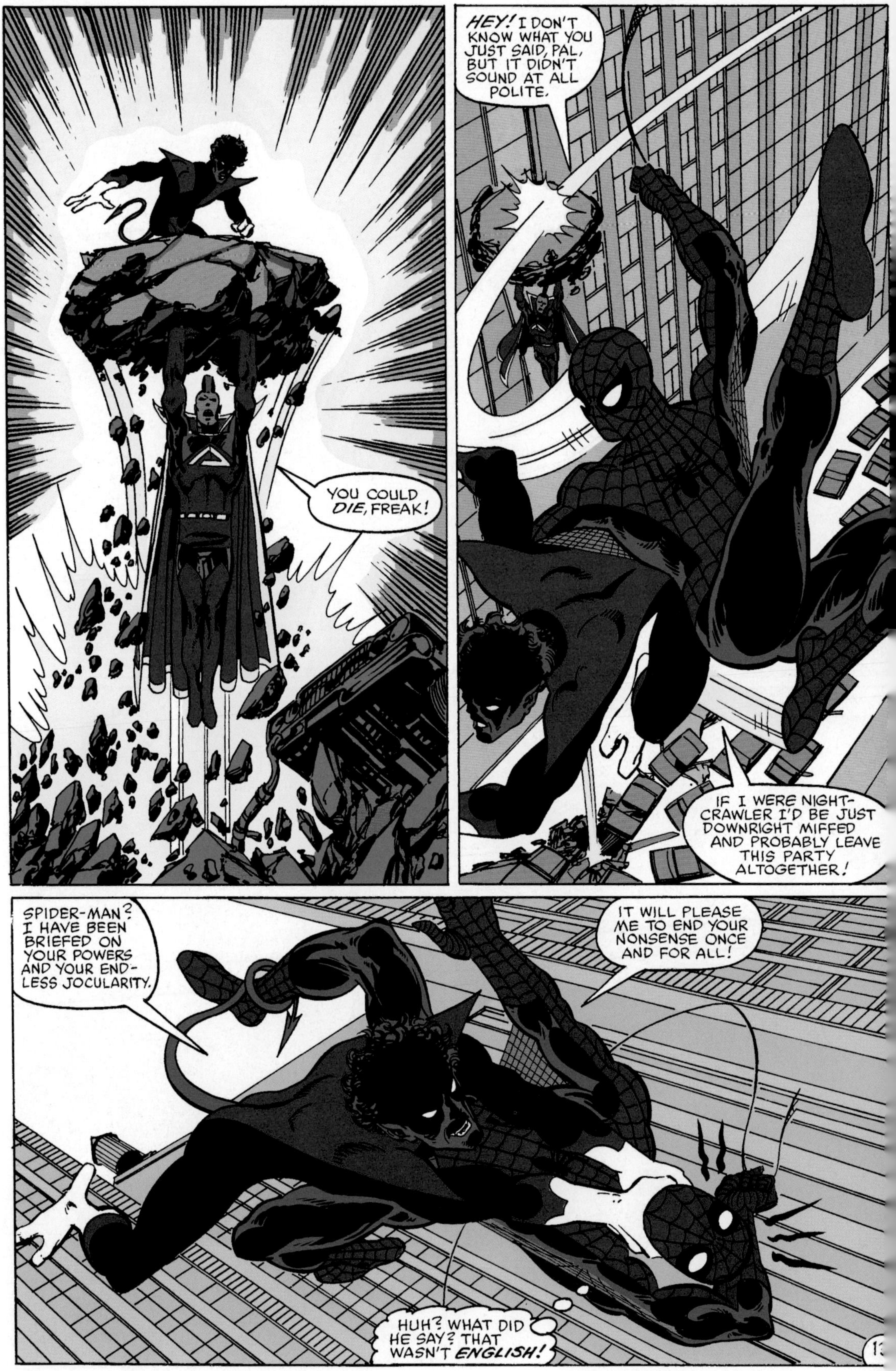
YOU COULD DIE, FREAK!
HEY! I DON'T KNOW WHAT YOU JUST SAID, PAL, BUT IT DIDN'T SOUND AT ALL POLITE.
IF I WERE NIGHT-CRAWLER I'D BE JUST DOWNRIGHT MIFFED AND PROBABLY LEAVE THIS PARTY ALTOGETHER!
SPIDER-MAN? I HAVE BEEN BRIEFED ON YOUR POWERS AND YOUR END-LESS JOCULARITY.
IT WILL PLEASE ME TO END YOUR NONSENSE ONCE AND FOR ALL!
HUH? WHAT DID HE SAY? THAT WASN'T ENGLISH!

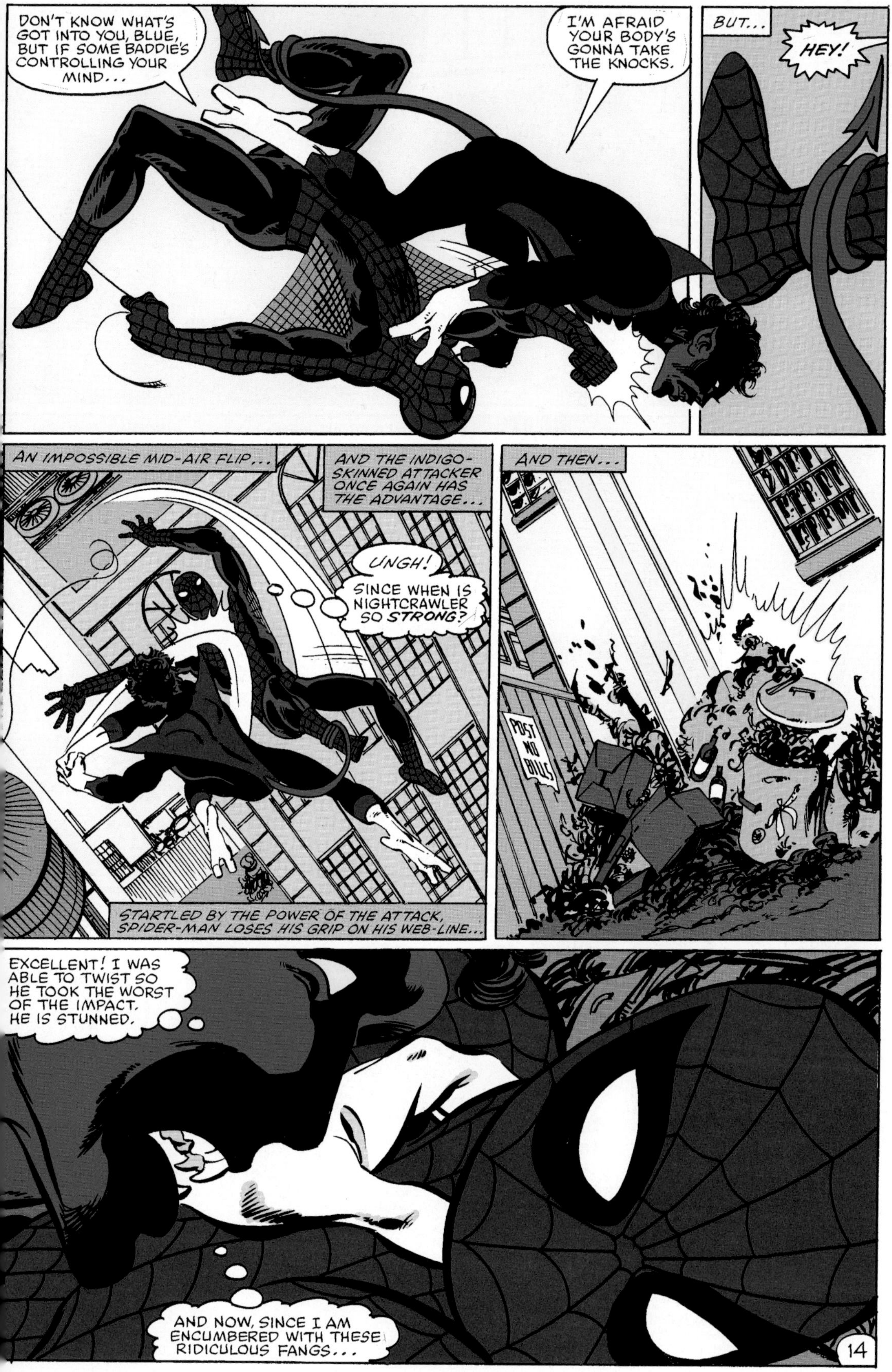
DON'T KNOW WHAT'S GOT INTO YOU, BLUE, BUT IF SOME BADDIE'S CONTROLLING YOUR MIND...
I'M AFRAID YOUR BODY'S GONNA TAKE THE KNOCKS.
BUT...
HEY!
AN IMPOSSIBLE MID-AIR FLIP...
AND THE INDIGO-SKINNED ATTACKER ONCE AGAIN HAS THE ADVANTAGE...
UNGH!
SINCE WHEN IS NIGHTCRAWLER SO STRONG?
STARTLED BY THE POWER OF THE ATTACK, SPIDER-MAN LOSES HIS GRIP ON HIS WEB-LINE...
AND THEN...
POST NO BILLS
EXCELLENT! I WAS ABLE TO TWIST SO HE TOOK THE WORST OF THE IMPACT. HE IS STUNNED.
AND NOW, SINCE I AM ENCUMBERED WITH THESE RIDICULOUS FANGS...
14

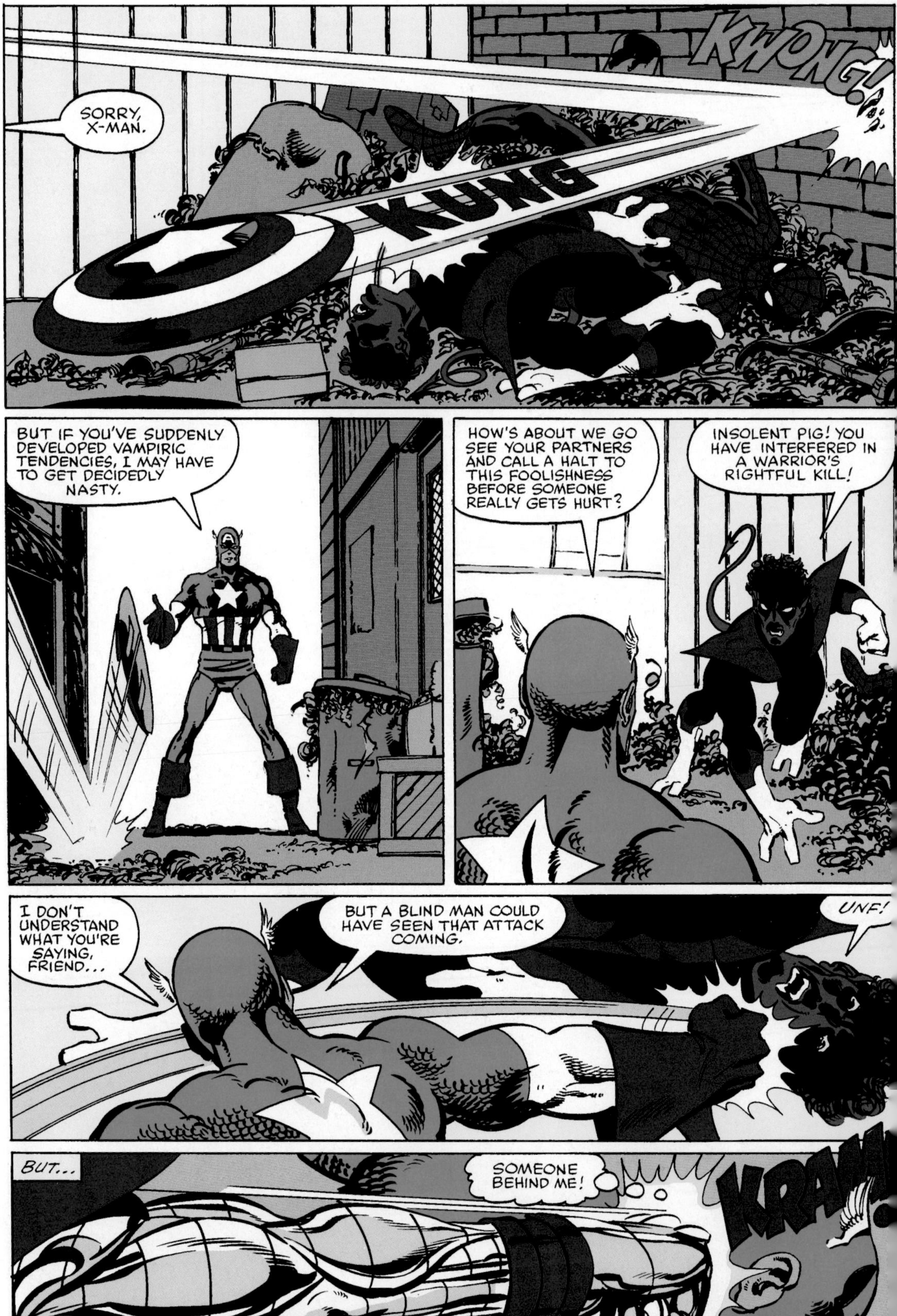
KWONG!
SORRY, X-MAN.
KUNG
BUT IF YOU'VE SUDDENLY DEVELOPED VAMPIRIC TENDENCIES, I MAY HAVE TO GET DECIDEDLY NASTY.
HOW'S ABOUT WE GO SEE YOUR PARTNERS AND CALL A HALT TO THIS FOOLISHNESS BEFORE SOMEONE REALLY GETS HURT?
INSOLENT PIG! YOU HAVE INTERFERED IN A WARRIOR'S RIGHTFUL KILL!
I DON'T UNDERSTAND WHAT YOU'RE SAYING, FRIEND...
BUT A BLIND MAN COULD HAVE SEEN THAT ATTACK COMING.
UNF!
BUT...
SOMEONE BEHIND ME!

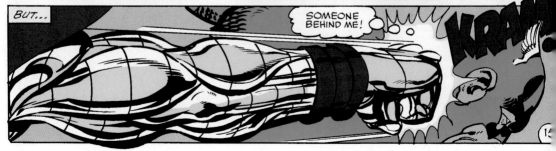

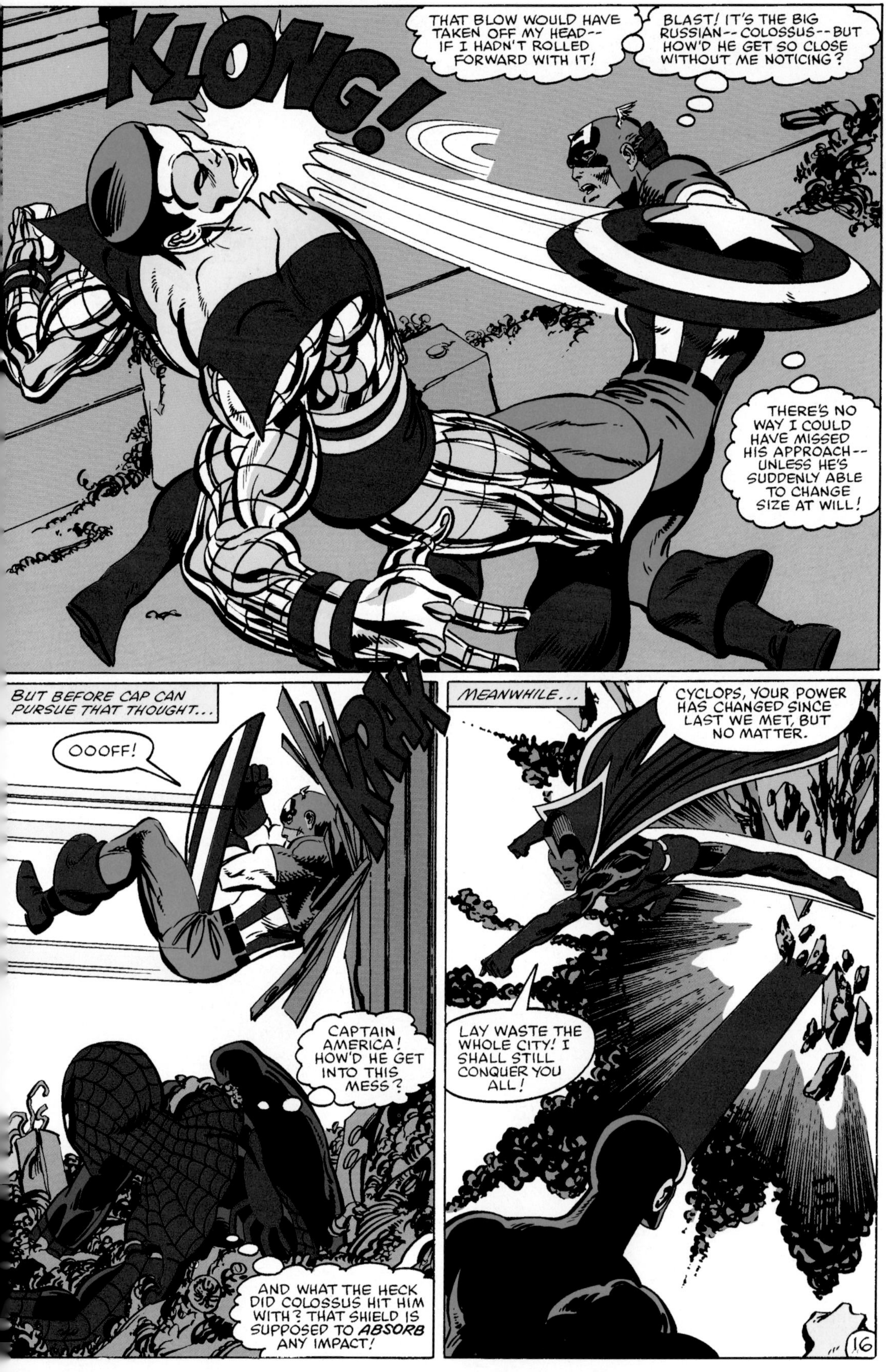
KLONG!
THAT BLOW WOULD HAVE TAKEN OFF MY HEAD-- IF I HADN'T ROLLED FORWARD WITH IT!
BLAST! IT'S THE BIG RUSSIAN-- COLOSSUS-- BUT HOW'D HE GET SO CLOSE WITHOUT ME NOTICING?
THERE'S NO WAY I COULD HAVE MISSED HIS APPROACH-- UNLESS HE'S SUDDENLY ABLE TO CHANGE SIZE AT WILL!
BUT BEFORE CAP CAN PURSUE THAT THOUGHT...
OOOFF!
KRAK
CAPTAIN AMERICA! HOW'D HE GET INTO THIS MESS?
AND WHAT THE HECK DID COLOSSUS HIT HIM WITH? THAT SHIELD IS SUPPOSED TO *ABSORB* ANY IMPACT!
MEANWHILE...
CYCLOPS, YOUR POWER HAS CHANGED SINCE LAST WE MET, BUT NO MATTER.
LAY WASTE THE WHOLE CITY! I SHALL STILL CONQUER YOU ALL!
16

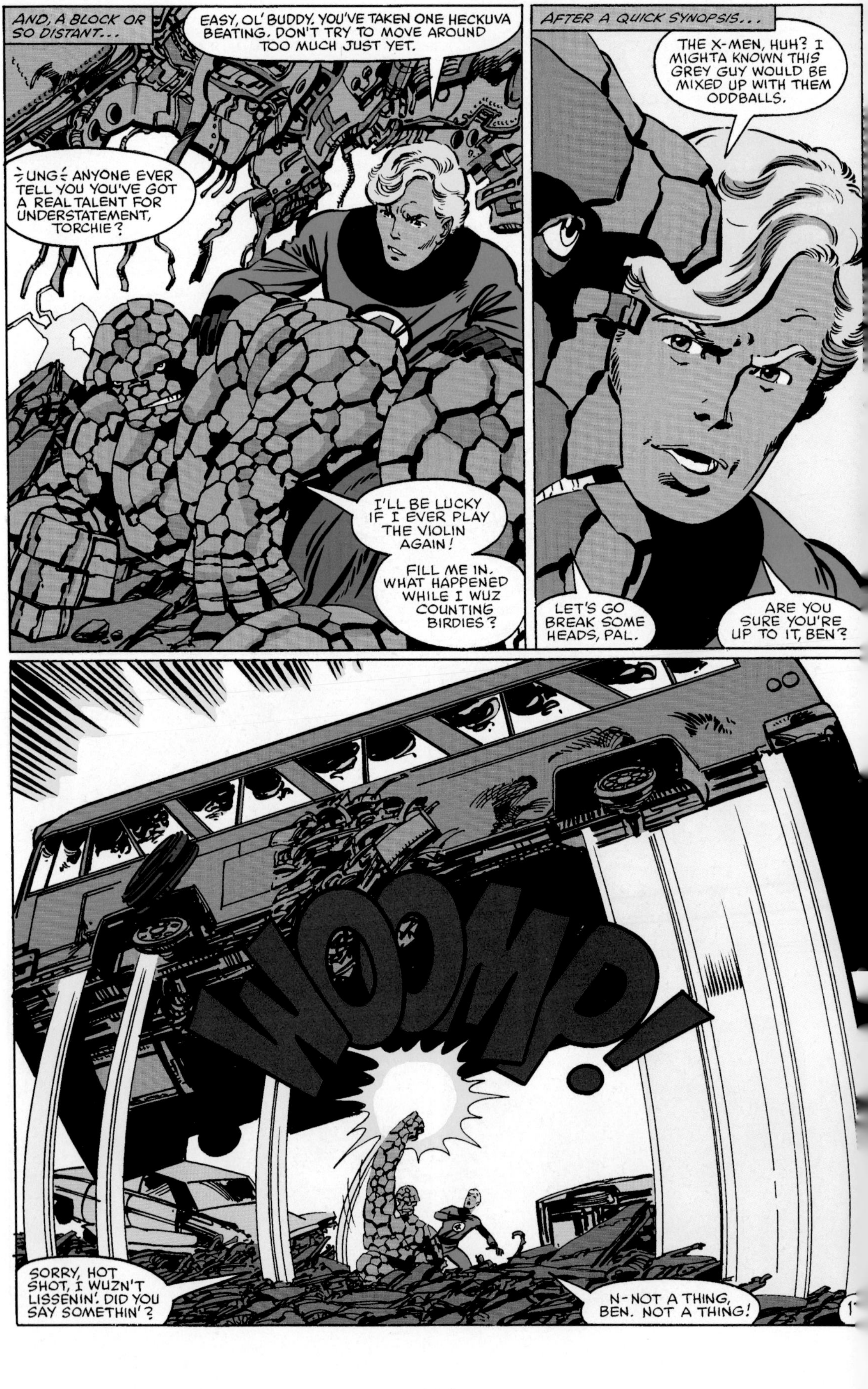

AND, A BLOCK OR SO DISTANT...
EASY, OL' BUDDY. YOU'VE TAKEN ONE HECKUVA BEATING. DON'T TRY TO MOVE AROUND TOO MUCH JUST YET.
=UNG= ANYONE EVER TELL YOU YOU'VE GOT A REAL TALENT FOR UNDERSTATEMENT, TORCHIE?
I'LL BE LUCKY IF I EVER PLAY THE VIOLIN AGAIN!
FILL ME IN. WHAT HAPPENED WHILE I WUZ COUNTING BIRDIES?
AFTER A QUICK SYNOPSIS...
THE X-MEN, HUH? I MIGHTA KNOWN THIS GREY GUY WOULD BE MIXED UP WITH THEM ODDBALLS.
LET'S GO BREAK SOME HEADS, PAL.
ARE YOU SURE YOU'RE UP TO IT, BEN?
WOOMP!
SORRY, HOT SHOT, I WUZN'T LISSENIN'. DID YOU SAY SOMETHIN'?
N-NOT A THING, BEN. NOT A THING!

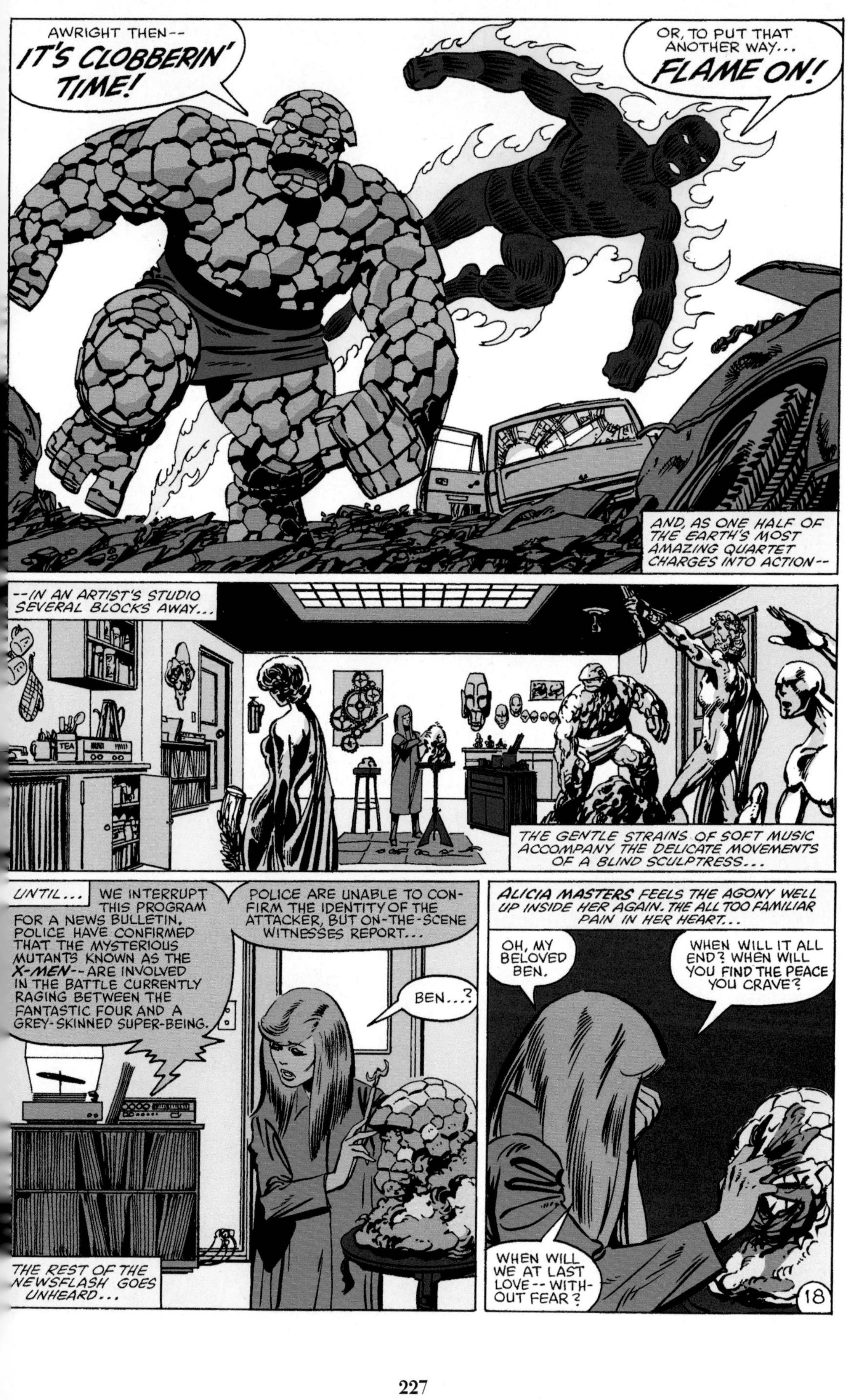
AWRIGHT THEN-- IT'S CLOBBERIN' TIME!
OR, TO PUT THAT ANOTHER WAY... FLAME ON!
AND, AS ONE HALF OF THE EARTH'S MOST AMAZING QUARTET CHARGES INTO ACTION--
--IN AN ARTIST'S STUDIO SEVERAL BLOCKS AWAY...
TEA
THE GENTLE STRAINS OF SOFT MUSIC ACCOMPANY THE DELICATE MOVEMENTS OF A BLIND SCULPTRESS...
UNTIL...
WE INTERRUPT THIS PROGRAM FOR A NEWS BULLETIN. POLICE HAVE CONFIRMED THAT THE MYSTERIOUS MUTANTS KNOWN AS THE X-MEN--ARE INVOLVED IN THE BATTLE CURRENTLY RAGING BETWEEN THE FANTASTIC FOUR AND A GREY-SKINNED SUPER-BEING.
POLICE ARE UNABLE TO CONFIRM THE IDENTITY OF THE ATTACKER, BUT ON-THE-SCENE WITNESSES REPORT...
BEN...?
THE REST OF THE NEWSFLASH GOES UNHEARD...
ALICIA MASTERS FEELS THE AGONY WELL UP INSIDE HER AGAIN. THE ALL TOO FAMILIAR PAIN IN HER HEART...
OH, MY BELOVED BEN.
WHEN WILL IT ALL END? WHEN WILL YOU FIND THE PEACE YOU CRAVE?
WHEN WILL WE AT LAST LOVE--WITHOUT FEAR?
18

LEAVING THE THING'S LADY-LOVE TO HER PRIVATE ANGUISH...

WE NOW TURN BACK TO THE FIVE STORY TOWER OF THE BAXTER BUILDING...

AND IN THE SMALLEST OF THE MANY LABORATORIES HOUSED THERE...

BUT, REED, I STILL DON'T UNDERSTAND.

HOW CAN A DEVICE--ANY DEVICE --BE OF USE AGAINST SOMEONE LIKE GLADIATOR?

I DON'T HAVE TIME TO EXPLAIN IN DETAIL RIGHT NOW, HONEY. JUST REMEMBER WHAT I SAID WHEN HE PICKED UP THE WHOLE BAXTER BUILDING.

YOU SAID THAT SHOULD HAVE BEEN IMPOSSIBLE--THAT THE BUILDING'S OWN WEIGHT SHOULD HAVE TORN IT APART.

EXACTLY! THAT MEANS GLADIATOR MUST BE USING SOMETHING MORE THAN STRENGTH.

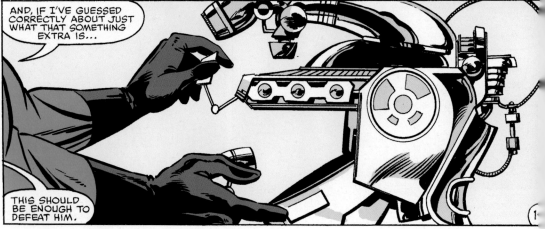

AND, IF I'VE GUESSED CORRECTLY ABOUT JUST WHAT THAT SOMETHING EXTRA IS...

THIS SHOULD BE ENOUGH TO DEFEAT HIM.

1

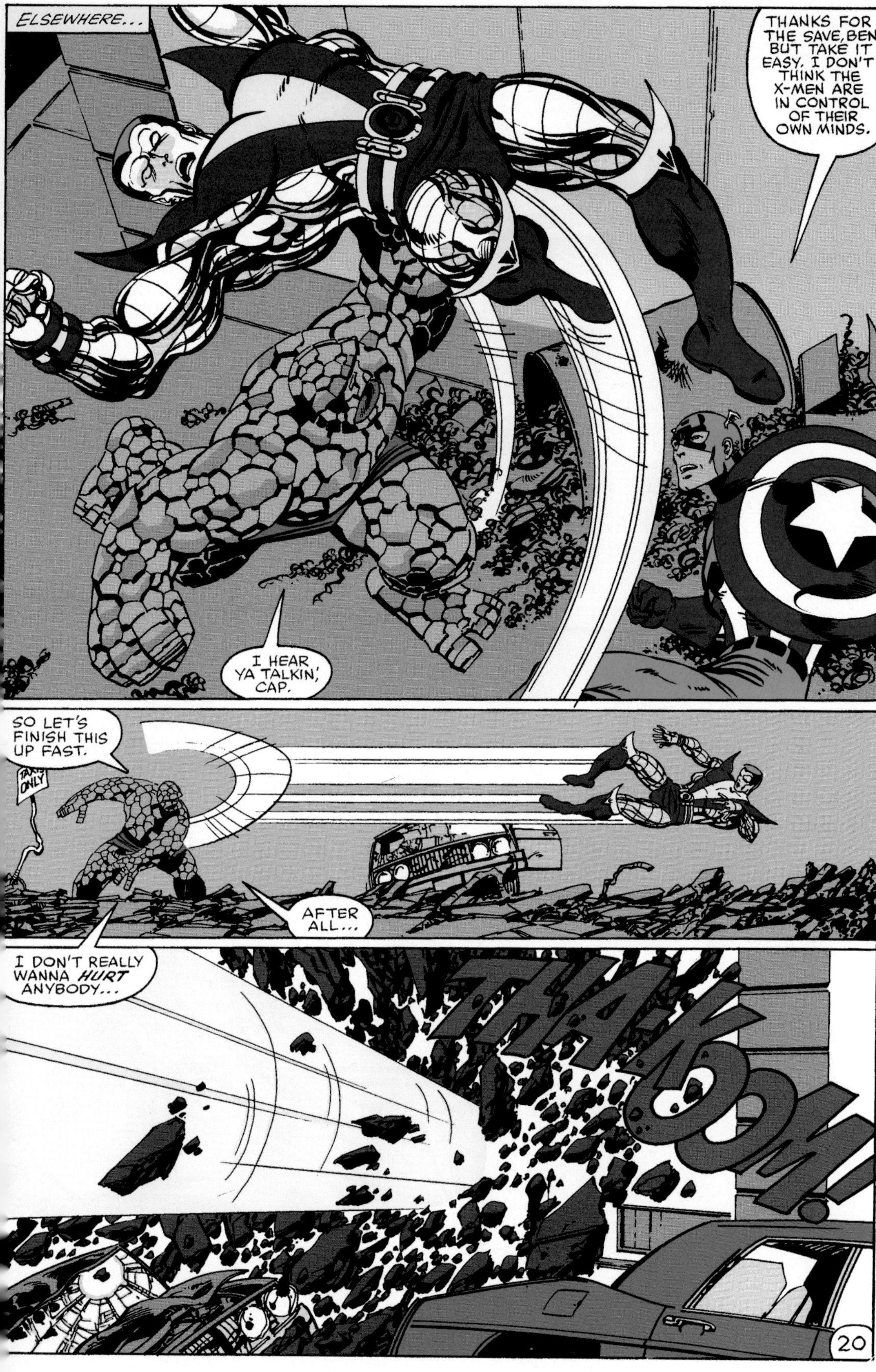
ELSEWHERE...
THANKS FOR THE SAVE, BEN, BUT TAKE IT EASY. I DON'T THINK THE X-MEN ARE IN CONTROL OF THEIR OWN MINDS.
I HEAR YA TALKIN', CAP.
SO LET'S FINISH THIS UP FAST.
AFTER ALL...
I DON'T REALLY WANNA HURT ANYBODY...
THA-KOOM!
20

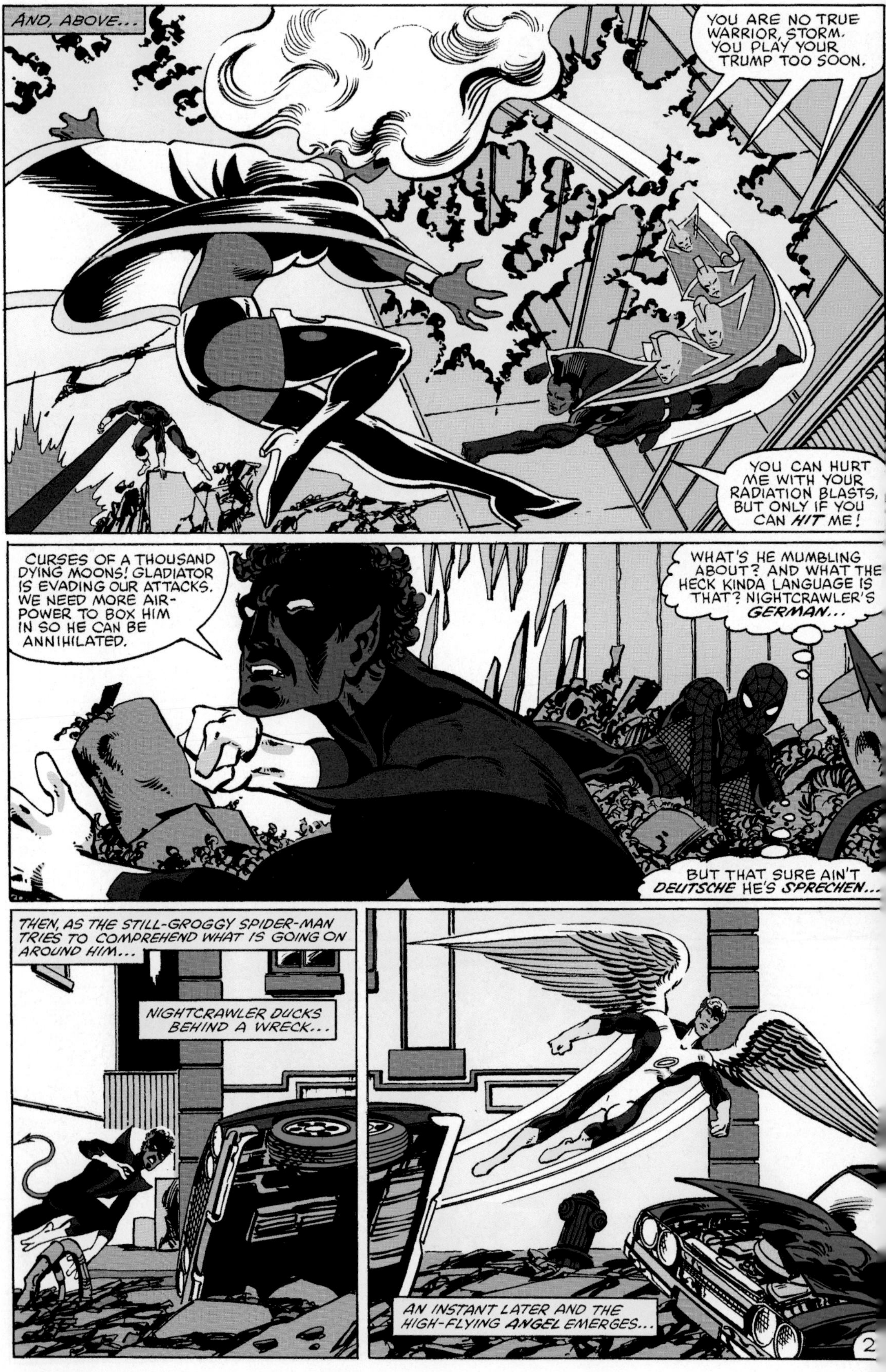

AND, ABOVE...
YOU ARE NO TRUE WARRIOR, STORM. YOU PLAY YOUR TRUMP TOO SOON.
YOU CAN HURT ME WITH YOUR RADIATION BLASTS, BUT ONLY IF YOU CAN HIT ME!
CURSES OF A THOUSAND DYING MOONS! GLADIATOR IS EVADING OUR ATTACKS. WE NEED MORE AIR-POWER TO BOX HIM IN SO HE CAN BE ANNIHILATED.
WHAT'S HE MUMBLING ABOUT? AND WHAT THE HECK KINDA LANGUAGE IS THAT? NIGHTCRAWLER'S GERMAN...
BUT THAT SURE AIN'T DEUTSCHE HE'S SPRECHEN...
THEN, AS THE STILL-GROGGY SPIDER-MAN TRIES TO COMPREHEND WHAT IS GOING ON AROUND HIM...
NIGHTCRAWLER DUCKS BEHIND A WRECK...
AN INSTANT LATER AND THE HIGH-FLYING ANGEL EMERGES...
2

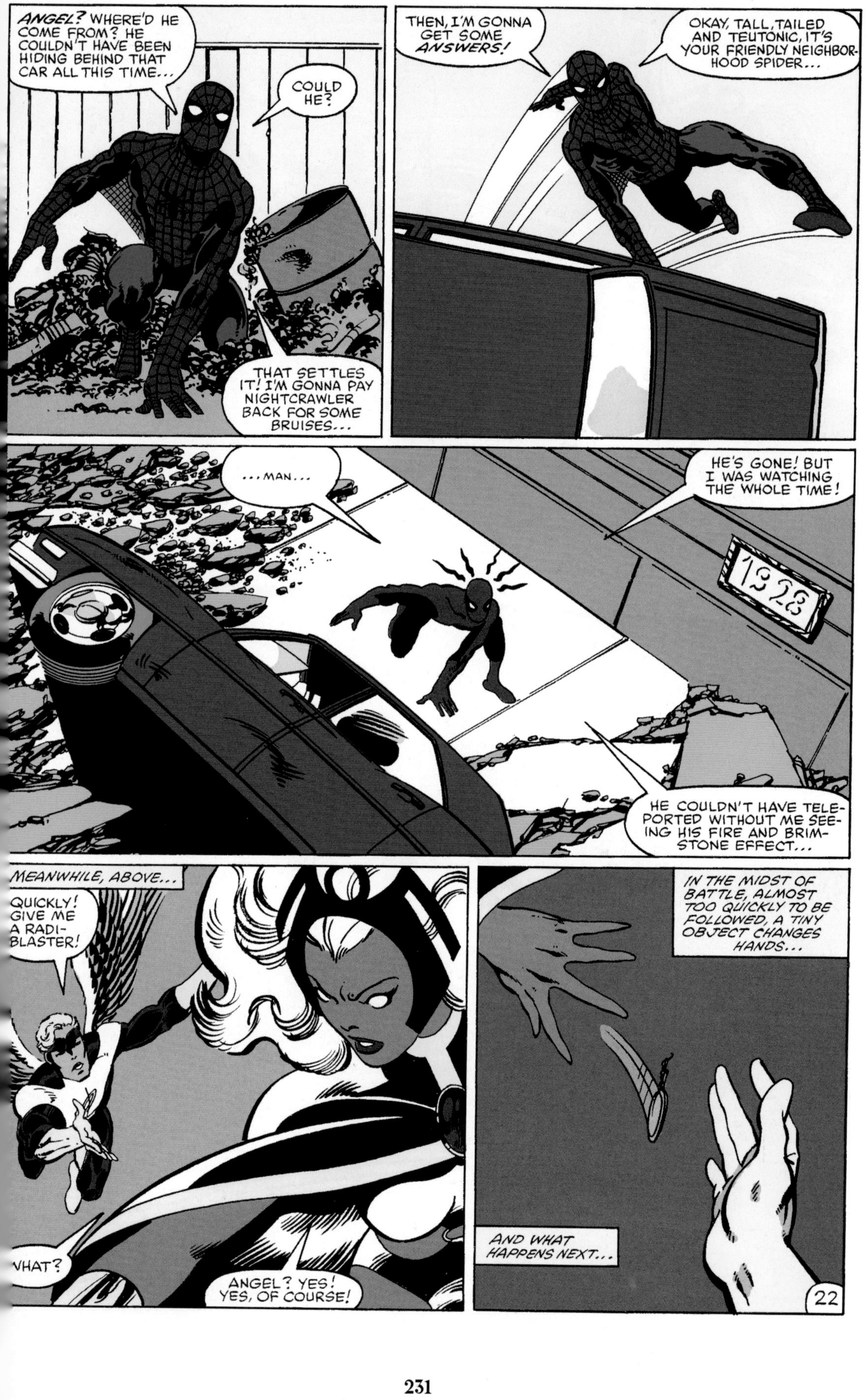
ANGEL? WHERE'D HE COME FROM? HE COULDN'T HAVE BEEN HIDING BEHIND THAT CAR ALL THIS TIME...
COULD HE?
THAT SETTLES IT! I'M GONNA PAY NIGHTCRAWLER BACK FOR SOME BRUISES...
THEN, I'M GONNA GET SOME ANSWERS!
OKAY, TALL, TAILED AND TEUTONIC, IT'S YOUR FRIENDLY NEIGHBOR-HOOD SPIDER...
...MAN...
HE'S GONE! BUT I WAS WATCHING THE WHOLE TIME!
1928
HE COULDN'T HAVE TELE-PORTED WITHOUT ME SEE-ING HIS FIRE AND BRIM-STONE EFFECT...
MEANWHILE, ABOVE...
QUICKLY! GIVE ME A RADI-BLASTER!
WHAT?
ANGEL? YES! YES, OF COURSE!
IN THE MIDST OF BATTLE, ALMOST TOO QUICKLY TO BE FOLLOWED, A TINY OBJECT CHANGES HANDS...
AND WHAT HAPPENS NEXT...
22

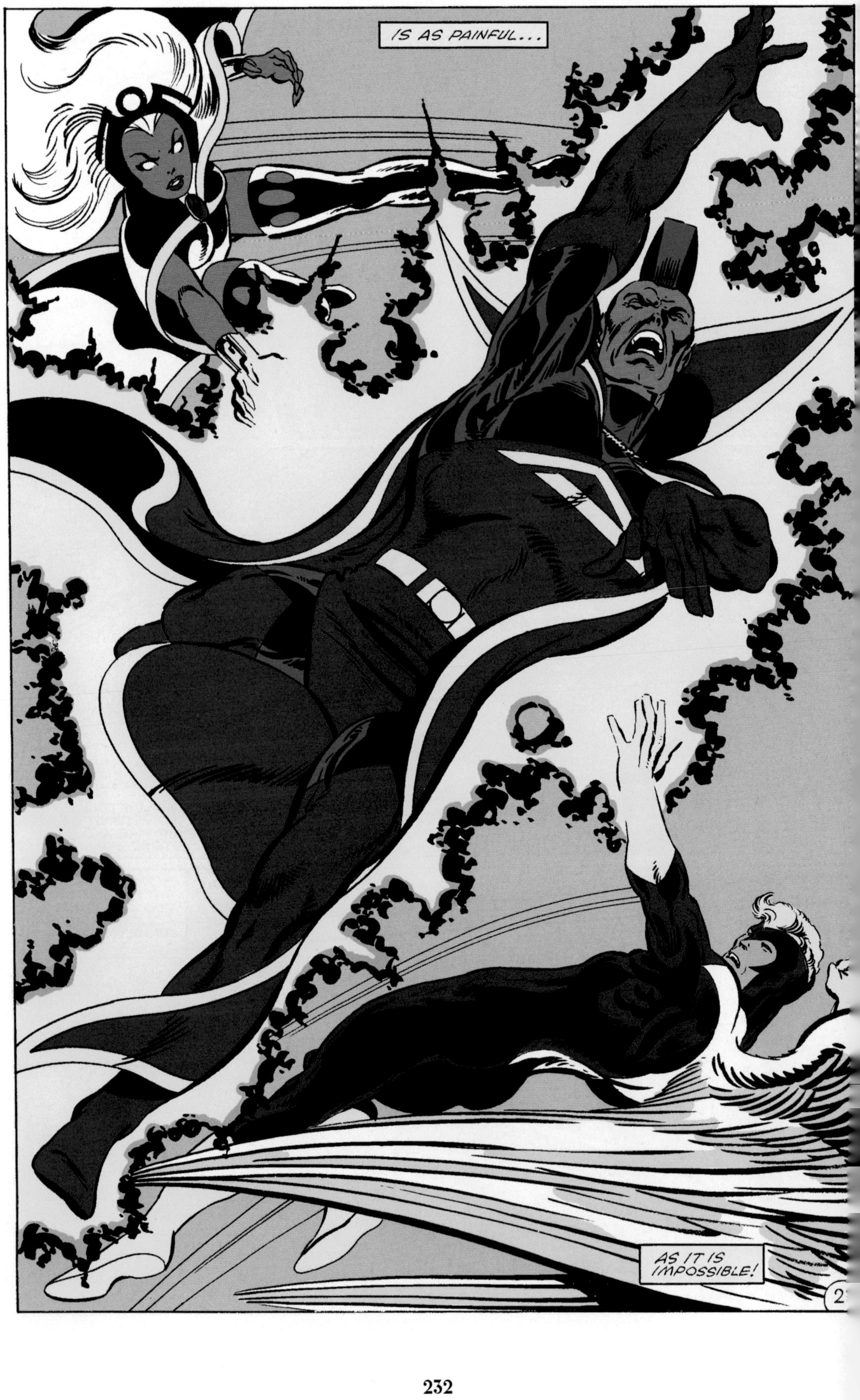
IS AS PAINFUL...
AS IT IS IMPOSSIBLE!
2

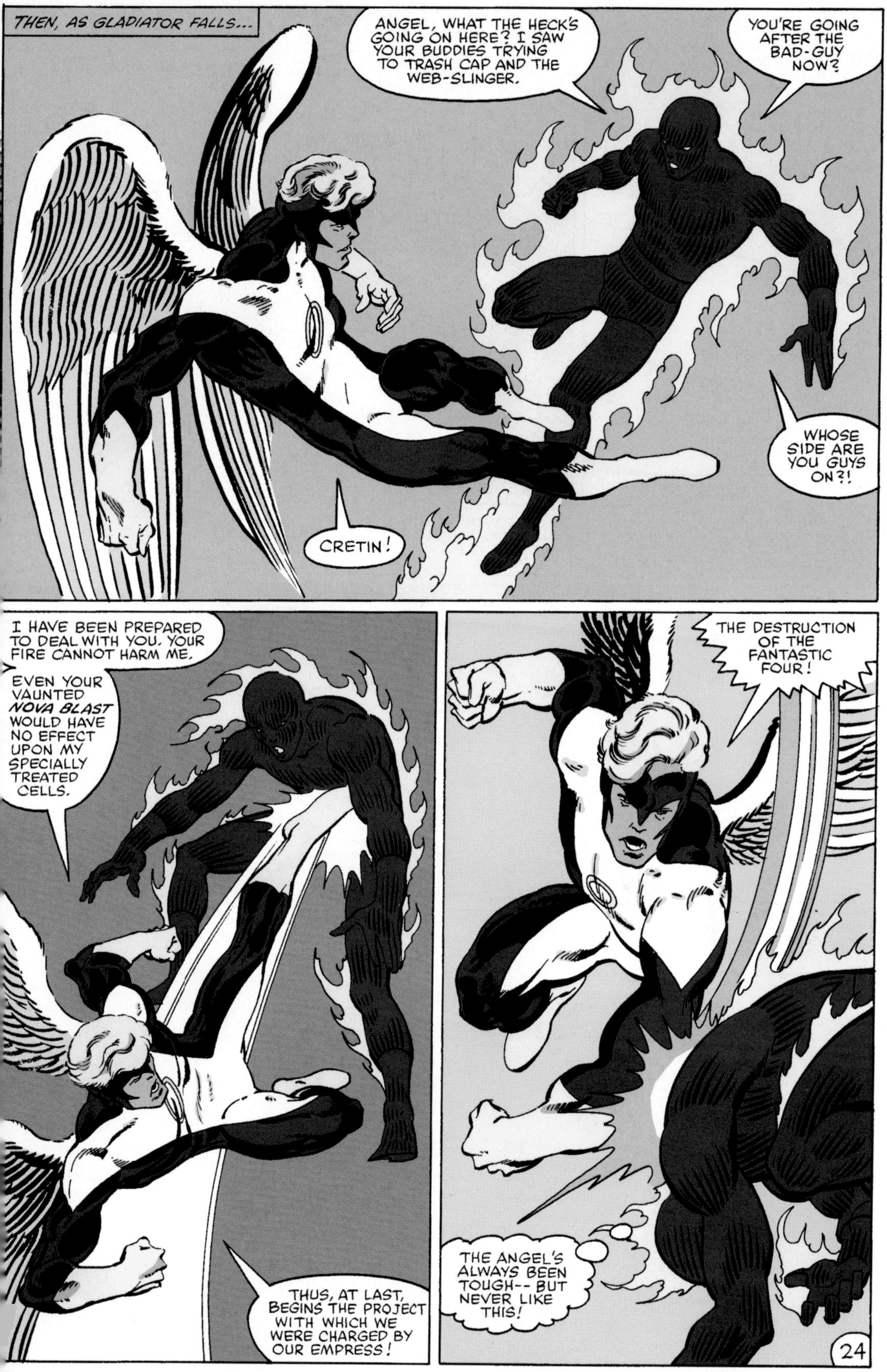

THEN, AS GLADIATOR FALLS...
ANGEL, WHAT THE HECK'S GOING ON HERE? I SAW YOUR BUDDIES TRYING TO TRASH CAP AND THE WEB-SLINGER.
YOU'RE GOING AFTER THE BAD-GUY NOW?
WHOSE SIDE ARE YOU GUYS ON?!
CRETIN!
I HAVE BEEN PREPARED TO DEAL WITH YOU. YOUR FIRE CANNOT HARM ME.
EVEN YOUR VAUNTED NOVA BLAST WOULD HAVE NO EFFECT UPON MY SPECIALLY TREATED CELLS.
THUS, AT LAST, BEGINS THE PROJECT WITH WHICH WE WERE CHARGED BY OUR EMPRESS!
THE DESTRUCTION OF THE FANTASTIC FOUR!
THE ANGEL'S ALWAYS BEEN TOUGH-- BUT NEVER LIKE THIS!
24

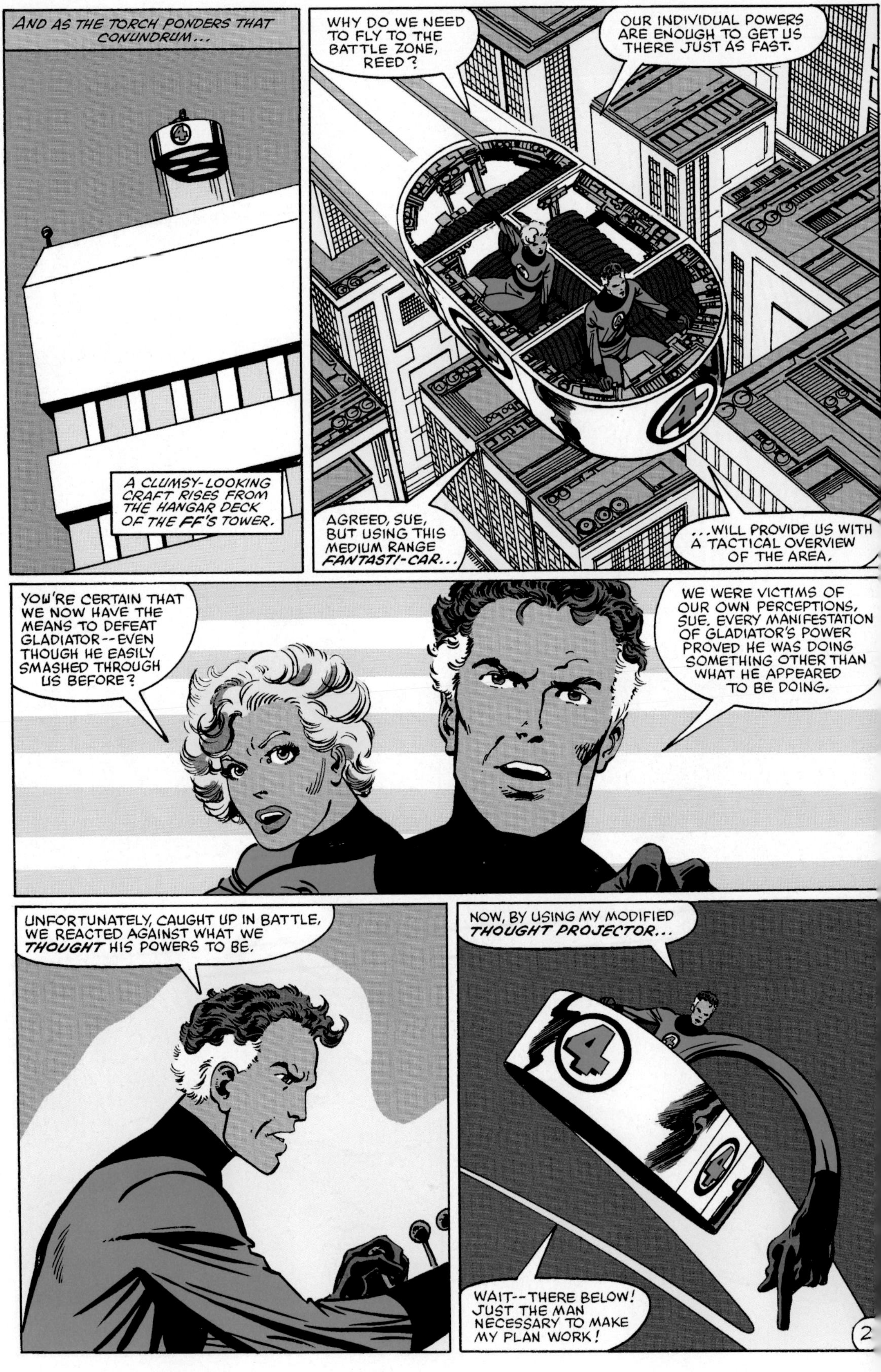
AND AS THE TORCH PONDERS THAT CONUNDRUM...
A CLUMSY-LOOKING CRAFT RISES FROM THE HANGAR DECK OF THE FF'S TOWER.
WHY DO WE NEED TO FLY TO THE BATTLE ZONE, REED?
OUR INDIVIDUAL POWERS ARE ENOUGH TO GET US THERE JUST AS FAST.
AGREED, SUE, BUT USING THIS MEDIUM RANGE FANTASTI-CAR...
...WILL PROVIDE US WITH A TACTICAL OVERVIEW OF THE AREA.
YOU'RE CERTAIN THAT WE NOW HAVE THE MEANS TO DEFEAT GLADIATOR--EVEN THOUGH HE EASILY SMASHED THROUGH US BEFORE?
WE WERE VICTIMS OF OUR OWN PERCEPTIONS, SUE. EVERY MANIFESTATION OF GLADIATOR'S POWER PROVED HE WAS DOING SOMETHING OTHER THAN WHAT HE APPEARED TO BE DOING.
UNFORTUNATELY, CAUGHT UP IN BATTLE, WE REACTED AGAINST WHAT WE THOUGHT HIS POWERS TO BE.
NOW, BY USING MY MODIFIED THOUGHT PROJECTOR...
WAIT--THERE BELOW! JUST THE MAN NECESSARY TO MAKE MY PLAN WORK!
2

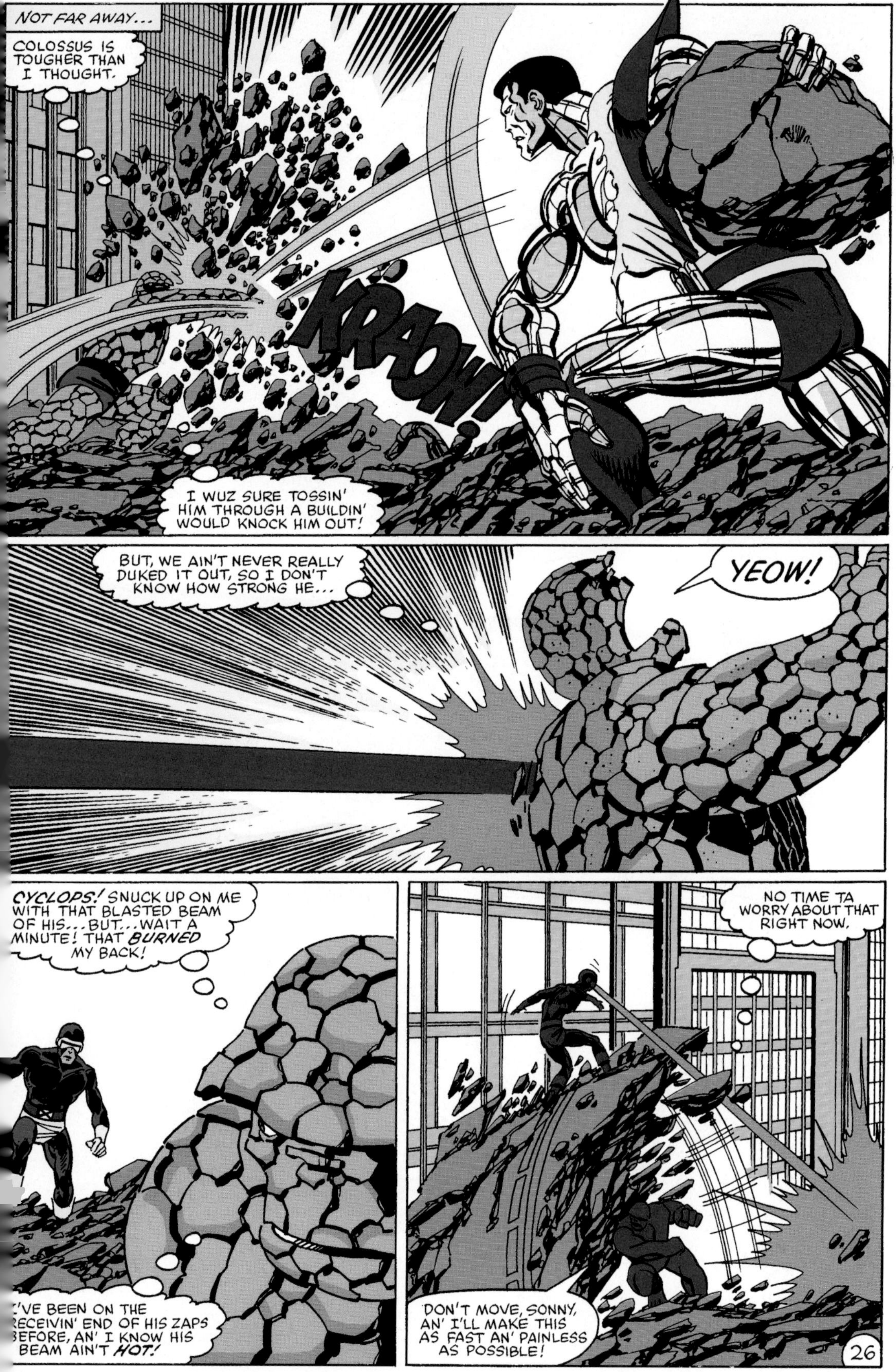

NOT FAR AWAY...
COLOSSUS IS TOUGHER THAN I THOUGHT.
KRAOW!
I WUZ SURE TOSSIN' HIM THROUGH A BUILDIN' WOULD KNOCK HIM OUT!
BUT, WE AIN'T NEVER REALLY DUKED IT OUT, SO I DON'T KNOW HOW STRONG HE...
YEOW!
CYCLOPS! SNUCK UP ON ME WITH THAT BLASTED BEAM OF HIS... BUT... WAIT A MINUTE! THAT BURNED MY BACK!
I'VE BEEN ON THE RECEIVIN' END OF HIS ZAPS BEFORE, AN' I KNOW HIS BEAM AIN'T HOT!
NO TIME TA WORRY ABOUT THAT RIGHT NOW.
DON'T MOVE, SONNY, AN' I'LL MAKE THIS AS FAST AN' PAINLESS AS POSSIBLE!
26

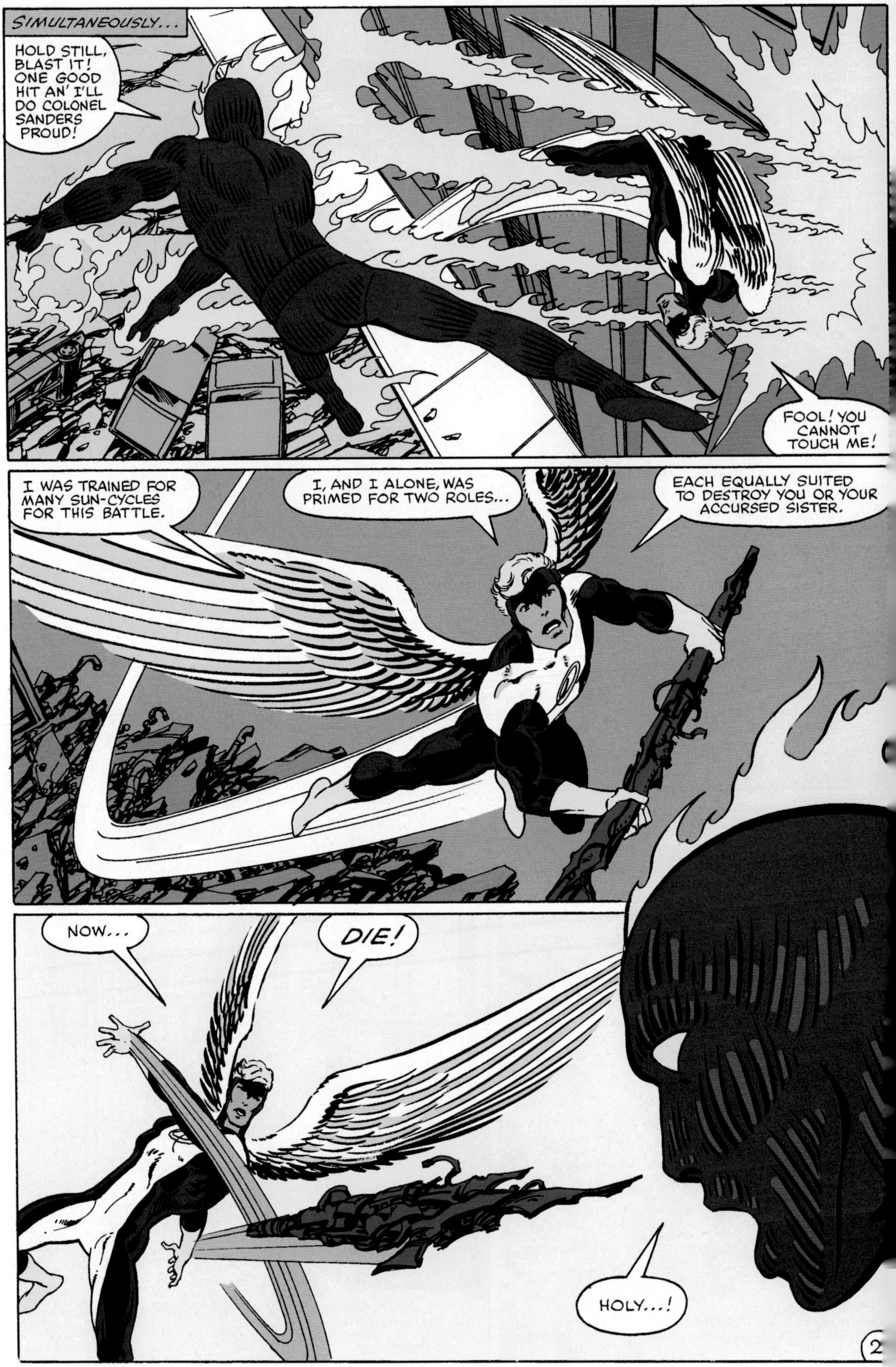
SIMULTANEOUSLY...
HOLD STILL, BLAST IT! ONE GOOD HIT AN' I'LL DO COLONEL SANDERS PROUD!
FOOL! YOU CANNOT TOUCH ME!
I WAS TRAINED FOR MANY SUN-CYCLES FOR THIS BATTLE.
I, AND I ALONE, WAS PRIMED FOR TWO ROLES...
EACH EQUALLY SUITED TO DESTROY YOU OR YOUR ACCURSED SISTER.
NOW...
DIE!
HOLY...!

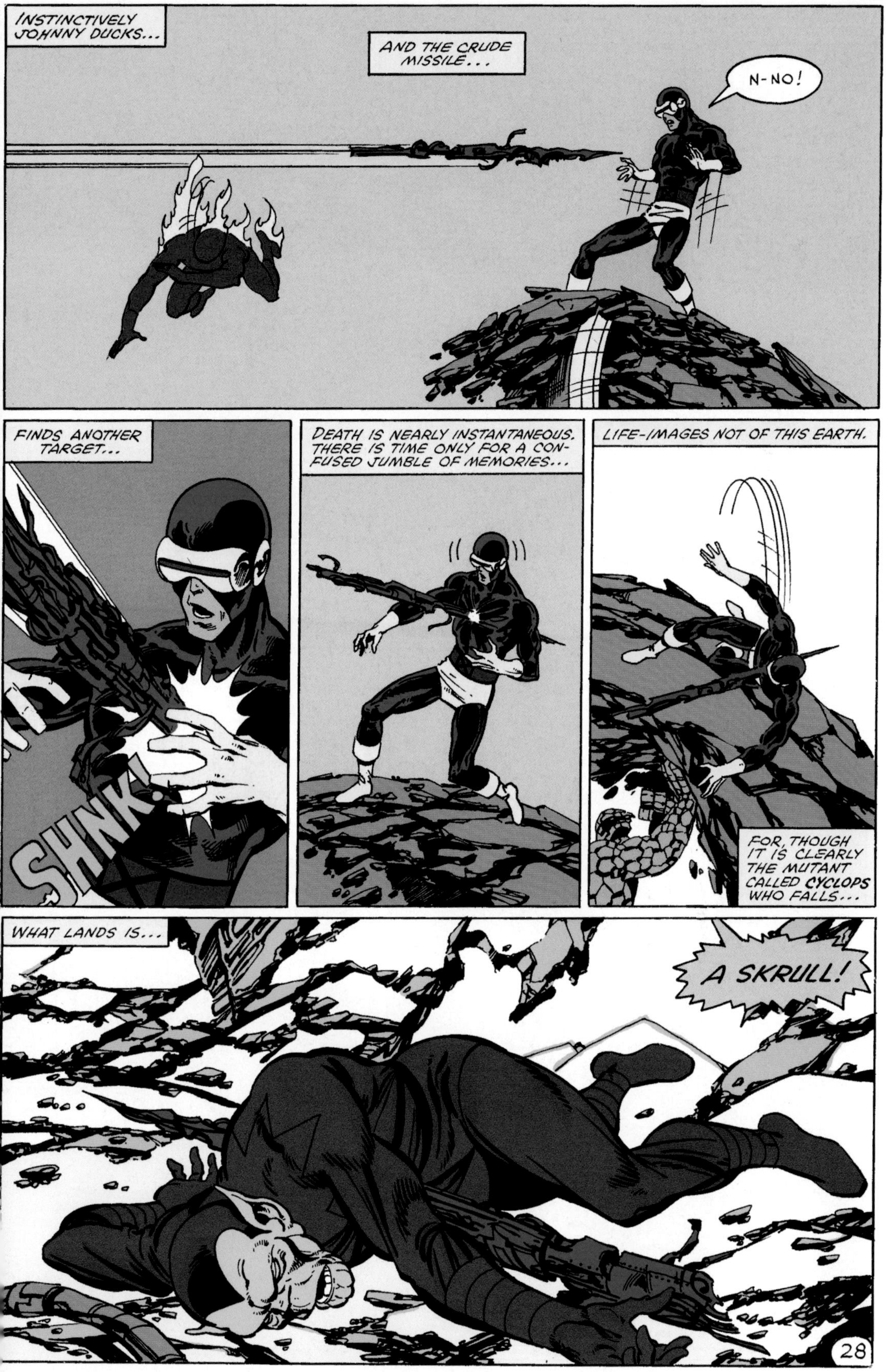
INSTINCTIVELY JOHNNY DUCKS...
AND THE CRUDE MISSILE...
N-NO!
FINDS ANOTHER TARGET...
SHNK!
DEATH IS NEARLY INSTANTANEOUS. THERE IS TIME ONLY FOR A CON-FUSED JUMBLE OF MEMORIES...
LIFE-IMAGES NOT OF THIS EARTH.
FOR, THOUGH IT IS CLEARLY THE MUTANT CALLED CYCLOPS WHO FALLS...
WHAT LANDS IS...
A SKRULL!
28

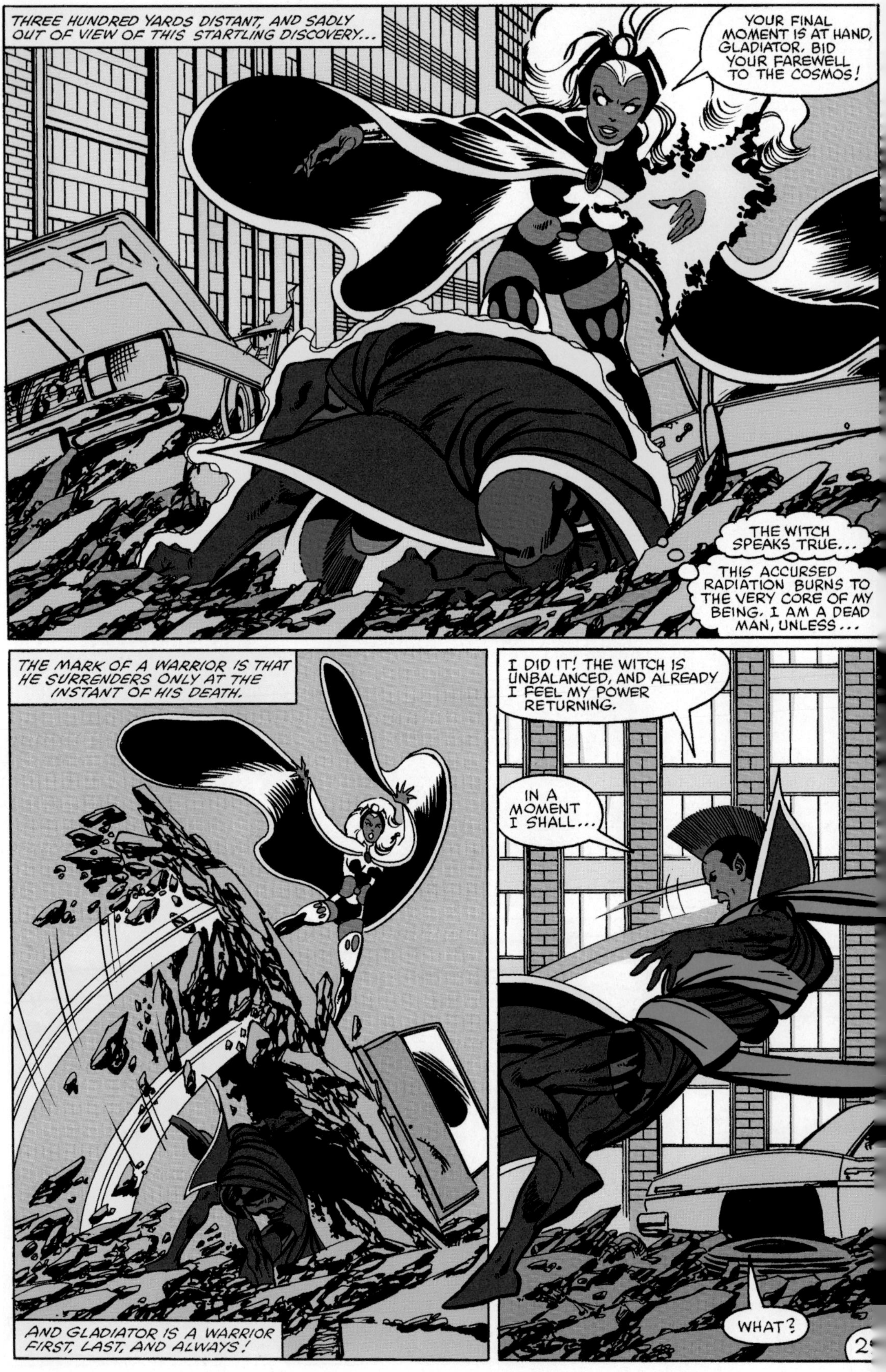
THREE HUNDRED YARDS DISTANT, AND SADLY OUT OF VIEW OF THIS STARTLING DISCOVERY...
YOUR FINAL MOMENT IS AT HAND, GLADIATOR. BID YOUR FAREWELL TO THE COSMOS!
THE WITCH SPEAKS TRUE...
THIS ACCURSED RADIATION BURNS TO THE VERY CORE OF MY BEING. I AM A DEAD MAN, UNLESS...
THE MARK OF A WARRIOR IS THAT HE SURRENDERS ONLY AT THE INSTANT OF HIS DEATH.
AND GLADIATOR IS A WARRIOR FIRST, LAST, AND ALWAYS!
I DID IT! THE WITCH IS UNBALANCED, AND ALREADY I FEEL MY POWER RETURNING.
IN A MOMENT I SHALL...
WHAT?

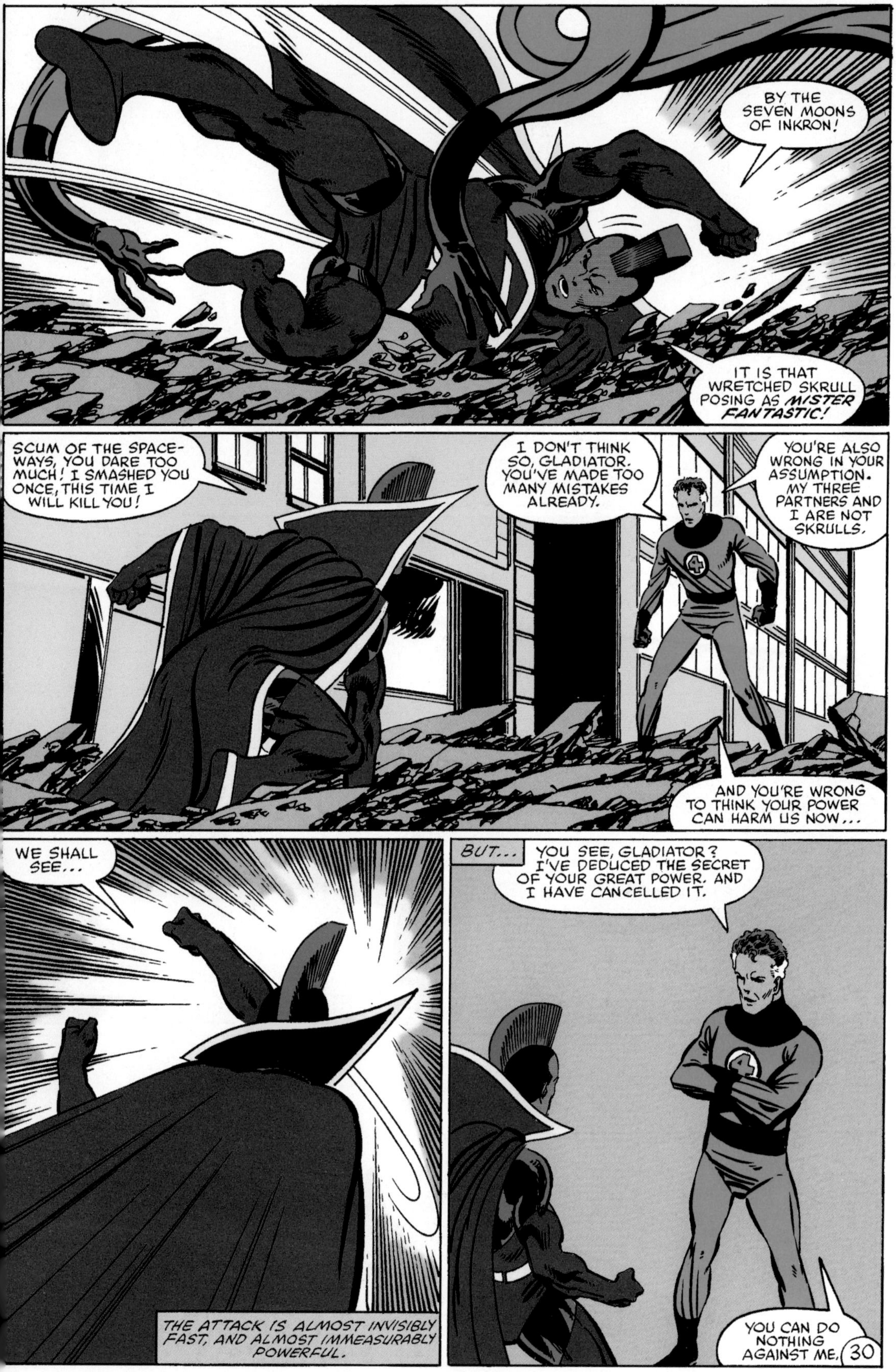
BY THE SEVEN MOONS OF INKRON!
IT IS THAT WRETCHED SKRULL POSING AS MISTER FANTASTIC!
SCUM OF THE SPACE-WAYS, YOU DARE TOO MUCH! I SMASHED YOU ONCE, THIS TIME I WILL KILL YOU!
I DON'T THINK SO, GLADIATOR. YOU'VE MADE TOO MANY MISTAKES ALREADY.
YOU'RE ALSO WRONG IN YOUR ASSUMPTION. MY THREE PARTNERS AND I ARE NOT SKRULLS.
AND YOU'RE WRONG TO THINK YOUR POWER CAN HARM US NOW...
WE SHALL SEE...
THE ATTACK IS ALMOST INVISIBLY FAST, AND ALMOST IMMEASURABLY POWERFUL.
BUT...
YOU SEE, GLADIATOR? I'VE DEDUCED THE SECRET OF YOUR GREAT POWER. AND I HAVE CANCELLED IT.
YOU CAN DO NOTHING AGAINST ME.
30

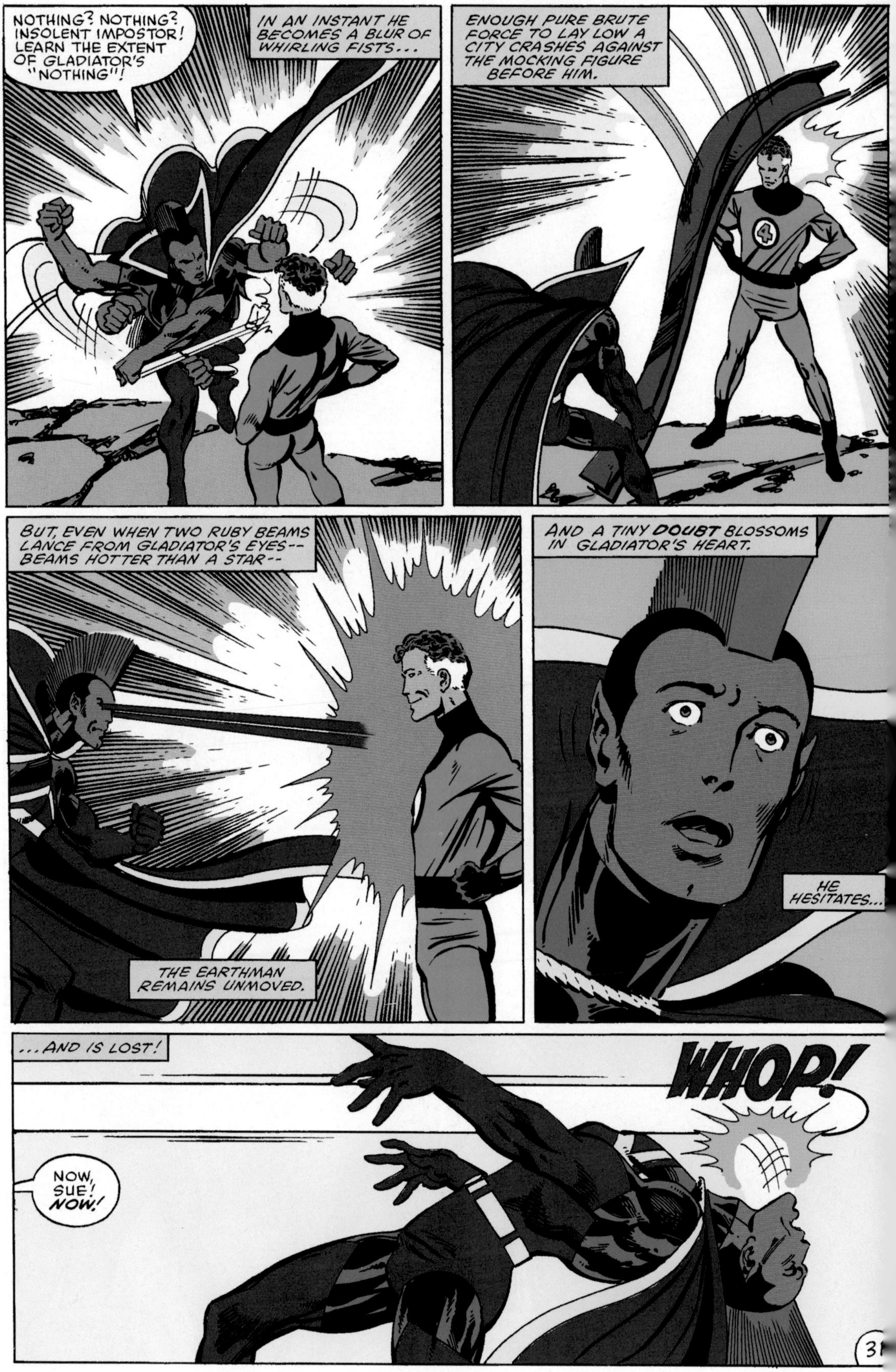
NOTHING? NOTHING? INSOLENT IMPOSTOR! LEARN THE EXTENT OF GLADIATOR'S "NOTHING"!
IN AN INSTANT HE BECOMES A BLUR OF WHIRLING FISTS...
ENOUGH PURE BRUTE FORCE TO LAY LOW A CITY CRASHES AGAINST THE MOCKING FIGURE BEFORE HIM.
BUT, EVEN WHEN TWO RUBY BEAMS LANCE FROM GLADIATOR'S EYES-- BEAMS HOTTER THAN A STAR--
THE EARTHMAN REMAINS UNMOVED.
AND A TINY DOUBT BLOSSOMS IN GLADIATOR'S HEART.
HE HESITATES...
...AND IS LOST!
WHOP!
NOW, SUE! NOW!

IT WORKED! OUR SUBTERFUGE FOOLED HIM JUST ENOUGH TO MAKE HIM DOUBT HIS OWN POWER FOR A MOMENT.

AND IN THAT INSTANT I WAS ABLE TO KNOCK HIM OUT WITH AN INVISIBLE FORCE FIELD!

CONGRATULATIONS, REED! YOU READ THIS FELLA EXACTLY!

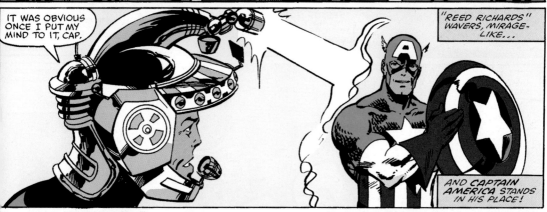

IT WAS OBVIOUS ONCE I PUT MY MIND TO IT, CAP.

"REED RICHARDS" WAVERS, MIRAGE-LIKE...

AND CAPTAIN AMERICA STANDS IN HIS PLACE!

ALTHOUGH GLADIATOR CLEARLY POSSESSES SUPER-HUMAN PHYSICAL TRAITS, IT WAS APPARENT THAT MUCH OF HIS POWER IS ACTUALLY PSIONIC IN NATURE--MENTAL POWERS SUCH AS PYROKINESIS, TELEKINESIS, AND LEVITATION.

KNOWING THAT, ALL WE NEEDED WAS A SCENARIO WHICH WOULD CAUSE HIM TO DOUBT HIS OWN ABILITIES, SO THAT WE COULD STRIKE THROUGH THEM.

SO I USED MY THOUGHT PROJECTION HELMET TO GENERATE AN IMAGE OF MYSELF OVER OUR STAR-SPANGLED FRIEND...

AND WHEN GLADIATOR THOUGHT HE WAS STRIKING AT YOU...

HE WAS ACTUALLY UP AGAINST CAP'S NEARLY INDESTRUCTIBLE SHIELD.

NOW, LET'S DEAL WITH THOSE SO-CALLED X-MEN...

32

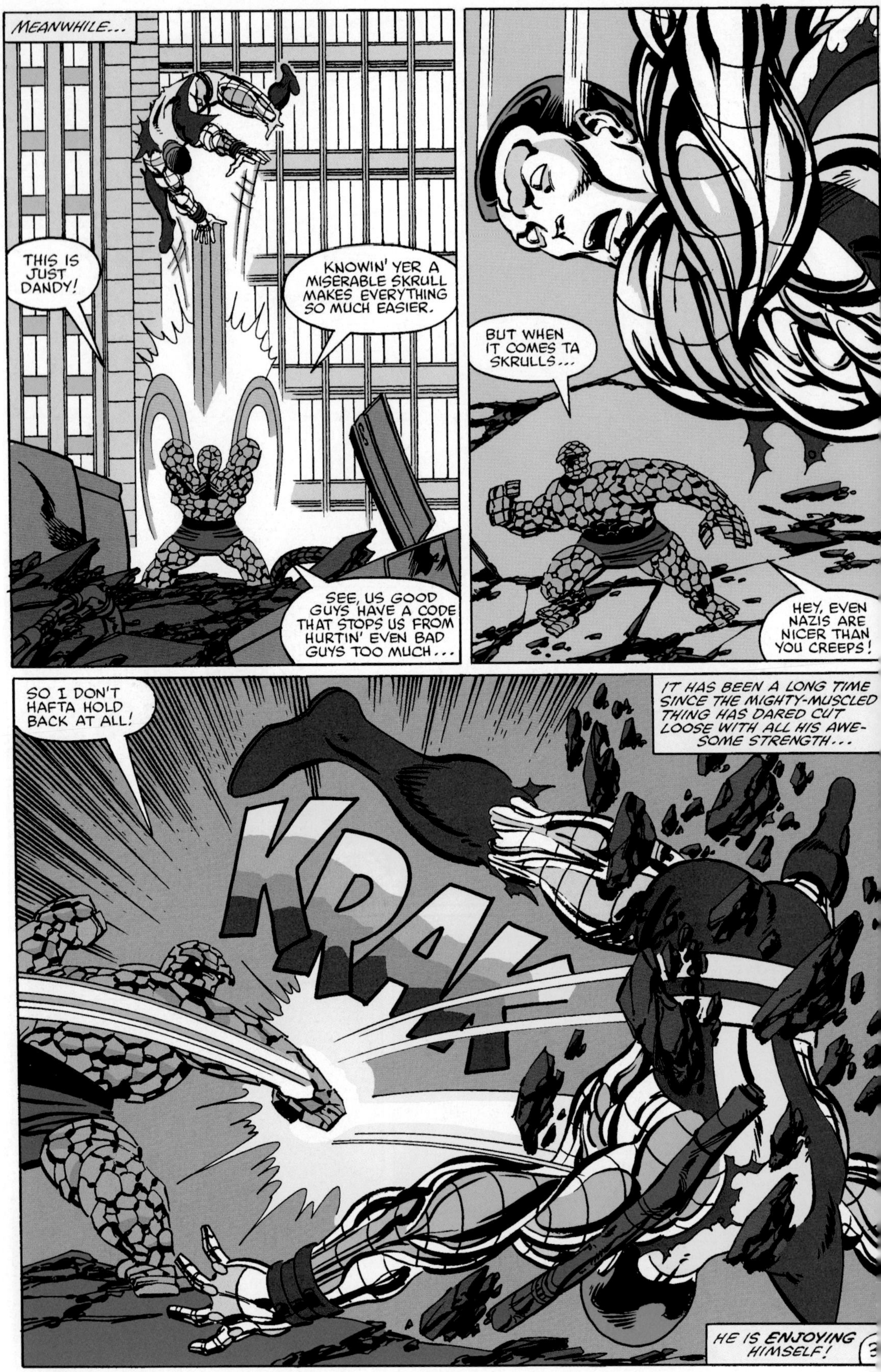
MEANWHILE...
THIS IS JUST DANDY!
KNOWIN' YER A MISERABLE SKRULL MAKES EVERYTHING SO MUCH EASIER.
SEE, US GOOD GUYS HAVE A CODE THAT STOPS US FROM HURTIN' EVEN BAD GUYS TOO MUCH...
BUT WHEN IT COMES TA SKRULLS...
HEY, EVEN NAZIS ARE NICER THAN YOU CREEPS!
SO I DON'T HAFTA HOLD BACK AT ALL!
IT HAS BEEN A LONG TIME SINCE THE MIGHTY-MUSCLED THING HAS DARED CUT LOOSE WITH ALL HIS AWE-SOME STRENGTH...
KRAK
HE IS ENJOYING HIMSELF!

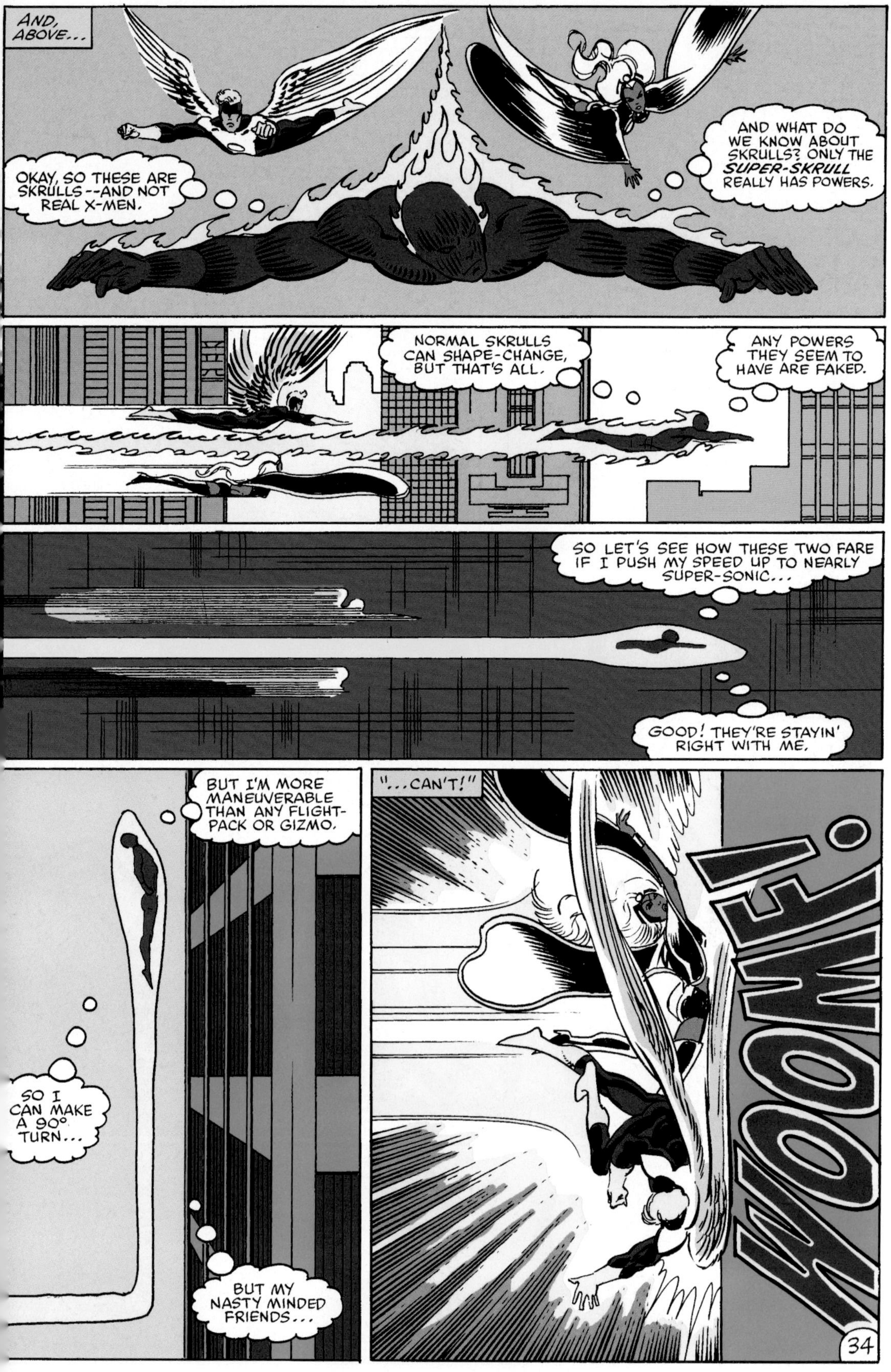
AND, ABOVE...
OKAY, SO THESE ARE SKRULLS--AND NOT REAL X-MEN.
AND WHAT DO WE KNOW ABOUT SKRULLS? ONLY THE SUPER-SKRULL REALLY HAS POWERS.
NORMAL SKRULLS CAN SHAPE-CHANGE, BUT THAT'S ALL.
ANY POWERS THEY SEEM TO HAVE ARE FAKED.
SO LET'S SEE HOW THESE TWO FARE IF I PUSH MY SPEED UP TO NEARLY SUPER-SONIC...
GOOD! THEY'RE STAYIN' RIGHT WITH ME.
BUT I'M MORE MANEUVERABLE THAN ANY FLIGHT-PACK OR GIZMO.
SO I CAN MAKE A 90° TURN...
BUT MY NASTY MINDED FRIENDS...
"...CAN'T!"
WHOOMF!
34

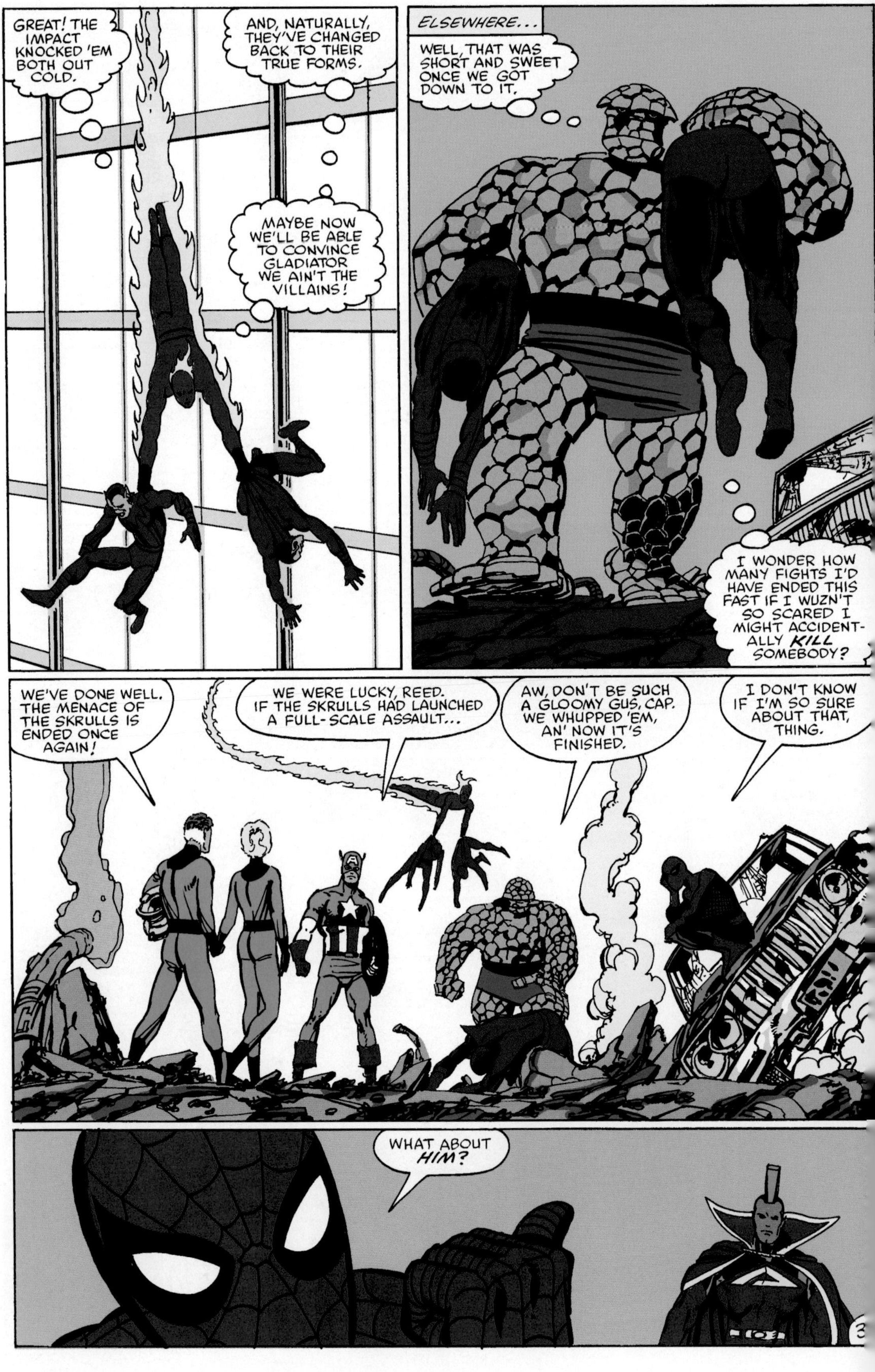
GREAT! THE IMPACT KNOCKED 'EM BOTH OUT COLD.
AND, NATURALLY, THEY'VE CHANGED BACK TO THEIR TRUE FORMS.
MAYBE NOW WE'LL BE ABLE TO CONVINCE GLADIATOR WE AIN'T THE VILLAINS!
ELSEWHERE...
WELL, THAT WAS SHORT AND SWEET ONCE WE GOT DOWN TO IT.
I WONDER HOW MANY FIGHTS I'D HAVE ENDED THIS FAST IF I WUZN'T SO SCARED I MIGHT ACCIDENTALLY KILL SOMEBODY?
WE'VE DONE WELL. THE MENACE OF THE SKRULLS IS ENDED ONCE AGAIN!
WE WERE LUCKY, REED. IF THE SKRULLS HAD LAUNCHED A FULL-SCALE ASSAULT...
AW, DON'T BE SUCH A GLOOMY GUS, CAP. WE WHUPPED 'EM, AN' NOW IT'S FINISHED.
I DON'T KNOW IF I'M SO SURE ABOUT THAT, THING.
WHAT ABOUT HIM?

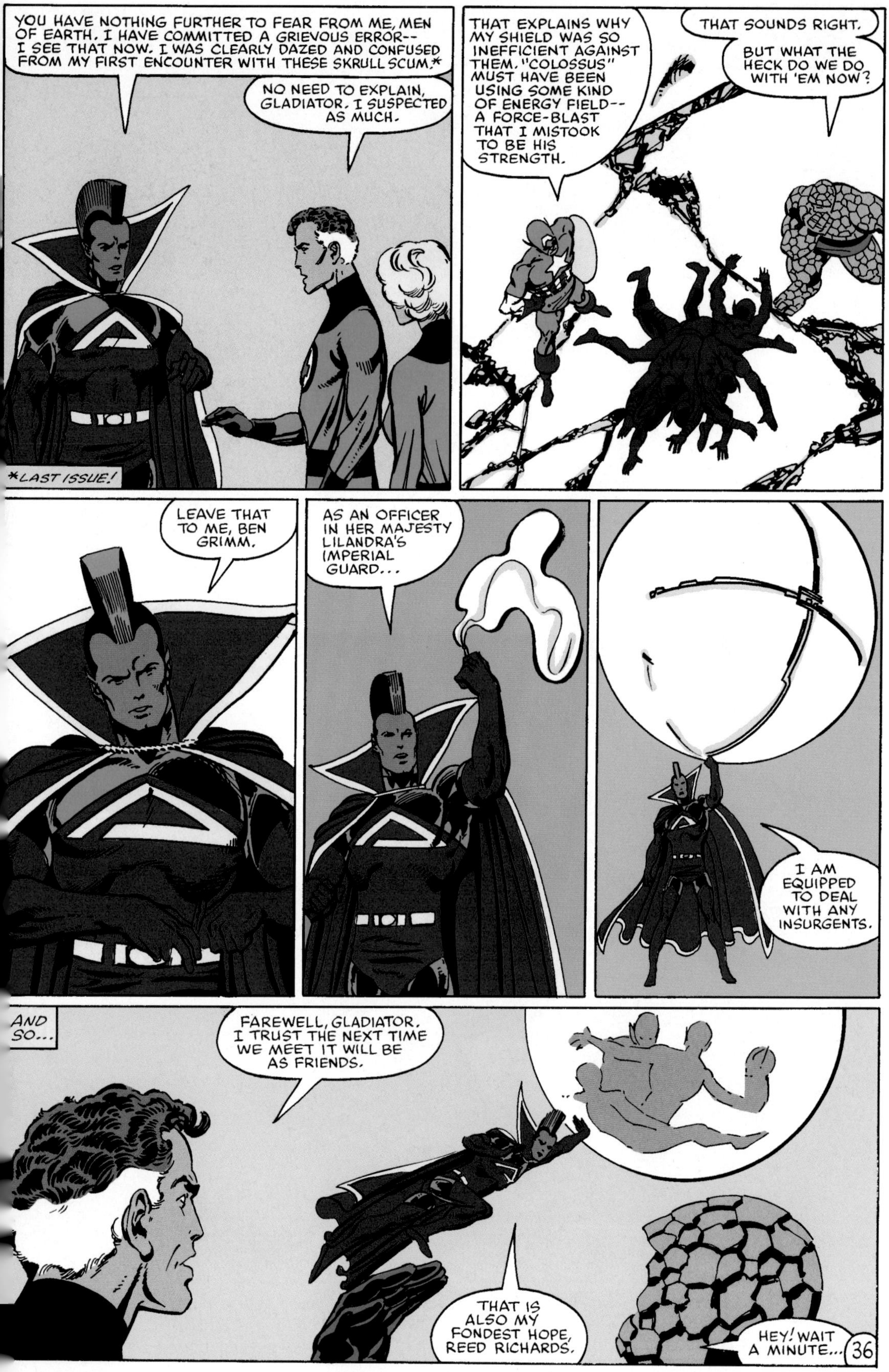

YOU HAVE NOTHING FURTHER TO FEAR FROM ME, MEN OF EARTH. I HAVE COMMITTED A GRIEVOUS ERROR-- I SEE THAT NOW. I WAS CLEARLY DAZED AND CONFUSED FROM MY FIRST ENCOUNTER WITH THESE SKRULL SCUM.*
NO NEED TO EXPLAIN, GLADIATOR. I SUSPECTED AS MUCH.
*LAST ISSUE!
THAT EXPLAINS WHY MY SHIELD WAS SO INEFFICIENT AGAINST THEM. "COLOSSUS" MUST HAVE BEEN USING SOME KIND OF ENERGY FIELD-- A FORCE-BLAST THAT I MISTOOK TO BE HIS STRENGTH.
THAT SOUNDS RIGHT.
BUT WHAT THE HECK DO WE DO WITH 'EM NOW?
LEAVE THAT TO ME, BEN GRIMM.
AS AN OFFICER IN HER MAJESTY LILANDRA'S IMPERIAL GUARD...
I AM EQUIPPED TO DEAL WITH ANY INSURGENTS.
AND SO...
FAREWELL, GLADIATOR. I TRUST THE NEXT TIME WE MEET IT WILL BE AS FRIENDS.
THAT IS ALSO MY FONDEST HOPE, REED RICHARDS.
HEY! WAIT A MINUTE...
36

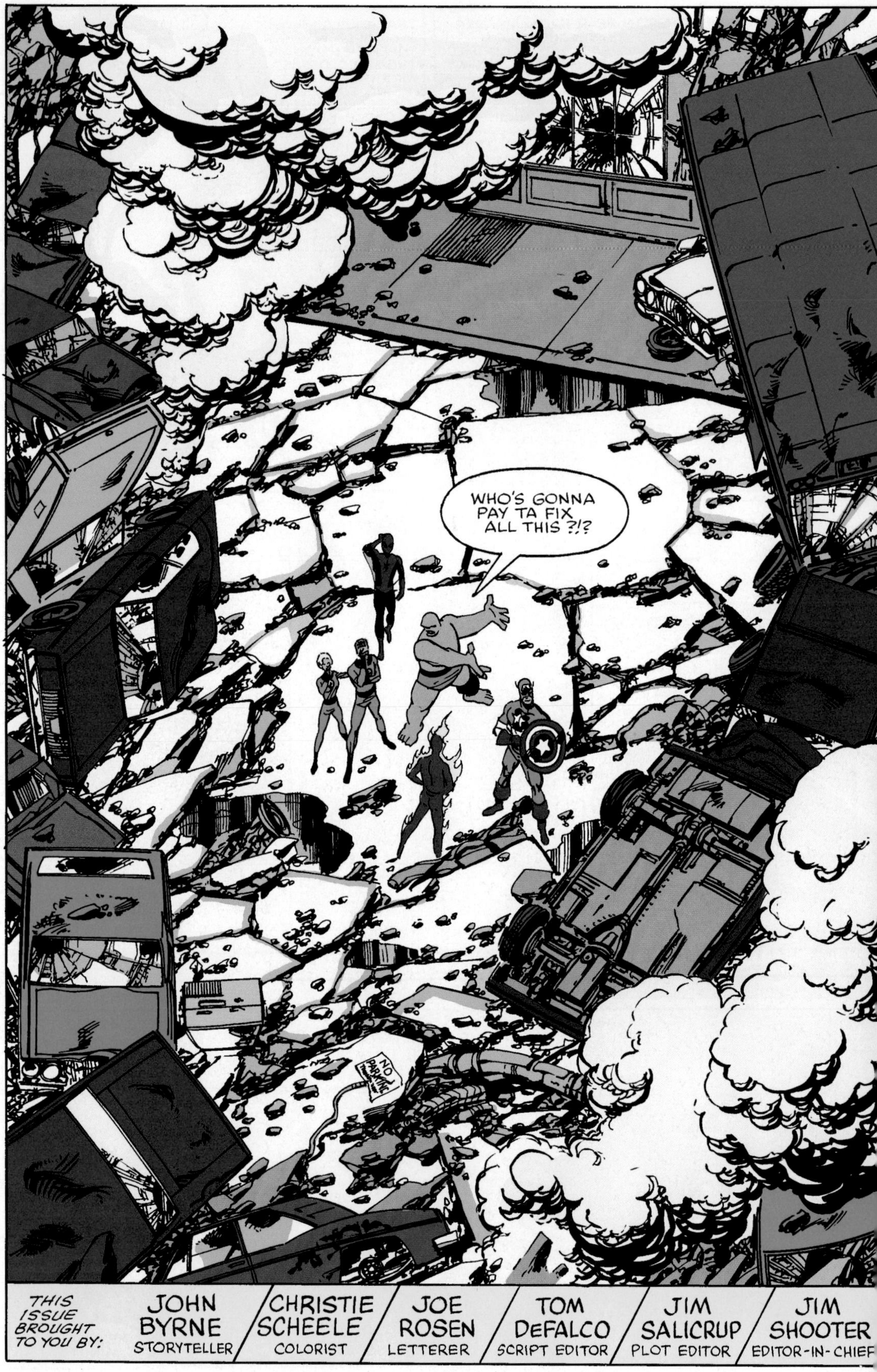
WHO'S GONNA PAY TA FIX ALL THIS ?!?
THIS ISSUE BROUGHT TO YOU BY:
JOHN BYRNE STORYTELLER
CHRISTIE SCHEELE COLORIST
JOE ROSEN LETTERER
TOM DeFALCO SCRIPT EDITOR
JIM SALICRUP PLOT EDITOR
JIM SHOOTER EDITOR-IN-CHIEF

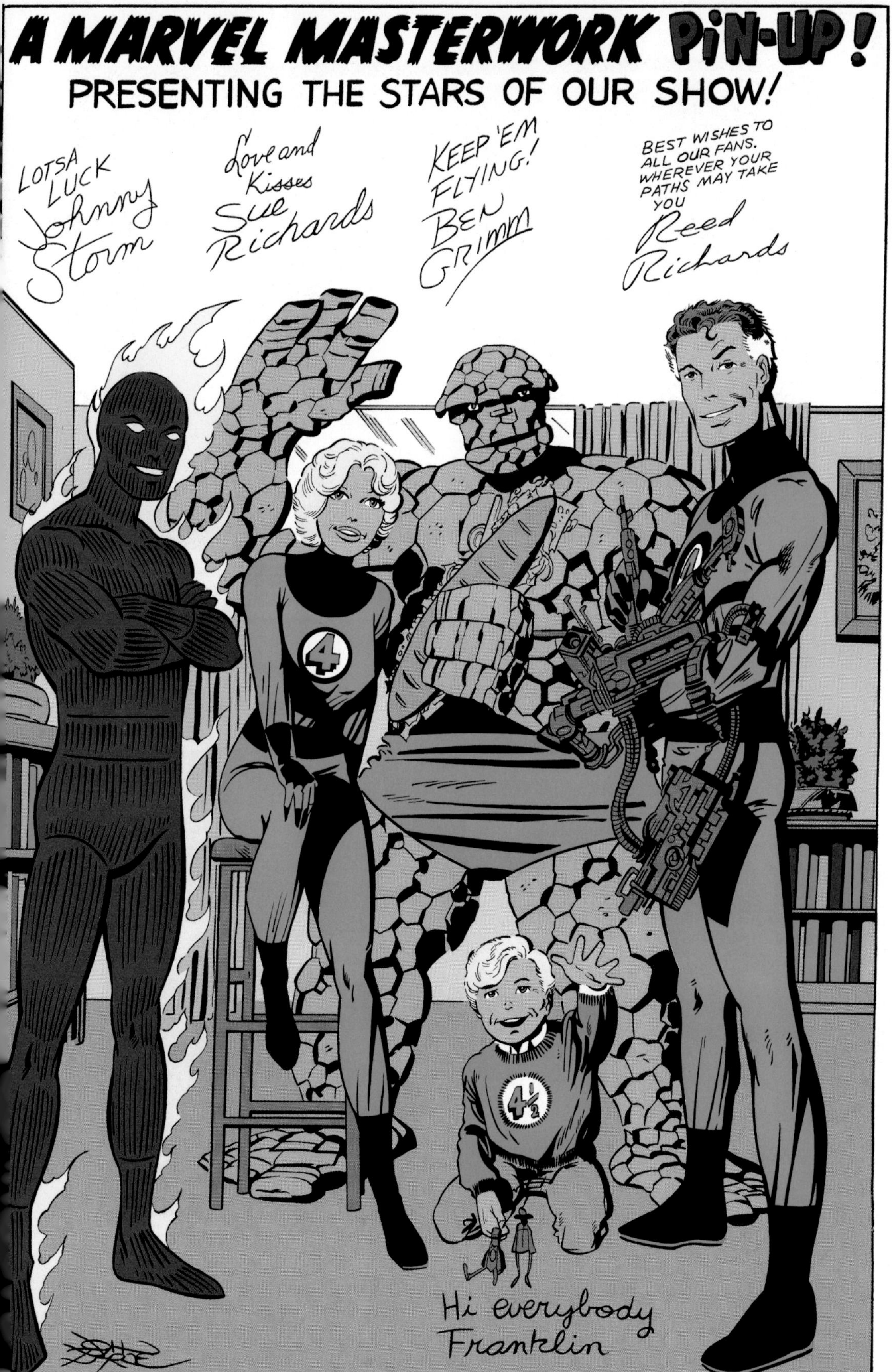
A MARVEL MASTERWORK PIN-UP!
PRESENTING THE STARS OF OUR SHOW!
LOTSA LUCK Johnny Storm
Love and Kisses Sue Richards
KEEP 'EM FLYING! BEN GRIMM
BEST WISHES TO ALL OUR FANS. WHEREVER YOUR PATHS MAY TAKE YOU Reed Richards
Hi everybody Franklin

MARVELS
10TH ANNIVERSARY EDITION

MARVEL®

CELEBRATE 10 YEARS OF MARVELS!
KURT BUSIEK • ALEX ROSS